D1577176

THE WAR THAT HITLER WON

By the Author

THE WAR THAT HITLER WON
ADOLF HITLER AND THE GERMAN TRAUMA
THE EVOLUTION OF WESTERN SOCIETY (co-editor, 3 volumes)
WESTERN CIVILIZATION
ADOLF HITLER AND THE THIRD REICH (editor)
THE HOLY ROMAN EMPIRE IN THE MIDDLE AGES (editor)

THE WAR THAT HITLER WON

THE MOST INFAMOUS PROPAGANDA CAMPAIGN IN HISTORY

ROBERT EDWIN HERZSTEIN

HAMISH HAMILTON

LONDON

First published in Great Britain 1979
by Hamish Hamilton Ltd
Garden House, 57-59 Long Acre, London WC2E 9JL

Copyright © 1978 by Robert Edwin Herzstein

British Library Cataloguing in Publication Data

Herzstein, Robert Edwin
   The war that Hitler won.
   1. World War, 1939-1945—Propaganda
   2. Propaganda, German
   I. Title
   940.54'887'43   D810.P7G3
   ISBN 0-241-10091-7

Printed and bound in Great Britain by
Redwood Burn Ltd, Trowbridge and Esher

Acknowledgments and Credits

I would like to thank many men and women for assisting me in my work over the past eight years. They have helped me obtain access to documents and films in a courteous and professional manner. Messrs. Robert Wolfe and John Mendelssohn of the National Archives, Professor Henri Michel, president of the International Committee for the History of the Second World War, Dr. Heinz Boberach and Dr. Kahlenberg at the Bundesarchiv, Mrs. Agnes Peterson and Mr. Charles Palm of the Hoover Institution, Mrs. Dina Abramowicz and Mr. M. Web of the YIVO Institute for Jewish Research, Mr. Marshall Deutelbaum of the International Museum of Photography, Frau Christiane Hoerter of the Bilderdienst in the Süddeutscher Verlag, Miss Gyernes of the Army Art Collection, Dr. Helmut Heiber of the Institute for Contemporary History, Mr. Pat Sheehan of the Motion Picture Section of the Library of Congress, the staff of the Mass Communications Center of the State Historical Society of Wisconsin, Mr. E. Hine of the Imperial War Museum, and Dr. Harriet Jameson of the Rare Books Department of the University of Michigan Library rendered valuable assistance in securing unique illustrations and documents. I wish to thank the Committee on Research and Productive Scholarship of the University of South Carolina for financial support, and the Department of History for granting me sabbatical leave. Both were essential to the completion of this book. My typists, Jill Swarz, Betsy Jones, Cindy Lewis, and Jami Bennett were efficient and pleasant.

Criticism and suggestions resulting from my presentation of papers on propaganda and related subjects have been most helpful. My thanks go to fellow panelists and audiences at the following meetings: American

Historical Association (1969 and 1975), the War and Peace Colloquia sponsored by the American Psychoanalytic Association (1970 and 1971), the Southern Historical Association (1975), the Duquesne History Forum (1974–76), and the Conference on War and Diplomacy (1977). Special thanks go to several of my colleagues and friends with whom I have, to my great profit, discussed aspects of my work over the past few years: Norman Rich, Robert Paxton, A. W. Salomone, Charles Sydnor, Burton Schepper, Jay Baird, Stanley Hoffmann, Bill Bradley, Peter Becker, Henry Huttenbach, Paul Blackstock, George Stein, William E. Griffith, Owen Connelly, Harry Cliadakis, and Donald Koenig. In addition, discussions with many individuals who lived through the wartime period as victims, "bystanders," and collaborators certainly influenced the nature of the questions I pose in this book. I wish to thank these men and women; I must do so abstractly, having agreed to respect their privacy. Yet, valuable as those discussions often were, the impressions and analysis which I offer the reader are based upon my own interpretation of documentary evidence. I alone am responsible for all opinions and statements of fact expressed in this book.

I would like to express my gratitude to the following institutions for graciously granting permission to print illustrations reproduced from materials held in their collections: The Army Art Collection, Washington, D.C.; the Dartmouth College Library (Myers Collection), Hanover, New Hampshire; the Hoover Institution on War, Revolution and Peace, Stanford, California; the Imperial War Museum, London, England; the International Museum of Photography, Rochester, New York; the Library of Congress Prints and Photographs Division, Washington, D.C.; the National Archives Collection of Foreign Records Seized, 1941–, Washington, D.C.; the Süddeutscher Verlag (Bilderdienst), Munich, Germany; Transit Film-Gesellschaft G.m.b.H, Munich, Germany.

I wish to thank this publisher for kindly granting permission to quote copyrighted materials: Excerpts from *The Goebbels Diaries* by Louis P. Lochner. Copyright 1948 by The Fireside Press, Inc. Reprinted by permission of Doubleday & Company, Inc.

I owe a special debt of gratitude to the photoduplication staffs of several institutions: the Süddeutscher Verlag, the Library of Congress, the Audio-Visual Department of the National Archives, the International Museum of Photography in the George Eastman House, the Hoover Institution, the Instructional Services Center of the University of South Carolina, and the Photographic Service of Dartmouth College.

R.E.H.

To the memory of my grandfather
Henry William Lewis

CONTENTS

English Equivalents of German Abbreviations Used in the Text

AC	Anti-Comintern
ALF	Central Film Office of the Nazi Party
ASA	Anti-Semitic Action
BPA	Illustrated Press Office
DAF	German Labor Front
DNB	German News Bureau
DPA	German Propaganda Studio
DW	German Weekly Newsreel
GPL	*Gau* Propaganda Central Office
HSA	Main Education Office
ID	Information Service
KONR	Committee for the Liberation of the Peoples of Russia
KPMB	Cultural-Political Communications Bulletin
NSDAP	National Socialist German Workers Party
OKH	Army High Command
OKW	Supreme Command of the Armed Forces
PK	Party Chancellory
Promi	Propaganda Ministry
RFK	Reich Film Chamber
RKK	Reich Culture Chamber
RMfVuP	Propaganda Ministry
ROL	Reich Organization Leader
RPA(e)	Reich Propaganda Office(s)
RPK	Reich Press Chamber
RPL	Reich Propaganda Central Office
RRG	Reich Radio Society
RS	Circular Letter or Instruction
RSHA	Reich Security Main Office
RSI	Speakers' Information
SD	Security Service of the SS
UK	Deferred by the Wehrmacht
WB	Wehrmacht Report or Communiqué

Note on translation of German terms: in all cases I have tried to render German terms into English in a manner both accurate and readable. I have included the original German in the text or the notes when I felt that the translation was unclear or did not convey the spirit of the original.

Despite his superiority, the enemy too is reaching the limits of his strength. This would not be the first time in history in which the stronger will triumphs over the greater battalions of the enemy. You can show your troops no other path than that which leads to victory or death.

—ADOLF HITLER *to Field Marshal Erwin Rommel, November 3, 1942*

Introduction:
The War
That Hitler Won

As soon as "victory or death" became a determining policy, and war actually aimed at the complete annihilation of the enemy, the Jews could no longer be of any use.

—HANNAH ARENDT, *The Origins of Totalitarianism*

I can only live in two different forms: as a mind in the service of lying or as a body in the service of murder.

—ALBRECHT HAUSHOFER, *1939*

During the Second World War, National Socialist propagandists made a massive effort to explain and justify Adolf Hitler's war to the German people. These men adapted Nazi ideology to their propagandistic needs and employed the mass media to reach the entire German population. The "coordination" of the media had progressed so far by 1939 that it was then possible to use proved techniques of public expression and control in an entirely new situation. Nazi ideologists and propagandists employed the enormous party propaganda apparatus and the directly or indirectly state-controlled mass media for intensive campaigns, blanketing the whole country with a single message.

War was the logical outcome and the ultimate test of National Socialism. For Nazi propagandists good popular morale and "decent" attitudes among the people were essential to total victory. German propagandists faced some of the same tasks which confronted public information specialists in other belligerent states: justifying one's own policy as peaceful and defensive, emphasizing enemy losses and one's own expectations of victory, keeping morale high, urging workers on to greater productivity, promising a better world after the war. The Nazis were in a unique position, however, for they represented a revolutionary movement which had arisen amidst the misery of a defeated nation. They promised revenge for the shame of 1918, and they achieved incredible, if brutal, successes between 1930 and 1944.

Triumphs had fueled the momentum of the Nazi movement, but the euphoria of the German people hailing every new German victory was in the long run a weak reed upon which to base one's propaganda. How would these men hold the allegiance of the nonparty majority in times of difficulty? Nazi propagandists, when they could no longer portray the *actuality* of victory as the vindication of National Socialism, responded to adversity by turning to a vision of a *future* but still total victory. Nazism did not grow through partial victories, but through the total destruction of the demons which opposed it: Jews or Communists, Social Democrats or Jehovah's Witnesses, the Polish Army or the French Army. A revolutionary movement whose claims and victory would change the world could never acknowledge compromise or retreat, even in 1944–45.

National Socialism was a purification ritual for millions drawn to its banners. It rendered respectable the public indulgence of private hatreds, as well as the moral and physical obliteration of one's chosen enemies. Resistance or opposition was a sign of evil, for the total claims of Nazi ideology made impossible permanent accommodation with opposing forces or nations. Nazi propagandists could glorify a *victorious* war by pointing to evil overcome and Nazism triumphant. They could justify a *losing* war by urging the nation on to greater efforts in the colossal struggle between Germany and total evil: Jews, Bolsheviks, plutocrats, "subhumans."

Through its own crimes Nazism turned much of the world into a bloc held together by the single common aim of destroying Hitler and National Socialism. Nazi propagandists pointed to this "conspiracy" as vindication of their original demonology. Defeat did not cripple wartime Nazi ideology; it reinforced its criminality by lending it the aura of desperate, crusading fervor. The greatest public hate and fear campaigns of our time took place in the "Greater German Reich" after 1942. Who were the objects of this propaganda? Over eighty million Germans. The main object of the Goebbels propaganda apparatus was the German civilian population, not the Wehrmacht and not the peoples of occupied or Axis-allied Europe. Goebbels was responsible for presenting a National Socialist interpretation of the war to the German nation. In that area he had wide-ranging powers. His control over armed-forces propaganda which was aimed at the other peoples of Europe was limited.

Nazi propagandists used the party-and-state propaganda apparatus to control the mass media. The term "mass media" refers to institutions of public expression through which a National Socialist message could reach the broad masses of the German population. The media included film, radio, the illustrated and word press, books, posters, placards, leaflets, brochures, coordinated campaigns by party speakers, and even "whisper" or "word-of-mouth" propaganda.

The resentments, strengths, and contradictions of Nazi wartime ideology found their most powerful and significant expression in the work of Paul Joseph Goebbels. The wartime ideology of National Socialism reached millions of Germans, party and nonparty members alike, through Goebbels' propaganda apparatus. An examination of the methods by which Goebbels and the party disseminated this message involves an analysis of the techniques of totalitarian thought control. It reveals the close relationship between ideology and totalitarian techniques in the transmission of attitudes and ideas. An ideology based upon force, command, and obedience found its natural form of expression within an apparatus which was both hierarchical and centralized. Within this structure there were many tensions, equally natural and even encouraged by Hitler within the "Führer state." The hierarchical structure of the propaganda apparatus was only as effective as the collaboration of its local branches with the Berlin and Munich policymakers. The men who directed the forty-two local propaganda offices were sometimes efficient, sometimes lazy, sometimes obedient to Berlin, sometimes under the thumb of a hostile local Gauleiter or Nazi big shot. When Goebbels received the total commitment of the party, as in his 1943 campaign against Bolshevism, the propaganda apparatus functioned smoothly, and the message effectively reached the German people.

The method I am using for a study of this propaganda is comparative, in that it involves parallel studies of different mass media during various propaganda campaigns. The method is also "vertical," for it analyzes the ways in which a message or an idea moved from the commands of Goebbels through the propaganda apparatus to realization in the media. This necessitates a study of the manner in which party and state institutions of propaganda functioned. Every party institution was a permanent instrument of propaganda. It would thus be a mistake to discuss techniques of control as the sole prerogative of the Propaganda Ministry. Goebbels reached the masses of party members through organizations such as the Main Educational Office of the party and the German Labor Front, as well as through his own employees and subordinate institutions. Goebbels felt confident about his control of certain mass media, particularly radio and film.

This book is not a history of German wartime cinema, but several films are useful in an analysis of Nazi war propaganda, particularly when one compares cinema, press, and radio. The Nazi vision of the war and of the Reich's enemies culminated in a series of large-scale film productions between 1940 and 1944. These films, often seen by millions of Germans, were ideal expressions of the National Socialist world view during the Second World War.

The unique nature of National Socialist propaganda lay in its combination of traits common to other nations' war efforts with a demonology and an idealism that made sense only in the context of historical experiences and cultural traditions shared by the German people. This uniqueness explains the discrepancy in effect between German propaganda intended for Germans and that aimed at enemy troops and civilian populations. Domestic propaganda was effective in mobilizing the nation even when Germany was on the verge of defeat. German wartime propaganda aimed at enemy populations was largely ineffective. Goebbels' mind and experience could only speak to Germans, and in the commanding tones and exhortations of Nazi ideology. Since this tone was real and not affected, it could not be dropped when addressing alien peoples for whom it had no attraction. German conservatives and diplomats of the old order sensed this failure, but they could do little about it, for the propaganda apparatus belonged to the National Socialists, not to technicians or cosmopolitans. Even when Goebbels finally began to speak of "Europe," he was speaking as a German to Germans. Self-interested fascist collaborators and a few duped idealists outside the Reich believed in this idea, but it had to fail. To National Socialists, "Europe" meant the organization of a vast territory under German control. Even this propagandistic concession to a deteriorating military situation had little appeal within the Reich. The battle cries of victory or death, triumph or Bolshevism, Germans or Jews, total triumph or total defeat, sacrifice unto death or the end of the German nation, were far more effective in mobilizing the German nation until early 1945. This was the war Hitler won through Goebbels, the man he chose as his successor. The Nazis appealed to the highest German values and perverted them. They used the lowest instincts of an unhappy nation, and built a successful campaign based upon "idealism" and hatred.

The war did more than reinforce the basic tenets of National Socialist ideology. This era proved how an apparatus of totalitarian media control could affect public attitudes and morale during a global conflict. Begun in 1939 as an attempt to explain rapidly changing diplomatic or military situations, wartime Nazi propaganda ended by projecting the final legacy of Nazi ideology. These visions reflected Nazi assumptions about symbols to which the German public would respond with a renewed commitment to total victory. Vindictive in victory, filled with fear and loathing in defeat, Nazi ideologists loaded their modes of expression with symbols and words which they believed would appeal to the German public: "heroism," "sacrifice," "Jewry," "capitalists," "Bolsheviks," "Frederick the Great," "Perfidious Albion," "mass murder," "hatred for Germany." Some symbols dated back to the eighteenth century; others emerged in the troubled years after the First World War. They formed a structure of word and symbol which was an essential instrument of Nazi propagandists. An infamous campaign of resentment and its result, murder and hatred, could thereby be justified as self-defense in total confrontation with alien doctrines. Victory could appear to the pious as divine grace, defeat, the result of devilish conspiracy. The wartime mass media thus reflected the cynicism, torments, and faith of Joseph Goebbels. In the end even Goebbels himself turned into a symbol. He ceased being an agent of control.

Henri Michel has commented with regard to waging total war: "Now, in total strategy, there exist many non-military means which can influence the decision ... I am thinking first of all of the part played by the mass media, of the press, but also and especially of the radio, which showed itself to be a powerful tool acting upon the morale of the populations engaged in the war." [1] This is true, but in the case of the Reich, the role of the media contained a sequel, unique to the German situation.

By 1944 the German propaganda apparatus and mass media were speaking as much to the Nazi elite as to the masses. When the war was clearly lost, a sense of Nazi justification and salvation permeated the media, for Goebbels deeply desired vindication "before history." The vulgarity of the phrases, often borrowed from the classics of German literature ("World history is the world court of justice," "It cannot have been in vain," "Man lives on in his deeds," adapted by Goebbels from Schiller and Goethe), concealed a real sense of longing for faith and redemption. In Goebbels one confronts a German will to believe in the midst of an age of disintegration, a desire for grace in an era of sickness and alienation. One medium, film, could present an ideal image of both the devil and salvation; hence it was perfect for Goebbels and his National Socialism. Some of the most powerful films ever produced emerged from this ideological and emotional cauldron: *Jud Süss, Ohm Krüger, The Dismissal, Rite of Sacrifice,* and *Kolberg.*

Joseph Goebbels, the cynical politician, the skilled propagandist, the romantic in search of salvation, was a far better Nazi than Hitler. Hitler was dead inside, lacking (as Speer put it) an emotional core, a man who wished to overcome his hatreds and resentments by sheer power and destruction. Goebbels wanted to *believe,* and in more than Hitler, though perhaps he never got beyond Hitler. Goebbels' romantic longing made him an expert in confronting the masses with Nazi ideology, for he could temper it to suit their tastes, even throwing in bits of Christian piety from time to time. Goebbels, even down to his crippled foot, which had its own symbolic appeal to the German imagination (Mephistopheles? Darkness without, light within? Materially bound, inwardly free?), combined brutality with a fear of pain, resentment with intellect, romantic longing with cynicism. This was a perfect German synthesis of decline and renewal, of modern chaos and romantic desire. War and the heroic ideal gave this little man his chance for greatness and redemption. It was for this struggle that he had helped create the propaganda apparatus which controlled the German mass media. Goebbels feared war in 1939 but achieved his greatest power as a result of that conflict.

An attempt to understand wartime Nazi propaganda in the German mass media presupposes several questions: Who was Joseph Goebbels, and how did he achieve his power? How did the party-and-state propaganda apparatus function at various levels and through what structures and individuals did it operate? How did Nazi propagandists use the mass media, particularly film and other visual media, such as posters and placards? What was the Nazi ethic of hatred and salvation, and how did it appear in the media? How did the German people react to this propaganda in terms of attitudes, and more intangibly but no less importantly, psychological, moral, and intellectual revulsion or attraction?

In a recent anthology on film and propaganda Gerhard Jagschitz noted, "The ultimate question about the effect of National Socialist propaganda cannot yet be definitely answered, since the relevant research has not yet been done." [2] In my concluding chapters I offer some tentative hypotheses about the nature of German popular reaction to the propaganda analyzed in this book. Important work remains to be done on the Nazi use of heroic myth, history, and language, particularly in the context of the regime's remarkably successful manipulation of people through symbolic images of German traditions and language.

We are about to enter a world which demanded self-abnegating heroism, a world in which the voices of men like Adolf Hitler and Joseph Goebbels appealed to many normal men and women as a "trumpet blast of freedom, a beacon light of faith," in the words of a popular slogan. This was a world in which brutal determination appeared in the guise of martial music and pathos-laden salutes to the fallen heroes of both world wars. This was an epoch when music encouraged men to suffer and die, yet offered solace and made men tougher; there was music sad and heroic, "The Song of the Good Comrade," "Raise the Banner," and famous old Prussian marches taken over by the Nazis because of their symbolic unity with an heroic past—the "Hohenfriedberger," the "Petersburger," the "March from the Time of Frederick the Great." Goebbels mobilized this spirit, and the German propaganda apparatus and mass media used it and conveyed it to receptive millions as the authentic voice of German greatness, a link with the pre-Nazi German past and culture.

A differentiation made by Hitler before the war when speaking of the Nazis is revealing. In 1934 at Nürnberg he declared that unlike for other Germans, "For us the mere proclamation of faith does not suffice, only the oath 'I fight!' " [3] The propaganda which addressed party members and cadres demanded that they *fight* as well as believe, for belief was assumed. In the instance of the general population, propagandists felt that a constantly repeated faith in Hitler and Nazi ideology would serve to buttress a German willingness to take orders and do one's duty. People would have to see that their fate and that of the Nazis were one and the same, that they too must *believe* in order to contribute to final victory. The apparatus could speak to Nazis directly and in ideological terms. In addressing the nation, greater caution was in order, but faith and belief were part of the media message, often skillfully disguised or sublimated. While Hitler was losing the war on the battlefield, Goebbels was salvaging a different kind of victory for his Führer.

If the Nazi propagandists were successful in inducing the population to wage an increasingly hopeless struggle, what does this say about Goebbels' audience? The Nazis knew their own people and could assume at least a minimal acceptance of the ideological propaganda which inundated the great mass media. The population consisted of three types of people. One type were Nazis who accepted the message and felt stronger when they emerged from a theater after seeing *Jud Süss* or *Ohm Krüger*. These were men and women who were electrified when they heard Goebbels speak in 1943 or when they saw a poster with an idealized portrait of Hitler over the caption "Adolf Hitler is Victory." Then there were the average types, the nonparty members or totally opportunistic "party comrades," the people who grumbled about shortages but did their duty in war, no matter who governed the nation. Keeping these people committed to victory was Goebbels' major task. The third group consisted of active and passive opponents of the Third Reich. These people concerned Goebbels greatly, but as an abstraction, since his propaganda was not directed toward winning them over to

Nazism, but rather at preventing the spread of their "poisonous" attitudes to the first and second categories of citizens. Himmler, not Goebbels, was in charge of dealing with dissidents: people in the Communist underground, graffiti writers, composers of anonymous hate letters to Nazi leaders, and antiregime activists.

Goebbels and his collaborators believed that transferring guilt for German crimes to the victims themselves was an effective answer to grumbling and privation. Anti-Jewish propaganda reached its peak in 1944, when most of the Jews of Europe had already perished. The Nazis continued to impute genocidal war aims to the Bolsheviks and the plutocrats, both of whom were fronts for "the Jews," even after the Allies had liberated several German concentration camps and showed the world what had taken place in such institutions.

The greatest success of the Goebbels propaganda apparatus was reflected in the continuation of the struggle by the German people into 1945 until practically every *Gau* was in Soviet or Western Allied hands. Even in 1945, German propagandists argued that the racialist and heroic ethos of Nazism was succumbing to a demented Jewish-Bolshevik-plutocratic coalition. Nazi believers saw this defeat not as a historical judgment, but as proof of their own righteousness, for their goodness had conjured up this anti-world of absolute evil, which was proof of the existence of good. This inversion of values represented a total repudiation of the bourgeois liberal world. The fatal attraction of this value reorientation for many Germans was the great discovery of Hitler and Goebbels, who could not have come to power nor maintained their control without it.

The reader may wonder why, in a book dealing with the dissemination of Nazi ideology, there is no single chapter on the Jews and anti-Semitism. The reason is that in the world we are about to enter, the Jews are everywhere and nowhere, deadly and subversive, the tie which binds the demonlike enemy coalition together. Goebbels' wartime phrase "The Jews are to blame for everything" summed up this view. Anti-Jewish feeling permeated every level of the Nazi propaganda apparatus and mass media, even after the Nazis had "evacuated" millons of Jews to the east. Since the enemy coalition was clearly a conspiracy, the arch-conspirator, the Jew, must be behind it. By 1943 the Jew was portrayed as the mind behind the "anti-world." The Jews were responsible for German misery and German defeats. To have a chapter on the Jews would be to acknowledge anti-Semitism as a part of Nazi ideology, whereas it was actually its ultimate moral and historical guide. Nazis such as Goebbels, Diewerge, and Taubert, measured good in terms of non-Jewishness, and evil as the concrete embodiment of Jewry.

Nazism was therefore the most pessimistic and optimistic of ideologies—pessimistic because of its murderous belief in the infection of humanity through anti-races, optimistic because the physical destruction of a people could salvage the world for an ideal Germany of goodness and virtue. Nazism was an ideology in which virtue consisted of the exorcism of inferior racial traits, the extermination of alien and Jewish-influenced elements.

This combination of idealism and brutality, of optimism and pessimism, typified the world view of the Nazi war propagandists. These men used their own confused yet comprehensible alienation to appeal through Nazi symbols to millions, yet they also could speak to one another as normal, logical, objective men. Such personality structures are difficult to describe in the abstract, but I believe that a study of Goebbels, the Nazi propaganda apparatus, and the German mass media will support these comments on National Socialist propaganda in its wartime incarnation.

I

Joseph Goebbels: The Politics

of

Propaganda and Faith

1

Joseph Goebbels:
The Mind of the Propagandist

For the last time Dr. Paul Joseph Goebbels addressed his senior employees in the shattered remnants of the "temporary" Propaganda Ministry in Berlin. The Bolsheviks were at most ten days from Berlin and scarcely a week away from the Americans near the Elbe River. When the Americans and the Russians linked forces, the Reich would be cut in two. This last ministerial conference was particularly eerie in that it was held by candlelight, owing to the loss of electric power. The light played off the wreckage in ominous flickers of shadows against the harsh edges of smashed walls and windows. The conference was small by the standards of earlier years, with perhaps a dozen men intently listening to the words of the minister. There was total silence in the room while Goebbels spoke, the only accompanying sounds being the occasional roar of artillery to the east and the shouted orders of Volkssturm unit commanders in the streets, often complemented by the noises made by weary refugees trudging on the torn-up streets through the desolate brick caverns of the blasted capital of the Reich.

Goebbels folded his arms as he looked intently at his colleagues: "Gentlemen, why have you worked with us? Now you'll pay for that with your necks!" [1] This brutal, almost sadistic realism struck the right note. For so long the incisive intelligence of Paul Joseph Goebbels had tried to overcome reality with the faith referred to in Hitler's famous slogan: "He who has faith in his heart possesses the strongest power in the world." But Hitler's call to heroism and faith had met with a betrayal at the hands of conspiracy and history; indeed, history had shown herself to be a "whore." As recently as the twelfth day of this same month of April, Goebbels had believed that history had justified the faith which he had spent more than twenty years acquiring. When Goebbels learned of the death of the hated archenemy Franklin Delano Roosevelt, he was ecstatic. "That is the turning point," he declared. Goebbels told his informant, General Busse, "Now, Herr General, it's up to you and your soldiers. You and your men must now perform the miracle of supreme bravery." [2] A bottle of champagne was opened. But within a short time, the minister's hopes faded, and he sadly concluded, "Perhaps destiny has once again become dark, and considers us to be fools." [3] So, at this last ministerial conference, Goebbels turned to his men and told them, "My family will not leave the capital of the Reich, come what may!" [4] If the Bolsheviks entered Berlin, Goebbels and his family would not survive.

Goebbels' thinly disguised talk of a murder-suicide pact should not have surprised one of his listeners, his aide Wilfred von Oven: The encirclement and destruction of the German Sixth Army at Stalingrad, and the surrender or capture of German generals and field marshals like Seydlitz and Paulus, had unleashed suicidal thoughts in Adolf Hitler. Imagine surrendering to the Bolsheviks when "with one shot of a pistol" one could have entered "national immortality"! Goebbels, always one to imitate and exaggerate Hitler's thoughts, had told von Oven: "I, in any event, do not fear death. If we are to lose this war, and with it our freedom, and if there is nothing at all that we can do to alter this fate, then my own life would not be worth anything more to me, and I would cheerfully toss it away. Certainly, it would be very difficult to choose the right moment to do so, the moment in which nothing more was to be salvaged, and one's own person had become useless to the cause." [5] Yet these words, so expressive of the maudlin and self-indulgent mood of late Nazi *Untergang* sentiment, concluded upon an ambiguous note, for Goebbels mused that the problem was choosing the right time and means, converting will into deed, not falling into the hands of the enemy . . .

Magda Goebbels was less intent than her husband upon maintaining an image of will and strength during these last months of the Third Reich. She may have harbored doubts about her second marriage, to Goebbels, but these she usually kept to herself. A fanatic Nazi, she did not question the wisdom of Goebbels' decision to commit suicide: "If our state collapses, then it is all over for us. My husband and I long ago came to terms with life. We have lived for National Socialist Germany, and we will die with her. The thought is one with which I am fully conversant, and it does not frighten me." [6] That was fine, but murdering their six children *did* disturb her. Goebbels tried to give her strength by mentioning Frederick the Great, whose way of avoiding depressing thoughts was to reflect that if one lived on a far-off planet, events on our little earth would appear insignificant. Magda looked at him and replied, "You may be right, but Frederick the Great did not have any children." [7]

When Magda Goebbels learned some days later that the Russians were only a hundred kilometers from Berlin, she at first could not believe the news, though it came from Joseph himself. When she realized that the story was accurate, she began to cry without restraint.[8] She wept because she still had not inwardly convinced herself that she would or could kill her six children. Early in February, with the battle for the Oder River and ultimately Berlin looming, Magda Goebbels mused aloud: "Doesn't it drive one to despair? We have conquered France, Holland, Belgium, Norway, the Balkans, and half of Russia and now we are not even able to destroy a couple of lousy bridgeheads [on the west bank of the Oder], which are a deathly threat to our own capital!" Her husband replied, "Yes, sweetheart, we are finished, bled to death, at our end. Nothing can help us." [9] Goebbels still offered a way out: She could take the children to the West and count upon the English to show mercy. Even when the final Russian offensive towards Berlin began in mid-April, Magda was capable of statements professing her belief in final victory. She did not believe her own words.

On April 18 Goebbels began to burn his papers. Shortly before this, as Wilfred von Oven recounts it, the long, painstaking work of making a microfilm copy (or copies) of the countless volumes of Goebbels' diary had been concluded. The diary, kept since 1920, was Goebbels' great treasure, his key to immortality, a guide to the twentieth century like none other. The pages of the diary were destroyed, and possibly as many as three microcopies remained, secretly stored in steel cases. Werner Naumann and Goebbels' stenographer hid the copies in secure places around the middle of April, probably right after the beginning of the Soviet offensive towards Berlin.[10] But the brave, heroic words still poured forth. For the last time, on the evening of April 19, Goebbels broadcast his annual celebration of Hitler's birthday, "Our Hitler." He even contrasted Hitler's favorable destiny with the doom accorded Roosevelt; fate had snatched Roosevelt away, while Hitler had survived the assassination attempt of July 20, 1944, "so that he could finish his work." He concluded, "I can only say that in the Führer our age, in all its dark and painful greatness, has found its only worthy representative." [11] Goebbels was still very much in charge of the defense of Berlin. In the newspaper *Panzerbär,* published by Goebbels "for the defenders of greater Berlin," the minister continued to tell the people that Berlin would be relieved, the Bolsheviks defeated on her outskirts, and the position of Germany changed for the better. Goebbels continued to use all the techniques of whispering campaigns and word-of-mouth propaganda to get these messages across. By April 24 ministry employees were strengthening the barricades around the ministry, using sandbags and rolls of newsprint in order to "further convert the ministry into a fortress." [12] The use of newsprint rolls, an increasingly rare commodity in the late stages of the war, possessed an irony of its own, for so much of Goebbels' life had revolved around the written word, journalism and printed speeches.

Two of Goebbels' last official acts as "Defender of Berlin" reflected major strains in his political life: deceit and heroic phraseology. On April 27 Goebbels ordered that Berlin be showered with leaflets. The Berliners could see that these leaflets were meant for the men of General Wenck's army, not for them. The sheets appealed to Wenck to hurry up and relieve the city, now that he was at the gates of Berlin. Actually, the leaflets *were* meant for the Berliners, as a way of boosting their morale. Wenck's army was no longer a factor, as Goebbels knew. Then came one of Goebbels' last proclamations, in which he told the Berlin defenders that "the hour before dawn is always the darkest." [13] Poetry and demagoguery, heroic words and tactical deceits until the very end: This was the world of Dr. Goebbels.

Adolf Hitler completed the final versions of his political and personal testaments on April 29. He appointed Dr. Paul Joseph Goebbels his successor as Reich chancellor, though he knew that Goebbels and his family, who had moved into the bunker, would stay in Berlin and probably die there within a few days. After frightening, emotionally draining scenes, the Goebbels children were put to death, though the agents and circumstances of their demise are still unclear. On May 1, 1945, Paul Joseph and Magda Goebbels, who had moved into the bunker on April 22, committed suicide. Following Goebbels' orders, the bodies were doused with gasoline and burned by an adjutant, a chauffeur, and an SS man.

He was the most cynical of men, an embittered idealist who was capable of sadistic words and behavior. Before the war Goebbels so humiliated a senior privy councilor accused of a ministerial security lapse that the man—and later his secretary—committed suicide.[14] Goebbels could brag about his own self-evident accomplishments as a propagandist and quote his wife in support of his assertions, only to follow this with the phrase "and she is not bright." [15] One day in 1941 he turned to his wife and guests at lunch and came out with this comment: "I think it is a happy dispensation that our children have all inherited your good looks and my brains. How awful it would have been had it happened the other way around!" [16] Such comments were suspiciously similar to the type of statements Adolf Hitler made when relaxing on the Obersalzburg. Goebbels often combined his vanity and need for love with comments calculated to make his company ill at ease. No one dared to look at his deformed foot, and he knew it, but Goebbels was capable of telling his aides that people loved cripples like Roosevelt and small men like Stalin. These aides had to suppress any tendency to associate Goebbels with those phrases. Goebbels liked to cultivate an atmosphere in which he could talk on and on, dominating a situation through his facility with words and his quick mind. Yet suspicion never was absent at Goebbels' long talk sessions. One of his closest aides once noted this suspicion when he was with Goebbels' family and received a phone call. After taking the call, the aide, Rudolf Semler, explained that it was a private call: "I am sure the idea has crossed his mind of checking up with telephone exchange in the house [to see] whether I have told the truth." Semler continued, "He sees the worst side of every human being and admits frankly that he had become an uncompromising misanthrope."[17]

Goebbels had contempt for the masses, as did Adolf Hitler. Possessing a good mind and superior education, the young Goebbels must have noted how much easier it was to move people by violence and cheap demagoguery than by clear ideas and reason: ". . . the rank and file are usually much more primitive than we imagine. Propaganda must therefore always be essentially simple and repetitious. In the long run only he will achieve basic results in influencing public opinion who is able to reduce problems to the simplest terms and who has the courage to keep forever repeating them in this simplified form despite the objections of the intellectuals." [18] Yes, including the intellectuals like himself, no doubt. When Goebbels was on his way to the Sportpalast on February 18, 1943, he bragged about the rhetorical and emotional performance which his colleagues were about to see. Goebbels would give the most famous speech of his career, on "total war." The crowd of convinced Nazis went wild, but the cynical Goebbels allegedly said of it afterward, "This hour of idiocy! If I had told those people to jump off the third story of the Columbus Building, they would have done it!" [19] Goebbels, whose greatest literary gifts were in the realm of biting irony and vicious satire, belived that irony was lost upon the simple masses. Mass media must not be elitist in its approach, though it must be directed by an elite: "Far and away the majority of those who listen to the radio have been roughly treated by life ... They have a right to genuine relaxation and recreation in their scarce hours of quiet leisure. The few who want to take their nourishment only from Kant and Hegel are very much in the minority." [20] The condescension of the elitist.

Goebbels, the idealist, was also Goebbels, the cynical materialist. Everyone, except Hitler, had his price. The minister thought to influence foreign correspondents in Germany's favor by classifying them as heavy laborers, which meant double rations of scarce goods such as meat, bread, and butter. The "Little Doctor," the man of letters, was obsessed with the idea of producing more tanks, more troops, total war: "Tanks are more important than operas." [21] Because of this acquired brutal materialism and contempt for the German masses, Goebbels never thought much of the idealist who spoke of a "crusade" against Bolshevism or the "idea of a new Europe." Late in 1942 Goebbels told his aides that there should not be too much talk of Germany fighting for Europe, since nobody would believe that she was not fighting solely for her own material interest. It was better to tell the German people that the Nazis wanted oil and wheat for the *Volk*.

Goebbels loved the language of heroism and idealism, but only as phrases descriptive of the German war effort, not as words defining all-embracing war aims. After Stalingrad the minister wrote: "Today every German soldier, worker, and peasant knows what we are fighting and working for. This is not a war for throne and altar; it is a war for wheat and bread, for a full table three times a day, a war for the achievement of the material means necessary for a solution of the social question, the question of the construction of homes and highways ..." [22] Germany could not go on forever fighting for ideals. Goebbels concluded that it might say a lot for the generous spirit of a nation that it was willing to go on being the source of much of the world's culture, but it hardly spoke well for its political sense. Goebbels, who had experienced the French occupation in the Rhineland after World War I, had no illusions about German patriotism: "Give Luxembourg power over Germany, and you will discover numerous Germans who will recognize that power, and will serve it." [23]

Goebbels was less prejudiced against the Slavic nations than most of his high-ranking Nazi colleagues. He mouthed some of the usual phrases about "colonial peoples" in eastern Europe, but these usually occurred early in the war: "The minister, pointing to an ice hockey match in Prague lost by Germany, said this confirmed that it was a mistake to contest colonial peoples in areas where we are inferior." [24] In the last stages of the war, Goebbels became an outspoken opponent of the policies of Hitler and Himmler regarding the "subhumans," the *Unter-*

menschen. This was not because of any humanitarian feeling, but rather because of a materialistic and realistic view of German self-interest. By 1943, spurred on by the Stalingrad debacle, Goebbels directed the German media that people of the eastern nations should not feel the Germans were showing contempt for them as Russians or Poles or Balts: "One cannot characterize these eastern peoples, who hope for their liberation at our hands, as beasts, barbarians, etc., and then expect them to show interest in a German victory." [25] Goebbels felt that it was sheer stupidity for Germans to talk about building colonies in the east and exploiting its inhabitants. Germany needed the labor and the support of these men and women, not their hatred. One of the reasons for Goebbels' reticence towards the "European" idea in German propaganda was his sense that it would give the other peoples of Europe the feeling that they would forever be subjects of the German Reich. At one ministerial conference in early March, 1943, Goebbels went on at some length about the miserable treatment of *Ostarbeiter,* or workers from the east. He quoted a German industrialist who had complained about this harsh treatment, and he strongly agreed that it was not in the interests of Germany. But Goebbels had his blind spots, though he loved to ridicule and curse the stupidity and corruption of much of the Nazi leadership. He never allowed himself to believe that the treatment of the eastern workers reflected Hitler's policies; yet it was Hitler, after all, who in 1942 had appointed as his forced labor commissar Fritz Sauckel, an "Old Fighter" in whom Hitler had total confidence. After the Germans had murdered millions of Poles and had savagely put down a revolt in Warsaw in 1944, Goebbels privately broke with a fundamental tenet of National Socialism when he waxed lyrical about the eternal Polish desire for freedom and nationhood: "What accomplishments and suffering a nation is capable of when it is fighting for its national freedom!" [26]

Paul Joseph Goebbels was not an open man, but one could at times disagree with him and even engage in spirited repartee, something his agile mind and wit craved. When the Luftwaffe field marshal Erhard Milch told him that he, Milch, would have saved the Sixth Army at Stalingrad even if this had meant disobeying Hitler, Goebbels rejected the argument but engaged in a long debate with him. Months later Milch went so far as to tell Goebbels that he thought the war was lost. While this statement infuriated Goebbels, he took his feelings out by a frenzied tour of bomb-devastated Hamburg, not by running to Göring or Hitler with verbal assaults on Milch.[27] Goebbels appreciated an acting liaison officer from the Armed Forces Supreme Command (OKW) who gave him the military report of the day in unvarnished terms, without the usual cover-ups and wordplay favored by Hitler and press chief Otto

Dietrich.[28] Yet Goebbels would reject potentially useful information if accepting it implied that he was not fully knowledgeable in an area of alleged expertise. When valuable information on the Soviet Union was available from a Corporal Thielscher, who had been there for two and a half years, Goebbels refused to receive him. Dr. Gast, director of the propaganda section of the ministry, told his correspondent, "The minister does not wish to receive Corporal Thielscher, since he is sufficiently informed about the situation in the Soviet Union." [29] Goebbels liked private bluntness; he did not want subordinates to know of his receipt of information from external sources. This was vanity and a certain know-it-all tendency, qualities Goebbels shared with Adolf Hitler.

And how much vanity there was in the Little Doctor's personality! He was in constant need of praise, and if he did not receive enough during the day, he praised himself to his recording machine or private secretary when dictating a diary entry. The diary would appear some day in print, so Goebbels was speaking to posterity. As he stated in the February 15, 1942, entry, "What I do personally continues to meet with general approval. What I've done with the radio as well as the newsreel is lauded in terms of highest praise. My articles are having the greatest effect throughout the world, nor need I complain of their echo among the German people." On March 29, 1942, he exulted, "Our navy journals have asked me to let them have my editorials a little sooner. . . . I am happy that my editorials are held in such esteem by the fighting forces." [30] And on August 10, 1943: "I am convinced that we would have won the war long ago if the leadership had been in the hands not of the generals but of the party." "Why should not party leaders, for example, who have proven themselves in the bombing war, not lead an army at the front?" [31] Goebbels was one of the few such leaders in the top Nazi hierarchy who visited bomb-blasted cities, and his popularity thereby increased. He was thinking of himself when he made this last statement, satisfying his vanity and his military fantasies, seeing himself as the heir to two of his heroes, Frederick the Great and the Prussian general Gneisenau.

Literary vanity infused much of Goebbels' love for the German word. When he published anthologies of his articles and speeches from the Weimar "Era of Struggle" in the 1930s, Goebbels made sure that each book contained full-page ads for his earlier works, replete with lavish praise from Nazi press reviews. Yet Goebbels, the man of the pen, wanted more than the praise of party hacks. On May 19, 1943, he noted that Knut Hamsun, the great but possibly senile Norwegian writer, was moved to tears when he set eyes upon Goebbels! In his diary entry for the day, the minister referred to this "precious encounter." He took much pride in the fact that he, an aborted novelist, had received tribute from Hamsun.

Goebbels had many of the concerns and conceits of the professional writer, and in this he was almost unique in the top Nazi hierarchy. When he tried to trick the Soviets into thinking that an invasion of Britain was imminent in June 1941, he mused that the affair "would make a good subject for a student writing his doctoral thesis." [32] Such a dissertation would glorify Goebbels, and perhaps he would have considered it a special case under his March 1940 decision that there would be "publication of dissertations during the war only with special permission."[33] Goebbels constantly bickered with his publisher, the Nazi Franz Eher Verlag, over royalties and advances. Semler wrote in 1941, "The Eher house has offered Goebbels 13 percent of the selling price as royalty on his new book. Goebbels has accepted it with reluctance and abuse." [34] Goebbels saw his secret diaries as a potential gold mine as well as a work of genius. He claimed that the party publisher Max Amann had offered him two and a half million Reichsmarks for them and that he had turned him down. Goebbels saw himself as a great writer. In fact, he was facile, clever, and witty, but hardly profound. He authored much journalistic output and a failed novel which bears all the marks of adolescent immaturity. In this sense, he never wrote a book, certainly not one worthy of his grandiose aims for after the war: a biography of Hitler, a study of Christianity, a treatise on film that would be as vital as G.E. Lessing's work had been for the theater, and a history of Germany since 1900 that in large part would be autobiography.[35]

The man's personality contained inconsistencies which at times took on the quality of hypocrisy. Late in 1942 Goebbels claimed, "I am glad that I have always lived in wartime style, so that I need now change nothing in my personal habits." [36] Wartime style! Goebbels acquired beautiful homes, valuable art works, a fortune in royalties, a wife with a parvenu style, and all the arrogance of a resentful but smug nouveau riche. He liked having a prince in attendance upon himself and a steward who had kept house for aristocrats. Goebbels possessed a beautiful wardrobe. If he lacked gluttony and was uninterested in alcohol, it was only in these virtues that he differed from the ostentatious life-style of many other Nazi arrivistes.

Goebbels rode a wave of popularity unique in his life when he visited bombed areas of Germany after 1942. He seemed to care about the homeless victims of the Allied air terror war. Yet he told an aide that, while it was too bad about the destruction, such devastation would make it easier to build new, better cities after the war. This comment was vintage Hitler, circa 1943, but it reeked of hypocrisy and cynicism when coming from the "concerned" Goebbels. Goebbels, the intellectual and the cripple, loved to appear strong, a study in will and decisiveness. During the first Russian winter he noted, "In times of crises ... there is but one sin, as Nietzsche put it; namely, that of cowardice." [37] Yet this was the same man who admitted that he could not bear physical pain, the self-indulgent cynic who once stated that even the smallest toothache incapacitated him.

Because of the contradictions in his character, Goebbels combined blunt insights with equally impressive blind spots. Early in 1941 this born journalist noted that no self-respecting journalist wanted to spend his professional life taking orders from Hans Fritzsche about how to write an article and about what not to say. Goebbels viewed most German journalists as hacks or as unhappy men doing their job. Yet in 1942 he exploded over the lifeless, boring, repetitive, hack nature of the German media, not seeing any connection between this situation and the constraints placed upon the media by National Socialism. He blamed men rather than the system. Adolf Hitler took a somewhat different view in this same year: "... what is called liberty of the press does not in the least mean that the press is free, but simply that certain potentates are at liberty to direct it as they wish, in support of their particular interests and, if need be, in opposition to the interests of the state. ... Today the journalist knows that he is no mere scribbler, but a man with a sacred mission of defending the highest interests of the state." [38] Goebbels knew this was not true, but he never made the connection between unfreedom and a dull press. He dared not do so. Quoting an old German saying, "Politics ruins the character," Goebbels was really speaking of himself, of the disappointments of a quick mind forced to immerse itself in the mediocrity of totalitarian media. So this unhappy man, so critical of the Nazi big shots with their backbiting and cabals, spent much of his time in conspiracies, undercutting his colleagues and denouncing the very media which he did so much to coordinate and castrate.

Yet these unattractive qualities can be misleading. Paul Joseph Goebbels needed to believe; he needed to sense that his feelings were real so that he could feel justified through faith alone. By the time he had come to devote his whole life to the seizure and use of political power, Goebbels was a human failure, a man who believed that faith and romantic art had failed him. Perhaps he sensed that through some flaws in himself, physical and emotional, he could never become a whole being; so, the moral aspect atrophied, while the cynical and manipulative instincts came to dominate.

Paul Joseph Goebbels was born in the Rhenish town of Rheydt in

1897, the third son in what was to be a family of four surviving children. His parents were devout Catholics, his father a bookkeeper of less-than-modest means. Fritz Goebbels was struggling to enter the German bourgeoisie, and this man of proletarian origins spared himself no sacrifice in order to improve the prospects of his children. Young Paul Joseph suffered from a humiliating deformity, a clubfoot or crippled leg, either the result of childhood disease or, more likely, a congenital deformity. The suffering this must have caused him in his formative years can only be imagined, and a militarist society with its cult of soldierly physical fitness was not the ideal social context for the healthy development of a young man such as this. Anyone familiar even today with the rough, almost sadistic games of preadolescent German youths can only wonder about what his suffering contributed to Joseph Goebbels' later development.

As a patriotic young German, Joseph Goebbels wished to serve his nation in the First World War. This brought laughter from the examining Army physician—and a trauma of rejection, tears, abstinence from food, and misery for this skinny, tiny, deformed youth. The mature Goebbels had a way of distorting the truth that was sometimes more revealing than he intended. In 1943 he stated, ". . . we *today* must atone for the sins of our fathers of 1918." [39] "Our fathers," or his own sins? Goebbels never served during the Great War, and his heroic "Prussian" service as propaganda minister in World War II was his own atonement for that omission. He had at least progressed beyond the lies of the 1920s, when he often began a political speech with the phrase "Those of us who were shot up in the war . . ." To the end of his life Goebbels dreaded public appearances where his deformity would be obvious. Subordinates dared not be caught staring at his foot during an audience (he usually sat behind a large desk, at any rate). Goebbels liked to be surrounded by beautiful, healthy men and women. He bragged about his superior brains, but as a *völkisch*, or German racialist self-induced believer, Goebbels equated physical health and beauty with faith and will, critical intellect with Jewish sickness and inorganic thought and personality. Yet intelligence and sharp wit were Goebbels' only assets as he entered the grim world of the Weimar Republic as a young man.

Paul Joseph Goebbels was one of the best educated of the Nazi leaders, certainly in the humanities. Thanks to the Catholic Albertus Magnus Society, Goebbels was able to scrape together enough money to visit several German universities and ultimately earn a doctorate in literature at Heidelberg in 1921. By this time his break with Catholicism was complete. He even defrauded his clerical benefactors by offering to repay his loans to them (the last having been received in 1920) in inflated

1923 marks! They sued him, and ultimately Goebbels was forced to repay some of the money. The Little Doctor had literary ambitions, but he had to earn a living. For a time he worked as a trainee at the Cologne branch of the Dresdener Bank. Helmut Heiber comments in his excellent Goebbels biography, "During this period his resonant voice was put to good use—not at political meetings, however, but in calling out stock prices on the Cologne exchange." [40] Goebbels later politicized this time of his life, making it appear as if he had been a Nazi from the primeval days of the movement, as if he had fought against the French when they occupied the Ruhr in 1923. He was becoming politicized, but as much because of personal frustration and professional failure as because of the situation in Germany. It would be several years before he would have close contact with Adolf Hitler.

In an interesting conversation one evening in April 1944, Joseph Goebbels looked back on his early years.[41] What he left out of this verbal autobiography was as significant as its contents. He said almost nothing about his mother or her concern for pitiful, crippled little Joseph, a love which contributed much to his later quest for faith and life in the great world beyond Rheydt. He also said little about the Jews, thereby implicitly admitting that his hatred for them developed later and was perhaps the result of political opportunism and his love for Hitler. Goebbels described his father as meticulous, incredibly hard-working; indeed he may have acquired these qualities from him, for he possessed them in abundance. Goebbels recalled a warm home life, one in which the rare luxury took on more luster because of the sacrifices necessary for its acquisition. Young Joseph far outstripped his two older brothers in mental and artistic ability. In 1944 Hans, the oldest, was director of an insurance company in Düsseldorf, while Conrad ran the party press in Frankfurt-am-Main. Both were longtime members of the Nazi party. Even without his personal frustrations and desires, it is logical that young Joseph Goebbels believed in life as struggle. He grew up in an environment where the dominant social theme was a sort of controlled frenzy, an attempt to claw one's way into the respectable middle class. And just when he "made it" as a young doctor of philosophy, the world of central Europe was in total collapse.

Paul Joseph Goebbels was to be his father's instrument in this process of becoming comfortably bourgeois, but the whole effort was cut short by the collapse of the secure world which the Goebbels family was fighting to enter. What a graphic scene Goebbels described in 1944, when he recalled the ecstasy in his father's house when a piano was delivered, the "symbol of the bourgeoisie," as the minister called it. How much scrimping and saving it took to be able to buy the instrument, and it was all done for young Paul Joseph! He practiced even on the coldest winter days, a cap pulled down over his ears, his little fingers freezing, his hands shaking from the cold of the Rhenish winter. The family even gave Joseph enough money to go to Cologne to see a real opera, an unheard-of luxury. The family could only prepare one child for the university, and that was Joseph. He excelled in history and German, though he was hardly outstanding in his preparatory studies. Goebbels remarked ironically in 1944 that his father wanted to prepare him for a career as a civil servant, which is what he became—in a sense.

Joseph Goebbels arrived in Heidelberg with little money, too proud to accept the culinary offerings of his landlady, who took pity on the thin little man with the limp, who would reply, "Thank you, but I have already eaten," or "No, thank you, I have no appetite." Even in 1944 Goebbels did not conceal his petit bourgeois resentment of more fortunate students. He hated them, had contempt for them. Goebbels was a pariah, though he later denied that he envied the wealthy, gallant youths who strutted around in their fraternity caps and fought aristocratic duels. Goebbels claimed to have made the acquaintance of the "National Socialist Idea" as early as this era, perhaps around 1920. He may also have flirted with movements such as national Bolshevism; he claimed to be a burning patriot, filled with patriotic feelings. For this reason he rejected Marxism, though socialism appealed to him. Goebbels was looking for a "national socialism," though it is doubtful if he really knew National Socialism at this point. The dates are unclear, but by 1924 Goebbels had probably became active in the National Socialist movement in his hometown of Rheydt. He had failed to achieve meaningful employment, and friends may have influenced his choice of political activity.

In his reminiscences of 1944, Goebbels painted a poignant scene of the father-son relationship from the early 1920s to the death of Fritz Goebbels in 1929. Even twenty years later, Goebbels was anxious to convince his audience that his father had accepted him and approved of his Nazism. Fritz Goebbels was a pious Catholic and a follower of the Center party; he had no use for the Nazis. A candidate for a minor municipal office on the Nazi ticket, Joseph was also a poll inspector for the party. He recounts that he went from polling place to polling place and at one location noticed his father about to mark his ballot. He sneaked up behind him and, in his words, ". . . saw to my satisfaction that he marked his X next to the NSDAP and its candidate, Dr. Joseph Goebbels." When Goebbels gave his first public speech in Rheydt, he asked his father to attend. Fritz Goebbels responded that no one, not even his son, would drag him to a Nazi meeting. "Nevertheless," said Goebbels, "during the meeting my sharp eyes detected him standing behind a column at the end of the hall, and from this position he listened to his son's speech with great fatherly pride, and when applause shook the hall, he even joined in." Goebbels concluded his reminiscences on a typical note of self-deception and distortion, qualities which this "shrewd intellectual" possessed in abundance. He says that it is too bad his father died in 1929 and did not live to see the real rise of his son—this on April 24, 1944, with doom confronting the Greater German Reich! More extraordinary still was Goebbels' attempt to convince himself that he was already one of the best known politicians in Germany in 1929. This fantasy allowed Goebbels to believe that his father died in full knowledge that his life had not been in vain, for his son had "made it."

It always amused Goebbels to note that both he and Adolf Hitler still paid their church taxes to the Catholic Church. When he married Magda Quandt on December 19, 1931, Hitler was their witness. Magda was a "heretic," as Goebbels put it, a Protestant. By witnessing the union, Hitler was also culpable in the eyes of the Church; both men were excommunicated. Since they did not willingly leave the Church, they had to pay their church taxes until their death, which they did. "What is grotesque about this is that the income which the Catholic Church receives in this way stems largely from our books, which are on the Index, . . ." commented Goebbels. "The ways of the Lord are indeed sometimes wondrous . . ." [42] But there is also something wondrous about Goebbels' story. Although a convinced National Socialist by 1924–25, he had not formally left the Church as of late 1931. Why? Probably for a reason he did not wish to acknowledge to his listeners: the memory of his recently deceased father, who could accept almost anything, but not that.

In his famous essay, *The Betrayal of the Intellectuals,* the French philosopher Julien Benda analyzes the problem of the modern nationalist intellectual, the passionate trafficker in the ideas of the marketplace.[43] His insight into the uprooted intellectual's abandoning of the ivory tower for politics is brilliant and can be applied to the case of Dr. Goebbels. Benda writes, "Our age is indeed the age of the *intellectual organization of political hatreds.* It will be one of its chief claims to notice in the moral history of humanity." The young Goebbels made the transition from academia to politics between 1921 and 1924. But his odyssey was not merely a contemporary phenomenon (Benda developed his idea in the late 1920s): "Now, at the end of the nineteenth century a fundamental change occurred: *the 'clerks' began to play the game of political passions.* The men who had acted as a check on the realism of the people began to act as its stimulators. This upheaval in the moral behavior of humanity operated in several ways." The intensity of political passion was a sign of realism, an abandonment of faith. Paul Joseph Goebbels took the road from literary romanticism to the manipulation of the masses through modern propaganda, of which he was a major inventor. Benda continues, "Formerly man was divine because he had been able to acquire the concept of justice, the idea of law, the sense of God; today he is divine because he has been able to create an equipment which makes him the master of matter."

Goebbels was never more than a quasi-intellectual, for his purely German cultural sensibility was acquired when he was emotionally immature, and intellectual inquiry stopped for him at an early age, however much he continued to read. He kept reading but he stopped studying. He became utilitarian in his mental development. He could have been describing himself (but he was not) in a speech given in Weimar in 1942 when he scornfully said, "By intellectualism we mean that type of semiculture which knows too much to believe out of instinct, and knows too little to believe out of knowledge." [44] From romantic dreams to manipulation of the masses, from intellect to nationalism, one factor remained constant in Goebbels' personality: the need to believe.

Young Dr. Goebbels was a failure in life, in his own eyes, until he found National Socialism. His failure was connected with his romanticism, his dreamy idealism, all out of place in a miserable world of struggle and crudity. The great expression of the early Goebbels was his failed novel *Michael*, probably written in 1921-24, but not published until 1929, and then only by the Nazis. Goebbels may have added materials in the intervening period, turning the hero from a confused, romantic late adolescent into a budding Nazi who finds salvation in the *Volk*. Yet the book is revealing. Michael, the hero of this novel-as-diary (the diary always remained Goebbels' favorite literary form), reflected the author's quest for meaning in life. *Michael, a German Destiny in Diary Pages* showed the influence of Goebbels' friend Richard Flisges, a leftist activist.[45] Although Goebbels probably ended his friendship with Flisges in 1922, *Michael* was the Little Doctor's verbally ambiguous fantasy of what should have happened: The Communist becomes a Nazi and dies a hero's death, fighting the French in the Ruhr. The idea of a tragic German destiny, *ein deutsches Schicksal*, appealed to Goebbels, and he used this same concept in his treatment of the Nazi "martyr" Horst Wessel, killed in 1930.

The dedication of Goebbels' novel, besides the mention of its inspiration, Richard Flisges, shows that even from 1921 to 1929 Goebbels remained imbued with a postadolescent romanticism that thrived upon fantasies and the quest for total belief: "1918: Our answer was: revolution! ... 1920: My answer was defiance! ... 1923: Your answer was: death! ... 1927: My answer was resurrection. ... This book is dedicated to the memory of my friend Richard Flisges, who died a difficult death as a brave soldier of labor in a mine at Schliersee on July 19, 1923." The implication is that Flisges died in a workers' strike against the French, but no more specific information is given by Goebbels. In his foreword Goebbels writes, "Disintegration and dissolution do not mean decline, but rather rise and advent. . . . Youth is livelier than ever today. It believes. In what—that is what the contest is all about. . . . Faith, struggle, and labor are the virtues which unite the German youth of today in its Faustian creative drive." Goebbels goes on to say that the spirit of resurrection, the renunciation of the ego, the drive to another, to the brother, to the *Volk,* are the bridges from the present to the future: "We will at the right moment have the courage, the will to pull ourselves together for a deed on behalf of the fatherland. We want to live: therefore we will gain life." Youth, faith, fatherland, resurrection, comradeship, all the virtues of the old German youth movement inspired this novel, and for Joseph Goebbels they were the faith of National Socialism. In this sense he was indeed, in a favorite phrase, "one of many, a German destiny." But those phrases come from his foreword, written when he was a convinced Nazi; much of the novel itself may have dated back to 1921 or even earlier.

The language of Nazi propaganda during the war owed something to this obscure novel. Goebbels did not invent the language he used in *Michael* but its impact upon his own mind and his dissemination of it colored much of the phraseology which dominated German propaganda during the 1939–45 war. It is therefore useful to consider some examples of language and themes from *Michael.*

On the loss of World War I by Germany: "Useless? Oh no! It only appears thus. The war was the great demonstration of our will to life."

On the future Leader: "It seems to me if another, one greater, is already in our midst; he will one day rise up from among us and will preach faith in the life of the fatherland. . . . Such a one will come! If I lost this faith, I would no longer have any reason for living. . . . Geniuses devour human beings. But . . . not for themselves, for their mission."

On youth and sacrifice: "Youth which is not ready to silently and with a ready sense of sacrifice offer up its life for the future, is no longer youth."

On the German woman: "Woman has the task of being beautiful and bringing children into the world. . . . How reactionary! . . . What does that mean, reactionary? That is only a slogan. I despise loud women who meddle in all the things they know nothing about. . . . If modern means unnatural, demoralizing, corrupted morality and planful disintegration, then I am indeed a conscious reactionary."

On man, God, and faith: "We have lost our real relation to God. We are neither cold nor warm. Half Christian, half pagan. Yes, even the best stumble around in the dark . . . A nation without religion is like a man without breath. The organized religions have failed. Totally failed. . . .

With their resentments they terrorize any development of a new religious will. Millions are waiting for this, but their yearning remains unfulfilled. . . . But one should leave to the broad masses their idols until one can give them a new God. . . . I pick up the Bible and through an entire evening read the simplest, greatest sermon which was ever preached to humanity: the Sermon on the Mount! Blessed is he who suffers persecution for the sake of righteousness, for his shall be the Kingdom of Heaven!"

On comradeship and war: "I love as comrades . . . simple, straightforward, strong men. . . . All say *du* to me, and I say *du* to all of them, just as in the field, in the trenches. . . . This is what the fatherland must become. Not all equal, but all brothers."

On the German destiny: "If we succeed in creating a new type of German, then we will mold the next millennium. . . . Pan-Slavism! Pan-Germanism! . . . Who will win the future? No, I'm no turncoat. I believe in us, Germany!"

On labor, intellect, and struggle: "The law of work, which means struggle, and of intellect, which means work. The synthesis of these three makes us free, inwardly and outwardly. Work as struggle, intellect as work, in that lies the solution! . . . If we become ourselves again, then the world will learn to shake in our presence. The earth belongs to him who seizes it."

On the Advent of the Leader, the messiah: "In the evening I sit in a large hall among thousands of people and see again him who awakened me. Now he stands in the middle of the commune of believers. I scarcely know him any more. His being is greater, more contained. . . . This sea of light shining from two blue stars. I sit in the midst of all the others and yet it seems as if he is speaking only to me. On the blessings of work! That which I felt, suffered, and bore, he sums up in a word. My profession of faith! Here it takes on form. . . . Around me sit men I have never seen before, and I feel as ashamed as a child as tears come to my eyes."

On Michael's love for Hertha Holk: "Hertha Holk has an impulse towards the new, but she remains too mired in little prejudices, old views, in a word, a superannuated bourgeoise. She does not have the courage to become somebody."

On life and struggle: "We must be grateful to men who give us the opportunity for sacrifice."

"The war awakened me out of a deep sleep. It brought me to consciousness."

"Mind tortured me and drove me to catastrophe; it showed me depths and heights."

"Work redeemed me. It made me proud and free."

"And now I have formed myself anew from these three. The conscious, proud, and free German man, who wants to win the future!"

"The life of the individual is not everything. It is not a thing in itself. We must overcome it and ascend to a new, fructifying power. As long as man clings to life, that long is he not free. . . . We are not put into the world to suffer and to die. We have a mission to fulfil. . . . Struggle demands blood. But every drop of blood is a seed. . . . We must all make sacrifices."

By an incredible, almost mystical foresight, the character Michael, now a worker in a mine, dies in an accident on January 30. Goebbels could not have known at that time that Michael's hero would come to power on that day in the future.

In describing the death and burial of Michael, Goebbels depicted some of his most intense fantasies. Michael, surrounded by comrades, meets his tragic death. His funeral is heroic; he is a "pioneer of the new Reich," a "worker, student, and soldier," the progeny of the Bible, Faust, and Zarathustra. Goebbels used the enthusiastic romantic language of the German youth movement. *Michael* embodied dreams of a pure, new Reich, the intense yet clean eros of comradeship, the desire for idealistic sacrifice, and the worship of the Leader. Much of the language used by Goebbels became part of the National Socialist cult of death and transfiguration, of heroism and sacrifice.

Terms constantly repeated in the novel or used in crucial contexts include these: *Tod* (death); *Auferstehung* (resurrection); *Kampf* (struggle, battle); *Glaube* (faith, belief); *Schöpferdrang* (creative drive); *Volk* (people, nation); *Krieg* (war); *Vaterland* (fatherland); *Genie* (genius); *Opferbereit* (readiness to make sacrifices); *Jugend* (youth); *Kamerad* (comrade); *Arbeit* (work, labor); *Glaubensbekenntnis* (profession of faith); *Opfer* (sacrifice); *stolz* (proud); *Mission; Blut* (blood); *Soldat* (soldier).

Paul Joseph Goebbels did not make a great literary or academic impression in Heidelberg, though he had worked with the famous Friedrich Gundolf (of the Stefan George circle). He was not temperamentally suited to an academic position; there is no evidence that he seriously longed for such a career. Goebbels approached leading newspapers and journals in Berlin, including the *Berliner Tageblatt,* but the response to his work was negative. Ambitious, gifted with wit and verbal facility plus a critical, if superficial, intelligence, young Dr. Goebbels would appear to have been a natural in the world of literary journalism. The German-Jewish intelligentsia, which played such a dominant role in this area, rejected him. A Rhenish provincial, personally unhappy, Goebbels never forgave this slight. His adolescent romanticism and immature literary style—not yet disciplined or worldly-wise—probably offended the journals and newspapers to which he submitted his work in the early 1920s. Goebbels retained a special hatred for the *Berliner Tageblatt.* In 1929, for example, when he was already a rising figure in the Nazi party, Goebbels declared on placards and in party literature that international Jewish financiers controlled German reparations payments, and that if Germany defaulted she would have to export young men and women (except Jews) as slave laborors.[46] He gave as his source for this lie the *Berliner Tageblatt.* More than a decade later, in the famous Emil Jannings film *Ohm Krüger,* the "heavy" in the first scene is an obnoxious, pushy Jewish photographer—for the *Berliner Tageblatt.* In an article written in the early days of World War II, Goebbels still recalled the attacks upon him by the "Berlin Jew press." [47]

Goebbels' unstable "radicalism," in part the legacy of his late friend Richard Flisges, led him to the radical North German wing of the Nazi movement. By 1926, as Hitler was struggling to rebuild and extend the fragmented, small Nazi movement, Goebbels had betrayed the Strasser brothers, Gregor and Otto, leaders of Rhenish and North German National Socialism, and had gone over to Hitler and the Munich Nazis. His dedication to the new Leader, combined with his intellectual background and gifts, marked Goebbels as a rising star in a movement generally devoid of men with real ability as journalists, speakers, and organizers. Goebbels became Gauleiter or *Gau* leader of greater Berlin, in itself a thankless task in that "Red citadel," but not without prospects for an ascending star in the Nazi firmament. Berlin cried out for a Nazi agitator who would reorganize the tiny Nazi party in the capital of the Reich, build a base of loyalty to Hitler, and gain publicity by taking on the Reds and creating a new type of political journalism—the printed word and picture as pure agitation and demagoguery. Surrounded by a few hundred Nazis in 1926–27, Goebbels proceeded to create a Nazi legend in the next six years, the legend of the Little Doctor with the big heart, the peerless speaker and agitator, the "Conqueror of Berlin" who smashed the Reds, the propagandist without equal, the beacon of light, the trumpet blast of freedom announcing the end of the "Jew Weimar Republic" and the advent of Hitlerism.

Goebbels never conquered Berlin, but he did build a party there, and he did cause a constant uproar. He took the battle to the enemy: On February 11, 1927, for example, the Nazis held a meeting in Wedding, a Red district of Berlin, in the Pharus Hall. The Nazis outnumbered the Communists, who had come to disrupt the meeting, and fought the greatly outnumbered Reds for a few minutes in a pitched battle. To Goebbels this proved that the bourgeois state, which could not take on the Reds, was collapsing before the Nazi movement, which had the will to smash the Red Front. Goebbels created a legend out of this brawl; his heroic use of words and music were the products of an uncanny sense of propaganda.[48] He invented the "Unknown SA Man"—a phrase that might stir German hearts with memories of the Unknown Soldier of 1914–18—"who does his duty day after day, obeying a law which he doesn't know and scarcely understands." As a 1928 Nazi election poster put it, against the background image of a fallen soldier of the Great War, "National Socialist—or the Sacrifices Were in Vain." Goebbels knew that man does not live by bread alone, that Germans would be moved by pathos and heroism more than by appeals for a new economic order. In the early days of the movement in Munich, Hitler had intended to frighten away cowardly, "respectable" bourgeois elements. They would follow later, when a militant party showed that it alone would battle the Reds in beer halls and streets. Goebbels now used the same methods. A meeting without a brawl was a failure, for verbal violence needed at least

Nazi ridicule of the respectable "liberal" middle class. S. Bergmann, a Jewish banker, picks the pocket of the dumb Aryan bourgeois who smugly reads the liberal *Morgenpost,* here turned into *Morgenpest,* or "morning plague." The reader is pleased by an unpatriotic editorial demanding, "Down with Wilhelm!" (former emperor Wilhelm II).

CREDIT: "Der Angriff"

a touch of physical brutality in order to sustain the growth of the movement. Hecklers were beaten up, Reds set upon, the police and "Jew press" denounced, and the state itself challenged. If the small Berlin party was banned, so be it. It would boldly reject the *Verbot,* reorganize, agitate—and become legal again.

Goebbels' journalistic mouthpiece was *Der Angriff,* a short newspaper which was more an agitational pamphlet than a journal. Goebbels sensed the value of brilliant placards and biting, satirical cartoons, the more outrageous the better. His collaboration with the artist and cartoonist Hans Schweitzer ("Mjölnir") proved fruitful and lasting. By the time he was eighteen years old, Schweitzer had already published his first anti-Semitic cartoons; he was a child prodigy in his chosen field of work. As Goebbels wrote to Schweitzer, "Only you can draw like that." [49] The drawing as a hate-filled call to battle: This was Schweitzer's forte. The work of Goebbels and Schweitzer took them in and out of court, but they made an impact which by 1930 extended far beyond Greater Berlin. A good example of their work was *The Book of Isidor: a Contemporary Portrait Filled with Laughter and Hate,* written in 1931.[50] Vicious, outrageously "funny," cheap, direct, and sick, this kind of effort showed that Goebbels had matured into an emotionally retarded but intellectually clever political propagandist.

Joseph Goebbels considered himself one of the greatest propagandists of all time. During the Second World War Goebbels took time out to reflect upon his earlier accomplishments in this area. He claimed credit for four developments: (1) The creation of a base for National Socialism in the working-class areas of the Rhineland (presumably as a collaborator of the disgraced Strassers, whom he had betrayed and whom he did not mention in his account); (2) The conquest of Berlin: "Without control of Berlin the party would have remained a provincial movement"; (3) The working out of "the style and technique of the party's public ceremonies"; (4) The creation of the Hitler myth.[51] The second point was the heart of Goebbels' view of his role during the *Kampfzeit,* or Era of Struggle. After he became propaganda minister in 1933, Goebbels summed up his opinion in regard to that effort: "In itself propaganda does not possess any set of fundamental methods. It has but one goal, and in politics this goal always revolves around one point: the conquest of the masses. Every method which furthers this goal is good. And every method which misses this goal is bad. . . . The methods of propaganda emerge in a causal sense out of the daily struggle. None of us is a born propagandist." [52] Goebbels went on to say that revolutions are made not by great writers, but by great speakers. He proudly referred to himself and his comrades on the Rhine and in Berlin as agitators.

Kaufmann, Handwerker!
Nur einer kommt Dir zu Hilfe!

Goebbels' grotesque political humor during the Weimar Republic era. A ludicrously bloated Jew strangles the German lower middle class and small merchants. A stalwart Nazi comes to rescue this *Mittelstand,* while Communists, Social Democrats, and German Nationalists look on. The leftists smile at the destruction of this class, while the reactionary Nationalist is disturbed—but does nothing. The appeal: "Merchant, artisan! Only one man comes to help you!"

CREDIT: "Der Angriff"

How far Goebbels had come since the dreamy days of *Michael* and the studious, if frustrating, years as a student! That baggage was thrown away, and the cynical manipulator now emerged. Goebbels discovered the agitational power of vicious "black humor," and he and Schweitzer exploited it to the full, especially among the Berliners, who, uniquely among Germans, had a reputation for wit. They might not vote for the Nazis, but they were beginning to notice them. As another Nazi journalist, Hans Schwarz van Berk, later put it, *Der Angriff* taught Berlin how to laugh again.[53] And if the paper seemed brutal, was this not merely "German honesty" in the tradition of Martin Luther? When the party was outlawed in Berlin, its members went around in outrageous but funny outfits, as in a Halloween masquerade. One *Angriff* journalist,

Dagobert Duerr, reminisced that the *Angriff* of the *Kampfzeit* "might well have had a fatal attraction for every patient released from Wittenau Insane Asylum." [54] But just as Goebbels knew how to use Schweitzer, so he made good use of the bums, degenerates, drifters, and idealists, proletarian or bourgeois, who began to pour into the Berlin party in 1929–30. Schweitzer idealized these SA men as mindless fanatics whose brutality was in the holy cause of German freedom. They were "freedom fighters," and if the party was outlawed in Berlin from 1927 to 1928, then *Der Angriff* became the "voice of the persecuted." Goebbels challenged the Weimar Republic with self-pity and derision, with violence and hatred, with glaring posters and endless agitation, with ridicule and brass knuckles. No other Nazi *Gau* was in such a constant uproar as the capital of the Reich. And if Weimar could not maintain order in Berlin, where could it do so? In many a small German town and village, in farms and in great cities, middle-class people and peasants began to wonder, not about the Nazis, but about the weak, Red-coddling state. Goebbels did not conquer Berlin, but Hitler conquered Germany.

This was the first war that Goebbels helped Hitler win, but it was merely a prelude to a far greater victory—in defeat.

Sometime late in 1929 or early in 1930 (the precise date is unclear), Dr. Goebbels, so famous in Berlin, became Nazi Reich propaganda director. He ran the campaign in the crucial 1930 Reichstag elections scheduled for September 14. By this time Goebbels was a controversial figure both within and outside the party. He was constantly embroiled with units of his own SA in a struggle for political power. He still had to live down his betrayal of his patrons, the Strasser brothers. Goebbels, with all his heroic vocabulary and cult of violence, was an intellectual among thugs, a secretive Mephisto-like figure. One former Gauleiter remembered him as a "half–French-Jesuit pupil," and recalled his "slick dialectics, his Latin attitude and diction, his wit, and his icy irony."[55] Yet even this enemy, Albert Krebs of Hamburg, unknowingly revealed another side of Goebbels in the following anecdote. A young, idealistic SA man, referring to the corrupt Reeperbahn (the Times Square of Hamburg), asked Goebbels what would happen to it after the revolution. Goebbels eloquently but forcefully told him that the Nazis would sweep it away like garbage. As he departed, the young man looked at the Little Doctor with eyes filled with tearful rapture.[56] Goebbels' forgotten words to an unknown SA fighter foreshadowed the mass "sexual climax" that seemed to erupt during and after his "Total War" speech of February 18, 1943. Enemies outside the party could never appreciate this appeal, a hold upon subordinates' emotions which Goebbels retained to the end of his life. Ernst Niekisch, an independent leftist, only saw in Goebbels "the slickness of an eel," "little substance," "theatricality." [57]

The best indication of what Goebbels had become in these years of political struggle emerges from his work as a Berlin propagandist. His style was his substance; objectivity had nothing to do with propaganda, and propaganda had nothing to do with truth. Not intellectual elevation but mass appeal was the key to journalistic success for the party. Hitler, reminiscing about the Munich-based *Völkischer Beobachter* in 1942, recalled that the "intellectual" Alfred Rosenberg was a failure as editor during the Era of Struggle because of his lofty concept of the job: "... his contempt for mankind was only increased when he found that the more he lowered the intellectual level of the journal, the more sales increased!" [58]

The foreign minister Gustav Stresemann, a German nationalist, but a moderate man, appeared thus in the pages of *Der Angriff:* "... eyes bedded carefully in cushions of fat, a smooth, rectangular forehead topped by an enormous expanse of bald head, there he stands, in the midst of his beloved Jews. The beer bottle doctor, the democratic arriviste, the risen shyster, the citizen gone wild." [59] Goebbels referred to

Unter „Brüdern". . .

„verständigt" man sich leicht

Goebbels' view of Weimar Foreign Minister Gustav Stresemann: "Among 'brothers' one hits it off immediately." Austen Chamberlain, Stresemann, and Aristide Briand are at the League of Nations in Geneva. Instead of a halo, Stresemann wears a Star of David.

CREDIT: "Der Angriff"

the German people as a nation of slaves, which ranked behind the lowest black colony in Africa. Writing in an area which contained many bourgeois German Jews, as well as newer arrivals from Poland and Russia (the *Ostjuden*), Goebbels contrasted these types, "speculators and parasites," with suffering former soldiers. "Everyone has a say in Germany, the Jews, the Frenchman, the Englishman, the League of Nations, the conscience of the world, and God knows who else, everyone except the German worker. . . . Therefore we demand the destruction of the system of exploitation!" In August 1927 Goebbels wrote: "Every blow makes us tougher and more defiant! We will not capitulate!" [60] The first sentence reflected the inspiration which Goebbels was to discover in Frederick the Great and Friedrich Nietzsche: "What does not destroy me makes me stronger," and "Praised be that which makes me tough!" The second proverb was an appeal to overcome the shame of 1918, the agony of capitulation, which to many Germans of Goebbels' generation had been a form of castration. It was a phrase used over and over again by Hitler and Goebbels until 1945, and they did not capitulate.

How cleverly Goebbels combined black humor with idealistic appeals! He cursed the "Jew speculators" and influence peddlers—Barmat, Goldschmidt, Petschek, Sklarek—and connected them with those who supported the German republic, whom Goebbels called "Schadres." This term was his comic Hebrew-sounding abbreviation for the slogan "Everyone defend the Republic!" which supporters of Weimar used as a rallying cry. Gloating about the economic crisis early in 1930, Goebbels saw 1929 as an "uprising of the nation," and foresaw this year as the time of revolution, as the *Sturmjahr*. The Führer would lead, for he embodied "character, will, ability, and luck. . . . The leader must be able to do everything." Goebbels applied this dictum to himself: "A revolutionary must be able to do everything." [61] And indeed, the Little Doctor could speak, agitate, write, organize a *Gau*, break dissident SA forces, and direct a national propaganda campaign. In this junk heap of moral confusion and social decay, Goebbels appeared a Renaissance man, and his vanity was, if not fully slaked, at least pampered. And how well he knew to build up the Hitler mythos! "When Hitler speaks, the magic effect of his words breaks down all opposition. One can only be his friend or his enemy. . . . That is the secret of his strength: his fanatic belief in the movement and thus in Germany." [62] *Das Geheimnis seiner Kraft,* an interesting phrase, was one which Goebbels himself may have inserted in slightly altered form into the script of his last film production, *Kolberg* (1945). Mystic wells of strength sustained by faith, justified in the spoken word and the epic deed—*this* idealism, at least, Goebbels could take with him into National Socialism.

The Nazi cult of death and transfiguration drew upon various traditions, some reaching back to the Napoleonic wars, but Joseph Goebbels made mighty contributions to this religion in the Era of Struggle. In 1927, on the eve of the commemoration of the fallen martyrs of the First World War, Goebbels sounded a trumpet blast of memory and hate: "We think of the two million who grow pale in the graves of Flanders and Poland. . . . We think of the soldiers of the *German* revolution and of all those who gave their lives upon the altar of the future so that Germany might be established again. . . . Retaliation! Retaliation! The day is dawning! . . . We greet you, dead ones. Germany is beginning to glow anew in the dawn of your blood . . . Let sound the march-beat of the brown battalions: for freedom! The army of the dead marches with you, you storm troop soldiers, into a better future." [63] Goebbels refined his words in the succeeding years and improved his techniques, but the thought and the appeal were the same until the end in Berlin almost eighteen years later.

Joseph Goebbels was in the vanguard of those Nazis who turned such symbols into the emotional fertilizer of the movement. When seven hundred members of the small Berlin party marched to Nürnberg for a rally in 1927, the Gauleiter wrote of the holy banner waving before them as they passed in review before the Führer. The Berlin contingent marched first because it had already gained a reputation for heroism in its battles in streets and meeting halls. Goebbels' prose still showed touches of adolescent pathos and enthusiasm in this period. By 1928–30 the mature Goebbels prose style was emerging, more taut and disciplined. No one could create martyrs with words the way Goebbels could. In 1928 he celebrated the martyr's death of the Nazi Kütemeyer, killed in ambush by a Red mob, at least according to Goebbels: "This dead man too has a right to make demands." [64] Goebbels attacked the press for saying that Kütemeyer had either drowned, or was drunk, or had committed suicide, or was killed in an accident. When Goebbels smelled the blood of a possible martyr, objective truth meant little to him. For him the dead man became a battle cry for heroism and revenge—"A dead man calls upon us to act! —as)in the case of the far more famous Nazi martyr, Horst Wessel. The comradeship of the SA was the "revitalizing strength of the movement, the living presence of the Idea. The blood of martyrs gave sustenance to the living body of the party. When Horst Wessel—the sometime student and drifter who wrote the words to the Nazi anthem "Raise the Banner!"—met with a violent death early in 1930, Goebbels' words reflected a heroic mourning and an emotional salute that showed his mastery of the martyr technique. He had Wessel die with a tranquil smile on the lips, a believer until the end, "marching in spirit in our ranks. . . . His song makes him immortal! Thus he lived, and thus he died. A wanderer between two worlds; between yesterday and tomorrow, that which was and that which is to be. A soldier of the German revolution!" [65] Goebbels memorialized a Wessel killed by the Reds; in fact, it is more likely that he was the victim in a brawl involving another thug and a prostitute. There is also the strong possibility that he was drifting away from the party in the last weeks of his life. No matter: Goebbels knew what needed to be done, and he did it well.

Much of Goebbels' agitation in 1929–32 sprang from both a need to come to terms with his own past, and the political context within which he worked. Goebbels had a "radical" past from his days with Richard Flisges down to the association with Gregor and Otto Strasser, from about 1919 through 1925. This leftism was more petit bourgeois resentment and idealization of the "Worker" as abstraction than a concrete Marxist approach to the world. Goebbels had no use for "reactionaries" and conservatives, for the comfortable bourgeoisie. He felt at home attacking Prussian reactionaries and welcomed the line in Horst Wessel's song which celebrated the martrydom of "comrades shot by the Red Front and the Reaction." Goebbels believed in 1929 that the "idols and illusions" of a bourgeois-republican Germany had been smashed. He greeted the sight of the wreckage with glee, for from it would surge the Third Reich. Goebbels accused the nationalist-minded bourgeoisie of ruining Germany, for this class paraded its patriotism in order to disguise its real passion, making money. He wrote: "We were the drummers, and they the politicians. We make up the vanguard, and they the rear. . . . A revolutionary idea . . . will make no compromises." [66]

Goebbels felt unhappy about Hitler's tactical alliance with the Nationalists, which prevailed intermittently between late 1929 and early 1933. Since he had no firm radical ideology, however, he could live with this opportunism and change his tune. Now he would speak of the unified "National Opposition" as if he had never attacked the reactionaries, just as he had praised Hitler after 1926 as if he had never attacked him as a "petit bourgeois betrayer of socialism." Goebbels retained touches of his old "radicalism" because it coincided with his own resentments and his activism, with his tough-guy image on the streets of Berlin during the Weimar days. But he was not an ideologue like Alfred Rosenberg, who had a real crisis of conscience over the Hitler-Stalin Pact of 1939. Goebbels was not a systematic thinker; his world view was expressive of his own moods and frustrations and was thus fragmented. He never tried to get outside of himself and use his reason to organize a world view or an ideology which would turn that *Weltanschauung* into a force for historical change.

In the last years before the "Seizure of Power" in 1933, Joseph Goebbels worked closely with Adolf Hitler in coordinating national propaganda. The party was now national in scope. As the Weimar economy collapsed, so did the republican political system. Yet the growth of the Nazi movement did not put Hitler in the shadows—as some conservatives had hoped. Goebbels worked at the creation of what he later called the Hitler mythos. Goebbels' propaganda was the bridge between Hitler's public personality and the broad masses. Albert Speer later recalled his reaction to Hitler before and after a Nazi rally: "Three hours later I left that same beer garden a changed person. I saw the same posters on the dirty advertising columns, but looked at them with different eyes. A blown-up picture of Adolf Hitler in a martial pose that I had regarded with a touch of amusement on my way there had suddenly lost all its ridiculousness." [67] In building the Hitler mythos, Goebbels quenched his own thirst for belief. During the war he quoted Hitler's adjutant Schmundt as enjoying ". . . the greatest happiness that a contemporary can today experience; namely, that of serving a genius." [68] In May 1942 Goebbels noted, "[Lt. Col. Scherff] has sent me a compilation of quotations on the nature of genius by great Germans. . . . Taken as a whole they almost give one the impression of an apotheosis of the Führer." [69]

Goebbels as propaganda director appealed to the workers more intensely, and he tried to root National Socialism in the Prussian glories of the past. But Hitler was the key to Goebbels' work, for he alone tied the whole incoherent Nazi mishmash of impulses, feelings, and resentments together. "Hitler over Germany"—what a propaganda coup! Hitler's flying from town to town in one day and addressing tens or hundreds of thousands, the banners and placards everywhere, the screaming *Angriff* headlines, the SA versus the Reds in the streets—all was orchestrated by Reich Propaganda Director Joseph Goebbels. As Goebbels grew greater, he did so through Hitler. In April 1932 he said of the Leader, "The true politician stands in the same relationship to his nation as does the sculptor to marble." [70] Some would say that Hitler and Goebbels were working with clay, but Goebbels successfully fostered the image of Hitler bringing together a shattered people in order to create a nation imbued with greatness and will. Goebbels' image of Hitler did not stop with the heroic aspect of his personality. His portrait was a potpourri with something for everyone. For students and intellectuals he presented Hitler, the artist and architect, torn from his studies by the need to serve his nation in 1914. For sentimentalists, he had Hitler, the man who loved children. To the workers Goebbels gave Hitler, the worker; to veterans, Hitler the Unknown Soldier of the Great

War. Where did the money to finance this propaganda orgy in 1932–33 come from? Goebbels and Hitler were highly sensitive in regard to such inquiries, but Goebbels dealt with the problem with one of his best techniques. He lied. On June 9, 1932, he solemnly declared that "We receive no means from banks, stock markets, and rich fat cats. As a workers' party we have to finance ourselves." [71] Goebbels knew that five months earlier large amounts of money from precisely such sources had begun to flow into the party's coffers.

By 1932 Goebbels had acquired total self-confidence as a speaker. He no longer addressed a few hundred supporters and hecklers in a meeting hall; he now faced tens of thousands in the Berlin Lustgarten. The mellifluous voice, the clever denunciations of the incompetent government, the ironic or "dialectical" twists of phrase, the appeals to idealism and heroism, all these characteristics made Joseph Goebbels the second most famous speaker in the Nazi hierarchy. His voice did not break (as did Hitler's) nor did he leave his audiences in a state of ecstatic exhaustion (as did Hitler), but he achieved his objective. Goebbels acquired another technique during these last years before the Seizure of Power. He manipulated the German past in such a way as to strike a responsive chord in millions of Germans longing for communion with their national heritage. It was not that Goebbels knew German history in any profound way, for he did not. Rather, he sensed the meaning of symbols from the past, symbols which evoked myths of heroism. He began to play upon these symbols in 1930, and by 1944 the orchestration of historical myth reached its crescendo. In 1932 Goebbels told his audience that the Nazis were appealing to the nation for a new war of liberation, an uprising of the people *(Volkserhebung)*. He quoted Theodore Körner, the great German poet of the wars against Napoleon: "The nation rises up, the storm breaks loose!" [72] These images evoked the grandeur of the struggle against the French between 1806 and 1814, when modern German national consciousness emerged. Goebbels cleverly contrasted such symbols with the misery of the present time: "fourteen years of deceit," hunger, and foreign domination, with miserable bourgeois, reactionary politicians, and voracious Marxists and Jews. Goebbels himself was affected by the response to his words, and he read more widely in the literature of the "Liberation" period in the years ahead.

Joseph Goebbels accommodated himself to Hitler's alliance with the reactionary Nationalists, but he did not like the situation. When the coalition of Nazis and Nationalists temporarily fell apart before the elections of November 1932, Goebbels reverted to his natural hostility towards Alfred Hugenberg and the DNVP (German National People's

Party). The break cost the Nazis votes and helped the Nationalists and the Communists. On November 6 Goebbels noted, "A government of reaction is always the pathfinder for Bolshevism." [73] When the Nationalist Reichstag deputy Schmidt-Hannover defended the conservative Nationalist position, Goebbels published an attack on the Nationalists in the *New World.* He argued that the DNVP was part of the Weimar System, that it had shared power from 1925 to 1927. Goebbels defended National Socialism against the elitist Nationalist charge that the Nazis appealed to the majority with posters and propaganda "as loud as the marketplace." "Obviously," he stated, "we desire to win over the majority; and not only that, we have the intention of conquering the entire German nation." [74] Goebbels lied when he responded to the next objection of the Nationalists. Schmidt-Hannover wanted to know where all the Nazis' money came from; Goebbels answered that it came from simple, poor SA and SS men. Goebbels bitterly attacked the German Nationalists for having allowed their minister of justice, Gürtner, to send Adolf Hitler to prison for a year in 1924. Goebbels then turned to another, hypocritical Nationalist objection to the Nazis: Now they were just another legal party. "In past years people criticized us for being illegal. Now things are turned around, and we are criticized for being legal. In the past they wanted us to be legal because they thought we could never come to power that way, and today they want us to be illegal because they think if we were, we could be excluded from gaining power." [75] This last phrase was a good example of the clever Goebbels wordplay and dialectics at work.

When the "Harzburg Front," or Nazi-Nationalist coalition, fell apart, Goebbels came close to attacking Hitler's tactical alliance with the Nationalists. He argued that the Nazis fought for the rights of the poor and that "Any asocial, reactionary policy always means the preservation of Bolshevism." [76] Goebbels believed that the Nazis were the only nationalist group which could unite all German patriots. He compared Hitler's eventual unification of German nationalism with Bismarck's unification of the German states. Using Bismarck in this manner was a calculated insult, for the Nationalists considered him their property. Goebbels repeated Hitler's belief that the collapse of 1918 was as much the result of the failure of the right as of the activism of the left, for the conservatives' asocial reactionary policies had led to class struggle and social dissolution. The Goebbels wit was at work when he rejected the Nationalist argument that the Nazis had no "heads" or trained brains and therefore could not govern. Goebbels pointed out that without these brains the Nazis had created a mass party, while the Nationalists, who presumably possessed such talent in abundance, had grown into a small party! Goebbels repeated a phrase he used in *Michael* in order to describe the appeal of National Socialism: It was a profession of faith, and that is how it could survive its early days as a "small, ridiculed, attacked, and persecuted sect." Such a party could not support the conservative chancellor, Franz von Papen, because, he said, "We see in him a chancellor without a nation." Goebbels dredged up his Nazi martyrs in an effective riposte: "These men have fought and suffered. We have buried twenty-six SA men in Berlin. Where are the dead who could witness for you? . . . Where are the blood witnesses of your party?" And then the final insult to the monarchist-minded Nationalists: "You had the opportunity of defending the emperor's crown . . . not only did you not defend the crown, you made the kaiser the only German who could not return to Germany." [77] Goebbels, who despised reactionary monarchism, was using one of his most cynical techniques, one at which he was a past master. He accused his enemies of not living up to ideals in which they supposedly believed, ideals which were repugnant to Goebbels. He taunted the Social Democrats for not being Marxist enough, and the Catholic Church of Germany for not being Christian, though he was himself neither a Marxist nor a Christian.

The main sources of Goebbels' propaganda techniques during the Weimar period were Adolf Hitler and the daily nature of the actual situation in Greater Berlin and the Reich. Yet between 1928 and 1933 Goebbels acquired some knowledge of the history and theory of propaganda, and he put this information to good use. The main source of the theory was the late–nineteenth-century French sociologist Gustave Le Bon, whose work *The Crowd* made a profound impression upon Goebbels. He admired Le Bon until the end of his life. As one of the minister's aides recorded in his diary during the Second World War: "Goebbels thinks that no one since the Frenchman Le Bon has understood the mind of the masses as well as he." [78] Le Bon was an elitist who had a scarcely veiled contempt for the masses, but he lived in an age of mass democracy, so he tried to come to grips with the emergence of an age of the people by a study of crowd motivation.[79] Le Bon's detached, ironic view of the crowd appealed to Joseph Goebbels, as did his great insights into manipulation of the masses. He wrote: "The substitution of the unconscious action of crowds for the conscious activity of individuals is one of the principal characteristics of the present age. . . . Men are ruled by ideas, sentiments, and customs . . . crowds display a singularly inferior mentality . . . The part played by the unconscious in all our acts is immense, and that played by reason very small." Goebbels combined Le Bon's contempt for the masses with his own fascination for the manipulation of the people. Le Bon stated:

"Crowds are only powerful for destruction. Their rule is always tantamount to a barbarian phase." Le Bon's words were an uncanny prophecy of Nazi rule, though Goebbels and Hitler would not have admitted this fact so openly.

Le Bon argued that successful politicians possess "an instinctive and often very sure knowledge of the character of crowds, and it is their accurate knowledge of this character that has enabled them so easily to establish their mastery." Crowds make "normal" people capable of savage actions: Goebbels exploited this insight of Le Bon to the full. Yet crowds are also conducive to great acts of heroism. Goebbels understood this even better than Le Bon, and his idealistic appeals to sacrifice and struggle had a tremendous impact upon the German nation up to 1945. Le Bon stated, "A crowd thinks in images, and the image itself immediately calls up a series of other images, having no connection with the first. . . . A crowd scarcely distinguishes between the subjective and the objective. It accepts as real the images evoked in its mind, though they most often have only a very distant relation with the observed fact." Goebbels believed in these truths, and acted upon them throughout his political career. The crowd or even the entire nation—which was just a vast crowd that could now be reached through radio, the press, and film—would respond to symbols which evoked the greatness of the past or hostile conspiracies in the present. As Hitler wrote in *Mein Kampf:* "All propaganda must be popular and its intellectual level must be adjusted to the most limited intelligence among those it is addressed to. Consequently, the greater the mass it is intended to reach, the lower its purely intellectual level will have to be. . . . The people in their overwhelming majority are so feminine by nature and attitude that sober reasoning determines their thoughts and actions far less than emotion and feeling." [80] The idealization of the abstract *Volk* in Goebbels and Hitler was the complement of a contempt for the masses as the physical embodiment of the nation.

When Goebbels manipulated the symbols of the German past, he appreciated the truth of Le Bon's great dictum: "It is not even necessary that heroes should be separated from us by centuries for their legend to be transformed by the imagination of the crowd. The transformation occasionally takes place within a few years." Goebbels helped create the myth of the Nazi Era of Struggle within ten years of the end of that period in German history. The crowd was endlessly impressionable, "like a woman," thought Le Bon, and, he believed, "An orator wishing to move a crowd must make an abusive use of violent affirmations." Le Bon brilliantly analyzed the conservatism of crowds, their fear of change. The uprooted, disoriented German masses were putty in Goebbels' hands. Crowds could be best motivated by an appeal to their collective idealism. Le Bon stated, "Personal interest is very rarely a powerful motive force with crowds, while it is almost the exclusive motive of the conduct of the isolated individual." Goebbels knew all this, but he possessed a quality which National Socialism rejected, at least in theory—the critical intellect. This made him a master manipulator of crowds, since crowds, according to Le Bon, show a "complete lack of the critical spirit." Here Goebbels' oratorical techniques differed in their effect from the speeches of Adolf Hitler. Hitler left his audiences in a frenzy, but a reading of his speeches confirms Le Bon's comment, "Astonishment is felt at times on reading certain speeches at their weakness, and yet they had an enormous influence on the crowds which listened to them." Many of Goebbels' speeches, in contrast, can still be read with interest because of their intellectual content.

Le Bon said of the masses that ". . . they turn instinctively, as the insect seeks the light, to the rhetoricians who accord them what they want. . . . Whoever can supply them with illusions is easily their master; whoever attempts to destroy their illusions is always their victim." Le Bon's racialism appealed to Goebbels, and he agreed with the Frenchman's argument that "Every race carries in its mental constitution the law of its destiny . . ." This was Goebbels' assumption when he used so many symbols of the German past in his appeals during the Era of Struggle and during the last war years: honor, sacrifice, faith, readiness for combat, love of fatherland. As Le Bon said, "It is not by reason, but most often in spite of it, that are created those sentiments that are the mainsprings of all civilization—sentiments such as honor, self-sacrifice, religious faith, patriotism, and the love of glory." Most remarkable in Le Bon's treatise were his insights into the masters of crowds. At times his descriptions seemed to foreshadow Adolf Hitler: "The leader has most often started as one of the led. He has himself been hypnotized by the idea, whose apostle he has since become." The leaders "are especially recruited from the ranks of those morbidly nervous, excitable, half-deranged persons who are bordering on madness. . . . Contempt and persecution do not affect them, or only serve to excite them the more. . . . To endow a man with faith is to multiply his strength tenfold." When Goebbels read Le Bon, he saw Adolf Hitler, the Hitler who loved to state, "He who has faith in his heart, possesses the greatest strength in the world." Goebbels felt justified by his faith in Hitler after 1926, and he preached this faith to the German people. He was thus the herald of redemption, and in the process he deified Hitler, all the while praising his "human" qualities. As he had learned from Le Bon, "The gods and men who have kept their prestige for long have never tolerated discussion. For the crowd to admire, it must be kept at a distance."

In 1928 Gauleiter Joseph Goebbels delivered a speech with the pretentious title "Knowledge and Propaganda." [81] The address tells us what he had learned about propaganda from his activities in Berlin and his study of the relevant literature. Goebbels started out from the premise that the aim of propaganda was political success, not intellectual depth. The role of the propagandist was to express in words what his audience felt in their hearts. The propagandist must feel the totality of the National Socialist idea in every aspect of his perceptions. His desire is to transmit this idea to his listeners. Party organization is necessary for the victory of an idea. Goebbels declared that the racialists had the better idea in 1918, but the Marxists triumphed because they were better organized. Goebbels believed that being in power gave a party or an idea the right to use that power. With the "Jesuit" or "French" or "Latin" logic that his enemies imputed to him, Goebbels ridiculed the Marxists for not using their power, and attacked his persecutors in the Berlin police not for harassing him, but for doing so while calling themselves democrats! "In politics power prevails, not moral claims of justice," Goebbels stated. He thus saw propaganda as a pragmatic art, the means to an end, the seizure of total power. Because methods and situations change, the propagandist must be an organizer and writer as well as a speaker. He must be able to appeal to "the broad masses of educated people" as well as to "the little man." The propagandist of the totalitarian party bears an evangelical message to the masses: "No one is willing to die for the eight-hour day. But one can die so that Germany might belong to the German people." Idealism and pragmatism were the keys to Goebbels' concept of propaganda during the Weimar period. And a large dose of cynicism: "As long as our propaganda did not lead to a *Verbot* by the Jewish police presidium, it was false, because it was not dangerous. That [decree of dissolution] is the best proof that we are dangerous."

Goebbels used Hitler's phrases about the spoken word as the key to past revolutionary movements. When listing revolutionary propagandists, Goebbels lifted some names from Le Bon and added others of his own: Christ, Mohammed, Buddha, Zarathustra, Robespierre, Danton, Mussolini, Lenin, Napoleon, Caesar, Alexander. All of these men combined great ability as speakers with a revolutionary idea and brilliant organizational talent. Goebbels might be an organizer and a speaker, but Hitler alone had created the Idea. He could advance Hitler's revolution, but could not make one of his own. As Albert Krebs, a Nazi who knew Goebbels during the Weimar era, later put it: "Goebbels possessed an infinitely acute sense of these forces and an equally vast ability to appeal to them as conscious factors and set them in motion with words. But since he himself, in my estimation, was largely lacking in such vital elementary forces, he was not in a position to establish courses and goals for himself. On the contrary, he needed the forces of others to be himself." [82]

"He needed the forces of others ..." Goebbels' ideological propaganda, in all of its aspects, always contained one theme: The Jews were to blame for everything evil, everything gone wrong. Joseph Goebbels openly bragged about the destruction of European Jewry during World War II. He was the man most responsible for the "Crystal Night" pogroms of November 1938. Hitler and Goebbels would get together to gloat about the indignities inflicted upon Jews on the streets of Berlin. Yet Goebbels was the most "Jewish" of the Nazi leaders in terms of characteristics considered "Semitic" by National Socialists. He was physically inferior, a cripple; possessed of a sharp, deceitful intellect; a maker of cabals and plots; a rationalist "Levantine" (Rosenberg). A close aide wrote, "I can see that criticism is the salt of life to him." [83] His brilliant anti-Semitic, anti-Weimar journalism contained black humor and satire reminiscent of Lenny Bruce; hence, it was "Jewish." Goebbels had approached Jewish publishers in Berlin and had studied with at least one Jew at Heidelberg. He may have at one time been engaged to a partially Jewish girl. He was the only Nazi leader to constantly use Yiddish words.[84] He envied the Jews their sense of humor, which he in part shared. His private conversation contained but a fraction of the anti-Semitism of his speeches. He was capable, when dissatisfied with their work, of telling his subordinates that the job would be done competently if he could replace them with Jews. He referred to Bolshevism as a typical example of Jewish chutzpah, and ridiculed the goy who believed that *his* Jew was decent, even if the others were bad. Goebbels used half-comic Yiddish or Hebrew terms all the time. He declared that Churchill's son-in-law was "of the Mishpocheh," or the [Jewish] clan.

There is no evidence that Paul Joseph Goebbels grew up in an anti-Jewish home. As a student after the Great War he lived in anti-Semitic environments, where he no doubt heard of and perhaps read the *Protocols of the Elders of Zion* and experienced the wave of anti-Semitism which swept much of Germany in 1918–20. By 1927 ridicule and hatred of the Berlin Jews was Goebbels' chief stock-in-trade. What had happened during the intervening years? Goebbels had met Hitler, had attached himself to him, and had begun to parody and exaggerate the Leader's anti-Semitism. This anti-Jewish sentiment had always been stronger in the Munich Party than in the Strasser, North German wing, and when Goebbels went over to Hitler, he overcompensated for his earlier anti-Hitler lapses by absorbing Hitler's great obsession, the Jews, and by building upon it. He went so far in later years as to go around saying that Strasser's mother was a Jew. Goebbels never forgot his humiliations at the hands of the "Jew press" in Berlin, a city with a large professional Jewish middle-class population as well as many poorer Jews, recent immigrants from the east. It is significant that Goebbels did not dwell so much upon these "alien" Jews as upon the successful German-Jewish bourgeoisie. He hated the bourgeois Jews more because they embodied liberal bourgeois values, and "their Jew press" had rejected his literary and journalistic work. Joseph Goebbels was hardly the model Aryan in physique. Moreover, his intellect was suspect in a party largely devoid of doctors of philosophy (at least in 1928), and his analytical cast of mind was considered "Jesuit" or "Jewish" or "Cartesian." Goebbels, the little man with the big head, projected these qualities back onto the Jews, thereby sadistically cleansing himself of the impurities. He ridiculed the Jews with the type of humor one might associate with a Jewish "stand-up" comedian, with put-down wisecracks. Behind such vindictive humor usually lies a disappointed idealist, a man who laughs out of anger at the world and its stupidity because it does not live up to his beautiful adolescent ideals.

Goebbels in many ways remained an emotional adolescent. Norman Cohn has said this about such types: "The trouble is that many men who never cease to be small boys in their emotional lives continue to see ... monsters around them, incarnated in other human beings." [85] Jean-Paul Sartre suggests that anti-Semitism is a passion among those "afraid of reasoning." It appears among those who seek what they already have, who do not wish to become anything other than what they are. It is a lower-middle-class phenomenon, urban in nature, belonging to a mentality which sees events as the result of petty intrigue rather than as the products of collective social change. Yet one may wonder if Goebbels indeed saw the Jews as monsters. His cynicism and desire to prove his love for Adolf Hitler were more important in his formation as Jew hater than was his adolescent emotional makeup. Goebbels' desire to believe in something was an extension of his earlier fantasies and ideas and thus was "adolescent," but his Jew-baiting was both political opportunism and proof of his love for the Führer, who was entirely consistent in his murderous hatred. Goebbels hated the Jews as "rationalists" because as a demagogue and agitator he had prostituted his own reason. Goebbels was not "afraid of reasoning," but he had been rejected as a scholar and journalist, so he gave up free intellectual inquiry and with it any decent sense of toleration he may have acquired before 1919. In his own life, where so much hinged on one accident, the deformity of his foot, Goebbels saw a twist of fate equivalent to the nefarious destiny that the presence of the Jews had inflicted upon Germany,[86] an internal bacillus that could only be stamped out by radical measures. When he looked at his hideous foot, he saw the Jews, and Goebbels' occasional bursts of nihilism, his hatred for life, reflected this distorted personal fate.

Yet Goebbels' hatred of the Jews was carefully cultivated. In emulating Hitler he found a role for the Jews in his own life and in the fate of Germany and Europe. Years of practical anti-Semitism led to the creation of Goebbels, the existential anti-Semite. Yet Goebbels was still a man with an alert, calculating, opportunistic brain. When it suited him to do so, he could do a favor for a foreign correspondent and obtain exit papers for a Jewish woman.[87] Goebbels' Weimar Republic career as an anti-Semite represented a synthesis of his propagandistic methods. These included vicious satire, concentration upon single individuals as symbols of the Jews, and denunciation of the Jews as being to blame for everything wrong in Germany. Goebbels' particular hate object was Bernhard Weiss, deputy police president of Greater Berlin, a German patriot and more-than-competent criminologist whom the Little Doctor turned into the Jew "Isidor," a pompous, ridiculous figure protecting shady Jews from prosecution and tormenting nationally minded Nazis. The cynic Goebbels, in bragging about this campaign in later years, readily acknowledged that he chose Weiss as his private target because he was so easy to ridicule. This was Goebbels' answer to those who asked, "Why pick on Weiss; he's a decent fellow and fought in the Great War?"

When Weiss and his supporters objected to Goebbels' attacks upon "Isidor," Goebbels struck back by a clever use of satirical metaphor. He turned Weiss into Hare, placed him in China, and portrayed a creature who got mad if one called him Hare, since he had changed his name to Wukiutschu and had grown a Chinese-style pigtail.[88] In another satire Goebbels turned Weiss into Fridolin, who, he said, "plays a role in this republic." But people call Fridolin Max when they meet him on the street, saying, "The way you look, one is called Max. What can I do about the fact that your father did not give you an appropriate name?" They continue, "Why did the Berlin police president, Dr. Bernhard Weiss, drag us before a judge just because we call him Isidor? Does he imagine that this name does not fit him? Or does it fit him all too well? Because Isidor is the description of a Jew? Yes, is being a Jew something unworthy?" Goebbels went on to portray Weiss as a "German citizen of the Jewish faith and appearance," adding the last word as a takeoff on the proud self-description of many German Jews. When Weiss objected in court to being called a Jew by the Nazis, Goebbels responded that he would be proud to acknowledge that he was a German if someone "accused" him of so being.

Goebbels commented in 1929, "The Jew is immune to all verbal injuries: bum, parasite, cheat, profiteer, that goes over him like water off a duck's back. Call him a Jew and you will note with astonishment that you have touched a raw nerve, that the Jew withdraws into himself and becomes quite small: I have been found out!" [89] Goebbels accused the Jews of projecting their qualities onto their enemies. Thus, they turned the Nazis into liars, agitators, and terrorists. Goebbels was projecting upon the Jews his own political techniques, a mark of his clever cynicism. In the end he came to believe the trash which his own opportunism and personal misery had created. Quoting Mussolini (out of context), Goebbels declared that to fight the Jew was social hygiene, a struggle against a bacillus.[90] This metaphor was one of Hitler's favorites, and Goebbels made occasional use of it until the end of the war. Goebbels also depicted the Jews as social parasites and thieves. He seized upon every Weimar financial swindle and implicated the Jews: Kutisker, Barmat, Schlesinger, Sklarek. And he charged in 1931 that Jews dominated the Prussian government of Braun and Severing, pointing to the speculators Sklarek and Helphand. No connection was too tenuous, no charge too crazy so long as Goebbels could get some journalistic mileage out of his distortions. In attacking the *Berliner Tageblatt* in 1932, Goebbels ominously used a phrase which was to recur after 1940, "The Jews are to blame," to which he occasionally appended "for everything!" [91]

2

Joseph Goebbels: The Ideologist of Total War

Joseph Goebbels avenged himself upon the Jews after 1933. At times even the vulgar pornographic newspaper *Der Stürmer* could not surpass the Little Doctor in anti-Jewish hate. The propaganda minister had this to say at the 1937 Nürnberg rally: "Look, there is the world's enemy, the destroyer of civilizations, the parasite among the peoples, the incarnation of evil, the ferment of decomposition, the demon who brings about the degeneration of mankind." [1] Despite its vehemence and its attempt to portray Goebbels as a born Jew-hater, one notices in that sentence a cynical pasting together of phrases from Julius Streicher, Hitler, and Theodor Mommsen. A year later Goebbels orchestrated the "Crystal Night" pogroms against thousands of German Jews, their synagogues, and their property. When the war broke out, Goebbels was one of the few Nazi leaders to allude openly to the destruction of the Jews. He stated in 1941: "If the Jew loses this struggle, then he has lost for good. He knows this, too. The Jews of the City [London] and the Jews in the Kremlin are hence united in this question. They play capitalism and Bolshevism, Christianity and atheism, democracy and autocracy, liberality and terror, whatever is necessary to save their necks." [2] While the battle of Moscow raged and the Jews of Poland were being herded into cramped ghettos for eventual extermination, Goebbels quoted Hitler's statement of January 30, 1939, which threatened that in the event of war, not the Aryan peoples, but the Jewish people would be destroyed. At this time Goebbels thought back to Weimar and entitled his weekly *Das*

Reich article "The Jews Are to Blame!" Goebbels, so skillful at project-ing Nazi fantasies and plans onto the Jews, declared that Germany's enemies intended to sterilize and exterminate the German nation.[3] As Dr. Robert Ley, head of the German Labor Front, publicly stated at Karlsruhe in May 1942, "It is not enough to isolate the Jewish enemy of mankind—the Jew has got to be exterminated." [4]

When Joseph Goebbels gave a speech before the German Academy in December 1941, he convincingly showed how the whole Nazi world view had one central aim: killing the Jews. Goebbels surveyed the tasks of propaganda, the work of newsreels and the press in wartime, the dangers of Bolshevism and plutocracy, only to conclude with this central theme: The Jews were to blame, and they had to die. He described a fate for them which, he said, "is hard, to be sure, but more than deserved. Pity or even regret would be out of place. . . . Now is the time for the old law, 'An eye for an eye, a tooth for a tooth.'. . . All Jews, on the basis of their birth and race, belong to an international conspiracy against National Socialist Germany." [5] Goebbels referred to Nazi measures as "hygienic prophylaxis." The Jews were to blame for the war, he insisted. Goebbels had this to say after the Battle of Stalingrad: "If we lose the war, we do not fall into the hands of some other states; we will all be annihilated by world Jewry." [6] Goebbels reiterated that the Jew used two methods to control other peoples: capitalism and Bolshevism.

As Germany's military position deteriorated early in 1943, Joseph Goebbels demanded an increase in anti-Jewish hate propaganda. It is interesting that he was afraid that intellectuals were vulnerable to the Jewish virus. This reminds one of Goebbels' fear that the same people were too sentimental in their attitudes towards America. Once again, Goebbels inverted the qualities of subject and object. He himself was fascinated by Hollywood; he too was an intellectual of sorts. At any rate, in May 1943 Goebbels noted, "There is therefore no other course left for modern nations except to exterminate the Jew. . . ." [7] Goebbels felt that he had to *prove* his anti-Semitism. Yet even during the last two years of his life, when Goebbels brought his Jewish propaganda to the outer limits of paranoid hysteria, he said relatively little about the Jews in his diary or in private conversation. Goebbels began his new campaign against the Jews in the spring of 1943. His party bulletin, "Current Information for Speakers," bemoaned the lack of public concern with the Jewish question. The issue of May 5 declared that the Nazis had to solve the Jewish issue in Europe just as they had done in Germany: "We have made the whole nation anti-Semitic." Now, use could be made of "anti-Semitic" voices in the enemy camp. "The Jews are to blame for everything!" [8] While the mass extermination of the Jews was taking

place from the Ukraine to Latvia, from Croatia to Poland, the issue of
May 18, 1943, bore the headline "Sunset of the Jews Throughout the
World!" [9] The party line now suggested that anti-Semitism was growing
in Great Britain and that the Jews themselves, in various articles and
books, had admitted that they caused wars and profited from them and
that they intended to exterminate the Germans.

Less than a month later Goebbels synthesized these points in a major
speech: "Take a look at the enemy camp. Wherever you look, Jew after
Jew. Jews behind Roosevelt as his brain trust. Jews behind Churchill,
puffing him up, Jews as agitators and hatchet men in the entire Anglo-
American-Soviet press, Jews in the dark corners of the Kremlin as the
real bearers of Bolshevism." [10]

A year later Goebbels saw the English as bleeding themselves to death
to achieve a goal which was not in their interest: the annihilation of the
German people. He asked, "Have we ever threatened the English with
anything like that?" [11] As the Allies prepared to cross the Rhine and the
Oder, Goebbels foresaw an Allied victory as the ultimate victory for
international Jewry. The acceleration of the anti-Jewish propaganda
campaign was to be proof of Goebbels' loyalty to Adolf Hitler. Indeed,
anti-Semitism was public demonstration of this attachment. And Goebbels was rewarded. He was closer to Hitler in the last months of their
lives than was any other Nazi except the ubiquitous personal secretary
and party chancellory director, Martin Bormann. Hitler made one of his
rare social calls early in 1945 when he visited the Goebbels home; he
later permitted them to join him in his bunker and share his death. But
first he paid Goebbels the compliment of naming him his successor as
chancellor. In his testament Hitler finished where he began in 1919: with
the Jews. They were the thread that tied everything together in his world
view, something which Goebbels had sensed and acted upon since 1926.
As Hitler put it in 1945, the Jews had started the war, the Allies had
served Jewish interests, the Jews had planned this destruction of the
Reich. When Hitler emitted these last groans of hateful agony, he was
repeating the lines of Goebbels' propaganda, words which themselves
represented an expression of Hitler's fundamental hatred of the Jews.[12]

Goebbels' anti-Semitism began as a more calculated political move,
reinforced by personal resentment, accelerated by his perception that it
was the key to Hitler's allegiance. How ironic—yet how logical—that
Goebbels should have loved to use Yiddish words and employ Jewish-
style wisecrack humor. His satirical bent led him to this style; had
Goebbels not become a Nazi he might have wound up in Berlin
anyway—as a comedian in nightclubs and cabarets catering to the newly
rich or newly poor around 1930. Goebbels alone among Nazi leaders

could have told a ministerial conference (as he did in 1940) that he would seize any newspaper that printed ads for antigas pills with the heading "*Mein Kampf* against flatulence." [13] While he ordered the media to play up the visit of Japanese foreign minister Matsuoka in 1941, Goebbels privately commented that the gentlemen reminded him "of a yellow ape from the primeval jungle." [14] Goebbels shared the sadistic element in his humor with Hitler. The Führer's idea of a joke was to make his terrified personal steward believe he had been drafted or to listen to the economic minister, Walther Funk, imitate Robert Ley's stutter. When a son was born to Rudolf Hess, that eccentric and mystic wanted bags of soil from each Gau. "This soil was spread under a specially built cradle. Goebbels added that he himself had thought seriously—as Gauleiter of Berlin—whether it would not be better to send a Berlin pavement stone. . . . In the end his gardener brought him a little heap from the manure bed which he then sent in a sealed official package." [15]

Goebbels, the stand-up comedian, reached the peak of his career when he attacked Winston Churchill. "When Churchill plays his Napoleon card and says, 'Nevertheless, one must always remember that the armies of Napoleon bore the spirit of freedom, of equality, of the French revolution,' it is fitting to state 'that's why England fought Napoleon.' " [16] On Churchill he commented: "He has a mind like a Nile hippo," and only a few "intellectual schmucks find anything in him." [17] This pejorative term did not exist in the public (or probably the private) vocabulary of any other Nazi leader. Goebbels stated elsewhere: "His [Churchill's] secretary recently published a book about him in the U.S. which is supposed to bring him closer to us in a human sense. There he is portrayed as an old whiskey guzzler who is so drunk in the evening that he can't stand up. He consumes, according to the report of this colleague of many years, unbelievable amounts of the most carefully selected Schnapps and food delicacies . . . He drinks from the moment he gets up, while smoking luxury cigars especially prepared for himself. . . . It does not matter to us how Mr. Churchill structures his private life, and an eternal whiskey drinker is more welcome from our viewpoint as English prime minister than a teetotaler." [18]

Early in 1942 Goebbels wrote, "Too much is too much. When one has as many credits as Mr. Churchill, he should really be forbidden by the police from putting on such a witless performance before the world as he enlightens us with explanations of his long series of his failures. A man with such many-sided talents belongs on the variety stage or in a cabaret, not among the leadership of an empire." [19] The last sentence was a good description of Goebbels himself. Two months later Goebbels played the comedian before a receptive audience that was overcome by laughter. He told his listeners that Germany was lucky to have Churchill as British premier: "We cannot imagine a *more ideal* leader from our point of view." [20] Goebbels declared to applause that if Germany had to destroy the British empire to win the war, then she was fortunate in having the aid of Churchill! Churchill "had said: 'I bring you sweat, tears, and blood.' That still holds true [laughter]." Goebbels compared Churchill to a doctor who visits a patient and says, "Yes, he will die." If he doesn't die, the relatives of the sick person will not get mad at the doctor, and if he dies, the doctor can say, "Well, didn't I tell you?" [21]

Goebbels continued his treatment of Churchill as a British "Isidor" into 1943. The personal attacks diminished as the war turned against Germany, since it was hard to ridicule Churchill, when, for example, the Royal Air Force leveled Hamburg. Moreover, as E. H. Gombrich has observed, "However effective the shouts of 'criminal' may have been during the *Blitzkrieg,* listeners must have wearied of this artificial frenzy." [22] Goebbels changed his line only reluctantly, perhaps because both the nature of his mind and the advice of Hitler caused him to wish to continue his personal attacks on the British prime minister. In April 1942 Hitler declared, "Our stations must . . . go on talking about the drunkard Churchill and the criminal Roosevelt on every possible occasion." [23] Goebbels received the message, for two weeks later he wrote of Churchill: "He is an alcoholic, a raving maniac altogether. He really is not to be taken seriously, because his policy belongs more to the pathological than to the rational world." [24] On the tenth anniversary of the Hitler Seizure of Power, Goebbels told a wildly cheering throng, "A nation which is led by Adolf Hitler does not need to take as its model a drinker like *Churchill!*" [25] Yet ten days later, Goebbels told his ministerial conference to beware of cartoons and satires that reduced the stature of Germany's enemies, since they would diminish the ability of the German people to see the enemy as he was and to combat him in the interest of German survival. Stalingrad was killing a good part of the Goebbels humor, though occasional—and less personal—flashes continued to find expression, as in late November 1943. Goebbels noted then that the English reports about a million dead from the RAF raids on Berlin were nonsense, adding, "But I don't issue a denial of these exaggerations. The sooner the English believe there's no life left in Berlin, the better for us." [26]

By this time, when the RAF was pounding much of Berlin into rubble, Joseph Goebbels had become one of the most powerful men in Germany and perhaps the most popular. His strength and prestige rose as the fortunes of Hitler's Reich sank. Few observers would have predicted Goebbels' rise in 1939 or even 1940. Never a beloved figure to other Nazi leaders, Goebbels weakened his political position in the late 1930s and gave his many enemies abundant ammunition for personal and political sniping. He did this by having a passionate love affair with a Czech actress, Lida Baarova. Magda Goebbels reacted in a predictable fashion, and in her hurt and her rage she found willing allies, among them SS Oberführer Karl Hanke, state secretary in the Propaganda Ministry. The series of international crises after 1936—the Rhineland, Austria, the Sudetenland, Danzig, the outbreak of war—also diminished Goebbels' standing because his role was a domestic one, while most Germans now saw their own fate and that of Germany in terms of foreign involvements. Goebbels' orchestration of the "Crystal Night" programs of November 9–10, 1938, was a bid for moral reinstatement, his message of love to Adolf Hitler.

Goebbels' philandering, a product of his lechery and his longing for female love, nearly cost him both his marriage and his ministry. Nazi puritans like his old enemy Alfred Rosenberg were offended by a man who used his position to force an employee (or actress partially dependent upon him for work) into his bed at the ministry. Goebbels' behavior represented a betrayal of the Führer's confidence. Rosenberg noted that Himmler told him early in 1939: "You know that a character like Goebbels is distasteful to me, but I have always refrained from passing judgement on him. But today he is the most hated man in Germany. We used to curse the Jewish managers who put sexual pressure on their employees. Today Dr. Goebbels does it. It is clear that this takes place not out of love, but because he is the propaganda minister. In the Führer's view, this was terrible. I told Himmler the story that Göring narrated to me, without mentioning him. Himmler: the cases are *legion*. . . ." Rosenberg concluded that Goebbels was "morally isolated in the party, despised." [27] He even declared that "Crystal Night" had damaged the state. Rosenberg claimed to have seen through Goebbels as early as 1927, and described him as a man without comrades, surrounded by flunkies and by people just doing their jobs. Rosenberg grudgingly admitted that Goebbels was a tough character and that the minister actually believed that he would prevail. Here, too, Rosenberg was right.

At a reception in Munich commemorating the adoption of the Nazi program in 1920, Goebbels supposedly told two guests that if Hitler did not like his life-style, he should have told him in 1924, and Goebbels would have joined another party! This type of comment has also been attributed to Dr. Robert Ley.

Goebbels' enemies accused him of financial corruption. Rosenberg reported that Goebbels tried to take over 3,200 hectares of forest land outside Berlin, an area used by Berliners for relaxation and recreation.[28] He wanted to build a private house and fence in the forest. Evidently, a courageous party official blocked Goebbels' move and threatened to go to Hitler if the Gauleiter of Greater Berlin, Goebbels, pursued his arrogant course. Rosenberg noted, "Dr. Goebbels costs us the confidence of the country ..." He quoted Hermann Göring as agreeing that Goebbels was a disaster. Now that Germany was at war, Goebbels would have to shut up. Göring told Rosenberg that Hitler agreed that Goebbels' attacks on Churchill were harmful to the German cause.[29] At a dinner in December 1939 Hitler criticized the "German Weekly Newsreel" in the presence of Goebbels, for these films lacked any feeling for the mobilization of the National Socialist nation. Hitler went on for twenty minutes, denouncing German films as, at best, patriotic but not Nazi in inspiration. Goebbels said not a word, and Hess later told Rosenberg that he himself disliked Goebbels. Rosenberg indignantly noted that Goebbels in his arrogance later dared to curse that unpleasant midday meal with the Führer's entourage.[30]

Goebbels' early wartime propaganda was not particularly successful, and some of it was disastrous. In January 1940 Max Amann, Nazi party publisher and entrepreneur, denounced Goebbels and his ministry to his face for two hours, while the Little Doctor just sat there and took it all without responding. Goebbels finally whined that he had offered Hitler his resignation a year earlier.[31] Rosenberg was still bad-mouthing Goebbels on the eve of the *Blitzkrieg* against the Low Countries and France. He came close to calling him a racial alien: "Dr. Goebbels, who speaks so much of the intellectual aspect of waging war, can perhaps hit the right note among Levantine types, but not with the German people." And Rosenberg quoted another source to indicate that Goebbels was a cultural philistine who understood nothing of film production: "Next he'll leave out the fourth act of a Shakespeare drama because it deals with a disturbing theme." [32] When Rosenberg noted these sour comments in his secret diary, a change in Goebbels' fortune was in the making. Yet as late as December 1, 1940, a shrewd foreign observer noted, "[Goebbels,] who used to be Number Three, has lost ground since the war, partly because he has been swept aside by the military and the secret police, partly because he has bungled his propaganda job at crucial moments, as when he ordered the press and radio to celebrate the victory of the *Graf Spee* the day before it was scuttled." [33]

Goebbels' fortunes did not merely change for the better because of luck or the evolving course of the Second World War. His mental attitude and the nature of propaganda in war prepared him for the

Goebbels at Hitler's Field Headquarters, 1940

activist role which became available between late 1940 and the end of
the Third Reich in 1945. Goebbels had studied the history of World War
I propaganda and he had absorbed Hitler's teachings. In *Mein Kampf*
Hitler had written in 1924:

> Ever since I have been scrutinizing political events, I have taken a
> tremendous interest in propagandist activity. . . . And I soon realized
> that the correct use of propaganda is a true art which has remained
> practically unknown to the bourgeois parties. . . . But it was not until
> the war that it became evident that immense results could be
> obtained by a correct application of propaganda. Here again,
> unfortunately, all our studying had to be done on the enemy's side,
> for the activity of our side was modest, to say the least. . . . If, as in
> propaganda for sticking out a war, the aim is to influence a whole
> people, we must avoid excessive intellectual demands on our public,
> and too much caution cannot be exerted in this direction.[34]

German nationalists after 1918 believed that the collapse of Germany had in large part been caused by the failure of German propaganda and by the success of the Allies' subversion of the German war effort. Allied propaganda directed at the German soldier was more effective than domestic German propaganda, and the Allies were also more clever in addressing their own soldiers. This belief, so dear to the German right, was closely related to the "stab in the back" legend, according to which Germany had not lost the war in 1918, but had collapsed because of subversion, both domestic and foreign. This assumption led to some important books and articles in the days of both Weimar and the Third Reich.

In his *World War Without Weapons: The Propaganda of the Western Powers against Germany, Its Effect and Counter-Measures*, Hans Thimme wrote in 1932:

> After America's entry into the war one had to foresee the eventual defeat of Germany, unless she succeeded quickly in ending the struggle by delivering a knockout blow. That the collapse of Germany's capacity to fight occurred so rapidly and in such an unfortunate context, even earlier than her enemies had expected, was due to the rapidly accelerating breakdown of Germany's will to fight.... This breakdown became more profound and widespread and took on the character of a mutiny and of self-laceration due to the decisive contribution of enemy propaganda.[35]

In late 1933 Eugen Hadamovsky, a Nazi "media expert" and a then admirer of Goebbels, published his outspoken work, *Propaganda and National Power: The Organization of Public Opinion for National Politics.* Hadamovsky, a loud, eccentric, ambitious man who later was an object of Goebbels' contempt, saw fit to dedicate his book to the new propaganda minister. He wrote of the Allies that their "... propaganda succeeded in spreading the fateful belief that by accepting voluntary defeat and by laying down arms the enemy could be brought into a mellower mood...."[36] German writers preferred to ignore another major lesson of this propaganda, namely, that it would not have made so great an impression upon Germans in 1918 if divisions in German society and war weariness had not made the German people vulnerable to the Allied message. As Harold D. Lasswell put it, "Success in propaganda of this kind depends much more upon the existence of strains and stresses in an enemy state than does success in propaganda among neutrals."[37]

German writers preferred to play up the nefarious cleverness of the

Allies. This line continued right up to the Second World War. In August 1939, for example, Hans Baehr published an unusually long article on "English World War Propaganda and the German People" in a prominent Nazi journal.[38] Baehr reiterated the views examined above. The work of these Germans in the area of propaganda theory—Hitler, Thimme, Hadamovsky, Baehr—culminated in Goebbels' cynical conclusion that propaganda has nothing to do with truth, but everything to do with victory. But Goebbels knew something else, a factor ignored by other writers. The Germany of 1918 was a class state, a nation ready to bleed and sacrifice, but a people without leadership rooted in the *Volk*. Goebbels believed that he could have saved Germany in 1917–18 had he grown up a generation earlier.[39] Even the snobbish imperial German elite would have turned to the man of the hour for salvation; *Volk* and leadership, one and together, would have overcome the hardships of the home front and the trenches, in addition to the challenge of Allied subversion. Goebbels knew that clever propaganda, rooted in the moods and symbols of the nation, could strengthen the National Socialist "people's state" and guarantee, if not victory, then at least, in his words, "never again another 1918, no capitulation, we will never give up! . . . There is nothing before which we will capitulate." [40]

Between the beginning of the war in September 1939 and the Battle of Britain late in 1940, Joseph Goebbels oscillated between two concepts of propaganda. Should the German media be facile, optimistic, and snide about the enemy, or should they convey a sense of cautious pride, realism, and toughness, even in adversity? The cheap, slick Goebbels of the *Kampfzeit* was drawn to the first approach; the more experienced, fatalistic man in his early forties believed in the second path. Goebbels' propaganda often blundered early in the war. It bragged and celebrated victories that did not exist, such as the sinking of the British carrier *Ark Royal* or the expulsion of the British from the South Atlantic late in 1939. Credibility was undermined, the armed forces were furious, the people felt deceived and let down when the British navy did not disappear.[41] Goebbels' work often had the mark of incompetence in 1939–40. In late 1940 he told the German soldier that Germany then enjoyed "advantages over England greater than any land which ever took up arms against Britain." Churchill was grasping desperately at illusions, he claimed.[42] This statement was made after Britain had survived the first great Luftwaffe challenge to the RAF. At the end of the year Goebbels predicted a fate for Churchill similar to that of Bruening of Weimar or Schuschnigg of Austria or Beneš of Czechoslovakia or Beck of Poland or Reynaud of France, all enemies of National Socialism, all in exile or disgrace.[43]

The war did not end quickly, and a wiser Dr. Goebbels seized his opportunity. No more promises of victory in sight, no more suppression of many harsh truths. Soon after the Russian campaign began, the minister was bitter about his past work. He felt that he had spoiled and misled the German nation; he had treated Germany like a pampered, protected child. Yet the optimistic strain did not totally disappear. It continued to appear in its old, crude form: Goebbels did not want to call the campaign against Russia a "crusade," because that term had negative historical overtones—the Crusaders ultimately lost. On June 22, 1941, Goebbels predicted that the Russian campaign would last eight weeks. On April 6, after all, he had correctly predicted that the Balkan campaign against Greece and Yugoslavia would be over in less than two months. While the battle for Stalingrad raged, Goebbels was so foolish as to believe that, in his words, "A catastrophe such as we faced last winter is simply out of the question this winter." [44] As Soviet victory sealed the doom of the German Sixth Army, Goebbels warned his staff against pessimistic slogans like "Fortress Europe" and "Life or Death." The German people must realize that it possessed the ability to win the war. While the Sixth Army died, Goebbels, in a phenomenally stupid ploy, told his media people to compare the Soviet offensive to the abortive Russian [Brusilov] offensive of 1916. With a touch of bravado reminiscent of the Era of Struggle, Goebbels had this to say about Churchill's reference to an Allied invasion of Europe: "They shouldn't talk so much, they should just come." [45]

Goebbels' wartime propaganda became a personal and political success only after 1940, despite occasional blunders. There were signs of this ascent in the early days of the war, but they were scattered among the boasts and the bragging, the misjudgments and the misleading communiqués. Goebbels came to believe that a nation like Germany, which had gone through a "school of suffering" since 1914, could take the truth, could accept some bad news, could measure up to the "challenge of destiny." [46] Destiny, fate, tragedy, necessity—Goebbels was becoming more detached as he became more committed to the Nazi Idea, more serious, less a slick confidence man, more a domestic leader. As early as December 1939 he told his staff, "The war which looms before us will not be child's play." [47] The enemy wished to destroy Germany. On New Year's Eve, 1940, Goebbels told the nation: "It will be a hard year and it will be well to be prepared for it. Victory will not be given to us as a gift. We must earn it ..." [48] When the Wehrmacht attacked in the west in 1940, Goebbels wanted the press to "indulge neither in exaggerated optimism nor in a wild panic" [49] when it covered the campaign. A month earlier Goebbels, disturbed about the optimism dominant in the press, had warned against reports that would result in a lessening of media credibility.[50] After France fell, Goebbels kept his feet on the ground and instructed the Reich Propaganda Central Office (RPL) of the party to make sure that party cadres realized the serious nature of the continued war against Great Britain.[51] When the Balkan campaign against Greece and Yugoslavia began in April 1941, Goebbels warned against quoting reports from Budapast which exaggerated factors favorable to the Reich.[52] A month later the minister warned the German press against making too much of a speech in the House of Commons by the former British prime minister David Lloyd-George, since its defeatist and pessimistic tone did not correspond to British public opinion and would awaken premature hopes in Germany.[53]

When the campaign against Soviet Russia began, Joseph Goebbels maintained a cautious attitude despite the reports of great German victories: "There can be no assertion that the Soviets have used up their last reserves. They have enormous numbers of soldiers at their disposal . . ." [54] Seven weeks later Goebbels believed, "It is now clear to all sober observers that this war cannot be won quickly." [55] Yet Goebbels made a disastrous mistake at this point, one reminiscent of his earlier optimistic guidelines to the media. He refused to appeal for donations of winter clothes for the soldiers fighting in Russia, believing that to issue an appeal to the German people to give up their winter clothes would "go against the grain." On Pearl Harbor day, December 7, when the great Soviet counteroffensive had already begun before Moscow, Goebbels reiterated his belief that the media should continue to display "justified optimism" about the outcome of the war, even as German propaganda became "more realistic." [56] Goebbels tossed in the "optimism" phrase in order to put across his comment about realism, which was his cautious way of telling the German people that they would have to make some more sacrifices.

The first winter in Russia loomed before the German people. Goebbels now publicly predicted a "hard and bitter struggle," and even went so far as to admit that Germany might suffer setbacks.[57] Events during the hard winter struggle on the eastern front justified him. Even when the German summer offensive was in high gear, on July 22, 1942, Goebbels warned his media not to single out for public comment enemy news reports which were pessimistic about the Allies' chances for victory, but rather to mix pessimistic and optimistic reports. The German people must not receive the impression that the Soviet armies in the south were about to crumble. Three weeks later Dr. Goebbels warned against undue optimism and predictions of a rapid conclusion to the war. In his propaganda guideline Number 40 for the week of August 18, 1942,

Goebbels admonished against a widespread tendency on the part of the public to believe that the war would soon be over. This popular optimism was based upon three factors: German successes in the U-boat war, the rapid progress of the German offensive in southern Russia, and the supposedly critical raw-material shortages in the American war economy. In September the name Stalingrad began to dominate German news reports about the eastern front. On September 21 Goebbels was a study in realism compared to Hitler's bragging and told the media that Stalingrad was not about to fall to the Germans. He ordered his men to de-emphasize the name Stalingrad in German news reports. When the Soviets had long since surrounded the German Sixth Army and were pounding it to pieces early in January, Goebbels saw his policy vindicated. He now dredged up a slogan he had earlier rejected as too pessimistic, "Life or Death." Goebbels even acknowledged the falseness of the propaganda statement "We cannot lose the war." "Of course we can lose the war if we do not mobilize and activate all our strength," he asserted.[58] This was Goebbels' way of preparing the public for the news of a total war effort.

The German people would now be told the blunt truth: victory or death. Goebbels astonished his colleagues by pointing to Churchill, formerly the butt of every foul Goebbels joke, as the man who had understood England's desperate situation in 1940, drawn the necessary conclusions, and told the truth to the British people. During the last days of the Sixth Army, Goebbels returned to Winston Churchill in 1940, but he commented that the Nazis could not use the words "blood, sweat, and tears"; they would have to invent their own slogan. One month later, after the Sixth Army had been destroyed at Stalingrad, Joseph Goebbels remarked: "I regard it as my task to train the people in the coming months to be tough. To applaud a *Blitz* campaign needs no toughness. But I have the feeling that this war will not come to an end quickly. So we must prepare our minds and hearts for bitter experiences." [59] Even when the German armies were rolling through western Russia in August 1941, Goebbels had realized that persistent Soviet resistance surprised the German people.[60] Now, in 1943, he acknowledged that the Soviets had a great reservoir of men and material, and that this meant a long war.[61]

In 1943 Joseph Goebbels was nearing the pinnacle of his power. His daily routine, however, did not change. The minister appeared at his office in the morning freshly shaved, beautifully dressed, and carefully groomed. The fresh scent of a decent cologne emanated from his skin. It was said of Goebbels that he had a perfectly tailored suit for each day of the year. However exaggerated, this observation reflected Goebbels' own concept of his office: "Today we bear the dignity of the state; we are its representatives. We are no longer rowdies who spit on the floor." [62] He was always in a bad mood in the early morning hours. Goebbels' office in the ministry on the Wilhelmsplatz was modest and businesslike; when he worked in his Berlin home on the Hermann Göring Strasse, he used a more sumptuous office. Whether at home or at the ministry, Goebbels was an autocrat; when he relaxed, he talked endlessly and brilliantly, dominating his family or his underlings with his verbal ego trips. He ate little for lunch, even at midday preferring the delights of his own words. One aide noted, "His mind is sharp, his wit blinding, and his culture all-embracing." Like his idol, Frederick the Great, Goebbels took a nap after lunch by sitting in an armchair with a cover over his knees. At five he served tea in his office, though bread and coffee were also available, and took three different pills. No matter what else he had to do or where he was, Goebbels called his wife Magda once or twice a day.

The major structured event of Goebbels' day was his late morning ministerial conference with heads of departments and representatives of other ministries. He often seized upon this occasion to express some of his strong personal opinions. At one such conference, Goebbels mentioned that he had recommended that a senior ministry official be sent to a concentration camp for half a year. It appears that the official, while drunk, ordered an equally drunk chauffeur to drive a married secretary to his home. The driver got into a terrible accident, and the secretary was killed. Goebbels forbade any ministry official to get drunk, even while off duty. When a drunk Karl Boemer, head of the foreign press division, bragged before the invasion of Russia that he would be the Gauleiter of the Crimea, word of this got back to Goebbels. He was fond of Boemer and tried to protect him, but Boemer was forced to put in a year at the front, where he died from wounds incurred in battle. Goebbels despised drinkers, whether Churchill, Ley, or people in his own entourage. Once in a while the minister would have a glass of wine, beer, or liqueur. The Gauleiters did not like to visit Goebbels' house because they could not get roaring drunk, as was their wont. Revolted by the behavior of the Gauleiters at a conference in Posen, Goebbels declared that in the future they would be limited to two cognacs per man.[63]

Goebbels was a hard, methodical worker. He mercilessly exploited the men around him, expecting intelligence, obedience, and hard work. Yet he could be a charming man. Semler admitted, "I was surprised by the charm of Goebbels' manner." [64] But more to the point was another comment: "Goebbels wants no real personal contact with his staff. He prefers them to be working machines, without personality, which can be switched on and off as he pleases." Goebbels did not believe in social intimacy between colleagues or between an official and his subordinates. He commented that he did not use the familiar *du* form either in the office or in the party.[65] One aide, von Schirmeister, commented, "The Doctor has squeezed me like a lemon, but nevertheless I would still go through fire for him." [66] Goebbels' intelligence and his selfless dedication to his work had won his loyalty. While Hitler's adjutants had major duties, those around Goebbels were lackeys, men who were to make sure that a new film was available for evening viewing or that the minister's collars and cuffs were not overly starched. Goebbels lived well, with country houses, aristocratic valets, and a large income. He supposedly had paid over three million marks for his two country homes, Schwanenwerder and Lanke, though he asserted that after his death Lanke would be handed over to the state.[67] When he was at home in the evening, Goebbels loved to watch movies, read, listen to records, or talk.

Though not close to Himmler, Goebbels cultivated good relations with the Gestapo. His favorite and successor in the ministry was Werner Naumann, a high-ranking SS officer. This collaboration with the SS was fruitful to Goebbels on many occasions. Late in 1939 Goebbels persuaded Himmler to release the astrologer Karl Ernst Krafft,[68] who had evidently predicted the November 8 attempt upon Hitler's life. Goebbels put Krafft to work editing the prophecies of Nostradamus in such a way as to demoralize the Allies. At his ministerial conferences, Goebbels used his rapport with Heinrich Himmler to demand that aides make inquiries with the Gestapo about this or that person or situation. Upon occasion, he even felt that he had the personal right to threaten arrest. A Potsdam clergyman had publicly prayed for German youth, "Which goes through life without a goal." Goebbels ordered the state secretary Leopold Gutterer to inform the gentleman that repetition would bring about a term in a concentration camp.[69] Despite this authoritarian streak, one could contradict Goebbels or bring him unwelcome news, so long as this was done privately.[70] His ministerial conferences were generally monologues, but there were times even then when Goebbels would seize upon a comment and adopt it as his own.

Goebbels had the broadest interests of any Nazi leader. He was extremely musical, loved the written and spoken word, supervised a vast propaganda apparatus, and dominated the politics of the German war effort through a weekly newspaper column. A clever and intense dilettante, Joseph Goebbels involved himself in areas which surprised observers. In June 1941 he put together the official march tune for the Russian campaign, synthesizing the work of several authors and composers. No matter how busy he was or how desperate the military situation, Goebbels continued to dictate his precious political diary. Only his trusted private stenographer, Richard Otte, and Otto Jacobs knew the details of this work, which Goebbels now dictated each day without fail (July 1941–April 1945). The diary was then typed on a "Führer type-writer" (large type), possibly for Hitler's perusal. When Goebbels had to deliver a speech, he dictated it to Otte, who wrote down the text. Sometimes Goebbels would dictate the speech to Otte over the phone, using him for rehearsal purposes.[71]

The great journalistic obsession of Goebbels' war years was the weekly newspaper *Das Reich,* the first issue of which appeared on May 26, 1940, the last, on April 15, 1945.[72] Goebbels, who often complained about the unimaginative and monotonous nature of the German press, saw this new journal as his vehicle of political and cultural influence. The newspaper would have "class" and would be influential both at home and abroad. Actually, Goebbels' interest in the paper was pretty well limited to his own weekly lead article. By 1944 the newspaper had a readership of almost one and a half million persons. As the tides of war began to run against the Reich, Goebbels found his lead article more and more difficult to write. Who could foresee what the military situation would be in a week, or even in a few days?

The last two years of the war showed a marked transformation of Goebbels' personality. He wavered between ice-cold "Prussian" military realism, tearful pathos, and a sense of tragic destiny. Goebbels' work pattern remained the same. He insisted on being warned an hour in advance if Allied bombers were heading toward Berlin, as they did so often after 1942. This would give him time to shave, dress carefully, pack a briefcase filled with paperwork, and head for the shelter under the Wilhelmsplatz or the Hermann Göring Strasse. The former shelter was indeed sumptuous and even contained some valuable paintings. After Stalingrad Goebbels became more of an insomniac, often resorting to pills to fall asleep for a few fitful hours. Like many other Berliners who spent a lot of time underground, Goebbels suffered from constant colds and grippe, with symptoms such as fever, headaches, watery eyes, and a runny nose. Hitler recommended his own physician, Dr. Morell, who was enthusiastic about pills and injections, and Morell sent Dr. Weber to the minister. Weber would give Goebbels a shot to alleviate his symptoms, and the "workaholic" minister would soon be back at his desk, whether in his office or in a bunker. Early in June 1944, Goebbels gave up cigarette smoking (he had never been an excessive smoker), but the pressures caused by D Day (June 6) led him to return to this habit around July 1.[73]

Despite these personal problems, Joseph Goebbels reached new heights of power and popularity by the summer of 1944. Alone among the major Nazi leaders, Goebbels had been calling for a total war effort since the end of 1941. The minister forced much of Nazi domestic propaganda into the mold of his own cautious realism. As the German armies were pushed back towards the Reich, as Allied bombs leveled one German town after another, the policies and attitudes of the Little Doctor appeared vindicated. Goebbels did not coin the phrase "total war" (the late General Erich Ludendorff had popularized it after 1918), but he was its apostle, indelibly associated with that concept in the eyes of the German people. Since early 1940 Goebbels had become the spokesman for sacrifice and for total war. His was the voice calling for selfless donations to the metal collection in April 1940, requesting private gifts to the state for the sake of the war economy.[74] It was the voice of Joseph Goebbels which, on the very eve of the first horrible Russian winter, belatedly appealed to the nation for donations of furs, warm clothes, socks, sweaters, and all items which might aid the fighting Wehrmacht forces ·in the east.[75] "I myself hope that during this momentous struggle I can play a political role as spiritual physician to the nation," he said.[76] Goebbels was becoming more disciplined and "military." A journalistic colleague, Hans Schwarz van Berk, described him late in 1941 as a master polemicist, a revolutionary, a man who runs the propaganda war effort the way a general's staff deals with maps of the front.[77]

After the first Russian winter Goebbels became more obsessed with the idea of total mobilization and a radicalization of the German economy. He was irritated by the bureaucratic morass surrounding Hitler that was created by Martin Bormann, Hans Lammers, and Field Marshal Keitel. Goebbels attempted to see more of Hitler at his field headquarters and he tried to cultivate Bormann, all in the interest of total war and more domestic power for himself. Hitler took little interest in the home front; he was obsessed by the daily pressures of the war, particularly in the east. Hitler's absence from the German people made the task of propaganda more difficult, since so much of it had been built around the Hitler mythos. Yet Hitler's growing remoteness also presented an opportunity, since it left a moral and political vacuum in the German public and in the Nazi leadership. Goebbels sensed the appeal of calls for selflessness and sacrifices such as he had foreseen in his novel *Michael*. People wanted a goal, they wanted to participate, they wanted to help Germany win, they wanted total war. As the bombing of German cities increased sharply in 1942–43, Goebbels saw his great chance.

Hitler never visited the affected areas; the interior ministry under the hapless Wilhelm Frick had no policy; people were confused and frightened. Goebbels accepted what appeared to be a thankless task: He received authority for caring for civilians bombed out of their homes by the RAF. As he commented, "It is a characteristic thing that during the war almost nothing has been done with domestic politics by the Ministry of the Interior. Whatever there is in Germany in domestic policy stems from me." [78] Goebbels openly told his media colleagues that London in 1940–41 was a good example to follow. The British had turned the bombed, sorely tried capital into an heroic myth, and that reinforced the will to victory of the British people. In his drive for total war Goebbels formed shifting political alliances. At times he tried to revive the party on the *Gau* level, thereby circumventing the Führer headquarters and Bormann. But as the fortunes of war turned against the Reich in the middle phase of the war (1941–43), the party grew increasingly unpopular. One reason for this decline was the widespread feeling that the party was soft-living, corrupt, not doing its part. In some places the party emblem was called the "Bird of Death," since party officials were responsible for informing relatives of a death at the front.

Stalingrad presented Goebbels with his great opportunity. He could offer total war to a people frightened by that disaster, and he could reinforce their commitment by scaring them half to death with a gruesome portrayal of the meaning of Bolshevik victory. In January Goebbels proclaimed a new labor requirement for all women between seventeen and fifty, and all men between sixteen and sixty-five years of age. Women with a child under six or two children under fourteen and women who had to support a household were exempt. But Goebbels had no power to carry out the measure; he could only recommend and announce it. Within weeks people were snickering at the biased manner in which the decree was being executed, at how limited and meaningless it was. On January 28, 1943, Goebbels commented that the German people were not losing heart, that what they wanted was a tougher prosecution of the war. He believed in shaking people up by portraying the true danger of the situation, though without any hint of despair. At the same time, Goebbels did not want total war to become a front for mindless radicalism or class warfare against the rich, nor was it to be an excuse for putting an old lady who sold flowers on the street out of business. Manpower, work, sacrifice, common sense, these were the minister's guides.

On January 30, 1943, Joseph Goebbels read to the German people Hitler's proclamation for the tenth anniversary of the Nazi Seizure of Power. The Sixth Army was in its death throes at Stalingrad. Goebbels then gave a speech of his own, a key to his total war ideology. The symbolism of total war, juxtaposed against Hitler's absence and his replacement by Goebbels, had a powerful effect upon the German public. During the next two days the German media gave tremendous play to Goebbels' speech. Some of the headlines: "Goebbels: Alarm Signal for Total War"; "What Would Have Become of Germany and Europe . . ."; "The Heroic Struggle of Our Soldiers in Stalingrad Must Persuade Everyone to Do His Utmost"; "On the Tenth Anniversary of the Seizure of Power a Glowing Profession of the Readiness to Make Sacrifices—Führer, Give Us Our Orders, We Will Follow!" "The Proclamation of Adolf Hitler: Battle until Unambiguous Victory—Neither Time nor the Force of Weapons Will Overcome the German Nation!" [79] One journalist, Hans Liebscher, referred to Goebbels as the "Speaker of the Nation," and described his speech in ecstatic terms. Goebbels' January 30 performance was a mere rehearsal for his great effort in the Sportpalast on Februrary 18. Indeed, the hunger of the German people for Goebbels' themes encouraged him to give the famous February address before a nearly hysterical throng of party loyalists.

Goebbels' speech on February 18, 1943, was the greatest of his life. He asked his audience, in many different contexts, if they wanted total war,

Joseph Goebbels' greatest wartime speech, the Sportpalast, in Berlin, February 18, 1943.

CREDIT: The Library of Congress

and each time the screaming response "Ja!" was more deafening. "Now, Nation, arise, let the storm break loose!"—Goebbels ended on this note reminiscent of the Wars of the Liberation and the struggle against the French in the time of Napoleon.[80] The German media went wild in their reaction to the speech, not merely because Dietrich and Goebbels wanted them to do so, but because radio, newsreel, and press sensed that Dr. Goebbels was responding to the hopes and fears of the German people. Some of the screaming, huge headlines on February 19: "Mass Rally in the Berlin Sportpalast: Referendum for Total War. Reich Minister Dr. Goebbels: 'We Would Rather Apply Too Much Energy Toward Securing Victory than Too Little' Yes—Yes—Yes!" "Dr. Goebbels Gave the Signal, the Nation Will Follow. 10 Questions—A Popular Referendum. Representatives of All Strata Gave a Determined Answer Yesterday!" "Dr. Goebbels in the Berlin Sportpalast: Now, Nation, Arise! Total War the Commandment of the Hour"; "Dr. Goebbels Showed the Serious Meaning of the Hour. The Will of the Whole Nation: Total Commitment to Victory. Our Hearts Are Moved. Rally of Fanatical Will to Victory in the Sportpalast"; "Total War—Total Victory. Fanatical Agreement with the Ten Questions of Dr. Goebbels." [81]

Goebbels' speech was an act of pressure upon Adolf Hitler. What followed profoundly disappointed the minister and most of the German people. Hitler made Goebbels an advisor to Bormann, Lammers, and Keitel on total war mobilization. He had no specific authority to carry out radical measures. The closing of some luxury institutions and the promulgation of easily evaded decrees were not what Goebbels had in mind as the key to total war. If one *Gau* closed its beauty parlors, rich women went to a neighboring *Gau* to have their hair set. Nazi officials generally opposed radical change. Goebbels was unique in that he actually invited the public to make suggestions for the total war effort. He received thousands of letters, most of which indicated a willingness to make sacrifices but frustration at the manner in which so-called total war was being carried out. A journalist who worked in the foreign office, and hence for Ribbentrop, Goebbels' enemy, commented in 1943 that Goebbels was the only government leader who invited the help of the public and did not shield himself from criticism behind the "Führer principle." This same man, Hans-Georg von Studnitz, noted almost two years later, "The National Socialist 'People's State' is full of ... anomalies. The preferential treatment which it accords to the few far transcends the privileges enjoyed by the ruling classes in any other country." [82]

In an important address at Heidelberg University on July 9, 1943, the propaganda minister spoke on "The Intellectual Worker in the Reich's

One day after Goebbels' "total war" speech, German newspapers were filled with headlines such as "Program of victory the vital law of every German! Commitment of the nation to total war. Faith and will are unshakable. Community of struggle." The illustration shows a German against the background of the flames of war. But he will prevail, nevertheless!

Battle of Destiny." Among his comments occurred this phrase: "The longer the war lasts, the more it makes all of us equal." [83] Goebbels did not want to break down class lines in mobilizing for total war, he wanted to *ignore* them and require each individual to make a full commitment to furthering the war effort in a relevant manner. In a pamphlet widely distributed in late 1943, "Thirty Articles of War for the German People," Goebbels spoke of the war as one forced upon the Germans, as a defensive war, the loss of which would mean the end of Germany.[84] He appealed in Article 5 to the "sense of community" of the German nation. He warned against spreading rumors and reminded his readers, "What is routine for us today will in a few decades be a source of the greatest awe among our children and grandchildren" (Article 16). "This is not a war of the regime or of the Wehrmacht, but rather a war of the nation," he concluded in Article 18. Every German was therefore to make his or her utmost effort to secure victory and the future of the nation (Article 30). "There are people who are not interested in such things. These are the materialists, who only think of their creature comforts and the pleasures of life, who have no sense of the claims of history . . ." (Article 29).

Yes, Joseph Goebbels was offering something to which the German nation responded. In October a girl living in Baden, a leader in the Nazi League of German Maidens, presented a donation of RM 65 to a local child whose father had fallen at Stalingrad. Soldiers in the field donated money to the victims of the bombings at home. When a woman sent Goebbels RM 5 for his birthday, his secretary wrote back to her indicating that all such donations went into the ministry fund for the victims of the bombings. Italian workers under the control of Albert Speer's Berlin Office of the General Building Inspector for the Capital of the Reich donated RM 650 to the survivors of the German special forces (SS) troops who had fallen in the recent "rescue" of Mussolini. They also made a greater sacrifice, donating their entire stock of Chianti to wounded German soldiers.[85] The German media played up all these moving examples of personal sacrifice. By the end of 1943, despite all this, Goebbels was profoundly depressed about the total war effort. Though impressed by the ever-increasing production figures of munitions minister Speer, Goebbels did not perceive the total war effort of which he had been the prophet. He was a prophet with high honor; his popularity reached an all-time high in 1944, but the total mobilization concept was not being realized.

Goebbels' popularity increased in part because of his public visits to bombed cities and their victims. After heavy bombing raids on Berlin in late 1943, Goebbels noted, "Women come up to me and lay their hands on me in blessing, imploring God to preserve me. All that is very

Dr. Goebbels and the unity of homeland and front. The minister received SS and Wehrmacht heroes of the Battle of Cherkassy (Russia), where in early 1944 some of the German forces broke through Soviet lines and avoided a "little Stalingrad."

CREDIT: The Suddeutscher Verlag, Munich, Germany

touching. . . . We shall never lose the war for reasons of morale." But even here the old cynicism had to flash through: "Show these people small favors, and you can wrap them around your finger." Goebbels visited the working-class Berlin area of Wedding, scene of some bloody Red-Nazi battles in 1929–32. Though uncomfortable in the presence of back-slapping familiarity, Goebbels bragged, "The people wanted to carry me on their shoulders across the square, and I had difficulty preventing it." [86] Goebbels shrewdly ordered that such incidents not be reported by the press, which did not have much credibility, but accounts were spread by word of mouth.

Goebbels knew that the key to power over a total war effort lay with Hitler. The minister wanted to raise a hundred more divisions by cleaning out rear-echelon and auxiliary units and cutting army deferments.[87] In a rather simplistic analysis he believed that a hundred new

Dr. Goebbels as the patron of bombed-out Berliners, 1944. He attends a concert in the Berlin cathedral directed by Wilhelm Furtwängler, the great German conductor, a favorite of the propaganda minister.

CREDIT: The Suddeutscher Verlag, Munich, Germany

Dr. Goebbels, spokesman for total war, comforter of the nation. The minister greets wounded flak and auxiliary defense personnel late in the war (H.I.A.)

CREDIT: The Hoover Institution on War, Revolution, and Peace, Stanford, California

divisions meant total victory. To cut through the red tape, he needed
Hitler. Goebbels visited Hitler's headquarters more often, taking with
him lists of points to discuss. Sometimes he would leave Hitler at 4:00
A.M., after having agreed to make at least one weekly visit to Headquarters. Goebbels was growing closer to Hitler, but he did not receive the
authority which he sought; indeed, in some ways these visits were
harmful to his goals, for he would come away moved and entranced,
temporarily having forgotten his original goals.

On July 17, 1944, Goebbels wistfully noted that the pendulum of war
might soon swing back to the German side.[88] New weapons were in
production. Yet total war, in its 1943–4 form, had been a failure: The
Soviets were destroying the German armies in the center of the eastern
front, the Allies had made good their invasion of Europe in the west, and
the air war had left much of Germany wrecked and defenseless. Three
days later, Colonel Stauffenberg tried to kill Adolf Hitler.

A German town, about July 21, 1944. Goebbels turns the attempt upon Hitler's
life into a propaganda spectacle intended to boost morale through moving
demonstrations of loyalty to the Führer. Women and elderly men comprised
most of these crowds, the largest of which assembled in Vienna. (H.I.A.)

The attempted revolution of armed-forces personnel and civilians aided Goebbels in his plans for total war. His own courage and nerve in the face of "treason" in Berlin further bolstered his standing with Hitler. Goebbels as a National Socialist had long been suspicious of the commitment of the Wehrmacht to the Nazi Idea, and the revolt seemed to bear out his concern. Nine months earlier, Goebbels had noted, "The English and the Americans are again talking about a generals' plot in the Reich which is to overthrow the Hitler regime. It is very suspicious that, whenever the enemy speaks of a domestic crisis in the Reich, he always thinks of the generals." [89] When he spoke to party people after the attempted coup, Goebbels emphasized that the generals did not want victory in the east, because that would be a victory for National Socialism. After the attempt of July 20, Hitler decided to vest far more domestic authority in the hands of both Himmler and Goebbels. Goebbels became plenipotentiary for waging total war on July 25, 1944. He established a planning committee under state secretary Naumann and an executive committee under Gauleiter Paul W. Wegener. Goebbels announced that total war would now have meaning, no more of this "Wash my fur but don't get me wet" business! Goebbels undertook radical measures, raised much manpower for Himmler's Home Army and panzer grenadier divisions, and later for the Volkssturm, or people's militia. Total war became less of a slogan and more of a reality—but it was too late. And Goebbels could not touch the Wehrmacht with its bloated staffs and bureaucratic, manpower-consuming mazes. As Wilfred von Oven noted, Goebbels understood the weaknesses of the Wehrmacht, but alienation and hostility between the minister and the Army made it impossible for much to be done in this crucial area.[90]

Suggestions poured into the Wilhelmsplatz telling Dr. Goebbels how to wage total war. One such letter, which exists only in part and in German translation, allegedly arrived from Benito Mussolini. One wonders if the humor was intentional. The Duce congratulated Goebbels upon his appointment and told him that if he needed more manpower for the German war effort he should look to Italy, where there were hundreds or even thousands of Germans who could better be used elsewhere! Even in the area of civilian labor mobilization Goebbels' powers were limited. He had to confront Albert Speer and the armaments ministry, Fritz Sauckel and labor allocation, various Gauleiters, armaments manufacturers, and Martin Bormann and the party chancellory. In October Goebbels and Naumann tried to convince the chancellory to initiate a new decoration for bravery on the home front. State secretary Meissner, presumably supported by Lammers and Bormann, turned down the idea, and that was the end of it. By this time Goebbels was becoming more realistic about what he could accomplish. He now told his audiences that they should hold out (a phrase he had earlier rejected as being depressingly reminiscent of the last years of World War I) and win time until new divisions and new weapons were put into action. Here Goebbels indirectly touched upon one of the more controversial questions of his late war propaganda, the problem of "miracle weapons" and "retaliation" *(Vergeltung)* against the enemy for the destruction of German cities.[91]

Goebbels could not blame anyone else for raising false hopes for re-taliation in the German people, though he later tried to do so. As early as May 1942, the minister, speaking through state secretary Gutterer, ordered that the successes of the German retaliation attacks against England be played up more strongly in the German press. This represented a change in context from Goebbels' use of the term "retaliation" in 1940, when he had felt constrained by world opinion to justify German attacks on London by pointing to English attacks on Hamburg.[92] Germans cheered loudly when Goebbels, reacting on their behalf to the attacks on German cities in the hard year 1943, promised revenge while bluntly admitting that bombed-out Germans were having a hard time surviving. He screamed out to stormy applause, *"One day will come the hour of retaliation!"* A few months later Goebbels promised that retaliation would burst over England *"like a raving demon."*[93] By visiting bombed cities and civilians, by becoming the heroic spokesman for feelings of hate and revenge, Goebbels further increased his popularity. Göring had lost most of his 1940 luster as one German city after another was destroyed from the air. When Goebbels went to the bombed town of Dortmund he spoke of an "armada of revenge" and his listeners went wild with enthusiasm.[94] Goebbels summed up the feelings of many when he described how moved he had been by this notice, posted on a wall of a badly bombed town: "Arthur, dear Arthur, I am alive with both children and am looking for you. Where are you?"[95] Solidarity with the victims and the promise of revenge dominated much of Goebbels' work and talk late in 1943.

But retaliation did not occur. The German armies were being pushed westward in Russia at an alarming rate. In the summer and autumn of that year, more cities (Hamburg the most drastic case, then Berlin) fell victim to the "terror attacks." False hopes had been raised. Goebbels now did a complete about-face and ordered the press and radio to avoid talk of retaliation. His reason told him he had made a mistake, but when he came back from a visit to Hitler's headquarters early in January 1944, he was once again buoyed by hopes for new "wonder weapons."[96] Goebbels ardently wished for this retaliation, for despite his better judgment he had often told bombed-out civilians that retaliation would occur. He had pledged his word; he would be dishonored if retaliation did not occur.[97] Goebbels showed what his concept of honor was right before D Day when he told a hysterical crowd, ". . . naturally the German Wehrmacht and the German police *do not exist* to hold the German public in *check if it acts against such murderers;* that is not their task!" [98] Goebbels was referring to the lynching of parachuted Allied bomber pilots. All the months of disappointment had so lowered the value of "retaliation" that the only outlet was murdering a few prisoners of war.

Soon after D Day, pilotless German buzz bombs were launched against Britain from bases in Holland and Belgium. Was this the beginning of the great retaliation? Goebbels himself suggested the name V1 (Vergeltung-1) for the bombs, and Hitler approved the designation. Yet Goebbels could not be sure about the scope and effect of the bombs (actually too limited and too late), so he ordered the press to avoid the term "retaliation." The eyes of the nation were riveted upon the new front in France, and it would make no sense to say that Britain was about to collapse because of the V1s if the German people saw Allied armies heading towards the Reich. The OKW communiqué was modest and did not mention retaliation. Goebbels and Hitler appeared to agree that it was best to avoid the term. Then how did it happen that an early-afternoon edition of the *Berliner Nachtausgabe* contained in June 1944 an article by the famous Nazi journalist Otto Kriegk which began with the words "The day for which eighty million Germans have been waiting with such desire is here . . ."? Kriegk spoke of the V1s as the realization of retaliation. Goebbels went into a rage, then finally realized that Otto Dietrich had given his daily instruction to the press in such a way as to encourage formulations such as that of Otto Kriegk.[99] Goebbels wanted to have Kriegk arrested for treason, but since Dietrich was the real culprit, little could be done. Raving to Wilfred von Oven, one of his press officers, Goebbels made one of his better puns, "Nie Wieder Kriegk!" One of the slogans of pacifists in the Weimar Republic was "Nie Wieder Krieg!" ("Never again war!"). Goebbels ordered his leading radio commentator, Hans Fritzsche, to counteract any overly optimistic impressions that the press may have left with the German people. The war would not be won tomorrow. Yet it was Goebbels himself who had built up the great hopes for retaliation in 1943; so, much of the blame was his. Goebbels' relations with Reich Press Chief Otto Dietrich were symptomatic of another factor limiting his success in waging a truly total war: his disastrous or unstable relationships with other Nazi leaders.

When war broke out in 1939, Hitler took less interest in the daily domestic workings of the Reich government. He tended to delegate authority in this area, often in such a way as to encourage competition and even chaos among his colleagues. On August 30 Hitler had established a ministerial Council for the Defense of the Reich.[100] It included as permanent members Frick, Göring, Funk, Keitel, Lammers, and Hess. This group itself promulgated little legislation, Göring pleading the pressures of war as an excuse. By 1942, sensing the void in leadership on the home front, Joseph Goebbels believed that a revival of the council could augment his own power. He might become a kind of "chancellor for total war." Hess was gone, Keitel involved in the daily conduct of the war, Lammers an increasingly powerless bureaucrat, and Frick a nonentity who would soon lose his cabinet post as minister of the interior. Goebbels had good relations with the economics minister Funk, who had been an employee of his ministry before the war. The key figure in Goebbels' scheme was Hermann Göring. It took some time for Goebbels to realize that Martin Bormann could make or break his plans. The personal secretary of the Führer had control over all party matters and correspondence intended for Hitler. Eventually, Goebbels realized

Hermann Göring with Albert Speer, inspecting some architectural models (1941). From Göring's photograph albums.

that the secretary of the Führer had taken control of the government, but through much of 1943 he spun his conspiratorial webs without understanding that Martin Bormann was a very big spider. By 1944 Goebbels had learned to work with Bormann when necessary.

Joseph Goebbels believed that Albert Speer and Herman Göring were vital to the success of the total war concept. By March 1943 Speer had been armaments and munitions ministers for a year, and his policies were achieving striking results in arms production. Goebbels bragged, "Speer is entirely my man," and mobilized him to bring Göring into the total war camp.[101] But no Nazi leader was another leader's man; they all belonged to Hitler, and he had set up their offices in such a way as to guarantee rivalry and friction. Despite Magda Goebbels' dislike of Speer ("He walks over corpses"),[102] Goebbels was impressed by the competence of the arrogant, cool young architect, long a Hitler favorite. Speer believed in quality as well as quantity in armaments production and he was less concerned with sheer numbers, whether of planes or of divisions, than was Goebbels. Goebbels perceived that Speer was totally dependent upon an often-distracted Hitler, that he was not an "Old Fighter" or a relatively invulnerable Nazi eminence such as Himmler, Ley, or Göring. Goebbels was jealous of Speer's closeness to Hitler, based upon the Führer's delight in the architect's profession and the almost fatherly friendship which Hitler lavished upon the munitions minister. By 1944 Speer was increasingly isolated, even from Hitler, for the fortunes of war had not vindicated his policies. He became the victim of conspiracies in which Bormann, Himmler, and Goebbels participated. Economics minister Funk later told Speer, ". . . he [Goebbels] turned openly against you, in the Führer's headquarters, at meetings of Gauleiters, everywhere." [103] In October Goebbels commented that he no longer believed a word Speer said. Goebbels, disappointed by the failure of "retaliation," blamed Speer for the lack of truly effective miracle weapons.

How effective could total war be if Goebbels could no longer work with Albert Speer? Until early 1943 Goebbels had underestimated Speer's importance, just as he overestimated that of Hermann Göring until early 1944. Goebbels believed that despite the loss of the Battle of Britain, the failure to adequately supply the Sixth Army at Stalingrad, and the inability of the Luftwaffe to defend German cities, Göring still retained great popularity and potential political power. Göring was tired and apathetic. Goebbels commented, "It is therefore all the more necessary to get him straightened out. For he is a first-rate factor of authority." And early in March 1943 Goebbels noted, ". . . it is equally essential that we succeed somehow in making up for the lack of leadership in our domestic and foreign policy. One must not bother the Führer with everything." [104] What Goebbels failed to appreciate was that this "lack" existed with the full approbation of Hitler, and if there was any gap to be filled, it would be filled by Martin Bormann, not by the increasingly disgraced Hermann Göring. "Göring is unfortunately somewhat inactive and resigned, and it will take a lot of work to gear him up again ... ," Goebbels stated.[105] He believed that he had good allies in Robert Ley, Walther Funk, and Albert Speer. He continued to attempt to breathe new life into Göring's image and authority, building him up in the "German Weekly Newsreel," consulting with him, flattering him. Goebbels believed that if these men could work together, he would have great domestic authority to wage total war, to mobilize the whole society. In November Goebbels made this comment: "Göring, thank God, is showing himself oftener in public. I am very happy that he is again in evidence and that thereby his authority is gradually being strengthened." [106]

By 1944 Goebbels realized that his hopes in Göring had been misplaced. That Goebbels held such hopes at all was a tribute to his vanity and to his powers of self-deception. He now saw Göring for what he was: incompetent, apathetic, a soft-living, powdered, and perfumed shell of a man, a total failure. Goebbels now had contempt for Göring, but it was contempt tinged with pity and regret, for the fall of Hermann Göring was closely related to the fall of National Socialism and the Third Reich. Goebbels reminisced with affection about their days together in the Era of Struggle.[107] He continued to see sympathetic qualities in Göring, such as the Reich marshal's considerate behavior when Magda's son Harald Quandt was reported captured by the Canadians. Goebbels despised gluttony, but he chuckled when he remembered Göring's exploits around 1930, when the former fighter pilot would buy enormous amounts of chocolates and other candies before boarding a train for a campaign trip. "Decent," "honorable," "human," these were some of the adjectives that Goebbels continued to apply to the fallen Hermann Göring until 1945.

Joseph Goebbels had no such patience when he thought of Alfred Rosenberg, the Nazi ideologue and minister for the occupied eastern territories. Goebbels considered Rosenberg a crackpot, a man whose policies in Russia had harmed the German war effort. The bad blood between Rosenberg and Goebbels went back to at least 1934. Rosenberg was head of the Nazi Foreign Policy Office, and he believed that the anti-Semitic policies of Goebbels' ministry had harmed Anglo-German relations. Rosenberg, viewing himself as a deep thinker, resented Goebbels' role as president of the Reich Chamber of Culture. He felt that Goebbels' speeches were slippery, without structure. Rosenberg coveted that czardom over cultural affairs which the upstart Goebbels exercised. In his diary Rosenberg constantly sniped at Goebbels, portraying him as a sniveling beggar who had latched on to an overly indulgent Hitler. Rosenberg, along with other old Nazis, was repelled by Goebbels' self-serving attacks upon his old patrons, the Strasser brothers. Rosenberg spoke of the great reaction to a speech he had delivered in Eisenach: "Only one man did not react: Dr. Goebbels. I understand that, he *cannot* do otherwise." [108] Rosenberg considered Goebbels a catastrophe for the Nazi movement and for German foreign policy, believing he had exchanged his role as a Reich minister for that of a "suburban agitator."

When Goebbels was in deep trouble on the eve of the war over the Lida Baarova affair, Rosenberg let it be known that he was available as a replacement for the Little Doctor. Goebbels' reaction to Rosenberg was compounded of contempt and some grudging admiration. Even in the Weimar days Goebbels referred to Rosenberg as "almost" Rosenberg: "almost adequate as a scholar, as a journalist, as a politician, but just almost." [109] In 1942 Goebbels noted that Rosenberg was "A good theoretician but no practitioner; he is completely at sea as far as organization is concerned, besides has rather childish ideas." [110] Goebbels resented Rosenberg's humorless pseudo profundity: He was a shrewd judge of the written word, and it is surprising that he had something positive to say about Rosenberg's murky prose and plagiarized "depth": "He can write, that one has to grant him. Among us National Socialists who disseminate our idea with the pen, he is without doubt the most capable." [111] But almost in the same breath Goebbels lumped Rosenberg with Ley and Ribbentrop as "beauty marks" of leadership, inmates of an insane asylum, crazy men. He commented that he could not understand how the Führer could leave such an "obstreperous nincompoop" in his job.

Dr. Robert Ley, Reich organization leader of the party (ROL) and head of the German Labor Front (DAF), was a man whose personal and political fortunes were in eclipse by 1943. Goebbels thought that Ley, because of his status as an "Old Fighter" and holder of two important offices, might be of use in the total war effort. At this point, in fact, Ley was of little use to anyone. An alcoholic, incoherent much of the time, contemptible personally in Goebbels' eyes, a recent widower because of his wife's suicide, Robert Ley had lost his power in the party to Martin Bormann, and his role in the German Labor Front meant less in war than in peace. Goebbels had seen through Ley years earlier, as in 1940 when he had warned his ministerial conferees against disseminating Ley's "exaggerated social promises." [112] Goebbels thought that Ley could be useful in circumventing Bormann's growing authority: "Ley weeps on my shoulder about the inactivity of the party, which is a thorn in his flesh. . . . Bormann is not a man of the people." [113] Goebbels was nevertheless so repelled by Ley's crudeness that he forbade admitting him to his residence on the Hermann Göring Strasse. Goebbels noted with satisfaction in March 1943 that Hitler was going to forbid drinking at any party function for the duration of the war.

Ley had taken over *Der Angriff* and turned it into the voice of the German Labor Front. He published eccentric articles which, much to his fury, Goebbels was powerless to censor: "The minute he opens his mouth he gets his foot into it," Goebbels said. Yet however much his power had declined, Robert Ley remained a Nazi big shot. In the structure of the Third Reich, with its competing empires and feuding personalities, this gave him a degree of autonomy. "A madman speaks!" was Goebbels' comment about the Ley article "Jewry will die, Moscow must burn, Germany will conquer." [114] After the 1944 attempt on Hitler's life, Ley screamed out in a factory that the mother of the traitor Stauffenberg was an "English count" (sic). By 1945 Ley was half dead from drink and brain damage, now reduced to preparing for guerrilla warfare against the Allies, suggesting that the Germans confront the Russians with their bare bodies and without weapons. Without power, a mental and physical wreck, Ley somehow wormed his way back into Hitler's confidence in 1945 by his show of pathetic loyalty. He was of no use to Joseph Goebbels.

When Goebbels organized his total war propaganda, he felt that the biggest thorn in his side was Dr. Otto Dietrich, Reich press chief and state secretary in the propaganda ministry. Unlike Goebbels, Dietrich lived in Hitler's headquarters. Until at least the middle of 1944 Dietrich at times had more authority over the headlines of the German newspapers than did Goebbels. Dietrich's voice was that of Adolf Hitler, so Goebbels had to be cautious about contradicting the "daily slogan" which Dietrich's man, Helmut Sündermann, gave to the German press. Goebbels saw Dietrich as a clever, opportunistic worm, devoid of real intelligence, disloyal, a disaster in his job. Two of Dietrich's blunders especially enraged Goebbels. In October 1941 Dietrich told the German press to print headlines indicating that the campaign in Russia had been decided. Actually, the slogans came from Hitler, who wanted to reassure the German people that a fighting winter in Russia would be unnecessary. Hitler also saw the victory message as a warning to the United States to stay out of the war. Goebbels probably knew all this, but he could not blame Hitler for the mistake, so he blasted Dietrich. As Semler commented, "Goebbels thinks we have seen today the biggest propaganda blunder of the war." [115] By this time, after all, Goebbels was cautioning the nation against undue optimism. Late in 1943 Goebbels and Dietrich were supposedly working in harmony. The minister still liked to think that he could have Dietrich fired at any time, but this was a sign of his self-delusion. Hitler knew how to deal with Goebbels, and he solemnly explained to him that he would get rid of Dietrich but the man was so incompetent that it would be impossible to find another position for him. This assuaged Goebbels' ego—and Dietrich stayed by Hitler's side. When Dietrich dared to bring up the "retaliation" canard again in June 1944, Goebbels went wild with rage.[116] He was still raving in March 1945 about Dietrich's "inferiority complex, his envy, his sick ambition." Hitler fired Dietrich at the end of the month, when the Third Reich had four weeks more to live.

During the last two years of the war Joseph Goebbels became obsessed with the hope that Germany might arrive at a compromise peace or that the Allied coalition would fall apart. In his propaganda the minister portrayed Western capitalism and Eastern Bolshevism as two sides of the same coin. He followed Hitler in urging the German people to fight on to victory in east and west. Privately, Goebbels felt frustrated

Otto Dietrich, Reich press chief of the NSDAP and state secretary in the propaganda ministry.

by the lack of creative Nazi diplomacy. More and more he fantasized about the Era of Struggle, about how a seemingly hopeless situation had turned around in favor of the Nazis during the years 1926–33. Goebbels had been afraid of the two-front war which engulfed Germany in 1941–45. Hence in April 1941 he was elated by the prospect of continued peace with Stalin.[117] By 1943 Goebbels sensed catastrophe in the air, especially in the light of Stalingrad, the fall of Tunis, and the collapse of the fascist regime in Italy. The air war was becoming disastrous for Germany, and the Soviets were moving westward at an alarming rate in the Ukraine. Goebbels noted that Germany could not stand this two-front war much longer. "I pointed out to the Führer that in 1933, too, we did not attain power by making absolute demands," he stated.[118] But Hitler had no intention of making a compromise peace with Russia, even in 1943–44. Goebbels wistfully thought otherwise. Stalin could decide upon such a course in a moment, whereas the Western politicians were accountable to their parliament or congress. By early 1944 Goebbels thought intensely about a peace with the Soviet Union which would leave German divisions free to repel an invasion of France. Goebbels criticized German diplomacy for not realizing that peace with the Soviet Union was vital to Germany's confrontation with Britain. Now, Germany was "bleeding to death in the east" and losing the air war at home.

The Anglo-American landings in Italy, in July–September 1943, had made the question of a compromise peace an urgent one in Goebbels' eyes. "The problem begins to present itself as to which side we ought to turn to first—the Muscovite or the Ango-American," he wrote.[119] Goebbels, unlike Hitler, felt that it would be easier to make a deal with Stalin than with the "romantic" adventurer Churchill. The British leadership that might follow the fall of Churchill could even be worse (Anthony Eden?). Churchill wanted the Germans and the Russians to bleed each other to death so that he could dominate Europe. It was true that he was an old anti-Bolshevik, and his collaboration with Moscow only a matter of expediency, but Goebbels was dubious about any immediate change in British policy. Hitler believed that Churchill was guided by hatred, not by reason. Hitler knew that his own compulsion to divide up Russia and destroy Bolshevism made a deal with Stalin impossible. In late September Goebbels told Hitler that Germany could not win this two-front war.[120] Goebbels at times felt that Germany would receive better terms from democratic Britain than from Communist Russia. But he was realistic about the limits of Germany's freedom to negotiate. At times the old "radical" Goebbels waxed almost lyrical about Stalin, admiring him for killing off much of the officer corps of the Red Army in the late 1930s and for replacing those purged with fanatical young officers with total faith in Stalin and victory.[121]

In the midst of this frightening situation, Goebbels deluded himself with a peculiarly optimistic analysis. He concluded that the Grand Alliance formed to defeat the Reich would fall apart as the Allies got closer to their goal. If Germany disappeared—and Goebbels fervently believed that this was an Allied war aim—east and west would clash in a third world war. They would soon realize this; hence, Germany would hold the balance of power. Following a thought to which Hitler remained loyal until his death, Goebbels told an aide that Germany had to fight hard on all sides while the contradictions in the Allied camp rose to fever pitch. Goebbels admitted that one aim of his lead article in *Das Reich* was the transformation of British policy; yet he looked mainly to Russia. Goebbels knew that all of eastern Europe would fall to the Soviet Union in a compromise peace.[122] And in his heart Goebbels must have realized that Hitler would never agree to such a plan.

Early in 1944 Goebbels believed that there would be no salvation for Germany, no compromise peace, until after an attempted Allied invasion in the west. If the landings were beaten back, all sorts of possibilities opened up. If they succeeded, however, Germany might be destroyed by the Grand Alliance. By March no invasion attempt had occurred, and Goebbels grew increasingly frustrated with the obstinate British. Had they not gone to war to preserve the balance of power? Then why turn Europe over to Bolshevik Russia? Germany, Goebbels continued, had made no demands which threatened the vital interests of the British empire. Why did England want to bleed to death in Europe, hand it over to the Reds, and lose her empire to America? In a shrewd commentary Goebbels acknowledged that Churchill, though not beloved by his people, was supported by them for reasons of self-interest. The minister predicted that this support might be withdrawn after the war. Goebbels clung to the hope that the British would belatedly realize that the Bolsheviks, who were nearing Poland and Rumania, were a real threat to British interests. If only Churchill would come down with a mortal case of pneumonia . . .

Goebbels knew that German diplomacy had reached a dead end. The Reich was no longer master of its own destiny. But even if an event occurred which presented new opportunities to Germany, the nation did not have a foreign minister with the ability to seize upon such a last chance. As Goebbels stated, "Our foreign policy today has become completely sterile and frozen." [123] Goebbels himself would have liked to have become foreign minister, chancellor, total war commissar, and minister for the occupied eastern territories, at least in the sense of setting broad policy. All of this was not merely the result of personal ambition, but was caused by his frustration at seeing the way in which

Ribbentrop, Rosenberg, and Bormann were leading the Reich to ruin. Even Hitler did not escape Goebbels' criticism. But there was no one whom the minister despised more than Joachim von Ribbentrop. Ribbentrop had few defenders in the last years of the Third Reich, but he had one who counted—Adolf Hitler. Albert Speer remembered an early encounter with Ribbentrop: "This tall, fair-haired man, who always held his head very high, struck me as arrogant and inaccessible." Ribbentrop's own mother-in-law referred to him as "her dumbest son-in-law." [124] The competition between Goebbels and Ribbentrop extended to the absurd. They ran competitive dining clubs for the foreign press, Ribbentrop supporting the Foreign Press Club, Goebbels the Foreign Club.[125] Goebbels had this to say late in 1943: "If Ribbentrop is as clever in his foreign policy as he is toward his colleagues . . . , I can well understand why we don't achieve any notable successes in our dealings with foreign nations." [126] In the following March Ribbentrop became a "blockhead." Goebbels never forgave Ribbentrop for their violent dispute in 1941 over the question of authority in the field of foreign propaganda. Hitler had forced both men to compromise, but the peace was a compulsory, uneven one. When Goebbels wrote long memos on foreign policy, Bormann suppressed them before they went through to Hitler. Hitler did not want to change the leadership of the Foreign Office, at any rate, and Bormann knew this. Hitler had a much more profound understanding of Germany's position after 1942 than did Goebbels. Hitler really did not believe that anything but force would end the war, one way or the other.

After the Allies landed in France on June 6, 1944, Goebbels and Hitler seized at the following straw.[127] The capitalist West was basically weaker than Bolshevik Russia, more decadent. If the Western armies were driven back into the Channel with bloody losses, they would be willing to negotiate with the Nazis, especially since the Bolsheviks were pouring into eastern Poland. The new VIs, raining ruin upon London, would help bring the British to their senses. Goebbels believed that the British working class was turning against Churchill. By July 15 he was thinking in terms of holding a line in northern France, not of hurling the Allies back into the sea. Nevertheless, if that position could be held, perhaps other possibilities would turn into reality, especially if Germany was able to stall the Red offensive against Army Group Center. On June 10 Hitler and Goebbels thought that the gradual Red advance played into their hands in terms of bringing the West to "its senses." After June 22 the Bolsheviks smashed through the center of the German front deep into formerly Polish territory. By July 15 Goebbels knew that the deadly crisis in the east would have to be mastered if Germany was to survive at all. He created new delusions in an ever-shifting scheme to justify his wishful thinking and enable the Nazi regime to survive.

Early in September Goebbels came to the conclusion that the British must have recognized the Soviet threat. The reason that the Churchill government did not change its policy was the inherent weakness of the executive power in a parliamentary system. Goebbels was beginning to change his opinion of Winston Churchill, a man who might alter his course if he could ignore parliament. Within four months Goebbels would marvel at the old British prime minister, who even journeyed to Athens when turmoil there so necessitated. What a contrast with the isolated nature of the German leadership! Using a sadomasochistic analogy, Goebbels fervently hoped that the ponderousness of the parlimentary system would not prevent the British from reacting more rapidly to the moves of the Kremlin than they had to the expansion of Nazi Germany between 1936 and 1939! With a characteristic touch of vanity, Goebbels believed the rumor that Churchill might negotiate with him. Yet Churchill remained committed to the formula of unconditional surrender first enunciated by President Roosevelt in January 1943, and by the end of September 1944 Goebbels despaired of any change in British policy. Churchill was a "blind hater"; even worse, he did not seem ready to die or to be overthrown. "I lean more and more to the viewpoint that we would have a better chance to reach an agreement with Russia," stated Goebbels.[128]

In December 1944 Hitler launched his ill-fated Ardennes offensive, the Battle of the Bulge. His aim was to strike a hard blow at the Western Allied armies, thereby buying time and bringing them to their senses. They then might join him in a war against Bolshevism or at the very least cease their offensives against the Reich. When this last Hitler offensive failed, Goebbels ceased to believe in Hitler's political strategy. Hitler held to his course until his death, calling for resistance in both east and west. Goebbels changed his view and in early February recommended that Germany use all her forces against the Russians, believing it no longer made sense politically to resist the Western powers. Goebbels had an interesting conversation with Himmler late in February. The two men, never close, spoke in two different ways. Himmler, who was thinking of "treason" (negotiations with the West behind Hitler's back), expressed himself cautiously, while Goebbels, who disagreed with Hitler's continued war against the West but never considered "betraying" the Führer, spoke bluntly and honestly. Goebbels argued that Germany's only remaining gamble was to let the Western Allies into the Reich while the Nazis continued to struggle against the Bolsheviks. Himmler coyly commented on the poor state of Hitler's health, only to hear Goebbels respond that in the wreck of the body lived a "fiery spirit." [129] Himmler reflected pressures upon him from within the SS, from men such as Walter Schellenberg and Gottlob Berger, who believed that "The ultimate aim of political leadership is to raise a people up, not to bring it to a proud and heroic end." [130]

When speaking to more common personalities, such as German journalists, Goebbels kept up the Nazi front. As late as April 1, 1945, one editor commented, "Goebbels holds to the view that the nearer the military debacle of Germany, the stronger her political position, for the Allies will fall apart in proportion as the Russians advance westward." [131] Privately, Goebbels had long since recognized that Hitler's policy of holding out in the west *and* the east was catastrophic. On April 22 an excited Goebbels reported to Hitler that the West was joining the Nazis in an offensive against the Russians. More wishful thinking: Goebbels hoped to interest Hitler in a plan which would represent a complete turnabout in German policy. The German armies in the west would cease firing, he said, and "We will see if the Americans shoot us in the back in these circumstances." [132] Nothing came of the plan, and within nine days both Hitler and Goebbels were dead.

When Goebbels committed suicide on May 1, 1945, a myth died with him. In the last years of the war Goebbels had consoled himself and his listeners with two intellectual formulations. The first concerned the collapse of the Allied coalition, a compromise peace, and the salvation of Nazi Germany. The second was based upon a beloved historical analogy. Hitler had set the tone for this in 1941, on the eve of the first Russian winter: "Our present struggle is merely a continuation, on the international level, of the struggle we waged on the national level." [133] Goebbels was convinced that the war against plutocracy and Bolshevism was a replay of the struggle of the Nazis in the Weimar Republic when they fought both the Red Front and the Reaction, and won. So much heroism, so much despair, in those years of the *Kampfzeit,* or Era of Struggle, not least of all in the Little Doctor himself: Just as the hopeless political situation of 1923 or 1927 or late 1932 had culminated in the Seizure of Power, so the military debacles of 1944 would ultimately be transformed into final victory. The same foundations for victory were present: fanatical faith and the Führer. In Goebbels' words, "How many of us, for example, thought that after November 9, 1923 [the date of the failed "Beer Hall Putsch"]: Yes, everything is lost. But *despite* that there was a way out." [134] Fourteen years of struggle against Weimar and almost seven years of peaceful development had made National Socialism equal to the task of winning the war, the minister believed.

Late in 1940 Goebbels ordered the press to compare the present situation of uneasy anticipation with the frustrating period of waiting that took place late in 1932 when the Nazis lost seats in the Reichstag and were troubled by internal dissension and "treason." When the British press spoke of war aims of a progressive nature, Goebbels contemptuously dismissed this as an attempt to steal the slogans of the Nazi "people's community." He compared the behavior of the London *Times* to that of the German Nationalist reactionaries in 1932: They too could do little except steal the slogans of the Nazis. If Hitler seemed increasingly isolated and headstrong at the end of 1941, at the beginning of the terrible Russian winter, one need only recall late 1932. If Hitler had listened then to the mood of the party, everything would have fallen apart. Early in 1942, when Britain had lost Singapore to the Japanese but showed no sign of yielding to Hitler, Goebbels compared the British empire to the position of the Social Democratic party of Germany in 1932. Despite all blows, that party was not broken, yet it had lost all of its offensive power.[135] If Goebbels and Hitler belittled Roosevelt and Churchill, this was because they saw in these "plutocratic reactionaries" images of Chancellor Heinrich Bruening (1930–32) or other victims of days gone by. Stalin would suffer the same political fate as the leftists of Weimar, the Socialist Otto Braun and the Communist Ernst Thaelmann. The Era of Struggle gave Goebbels hope, for its main link with the present was the fanatical idealism of the Nazi movement and the "statesmanlike genius" of Adolf Hitler. When Goebbels spoke in the Berlin Sportpalast during the war, his ecstatic demeanor stemmed from memories of speeches of bygone days, of Nazi rallies during the *Kampfzeit,* especially between 1930 and 1932.

In constructing his analogical myth of the Era of Struggle, Goebbels took incredible liberties. Two days before the Red Army began its fateful Stalingrad offensive, Goebbels made a speech in which he declared that the enemy alliance was the same as the one faced by the Nazis between 1919 and 1933: "The same coalition faces us, from the bourgeois-nationalist-plutocratic camp to Bolshevism." [136] In 1932 this had hardly been the case, for the Nazis had faced a corrupt conservative right, a divided left, and a basically nonexistent center. Goebbels told a half-truth when he asserted that the setbacks of late 1932 (Hindenburg's rejection of Hitler's terms on August 13, the Reichstag election of early November) had brought out the combative spirit of the movement and spurred it on to victory. In fact, a series of conspiracies and deals had brought the Nazis to power, not "inner concentration" and "moral strength of resistance." To say that the conservative People's party had marched arm in arm with the Communists was absurd, but it gave hope to Nazis puzzled by Churchill's alliance with Stalin.

After the Stalingrad debacle Goebbels developed a new aspect of his *Kampfzeit* analogy. The minister claimed that Stalingrad showed the fearful threat that Germany and Europe hàd escaped because of Germany's "preventive" attack on Russia in 1941. Goebbels then compared this last-minute salvation with the Nazi Seizure of Power in 1933. How could the Germany of Chancellor Kurt von Schleicher have prevented the accession to power of Communism? The Communists had "150 seats in the Reichstag" (the actual number was 100), and a fragmented, weak Germany would soon have fallen prey to these "Subhumans." The cynic Goebbels told his "total war" audience on February 18, 1943, "In our Era of Struggle we were *quite poor Nazis! And when we won, everyone courted us!*"[137] If Germany seemed isolated at the moment, the Nazis had been *more* isolated before 1933. This, too, was a false analogy, for before 1933 the Nazis had had intermittent alliances with the German Nationalists. Conservatives had not merely flocked to the party after the Seizure of Power, but many of them had actually connived to put Hitler in power (though not in total power) before that event. There might be an analogy between Neville Chamberlain at Munich in 1938 and Alfred Hugenberg in Weimar early in 1932, but not between Germany after Stalingrad and the Nazis late in 1932. Goebbels, following Hitler, believed that Bolshevism and Western capitalism were two sides of the same Jewish-liberal coin. He believed that before 1933 the Communists and the stock market were collaborating against Hitler. "Everything that happened then is being repeated today . . . ," said Goebbels in May 1943.[138] In August 1943 the German press was sharply reprimanded by Dietrich for occasionally portraying capitalism and Bolshevism as opposing forces.

In Goebbels' mythology he himself was the "Conqueror of Berlin," the man who had organized a small, fanatic band of followers in the 1920s and won the capital. He had done the same thing earlier in the Rhineland, between 1924 and 1926, according to his own account. The fanaticism prevailed over all adversity, just as it would in 1943. Goebbels was convinced there would be no 1918, no shameful capitulation, for now there was no Jewish leadership for it. By the middle of 1943 the *Kampfzeit* was Goebbels' main private obsession as well as his consolation: "In seven years I won the title of honor of 'Conqueror of Berlin.' I have decided to earn the title 'Defender of Berlin' in just as many weeks." "I came to Berlin in November 1926 with three hundred Berliners on my side, and with them I conquered Berlin. Today three million would cheer me, if I put them to the test."[139] After Stalingrad, after Tunis, after increased terror bombings, after the fall of Mussolini, Goebbels did not despair; he enveloped himself in mythos: "But just think of the Era of Struggle! How did we come to power then? Not at the height of our success, but after a period of profound setbacks. . . . Why? Because those in power at the time realized that the voters who were leaving us would not go back to the bosom of the bourgeois parties, but would turn to Communism, that our setbacks were not victories for them, but for Communism." [140] Despite his assertion that capitalism and Bolshevism had emerged from the same Jewish cocoon, Goebbels inconsistently developed this analogy: When Roosevelt and especially Churchill realized that German defeats meant Red victory, they would act like Hugenberg and Papen in 1933 and turn to Hitler! "We are angels of innocence compared to the Bolshevik monsters," he stated. [141] Goebbels' problem, however, was twofold: Germany might collapse before the Grand Alliance fell apart, for German diplomacy was nonexistent. And German propaganda about the plutocratic-Red alliance made it difficult for the media to switch course and exploit differences between Stalin and his Western partners.

Goebbels took solace in his sense of living in an heroic age "without precedent." Despite the agonies of the present, he insisted in September 1943, ". . . we must never forget that, once these anxieties are a thing of the past, they will constitute our most beautiful memories." [142] Just as Goebbels romanticized the *Kampfzeit* in 1943, so he expected to romanticize the present war in 1960, believing Germans were again living in an Era of Struggle. Joseph Goebbels did not exude the comradely warmth and drunken fellowship of so many of the other "Old Fighters" of the party. To many of these men he was an object of suspicion, a clever, opportunistic intellectual, a disloyal conspirator, a vindictive Mephistopheles to Hitler's Faust. Goebbels compensated for this problem by throwing himself heart, brain, and soul into the memory of the *Kampfzeit*. By creating his own, carefully doctored myth of the *Kampfzeit,* he cultivated the image of the loyal "Old Fighter," however alien the social trappings of that role were to him.

Late at night on October 28 of each year, some of the Berlin Old Guard got together with Goebbels so they could celebrate the first hours of his birthday, which fell on October 29. During the 1943 celebration Goebbels told his comrades how much he admired the French premier Clemenceau, who had saved the mutinous French Army in 1917: "That was the greatest deed of his life, and France was saved at the last moment from defeat." [143] Goebbels' mind was on the shameful surrender of Germany in 1918. Thanks to National Socialist loyalty and the fanaticism of men like his Berlin Old Guard fighters, such a shame would never recur. Goebbels would be the Clemenceau of 1944.

The last great public celebration of Hitler's accession to power took place on January 30, 1943. One year later an aide to Goebbels noted the ironic contrast with 1933: Then, torches had been lit to hail the new ruler of the Reich; now, in 1944, Berlin itself burned like a giant beacon, illuminating the death throes of the Third Reich. But Goebbels clung ever more intensely to positive analogies with the Era of Struggle and its happy ending. On March 31 he told party leaders that the nation still possessed Hitler, who had defeated the Reds in 1933 and would do so again, as the living promise that there would never again be a 1918. The situation today was like that on the eve of the Seizure of Power. By 1944 Goebbels was making propaganda as much for himself and the leadership as for the masses: It was a consolation in the midst of despair and destruction. If Germany could play upon the contradictions in the Allied camp, as the Nazis had done with their enemies in Germany before 1933, much could be salvaged. If the situation seemed desperate in June 1944, how much more desperate had it been in 1919, when seven men founded the Nazi movement! [144]

The Allied invasion in the west might have upset Goebbels' *Kampfzeit* myth, had not the attempt to murder Hitler taken place on July 20, 1944. Goebbels saw in the Stauffenberg revolt a confirmation of his historical analogy.[145] When Otto Strasser broke with the Nazis in 1930, when Gregor Strasser considered "treason" late in 1932, and when Ernst Röhm launched his "revolt" in 1934, the Nazi party had shaken to its foundations. Yet it had recovered more determined than ever and had gone on to victory, led by a man of indomitable will and divine good fortune. Goebbels believed that Hitler, hardened and decisive, would draw the necessary consequences, as he had in 1930–34. Now that Goebbels had some authority in the waging of total war, Germany would salvage the situation. Goebbels built analogy upon analogy. If Germany could hold out—and it was five minutes before midnight, in Hitler's melodramatic phrase—the Allied camp might break up, and the West would allow Germany to destroy the Bolsheviks. Had this not occurred in 1933, when the bourgeois reactionaries came over to Hitler in order to prevent the Reds from coming to power? Early in 1943, when a German victory still seemed possible in Goebbels' eyes, he had argued a somewhat different analogy: The Grand Alliance of Reds and capitalists was *natural* and was similar to the opposition faced by Hitler in 1932. In 1944 when Goebbels hoped for some way out of the present war, he changed the analogy, emphasizing that the victory of the Nazis in 1933 was in part the result of the anti-Communist attitude of the German conservatives and bourgeoisie.

When Goebbels turned against Hitler's strategy of continued resistance in the west after the disastrous Ardennes offensive, he developed a

Kampfzeit analogy in order to convince Hitler that he should change his mind. Goebbels' argument was that just as Hitler had not come to power by making absolute demands, but as part of a conservative coalition, so he would have to modify his total confrontation strategy in 1945.[146] When the Nazis had made absolute demands upon President von Hindenburg on August 13, 1932, they had been rebuffed. Complete victory could only come after compromise. The salvation of Nazism in 1945 presupposed a compromise peace, probably with the West, as a prelude to an alliance against Bolshevism.

Did Joseph Goebbels really believe in such an analogy and in such a possibility early in 1945? In his moments of despair, of which he now had many, the minister fell back upon the nihilistic "bottom line" of Nazi analogy. Imputing to the enemies of the Reich the aim of annihilating Germany, Goebbels could morally justify his willingness to see the nation destroyed before it surrendered to Russia and the West. There would never again be another 1918 even if it meant the total destruction of the German nation. "The Germans were not capable of resistance in 1918 because they did not have a government capable of resistance," Goebbels stated.[147] "... *the word capitulation does not exist in our vocabulary!*" [148] On the eve of Hitler's last birthday, amidst the ruins of Berlin, he insisted, "What we are today experiencing is the last act of the tremendous tragic drama which began on August 1, 1914, and which we Germans interrupted on November 9, 1918, at *precisely* the moment when it was nearing its decision." [149] The situation in 1945 was atonement for the sin of capitulation in 1918. Joseph Goebbels took grim satisfaction in the contrast with 1918. Now there would be no cowardly surrender, only ruin in heroic defeat.

Although Germany was losing the war by 1943, Paul Joseph Goebbels continued to believe that victory was possible. As one German town after another suffered the fate of Berlin, Lübeck, and Hamburg, Goebbels, speaking to the party leadership in Essen, offered this consolation to both the nation and to himself: "New streets will arise from the ruins, towns of a new character will emerge ..." [150] The leadership would repay the populations of the bombed cities for their trust. After the war the devastated towns would be more beautiful than ever. Monumental buildings, new, wider streets, and clean, spacious apartment buildings would replace the rubble. Two weeks before the end of the Third Reich Joseph Goebbels was still making such promises to the German people. The rubble would indeed be cleared, but not by the Nazis. Reconstruction was the materialistic aspect of Goebbels' fantasies late in the war. In his more detached moments the minister reflected upon history and the manner in which history had betrayed him and National Socialism. Closest to his heart in the closing months of the war was a tragic sense of heroic idealism, a feeling that perhaps the blood and the sacrifices which so many had made for the Nazi movement had indeed been in vain.

Joseph Goebbels was obsessed by power as perceived through the greatness of the modern state. Historical greatness meant a strong state, power over individuals and other nations. However much he mused about his "real heroes," poets and other creative people, however often he asserted that it was better to win the heart of a nation than to govern it, Joseph Goebbels possessed a full measure of German state worship. The year 1918 was terrible because it humbled German power. "After 1918 we ran the danger of sinking into an ahistorical existence. That would have been the greatest misfortune not just for us, but for the whole world," he stated.[151] Goebbels was no expert on modern history, but he, like so many other Germans, was the product of a historiography and a concept of historical significances which were rooted in the equation of greatness, power, and the state. World War II was Germany's last great chance, her bid for world power, to use Fritz Fischer's phrase. "The present is the great, *decisive,* but also the last chance! *For this reason* it is so hard, filled with sacrifices, and so bitter." [152] When Goebbels spoke these words late in 1943, he was filled with contempt for the Italian people, who by their performance in the war had forfeited any chance for historical greatness. After the Allies landed in Normandy, Goebbels turned to history for consolation. Germany was a young nation, outnumbered in manpower and inferior in material, but it would prevail as had outnumbered Athens, Sparta, Rome, and Prussia. Quoting novelist Theodor Fontane, Goebbels liked to say, "Perseverance is better than courage." [153] A month later Goebbels warned the German nation that if it did not meet the challenge of this war, it would fall into an "ahistorical existence," much like France after May 1940.[154] The right to life of a nation was less important in Goebbels' mind than a struggle for historical greatness, measured in terms of sheer power. Here, too, he was only the reflection of Hitler's personality, which in turn was a hideous caricature of modern Germany.

Joseph Goebbels felt betrayed by the course of contemporary history. As early as 1941 he had declared that history would have showed itself devoid of meaning if Germany lost the war.[155] In the bitterness of total defeat early in 1945 Goebbels abandoned his worship of the "goddess History," and declared that if Germany did not prevail History was a "whore," selling herself to the largest armies for the most money.[156] If History allowed the devil to triumph, History was without meaning, cheap. All the idealism, all the sacrifices of the Nazi movement had been in vain, betrayed by the whore History. In the late 1920s Goebbels, the poet of death for fallen comrades, had begun to speak of the majesty of death: Goebbels cried in 1931 that out of the blood of those who had been killed would one day arise their avengers. But sacrifice and idealism only made sense if vengeance and triumph followed. Otherwise, history had no meaning, history was a cheat. In 1940 Goebbels had called for more sacrifices by the German people. Victory and the "social community" of the nation would justify and sanctify those sacrifices, he had believed.[157] In 1941 the minister had proclaimed that out of the sacrifices and cares, the heroism and needs of this hour, would emerge a new, beautiful Reich in the coming days of a victorious peace.[158] The victorious peace was not to be, but Goebbels gave Hitler his greatest victory of the war, the final conquest of the German people. There was no "1918." Those who claim that the Germans fought to the end because of the Allied "unconditional surrender" formula have a weak case. Nazi propaganda emphasized the alleged "extermination plans" of the Allies from 1941 on. This propaganda reached its effective peak after Stalingrad—because of the military situation, not because of the Allies' declaration.

In *Michael* Joseph Goebbels described his protagonist as being overcome by tears when he heard Hitler. Here was Michael's confession of faith. Upon this need to believe, which his faith justified through history, Joseph Goebbels built his world view. During the war the minister fondly recalled how National Socialism emerged out of the ruins of defeated Germany because of a small group of believers. Early in 1945 Goebbels wrote his own epitaph in the same spirit. He acknowledged the "little faults, human weaknesses, and mistakes" of the believers, but convinced himself that posterity would see in men like himself "a glowing model of courage, steadfastness, and all national virtues." [159] Yet even at the very end of his life, with Berlin in ruins around him, Goebbels showed his entourage old flashes of his brutally frank insight. On April 16, for example, he acknowledged the good motives of some of the July 20, 1944, conspirators.

What prevailed in these last weeks was the sense of loss, a feeling that all the idealism had been for naught. In 1945 Goebbels became more like Michael, a man moved by the frustrations of life: "But tears come to my eyes when I think that this movement, built with so much idealism, so many sacrifices, privations, so much blood and sweat, is now going to the dogs like refuse . . ." [160] Tears rolled down the minister's cheeks as he finished his thought. When he recovered, Joseph Goebbels declared that he faced posterity with a clear conscience. He admitted to temptations and moments of indecision, but justified himself by the fact that he had emerged unscathed from these times of doubt, these inner struggles. Goebbels spoke in idealistic terms as he stated his belief that man lives on in his deeds. Here the Heidelberg Ph.D. in literature may have recalled Goethe's line in *Faust II:* "The traces of my earthly days/cannot fade into the aeons." [161]

In the 1944 spectacular feature film *Opfergang (The Rite of Sacrifice)*, the pearly gates of heaven open for the dead protagonist. Goebbels was profoundly moved by this scene and may have viewed it as a glimpse of his own immortality. At the end of his life Joseph Goebbels saw himself justified before God and man by his earthly deeds, by his faith, and by his participation in an era of unprecedented misery and unheard-of greatness, truly a "time without example." History had shown herself to be a fickle woman, so Goebbels had to seek out his own death. He saw his suicide as a confirmation of his triumphant faith and deeds, a blood sacrifice of his body, but not his soul, to history, which had become an agent of Lucifer. Goebbels' last act would be eternal proof that his tortured quest for faith had ended in success. His self-destruction was symbolic both of the perversity of National Socialist emotions and of the distortion of Christian values in the twentieth century. Joseph Goebbels' suicide, a mortal sin in the eyes of his former church, was the final profession of his faith that grace comes to those who believe.

II

Wartime Propaganda

And the Mass Media:

Techniques of Control

And Dissemination

3

The Propaganda Apparatus in State and Party

Early each morning Joseph Goebbels appeared in his office at the Propaganda Ministry on the Wilhelmsplatz. He was not in a good mood, but the work was of such importance that he quickly began to concentrate upon the reports and documents placed before him. The minister was preparing for the central event of his day, the ministerial conference. Before the conference took place, Goebbels read extracts culled from enemy broadcasts and newspapers. Thick folders lay before him on the large desk, and their contents often necessitated quick action by the minister. These documents were memoranda or official acts which required a signature here, initials there, outright rejection, or an indication that they were to be reconsidered or redrafted. Goebbels intently studied the secret reports on German and foreign public opinion prepared by the Security Service of the SS, as well as the "Activity Reports" of the Reich Propaganda Offices (RPAe). Few details escaped his notice. If Goebbels learned from the Gestapo that some "Communists" or Austrian separatists had been sentenced to death, he might well use this information in his ministerial conference. The minister then received the director of his personal office, the man responsible for selecting the documents on the desk. The director gave an oral report containing an estimate of the relative importance of various pending matters. Following this, the liaison officer of the Supreme Command of the Armed Forces (OKW) appeared and informed Goebbels of the latest military events and their significance. The minister had his own phone line to Hitler's headquarters and often made use of it to obtain confidential military information.[1]

Goebbels used the ministerial conference to give specific directives to high-ranking officials of the various divisions and offices of the propaganda ministry. The origins of the conference went back to the last years of the *Kampfzeit,* but its wartime form emerged only in October 1939. As Goebbels widened the scope of his propaganda work during the war, the conference expanded to include representatives of other ministries. At its peak, in the middle war years, it involved about fifty listeners. Until the onset of the Russian campaign, there were about twenty participants. The hour of the start of the conference varied from 10:00 to 11:00 A.M. There is even a record of one conference, possibly the last one, commencing at 12:15 P.M., but that was at the end of the war, when Russian artillery and Allied bombings made scheduling an unreliable process. The hour of the conference was dependent upon two factors, the arrival of the OKW communiqué, and the need of the press department of the ministry to hold its "major press conference" in time for the newspapers of Germany to prepare their evening and morning editions. Since the military communiqué arrived later and later, thanks in large part to Hitler's meddling, Goebbels had to content himself during most of the war with a draft communiqué.

Goebbels always arrived promptly for the conference, which was held in the conference hall of the ministry. His audience, seated in upholstered chairs around a U-shaped table, watched the perfectly dressed and groomed minister walk into the hall, his hand upraised in the Hitler salute. Goebbels showed a certain degree of excitement or anticipation. The ministerial conference was a performance, not a dialogue. Goebbels spoke clearly and mellifluously, using his hands to emphasize a point with eloquent gestures. As Willi A. Boelcke has commented, even in these small meetings the style of the mass-rally speaker sometimes broke through. Goebels' faithful secretary, Richard Otte, formerly a stenographer with the German News Agency, took down the minister's words. Otte's protocols have only been recovered for the period to May 31, 1941, but other sources, such as the notes of a representative of the foreign ministry, have preserved a reliable record of later conferences, at least through much of 1943. At these conferences, which lasted for half an hour to forty-five minutes, Goebbels was the dominant figure. The only other regular speaker was the OKW liaison officer, who gave a brief account of developments at the front(s). If anyone raised a question or hesitantly contradicted the minister, it was generally Hans Fritzsche, Dr. Karl Boemer, or Dr. Ernst Brauweiler, three of the highest-ranking officials in the ministry. Such interruptions or objections were rare, as were suggestions. Occasionally, the OKW liaison officer, a man not totally dependent upon Goebbels, would intersperse a comment or two.

If Goebbels was absent, he made sure his directives to the departments and divisions of the ministry reached the conference. His state secretary, Leopold Gutterer (later Werner Naumann), and Hans Fritzsche, if the latter was unavailable, received stenographic instructions from the minister and communicated these to participants in the conference. Though careful about limiting the time, Goebbels enjoyed these conferences and missed few of them. Through the conference he exercised broad control over the German mass media, though more effectively over film and radio than over the daily press. Sitting to Goebbels' right was his state secretary, in effect the chief administrative officer of the ministry, and then to his right the OKW liaison officer. When he wanted information or reactions to an idea, Goebbels usually turned to one of these men. On July 1, 1942, Goebbels turned to Hans-Leo Martin and obtained a fairly detailed comment on the uses of anti-Jewish propaganda among the Arabs in Palestine. After the conference the minister received important department officials in his office for private conferences. The topics were either of a technical or specialized nature, or concerned personnel questions. Both types of subject matter were not considered proper topics for the full ministerial conference.[2]

The highest officials of Goebbels' ministry comprised two types of individuals, the "Old Party Fighters" and the technicians. The *alte Kämpfer* usually held the major positions, though Goebbels demanded competence and a dedication to work from all his associates. Karl Hanke was state secretary until 1941, though in August 1939 he had entered military service, achieving the rank of SS-Oberführer. Goebbels hated Hanke, for the future Gauleiter of Lower Silesia had defended Magda Goebbels and had schemed to retire the minister during the troubled days of the Lida Baarova sex scandal. Hanke had the support of the SS, thanks to Himmler's aversion to Goebbels during that period, and even in his absence Goebbels could only replace him in fact, not in title. By 1940 Dr. Leopold Gutterer, aged thirty-eight, was the leading candidate for Hanke's job. When Hanke accepted Hitler's offer of the *Gauleitung* of Lower Silesia, Goebbels wasted little time in naming Gutterer to his post.

Leopold Gutterer was an "Old Fighter" who had joined the party in 1925 and wore the Golden Party Badge, an honor accorded after 1933 to Nazis who had suffered because of their political activity during the Weimar days. Gutterer was effective in arranging mass marches and reviews, and in 1930 became *Gau* propaganda director of Hannover. He had had experience as editor of a party paper in Göttingen. Gutterer was an early employee of the new propaganda ministry, joining Goebbels in 1933. Between 1930 and 1933 Gutterer had specialized in election rallies and demonstrations; he now continued that work as specialist for rallies and state occasions in the ministry. By 1937 ministerial councillor Gutterer was head of the propaganda division of the ministry, its most important section. A year later he was promoted to ministerial director. In May 1941 Goebbels surprised no one by appointing Gutterer state secretary, making him the second most important figure in the ministry, at least on paper.

Gutterer was a mediocre personality, described by Boelcke as a man whose "willingness to serve without contradicting" and "flattering obsequiousness" accounted for his success.[3] Another source described him as "a crude and platitudinous speaker and an uninspiring personality," but gave him credit for "dogged energy and painstaking care for detail."[4] Goebbels did not greatly respect Gutterer, but he liked these aspects of his personality and work habits, his slavish devotion to his job. One Goebbels colleague saw Gutterer as "not overly competent, but a basically decent, straight-shooting guy." Gutterer was not the only man near Goebbels whose career came to an end because of black marketeering. The irony is that Goebbels had an official assignment from 1942 on, to suppress such illicit trade. Even if Gutterer had not become involved in shady dealings, however, his days as state secretary were nearing their end by 1943. In July, Wilfred von Oven[5] noted that Gutterer's days seemed numbered.

A hard, charismatic, talented and ambitious man loomed like a shadow across Gutterer's path: Dr. Werner Naumann, since early 1941 Goebbels' "right hand." At that time Naumann was only thirty-one years old, a Silesian "Old Fighter" who had joined the party at the age of nineteen. He rose to a high rank in the SA, but cultivated close connections with Himmler and the SS. This patronage perhaps saved him from the fate of Ernst Röhm during the blood purge of the SA in June 1934. Naumann had met Goebbels before 1933. Naumann had studied at Breslau University and received a doctorate from the University of Jena in 1934 for a dissertation on the German Labor Service. Naumann became director of the Breslau Reich Propaganda Office and showed his organizational abilities as a district leader, and then as a top aide to the Gauleiter. He had accomplished all this while in his twenties. In 1937 Goebbels brought the talented, ambitious young man to Berlin, where Naumann became director of the minister's personal office. Naumann rose to the rank of Hauptsturmführer in the SS, and served on the eastern front with an artillery battery, where he was badly wounded. In October 1941 Goebbels named Naumann ministerial manager, and in the following year this young man on the way up became ministerial director.

Werner Naumann was the perfect young Nazi, almost a trophy for Goebbels to display. He combined modesty, steel-like determination, and military bearing, with apparently fanatical devotion to Hitler and Goebbels. Naumann cut an impressive figure: tall and wiry, he strutted about the ministry bedecked with medals and ribbons symbolic of party and military heroism. The secretaries loved him; even Goebbels' wife wrote Platonic love poems to him in 1944–45. In March 1942 Goebbels noted, "Naumann has already mastered his tasks very well and is an indispensable assistant to me. He has taken hold energetically of my prospective purchase of land in the neighborhood of Berlin." [6] Such planned purchases had embarrassed Goebbels with the party before the war, but now he had the tactful but forceful Naumann at his disposal. When von Oven joined the ministry early in 1943, wise men told him to make sure he got along well with Naumann. Von Oven quickly came to realize that, in his words, "He is the closest confidant of the minister, his only advisor, discussing all questions with him and receiving plenipotentiary authority." [7] Von Oven saw in Naumann cleverness, diligence, and energy, besides good looks. Both Boelcke and von Oven viewed Naumann as a figure worthy of respect, but hardly a likeable man. Naumann became a favorite of Hitler, who in his will made him Goebbels' successor. Despite his apparent devotion to the ministry, it is not inconceivable that Naumann intended to succeed Goebbels even if the Third Reich emerged from the war intact. He maintained his close ties with Himmler and may have been collecting a negative dossier on the minister.

Naumann was the devoted superman, the fanatical Nazi who shored up Goebbels' will to victory or death. Behind this facade of will and belief existed a scheming, ambitious soul. Naumann undermined Gutterer in every way he could. Naumann ran to Goebbels with stories about Gutterer's drinking (a tale calculated to infuriate the minister), or gave him accounts of Gutterer's sloppy administrative work. When Gutterer's black marketeering was exposed, Naumann's hour struck. In April 1944 Goebbels appointed him state secretary.[8] Longtime participants in the ministerial conference almost wept at the sad departure of Gutterer, but Naumann now had a title more in harmony with his actual power. Goebbels covered up Gutterer's corruption, since he did not wish to embarrass the ministry. When he had appointed Gutterer state secretary in 1941, the ministerial conferees applauded; when Goebbels announced the appointment of Naumann, the men felt sorry for Gutterer, and perhaps for themselves. Naumann worked all the time and was a man of some intelligence, but he expected similar attributes in his subordinates. Goebbels' rise to greater power in the German war effort was partially due to the efficient and untiring work of this state secretary.

Goebbels met Major Hans-Leo Martin at a ministerial conference early in 1940.[9] He later agreed to General Keitel's suggestion that Martin become liaison officer between the OKW and the ministry. Martin was a group director in the propaganda division of the Wehrmacht, and he retained this responsibility even after his appointment to the liaison post. Martin's specialty as an army propagandist was warding off the enemy's propaganda and subverting his will to fight. Martin later described Goebbels as a man who wanted a truthful account of the military situation, even when things were going badly at the front. Like Gutterer, Martin was caught while involved in black market activities, and at the end of 1944 he lost his position and returned to active service as a soldier. Goebbels' basic information about the war came from three sources, to which he added his own insights: the OKW report, Martin's private oral report (or that of his deputy), and the occasional "secret" news from the Führer's headquarters. Relying heavily upon the official report at his ministerial conference, Goebbels rarely went beyond Martin's prior account of the OKW communiqué. Goebbels usually respected military expertise, though he suspected a lack of National Socialist commitment in many German generals.

Brief portraits of a few more of the minister's colleagues give some sense of the nature of Goebbels' empire. Specialists with an intellectual background, belated National Socialists, coexisted with old Nazis who were proud to abide by the 1941 internal decree that National Socialists in the ministry had to wear the party badge while working. Such a specialist was Dr. Rudolf Semler, born in 1913, and a member of the party only since 1937.[10] Semler had earned a doctorate at the University of Berlin in 1939 with a dissertation on "France's Radical Socialists and Their Press." Goebbels liked to affect the sentimental toughness and image of the "Old Fighter," but he preferred Ph.D.'s as his closest collaborators. The best background for a successful career in the Goebbels ministry was a doctorate in the humanities or social sciences, combined with a past history as an old Nazi. If one had these qualifications and was under forty, so much the better. Naumann combined these attributes, and he made it to the top.

Goebbels' personal press aide, the East Prussian M.A. von Schirmeister, was totally devoted to Goebbels, worked hard, and was always available to the minister.[11] Von Schirmeister had been a member of the party since 1931, and had experience as a news editor with a Silesian newspaper. He was responsible for keeping protocols of the wartime ministerial conferences. He was known as Goebbels' memory, since the minister used him constantly to check references and look up facts and names. Goebbels authorized von Schirmeister to edit the second volume of his wartime speeches and articles. Von Schirmeister did not have the intellectual or technical background of Semler, or the National Socialist élan of Naumann, but his painstaking devotion to duty and his self-abnegation guaranteed his place at Goebbels' side until 1943, when, for reasons which are still unclear, the minister dismissed him.

Goebbels replaced von Schirmeister with Wilfred von Oven.[12] Goebbels expected great things from his political diary; how upset he would have been if he had known that press aide von Oven was also keeping a diary! Von Oven used every spare moment to write down his impressions of the ministry and of Goebbels, but more importantly, the new press aide jotted down Goebbels' own words, his reminiscences and outbursts of anger, his pathos, and his sarcastic egotism. If Goebbels or Naumann entered his office unannounced, von Oven quickly covered up his diary page with telegrams, envelopes, or anything else at hand. The Goebbels voice has the ring of authenticity in von Oven's pages. Wilfred von Oven was born in South America; after the fall of the Third Reich he again took up residence there, in Argentina. At eighteen years of age, von Oven became an SA man. Frau von Oven later claimed that her husband left the party in May 1932; she does not mention whether he rejoined, but it is highly unlikely that Goebbels would have had a nonparty member as his personal press aide. Von Oven served as a war reporter in a propaganda company. He later fought on the eastern front, and in 1943 was called to the ministry to replace von Schirmeister. Von Oven's work overlapped with that of Rudolf Semler, and there was no love lost between the two men. Semler was a career official, and he viewed von Oven as an outsider who had wormed his way into Goebbels' confidence. Von Oven admired much about Goebbels. Rarely do hints of criticism come through his diary. Goebbels so captured von Oven's imagination that the pages of his journal reveal a lot about Goebbels, but nothing about von Oven beyond a few autobiographical details. The diary is an extraordinary historical document.

Until April 1940 Georg Wilhelm Mueller was personal aide and advisor to Goebbels in the minister's office. Mueller seems to have been an unpopular figure among his colleagues, and there was relief when he was replaced by Karl Frowein. Mueller, born in 1909, wore the Golden Party Badge and was a loud-mouthed party activist. In 1933 he declared in Frankfurt that German youth did not need learning, but rather, it needed to know how to handle a Carbine 98. After the conquest of Norway, Mueller became the ministry's liaison with the commissar for the occupied Norwegian territories. His successor, Kurt Frowein, born in 1914, was the son of a Wuppertal artisan. He was a graduate of the Reich Press School. During the Polish campaign, Frowein, who had already written a book about the daily life of the new German soldier, served as a war correspondent at the front. In 1940 he published *Fortress France Fell.* Goebbels approved of his work in the office, and Frowein rose to the rank of senior governmental councillor.

Goebbels' adjutants had little or no power, quite unlike their colleagues who worked for Adolf Hitler. Goebbels treated these aides as domestics, just the way he treated von Schirmeister. Herbert Heiduschke, a high ranking SA leader who fell in the German attack upon Crete in 1941, served Goebbels until his ill-fated return to the service. Goebbels gave him the most thankless tasks to perform, yet treated him as a menial servant. When Heiduschke was killed in action, Goebbels said of him, "I lose in him not only one of my most loyal and reliable colleagues but also a good friend." [13] This eulogy would have surprised the deceased, but it would have moved him as well, and therein lay a good example of Goebbels' hold over the men and women around him. In Prince Friedrich Christian zu Schaumburg-Lippe, born the son of a reigning prince, Goebbels found an aristocrat devoted to the party and to the SA. In 1933 the twenty-seven-year-old prince became Goebbels' chief adjutant and taught the new minister the secrets of etiquette and ceremonial functions. The prince was a man of "disarming naiveté," endlessly credulous. Goebbels valued his services to the extent of recalling him to his personal office for special assignments even after the prince had departed for a position in another section of the ministry. The Nazi reaction against the aristocracy after the attempt on Hitler's life in 1944 cost the prince his position.

The ministry which these men served was founded on March 12-13, 1933. Ten years later Joseph Goebbels looked back upon a decade of propaganda, and he described the success of the ministry in glowing terms.[14] The ministry had succeeded in uniting the German people, and it had increased respect for Germany throughout the world. Goebbels declared to the ministry's employees that their diligence and sense of responsibility had made possible these accomplishments. The proof of the ministry's success lay in its having gained the respect of Germany's friends and the hatred and impotent rage of the Reich's foes. More objective views of the ministry's aims and work must be sought elsewhere. A foreign journalist observed late in 1939, "Whether it be in the press, films, radio, schools, party organizations or industrial organizations, the specific policies that the government is pursuing at a particular moment are constantly paraded before the people in their most favorable light, while opposing views—for example, those which might seep in through foreign broadcasts—are either buried in an avalanche of positive propaganda or submitted to the type of dissection that is designed to render them false or ridiculous." [15] One of the Nürnberg judgments in 1946 concluded, "The Nazi Government endeavored to unite the nation in support of their policies through the extensive use of propaganda. A number of agencies were set up ... All these agencies came under Goebbels' Ministry of the People's Enlightenment and Propaganda ..." [16]

The ministry constantly expanded from 1933 to 1942. In its early days, the Propaganda Ministry (Promi) had five divisions: propaganda, radio, press, motion pictures, and theater. In 1934 a music and art division was created; these disciplines each received divisional status in 1937. A separate literature division emerged in 1934. The press division grew rapidly, so in 1938 Goebbels divided it into a German press section and a foreign press section. In 1941 a periodical press section made its appearance, and in 1944, a periodical and cultural press section. The ministry went from five divisions in 1933 to seventeen in 1941, though there was some consolidation during the war years. The ministry was still not completely organized at the time of the promulgation of the operational plan of February 10, 1936. The propaganda division, however, had emerged as the most important division in the ministry. This section was concerned with means of propaganda, the promulgation of the Nazi world view, mass rallies, and conducting a unified propaganda campaign throughout Germany. It was to take into account both National Socialist ideology and the existence of hostile ideological enclaves among the population. Dr. Eberhard Taubert was the ministerial expert on hostile world views (Bolshevism, Judaism, democracy, the churches, Freemasonry), a position he maintained through the war.[17]

In 1940 G. W. Mueller wrote an official description of the ministry in which he described the propaganda division as "the great division whose initiative and work can be perceived everywhere ..." [18] Within the division were sections concerned with the following specialities: rallies, expositions, liaison with the party Reich Propaganda Central Office (RPL), liaison with the party chancellory, liaison with the local Reich propaganda offices, cultural-political propaganda, propaganda among ethnic Germans outside the Reich or newly settled in Greater Germany, censorship of the media, the furthering of German ethnicity *(Volkstum)*, and propaganda in the areas of health, racial policy, and social measures. The specialists who ran these offices were responsible for maintaining close ties with the relevant government ministries and for furthering the work of those agencies through propaganda. The propaganda division had other important functions. Under Dr. Schaeffer, it was responsible for evaluating reports on civilian morale and suggesting countermeasures to be taken in this area, should they be necessary because of the state of public opinion. The division published the "Confidential Information for District Leaders," an information bulletin mailed to Gauleiters, deputy Gauleiters, the Reich propaganda offices, and district leaders.[19]

When the minister was drafting a speech, his personal ministerial office often turned to the propaganda division for specific materials.[20] Early in 1943 Goebbels was preparing a speech for the tenth anniversary of the Seizure of Power. His personal press aide, von Schirmeister, wrote to the director of the propaganda division requesting material about the social accomplishments of the last ten years. A month later, while Goebbels mulled over a speech to be delivered before the forty-two directors of the regional Reich propaganda offices, the radio division provided relevant information to the director of the propaganda division. This material was transmitted to the personal office of the minister. This office, with its adjutants, made up the liaison staff which coordinated the many divisions and sections of the ministry and dealt with other ministries. The three state secretaries of the ministry were responsible for this personal office (Ministeramt) of the minister, but adjutants, press aides, and stenographers carried out the difficult vital tasks stemming from Goebbels' daily work schedule. Werner Naumann quickly discovered that control of this office was a path to power. The propaganda ministry was also responsible for entertaining foreign dignitaries, through Herr Zippe, down to providing food, drink, accommodations, and flowers.[21]

Although Nazi leaders such as Himmler liked to denounce the "bureaucratic spirit," Goebbels' propaganda ministry exemplified a major quality of bureaucracy, its tendency to grow. Adolf Hitler had written, "The better the propaganda has worked, the smaller the organization can be; and the larger number of supporters, the more modest the number of members can be; and vice versa: The poorer the propaganda is, the larger the organization must be, and the smaller the host of followers of a movement remains, the more extensive the number of its members must be, if it still hopes to count on any success at all." [22] In expanding his ministerial responsibility, Goebbels ignored this dictum. The great growth of the ministry after 1939 was due to the role which his perception of the war assigned to it. The total war effort and the exigencies of military service forced some reductions upon the ministry, but its history from 1933 to at least 1943 was a story of expanding budgets and a growing number of employees. The ministry employed about 350 people in 1933; by 1941 the number had grown to over 1,900 men and women.[23]

Goebbels' ministry was a reflection of the National Socialist youth cult.[24] The average age of senior officials was under forty-five, and the future seemed to belong to men born around 1910. While Goebbels fought vigorously for draft deferments for artists and actors not directly employed by the ministry, he was very cautious about seeking such deferrals for his own people, unless they were either totally necessary for his work or had already proved themselves in battle. The minister was the prophet of total war, and he could hardly avoid setting a good example of willingness to simplify structures and provide manpower for the armed forces. Lammers, head of the Reich chancellory, congratulated Goebbels for having so few UKs (draft-exempt men) who were under thirty-five years of age. This happy situation did not prevail in many other Reich ministries.[25] Despite such window dressing, the ministry, though efficient, was a huge empire by 1942. Nevertheless, foul-ups did occur, though they were rarely the fault of the ministry. Classic bureaucratic confusion prevailed for almost a year in 1941–42, when the Reich League for the German Family, following a request from the ministry, tried to convince its members not to use the initials RPA (Reich Propaganda Office) when they were referring to the Racial-political Office *(Rassenpolitisches Amt)* of the party. This confusion was causing mistakes in mail delivery. As late as April 1942 the RPA in Bayreuth complained that agencies, including the Racial Office itself, were still using the letters "RPA." For several months late in 1944 nobody in the ministry could find out what the "Europe Press and Advertising Service" was, or whether it even worked for the ministry.[26]

The growth of the ministry was reflected in its constantly rising expenditures. It expended about RM 14.25 million in fiscal 1933 and RM RM 28 million in 1934, while the figure for 1942 was up to over RM 187 million. Even if one takes moderate inflation into account, the rise was enormous. On the eve of the war the ministry was probably spending about RM 95 million, so the great acceleration in expenses occurred between 1939 and 1942. The ministry differentiated between "regular" and "special" expenditures, and during the war the latter outstripped the former. Regular income and necessary state subsidies from the finance ministry covered the deficits. The "special expenditures" and Goebbels' almost unrestrained use of funds for his own political purposes were logged in such a way as to avoid accountability to the party and Reich accounting and audit offices. This was a legal procedure, but it involved careful work on the part of the ministerial office. Goebbels managed to cover the regular budget of the ministry from audited income. Because of his stature as a Nazi eminence, he was able to turn to the finance ministry for funds to cover the special expenditures for which he provided little or no explanation.

The main source of ministry income was the Reich Radio Society (RRG). The ministry received 55% of the income derived from the Society's collection of listeners' fees. When the number of subscribers to the German radio passed seven million, as occurred by wartime, the ministry's share automatically rose to 75%. Its income was further augmented by the sharp rise in certain categories of listeners' fees after 1939. From 1933 to 1943 the ministry turned over to the Reich Radio Society approximately 41% to 42% of its radio income. This was the basis of Goebbels' somewhat inaccurate boast that the ministry paid its own way out of "its" funds. Over 98% of the ministry's audited budget for the ten-year period 1933–43 came from these radio fees. Goebbels gave the ministry's employees the following account of the audited expenditures for the same era, though he omitted any account of his use of personal or discretionary funds: active propaganda (21.8%); news and communications services (17.8%); music, fine arts, literature (6.2%); film (11.5%); theater (26.4%); buildings and equipment (4.3%); salaries and business expenses—ministry (7.5%), film inspection offices (0.1%), Reich propaganda offices (4.4%).

Goebbels claimed that 88.5% of these expenditures had been covered by the ministry's own sources of income. The growth of the budget division (Bureau G, under Dr. Karl Ott) reflected the expansion of the ministry. In 1933 the budget staff had 8 employees, of whom 4 still worked in Bureau G. The budget for 1933 accounted for 473 officials, employees, and workers. The 1942 budget showed that the ministry was responsible for 3,441 persons.[27] Bureau G alone now had 73 employees. The figure of almost 3,500 employees does not contradict an earlier figure of almost 2,000 for the same era. Goebbels included employees of subordinate offices and agencies in the higher statistic. These agencies were not part of the ministry, but were fully or largely subsidized and controlled by it. They included groups such as the Reich Culture Chamber, the Office of the Leipzig Fair, the German Library, the German International Affairs Institute, and the Reich League of the German Press.[28]

Goebbels and his state secretaries kept employees of the ministry informed of personnel and organization matters through a minutely detailed "News Bulletin." Thousands of regulations, from the insignificant to the petty, appeared in its pages, which were mimeographed and appeared on the eighteenth of each month. A brief description of some of these notices gives an indication of the daily work and concerns of the ministry. A notice in the "Bulletin" on September 18, 1941, ordered all employees of the ministry and its subordinate agencies to follow local police instructions when summoned to air raid duty. An

October ordinance warned employees against throwing razor blades or other hazardous household or office implements into wastepaper baskets, since the cleaning people were complaining about injuries caused by such carelessness. The ordinance warned that anyone violating its dictates was required to compensate an injured person if proven negligent and liable. The "News Bulletin" often contained obituaries for ministry personnel who had fallen at the front. On January 18, 1943, the "Bulletin" noted that P. Carstensen, who had been killed in Africa, was posthumously promoted to the rank of ministerial councillor by Hitler. This qualified his survivors for a higher pension. To us the promotion may appear ironic, but it possibly appealed to ministry personnel. There but for the grace of Goebbels . . .

A July 1943 regulation pointed out that the ministerial library was strictly for the professional use of Promi employees. Only in special cases could employees of the subordinate agencies use the books. The employees could check the books out for three weeks, but this time could be reduced in the case of volumes for which there was a heavy demand. Upon occasion the "Bulletin" contained important statements by Goebbels himself. The minister once warned his employees that they would have to set an example in waging total war. Simplicity and efficiency in both public and private life would typify ministry workers. It was their duty to avoid giving the impression that leadership circles needed to pay less attention to the total war ordinances and decrees than the broad masses of the population. Goebbels was ostentatious about his austerity long before the proclamation of total war in 1943. In 1941 Goebbels made his old party comrades bring their own bread and meat ration cards to the fifteenth-anniversary celebration of his accession to the Gauleitership of Berlin. None of Hermann Göring's sybaritic lifestyle for the Little Doctor!

The efficiency of the ministry was due in no small way to its good fortune in escaping major damage from the worst Allied bombings of Berlin, although the great raids of November 1943 caused heavy damage to parts of the building. State secretary Gutterer effectively led the fire-fighting brigade; this did not save his position in the long run, but his work impressed Goebbels. The damage to the building, a former princely palace, was not incapacitating to the work of the ministry. Goebbels always believed that the relative lack of destruction was a good omen for his work. But by early 1945 fortune had deserted him. Hotels which formerly housed visiting Reich propaganda office personnel were demolished in the bombings. On March 13, 1945, the ministry was so damaged by Allied air attacks that it could no longer house the offices of its personnel. Goebbels then turned his residence on the Hermann

Göring Strasse into the ministry. The greatly reduced number of employees in the last weeks of the war made this a feasible move. Goebbels himself kept functioning, but Magda showed signs of losing her grip on reality. After Hitler paid them a rare social call in January, she took satisfaction in noting that he would never have gone to the Görings'! On March 14 she inspected the damage on the Wilhelmsplatz, dressed as if ready to go to an elegant cocktail party.[29]

During these harsh last years of the war Joseph Goebbels had little time to devote to several of his great loves, music, fine arts, literature, and theater. From 1933 to the crisis year 1938, Goebbels saw one of his tasks as minister as promoting the return of the arts to the *Volk*. Just as Goebbels' *Michael* had found his way back to the nation, so German art must rid itself of alien and egotistical influences and must be *volksgebunden,* tied to the nation. In August 1933 Goebbels spoke about Richard Wagner in this sense, choosing a figure whom he knew Hitler revered. The young minister made Wagner's comic music drama *Die Meistersinger* the model of everything great in German art: profundity and wit, romanticism, tragedy, jubilance in triumph, the "ringing pathos of the festival of the nation." Goebbels borrowed a phrase from Hitler and referred to Wagner as "one of the greatest musicians of all time." Bringing art back to the nation: in Goebbels' eyes this involved purging the Jews, getting rid of the "cosmopolitan" influences, and increasing the role of the state so that national interest and not individual egotism and money lust dominated an area so vital to the psychic health of the German people.[30]

A few months after his talk on Wagner, Goebbels described the old system as "liberal." The new system overthrew it by putting the common good before the good of the individual. Building the folk community of racial brethren took precedence over individual egos: "The more free a nation is, the more freely its members can move about."[31] Goebbels declared that the new art represented a spiritual rejection of decadent modern anarchy. Truly *voelkisch* artists could now emerge into the light of a new era; they could return to the *Volk*. Goebbels wanted to be the good patron of the new art, an art which would satisfy the spiritual hunger of the nation.

The Nazis intended to carry out this task through a centralized cultural institution called the Reich Culture Chamber (Reichskulturkammer, or RKK), which was authorized by a law of September 22, 1933. Goebbels described this organization as bringing together all creative individuals in a "spiritual-cultural unity." Workers of the hand and of the head would join together under the protective shelter of the state. The

RKK consisted of seven chambers: music, fine arts, theater, literature, press, radio, and film. The radio chamber was eventually dissolved. A Goebbels decree of May 31, 1938, clarified the relationship of these chambers to the ministry. The Promi was the central overseer of the RKK and its individual branches, while the central office of the RKK, whose president was Joseph Goebbels, coordinated the work of the various chambers insofar as it involved common responsibilities. From 1938 the individual chambers reported to Goebbels directly, not to the RKK or via the RKK. The individuals who ran the RKK and its branches were usually Promi people, and in the long run Goebbels probably intended to absorb the RKK into the ministry. No artist or painter, writer or poet, to take some obvious examples, could practice his art and profession in the Third Reich unless he was a member of one of the chambers. By 1939 there were 65,000 members of the various chambers. Goebbels used this system as a means of dominating the arts in Germany. Through it he manipulated employment and benefits as well as blacklists and prospective Gestapo actions. As Germany's borders expanded, so did the membership of the RKK. Affiliated groups and subordinate organizations contributed to its swollen membership rolls. One wartime document claimed that 410,000 people were active in the arts in Greater Germany, and that they were all "supported and advised" by the state.[32]

Hitler had a certain degree of condescending tolerance for egotistical or political deviations among artists and actors. After all, they were eccentric Bohemian types. Goebbels did not share this attitude and ruthlessly used his powers to control or even destroy individuals. Actors might call him "Mickey Mouse" behind his back, but they usually yielded to his demands that they play a certain role or agree to a new contract. Rumors abounded that the minister took advantage of actresses by forcing them to trade sex for starring roles, better contracts, or good publicity for a forthcoming film. A new problem arose for Goebbels from early 1942. It was extremely difficult to retain or obtain draft deferments for RKK artists; at best many were inducted into the armed forces to provide cultural entertainment for the troops. Equally troublesome, Fritz Sauckel, Hitler's new labor commissar and hardly a man of the arts, possessed powers of conscription through a decree of July 30, 1942. The armed forces had the last word in deferment appeals, and if one UK was granted, another might be lifted in compensation.

When the war broke out, Goebbels praised the many ministry employees who requested leave so that they could go to the front. He told them to remain at their desks. Early in 1940 it became clear to the minister that the Promi contained opportunists as well as heroes. He warned everyone that nobody could resign to accept a position in another ministry, even if the offer meant a promotion or higher pay. The call-up of reserves prompted this situation. The files of the ministry and the Reich Culture Chamber were filled with documents illustrative of the deferment situation. By 1943 the party propaganda central office was even losing many of its middle-aged men to the draft, and the ministry was powerless to prevent this. Even when the OKW yielded in a specific case, the Army demanded that the requesting agency substitute another employee for the man now given UK status. The OKW would rarely give up a man once he was inducted, though *Arbeitsurlaub,* or work leave, might be approved for specific time periods. The ministry had a special list of absolutely essential personnel, but the party offices were losing musicians and designers of posters to the Army in increasing numbers. A rare amusing note was struck in 1944, when the ministry discovered that the draft status of one Hans Albrecht was no longer a problem. He had been arrested after the attempt on Hitler's life. Hitler himself occasionally intervened to secure a deferment or a release from the Army. The importance that Hitler and Goebbels attached to the cinema was reflected in the fact that as late as 1944–45 the film industry had 1,944 men with deferments.[33]

Another cultural problem emerged during the war, one related to the overly ardent attempt of local Nazis to edit plays, oratorios, and operas. They did this on their own, with no authorization from the relevant culture chamber. Local Nazi thugs or self-appointed purifiers of culture were capable of carving up Shakespeare, rewriting Schiller, changing the text of a Handel oratorio, or altering Mozart's Requiem. Martin Bormann agreed with Goebbels that this was impermissible, at least during the war (religion could be taken care of after the victory). Local theaters were forbidden to make such changes in text. If they found something offensive, they were to report this to the Reich Theater Chamber, through its Commission for the Translation of Foreign Stage Works, or to the Reich Agency for the Adaptation of Music.[34] Despite his attacks upon intellectualism, Goebbels had contempt for the semiliterate types who produced so much of the Nazi literature. He considered himself musically gifted and a fine literary stylist. More importantly, Goebbels alternated pressure with flattering patronage in his quest for an image as the man who protected and fostered German arts and German artists.

Joseph Goebbels worked hard during the war to create an image as a leader who cared, a minister who supported victims of the Allied terror bombings and who aided artists and actors in need. In this way, the minister increased his popularity by building a structure of patronage and moral debt. The masses would not spontaneously turn to a man of

Goebbels' character and intellectual coldness, but if he protected the German nation and its artists, he might transform his image into that of a man of the people. Perhaps Goebbels never allowed himself the thought, but his wartime patronage activities almost seemed calculated to put him in a good position, should a struggle for power ensue "after the victory" or after the departure of Adolf Hitler. Joseph Goebbels used his discretionary "Dr. Goebbels-Fonds" for the purpose of aiding those in need. Goebbels donated funds to the survivors of fallen war correspondents and photographers. In 1942 Goebbels gave RM 100 each to surviving relatives of those Nazis who had fallen in the Era of Struggle. He also donated from RM 50 to RM 500, depending on the size of the family, to those who wore the Badge of Honor and who had been severely wounded during the *Kampfzeit*. Each local Reich propaganda office was urged to submit up to sixty-five names in these various categories. Goebbels thus combined political patronage in the Tammany Hall manner with his image as protector of Nazi martyrs and their surviving loved ones.[35]

The money which went into the Dr. Goebbels-Fonds came largely from money earned by the "German Weekly Newsreel" operation. This *Deutsche Wochenschau GmbH.* paid RM 1 million to the treasury in 1941, money earmarked for the Goebbels fund. When Julius Streicher's newspaper *Der Stürmer* inquired about publication of a propaganda company report from the front, it learned from the ministry that it could reprint the material at no cost, but that it might wish to contribute something to Goebbels' fund for survivors of fallen propaganda company soldier-correspondents. In a similar case, the ministry official Werner Stephan informed a book dealer and publisher in Minden that he might wish to donate RM 25 to the Goebbels fund. A memorandum by an armed forces propaganda official in 1940 stated that picture news services were paying a not inconsiderable amount per month into the Dr. Goebbels-Fonds. The minister was fearful that private publishers and newspapers would try to gain exclusive and unfair advantages by monopolizing the work of former employees who were now serving in the propaganda companies. Goebbels moved toward taking over the responsibility of subsidizing the families of these men, thereby eliminating any appearance of favoritism while gaining more patronage for himself. The *Deutsche Wochenschau GmbH.* paid special subsidies to free-lance reporters serving in the propaganda companies, but Goebbels viewed that as an acceptable procedure, since he controlled that corporation. Ten percent of the rental income from the popular documentary films *Campaign in Poland* and *Baptism of Fire,* or RM 270,000, had gone into the Goebbels discretionary fund by June 1940.[36]

Whenever Dr. Goebbels visited the front, he distributed generous supplies of cigarettes and cognac to the boys in uniform. General Dietl, whose exploits made him a Goebbels favorite for newsreel exposure, saw his troops receive RM 600,000 worth of alcoholic beverages in 1942. The bottles were distributed to the general's army by way of the Reich Culture Chamber! Goebbels, clever man that he was, calculated that troops serving in the far north of the eastern front would be grateful for something which would warm them up. Goebbels also distributed some of his funds to the National Socialist Welfare Organization (NSV) as a way of augmenting his influence. Goebbels' use of money was similar to Heinrich Himmler's technique of placing high-ranking SS officers in various ministries, while at the same time flattering non-SS men in key positions by giving them SS titles. In the competitive world of National Socialist fiefdoms, each leader schemed to retain and augment his own power and influence.[37] It was impossible to maintain one's status without increasing one's power. Ribbentrop and Rosenberg had discovered this by 1943.

Goebbels used his ministerial position to gain popularity among those who served in the mass media and the fine arts. He created the Dr. Goebbels Radio Donation, the purpose of which was to give free radios to those in need. From 1933 to 1942 he collected many thousands of radios from men involved in the broadcasting industry. During the war Goebbels gave the radios—items in short supply—to wounded soldiers and to the survivors of men fallen at the front. On one day in 1942 Goebbels donated five thousand radios in this manner.

Goebbels had millions of Reichsmarks at his disposal through his control of the Dr. Goebbels Foundation for Actors, or the "Thanks to Artists" (Künstlerdank). Goebbels used this money to help artists and actors who were in financial need. His ministry made much of this in its propaganda, contrasting the social conscience of Germany with the harsh attitude of England towards its many bombed-out, unemployed, and needy people in the arts. In 1943 Goebbels channeled almost a million Reichsmarks to such individuals through the Reich Culture Chamber. The Goebbels Foundation for Those Active in Cultural Pursuits offered a three-week cost-free recuperation period to member artists who had been injured or made homeless by Allied bombings of their towns.

Joseph Goebbels built much of his growing popularity upon his role in consoling bombed-out people and refugees. He organized and paid for a "Reich Music Train" in 1943. The train took performing musicians to various areas in northern and western Germany, where they offered concerts and diversion to sorely tried people. Goebbels believed that films would boost morale in such areas, and in the same year he requested that all Reich authorities try to come up with projectors, which would then be turned over to the affected communities—by Goebbels or his agents.

Goebbels emphasized in his public statements at this time that the population in the north and west was suffering badly from the Allied bombings. People elsewhere in the Reich should not gripe about shortages; 7 million people in the north and west lived in the shadow of major terror bombings. Goebbels referred to this problem as a greater challenge than Stalingrad. It was a problem, but also an opportunity for Goebbels, the patron and protector. He had acquired experience for this role by his earlier work on behalf of ethnic Germans who had settled in the Reich between 1939 and 1941. For the Christmas season of 1941 Goebbels supervised the distribution of gifts to almost 165,000 such settlers. The action cost Goebbels about RM 400,000, money used by local propaganda offices for a variety of purchases, including rum, vodka, song sheets, and tens of thousands of photographs of Hitler in various war zones.[38]

Joseph Goebbels took a profound personal interest in the cultural needs of those Germans who participated in "This greatest migration of all times," as he called the resettlement of individuals because of the effects or the threat of Allied bombings. In 1943 Goebbels assigned responsibility for this cultural and propagandistic activity to the Main Cultural Affairs Office of the Reich Propaganda Central Office (RPL). An internal bulletin late in September 1943 declared that providing for the broad needs of such refugees and bomb victims was the most important work of the party. Some of this work consisted of showing movies, presenting plays, and displaying the work of important artists. Cultural work, the bulletin said, could preserve and strengthen the inner strength of resistance in the nation. Goebbels' empathy for the victims of massive dislocation led him on several occasions to propose that a new military decoration be created, one which recognized bravery and meritorious service by civilians on the home front. As late as October 1944, Goebbels and Naumann pushed for such a medal, but the party chancellory rejected the idea.[39] Bormann and Hitler probably felt that attendant publicity would only make more evident the suffering of millions and the changed fate of Germany in the war. Goebbels realized that such reasoning was absurd, but his powers to alter it were limited.

The ministry controlled its propaganda apparatus through the Reich propaganda offices situated in each of wartime Greater Germany's forty-two *Gaue,* or regions. These offices owed their origin to a July 1933 decree which established thirty-one provincial offices of the new ministry. In 1937 these branches became the RPAe, or Reich propaganda offices.[40] Throughout the war Goebbels and the officials of the propaganda division of the ministry worked at strengthening the authority of the forty-two offices. A memorandum in late 1942 stated, "The leader of the propaganda office is, in his official function, the representative of the ministry. Accordingly, he must possess the means to make visible his role upon the occasion of special events (receptions, state ceremonies, jubilees, etc.) . . . "[41] Goebbels encouraged a certain degree of autonomy and decentralization in order to strengthen the RPAe. If a local office was inactive or was dominated entirely by the regional party bosses, the power of the ministry suffered.

In 1944 an internal memorandum in the ministry addressed this question.[42] It recalled that under the decree of February 26, 1941, all divisions of the ministry were to keep the RPAe informed of their work, and they were to use the local offices in carrying out cultural and political work in the *Gaue.* The directors of the cultural divisions of the ministry had been under orders since October 1941 to work with the cultural officials of the local offices. The memo noted that ignoring the local offices would erode their prestige. Goebbels saw the RPAe as a local tool for carrying out the ministry's policies. No Gauleiter, however, would pay much attention to a weak local office. Goebbels never solved this problem, since most directors of the RPAe were old cronies of the Gauleiter. These directors were also the Gau propaganda directors of the party, and in this sense were subordinate to the Gauleiter in matters of rank and discipline. The RPAe were divided into four sections: administration, propaganda, press, and culture. By 1941 the total number of RPAe employees had almost reached fourteen hundred. Their budget had risen to ten million Reichsmarks, twice the figure for 1939. The Berlin office was of particular interest to Gauleiter Goebbels; Werner Wächter directed it until 1941, to be followed by Erich Boeker.[43]

One of the major sources of information for the ministry was the *Stimmungsbericht,* the RPAe report on morale and attitude among the civilian population. Each local office was responsible for sending such a report to the propaganda section of the ministry's political division for evaluation. These reports were sometimes the basis for policies formulated by Goebbels and his associates. At his ministerial conference Goebbels often expressed an opinion or ordered actions to be taken on the basis of one or more of these reports. In September 1942 he feared that a rumor reported in several RPAe *Berichte* would turn the German people against Berlin. The gossip concerned an alleged pact between Britain and the Reich to spare each other's capitals. In this instance the minister, flashing his sardonic and mordant wit, pointed out that later in the autumn the British would probably bomb Berlin heavily, and that should put a stop to the rumor. The local offices were responsible for a further report, the "Activity Report" *(Tätigkeitsbericht)*, in which they were to provide information to Berlin about the local situation in terms of politics and propaganda, and to make relevant suggestions to the ministry for dealing with these trends.

By late 1944 Schaeffer, who received and evaluated these reports, was dissatisfied with them. They were too long and lacked good suggestions. He indicated that from then on, the reports were to make practical suggestions which could be immediately implemented. Many local RPAe officials were hesitant about making such suggestions, since Dr. Schaeffer so often slapped them down. In September 1944 an official of the Dresden RPA, Elsner, complained about the way the press was handling the Soviet-Finnish armistice. The newspapers seemed to imply that the terms were rather mild. This might start Germans to thinking that the Bolsheviks were not so bad after all. Schaeffer replied to Elsner that if he had been paying closer attention to the situation, he would have seen that the necessary measures had already been taken. A month later an RPA official in Oldenburg suggested that the ministry put out a pamphlet showing who was really to blame for the origins of the war. Schaeffer replied that this was hardly a top priority item at the moment.

Many of the RPAe reports to Schaeffer consisted of bizarre suggestions, self-serving gossip, or factual information. In June 1944 (on June 6, D Day) one correspondent had an idea on how to respond to the Allied terror bombings of German cities: put Allied POWs in German buildings of cultural significance and make them stay there during air raids. This suggestion was not seriously considered, despite Goebbels' "lynch them" mentality late in the war. In October a former ministry employee reported on Army corruption in occupied Norway. He alleged that officers lived an easy life and made use of their good connections. Especially after the attempt on Hitler's life by Army officers (July 20, 1944), anything of an antimilitary hue was attractive to Goebbels and Schaeffer. A few months later a correspondent from the RPA in the Moselland gave the ministry some information that could be used in German atrocity propaganda. It seems that the Allies had bombed a German military hospital train. Some of the RPAe reports suffered from a common defect. When they reported on civilian reaction to a speech by a Nazi eminence, they invariably spoke of the enthusiasm and inspiration which gripped the populace.[44]

Schaeffer provided the local offices with information which could prove useful in carrying out the ministry's propaganda aims. In 1943 he and his colleague Dietze obtained thousands of names of professional people from the RPAe and considered drawing up confidential, frank reports that could not be broadcast or printed in the mass media. These men were doctors, lawyers, druggists, engineers, architects, chemists, and generally people of status in their communities. They would receive reports dealing with the situation in Italy, defensive measures in the air war, the situation in America, and the spreading of rumors. Not much was done along these lines, however, although some information was sent to leaders and active members of Nazi professional organizations. In the same year Schaeffer sent long translations from Wendell Willkie's book *One World* to the RPAe, the aim of the operation being to show how the West had sold out Europe to Bolshevism. In May 1943 the RPAe received confidential material relating to Stalin's recent dissolution of Comintern, which was treated as an example of the old Communist "United Front" tactic. The propaganda machine still functioned in late February 1945, though signs of collapse were everywhere. An irate ministry official wrote to a resident anti-Jewish expert that his proposed anti-Semitic material could not be distributed to the RPAe directors: "For what RPA director, faced with the burdens of the moment, has time to read an essay of seventeen typed pages?" [45]

The directors of the RPAe convened from time to time in Berlin in order to discuss their work and their problems. Goebbels was the host. The program of such a meeting, held on February 28–29, 1944, gives some sense of the theoretical responsibilities of the local office director. These men heard papers on economic policy, the food situation, recruiting questions in the Wehrmacht, air raid measures, "contemporary questions in German cultural life," and the German Luftwaffe. There were two special treats in store for the directors: a talk by interior minister Reichsführer Heinrich Himmler on "questions of internal policy," and a discussion by Alfred Rosenberg of "philosophical questions." The exigencies of the military situation, particularly the worsening air war, forced the ministry to make this conference briefer than one which had been held in June 1943. These meetings concluded with an address by Joseph Goebbels.[46]

Goebbels' great interest in the victims of air attacks inspired a memorandum to him from the director of the propaganda division in April 1942. Entitled "Cultural Support of the Population Affected by Air Attacks," the memo briefly described measures which had been taken by the RPA in Kiel after heavy British bombings.[47] Choirs and Wehrmacht bands gave concerts every Sunday, and a theater was being set up outside the city. All this cheered up the population and restored a sense of social cohesiveness. The Kiel operation was paid for by specially allocated ministry funds. The growing catastrophe of the air war forced a change in emphasis in the work of the RPAe. Their original function was threefold: (1) carrying out the propaganda policies of the ministry through "active propaganda"; (2) strengthening the sense of German ethnicity; (3) handling special expenditures. In some regions badly affected by the air war, the RPAe became absorbed in local efforts at survival. In areas remote from the danger zones, the RPAe often became dormant, neglected by the Gauleiters.

The most significant single project of the RPAe in the early and middle war years was *Volkstumsarbeit,* or work to strengthen German ethnic self-consciousness, a form of National Socialist nation building. In the annexed formerly Polish territories of the Reich, the needs of German settlers were of paramount concern. Many of them did not like West Prussia or the Wartheland and were moving westward. If this continued, the areas would be largely Polish. One suggestion to Goebbels was that the Germans build clubs and cultural centers in the east ("like the English"!). Bookstores should be established, and all towns of more than two thousand inhabitants must have a weekly film show, even if this was done by means of a mobile van. Fifty-five of these touring vans were necessary, in addition to service personnel. The vans were hard to come by, as were radios, despite the seizure of many Polish receivers. Banners and pictures were needed for the new German clubs and social centers. Mobile exhibitions should present traveling shows illustrating cultural, economic, and political themes; perhaps they could be taken from one community to another by train. The same principle might prevail in presenting concerts, plays, lectures, poetry readings, choral groups, and community evenings, including celebrations of days sacred to the Reich and to the party. Such events might raise the consciousness of German *Volkstum* in the east. The memorandum to Goebbels which contained this program assumed a coordinated campaign by the ministry and the local RPAe in cooperation with other party authorities and offices. The image of the new lands of the east should be improved in the press; posters and placards must show Germans in the "old Reich" that the eastern provinces would be nice places in which to live. Newsreels and travelogues could do a lot for the settlement program. The eastern division of the ministry requested over eleven million Reichsmarks for fiscal 1941, though most of this money was to be used in the new provinces rather than in the old Reich for image improvement.

The propaganda ministry was particularly interested in strengthening the ethnicity work of the RPAe in "borderland" areas, that is, of offices in regions which had large ethnic non-German minorities or which bordered formerly French, Belgian, Italian, Polish, or Czech territory.

The *Volkstum* advisor in each RPA disposed of his part of the 1941 RPAe Reich *Volkstum* budget of RM 810,000. This money was earmarked for such work by Berlin, but its use by each office was largely subject to local conditions and discretion. In June 1941 a Dr. Hopf of the ministry told the RPAe directors that the tasks of the *Volkstum* advisors were fourfold: to support all efforts at strengthening Germandom; to second Himmler's efforts as commissioner for the strengthening of German folkdom; to raise the cultural level and national consciousness of the citizenry; to warn Germans about contacts with foreign workers, without defaming those people. The peak of this *Volkstumsarbeit* came in 1941–42; the budget allocated to the advisors began to drop by 1943. Even in 1943, however, the budget for this type of work was a large part of the total RPA allocation, especially in the case of border regions. In border areas such as East Prussia, the Upper Danube, the Lower Danube, Carinthia, the Tirol, the Sudetenland, Danzig, the Wartheland, and Upper Silesia the money allocated to an RPA for ethnic work ranged from about 44 percent to about 77 percent (Danzig-West Prussia) of its total fiscal 1943 budget. The average figure for all RPA offices was more like 38 percent.

The RPAe asked for their budgetary allocations for the next fiscal year in March and April. The Brandenburg office requested additional funds in 1942 because of demographic changes in the region since 1939. Formerly rural, the *Gau* now contained many German and foreign laborers, and this necessitated more *Volkstum* work. The office conveyed the negative impression of men having difficulties coping with the challenges that faced them. For such an office Goebbels' decentralization program was a mixed blessing. The major problem which confronted the RPA in Main/Franconia was resurgent ecclesiastical opposition to Nazism. The acting director, writing to Goebbels from Würzburg in March 1942, suggested a special RM 24,000 subsidy for efforts to combat Christian influences. This campaign would include subsidizing Nazi clubs and singing groups, lectures, puppet shows, and village bookshops. The RPA could mobilize veterans' associations, sporting groups, and village meetings of the Hitler Youth and the League of German Girls.

By 1941 every *Gau* office had a special department concerned with ethnic work. Monthly allowances for special projects, such as film presentations by the *Gau* film office, gave way to a more unified budgetary approach. The problems of a society at war plagued many offices, however, and complaints about lost records and red tape abounded. Such confusion was evident when the RPA of Danzig-West Prussia ordered 1,400 copies of the brochure "Return of the Banners" for female worker-settlers, of whom 500 were from Berlin. Some RPA offices used the excuse of pressing *Volkstum* work in order to augment their budgets or prevent reduction in monies allotted to them. In 1940–41 the RPA director in the Bavarian Eastern March (Bayreuth) admitted that Bavaria was no longer a borderland, given the absence of the old Czech-German frontier, but that it contained many Czechs, 17,000 resettled children from Hamburg and Berlin, and 11,000 ethnic German newcomers from the east. For these reasons the director requested more than the current RM 1,000 per month for *Volkstum* propaganda. The ministry increased the RPAe budget for this office, but not as much as the local director wished.

Early in 1941 the director of the Lower Danube RPA office (Vienna) asked for a special fund in order to produce a pamphlet, "Keep Your Blood Pure." The director argued that the influx of alien farm workers made such a measure urgent, since German workers viewed these foreigners as peasants equal to themselves. The ministry agreed to the request. Wartime conditions made other demands more difficult of fulfillment. Early in 1942 the ministry informed all local offices that there was not enough fuel or film wagons to meet the needs of resettlement camps for movies. By 1943 the total budget for all RPA offices was dropping. The allotment for *Volkstum* work was down by RM 100,000 from 1942, though it was 8 percent higher as a proportion of the total RPA national budget. Clever RPA directors got around these reductions by playing upon ministry fears. In May 1944 the East Prussian office reported strong pro-Bolshevik agitation, especially among foreign workers. The press was not effective in combatting this trend; what was needed were posters and placards showing Bolshevik atrocities in the most graphic manner. Slide shows would also be useful. A month later Schaeffer approved an extra allotment of RM 60,000 for this campaign. An unstated premise of the request was that East Prussia might soon be part of the eastern front.[48]

Joseph Goebbels took a personal interest in cultural propaganda in the formerly Polish eastern territories. He was the official patron of the *Deutsches Ordensland,* or Land of the Germanic Order, an organization formed in Danzig-West Prussia to promote Germanization. By early 1942 about half a million Reichsmarks had been raised for the local RPA efforts in this field, money which Goebbels helped provide through his own connections. This cultural work was a joint effort at Germanization by the minister, the *Gau* administration, German communities, and the RPA office. The propaganda section of the ministry considered it so successful that it fostered similar organizations in the Wartheland, Köln-Aachen, and the Moselland. The beginnings of Germanic Orders were apparent in these areas by 1942, though most of the work there would have to wait until after a German victory. In October 1942 state secretary Gutterer praised the work of Germanization in the east, declaring that it was a typical National Socialist achievement to be able to carry out such a project while the battle raged in Russia: "We no longer live in the cloud cuckoo land of the poets and thinkers, laughed at by the whole world." [49]

Germanization work was funded by ministries and agencies other than Goebbels' office. In the case of recently annexed territories or border areas, funds for banners, decorations, and the establishment of Hitler Youth hostels often came from the interior ministry or from the Germandom Fund. The ministry had made clear to the RPAe that it would not provide money for certain types of "active propaganda": Decorations for party rallies (banners, busts of Hitler, podiums), sports events, welfare payments. RPA offices which wanted to finance sports competitions were to turn to the interior ministry or to the office of the Reich sport leader, while allocating funds for welfare was the province of the NSV. Party rallies belonged to the financial obligations of the Reich Propaganda Central Office. The RPAe offices thus accounted for a relatively small fraction of Goebbels' expenditures.[50]

The Nazi propaganda efforts which had made possible Adolf Hitler's accession to power were the work of the Reichspropagandaleitung, or Reich Propaganda Central Office. The *Party Organization Book* noted that the propaganda of the NSDAP, its branches, and affiliated groups was the responsibility of the Reich propaganda director. The NSDAP was organized along hierarchical lines, consisting of political leaders, or "bearers of sovereignty" (Hoheitsträger), descending from Hitler, the party chancellory, and the Reichsleiters, to the Gauleiters, the district leaders, local branch leaders, cell leaders, and block leaders. In a practical sense, the designation "political leader" commenced at the local branch *(Ortsgruppen)* level. The heads of important party branches, such as the NS Student League, were put into the "bearer of sovereignty" category. There were eight official branches of the party, including the SA, the SS, the Hitler Youth, and eight affiliated organizations, including the German Labor Front. The *Organization Book* stipulated that the RPL was to determine the entire propagandistic manifestation of the movement, including its branches and affiliated groups. The *Gau* propaganda office (GPL), presided over by a *Gau* propaganda director, was the representative of the RPL in each *Gau* and was responsible for carrying out national party policy in four areas: active propaganda, film, radio, and culture. The district *(Kreis)* propaganda office had these functions the next level down, and subordinate to it was the local branch propaganda director.[51]

The main figure in the RPL, after Goebbels and the state secretary, was the staff director. Until April 1942 Hugo Fischer held this post. Born in Munich in 1902, Fischer studied business with the intention of becoming a merchant. He became an activist in the party instead, joining in 1922 and taking part in the Beer Hall Putsch the next year. He distinguished himself after the murder of foreign minister Walther Rathenau in 1922 by writing a pamphlet praising the murderers. In 1927 Hugo Fischer became an adjutant of Himmler. Fischer attracted Himmler's attention in part because he was active in the SA, associated with the notorious Edmund Heines. Fischer's crudeness and personal corruption made him more useful in the struggle for power than in the administration of a bureaucracy, so Goebbels finally pensioned him off with a sinecure.

The minister replaced him with Eugen Hadamovsky on June 8, 1942. This man was no favorite of the minister either, so Goebbels ordered his former head of the ministry's radio division to spend his time at the Munich headquarters of the RPL. Munich was the "cradle" and "capital" of the movement. Goebbels wanted to avoid bureaucratizing the propaganda of the party; thus he decreed late in 1941 that all offices of the RPL not essential to the war effort were to be located in Munich. This was somewhat of an illusion, for Goebbels and his ministry aides in Berlin determined what the RPL did. All the important offices of the RPL remained in Berlin despite the Goebbels order and were so listed in the 1942 edition of the *National Socialist Yearbook*. Werner Wächter, chief of the propaganda staff of the RPL, played an important role in its work after 1941. Goebbels was not amused when he learned of Wächter's brilliant gift of mimicry, a talent which enabled him to imitate the minister's speech and gestures perfectly. One of the problems of the RPL was that it was notorious for attracting inefficient or lazy party hacks to its offices, men whom Goebbels would not have admitted to the ministry.[52]

The Main Cultural Office of the RPL, directed by Karl Cerff, had many responsibilities, among them the formulation of sample programs for the celebrations of the Nazi movement. This office published a monthly "Suggestions for Structuring National Socialist Ceremonies," and was concerned with the promotion and supervision of the National Socialist spirit in the arts. By 1944 the Cultural Office had taken on many other tasks, including providing for the cultural needs of wounded soldiers, refugees, and survivors. The work of the main RPL offices was complicated by the propagandistic ambitions of men in the Nazi branch organizations or the affiliated groups. In 1940 Goebbels directed Hugo Fischer to make clear to the "Strength through Joy" organization that if it wanted to avoid presenting "senseless and damaging" lecture programs in the future, it had better clear its efforts first with the RPL.[53]

The leadership of the RPL, Goebbels, Naumann, Tiessler, Fischer (or Hadamovsky), and Wächter, regularly exchanged memos and ideas in preparation for seasonal propaganda campaigns. Late in 1941 several plans and slogans for the winter RPL effort were discussed. Once agreement was reached, the plan would be printed and distributed for use as a guide to party speakers throughout the Reich. For the winter campaign of 1941–42 some of the ideas and phrases considered were: "Through sacrifice to victory"; "The German people is winning the war of nerves"; "More humor!"; "Germany's inexhaustible reserves"; "Our allies." Too many Germans believed "Germany is conquering herself to death," and "England loses all the battles but wins the war." [54] Goebbels and his colleagues knew this because they paid close attention to the confidential Security Service reports on civilian opinion as well as to their own RPAe accounts of local morale. The plan for 1941–42 envisaged the use of agents to counter such feelings by planting counterrumors. Another possible ploy for boosting working-class morale was to have famous actors appear in neighborhood theaters during the presentation of their films. A second draft of a plan for this period more clearly expressed Goebbels' own approach, stating that Europe was at war with the Jews, who had been overthrown in Germany after 1933.

The plan, drawn up by Goebbels, was subject to later changes by the minister, but it summarized the methods of the RPL quite well. The propaganda campaign would make use of rallies and meetings, film presentations with speakers, slide shows, presentations by the *Gau* film offices, cultural celebrations, lectures on the political-military situation, exhibitions, posters, slogans of the week, the weekly quotation of the NSDAP, the picture of the week, and propaganda by word of mouth. Some of the slide-lecture themes included "Betrayed Socialism," "The German Woman in the War," "The U.S.A., Disturber of the Peace," and "The Mediterranean, Area of Decision." "The German Mission in Europe" and "Politics and War in Caricature" were in preparation. The campaign was to begin on October 1, 1941, and be concluded on March 31, 1942, with a long break from December 15 to January 15. Goebbels, obviously annoyed by prior slipshod work, demanded careful preparation and prompt mailing of materials to the local offices.

In suggesting a slogan for the campaign of 1942–43, Tiessler came up with "The Führer can depend upon us!" Goebbels decided upon the old *Kampfzeit* slogan "For freedom, justice, and bread," but changed his mind and rejected both ideas in favor of the tried-and-true "Führer, give us our orders, we'll follow!" Only then was the slogan given out to the many agencies and individuals who would publicize it all over the Reich. By July 1944 Naumann and Goebbels were so desperate for a fresh, good slogan that they used the Bolsheviks as a model. Naumann recalled that when things were going badly for the Russians, they had made use of the slogan "Better to die standing than to live kneeling!" He wanted something fitting for the hard battles lying before Germans in the coming year. The director of the ministry's propaganda section and the staff director of the RPL solicited slogans from their people and came up with quite a potpourri: "Any sacrifice for freedom"; "A nation which wishes to be free cannot be subjugated"; "There is only one sin: cowardice!"; "Don't pay attention to the hardships, only to the goals." These last suggestions were taken from the works of E. M. Arndt, Friedrich Nietzsche, and Ernst Juenger. The propagandists wished to bring out the "deadly seriousness" of the situation, while at the same time encouraging the nation with talk about miracle weapons and higher rates of arms productivity. Some of these suggestions were used by Goebbels and Naumann, most rejected. Goebbels was hostile to slogans containing phrases about Europe. He also felt at this time that themes like "It's life or death!" were too pessimistic, and usually changed them to "For freedom and life!"

The central RPL office kept *Gau* officials and speakers informed of relevant slogans and information by mailing them a variety of bulletins and news summaries. The "Special Service" *(Sonderdienst)* of the RPL was regularly sent to all Gauleiters, deputy Gauleiters, *Gau* propaganda directors, district leaders, Reich speakers of the party, and *Gau* speakers ("Edition B"). They were forbidden to use this confidential information in their propaganda unless otherwise directed; the material was "only for personal information." The Special Service included material about the latest rumors, as well as facts to be used in propaganda. A "Special Edition" *(Sonderlieferung)* of the bulletin contained Goebbels' lead article from the forthcoming weekly edition of *Das Reich*. The implication was clear that propagandists were to make use of the latest Goebbels line. The Central Information Service of the RPL regularly mailed out a strictly confidential report named *The Situation (Die Lage)*, which dealt largely with the implications of the latest developments at the front, in the armaments situation, and in the campaign for total war.

The RPL supplied local propaganda offices with another regular bulletin, the *Propaganda-Parole*, which contained both confidential information and specific instructions for applying such knowledge to the creation of propaganda. In May 1942 the RPL altered this bulletin by removing all specific instructions for making propaganda. These guidelines now appeared separately as "Propaganda Instructions," and the information in them could be passed down to subordinate *Gau* offices in the propaganda apparatus. These two bulletins were not released until Tiessler had obtained the agreement of the party chancellory. By July 1943 a new agreement had been reached, by which the chancellory would not go over the entire text, but would only examine points raised by Tiessler for endorsement by the party office. The official journal of the RPL was *Our Will and Way,* a monthly magazine which published illustrated articles about the techniques, personnel, aims, and successes of Nazi propaganda.[55]

Hitler believed that all great revolutions owed their origins and success to the spoken word, to the men who could attract followers through powerful verbal expression. He placed Jesus, Lenin, and Mussolini in this category, and the Nazis often pointed to Frederick the Great and Napoleon as men whose inspirational words to their troops secured success in battle. The RPL followed this cult of the spoken word by organizing a Main Office for Speakers' Matters *(Rednerwesen),* which encompassed a Speakers' Organization and a Speakers' Information Agency. Speakers were divided into two categories, the "political speaker," whose function was to carry Nazi ideology to the people and to explain the measures of the regime to them, and the "specialized speaker," who was provided by Nazi branch and affiliated organizations for the purpose of speaking on a specific subject, for example, the labor policies of the government. Party speakers ranged from those of the highest rank, the Reich speakers, to the local district speakers, with the *Gau* speakers placed on an intermediate level. The speakers were selected and used on the basis of two criteria, the "principle of accomplishment" and their merits as "Old Fighters" of the party. One hundred fifty men directed the work of these speakers in 1940. The *Gau* speaker worked for the GPL office in his area, and the district speaker was active at the behest of his local *Kreis,* or district propaganda central office.

On the eve of the war various party authorities were concerned about the disruptions that military conflict might cause in the speaker system. Rudolf Hess's office of the deputy Führer worked with the *Gau* mobilization commissioners of the party in order to prevent the breakdown of the system in the event of war. Hess's office ordered a survey made of the draft status of the party speakers as well as of the minimal needs of each *Gau.* The office outlined procedures for deferment applications and indicated that it would cultivate close relationships with the relevant Wehrmacht authorities. While the party lost some of its best speakers to the war effort (out of about 9,800, more than a third were serving in the Wehrmacht early in 1941), their absence was not catastrophic to the speaker system. The party held about 140,000 meetings and rallies between September 1, 1939, and December 15, 1940, and another 50,000 factory rallies. *Our Will and Way* boasted that the war was again proving that the most important elements in propaganda efforts were the speaker and the meeting. These efforts were helped by the fact that the Wehrmacht was sending servicemen back home on furlough to attend party meetings and to appear on the platform with political speakers. Some RPL efforts were seriously hindered by the war, such as the plan put into effect in some areas by 1938, which would have eventually established loudspeaker pillars in every public square. The speaker system began to fade away with the ebbing of the Germany military tide in the middle war years. The growing unpopularity of the party and the demands of the hour made the system almost irrelevant by 1942, and even the partial revival of the party late in the war could not resuscitate it.

The *Gau* propaganda central office received materials and advice for speakers from the Enlightenment Service for Political Speakers, printed by the RPL. Speakers in Munich received these instructions if they were going to give speeches on world politics: Study your subject, be tactful in your approach, display a good sense of the audience, show depth and clarity in your presentation, and make the listeners see how petty their everyday concerns are compared to greatness of Germany's goals and tasks. Enlightenment Service bulletins tried to revive the old fiery agitational spirit of the Era of Struggle. Inspired by *Mein Kampf,* one bulletin told speakers how to behave at meetings. The nature of the advice indicates that the speakers were of varying moral and intellectual quality. First and foremost, they were not to drink before a meeting nor to sit around and consume alcoholic beverages after giving a speech. Speakers were not to play for applause; they were to stand up with their hands at their sides while speaking, not with their hands in their pockets or behind their back. They were not to pace back and forth while speaking, and their speech was to be natural, devoid of fake pathos. They were not to scream or employ trite phrases and wisecracks, but should make use of tactful humor. Nor should speakers be touchy about being criticized by the *Gau* office. Except for the part about drinking, these instructions were the opposite of every technique used by Adolf Hitler in his speeches. This apparent heresy was not accidental: Too many speakers tried to be little Hitlers, imitating the Führer style, even down to his moustache. The party mandated the use of flags and banners, as well as the two national anthems and military music, and suggested that meetings should not last more than ninety minutes.

Before the war an Enlightenment Service bulletin denounced the mechanical tone of many party speakers. "We are preachers" was the theme; speakers should put their "hearts" and "blood" into their talks. The party was groping for a happy medium between fake Hitlerian hysteria and apathetic speakers who merely read their dull talks to an uninterested captive party audience. It urged that the speakers be more careful in varying their routines in order to fit the audience. Speakers addressing the National Socialist League of Women must be subtle rather than bombastic in their approach, but they should not be unctuous in style. When speakers were giving talks on Nazi population policy, it was inadvisable to pick men who were bachelors. The party was often disappointed with press coverage of speakers' addresses, for such articles were banal and of generally low quality. One receives the impression that the party and its press and speakers suffered from an influx of hacks and opportunists, of people "just doing their jobs."

In Munich the Information, or Enlightment, Services for Speakers provided these men with detailed figures on party activities throughout the *Gau* Munich/Upper Bavaria, including film presentations, increases in party membership, activities of the German Labor Front, art exhibitions, and district rallies. Some of the immediately prewar bulletins contained thematic materials which did not reappear once war broke out on September 1, 1939. Anticlerical propaganda played a major role in Enlightenment Service bulletins in Catholic Bavaria before the war. One issue even asserted that in Prague, Jews, the Church, and the Comintern had all been in the same anti-German league. This type of propaganda, as well as violent anti-Bolshevik diatribes, faded from the pages of information bulletins as Nazi policy led the nation to war, with the Soviet Union as a benevolent neutral. Anticlerical fanaticism was not calculated to unite the German nation, which was one-third Catholic, and it was toned down in most *Gaue.*

In early and mid-1939, speakers were urged to accentuate the positive achievement of the Nazi regime against the background of the miseries of German history. They were to denounce earlier *Schandfrieden,* or peace treaties based upon the disgrace of Germany, such as the treaties of Westphalia and Versailles, and should describe how Hitler peacefully created Greater Germany and secured peace based upon victory in 1938–39. Pride in the party should lead speakers to give proud answers to the questions "Why are you a National Socialist?" when addressing rallies at district ceremonies of the party. They might answer by declaring that they were party comrades because of their German blood, love for the German land, their knowledge of German history, their belief in the German *Volk,* and their love for and belief in Adolf Hitler. On the eve of the war party speakers denounced the Poles as an uncultured, peace-destroying, immature people.[56]

When the war began, the various party informational bulletins for speakers contained suggestions calculated to harden the German will to victory. Speakers were urged to tell their audiences that the Germany of today was far stronger than the Reich of the First World War. In 1940 the RPL placed several new slide shows at their disposal, including material on "Our Führer," "The West Wall," "Germany Pursues a Racial Policy," "World Pirate England," "Plutocracy and Jewry," "Front and Homeland, a Community of Struggle," "On the Road to Victory," and "Battle and Victory in Norway." As the war dragged on into 1942, a new tone was evident in the sloganeering. Speakers were to use phrases such as "Victory at Any Price" and were to talk about Germany "after the victory," never "after the war" or "after the conclusion of peace." Late in 1942 one bulletin pointed out the necessity of combatting the widespread belief that the United States was invincible because of its rich reserves of food and raw materials. Speakers should emphasize the fact that the Axis would soon have greater reserves at its disposal in the Middle East and in Russia than did the United States. Speakers were to continue denouncing Britain as a retrogressive "plutocracy" where the workers suffered.

In the spring of 1943 bulletins urged speakers to make a great deal of the Soviet massacre of Polish officers at Katyn, where the Germans had recently discovered thousands of corpses. They could thus demonstrate the brutality of Bolshevism while underlining the hypocrisy of Stalin's "democratic" Western allies. When Axis resistance collapsed in Tunisia in May 1943, speakers received guidelines on how to deal with yet another disaster. They were to emphasize the heroic struggle of the outnumbered German forces (little note to be taken of the Italians), but were not to draw depressing parallels with Stalingrad. One anecdote might be useful for the speakers: A German regimental band, while being marched off to an Allied POW camp, defiantly played military marches and Nazi battle songs. The bulletin showed a certain aversion to reality in implying that such stories would cheer up the sorely tried German population. Perhaps they would have a greater effect upon convinced Nazis, the main audience of these speakers. A month later speakers received statistics calculated to prove that the Axis, though somewhat outnumbered by the Allies in population and workers, controlled " inner lines" of communication (Japan?) and better-trained, more highly motivated workers.[57]

In 1943 the RPL leadership made certain changes in the structure of its informational system for speakers. Speakers had been complaining that the material they received was too long and in need of improvement. Much of it read like boring press releases, for the bulletins did not contain lively information. Tiessler recommended to Wächter that a restructuring of the information services and bulletins be undertaken. Goebbels dominated bulletins such as the "Special Information for Speakers" and "District Leaders' Information" through the Propaganda Guidance Office of the RPL. One response to the growing criticism was that these bulletins pushed the much-criticized Enlightenment Service materials to the background after the summer of 1943.

The growing intervention of the party chancellory in propaganda work was motivated by the decline of the party propaganda apparatus, as well as by Martin Bormann's determination to revive an increasingly dormant National Socialist movement.[58] The liaison man between Bormann's party chancellory and the RPL was Walter Tiessler, director of the Reich Circle for National Socialist Propaganda and Popular Enlightenment. The function of the Circle (Reichsring) was the coordination of the propaganda of the party branches and affiliated organizations. It consisted of representatives of these branches and organizations on the Reich, *Gau,* district, and municipality levels. A major aim of the Reichsring was the avoidance of confusion stemming from the issuance of so many different propaganda directives by various angencies. The Ring offered courses in propaganda to members of Nazi organizations. In pursuit of a clear and unified propaganda policy, the Ring published bulletins on the *Gau* and district levels, and its mobilized branches, affiliated organizations, and other groups for handing out brochures and similar tasks. The Ring was a creation of the RPL, and it enabled that central office to reach beyond the *Gau* and local Reich propaganda offices in order to disseminate its messages and mobilize propagandists. The Reich and *Gau* circles had a censorship function as well, for they were empowered to examine propaganda writings suggested by branch, affiliated, and related organizations before these brochures were distributed. When this work came up against a determined Nazi eminence in another agency, however, the Ring often failed in this goal.

Walter Tiessler was born in 1903. He was an *älter Kämpfer,* having joined the party in 1922 or 1923; within a year or two he was a municipal branch leader, and by 1925, district leader in Bitterfeld/Dellitzsch. Tiessler gained experience as *Gau* speaker, pamphleteer, and newspaper editor, and in 1926 became the *Gau* propaganda director of Halle. Tiessler was active both in the SA and in the Nazi "Into the Factories!" movement, and he continued to publish pamphlets for the party during the last years of the Era of Struggle. Goebbels recruited him for the RPL in 1934, and in 1936 Tiessler became the director of the Reichsring. The rise of Martin Bormann's party chancellory made Tiessler's role as liaison man between the RPL and the party extremely important, and his influence within the RPL is evident in the documentation available for the post-1941 period. Tiessler sensed Bormann's growing influence with Hitler before most other Nazis perceived it, and he catered to the Reichsleiter's prejudices. In August 1941 Tiessler indicated to Bormann that he would be quite happy to hang Count von Galen, the bishop of Münster, if the Führer agreed with his suggestion. Galen had publicly denounced the secret Nazi "mercy killing" program.

Tiessler's office collected reports and questionnaires filed by speakers and other propagandists. The purpose of this activity was to find out what type of propaganda campaigns branches and affiliated organizations of the party were waging, and how effective they were. Lazy or inarticulate speakers seldom filed detailed reports on their activities. Most information about local party efforts during the war came from the general reports made by Reich propaganda offices. One *Gau* reported that only 5 percent of the chairmen of party meetings and rallies bothered to send a report to the *Gau* propaganda office. The Reichsring tried to remedy this, at least in terms of branch and affiliated organizations, by demanding monthly reports from groups such as the Reich Women's Leadership. Speakers and organizers were to answer questions like these: "Do you plan a propaganda campaign? When? By what means? What new placards, brochures, leaflets, as well as other means of propaganda do you plan to issue or distribute in the near future? Place and date? Manner in which they will be carried out? What enemy propaganda in the form of leaflets, word of mouth, and rumors have you noted in the last month (include copies!)? How have you supported the present RPL campaign during the past month?" [59] The answers to these reports were often incomplete and vague.

The leader of a Gauring was in a good position to have broad insights into propaganda needs, since he was in contact with so many organizations. One of his functions was to make suggestions to the central RPL, through Tiessler, for propaganda campaigns and improved techniques. In 1942 the leader of the Ring in Saxony wrote an interesting letter on the role of schools in total war mobilization. He based his suggestions upon their success in Saxony. The correspondent suggested that teachers and school officials were performing valuable work in aiding the families of men who were at the front and in protecting schools against air raids. These people sometimes performed auxiliary service in the countryside or in factories. They helped take care of wounded soldiers and participated in operations designed to remove school children in bomb-threatened regions.[60] The writer suggested that manpower hours might be saved by reducing the curriculum in classes one through eight of the higher schools. The man was clearly aware of Nazi ideological priorities, for he urged cutbacks in literature while pushing for more emphasis upon "contemporary history," by which he meant the building of Greater Germany since 1933, plus a study of geopolitical doctrine and "racial problems." The writer suggested more space in the curriculum for a study of Greater East Asia, the "mixture of races" in the United States, the "Negro question" there, and exploitation by the United States as an "imperialist power." Pre-1933 history would evidently be downgraded in this improved curriculum.

On the basis of information available to him from all these sources, Tiessler made major suggestions to Goebbels early in 1943. Using the "Old Fighter" slogan, "A bourgeois propagandist can only make bourgeois propaganda," Tiessler called the minister's attention to a major problem. The conscription of propagandists was endangering the work of the RPL, and essential workers would have to be protected from the draft no matter what their age. Agencies which had already lost large numbers of such men had to be defended against further depredations, or their work would cease. Such agencies would have to be strengthened by the RPL. For Tiessler it was vital to decide which offices were vital to the war effort, and to protect them. Tiessler appealed to Goebbels to undertake what could amount to a war with the Wehrmacht conscription office. He tried to encourage the minister by emphasizing a thought dear to Goebbels' heart: Propaganda was indispensable to victory, it was another military front. Tiessler overestimated Goebbels' authority in this area, for the minister had no intention of involving himself in a major struggle with the armed forces, a battle he would probably lose.[61] The memoranda of Tiessler made evident the decline in the party propaganda apparatus after 1939. Propaganda could not be revived by the RPL alone, but only by radical measures undertaken by Bormann to revive the fanatical will of the party.

Martin Bormann had growing influence upon Nazi propaganda from late 1941. He built his dual role as Hitler's personal secretary and director of the party chancellory into an effective base.[62] By 1943 nobody would have repeated the mistake corrected by an obscure bureaucrat in a "secret directive to the press" of the Reich Culture Chamber. The press should not, he wrote, confuse the Bormann brothers. Martin was in the party chancellory, while Albert was an adjutant of the Führer. Martin Bormann, implicated in the 1920s in nationalist terror activities, had been prominent in the party since 1934, when he was promoted to the rank of Reichsleiter. He was Rudolf Hess's staff director in the office of the deputy of the Führer. Secretive and ambitious, Bormann made himself essential to Hitler by anticipating and satisfying the Leader's whims and needs, whether political, financial, or personal. Hitler found Bormann so essential to his daily routine that he ignored his aide's occasional excesses in alcohol abuse and lechery. Bormann was a tireless and methodical worker, and by the time the war broke out, he had accumulated and extended most of what still passed for Hess's power. Bormann traveled with Hitler to his varying field headquarters and became a personal wartime chancellory for civil and party administration, responsibilities for which Hitler had little time. At the postwar Nürnberg trials a prosecutor asked Hans Fritzsche, ". . . what kind of influence did the absentee defendant Bormann have on German propaganda?" Fritzsche accurately responded that "the role was unusually great ... Dr. Goebbels was quite clearly afraid of Martin Bormann." [63]

Fritzsche had good reason to know of Bormann's growing power in the propaganda field. In August 1941 Reichsleiter Karl Fiehler wanted to write an open letter to Roosevelt. The letter would be propaganda against the Jews, Churchill, and FDR, the usual thing, and Fiehler obtained the support of Walter Tiessler, whose only objection was to the length of the letter. Tiessler, one of Goebbels' highest-ranking propaganda men, strongly urged the party chancellory to approve the Fiehler letter. The response came from Bormann at the end of the month: Hitler had killed the idea. This is precisely the type of matter which Bormann avoided taking to Hitler (why disturb him with petty problems?); it is likely that Bormann acted on his own. Fiehler had wanted his letter to appear in the press with a comment by Hans Fritzsche, director of the German press division in the propaganda ministry.[64]

Bormann based some of his actions upon reports received from *Gau* and district leaders, though their quality was far inferior to the SD reports, which Bormann also read. The director of the party chancellory embodied his decrees and criticisms in the "Confidential Information" bulletins which he sent out in increasing numbers and length from the beginning of 1942. Bormann soon widened the circle of those privileged to receive his decrees. In the last stages of the war, busy, disillusioned, or drunken *Gau* and district officials may have paid little attention to the "Confidential Information," but they served Bormann's purpose, for they had augmented his power by consolidating his control over the central party apparatus. Bormann was a bureaucrat who managed to keep his head above a sea of paper. He sensed changing popular moods, however tardy and incompetent district and *Gau* staff were in preparing their weekly reports on the mood of the population and its reaction to events and measures of the regime.

Hitler and Martin Bormann enjoy some photographs. By 1943 access to Hitler was usually possible only through Bormann.

CREDIT: The National Archives

Bormann received reports indicating that people were uninterested in educational and propagandistic lectures which contained too much *Weltanschauung* or murky Nazi philosophy of the Alfred Rosenberg type. Many such talks were repetitive and irrelevant to people, including active Nazis, who had to face the everyday privations of wartime existence. Echoing prewar complaints, some reports argued that many speakers were worthless. Perhaps lectures which dealt more specifically with themes of the war, politics, science, and contemporary history would be more effective. Bormann reached this conclusion, whatever the objections of the Rosenberg chancellory. In this attitude he had an ally in Joseph Goebbels, who mistrusted abstract ideology in public speeches and articles and who rarely talked *Weltanschauung* in his *Das Reich* essays.[65]

By February 1943 the activity of Martin Bormann had greatly enlarged the role of the party chancellory in propaganda. The *Propaganda-Parole,* edited by the *Gau* propaganda director, often opened its current issue with the phrase "In agreement with the party chancellory." Hitler's growing isolation, his almost exclusive obsession with the deteriorating military situation, enabled Bormann to reach out for influence in many areas. Bormann did not even bother to be polite when he informed General von Epp in November 1942 that he and his Colonial League were to cease all propaganda for a German colonial empire.[66] Bormann told Epp to resume such propaganda only after the war had been won; for the time being, personnel of the League could be used for more pressing tasks. Such propaganda generally came to an end within a month, but as late as February 1943 one *Gau* reported that a district leader permitted a meeting of the Reich Colonial League. Bormann probably found out about that meeting, and his reaction, in the anguished days after Stalingrad, can be imagined. No detail concerned with propaganda and the public mood seemed too minute for the attention of Martin Bormann. Three weeks after the end at Stalingrad, Tiessler reported to Goebbels that the party chancellory did not want POWs and German civilians to visit art museums at the same time.[67] The German population might not take kindly to such integration.

Martin Bormann was a crude man who had mastered only the essential social niceties. He had certain obsessive Nazi beliefs, such as the enmity between National Socialism and Christianity. It is surprising to see a man of Bormann's modest culture taking time during the battle of Stalingrad to write a long letter, later published in the party *Verordnungsblatt,* or "Ordinance Bulletin," about the role of art and cultural policy in the work of the party. The letter was a challenge to

Goebbels, who viewed such affairs as entirely within the scope of his own competence. Bormann stated his belief that culture was one of the "most important and meaningful instruments" of the party, even in wartime. Bormann knew of Hitler's artistic interests; his statements on art and culture were intended as reflections of the Führer's views. The letter would have pleased Hitler if he ever saw it. Bormann wrote that everything from a folk song to an obituary, from a lyric poem to a railroad station, expressed the mind and creativity of the *Volk*.

This was a cliché in the *völkisch,* or mystic-racialist movement, but it served as a bridge to Bormann's next thought. He stated that to sense and celebrate the renewal of the *Volk* by participating in the joy of a family over the birth of a child showed more culture than getting dressed up and attending a great opera. Not that Bormann objected to "high art"; he praised one of Hitler's favorite institutions, the House of German Art, in Munich. This praise occurred in passing, however, for Bormann's main interest was the local strength of the party, and popular culture rather than high culture. Involving people in party evenings by educating them and making them feel part of a community was better than hiring skilled lecturers or musicians for a cultural evening. Real culture for Bormann consisted of party propaganda that was successful precisely because it was not perceived as propaganda: sessions, discussions, exchanges of thoughts among party comrades which reinforced the Nazi will to victory and demonstrated the true leadership capacity of the party. As Bormann wrote, "Culture is not a mere affair for 'fine people,' and one certainly does not need a doctorate in order to pursue a National Socialist cultural policy in one's township. An honorable German heart is what is required, plus the healthy horse sense of an old Nazi." [68]

4

The Nazi Party, the Press, and the Radio

The strengthening and propagation of Nazi wartime ideology within party circles was a major function of German propaganda. The term *Schulung* referred to training, educating, and informing present and future Nazi cadres and party members for the tasks confronting the Reich during the war. The *Educational Service of the Hitler Youth,* a monthly magazine, performed this service for all Nazi youth organizations, including the League of German Maidens. Each issue was devoted to a special topic, for example: "World Power Germany," "Germany's Unity—Germany's Destiny," "Jews and Lords Hand in Hand," "The Ninth of November," and "The Jew as the Enemy of All Peoples." [1]

Dr. Robert Ley, Reich organization leader of the Nazi party and head of the German Labor Front, had major responsibilities in party training and education. If party cadres and members did not understand the ideology of the war, how would the German people grasp the nature of this world-historical struggle? One of Ley's techniques early in the war was to have "educational" and party speakers visit German factories, bringing the message of Nazism to the workers: "Only the best is good enough for the German worker." These "Political Shock Troops of the German Labor Front" (DAF) made wild promises to the workers about the social paradise awaiting them after victory. Such exaggeration was typical of Ley, but the frustrated Goebbels could do little to curb the excesses of the Reich organization leader. Ley used his "circular directives" *(Rundschreiben)* to disseminate this propaganda; the directives were published in the *Gaue* by the German Labor Front.

Most of Ley's educational efforts in the realm of ideology were devoted to the *Gau* educational offices, particularly the division concerned with the training of Nazi speakers, the Schulungsamt. These offices received both the *Training Bulletin* and *The Bearer of Sovereignty (Der Hoheitsträger)*. Ley was responsible for the education and training of the future Nazi elite, though he shared this task with many other agencies and organizations of the party, its branches, and affiliated organizations. He used some of the financial resources of the ubiquitous German Labor Front to support his educational efforts. Ley faced a problem on the vital *Gau* level, however, that was typical of the contradictory and chaotic Nazi system. *Gau* educational offices and speakers programs were at the mercy of the Gauleiters and district leaders, who could use or ignore the materials he sent them. Lack of interest in the training of cadres was understandable late in the war, when it was clear that National Socialism itself would survive or die on the battlefield, not in a *Gau* educational office.

Ley's publications and directives are a good guide to the manner in which the Nazi elite explained the war to party members in terms of ideology. They contained themes and materials supplied by Goebbels' men, as well as other resources. The *Training Bulletin,* begun in 1934, offered many versions of this ideological explanation in 1942–43: "The Reich and Europe Conquer," "Struggle and Work—Brothers in Victory," "Forward to Victory," "Mobilization of the Nation" (after the proclamation of total war early in 1943). The issues, complete with these striking slogans and "heroic" illustrations on their covers, reached educational and training personnel down to the municipal branch *(Ortsgruppen)* level. District educational speakers were expected to address at least twenty-four meetings a year. Until they had done so, these men were standby, or "probational," speakers. For each meeting or rally addressed, the speaker received five Reichsmarks, the same fee paid to propaganda speakers of the RPL. The speakers were required to hand in monthly reports to the *Gau* educational office of the party.

Robert Ley's Main Educational Office produced several bulletins in support of these efforts. *Communications (Mitteilungen)* published ordinances and regulations and explained the functions of various circular letters and bulletins. One such regulation concerned compensation for educational speakers involved in addressing teachers and officials who were party members on *Weltanschauung,* or Nazi ideology. Another decree concerned adaptation to wartime exigencies: neighboring municipal branch offices should feel free to exchange speakers. This would mitigate problems of transportation and personnel shortages. The *Political Selections from Books and Journals,* published in three versions, was for the instruction of educational speakers and officials, but it was also a response to shortages of reading matter due to later wartime paper rationing. "Edition A" and "Edition B" were basically similar, while "Edition C" was for speakers and political officials who were serving in the Wehrmacht. This material was intended to keep them informed so they would be ready to resume their political work after the victory. Selections concerned ideological topics such as "Einstein's Attempt to Turn Physics Upside Down," "Nietzsche and National Socialism," "England's Hypocrisy," "Jews in the Red Army," and other highly predictable themes.

Ley's various bulletins often contained ideological bibliographies, usually listing at least one of his own works, perhaps *Germany Has Become More Beautiful* or *Our Work Makes Us Free*. Most of Ley's published work consisted of speeches which contained material bragging about the accomplishments of the German Labor Front and promising a social utopia to the German workers. The *Educational Folders* contained materials for speaking and instruction and were concerned with a single theme, such as "Germany Organizes Europe Anew!" *Collections* sent to the *Gau* and district training offices contained two types of material: (1) included discussions of ideological and political themes and (2) advice about party ceremonies and educational guidelines. The "Discussion Evenings" of party cells on the municipal branch level had as their aim strengthening the political will and deepening the intellectual substance of all party comrades. The "Discussion Evening Work Community" published a bulletin for coordinators of these meetings. Ley's offices often warned such people that their leadership and instruction would be "dead and boring" if they did not study at least a good part of the material they received from the Reich training office. The intellectual contents of the "Evening Discussion Service" consisted of slogans such as "Only one command of the day—win the war!" [2]

The *Gau* training offices published lectures and selections from books and journals as material for party educators and speakers. Some of the material bore the sign of abstract unreality typical of Alfred Rosenberg's productions. How many local officials were concerned with the battle of Tannenberg (1410) or the invasion of the Roman empire by the Huns in 375? Few, but the publication of such information late in 1943 attested to the fanatical persistence of the Nazi elite in pursuing its goal of placing the present war in the context of Nazi ideology and the Nazi world view. This National Socialist consensus always returned to the Jews. In 1943 and 1944 the *Gau* educational office in Thuringia repeatedly published materials on the "Jewish question," instructional materials for party cadres, at a time when the Jews of Europe were being murdered by the Nazis. [3]

Alfred Rosenberg saw himself as the keeper of the holy grail of

National Socialist ideology. It was frustrating for him to have to compete in the area of ideological propaganda and training with a man so crude as Robert Ley or an immoral opportunist like Joseph Goebbels. At the Nürnberg trial Hans Fritzsche testified that Rosenberg had influenced German propaganda only to an extent which was not noticeable to Fritzsche himself. Yet a judgment handed down on October 1, 1946, declared that "Defendant Rosenberg played a leading part in disseminating the National Socialist doctrines on behalf of the Party." [4] The apparent contradiction was based upon differing perspectives. Fritzsche was thinking of Goebbels, his ministry, and perhaps the RPL when he made his statement. Here, Rosenberg's influence, particularly on the daily propaganda line or the seasonal propaganda campaigns, was negligible. Even during the war, however, Rosenberg and his "chancellory" were important in the educational programs directed at Nazi speakers, institutions, and schools. Rosenberg's ideological influence was still apparent on the eve of the war, but it declined rapidly from 1939. The Speakers' Information Service of the *Gau* Munich/Upper Bavaria in 1938 reflected much of the Rosenberg line. The information was anticlerical in tone and sounded much like Rosenberg's speeches and essays of an earlier day. The assertion that November 9, the commemoration of the Nazi Beer Hall Putsch martyrs, and Heroes Memorial Day in March were greater events than Catholic religious processions or more profound than religious services held in the trenches during the Great War was vintage Rosenberg.

Alfred Rosenberg was born in the Estonian town of Reval (Tallinn) in 1893. He studied architecture at the German Polytechnic Institute in Riga (later Latvia), and he accompanied other students to Moscow during the First World War when the school was transferred as German troops neared Riga. While in Moscow, where he earned his degree as an architect, the future Nazi theoretician was a witness to some of the early events of the Bolshevik revolution. For Baltic Germans like Rosenberg, the overthrow of the old social order and the onset of an era of Baltic nationalism and Communist terror represented the end of a stable world order. Rosenberg developed a hatred for Bolshevism, second only to his loathing of the Jews, whom he blamed for Communism. He became a condescending patron of subject nationalities of the old Russian empire, such as the Baltic peoples and the Ukrainians, and a determined enemy of the Great Russian nationality, which had led old Russia to ruin and Communism. When Rosenberg returned to Reval early in 1918, it was occupied by the German Army. He began to give public lectures on Marxism and the Jews, and would soon claim that a mysterious stranger had given him documentary proof in Moscow that the Russian revolution was part of the Jewish bid for world power—the "document" was the *Protocols of the Elders of Zion.*

Rosenberg, along with many other White Russian and German-Russian refugees, drifted to Munich, where he joined the Hitler movement in its earliest days. From 1921 to 1923 he, along with Dietrich Eckart, was editor of the Nazi newspaper the *Völkischer Beobachter.* After 1923 he became sole editor and he was publisher as well from 1938. Rosenberg continued to publish long articles in that paper during the war. In the 1923 Beer Hall Putsch, Rosenberg marched with Hitler to the Bürgerbräukeller, and the next day he was in the forward ranks of the ill-fated Nazis heading towards the Feldherrnhalle. Rosenberg founded the anti-Jewish journal *The World Struggle* in 1924 and in 1930 became editor in chief (later publisher) of the *National Socialist Monthly.* He established the League of Struggle for German Culture in 1929 and was elected to the Reichstag in the Nazi landslide of September 1930. After the Seizure of Power, Rosenberg became a Reichsleiter and head of the Foreign Policy Office of the party. In 1934 Hitler appointed Rosenberg "Commissioner of the Führer for Supervision of the Entire Intellectual and Doctrinal Training and Education of the NSDAP." In 1941 Rosenberg finally became a minister "for the occupied eastern territories." [5]

Alfred Rosenberg read widely, choosing selections which fit his National Socialist world view. Though not a plagiarist in the sense of exact copying, Rosenberg tended to lift ideas and insights from earlier authors and paste them together in a new Nazi *pastiche.* He was smug, felt himself to be intellectually superior to his fellow party comrades, and enjoyed high-level ideological discussions, since he felt he always won the argument. Such superiority accounted for the smirk for which this dour, humorless man was noted. Rosenberg was never popular among party men; some believed that his arrogance was due to a justified inferiority complex. Rosenberg saw himself as the synthesizer of Nazi ideology, and throughout the late 1920s he worked at this major task. He studied racial theory, art history, Jewish history, and anything he could fit into his mental set. Even his enemies granted Rosenberg an excellent memory, prodigious energy, and a prolific, if murky and abstruse, pen, but limited intellect and unlimited dogmatism pervaded his writings. A man who declared that Nazism "was not a dogma, but an attitude," Rosenberg was the most dogmatic of individuals.

Some of his theories and weaknesses would have embarrassed any other political movement, but in the case of the Nazi party they only eroded Rosenberg's influence, not his freedom to speak out. For example, around 1931 Rosenberg was convinced that Chancellor Heinrich

Bruening, a devout Catholic, wanted to Bolshevize Germany. Life would then become hell, and the masses would return to the Church! In doing his research, Rosenberg based most of his statements about the ancient Etruscans on the work of Albert Gruenwedel, a respected scholar in the field. The problem here was that the one book of his which Rosenberg used, *Tusca,* was the product of senile old age. Rosenberg was working on his "great work" at the time, *The Mythos of the Twentieth Century,* and a party colleague recalled, "Rosenberg used to do some of his writing in the Odeon Coffeehouse. There he would sit at one of the little round marble tables right next to the big front window, where all the people could see him writing or 'visibly' thinking. Three or four tables or chairs around him would be covered with books and papers. [Max] Amann repeatedly pointed him out to me when we would pass by, with words: 'Look at 'im squatting there, the fool-headed, stuck-up, undergraduate ninny! Writing 'works'—the Bohemian! Oughta be puttin' out a decent newspaper instead!' " [6]

The same observer, Albert Krebs, then a Gauleiter, further described Rosenberg in this manner: "My personal encounters with Alfred Rosenberg were rare. Furthermore, in view of his inability to engage in a proper conversation, which stemmed from his assumed arrogance and his actual insecurity, they were generally unproductive. Thus I have a precise recollection of only three conversations with him. . . . He was so wrapped up in his own opinions that he simply could not understand how anyone else could have different ones." [7]

By 1934 Rosenberg's publisher had sold and distributed 150,000 copies of the *Mythos,* and by the time war broke out the figure was up to 250,000. Rosenberg was delighted by the reaction of the hated Catholic Church, which placed the book on the Index of Forbidden Works. Rosenberg would not have been so happy if he had known Hitler's reaction: The Führer considered the book to be unreadable, plagiarized, murky, and not necessarily representative of the Nazi world view. In 1937 Rosenberg received the National Prize, the German answer to the Nobel Prize.

The onset of the war marked the decline of Rosenberg's influence, for a man with his interests and personality could contribute little to an elite intent upon conquering and mobilizing an entire continent. A wartime employee of Rosenberg's eastern ministry, an individual not devoid of sympathy for his patron, recalled in 1958 that Rosenberg was a man of theory, "lacking in healthy instinctive sense." Rosenberg was not driven by frenzied ambition or a search for political prestige. Rather, his ego found satisfaction in the number of copies of his books sold by his party publisher or in winning an intellectual argument. He did not hold a grudge nor was he vindictive, but he had serious human weaknesses. Rosenberg could not be counted upon to stand up for colleagues or aides under fire from powerful party big shots. Frustrated in his work during the war, Rosenberg became something of a nag, endlessly splitting hairs with anyone who would pay enough attention to him to engage in a struggle over competing jurisdictions. By 1945 he was a "tired, sick man," bitter over his fate; he drank heavily, something uncharacteristic of him in earlier days.[8]

Alfred Rosenberg lost much of his prestige and influence because of his abstruse, irrelevant interests, which he continued to pursue no matter what was happening at the front. He would give a lecture on Nietzsche even if the Americans were in Aachen or the Russians had invaded East Prussia. In 1941–42 Rosenberg engaged in a major dispute with the foreign office over an archaeological expedition to Hungary and Croatia. The Office for Prehistory, under Rosenberg's patronage, was sponsoring an expedition to find traces of the ancient Germanic peoples.[9] Hungary and Croatia had agreed, and Budapest was to pay for the whole operation. The foreign office refused to stamp the necessary passports, however, for it felt that the expedition should come under the control of its own cultural institute. This would have meant that operations would be supervised by German foreign office representatives in Agram and Budapest. Rosenberg replied that this was impossible on political and scientific grounds. And so the mess dragged on endlessly, an example of the unreal world in which Rosenberg functioned.

Rosenberg's productivity as an author diminished during the war years, not least of all because of a time-consuming dispute with Ribbentrop and Ley. Yet a rumor surfaced late in 1942 that Rosenberg had written another major work, *From Mythos to Prototype,* a sequel to *The Mythos of the Twentieth Century.* Himmler was so concerned about the book that he wrote to Bormann. Both Himmler and Bormann believed that no such volume should appear unless it was approved by the Führer (which might mean by Bormann). Even Rosenberg's intellectual stock was dropping to a low point.[10]

A large part of Rosenberg's wartime propaganda revolved around the "Jewish question." Rosenberg had been fascinated by the Jews since at least 1917. He had done what he called research on the books of Jewish law, the Talmud *(Immorality in the Talmud),* on the role of the Jews in history, and on the *Protocols of the Elders of Zion.* Rosenberg, head of the Foreign Policy Office of the party, fully subsidized the anti-Semitic publication *World Service (Der Weltdienst)* after 1937, when he took it over from the propaganda ministry. During the war it was published fortnightly in eighteen languages, Nazi Germany's anti-Jewish beacon for the world. Ulrich Fleischhauer, a disciple and friend of pioneer anti-Semites Theodor Fritsch and Dietrich Eckart, published the *World Service* out of a publishing house in Erfurt. He bragged in 1937, "Our work reaches to the furthest corners of the earth." During the war August Schirmer took over the bulletin, then Kurt Richter. By this time the *World Service* was part of the Institute of the NSDAP for Research into the Jewish Question in Frankfurt. Rosenberg built this institute out of a seized Judaica collection, and he intended to use it to develop themes and curricula for postwar "higher schools" or National Socialist universities. These institutions would produce pure doctrinal idealists for the Nazi movement, and Hitler had somewhat ambiguously authorized Rosenberg to make preparations for the day of their consecration.[11]

Rosenberg's wartime writings may have had some limited influence upon those who bothered to read them, probably a fairly small group by 1942. Rosenberg had more of an effect upon the educational structure of the party, upon the curricula used for promoting doctrine and for training the future Nazi elite. As commissioner of the Führer for questions of doctrine, Rosenberg's office came into contact with Ley's structure of district, *Gau*, and Reich institutions, from the district educational office to the *Ordensburgen,* which were to turn out the next generation of National Socialist leadership. The Rosenberg office contained a number of specialized departments; among their concerns were pedagogy, history, philosophy, the Aryan world view, Nordic questions, ideological information, and the assemblage and supervision of educational materials and curricula. Rosenberg's staff director during most of the war was the competent Dr. Helmut Stellrecht. Professor Alfred Bäumler, who had achieved some note as a Nietzsche scholar, was in charge of learning and scholarship, while the fanatical idealist Karlheinz Rädiger (who later fell on the eastern front) controlled relations with the press and wrote articles for Rosenberg's publications.

Party officials of "sovereign" rank received the *Bulletin on the Doctrinal Situation,* edited by the office for ideological information. This publication demonstrated Rosenberg's consistency and his remoteness from the realities of the day. While even Goebbels' agencies tended to avoid anti-Christian statements during the war, Rosenberg devoted most of his *Bulletin* to attacks on Catholicism and the Evangelical confession. He and his men looked on in impotent rage as they saw religion making gains among the German people. Rosenberg's office published *Idea and Deed,* which appeared "when necessary," and which contained "teaching materials for the entire doctrinal education of the NSDAP," as well as the "Bibliography for the Work of Doctrinal Education." Many of the works produced by the Rosenberg people were published by the Eher Verlag in Munich, official party publisher.

The *National Socialist Monthly,* published by Rosenberg, was the central political and cultural journal of the NSDAP. This magazine reached beyond the party cadres and educators to all Nazis intrigued by doctrine and history. It too lost influence during the war, though as late as the summer of 1939, the Enlightenment Service for Political Speakers had quoted it and recommended it to RPL propagandists. A selection of titles of articles from the *Monthly* gives a good sense of Rosenberg's ideological production: "Ten years of Adolf Hitler" (Rosenberg); "Twenty-five years of Bolshevik World Aggression" (E.H. Bockhoff); "Folkdom and the Structuring of NS Ceremonies" (Hans Strobel); "Racialist Socialism–European Socialism" (Werner Daitz); "The Mission of Reichsleiter Rosenberg" (Otto Biedermann). After disputes with Ley and Goebbels, Rosenberg emerged in 1942–43 responsible for structuring the sacramental ceremonies of National Socialism *(Lebensfeiern).* Reflecting a direct borrowing from hated Christianity, these ceremonies were meant for good Nazis upon the occasion of a birth, marriage, or funeral.[12]

The National Socialist Monthly, official journal of the party for political and cultural matters, was edited by Alfred Rosenberg. It reflected the "intellectual" voice of Nazi ideology.

CREDIT: The Library of Congress.

Rosenberg's greatest ideological impact occurred in the area of party education. He and his staff developed several "Reich themes" for quarterly semesters, themes which the educational speakers were expected to learn and to place in their own curricula and lectures. While Rosenberg had *Gau* representatives who provided the materials, his problem was the control that the Gauleiters and the *Gau* educational people exercised over the curricula. The weakness of Rosenberg's position was underlined by the requirement that individuals with suggestions should send them to him by way of the *Gau* educational staff, not directly. Party speakers and educators ignored much of the Rosenberg material, and they had the tacit support of Robert Ley in so doing. When *Gau* education people carried out their orders they learned about themes such as "The German Accomplishment in America," "The Greater the Accomplishment, the Closer the Victory," "Battle of Destiny in the East," or "Struggle as the Purpose of Life." Rosenberg provided material for party evening sessions where people discussed doctrine. One district had to stress the fact that these meetings were strictly for party comrades. It was not that the public was breaking down the doors to attend, but rather that certain local officials dismayed by lack of attendance admitted anyone who could be persuaded to show up.

Alfred Rosenberg gives a speech, 1942.

In the spring of 1944 Rosenberg bragged before a group of NS educators that the "Reich themes" had taught instructors and speakers about the great questions of the day: the Jewish world parasite, victory through faith, and struggle as the law of life.[13] Did even Rosenberg believe that instruction in the mission of the medieval Holy Roman Empire was vital to the war effort in 1944? The commitment to doctrine was the one remaining interest which gave structure and meaning to his life. Rosenberg's aide Stellrecht made sure that copies of the Reich themes were available, with one hundred thousand being an average printing. Rosenberg's office used some of these themes for press campaigns intended to reach the general public, but a good number of the educational brochures probably wound up in party wastepaper baskets. Ley blocked Rosenberg at every turn, claiming that Rosenberg had been given the right to supervise, not to carry out. He should not meddle in the actual instruction and the *Gau* curricula.

Rosenberg strongly disagreed; he saw himself as the conscience of the movement's idealism. He urged *Gau* and district educational people to request visiting lecturers directly from his own office. Ley strenuously objected, for he feared that this would transform Rosenberg's office from a publication center for easily ignored pamphlets into a police force for doctrinal purity. Bormann tended to side with Ley on this matter early in 1943, but the Ley-Rosenberg abrasion continued in an atmosphere of increasing unreality.[14] These were two desperate men, fighting in the midst of political and personal disintegration to maintain some semblance of respectable authority. Robert Ley had become a stammering, incoherent drunkard with a suicidal wife. Alfred Rosenberg was a failure as eastern minister, and by 1944 he had no access to Hitler. He was ignored by most other high-ranking Nazis—except Ley, who would talk to anyone by this time. All Rosenberg had left was his pure doctrine, the holy grail which, he would later claim, had been the content of his "active life." Rosenberg may have been "happier" at Nürnberg than the other defendants. For the first time in years he was being taken seriously: He was a man important enough to execute.

Rosenberg's disputes with Goebbels had both personal and political origins. Rosenberg did not believe that the propaganda minister should control the arts, and for years he waged a sort of bureaucratic guerrilla war against Goebbels. In 1934 the commissioner of the Führer combined the "German Stage" with the League of Struggle for German Culture, founding the "National Socialist Cultural Community." [15] In Rosenberg's office the division responsible for caring for the arts controlled the "Community." As might be expected, Goebbels outmaneuvered Rosenberg and emerged by 1940 with far more authority in this area, whatever Hitler's opinion of the artistic sensitivity of the propaganda minister.

Rosenberg was reduced to gloating in May 1940 that Otto Dietrich received unique authority to issue direct instructions to the German press.[16]

Rosenberg's relations with Foreign Minister Ribbentrop were not devoid of abrasiveness.[17] Early in the war Rosenberg was appointed the "Führer's Commissioner for Securing the National Socialist World View." The foreign ministry feared that some of Rosenberg's statements and publications would infringe upon its territory. Rosenberg, after all, lacked tact in dealing with foreign powers. He caused major embarrassment to the Reich when he visited London in 1933; in 1940 he made a statement in which he seemed to foresee a German invasion of Sweden. Ribbentrop's representative von Weizsaecker therefore demanded that Hitler's state secretary Hans Lammers make clear to Rosenberg that any statements about foreign affairs would have to be cleared by the foreign ministry. Lammers agreed with the substance of the objection, but he feared that if he put it into the decree stating Rosenberg's new appointment, every other minister, especially Goebbels, would demand a similar cautionary phrase. Lammers tried to mollify von Weizsaecker by arguing that it was obvious that Rosenberg would have to clear certain statements with the foreign ministry. If it was so obvious, von Weizsaecker countered, why not put it into the document? The phrase was not included in Rosenberg's notice of appointment; in itself this was a hollow victory, for the significance of the new office was not profound.

Ribbentrop fought many acrimonious battles with the Goebbels people, especially after 1939. He wanted to extend the influence of the foreign ministry to areas of foreign and domestic propaganda. In the summer of 1941 Ribbentrop established a propaganda committee in his ministry, directed by Luther and Kruemmer. Kruemmer, often Ribbentrop's representative at the Goebbels ministerial conference, had firsthand knowledge of the operations of the propaganda ministry. Dr. Schmidt of the press division of the foreign ministry was an ardent exponent of subsidizing journals such as *Volk und Reich* as a way of influencing foreign and domestic public opinion. This was done through the information division of the ministry. Schmidt pointed out to Ribbentrop that for RM 8,000 per month the ministry could take over this prestigious-looking journal. The information division had distributed ten thousand copies of the journal as of the autumn of 1940. Since the propaganda ministry used subsidies as a way of controlling various journals, such a move by the foreign ministry would contribute to curbing the ambitions of Joseph Goebbels. Subsidized journals, newspapers, and magazines appeared alongside the semiofficial and official foreign-ministry publications, *Dienst aus Deutschland* and the *Diplomatic-Political Correspondence.*

Goebbels despised Ribbentrop, a man he considered a sleazy opportunist and belated Nazi. The friction between the two ministries resulted in major clashes late in 1941. Early in October the press division of the foreign office suggested techniques for a major news and press offensive in coordination with its propaganda division. Later in the month, Goebbels made another foray into foreign affairs. He solicited reports on "The attitude of the German people to its allies" from local ministry offices. The responses indicated rather apathetic or hostile attitudes towards Germany's allies. Goebbels forwarded this information, with his circular questionnaire, to Lammers. The chancellory liked Goebbels' report and suggested he bring it to the attention of the Wehrmacht.

Even after Hitler had forced Ribbentrop and Goebbels to reach an uneasy agreement delineating their spheres of influence in the realm of propaganda, relations were hostile.[18] In the spring of 1943 Ribbentrop's ministry was making determined efforts to influence the German press by use of the press division of the foreign office. Goebbels had hopes of convincing Hitler to dismiss Ribbentrop, for he wished to become foreign minister himself. Lammers and Bormann played off one feuding Nazi potentate against the other, but Hitler had no intention of rewarding loyalty, no matter how incompetent, with dismissal. Goebbels continued to curse Ribbentrop, but he took some solace from the reports from the SS and his Reich propaganda offices. These proved that the German people's regard for the propaganda minister was increasing, while Ribbentrop had lost most of his prestige.

Goebbels found Robert Ley a constant embarrassment to his propaganda work during the war. By late 1943 Goebbels realized that Ley was a personal wreck and of no political use as an ally in the attempt to revolutionize Germany for total war. For years Goebbels had been hostile to the exaggerated promises Ley was making to the German workers. Now he saw in Ley a man in full disintegration. When Ley's fourth child was born in 1941, two days after the start of the Russian campaign, he insisted she be named Gloria, "in the sacred belief in German victory, in remembrance of the greatest epoch in German history." [19] After his wife's suicide Ley drifted into a permanent alcoholic stupor. Goebbels had this to say about Ley's work in 1944, as he looked at his bookshelves in anticipation of weeding out his collection: "Here, the collected works of Ley can disappear . . . Away with them! I no longer want to see any of this ideological manure in my library. I would like to have my library organized according to literary criteria and not according to the party badge." [20]

Ley's growing isolation and eccentricity were becoming apparent in the summer of 1941 when he took on Goebbels, Bormann, and Rosenberg all at once over an ideological issue which was more symbolic than real. On July 3 Ley issued a decree which claimed that Martin Bormann had given him full authority, broadly interpreted, over Nazi ceremonies within the party. Walter Tiessler of the RPL fired off a note to Bormann, who enjoyed mediating this type of induced chaos, asking if Ley was not aware of the fact that Rosenberg had the responsibility for supervising these Nazi ceremonies *(Lebensfeiern)* of life and death. Bormann clarified his position in August, when he indicated that the RPL was responsible for *Feiergestaltung,* or structuring the solemn public ceremonies of, among others, January 30, Heroes Memorial Day in March, April 20 (Hitler's birthday), and November 8–9 (Beer Hall Putsch martyrs memorial). The chief political leaders of the party within each geographical unit were responsible for actually carrying out these ceremonies pursuant to RPL decrees. Rosenberg was indeed to be responsible for the *Lebensfeiern.* Ley responded by declaring he would not withdraw his controversial ordinance until he had seen Hitler, an event which was not likely to take place for quite a while. Bormann was only willing to concede to Ley relatively unimportant German Labor Front and professional organization ceremonies. Ley had seriously miscalculated and lost the argument. Perhaps he confused Bormann with Rudolf Hess during his last months as deputy Führer.[21]

Robert Ley was able to cooperate with Goebbels in administrative and even political matters. In October 1941 he worked well with Gutterer on a program to straighten out the chaotic German fashion industry.[22] Goebbels' problem with Ley was in the all-important area of propaganda. Ley used the pages of his newspaper, *Der Angriff,* to make statements incredibly embarrassing to Goebbels. In itself this would have meant little, for few people paid much attention to this rag of the German Labor Front. Goebbels was annoyed because the newspaper brought back memories of the heroic Era of Struggle, when Goebbels published it, and Ley was discrediting its name. Goebbels was disgusted by the lack of self-discipline shown by a major Nazi leader. When Ley wrote that the war could last another four hundred years,[23] Goebbels went into a rage and ordered Hans Fritzsche to make sure that Nazi eminences cleared their writings with him before publishing them. This was easier said than done, for Ley did as he pleased. Goebbels might laugh at Ley's stutter or his drunken speeches, but the sight of his "wisdom" in cold print enraged the propaganda minister.

Joseph Goebbels was active as a journalist during the *Kampfzeit.* He believed in his ability to manage the news media, but his powers were limited by the exigencies of wartime censorship as well as by the competing authority of Otto Dietrich. After some early mistakes, Goebbels learned to cooperate with the Wehrmacht censorship officers, whose desks were either at OKW headquarters or in the propaganda ministry itself. Goebbels explained government news policy to the nation in July 1941, pointing out, ". . . it obviously cannot be the object of the OKW report to provide enemy military leaders with information they can use in preparing their countermeasures." [24] In a prophetic sentence regarding the silence of the Führer, Goebbels told the nation that when he spoke, it would be to announce victory. If Hitler was silent, there would be good reasons for this reticence. How ironic these words would appear to a German looking back at them in 1944, after Hitler had become a virtual recluse! Goebbels was even more blunt in his diary in May 1942: "News policy is a weapon of war. Its purpose is to wage war and not to give out information." [25] Goebbels enjoyed his own monopoly on vital information. While he was upset by Ley's crazy speeches, Goebbels smugly noted in 1943: ". . . it is a good thing that the men who frequently address the masses are free from any knowledge of unpleasant news. That gives them much more self-assurance when talking to the people." [26]

The OKW and the ministry cooperated in establishing a Propaganda Examination Commission in the Wilhelmsplatz. Sometimes the military censors would add their own "daily instructions for military censorship" to the "Confidential Information" (V.I.) or directives to the press. All these instructions and guidelines were transmitted to forty-two Reich propaganda offices. These local authorities were responsible for instructing and reprimanding newspaper editors within their geographical districts; they were also to respond to inquiries regarding the suitability of certain materials for immediate publication. It was essential that no instructions issued by the ministry and its local offices contradict the daily "Wehrmacht Report" (WB). This report enjoyed far more credibility than did Goebbels, at least early in the war.

One reporter, writing about German military communiqués, noted during the blitz against France and the Low Countries that the German land army had seldom misled journalists since the first days of the Polish war. One major aim of the report was to influence the home front. The chief of the OKW operations staff, Colonel-General Alfred Jodl, played a vital role in deciding and approving the contents of the "Wehrmacht (WB) Report." The Wehrmacht propaganda department provided much of the material for the WB, but usually failed when it attempted to alter a report once it emerged from Jodl's headquarters. Hitler had the last word, and he frequently delayed the issuance of the WB until he had made some typical linguistic changes. The report then went to Otto

Dietrich, who issued the WB to the German News Bureau (DNB) and the wireless service for appearance in evening newspapers and on afternoon radio broadcasts. The propaganda ministry and the office of General Hasso von Wedel, head of the Wehrmacht propaganda branch, were jointly responsible for interpreting the WB to the press, often through belated instructions from the ministry to the local RPA offices.[27]

Goebbels and the OKW had close ties in two other areas. Officers in the propaganda branch and other divisions of the OKW frequently reported to Schaeffer in the propaganda division of the ministry and sometimes to Goebbels himself. Some of these accounts were written, others oral. Their quality varied, as two examples demonstrate. Late in July, 1943, an OKW report to the ministry was blunt in describing Italian hostility to the German cause in Naples, though it claimed that people living in small towns and rural areas were friendlier. A report dated August 15, 1943, was blatantly misleading, claiming that the ill-fated "Operation Citadel" on the eastern front—which had been broken off on July 13—had achieved major successes, including the destruction of more than eleven thousand Red Army tanks. This dispatch asserted that the Soviet Ukraine offensive had failed. The statement was particularly absurd in that the Red Army would make major gains in the Ukraine until the end of the year. Goebbels' concern regarding the unity of homeland and front produced his yearly "New Year's Greetings to Our Soldiers," which were published by the Nazi Eher Verlag under the auspices of the OKW. Goebbels' themes, particularly during the last three years of the war, were the "brilliant military genius" of Hitler, the unity of front and homeland, the nature of the war as a defensive struggle, the need to hold out, and the slogan "We will never capitulate!"[28]

The wartime German press offered little to the reader in the way of editorial variety, but it did present newspapers differing in style and format. Party newspapers which traced their lineage back to the Era of Struggle (the *Völkischer Beobachter* and *Der Angriff*) contained traces of the crudeness indicative of the old Nazi belief "The press is only a tool." "The NS newspaper is supposed to be a means of propaganda, not exclusively an organ of information; it has to serve the movement and without it it loses its justification."[29] Many of these early sheets were little more than verbal placards and posters, provocative because of their outrageous charges and vicious caricatures ("The Jew press, it lies!"). Nazi press theoreticians argued in the 1930s that the old liberal press lacked life even in its format. One author contrasted the VB with the respected *Vossische Zeitung* (founded 1704), praising the power of the

Nazi newspaper's format and style, while denigrating the dry approach and lifeless structure of the older paper.[30]

The coordination of the German press by the Nazis was based upon the Editors Law of October 4, 1933, which required newspapers to "Regulate their work in accordance with National Socialism as a philosophy of life and as a conception of government. . . . The chief editor is responsible for the total content and attitude of the textual part of the newspaper." [31] The Nazis claimed that they were freeing the editors from the capitalist special-interest groups which their publishers represented. The organ of control was the Reich Press Chamber (RPK), of which Max Amann was president. Its means of pressure were varied, including fines and closings. Members of the official Association of German Newspaper Publishers and the Reich Association of the German Press could not appeal such penalties. In most cases the Nazis preferred to "coordinate" internationally famous newspapers rather than shut them down. Meanwhile, Amann built up the Nazi Eher Verlag into a major industry, and by the middle wartime period this party trust controlled 70 percent of the press.

Amann used the excuse of wartime exigencies to enlarge his empire. His RPK regulated the size and format of newspapers. When it closed down all weeklies of a purely entertainment nature in 1944, only two illustrated weeklies remained, both published by the Eher Verlag. The affiliated Deutscher Verlag, originally based upon property seized from the Ullstein company, was the largest single subdivision of the Eher trust. Newspaper circulation rose dramatically during the war, in part because of increased readership in the occupied territories. The growth was most dramatic among the illustrated weeklies, such as the *Berliner Illustrierte* and the *Illustrierter Beobachter,* which gained about nine million readers between 1939 and 1944. By 1944 the party controlled newspapers which had about 82.5 percent of the total German readership. The limited number of diversions available, the interest in coverage of the front, and the first-rate photographic work of war reporters accounted for the growth of a press that was, to say the least, unimaginative, unfree, monotonous, and often unreliable. Germans were buying more newspapers, but were reading them more skeptically.[32]

The German press division of the Reich government, located in the propaganda ministry, was directed by Hans Fritzsche. Fritzsche was loyal to Goebbels in the minister's constant battles with Otto Dietrich, and much of the material which Fritzsche gave to the press came from Goebbels. In March 1942 Fritzsche's deputy, Erich Fischer, succeeded him. Dietrich, whom Goebbels contemptuously referred to as a "field mouse," was Reich press chief of the NSDAP, as well as state secretary in the ministry and chief of the press division of the Reich government. Dietrich's authority over the party press was based upon a Hitler decree of February 28, 1934. This control was exercised through *Gau* and district press offices, of which there were 882 in 1942. These offices provided information to Dietrich's aides in Berlin and were responsible for posting party newspapers in prominent places as well as for recruitment drives for new subscribers.

At the beginning of the daily press conference in the propaganda ministry, Hans Fritzsche read Dietrich's "Slogan of the Day" (earlier, the "Confidential Information") and supplied the instructions and guidelines of different ministries and agencies. Fritzsche subtly put across Goebbels' line, usually without mentioning the minister's name. Representatives of the foreign office and the OKW were present, providing their own information to the roughly two hundred journalists present. Through Fritzsche and Fischer, Goebbels undermined Dietrich's directives. In 1942 an exasperated Dietrich secured a decree from the Führer intended to secure cooperation with Goebbels, but the old infighting continued almost to the end of the Third Reich. Dietrich's men, Werner Stephan and later Helmut Sündermann, were somewhat isolated in the ministry because of their connection with the Reich press chief. Stephan accomplished more in his role as technical supervisor and distributor of the written and photographic accounts of the front contributed by men of the propaganda companies (PK). Control over the party press was exercised by Dietrich's men in Munich, and insofar as they were free of ministry supervision and control, they had more authority than did their colleagues in Berlin.[33]

The conflicts in the ministry were over personalities and means, not over ends. While Hans Fritzsche was a relatively belated Nazi (May 1, 1933) and an experienced technician in wireless and press work, he was under Goebbels' control and had to contend with important party types such as Alfred-Ingemar Berndt, an abrasive loudmouth who had considerable administrative authority within the ministry. Fritzsche founded the "German Express News Service" (Schnelldienst) in the summer of 1939, which provided the German press with materials that could be used in responding to enemy news reports and speeches by foreign leaders. This service was particularly useful to smaller newspapers which did not have representatives at the daily press conference in Berlin. Their main sources of information on sensitive issues, however, continued to be the local Reich propaganda office, which received Fritzsche's daily ministry press report by teletype around 3:00 P.M. each day, that is, in time for next morning's editions. These offices also received confidential reports from the German News Bureau. DNB copy appeared in different-colored folders, but the only material which could appear verbatim in the press was in the so-called DNB green.[34]

The coordination of the German press for purposes of wartime propaganda was the aim of these various institutions. On the eve of the war, the RPA Berlin, in its press circular of August 30, indicated that the newspapers should play up DNB reports about Polish "atrocities" against ethnic Germans. Anti-Nazi statements by Roosevelt should be followed by the pro-German statements of Henry Ford. Polish violations of the German-Polish treaty were to be emphasized in the press. Three months later the same office warned the press to be careful in its economic reportage, lest it give sensitive information about German trade figures to the Reich's enemies. This sort of campaign, reflecting the total coordination of the media, occurred early in 1938, before the seizure of Austria, and again later that year, in the agitation against the Czechs for their "oppression" of the Sudeten Germans. Berndt, director of the German press division, played a crucial role in those campaigns.

The March 1939 agitation against the remnants of "Czecho-Slovakia" began when Fritzsche, who had replaced Berndt, received instructions from Dietrich and from Paul Schmidt of the foreign office ordering him to inaugurate a press campaign stressing the "anti-German" policy of the Prague regime and the strivings of the "oppressed" Slovaks for independence. In the summer of 1939 the press began its anti-Polish campaign, which consisted of these themes: the terror against ethnic Germans in Poland; the forced labor of ethnic Germans; Poland, land of disorder and slavery; Poland's provoking of border incidents; the aggressive intentions of the ruling clique in Poland. The same type of press campaign was waged against Yugoslavia after the invasion of that country on April 6, 1941, the difference here being that for military reasons, the press blitz occurred *after* the invasion, not before.[35]

In emergency situations directives to the press came from Hitler through Dietrich. In cases involving possible embarrassment to the party, Hitler talked first with his Reichsleiter and other "Old Fighters." The word then went out to the news media, and a coordinated program followed. Such was the procedure followed when Rudolf Hess, deputy Führer and charter member of the "old guard," suddenly left the country on May 10, 1941. This action might, it was felt, seriously impair the prestige of the party. Once it was clear that Hess had landed in Scotland and was now a POW of the British, the German press followed the line laid down by the highest authority. By May 13 newspapers noted that Rudolf Hess had "been involved in an accident," that he had earlier been forbidden to fly, and that he had been showing signs of mental illness. The next day newspapers continued to stress the mental illness argument, but gave the story an ideological twist in portraying the former deputy Führer as an idealist who was deluded into thinking the vicious British might be induced to make peace with Germany.

Hints of British manipulation of Hess through astrologers appeared in the press, but Hess was still portrayed as a National Socialist "idealist" and a "confused head." Censors managed to edit Hess out of the "German Weekly Newsreel," but the regime was embarrassed by illustrated weekly editions which showed Hess with Hitler at a recent Reichstag session. The Hess flight provoked the government into mass arrests and interrogations of seers, astrologers, mentalists, and Christian Scientists, allegedly the types of people who manipulated Hess. The party survived the Hess incident, in part because of the mental illness argument, in part because of Hess's apparent loss of power long before May 1941. German public attention turned toward the east after the attack upon the Soviet Union; while the Hess incident was hardly forgotten, it was no longer a major topic of conversation.[36]

Hitler himself on various occasions dictated the outline or even the words of a major theme. In October 1941 Hitler declared through Dietrich that the campaign in the east had been decided. Despite their misgivings, Fritzsche and Goebbels could hardly contradict this idea, and it dominated the press through much of October. At his trial Fritzsche declared, "I had warned the entire German press about taking this slogan without reservations. I did not believe in this decision which supposedly had already taken place." [37] An examination of the press contradicts Fritzsche, for as late as November 29 newspapers reported a speech by Fritzsche in which he declared, "The decision has already taken place." It was impossible for the press to follow Goebbels' more cautious guidelines when Hitler himself dictated a "daily slogan" to Dietrich.[38]

As the press became concentrated in the hands of the party, it developed a degree of monotony broken only by a rare discordant note sounded by a paper like the *Frankfurter Zeitung.* By 1943 the Nazis had fitted the war into a rigid ideological mold to which the press was expected to conform. The *Berliner Illustrierte Nachtausgabe,* a widely read sheet, printed many aspects of this explanation of the war in the dramatic month of July 1943. The photographs used by this and other illustrated newspapers were supplied by the illustrated press office (BPA) of the press section. By fiscal 1943 the illustrated press office had a budget of RM 843,000, almost RM 600,000 above the figure for fiscal 1941. Half of its budget went into administrative costs. The BPA was responsible for preparing materials for perusal by the political and military censors, and thereafter for distributing approved pictures to photographic services and to the "picture press." This office provided weekly propaganda company (PK) photographs for Hitler's own attention and was active in securing illustrations for exhibitions and books. In 1943 it was able to contribute a sum almost as large as its budget to Dr. Goebbels' fund for the men and families of the propaganda companies. Donations and fees accounted for this money. Press directives to illustrated papers contained detailed instructions regarding the use of the photographs. When a Berlin division returned home after the victory over France, the press was provided with photographs of the event by the German news bureau as well as by the eight major photographic services, and was told to contrast this joyful homecoming with the shameful atmosphere of defeat and betrayal prevalent in 1918-19. The work of the illustrated press office was largely concerned with the thirty-five illustrated newspapers and magazines still extant until 1944.[39]

Six themes played up by the *Berliner Illustrierte* in July 1943 showed it to be a clear voice of Nazi interpretation of the war. On July 1 the paper described "The British terror attacks on Cologne—criminal annihilation of European cultural monuments." The next day its readers learned about an "Interview with Bose—10 questions, 10 answers. Armed revolution and civil disobedience—from within and without." (Subhas Chandra Bose was an ally of the Axis as leader of an Indian freedom movement fighting British imperialism.) Another lead article emphasized the competition between Britain and the United States in North Africa and in the Far East. By July 22 headlines about German successes in the Kursk tank offensive in the east were replaced by forecasts that the British empire was to be absorbed by the United States, a major Nazi theme by 1943. At the end of the month the newspaper described how Germany was defending Europe against Bolshevism and its criminal agents and stooges.

Propagandists argued that the "coordinated" press represented a vital, young generation of editors free of the old Jewish, liberal, and capitalist pressures.[40] Yet one could use terse "Nazi German," numerous exclamation points, and enthusiastic verbiage—and still be a monotonous bore. Goebbels realized that the German press was intellectually on a low level, though he refused to acknowledge the role of National Socialism in creating such a sterile medium. The minister respected a "born journalist" such as Hans Schwarz (who later added "van Berk" to his last name, perhaps to distance himself after 1930 from the discredited Otto Strasser, for whom he had been active as a writer).[41] Clever and supple in his phraseology, Schwarz van Berk edited *Der Angriff* for a time from 1935, and he impressed Goebbels by breathing new life into that dying newspaper. Schwarz served as a PK reporter during the Polish campaign in 1939, and in 1940 he became the political editor of Goebbels' new paper, *Das Reich.*

Das Reich was Goebbels' attempt to fill the void created by the absence of a quality press in Germany.[42] He wished to influence foreign circles as well as those at home, and for these purposes Goebbels deliberately chose the low-key format, "intellectual" in style, of a literary weekly. Goebbels' lead article was a major political event, and from October 1941 it was regularly read on the radio and was disseminated by the Reich propaganda central office and the RPL. Goebbels put both Hans Fritzsche and Schwarz van Berk to work on the journal, even favoring Schwarz from time to time with space for a long article of his own. By 1943 the new weekly was selling over one and a half million copies a week. Editors were informed that they could use part or all of Goebbels' article in their own newspapers but, as Berlin told the Hannover RPA office, no pressure was to be brought to bear to secure such cooperation. Though not without internal stresses, the weekly continued to operate successfully almost until the end of the war. It profited from the growth of Goebbels' prestige and popularity after Stalingrad.

Joseph Goebbels exercised more direct control over radio broadcasting than he did over the press. This may be one reason why "During the war the radio was for Dr. Goebbels the most important instrument of propaganda. He did not keep such a strict watch on any department as he did on the radio department." [43] As early as 1933, fresh from the editorial office of *Der Angriff,* the young propaganda minister foresaw a greater role for the newer medium, the radio: "What the press was for the nineteenth century, the radio will be for the twentieth . . ." Goebbels acknowledged that without the radio and the airplane the Nazi seizure and use of total power would have been unthinkable. He described the radio as the "first and most influential intermediary between . . . movement and nation, between idea and man. . . . We want a radio that marches with the nation, a radio that works for the people . . ." With these words Dr. Goebbels opened the tenth German radio exhibition on August 18, 1933.[44]

The central command post of the Greater German radio network resided in the radio division of the propaganda ministry. Alfred-Ingemar Berndt directed this unit from August 1939. Berndt served in the armed forces from February to August 1940. Within a year of his return, the erratic Berndt had turned much of the daily work of his office over to his deputy, Wolfgang Diewerge, who succeeded Berndt in September 1941. Diewerge was a fanatic Nazi and an "expert" anti-Semite who had been in the ministry since 1934. Eugen Hadamovsky, described by Willi A. Boelcke as a man "of the uncontrollable enthusiasm of the born fanatic," was director of Reich broadcasting, which gave him authority over programming. Hadamovsky had joined the party in 1930 and even then had showed signs of a restless antisocial nature. In his 1933 book on propaganda, dedicated to Goebbels, Hadamovsky frankly, perhaps too frankly, stated the Nazi disbelief in the hobgoblin of objectivity. While Berndt was in the army, Hadamovsky replaced him, but he was not successful and it was Diewerge who succeeded Berndt late in 1941. Goebbels assigned Hadamovsky as an aide to Naumann in the minister's office, but this did not work out either, and in 1942 Hadamovsky was assigned to the RPL, where he couldn't "do any more damage." While Hadamovsky was still director of Reich broadcasting, Goebbels appointed Dr. Heinrich Glasmaier as Reich superintendent of the Greater German radio network, partially as a way of curbing Hadamovsky's excesses and neutralizing his incompetence. Glasmaier was no improvement, and by 1942 he too was deprived of most of his authority.[45]

The Reich Radio Society managed the German radio network. Its program division coordinated all broadcasts and arranged for exchanges between the twenty-six stations composing the Greater German radio. There were thirteen regional stations and numerous local outlets; the latter did not broadcast on their own, but were voices of the regional stations and for the national "Germany transmitter," which was the anchor of the whole system. Simultaneous nationwide transmission was provided by this *Deutschlandsender,* and regional stations had to suspend their independent programming when so directed by Berlin. When Goebbels appointed Hans Fritzsche head of the radio division of the ministry in 1942, he had finally discovered a competent man to run the German broadcasting empire, though in Nazi fanaticism Fritzsche could not compare to Berndt, Hadamovsky, and Glasmaier. No matter, for at this juncture, Goebbels wanted ability, not merely a Golden Party Badge.

Hans Fritzsche was born in Bochum in 1900 and began his career as an editor of the *Prussian Yearbooks* in 1923. He soon went to work for the telegraph company, part of the media empire of the Nationalist politician and businessman Alfred Hugenberg. Until 1932 Fritzsche was an editor for the Hugenberg telegraph combine. Part of this work involved writing articles on foreign affairs for German newspapers which subscribed to the Hugenberg service. Fritzsche was not politically active for most of this time, though his articles rejected the German Nationalist viewpoint. Late in 1932 Fritzsche became director of the radio news service (the "wireless service"), which was a division of the state-owned

Reich Radio Society. Fritzsche began to do his own broadcasting in September 1932 with a program on the "political survey of the press." In 1928 he met Joseph Goebbels, who liked Fritzsche because of his favorable comments about the Nazis. These comments, which he later claimed he had terminated in 1931, reflected the Hugenberg-Hitler alliance of that era.

Goebbels, understanding the role of the mass media in the Nazi struggle for power, was looking ahead to the employment of competent technicians such as Fritzsche. Fritzsche was a typical, if highly talented, "nonpartisan technician," a "national-minded" individual who would work for anyone on the right if offered scope for his ambitions and a certain freedom in his work. Fritzsche became head of the German News Service, now part of the new propaganda ministry, in 1933. Taking no chances, the careful Fritzsche joined the party on May 1, 1933. In 1938 Goebbels promoted Fritzsche to head of the German press division in the ministry, a post he held until 1942, when he put in a brief stint on the eastern front. Later that same year Fritzsche returned and reached the pinnacle of his career, becoming both head of the ministry's radio division and Goebbels' commissioner for the political structuring of the Greater German radio. In this capacity he "formulated and issued daily radio 'paroles' to all Reich propaganda offices . . ." [46]

Fritzsche's division contained an important "reconnaissance service" *(Erkundungsdienst),* which monitored and transcribed foreign broadcasts. The confidential information which was obtained in this manner was summarized and distributed to Goebbels and other high-ranking officials of his choice. German radio could then quickly respond to and defuse enemy transmissions, some of which were listened to by Germans in their basements or other secret places. They could thus undermine an Allied broadcast before German rumors developed. The reconnaissance service also provided Goebbels with military, economic, and political information about the Reich's enemies. The quality of these reports varied. A report issued on November 24, 1944, noted that foreign broadcasters were commenting widely on Hitler's silence and lack of public appearances. Goebbels appreciated such a summary, since it confirmed his own judgment regarding the importance of Hitler's public personality to the German people. The reconnaissance service also issued reports on "The Situation in the Soviet Union," "Developments in the Middle East," and "The Influence of Bolshevism upon Enemy Countries." Some of these were mere summaries, pasted together without imagination. They consisted of translations from foreign broadcasts and left analysis to leaders such as Goebbels. Other reports, such as one on "German Propaganda in the Criticism of its Enemies," were a carefully prepared anthology of quotations from German radio programs and writings as they appeared in Allied newspaper commentaries and radio broadcasts. The work of the reconnaissance service complemented information provided by the archival division of the foreign office, which supplied materials to the propaganda ministry for use in structuring its radio programs and newspaper themes.[47]

Wartime German radio contained two nationwide daily broadcasts of the OKW communiqué, as well as detailed reports based upon eyewitness work at the front or at sea carried out by PK personnel. Walter Wilhelm Dittmar headed the "wireless service," or news division of the radio, succeeding Fritzsche in that post in 1938. Goebbels made clear that the policies and guidelines enunciated at the ministerial conference and the daily press conference were in effect for the radio as well as for other mass media. Radio personnel were free to rework materials so that they were presentable in broadcasting form, but they were not permitted to advance viewpoints of their own or release forbidden bits of news without the permission of the minister. In order to secure total control over radio news broadcasts and commentaries, Goebbels required radio commentators and news editors to attend his ministerial conference. He established this policy in 1941, and it remained in effect when Franz Wildoner succeeded Dittmar in 1942.[48]

The most dramatic radio event of the early wartime years was the "special announcement," or *Sondermeldung.* All programs were interrupted. There was a blast of trumpets leading to a brief transmission of heroic music adapted from Franz Liszt's famous symphonic poem *Les Préludes.* An announcer then read the military communiqué, which contained news of the latest German triumph. When the broadcaster finished reading, the special announcement concluded with the singing of a stirring contemporary marching song, perhaps "We're Marching against England," one of the most popular in 1940–41. These special announcements began during the Norwegian expedition and continued through the great victories in Russia in 1941. Goebbels was furious in June 1940 when an illustrated weekly published a photograph of the recording which contained the fanfare used for special announcements. Such pictures could lead to the demystification of great national events, and the minister threatened further perpetrators with a stint in a concentration camp.[49]

Goebbels was aware of the fact that people listened to the radio for relaxation and music as well as for news from the front. As early as 1934, the minister decreed that after the intense emotional experience represented by the Nürnberg party rally, the radio should emphasize light music for several weeks. Programs intended for instruction of the masses should be rich in content but not overly didactic, while "good German conversation" must be provided for relaxation. The concerns of the war, especially the Stalingrad disaster and the worsening of the air terror, imparted an increasingly depressing and heavy-handed polemical tone to radio programs. By early 1943 Wolfgang Fischer, head of the RPL radio office, was telling Walter Tiessler that the German radio lacked a necessary human-interest touch.[50] More broadcasting oriented towards social, personal, and human needs and interests was necessary, and there should be perhaps fewer polemics dealing directly with the war and foreign affairs. Fischer even alluded to the Soviet radio, which spoke to the concerns of specific groups of people. He suggested that the Greater German radio encourage the total war effort by discussing war work carried out by old men and women, using a folksy human-interest approach. Fischer's critique, a slap at Goebbels and Fritzsche, led to little change in format. The radio became even more political after Stalingrad, dominated by news accounts and by the ideological voices or articles of Fritzsche, Goebbels, and Karl Scharping.[51]

The use of music by the German radio demonstrated the hold that party ideologues and fanatics had over the medium. Despite his own intellectual and cultural predilections, Goebbels encouraged the radio in its never-ending presentation of German military music. These marches probably stirred the most apathetic citizen during times of great victories or imminent German offensives, but their irrelevance during harder times left a broadcasting void. One would have to be a convinced and committed National Socialist to respond in late 1944 to a march made popular in 1931 by a Berlin SA unit. The only limitation that Goebbels put upon the playing of military music early in 1940 was that Austrian as well as Prussian marches be included in the program "German Marches from Every *Gau.*" Herms Niel, a famed bandleader, wrote the most popular German march of the war, "We're Marching against England," and it was played ad nauseam on the German radio between the end of 1939 and the spring of 1941. When Hitler attacked the Balkans on April 6, 1941, the German radio made much of the "Prinz Eugen March," with its evocation of an Austrian military hero of early eighteenth-century Turkish wars.

A new technique appeared on June 23, when the radio began its anti-Bolshevik crusade: Martial music was now played against the background of the roar of artillery and the screaming dives of *Stukas.*[52] Heroic music accompanied the Nazi movement from its beginnings. Martial tunes played a role in German society unthinkable anywhere else, and the Nazis capitalized upon this fact. Fanatical Nazis and Hitler Youth responded best to these heroic, musical invocations late in the war. For other Germans, the records were wearing out as the Allied bombs and the artillery of the Red Army drowned out the strains of "We March through Greater Berlin" and "Raise the Banner!"

Goebbels and his radio supervisors fell back upon this type of music because of difficulties presented by other musical forms. While respecting even ecclesiastical German music as part of the nation's cultural heritage, the minister banned the Mozart Requiem from radio transmission because of its "depressing and world-renouncing" text. By 1941 even Beethoven presented problems, since the German public was discovering that his Fifth Symphony had become an Allied victory signal. *Fidelio*, with its appeal for human freedom, was as suspicious as Schiller's play *William Tell*, though the Vienna opera received permission to produce it in 1944. One of the clever techniques used by Goebbels to keep cultured, pious Germans out of church was to present Sunday-morning programs that contrasted with most German broadcasts. These sessions included some of the finest German poetry and classical—even church—music. The problems of German musical programming were not limited to the classical repertoire. Since Goebbels and Himmler had forbidden swing and jazz music as alien and decadent, permitted dance music was old fashioned and lacking in appeal to the contemporary ear. In Germany soldiers' choruses and marching songs often took the place occupied by jazz and the big bands in the United States.[53]

In the spring of 1943, after Stalingrad, Goebbels, Wächter, Tiessler, and Hans Hinkel, leader of the "division for special cultural tasks" in the ministry, debated the problem of radio music. Hinkel pointed out that 80 percent of the letters received from the public indicated that people did not want radio programming to be infected by the generally depressed mood of the nation. Radio as a diversion and a "lift" was now more necessary than during the great days of victory. Tiessler strongly disagreed, and in some of the (unintentionally) funniest comments ever made by a Nazi propagandist, he declared that the radio must not play songs with themes like "I dance with you into heaven" and "Another beautiful day comes to an end." Goebbels ordered Wächter to go to the regions of western Germany most affected by the Allied bombings and to find out what people wanted to hear.[54] Little was done, and nothing changed.

Hans Fritzsche took over the radio division late in 1942. His commentaries, along with those of Lt. General Kurt Dittmar and Dr. Karl Scharping, went far beyond the earlier Fritzsche broadcasts. They became highly polemical, abandoning the pretense of an objective review of the foreign press, which Fritzsche had always affected on his program. The commentaries of Fritzsche and Scharping, despite protestations after the war, were an expression of the National Socialist world view in their attempt to explain and justify the war to the nation. Dittmar was the military commentator.[55] He avoided the polemical tone of Goebbels' lead article in *Das Reich* (which was read on the radio from late 1941), and he refused to adopt Fritzsche's supercilious irony. Kurt Dittmar was born in 1889, had risen to the rank of captain in World War I, and later had become commander of the Berlin military engineering school. During the Stalingrad catastrophe Dittmar prepared the nation for bad news; his frankness often annoyed Goebbels, who could not quarrel with Dittmar's assessment of the military situation. When Dittmar strayed into domestic policy in a broadcast, however, Goebbels sharply reprimanded him and demanded that he follow the ministry line or avoid such areas altogether. Fritzsche claimed at Nürnberg that he staunchly defended Dittmar upon such occasions, but the incomplete records of the ministerial conferences do not support this thesis.[56] Perhaps he came to the general's defense privately. Goebbels wanted caution, but not pessimism; he was willing to admit a defeat after it had happened, but he was not willing to openly *foresee* disaster.

Hans Fritzsche was the most important German broadcaster during the war. In his career he probably spoke a thousand times on the radio; he was also well known as a good public speaker. Fritzsche's weekly talks during the last war years were sharp polemics in the form of reviews of foreign press and opinion. As Fritzsche put it, he would "wield a sharp blade in dealing with enemy propaganda." Goebbels realized how important Fritzsche was to his propaganda efforts, but the commentator did not totally escape the minister's barbs. Goebbels told von Oven that a man like Fritzsche was fine in normal times, for he had great political insight and intelligence, but during the present time of crisis (1943) he lacked decisiveness and courage.[57] Perhaps the minister felt inferior to Fritzsche in technical training, or maybe he resented the commentator's belated Nazism. Publicly, Goebbels praised Fritzsche highly.[58]

Hans Fritzsche's basic material was supplied by the Express Service Archive; it consisted of clippings from papers, reports of news agencies, and reports from foreign broadcasts. Fritzsche had a certain latitude in these broadcasts, so long as he did not deviate from Goebbels' main guidelines. In his work as director of the radio division, Fritzsche was not so free. Karl Cerff, cultural advisor to the RPL, opposed any programming by Fritzsche which deviated from the Nazi world view (e.g., religious services on the radio), and he had the authority to enforce his viewpoint until November 1944, when Goebbels got rid of him. Even when defending himself at Nürnberg, Fritzsche admitted that his work was governed by two overriding factors: the constant interference of Goebbels, especially concerning political guidelines, and, in his words, "my task of disseminating the viewpoint of my government on the origins, nature, and goals of the war in Germany, the occupied territories, and abroad . . ." [59] When Fritzsche received his appointment in 1942, Wolfgang Diewerge quoted earlier words of approval by Goebbels: "No one knows better than I how much work goes into these [radio] addresses, how they are sometimes dictated in the very last moment, only to find willing listeners throughout the nation a moment later." [60]

In the early wartime broadcasts, Hans Fritzsche affected the sarcastic, ironic, supercilious tones that attracted many listeners to the commentator's wit and ridicule. It was easy to put down the Allies in this manner while Germany went from victory to victory. The post-Stalingrad Fritzsche "shows" became more polemical; while the sarcasm remained, most of the wit and ridicule disappeared. The remnants of the old sarcasm now appeared to be a know-it-all cynicism, and this began to grate on the ears of many Germans during the hard years that followed Stalingrad. Fritzsche's technique during the early war years was to seize upon statements or broadcasts in the Allied camp and build his clever justification of German policy around them. The average German was hungry for this type of news from the enemy camp, and even the fact that he or she was receiving it from a questionable source did not diminish his or her enthusiasm for the program. Fritzsche could use his broadcasts as a quick response to Allied statements that might embarrass the regime if allowed to go unanswered. By calmly dissecting enemy assertions before many Germans knew of them through friends who illegally listened secretly to Swiss or British (BBC) broadcasts, Fritzsche further served the function of defusing Allied propaganda before it had reached its target.[61]

Hans Fritzsche's radio address of April 20, 1940, was a masterpiece of its type.[62] He was an expert in pretense, speaking to the average intelligent German in an "objective" manner while furthering the policies of his employer, the Hitler regime. Seemingly devoid of ideology, anecdotal but omniscient in style, Fritzsche told his listeners about a British pilot who bragged that he had easily flown low over the Unter den Linden in Berlin, had observed the Berliners and could sense their mood, and had flown off before they or Luftwaffe defenses knew what had happened. Fritzsche used his irony: It was too bad this "English specialist on the mood of the German people" had not returned on the night of April 19, when he would have seen many banners celebrating the eve of the Führer's birthday and vast crowds awaiting a

glimpse of their beloved leader. Despite the early successes of the
German invasion of Norway, begun almost two weeks earlier, many
Germans were nervous about an operation so dependent upon naval
operations in "British controlled" waters. Fritzsche's ridicule was thus
comforting. His promotion in late 1942 coincided with a dramatic
change in the Reich's military fortunes. By 1943 a sharp alteration in his
style was apparent, though his voice maintained its inflection of arrogant
omniscience.

Fritzsche, speaking during the battle of Stalingrad, followed Goebbels'
guidelines and did not attempt to gloss over the challenges confronting
the Reich: "A hard year is coming to an end, and a year which also
promises to be hard looms before us," he said.[63] In his celebration of ten
years of the Third Reich, Fritzsche compared the Nazi revolution to the
"German uprisings" of 1813 and 1914. He repeated the theme of the
struggle against Bolshevism, the Treaty of Versailles, and plutocracy. At
the end of March 1943, Fritzsche denounced the British plutocrats for
their brutal air attacks on civilian centers and told his listeners that the
British, not the Germans, had begun the air war with attacks on
Hamburg and Freiburg in 1940. His style was to combine denunciations
of the enemy with a note of consolation. In the late winter of 1943
Fritzsche argued that the air was costing the enemy great losses, as was
the German U-boat campaign in the North Atlantic. He hinted at a new
offensive in the east. In describing the end of the Axis armies in Tunis in
early May, Fritzsche used the familiar Hitler *Heldenkampf* (heroic
struggle) obituary perfected after Stalingrad, but gave his account a
cynical twist reminiscent of Goebbels. Fritzsche argued that the Allies
had blundered by missing an opportunity to open a second front in
November 1942! Now the eastern front was stable, and that chance
would not recur. When the Allies landed in Sicily in July, Fritzsche
smugly announced that they were unable to land in Italy, so they
attacked a mere island.

By the end of July the Soviets had regained the initiative, Mussolini
was under arrest, and heavy new bombings rained destruction on more
German cities. Fritzsche now spoke of "tough resistance" by German
forces in Sicily and Russia and bragged that the Germans and Italians
were "young peoples" fighting for their future. The German people had
become a "community of destiny" in adversity, and if they did not
persevere they would suffer the fate of 1918–19. They would never
capitulate this time, however, for in the Third Reich, a sense of realism
was wedded to German idealism. Fritzsche's comment that in "war,
morale is decisive" foreshadowed the Nazi "victory through faith"
rhetoric of 1944. Though his cool tones were not those of the Nazi RPL

or Educational Office speaker, Fritzsche utilized all the ideological explanations of the party: Bombing will not break our will; 1939 was more dangerous because we were surrounded; Badoglio had betrayed the Italian people in overthrowing Mussolini; an Allied victory would mean handing over Europe to the Bolsheviks. Fritzsche now hinted at "miracle weapons"; faced with the frightening successes of the Soviets in the Ukraine, he argued that the German leadership was surrendering land in order to conserve German lives.

Late in 1943 Hans Fritzsche developed a new theme, one he would exploit into 1944. He commented that the Allies had disagreements among themselves, and that there was a growing fear of Bolshevism in the West. Fritzsche was subtle in making these statements, but he was offering a new straw to the depressed German people. At the end of the year the commentator admitted that these were holidays which gave little cause for celebration. People were now talking about a possible second front in France, so Fritzsche halfheartedly boasted that so far all the Allies could do was *talk* about it. He told Germans curious about what the Allies had in store for Europe to look at southern Italy, which Fritzsche described as a land of misery, chaos, and dictatorship. In January 1944 he played down differences among the Allies, arguing that the Jews and Bolsheviks would dominate Europe in the event of an Allied victory. Fritzsche correctly predicted that the various exile governments (Poles, Czechs, Yugoslavs) in London would never really regain power if the Allies won the war.

One could detect a hint of nervousness in Fritzsche's comment early in 1944 that the Allied air and propaganda offensives could not weaken the will to victory of the German nation. By March Fritzsche was gloating about the decline of the British empire and the concomitant gains made by American capitalism in Canada and Australia. Early in 1943 he had emphasized the stabilization of the front and the success of the nation in confronting the air war, but within little more than a year many of his consoling arguments had become threadbare and irrelevant, and Fritzsche was reduced to telling his suffering German listeners that things were even worse for the British empire.

Dr. Karl Scharping employed many of Fritzsche's ideological themes, but he was more extreme in his statements.[64] During the last stages of the Stalingrad disaster, Scharping told his audience, which was smaller than that of Fritzsche, that sentiment for the New Europe was strong all over the continent. He compared European labor reserves favorably with those of the United States. Scharping's praise for Vidkun Quisling of Norway as a pioneer of the New Europe must have amused those listeners who knew that Quisling was the most hated man in Norway.

Scharping had a full measure of the cynicism so prevalent among Goebbels' propagandists. He told his audience that the Allies lied when they claimed that the Germans mistreated and exploited the inhabitants of occupied territories. Scharping used areas like the Baltic states, Minsk, and the Ukraine to prove his point, blithely ignoring the murders, deportations, and torture which were normal occurrences in the east.

Fritzsche strengthened his own appeal by occasionally acknowledging that the Reich faced a difficult situation. Karl Scharping would have none of this. He was absurdly optimistic, so much so that irate listeners began to write him critical letters addressed to "Dr. Charlatan." Scharping was a great spokesman for the idea of the German reorganization of Europe in 1943; the prevalence of this theme in German propaganda became more pronounced as the military situation turned against Germany. Scharping declared that even the French were providing volunteers for the European struggle against Bolshevism and plutocracy. He was more directly ideological than Fritzsche, mouthing without irony the themes concocted by Goebbels and Hitler. He did so without even the pretense of objective commentary. Fritzsche's wide popularity as a commentator held up until well into 1943, while Scharping lost his credibility with every new German defeat. Yet because of the few sources of information available to the German public, millions of listeners tuned in to such broadcasts each week.

5

Publications, Posters, and Propaganda Campaigns

Wartime German propaganda campaigns did not merely mobilize the press and broadcast media. It made vast use of books and pamphlets, brochures and leaflets, window displays and slide shows, posters and placards, even postage stamps and cancellation marks. The Nazi leadership assigned a major role to the written word when it interpreted the Second World War for the German nation. By 1941 books on every conceivable wartime political, geopolitical, racial, and military subject flooded the German market with updates of National Socialist ideological themes. The popular hunger for information was a boon to the Nazi movement, and the party encouraged "reliable" writers to satisfy the nation's desire for relevant instruction. Joseph Goebbels wrote of his people, "We Germans can scarcely picture a life devoid of books." [1] Late in 1941 he described the two tasks of the German wartime book: It must give the *Volk* an understanding of the background of the conflict, and it should provide "strength and relaxation in the difficult weeks and months of the war." [2] By this time, party and private publishers had produced almost a quarter of a billion copies of wartime books and pamphlets. Almost 40 percent dealt directly with issues of the war. The average printing was eleven thousand copies.[3]

Party and state agencies commissioned works and listed them on bibliographies widely distributed to booksellers and libraries. The party publisher, Franz Eher Verlag, published in Berlin a "Series of Writings

Mobilization of the publishing industry for purposes of wartime propaganda: the cover of Dr. Landes' *What Is the German Soldier Fighting for?*

of the NSDAP" *(Schriftenreihe)* addressed to questions of the war. The price of the volumes was kept low so that they would be accessible to all citizens. The volumes of the Series were divided into various groups. Representative listings included "German Armed Forces," "German Labor," "European Politics Then and Now," "That Is England," "The War Experiences," and "The European East." The party also began publishing in 1939 a bibliography of works entitled National Socialist Educational Pamphlets *(Nationalsozialistische Schulungsschriften)* which were suitable for use in *Gau* training programs.

The office of Alfred Rosenberg, NSDAP "doctrinal supervisor," produced many bibliographies which furthered his interpretation of the Nazi world view. *Book Lore: Monthly for German Writings,* for example, edited and published by Hans Hagemeyer, reviewed and listed works contributing to an understanding of Nazi wartime doctrine. This journal had a tendency to praise Rosenberg's intellectual efforts above all others. The office also published an annual list of recommended books. The works of some of the best-known Nazi writers dominated its pages: Gunter d'Alquen of the SS paper *Das Schwarze Korps,* Wilfrid Bade, Alfred-Ingemar Berndt and Karl Boemer of the Propaganda Ministry, Philipp Bouhler and Walter Buch of the party, Kurt Daluege for the police, Walther Darré of the "Blood and Soil" peasantry, Otto Dietrich, Gauleiter Albert Forster, Hans Frank of the General Government in Poland, Karl Richard Ganzer, a Nazi historian, Goebbels and Hadamovsky, and (until May 1941) Rudolf Hess. Many works were collections of speeches. The German tendency to intellectualize and appear cultured infected even semiliterate Nazi eminences. Rosenberg's "Guide to Books" listed recommended works with brief reviews by members of the literary department of his office.[4]

Books favored by intense promotional efforts of the party and its agencies achieved printings in the hundreds of thousands. During and immediately after the great German blitz victories of 1939 and 1940, the popular desire for pictures of Hitler at the front further enriched his official photographer, Heinrich "Photo" Hoffmann. This man, who had years earlier introduced a young assistant named Eva Braun to Hitler, published in 1939 *With Hitler in Poland* partially as an antidote to film documentaries influenced by the armed forces, such as *Campaign in Poland.* Many party leaders felt that the Army emphasized its own role in Poland at the expense of Hitler's military genius and leadership gifts. Hoffmann's book was a photographic glorification of the Führer. Goebbels despised Hoffmann as a drunkard whose blue-red face was "shattered by alcohol" and as a crude lecher, but he had no control over a party publication deriving from Hitler and his entourage.

These five photographs demonstrate how the Nazis mobilized the Hitler mythos during the early stages of the war. From Heinrich Hoffmann, *With Hitler in Poland.*

CREDIT: From Heinrich Hoffman, *With Hitler in Poland.*

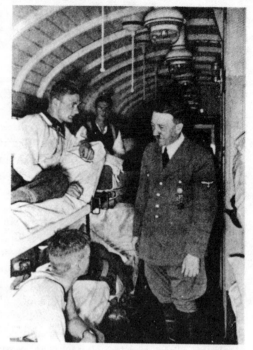

Hitler visits German soldiers wounded in the Polish campaign.

CREDIT: From Heinrich Hoffman, *With Hitler in Poland*

The Wehrmacht presents Hitler with a captured emblem of a crack Polish cavalry regiment. Himmler stands in the background.

CREDIT: From Heinrich Hoffman, *With Hitler in Poland*

Hitler sharing field mess with his troops in Poland. The thoughtful cook had removed the meat from the stew to please the vegetarian Chancellor. But you could not fool the Führer: After tasting the watery meal, Hitler asked if it was substantial enough for the fighting men!

CREDIT: From Heinrich Hoffman, *With Hitler in Poland.*

Hitler at the Polish front, September 1939.

CREDIT: From Heinrich Hoffman. *With Hitler in Poland*

Hitler the Liberator of Danzig, 1939.

The German Book for the Home was one of the most widely distributed party wartime publications.[5] It combined literature with the functions of a calendar. It was a clever blend of fine writing and Nazi ideology; the poetry of Goethe might appear next to a commemoration of November 9, 1923. The book was published by the Eher Verlag under the auspices of the Winter Relief Drive; in 1943 the main cultural office of the RPL cosponsored the work. This anthology was intended for the Nazi family. It was educational in that it contained stories and poems that could be read aloud to small children. The book explained the solemn ceremonies of National Socialism in a basic manner. For those interested in more "scholarly" approved works, the list of "Selected New Acquisitions" published by the Library of the Reichstag was a good guide.[6] In 1944 the bibliography included books by Heinrich von Sribik, Austrian historian of the "Total German" idea, Giselher Wirsing, Nazi journalistic expert on the United States, Viktor Bibl, a noted Austrian scholar belatedly converted to the Greater German idea in its Nazi form. Disseminating such "respectable" but reliable works was intended to impress German intellectual circles. Non-Nazis would, it was hoped, see the tie between the Third Reich and earlier traditions of German scholarship. Even on this list, however, there appeared a heavy sprinkling of more vulgar and blatantly Nazi works such as Fritz Debus on *The Deadly Sin of Liberalism: Jewry Receives Civil Rights.* Hans Hagemeyer and K. A. von Mueller, a "respectable" historian favored by the regime, collaborated to produce a major world atlas. One wonders how relevant or how great the popular demand for it was in 1944. The various RPL information bulletins for speakers were a major means of disseminating such approved works. Speakers sometimes received bibliographies with the suggestion that they consult works by Rosenberg, von Sribik, and Richard Suchenwirth, whose popular *Deutsche Geschichte (German History)* had been a best-seller since 1934.[7]

The party made intensive use of the written word through brochures, pamphlets, and leaflets. This was a legacy of the Era of Struggle, when men like Goebbels would do anything to catch the eye of passersby or to strengthen the will to fight of SA and party members. Nothing was too crude or too sensational for this work. In describing such publications in the 1930s, Franz Six still used early Goebbels pamphlets as the models for such efforts.[8] The later war years marked a return on a large scale to these early techniques, both in brochures and posters. In these media the work of 1944 resembled that of 1932 more than it did that of 1937. This reflected the growing reliance of men like Goebbels upon memories of the *Kampfzeit* to get them through the agonies of the last war years. Yet one had to be cautious: By 1943 the unpopularity of the party led

Wächter and the RPL to suppress the name of the publisher of many party brochures. Instead of seeing "Reich Propaganda Office" on the bottom, one might now read "Universum Verlag." [9]

In 1943 the RPL greatly increased the number of its brochures and pamphlets. Millions of copies of a single article by Goebbels were mailed to Germans throughout Central Europe. One brochure was printed in an edition of fourteen million copies (including copies for men at the front) late in 1943. By this time there was a growing urgency about RPL efforts. The air war was a disaster and Mussolini had fallen from power. The central RPL office breathlessly demanded that all GPL directors inform it within a week of the total number of copies necessary for every district in their *Gau*. The reason for this haste was the recent memory of a major failure. Some Gauleiters believed that distribution of Goebbels' famous February 18 "total war" speech would be useful, but they had run into typical bureaucratic wartime difficulties in obtaining the brochure. Goebbels kept changing the name; then he insisted that someone write a (flattering) preface describing the frenetic atmosphere that day in the Sportpalast; then there was trouble with the printer ... The pamphlet was not ready until the end of May, and then only in a much smaller edition than planned. By this time "total war" had proven to be a total farce, and the brochure lost much of its effectiveness. Another, but less important, brochure appeared in late June, again containing a speech by Goebbels in the Sportpalast. The lesson of the confusion surrounding the printing and distribution of the "total war" speech was not lost upon the RPL. In this case the first half million copies were ready within six weeks to go to party men serving at the front.

One of the most widely distributed brochures was Goebbels' folksy "Thirty Articles of War for the German People." [10] There was a tremendous demand for this little book on the part of *Gau* and district propaganda leaders during the last three months of 1943. It was probably the most widely distributed pamphlet since "German Soldiers See the Soviet Union," a collection of letters and comments published in 1942.[11] Two *Gaue*, Saxony and the Sudentenland, had ordered over 600,000 copies of that brochure. At the end of 1943 the Sudeten party cooperated with the German Labor Front and developed novel ways of publicizing Goebbels' "Thirty Articles of War." The pages were separated and posted on bulletin boards in factories, while 6,000 copies were displayed in store windows. The magazine *Der Propagandist*, published by the GPL, included the articles on the wrappers in which it was mailed. The Sudetenland officials reported that their work had been greatly aided by such promotions, which had been suggested by RPL headquarters in Berlin. By the winter of 1941 the RPL claimed to have distributed 2 million wartime brochures, 7 million placards, more than 60 million magazines, bulletins for public display, and handbills, as well as 67 million leaflets. It had sponsored about 30,000 slide presentations, and 200,000 meetings, demonstrations, and factory rallies.

The urgency of the military situation after Stalingrad, combined with a growing shortage of paper and difficulties in transportation, tested the ingenuity of Goebbels' propagandists. In May 1943 Scheffler (office of the RPL chief of staff) suggested to the minister that reading material be placed in barber shops and in the waiting rooms of physicians.[12] Scheffler claimed that this type of activity would cost less than RM 2,000 per week. By the end of the year many *Gaue* were receiving from 400 to 2,000 copies of Goebbels' weekly lead article in *Das Reich* for placement in the offices of physicians. Goebbels originally had misgivings about this program but after discussions with Dr. Conti, Reich health leader,[13] he permitted the RPL to go ahead with the program. Perhaps Goebbels, who could not stand physical pain, did not appreciate the thought of how sick people might react when they saw his "Thirty Articles" in their doctor's waiting room.

Nazi agencies directed their attention to every segment of the population when distributing their propaganda. Robert Ley intervened through the German Labor Front in an effort to hand out publications of the Eher Verlag in the factories, particularly the "standard works of the movement." [14] Ethnic Germans from eastern and southeastern Europe who were in resettlement camps in the Reich in late 1942 were the objects of Propaganda Ministry concern. Wächter and his aide Wernicke told Gutterer, "Our purpose is to provide settlers from the east and the southeast ... with written anti-Jewish material. The speeches of the Führer and the Reich marshal have reawakened the interest of the entire German people to the fact that our struggle for freedom represents a final accounting in the battle between the Aryan-Germanic race and the Jewish subhumanity." [15] Himmler and the SS had their own channels for book distribution, and their work increased sales of certain types of work. As the Reichsführer SS wrote to Ernst Kaltenbrunner, head of the Reich Security Main Office, "I have ordered a great number of copies of the book *Jewish Ritual Murder* and am distributing it down to the rank of Standartenführer." [16] The book concerned was written by Hellmut Schramm, and it may have impressed Himmler because of its scholarly subtitle, "Historical Investigation."

Martin Bormann's party chancellery began to send out large numbers of recommended titles from 1941 on. Political leaders began to wonder if they were to accept all these titles as the official party line. Early in 1944 Bormann issued a clarification, stating that these books were worthy of attention in terms of the great issues of the day, but that this recommendation did not mean a party endorsement of their every word. Bormann would send copies of these books to the *Gau* main offices, which were supposed to pass them on to the district leaders. In January 1942, when Japanese successes in the Far East opened up new possibilities for the war against Britain, the "liberation" of India was of interest to Hitler and Bormann. The book *India,* by Ludwig Alsdorf, which had appeared in a series advertised by the Rosenberg office, was sent to all Gauleiters by the party chancellory.[17] Karl Cerff, head of the main cultural office of the RPL, organized a party book week in 1941. Goebbels suggested such an exhibition, which was based upon book fairs that had in the past been organized by the state. This book week would be part of the effort to reinvigorate the party. Its model would be exhibitions outside of Germany sponsored for years by the literature section of the ministry.[18]

Censorship of the written word in wartime Germany took many forms. The literature section had most of the authority, particularly in allocating scarce paper for any given edition. The only living authors who could be published were those considered "reliable" members of the Reich Literature Chamber. The preliminary censorship division within this section examined about four thousand manuscripts a year during the war. It was responsible for weeding out objectionable books, articles, and pamphlets dealing with political and military affairs. This activity brought it into fierce conflict with the Official Party Examination Commission for the Defense of NS Literature (director: Philipp Bouhler). The commission gave its "imprimatur" to books, journals and even speeches which did not contain "misleading viewpoints and thoughts." It had been established in 1934 and published the "NS Bibliography." Other agencies also claimed authority in the area of censorship. Within two weeks of Rudolf Hess's sudden departure, Martin Bormann requested that Tiessler and the literature section forbid and seize an illustrated work (containing Hess's picture?) entitled *Our Hitler Youth.* By 1944 the bombings of Berlin had taken their literary toll. The ministry had to inform a Professor Kraeger that his work *Jewry in South Africa* had unfortunately been destroyed in a raid which leveled the Central Research Institute. Would he kindly send another copy to the ministry so that its literature section could take a position on the book? Nazi ideologists were nothing if not persistent.[19]

Max Amann directed the lucrative Franz Eher Verlag, which had offices in Munich, Berlin, and Vienna. By 1940 Amann had succeeded in convincing Bormann and Hess that party authors should be required to submit outlines or manuscripts to Eher before approaching "outside" publishers. Amann was thinking not of party purity, but of money. Imagine if he could some day publish Goebbels' secret diary or a book by Hitler on how he had won the war! Some party authors ignored the decree, so party treasurer Schwarz reminded them of it through Bormann in October 1942.[20] Goebbels fumed about the low royalties paid by Eher when he published his wartime articles and speeches, but there was little that he, of all people, could do about the situation. Goebbels was constantly concerned about his subordinates' embarrassing the ministry, so he made sure that anyone about to approach Amann with an idea for a book had to show the manuscript to him first. He also warned his literarily inclined subordinates not to use their positions to secure press publicity for their books.[21]

Despite all the censorship, embarrassment to the regime occurred from time to time. Late in 1941 or early in 1942 a publishing firm in Leipzig mailed a prospectus to a school in the Upper Danube *Gau*. As Tiessler pointed out in a note to the literature section, a book was being circulated which contained photographs of Rudolf Hess! The only permitted references to Hess after 1941 were those in internal party ordinances referring to earlier decrees by the "former Deputy Führer." [22] Hess's departure further eroded the position of the famed geopolitician, professor, and general Karl Haushofer, a teacher of the former Deputy Führer. Haushofer was already out of the good graces of the party leadership because of his "half-Jewish" wife and his politically dissident son, Albrecht. Goebbels decided by February 1942 to let Haushofer remain in the Reich Culture Chamber because the scandal of expelling a rather prestigious nationalistic author would disconcert too many intellectuals.[23] Bormann concurred, agreeing not to ban Haushofer's books. There was to be no public discrediting of the professor, but while Hess had promoted Haushofer's works, Bormann noted that he did not intend to continue doing that.

The Weimar Republic was a political battleground upon which parties made dramatic use of posters and placards. This was especially true of the Nazis in the last years of the Era of Struggle, 1930–33. Joseph Goebbels, dreaming of creating a campaign masterpiece early in 1932, referred first of all to "placards, leaflets, brochures." When he saw the sketches of the placards to be used in the presidential campaign (Hitler challenging von Hindenburg), he commented, "Our placards have become wonderful. The propaganda is being carried out in the best possible manner. The whole country has to pay attention." [24] The posters contained outrageous satire, brilliant drawings, striking colors; Hitler's enemies were evil incarnate, and Hitler was Germany's avenging angel.

The posters appeared everywhere, on building walls, kiosks, windows of party offices and those of Hitler sympathizers. These posters and placards had simple themes, but their appeal was always to two powerful emotions: hatred and idealism. Albert Speer commented after the war that a poster idealizing Hitler in a heroic pose no longer seemed ridiculous after he heard the Führer speak. Earlier Nazi caricatures had often made an enemy ridiculous ("Isidor" Weiss); by 1932 the enemy was brutalized and attacked. The party was no longer worried about being ignored. It now smelled power and needed more than laughter or the publicity stemming from a brawl in a beer hall or a day in the Berlin municipal courthouse. During the war Nazi posters reflected this post-1930 viewpoint. As Goebbels put it in 1941, the aim of these placards had to be to make the enemy look brutal, for you gained nothing in a life-or-death struggle by making him small and ridiculous. You frightened people into action by showing Bolshevik rapists and murderers looming over the Reich.[25] Nazi posters still appealed to idealism in 1944, but only in the context of this battle.

The Nazis made increasing use of leaflets, stickers, and handbills right before the Seizure of Power.[26] The same slogans were used again and again: "For Freedom and Bread," "Against Marxism and Reaction." The strident tones and powerful phrases, however vulgar, were the written equivalents of posters and placards. The musical parallel was to be found in the stirring marching songs of the SA. During the last two years of the war Goebbels and the RPL returned to many of those slogans and songs. What better way to revive the sluggish party than to appeal to it with the old techniques? The Nazi wartime propaganda apparatus thus made great use of the "slogan of the week," which was distributed in each region by the *Gauring* leader. The "picture of the week" was sent in duplicate to every local municipal branch leader, with the order to display it prominently, cleanly, and promptly. Some of these local leaders exhibited the picture of the week in a cluttered or unattractive setting, and they were reprimanded. Above all, the picture was not to remain there forever, but was to be removed upon receipt of the next edition. These pictures reflected the latest RPL propaganda campaigns. One wartime picture showed two men talking on a train under the large caption "Be Quiet!" This was a reference to the campaign against espionage and rumor mongering.

The Stalingrad disaster and Goebbels' appeal for total war unleashed a barrage of poster propaganda in 1943. The themes of the placards reflected Goebbels' priorities: "Victory or Bolshevik Chaos" and "Hard Times, Hard Work, Hard Hearts." Millions of these large (sometimes about three by five feet in size) posters appeared all over the Reich, on

A selection of German propaganda posters, 1939–40.

"Into the dust with all enemies of Greater Germany!" An early wartime poster showing the Reich smashing the French, the British (Churchill), and the Jews.

Nazi posters in a public place, middle war years. Clockwise from top left: a poster warning Germans not to blab because the enemy is listening in; a poster publicizing a cultural convention of the Hitler Youth in Salzburg; a poster glorifying "our infantry"; a famous anti-Jewish poster, "He is to blame for the war!"

CREDIT: The Suddeutscher Verlag. Munich. Germany

Goebbels, remembering the great propaganda success of "Mjölnir's" posters during the Era of Struggle, commissioned Hans Schweitzer to do these posters as part of the anti-Bolshevik scare campaign: "Victory or Bolshevism."

"Hard times, hard work, hard hearts." A "total war" poster dating from 1943. The theme was the unity of homeland and front, the combined efforts of armaments workers and soldiers. The image of the civilian taking up arms alongside the soldier was a hint of things to come late in 1944—the Volkssturm.

CREDIT: The Library of Congress

"Mjölnir" (Hans Schweitzer) designed this poster for the Reich Propaganda Central Office: "Total War—the Shortest War." The last crucial effort is demanded of the German nation.

An example of the work of the German Propaganda Studio (DPA): "Black out! The enemy sees your light!"

CREDIT: The Imperial War Museum, London, England

A poster designed by "Mjölnir" for the Reich Propaganda Central Office. "Front and homeland, the guarantees of victory."

buses, trains, kiosks, in shop windows, and on the outside walls of buildings. A new spate of Hitler posters—the last in the history of the Third Reich—bearing the caption "Adolf Hitler Is Victory" appeared that same year. At the same time Scheffler of the RPL announced to all *Gau* propaganda leaders that they would no longer receive the "slogan of the week." Goebbels made this decision, Scheffler noted, and the *Gau* offices that subscribed to the "slogan" would receive a refund. More money and effort was now being put into posters and brochures such as Goebbels' "Thirty Articles." A renewed drive to bring this propaganda to factory workers was undertaken in May with the cooperation of Albert Speer. Factories were targeted for the poster now renamed "Hard Times, Hard Work, Hard Hearts," a particularly appropriate theme for overworked and frequently bombed proletarians.

Since early 1940, the RPL had been distributing posters in the series named the "Weekly Motto of the NSDAP." This series featured heroic slogans taken from the writings or speeches of party leaders: Ley's German Labor Front had for years encouraged the posting of these mottos in factories. The growing concern about the morale of the industrial workers in 1943 was a reflection, intensified in these "hard times," of a long-held Nazi fear. Might not the workers return to their old alienated Marxism if consumer goods were difficult to obtain, if inflation eroded their incomes, and if the war went badly for Germany? The poster campaign of 1943 originated only ten days after the destruction of the German Sixth Army at Stalingrad, when Kurt Frowein of Goebbels' personal ministerial office presented the minister with a variety of suggestions for his approval or disapproval.[27]

The propaganda division of the ministry commissioned the German Propaganda Studio (DPA) to produce the posters and placards which went into such propaganda campaigns. The ministry believed that quality could only be maintained by a subsidized, highly professional central studio. It rejected requests by local RPA offices to design or commission their own materials. The propaganda division asserted that these local offices did not have the financial resources to maintain a quality program. During the war the ministry encouraged decentralization in budget and finances, but not in propaganda exhibitions and displays. The budget allocated to the DPA rose throughout the war, going from less than RM 1 million to over RM 1,400,000 in two fiscal years (March 31, 1940 to March 31, 1942). By 1942 almost half of the DPA budget was absorbed by the cost of exhibitions commissioned by the ministry. The 1941 DPA business report claimed that these presentations were highly successful. The exhibitions made use of materials created by the DPA graphics department. The displays used posters and

"Adolf Hitler Is Victory" (1943).

other graphics to create interest in a single theme, perhaps "The Enemy Sees Your Light" (for blackout propaganda), or "England, the Robber State." The DPA also did the posters and graphics for advertising the OKW film *Sieg im Westen,* which was a documentary about the defeat of France. Until 1944 smaller studios (e.g., Zerbst) competed with the DPA for ministry and related commissions. As part of the total war measures of that year, such studios were eliminated. Their personnel were either inducted into the Army or joined the DPA staff. In some cases former owners made financial demands upon the ministry or the DPA, but these were usually rebuffed.[28]

The propaganda apparatus overlooked no medium in its effort to reach the people. During the years of German military success, there was a great demand from local RPA offices for large maps that could be displayed in public squares. These maps indicated the advances made by the Wehrmacht. The last great effort in this area occurred during the late summer of 1942. Within three weeks of the Stalingrad debacle, orders went out to remove the maps because people were standing around discussing how much territory the Germans had lost. Another visual propaganda technique consisted of large cartoons and charts placed in front of prominent public buildings. The cartoons attacked the enemy, and the charts indicated why Germany was winning the war. *Gaue* that used this technique early in the war indicated great public interest in the medium, especially when a loudspeaker provided background music or commentary. The timing and nature of all these displays were greatly dependent upon the course of the war. At the end of August 1942 the RPL suddenly withdrew its "picture of the week" on conserving coal for the winter. At this time the German armies were making great advances in southern Russia, and it is conceivable that Goebbels wanted to spare the German people the thought of another vicious winter. Perhaps Soviet Russia would collapse. With the vast resources of the western USSR at its disposal, the Reich might not be short of energy sources.[29]

The RPL provided each *Gau* propaganda office with series consisting of twenty-five to thirty slides apiece.[30] These were distributed to district propaganda offices for public lectures. In September 1941 some of the topics were "Versailles Is Dead," "We Break England's Tyranny," "Prevent Accidents at Home," "The German Navy in Action," "Betrayed Socialism," and "USA—Disturber of the Peace." A technical problem appeared in this context, as it did in other efforts dependent upon the use of projectors: There were not enough machines available. It was easier to print handbills and leaflets, and thus more of this was done in later war years. There is little evidence of continued distribution of slide shows after 1942. Between 1940 and 1942 the RPL launched a major campaign to distribute handbills and leaflets which contained National Socialist maxims. Their purpose was to combat a tendency that was highly disturbing to the party. Germans, especially in rural areas, were fraternizing with POW laborers and other foreign workers. As the Reich was mobilizing enormous numbers of such people, the chancellory viewed fraternization as a dangerous subversion of the National Socialist Idea.[31]

The most upsetting aspect of the situation was the many reports coming in that described German girls as having sexual relations with foreign workers and POWs. As early as June 20, 1940, Bormann was so disturbed by this that he ordered that offending POWs be turned over to the Gestapo for execution. The problem became worse, however, for German peasants often found the French to be good workers; these men often became "members of the family," and in ways particularly offensive to the Nazi mentality. The number of cases accelerated as more German men left for the front, foreign POWs inundated the Reich between 1940 and 1942, and alien workers poured into the cities and countryside as a result of the Sauckel labor program after 1942. In one case a seventeen-year-old girl from a peasant family was sentenced to a year and three months in prison for having had intercourse with a French POW twice a week. Her excuse was socially revealing as well as touching in its naiveté. She declared that her lover was in the Wehrmacht, and she "needed to have intercourse." The authorities obviously rejected her argument. The party chancellory and the RPL decided in August 1940 that they would print millions of handbills, leaflets, and lists of dos and don'ts for Germans in contact with foreigners. The main points concerned the purity of German blood and the need to avoid intimate social contact with foreign workers. Tiessler was annoyed that so many Germans still reflected what he called the old German "humanity" and "self-indulgent emotionalism." Foreigners were to be treated with respect but sternly. Germans were warned against playing cards with working POWs, or sharing their rations with them. By early 1942, over two million handbills with maxims on racial purity and 85,000 placards had been sent out via the *Reichsring*. For the Nazis it was unpleasant to contemplate Germans dying at the front for a new, pure racial order, while some of their girls were enjoying sexual intercourse with men of inferior race.

By the middle war years a patron could not even pick up a restaurant menu without being bombarded with propaganda slogans.[32] "The soldier must often wait hours or days! Think about that, when you have to wait for a few minutes." "Be considerate, don't get excited! Think about yourself and your fellow men!" Shortages, inconveniences, mili-

A 1941 poster used to promote slide-lecture presentations by party speakers on the theme "We are breaking England's tyranny."

tary setbacks, and Allied bombings were making the Germans more irri-
table and "pushy." These maxims were part of Goebbels' "politeness"
campaign. Another way of getting this message across was the use of
party calendars.[33] Until 1944 the party, its branches, and affiliated
organizations all published their own calendars with different slogans
and pictures. In May 1943 Bormann authorized the RPL to publish a
unified party calendar for 1944. This would save paper and labor, but it
was also a way of unifying the propaganda message. In 1943, a typical
German civilian might awaken to radio propaganda, look at a calendar
covered with the same slogans, get dressed, have lunch after reading a
menu covered with propagandistic phraseology, then board a train
covered with posters and placards. When he reached his destination, he
might hear a loudspeaker blaring forth the Wehrmacht report of the day
while he peered through store windows at fewer consumer goods and
more "display window posters." The high point in this latter campaign
passed by August 1943,[34] however, because Allied bombs made urban
display windows a hazardous location for posters and placards.

One of the ministry's responses to the increased Allied air terror was
the mobilization of the German post office for the dissemination of
wartime propaganda. The intensification of this campaign began early in
1942. Some RPA offices worked with the postal authorities to produce
cancellation-mark slogans.[35] Vienna and Graz, formerly Austrian towns,
pioneered in this effort. Among the slogans were "With the Führer to
Victory," "Founders' Day of the European Youth Organization,"
"Georg Ritter von Schoenerer, Herald and Pioneer of the Greater
German Reich," "They Died for Greater Germany" (not used after
March 1942), "Führer, Give Us Our Orders, We'll Follow," and "Our
Führer Stops Bolshevism." In some cases the slogans were adopted
nationwide after success on the local level. One of the most optimistic
occurred in Munich for Hitler's birthday, April 20, 1944: "Germany will
Conquer." In the summer of 1943 the ministry and the RPL considered
issuing a series of commemorative stamps as "propaganda against the air
terror." Such stamps would contain pictures of cultural monuments
destroyed by the British, and would counteract the famous American
"captive nations" series. There may have been concern, however, that a
picture of a destroyed cathedral would not lift German morale. The idea
was dropped.

The distribution of leaflets continued almost until the end of the war.
In the Düsseldorf area of the lower Rhine alone, more than half a
million were distributed at the end of 1944. Their aim was to counteract
defeatism and its western German corollary, the hope and belief that the
"Anglo-Americans are not so bad as the Bolsheviks." The sheets bore
captions like "Is It Still Worth it?" and "The Anglo-Americans Are Not

So Bad." The brief texts answered the question affirmatively and refuted the widely held assertion about the Western Allies. Even toward the end the propaganda section under Schaeffer was commissioning 300,000 leaflets for the *Volksopfer* ("people's donation" of clothes, etc., for military use) in the Düsseldorf area, as well as 100,000 copies of a recruitment appeal for female Wehrmacht auxiliaries.[36] When the Wehrmacht moved into an area theatened by the Allied armies, RPA men were ordered to remain and put slogans on the houses, even if the civilian population was fleeing the region. Thus, some of the last Nazi propaganda efforts were in the form of graffiti.[37]

Coordinated propaganda campaigns could count upon a national press and radio, but their success or failure depended upon the efforts of party officials at the municipal branch *(Ortsgruppen)*, district *(Kreis)*, and *Gau* levels. The propaganda directors of these jurisdictions sent circular letters to their subordinates, guiding them along the lines of instructions, direct or indirect, from the RPL. The records of the *Kreis* Eisenach in the north central German *Gau* of Thuringia contain excellent examples of these propaganda campaigns and their techniques for the years 1940–42. In late March 1940 all municipal-branch leaders received leaflets entitled "German Men and Women" and "German Housewife." They were to distribute one copy of each to every house in their district. The leaflets appealed to the citizens to donate metals to the wartime collections. In May the same officials received a speech which they could use as the basis for their own statements on Mother's Day. It was a typically "Nazi-German" appeal, in which phrases about *Lebensraum* and struggle, the *Volk* and the front, replaced any false sentimentality about motherhood and the family.[38]

Eisenach's party educational programs were largely suspended during the spring and early summer of 1940. After the fall of France the district leader authorized a resumption of these curricula so that education of political leaders and potential party cadres could be resumed.[39] The themes would be "The Idea of the Reich" and "Political Questions of Today." The "greatest event of the year" for the Eisenach party occurred on December 9, when Gauleiter Fritz Sauckel himself addressed a large rally in the town.[40] A week earlier the district leader had nervously informed his subordinates that they better make sure that every party member in the district was present at the rally. These party comrades were also to bring their families with them. Local officials received placards advertising the meeting on December 3, and they were responsible for making sure that everyone saw them. They were to distribute the admission tickets to the rally.

Poor coordination undermined the effect of some propaganda campaigns. Early in August 1941 the RPL decided that the month should be devoted to meetings of party members so that they could better understand and explain the war against Bolshevism.[41] The RPL claimed that the time of year was not propitious for mass meetings involving the general public; hence, this was to be, at least at first, a purely party action. The real reason for this reticence may have been the decline of party prestige since late 1940. The decline was related to four factors: the failure to defeat Britain, the growing realization that German air space was not invulnerable to RAF attacks, the flight of Hess, and (after August 1941) the growing sense that the Soviet Union might not imminently collapse. Even this campaign among party members, the evangelists speaking to the converted, suffered from an unavailability of slides and displays relevant to the east. Materials on "We Break England's Tyranny" and "Our German Navy" would hardly lead to a better understanding of the war in Russia. Some of these slides had been around so long that they probably cracked in the August heat. The war also interrupted many of the educational programs of the NSDAP in Eisenach, but the lecture series for political leaders, leaders of the branch organizations, and party members was resumed during the winter semester 1941–42.[42] A fee of RM 5 was charged for ten lectures which dealt with Nazi law, German living space, and German history from Bismarck to Hitler. Cultural life was not totally neglected. In March 1942 the district party was to celebrate the one hundred fifteenth anniversary of Beethoven's death.[43] One would think that December 16, the day of his birth, might have been more fitting for a commemoration, but perhaps this was symptomatic of the death orientation of the Nazis. The idea for the ceremony came from Karl Cerff, the ardent National Socialist and idealist who was head of the main cultural office of the RPL.

The district of Eisenach participated in all the propaganda campaigns organized by the RPL. These "propaganda waves" usually had a title, such as "Everything for Victory" in May 1942. Speakers were paid RM 5 for the first speech of the day in their own town or village, and RM 2 for the second speech in the same area on the same day. If they spoke outside their home region, they received second-class rail fare. Speakers in the May 1942 campaign received detailed instructions about themes to be treated. Germany's enemies wished to deliver the Reich to Bolshevism; the "Jew Kaufmann" in America had written of the Allies' plan to exterminate the German nation. Then came Nazi words of strength and will: "The heroism of our soldiers is an example for us all"; "We must heroically bear the sacrifices demanded by the war effort"; "Everyone who sets a bad example on the home front . . . is a traitor to our nation and its soldiers"; "The Führer and his soldiers are our guarantee of victory." [44]

In many districts the propagandistic efforts of the party continued almost until the arrival of Allied troops. Grevenbroich, along the lower Rhine in northwestern Germany, was such a district. The new district leader organized a Christmas celebration for 1944, including poetry readings, expressions of thanks to the Führer and to the fighting men, choral singing of Christmas songs, and a reading of Goebbels' essay "Wartime Christmas." The district leader spent much time late in December composing leaflets both for local men who were at the front and for citizens of the district vulnerable to Allied "lies." The district leader's "greetings from the homeland" contained an appreciation of the soldiers' efforts and a promise that if their relatives had any problems, they could turn to the party for assistance. The leaflet addressed to the "Men and Women of the Grevenbroich District!" was more hysterical in its language, particularly in denouncing the Allied "poison of disintegration." The district leader denied that people were fleeing the area in fear of imminent Allied attack: "The Enemy Lies!" He was particularly bitter in denouncing Germans who believed Allied statements more than those of their own government. The leaflet seemed to be reponding to widespread disaffection from the party and a growing disbelief in German victory.[45]

The average German *Gau* contained about twenty districts, of which Eisenach was one in the *Gau* of Thuringia. The *Gau* propaganda director, who also ran the RPA, used the newsletter *Propaganda-Parole*, published often but at irregular intervals in Weimar, the *Gau* capital. Speakers and political leaders received guidelines for their propaganda from this bulletin. During the shock of the first Russian winter, the *Gau* office advised these men to use maps in order to show people the difference between Germany's present situation and that of 1914–18. The RPL was preparing a placard containing a model map and propagandists would shortly be receiving it. In February 1942 the director advised his men to warn people against using Allied phrases, including the "Allies' Flying Fortresses" and "Liberty Ships." The grumbling about Italy's military performance led the director to advise that propagandists point out the differences as well as the similarities between the fascist revolution and the National Socialist movement. What the RPL was trying to do was quiet anti-Italian gossip while preparing a way out for German propaganda if Italy fell apart completely. Many of these *Propaganda-Parolen* published not only regulations but also statistical information on the war economy and the occupied territories.

Though published by a *Gau* office for distribution to district and local municipal branch offices, the *Parole* was a precise reflection of the RPL line at all times. In Thuringia, in September 1942, people feared another Russian winter and grasped at straws offered by rumormongers. Among these illusions were stories that Russia was about to collapse or that Stalin was ready to sue for peace. The words used in the *Parole* of the *Gau* Thuringia in September were pure Goebbels: Propagandists must destroy such illusions but must at the same time reflect and inspire an unshakable faith in victory. Goebbels was capable of doing this, hence his rise as a popular and important figure, but one wonders about the success of the average *Gau* or district speaker in carrying out this difficult if not contradictory assignment.

It is useful to compare *Gaue* when discussing propaganda. The *Gau* of Munich/Upper Bavaria, the "Tradition *Gau*" of the movement, published a monthly bulletin for propagandists and political leaders simply entitled *Die Parole*. In 1943 the *Parole* contributed to the national campaign to revive the party by articles such as "Die Partei über alles!" This piece reiterated that the party was not just another political group, in power today and in opposition tomorrow, but was a movement and a world view. In this way the RPL hoped to disabuse any citizen of the idea of a transition to a post-Nazi government. As Goebbels had said in the early days of the Third Reich, "The only way they'll get us out of these government offices is by carrying us out in coffins!" Without the party in 1933, the *Parole* continued, Germany would have disintegrated because of the "Judaizing" of scholarship and culture, the general moral collapse, the seven million [*sic*] Communist votes, and the seven million unemployed.[46] This was the great Nazi apologia after Stalingrad, always beginning, "What would have happened to Germany . . . ?" and usually concluding, ". . . and to Europe, if the Führer had not acted in 1933 and in 1941?" [47]

Propagandistic publications on the *Gau* level reflected national guidelines, but local situations. The *Gauring* published the *Gau Circle Communications Bulletin* in each *Gau*. The local *Gau* propaganda director was responsible for distributing and supervising the publication, but Walter Tiessler, head of the national *Reichsring*, often told the *Gauring* publishers throughout the Reich what articles to reprint. He himself, along with Karl Cerff, wrote many pieces for the bulletin. By 1943 German moods were souring, and some *Gau* propaganda directors used abusive language that might win them some prestige in Berlin and Munich. Kuno Popp of Pomerania described the Reich's enemy in 1943 as "the most cowardly and inferior bastard on the face of the earth," comprised of the Jew and his Bolshevik-plutocratic helpers, all of whom would use lies, calumny, treason, terror, and murder to achieve their ends. This was another case of inversion: Popp's catalogue sounds like a description of Nazi techniques. The cultural fanatic Karl Cerff published an article in the same issue of the *Gauring* bulletin which sounded somewhat suspicious. Cerff, in defense of continued cultural work after Stalingrad, claimed that while riding a public conveyance he heard a citizen comment that after the fall of Stalingrad the radio had played three Beethoven symphonies; another passenger replied, "There's further proof of what it's all about." [48] This may have been fictional, an attempt to prove to Goebbels how important cultural work was even during hard times. It also could have been the comment of a party member who wanted to be overheard. If the statement was spontaneous, it represented one more success for Goebbels.

The *Gauring* bulletin of Bayreuth was far more dramatic in format than that of peasant Pomerania; perhaps this was due to its place of origin, for Bayreuth was the home of Wagnerian music drama. This *Gauring* publication contained drawings, cartoons, occasional photographs, and was more professional in journalistic format. In May 1943 it ran a lead article by Tiessler under the headline "What Our Enemies put Forth as War Goals, the Führer Put into Practice in Peacetime!" Tiessler's argument was that Germany's social gains under the Third Reich were better than the vague promises about "four freedoms" offered by the Western powers. The June issue of this *Gauring* bulletin was in part devoted to the memory of Victor Lutze, chief of staff of the SA, recently killed in an auto accident. The article, written by a Group Leader L. Schmuck, naturally did not mention what was common knowledge in the SA and the party, that Lutze had been heavily involved in black market operations.[49]

The party expected each *Gau* to establish an archive which would keep local and *Gau* records relevant to the history of the NSDAP. The sense of living in a "time without precedent," on the threshold of millennial greatness, spurred many *Gaue* into action by 1942. They wanted to have archives which reflected their work and faith during this heroic era (*Kampfzeit;* early Third Reich; war and victory). All levels and organizations were urged to contribute materials to the *Gauarchiv* of Magdeburg-Anhalt, which published its own bulletin on the subject.[50] The RPL placed a further burden on the *Gau* propaganda leadership, especially in the last years of the war. Its constant concern about morale in the factories led the RPL to demand in February 1943 that *Gau* propagandists work closely with representatives of Speer's armaments and munitions ministry.[51] The result of this collaboration was the distribution of numerous placards, handbills, and brochures in and around the industrial plants of the Reich. It was a sign of the decline of Ley's DAF that it was frozen out of this operation by early 1943.

The continuation of intense propaganda in 1944–45 on the *Gau* level depended upon the will and status of the Gauleiter. In Thuringia, "Old Fighter" Fritz Sauckel continued to expect propaganda campaigns and activity well into late 1944. The Thuringian Gau leadership proudly reported to state secretary Naumann on July 25, 1944, that it had sponsored almost 11,000 meetings and propaganda events in the spring, involving about 1.3 million participants. There had been exhibitions and slide lectures on the themes "The Air Terror," "Der Führer," "German Art against Bolshevism," "The Curse of World Jewry," "Our Navy," and "The Atlantic Wall." The *Gau* also sponsored a lecture campaign on how to save gas. The date of the report, July 25, was more than coincidental; it represented a confession of loyalty five days after the officers' attempt to murder Adolf Hitler.[52] While such major *Gau* propaganda campaigns became rarer after the summer of 1944, the "German Weekly Newsreel," a primary medium of ideological propaganda, continued to present the leadership's version of the war to the German nation almost until the destruction of the Third Reich.

III

Ideology and Propaganda
In Wartime German Film

6

War and Myth
in the "German Weekly Newsreel"

Joseph Goebbels viewed all the mass media, whether visual, aural, or verbal, as vital tools of National Socialist propaganda. Successful propaganda was achieved when the German masses renewed their commitment to victory after viewing, hearing, or reading the products of Goebbels' propaganda empire. For Goebbels, propaganda meant the successful unity of idea and medium. If the masses saw a film and felt that it was mere propaganda, they were misusing the word because such a film was a failure. It could not be propaganda. For this reason Goebbels forbade the German press to use the word "propaganda" in a negative sense, for example, "typical enemy propaganda." Any dissociation of message and medium by the masses meant that a film, radio program, or article had failed and was therefore not propaganda; it was merely a bad film, radio program, or article. Joseph Goebbels privately recognized areas of aesthetic appreciation that were divorced from the claims of the state or even from the will to victory in war. The intellectual and artistic elite craved such inward individual solace. Goebbels shared Hitler's contempt for the masses as a herd that needed to be molded and that could be shaped and inspired. Propaganda was for these masses. Goebbels himself possessed some of the aesthetic sensibilities of the elite, but his dubious achievement as an historical figure consisted of creating propaganda for the masses. This contradiction between the aesthetic value of inwardness and the manipulation of the herd was the product and reflection of Goebbels' dual personality, and it only reinforced his cynicism. The minister planned to devote some of his time "after the victory" to writing a study of film as aesthetically important as Gotthold Ephraim Lessing's famous work on drama, the *Hamburgische Dramaturgie* (1767–68). He could never have done this. Goebbels understood intellect but could only create works reflecting vanity, resentment, and a lust for power. Thus, his major literary achievement was a diary intended to glorify himself. It is valuable to us, not as a work of art or reflective intellect, but because of the factual material and the unintended revelations about the minister's personality.

Goebbels' task was the creation of propaganda. Since the film medium was closest to his heart, he could justify his constant attention to film on the grounds of its importance to the war effort. Goebbels played a major role in choosing subjects, editing, and distributing the "German Weekly Newsreel," the *Deutsche Wochenschau* (DW). This series, which reached great heights of technical and commercial success between 1940 and 1944, was the most effective Nazi medium of wartime propaganda. Far outstripping its Allied equivalents in visual power and in uniting music and image, word and deed, the *Wochenschau* was an institution of which Goebbels and his employees were justifiably proud. As Siegfried Kracauer commented, "... the emphasis they put on newsreels after September 1939 goes far beyond their former achievements and cannot easily be overestimated." [1] The DW brought the war home to the German people, but a war carefully, though unobtrusively, filmed and edited by good photographers and film technicians. While displaying its excellent battle sequences and occasional "human interest" stories, the *Wochenschau* managed, largely through Goebbels' constant intervention, to carry out two other vital tasks. It bolstered German morale, and it explained the war in the ideological terms delineated by the Nazi regime. Goebbels viewed the "Newsreel" as confirmation of a statement he had made publicly in 1934: "It may be all right to have power that is based on guns; however, it is better and more gratifying to win the heart of a nation and to keep it." [2]

Joseph Goebbels' home on the Hermann Göring Strasse was equipped with a film room, and it was usually there that he carefully studied the new DW before it was released. He viewed each *Wochenschau* in its entirety at least twice, the first time without narration, music or sound. "The texts are examined by the minister with extraordinary care, and none emerges without ... very significant alterations. In Germany no *Wochenschau* appears on the screen which has not been reworked by the minister himself," stated von Oven.[3] What von Oven was describing was not an oppressive task for Goebbels; rather, it was a pleasurable way to end the day. The minister could scarcely contain his enthusiasm in 1940 when he wrote, "The 'German Weekly Newsreel' is an incomparable contemporary document such as no other nation in the world has ever brought forth. It is the herald of a unique heroism . . . For us the war film is serious business; the incorruptible witness to heroic deeds of the young National Socialist Army. It goes beyond its propagandistic purpose. The lifelike pictures, the powerful marches, the songs, the music, and the language are the expression of a new age which was molded by the boundless will to life of a nation united in National Socialism." [4]

Goebbels repeatedly thanked the "PK" men who filmed the scenes at the front that made up a good deal of the DW, and told his Hitler Youth audience in October 1941 that the "Newsreel" was an area in which German film production was far ahead of its former competitors.[5] Hitler, who had doubts about some of the early wartime *Wochenschauen,* stated in 1941, "I've been thrilled by our contemporary newsfilms. We are experiencing a heroic epic, without precedent in history. . . . For the sake of the future, it's important to preserve the newsfilms of the war. They will be documents of incalculable value. New copies of these films will have to be constantly printed, and it would even be best to print them on strips of metal, so that they won't disappear." [6]

Goebbels gave a constant series of orders to his film people during the ministerial conference. Crowds poured into film theaters late in May 1940 to see scenes shot on the western front, where a "world-historical" German breakthrough was in progress. Goebbels instructed Fritz Hippler to make sure that theaters accommodated their patrons with extra showings of the *Wochenschau,* should the waiting lines prove this to be a necessity. If the theaters in the Berlin suburbs were receiving their copies of the *Wochenschau* too late, this was to be remedied immediately. On May 27 Goebbels told Hippler and Wächter to set up rooms in railroad stations for the presentation of the *Wochenschau.* Where this was impossible, posters were to be put up indicating when and where travellers could find the nearest theater presenting the "Newsreel." The minister suggested that the press might develop the theme "New waiting lines in Berlin," a reference to the *Wochenschau,* but also a sly comment upon civilian grumbling about queues.

Goebbels, like Hitler, became acutely aware of the emotional impact of the *Wochenschau* during the fall of France. He did not want the mood of awe, pathos, and enthusiasm, almost religious in nature, to be disturbed by the immediate projection after the DW of some mediocre musical or a cheap romantic film. Goebbels thus mandated an intermission of three minutes between the *Wochenschau* and a feature film. This later became a five-minute break, and theaters which did not cooperate were fined ten thousand Reichsmarks. Goebbels did not want the entry of late patrons to demystify the mood, so he decreed in 1941 that theaters were to keep their doors closed during the presentation of the *Wochenschau*. Latecomers could presumably enter after the DW, either during the pause or once the feature film had begun.[7]

The wartime *Wochenschau* varied greatly in length, but Goebbels did follow a certain formula. Heroic portrayals of the leaders and their allies, good battle footage, some human-interest stories, powerful march music, and martial airs made up most "Weekly Newsreels." Goebbels continued to be interested in learning from the foreign films available to him. At one point he commented that a Soviet film on the defense of Leningrad demonstrated effective improvisation and a sense of the involvement of the civilian population.[8] Of course, the minister was often willing to borrow a slogan or a cinematic idea from the Bolsheviks or the West.

Joseph Goebbels had not only "restructured" the German film industry by 1939, but he had effectively abolished any writing worthy of being called criticism. In the case of reviews and notices of the wartime *Wochenschauen*, Goebbels wanted more than praise for his masterpieces. He demanded enthusiasm, and he received it, even if the minister felt constrained to commission Fritz Hippler to write such reviews or "plant" them in the press. Here is a sample of what Goebbels liked to see and hear. The writer was Hans Joachim Giese, the year 1940: "The 'German Weekly Newsreel' has made a major contribution as part of the spiritual regeneration of the film industry, in that it has brought home to all strata and circles of the population in the most gripping manner the vital political necessity for the measures of the leadership, showing what fruits these measures can bring forth both in the present and in the future." [9] Goebbels warned against having blasé reviewers deal with the DW. He did not want his "works of art" and "documentary films" to be written about by bored hacks who saw a new film every day.[10] On August 5, 1942, the widely read *Deutsche Allgemeine Zeitung* noted, "The accomplishments of the 'Newsreel' deserve special mention." In 1943 the same newspaper claimed that these films were of special importance to the work of political and cultural enlightenment.

Goebbels manipulated the press in other, related ways. He forbade press discussion of the *Wochenschauen* during the first months of the Russian campaign, but this unusual step was taken for purely military reasons.[11] Typical was Goebbels' order in April 1940, when he directed Hippler to write an article about the "Newsreel" to make clear what was being accomplished in that field.[12] The next year, State Secretary Gutterer addressed a press reception in Berlin on September 16 and said that the DW's function was to bring "the unique achievements of the German Wehrmacht to the German people and to the Europe which is allied with it in a new community of struggle . . ." [13] Representatives of the German press assembled in the theater of the ministry once a week to see the new *Wochenschau* days or even weeks before it reached all of its audience. When Goebbels was particularly excited about a new *Wochenschau* that he had approved the night before, he ordered it to be shown to the press the very next day. The Propaganda Ministry encouraged film authorities and writers to put their impressions of the DW into their books.[14] One such volume, clearly inspired by Goebbels and his "Newsreel" people, contained the standard praise—"great art work," "unique technically." The authors, Braune and Koch, went further than this, for they claimed in 1943 that *Wochenschau* audiences were not merely seeking information about the war, but went to the "Newsreel" because viewing it was a "profoundly moving experience." They asked, "How often have we looked at the screen and seen not the face of infantryman M or Panzergrenadier S, but rather the vision of the eternal German unknown soldier?" [15] This was precisely Goebbels' intent . . .

The powerful battle scenes of the *Wochenschau* and related documentaries reflected the technical excellence of the propaganda company men. These PK men were trained soldiers who made use of their civilian occupations to become experts in war reportage. They bore military rank and were subject to military discipline. As Eric Borchert put it, "We, my comrades and I, have put aside our civilian clothes. We are no longer reporters or editors, we are soldiers of a new weapon of the Führer: the propaganda company." [16] Goebbels praised these men in 1941, "The PK man is not a reporter in the traditional sense; rather he is a soldier. Besides a pistol and hand grenades he carries other weapons: the film camera, the projector, the sketch pad, or a writing bench. He is trained and equipped like one of the troops; he lives as a soldier among soldiers, knows their milieu because it is his own, speaks their language, thinks and feels the way they do." [17] The professional expertise of these PK men, their courage in carrying out their work in the midst of battle, accounted for much of the excellence and popularity of the *Wochenschauen*, but it also resulted in an extremely high casualty rate. Goebbels could not praise their work highly enough: "Nobody, whether friend or foe, any longer doubts that Germany possesses the most modern, quickest, most reliable, and most current war reporting that we know of in the world . . . A future historical description of this war will make clear the specific reasons for this. Today we can only take account of this fact with satisfaction, knowing that such is the case now and will be the case until the end of this war." [18]

Other observers echoed these sentiments. A foreign correspondent noted in 1940 that a German officer told him that the victory over France owed a lot to "daredevil cameramen, uniformed reporters whose feats of courage often netted them iron crosses, radio commentators who stood in the thick of battle, and all modern technical devices for influencing public opinion." [19] In 1943 Ludwig Heyde claimed, "The just German struggle is its own best propagandist. The task is to convey this to all German comrades. This has been accomplished above all by the creation of the propaganda companies (PK) of the Wehrmacht. The war reporter of today is a trained soldier and a comrade in arms . . ." [20]

Hitler's adventuristic foreign policy made war an imminent possibility after the spring of 1938. In that year the OKW and the Goebbels ministry reached an agreement delineating their respective spheres of propaganda work. One result was the establishment in September of five PK companies. Their first assignment came in October, in the newly occupied Sudetenland. Both Deputy Führer Hess and propaganda minister Goebbels realized that the existence of the PKs would make a good impression upon the German public, so the mass media were allowed to acknowledge the existence of such companies. The structure of the PKs and the orders they received from the OKW and the ministry were secret. The leader of a PK unit was subordinate to a chief of staff of an army. In peacetime the companies were considered motorized reserve units of the Wehrmacht. Their work was divided into three categories, propaganda for the home front, for the troops, and against the enemy. Each company contained a variety of specialized personnel, consisting of about fifty men, ranging from photographers to broadcasters and laboratory assistants.[21] In planning the creation of Luftwaffe PKs in June 1939, Hess's staff reiterated that the party was responsible for checking out the "political reliability" of potential PK personnel. The Reich propaganda offices had a major role in such "security clearance" procedures, while the ministry itself was responsible for finding men for the PK units.[22]

During the early war years, only men who had already served in the armed forces or had completed their basic training were inducted into the PK companies. An exception was made in the case of Luftwaffe PKs for specialists who were willing to undergo that training in the immediate future, particularly those who knew something about flying. The rapid growth of the PK units, combined with manpower shortages, made these requirements more flexible after 1942. Anywhere from five to twelve local RPA offices were responsible for providing the personnel which made up the PK staff of a unit which was stationed in their region in peacetime. When war broke out, these offices were required to turn over camera equipment and trucks to the OKW for propaganda-company use. In peacetime the party film offices were responsible for maintenance of PK technical equipment. Wartime demands for specialized types of equipment needed by the PKs were directed to the German Propaganda Studio in Berlin-Lichterfelde. The armed forces maintained a central PK training and processing center in Potsdam, within easy distance of the German mass media and propaganda center, Berlin. It was in Potsdam that PK reports and films were processed for submission to the military censors and the Propaganda Ministry. By 1942 the PK companies of the various Wehrmacht branches were most in need of the following specialists: press stenographers, photographic laboratory technicians, cameramen (for the Navy), film projectionists (for the Army), radio and loudspeaker technicians, and radio broadcasters.[23]

Goebbels took a detailed interest in the work of the PK companies, since the success of so much of the ministry's photographic and cinematic propaganda was dependent upon those men.[24] He ordered that PK unit commanders receive the "Confidential Information" bulletins issued by the ministry, with the admonition that they make sure these sheets did not fall into enemy hands. The minister had no authority to issue direct orders to the PK men, who were under the military supervision of the Wehrmacht propaganda division, but through the provision of such bulletins he hoped to influence their work. At times he passed along specific requests, as when he told State Secretary Leopold Gutterer to see to it that PK reports and film footage contained more material on German workers at the front.[25] These workmen were civilians of the "Todt Organization," and they helped in the work of building fortifications and other types of military construction. At the same time, Goebbels was jealous of any other minister who attempted to create his own propaganda company, and he made sure that this did not happen. Fritz Todt himself discovered this in the winter of 1940.

Goebbels' comments and suggestions about the newest *Wochenschau* had the force of law for the many Promi employees concerned with the newsreel. By 1942 the final structure of the film division (F) of the ministry emerged. It was embodied in the organizational plan of the ministry, which was distributed on November 1, 1942. Dr. Gast and the senior councillor Eberhard Fangauf and Dr. Bacmeister were responsible for coordinating the censorship of the *Wochenschauen* with representatives of the OKW and Goebbels' ministerial office. Wächter, a general advisor on questions dealing with armaments and construction, monitored both the PK reports and the "Newsreels" from the viewpoint of these concerns. Specialists in different ministerial departments had authority to examine newsreels to see if segments conflicted with the propaganda line prevalent in their fields. Councillor Professor Starlitz, who was active in the propaganda division, was responsible for applying censorship rules to films, pictures, newspapers, and theater when these

Sketch of a naval PK photographer.

dealt with *Volkstum,* or German ethnicity. Councillor Dietz, who worked for Berndt and Gast in the same section, was in charge of coordinating the "*Wochenschau* team." Newsreel work touched upon several divisions of the ministry; it was a collective responsibility in both subject matter and censorship.[26] The OKW military censors in the ministry had the last word in determining the security priorities of the Reich: Their changes and suggestions were always accepted and carried out.[27] Nevertheless, the officers often prevailed only after lengthy and acrimonious discussion with ministry officials.

Each new *Wochenschau* was ready for distribution on Monday, but changes could still be made if Hitler was so inclined.[28] Until Stalingrad, Hitler studied the *Wochenschauen* with great interest, often in the company of adjutants and staff. This viewing took place in Berlin or at Berchtesgaden, generally on Monday evening. In 1944 the staff viewing was changed to Tuesday evening, though by this time Hitler had long since stopped watching newsreels. His earlier enthusiasm dampened as the military fortunes of the Reich declined. It took officials in the film division of the ministry a long time to realize that Hitler was no longer watching the newsreels sent to his aides, though Goebbels was suspicious as early as 1943. In late April, of that year Goebbels realized that something was wrong. He wanted to devote much of the latest *Wochenschau* to pictures of atrocities committed against Polish officers by the Bolsheviks in the Katyn forest, but was forced to concede, "The military men at the Führer's GHQ have actually succeeded in eliminating the pictures of Katyn from the weekly newsreel. Unfortunately, the Führer did not have time to see the reel personally." [29] There was consternation in the Wilhelmsplatz when Goebbels' men confirmed that last-minute changes demanded by "the Führer" were actually the opinions of aides and adjutants speaking in the name of "headquarters" or "the chief." When Hinkel and Goebbels found out what was going on, they put a stop to it by refusing to acknowledge any suggestions from headquarters unless they clearly came from Hitler. Goebbels was extremely possessive about the *Wochenschauen.* In 1944 Hasso von Wedel, chief of the Wehrmacht propaganda staff, demanded that the ministry make a personnel change.[30] He alleged that the "Newsreel" was playing up the Luftwaffe at the expense of the Army. The director of the film division, the state secretary, and the minister put together a forthright statement to the effect that von Wedel had no right to meddle in the personnel affairs of the "German Weekly Newsreel."

The UFA (Universum-Film Aktiengesellschaft), part of Alfred Hugenberg's media empire, put out its first silent newsreels under the name *Wochenschauen* in 1926. The following year UFA took over the Deulig-Woche newsreel concern. The first sound *Wochenschau (UFA Tonwochenschau)* appeared on German cinema screens on September 3, 1930. It was ominous but coincidental that this premiere took place less than two weeks before the first great Nazi electoral breakthrough. By 1933 UFA had produced 103 *Tonwochenschauen*. During these years the Nazi party, under its propaganda director, Joseph Goebbels, pioneered in the use of sound "documentaries" for political propaganda. The first NS sound film opened in Munich on October 23, 1932; it focused on Hitler's electoral campaign earlier in the year and was entitled "Hitler over Germany." The name made reference to Hitler's breathless pace, flying from town to town in a single day. The Nazis were political pioneers in two media that were united in this propaganda film, aviation and political cinema. Recognizing the growing importance of film for politics, Goebbels encouraged the formation in 1932 of a Nazi film theater owners' association.

After the Seizure of Power, the important trade newspaper *Film-Kurier* wrote that the latest *Wochenschauen* often gripped people more than the feature films which they preceded on the screen.[31] When Hitler came to power, the *Wochenschau* employed ninety-eight men and women and used over fifty cameras in the field. These Newsreels, produced in batches of about one hundred copies, ran for twelve weeks in different parts of the Reich, reaching an average audience per film of about six million persons. The growing concentration of the newsreel and film industry between 1929 and the early days of the Third Reich meant that only four newsreel production companies survived. Cameramen sent their material to Berlin, where all four companies exchanged footage, which was then edited so as to avoid duplication. This "coordination" made easier Goebbels' creation of a state monopoly.

Until late 1940 the head of the ministry's film division directed the work of the German Weekly Newsreel Central Office, which produced the *Deutsche Wochenschauen*. This office had absorbed UFA's newsreel industry as part of Goebbels' coordination of the film world. At the end of 1940 a "German Weekly Newsreel, Inc." replaced the old Central Office. Goebbels believed that this change of status from state monopoly to "private" firm would enable him to dominate the European newsreel market and influence foreign opinion. Newsreels using *Wochenschau* material appeared in many languages and were distributed throughout Europe. By June 1944 these *Auslands-Tonwochenschauen* appeared regularly on the screens of 2,540 theaters outside Germany and before audiences totaling of four and a half million persons per week.

After the 1940 reorganization, the German Weekly Newsreel, Inc., became part of the UFA conglomerate. Goebbels hoped to capitalize upon the prestige abroad which the UFA name promised. In fact, UFA was itself entirely state-owned when Goebbels reorganized the German film industry between late 1940 and early 1942. The board of directors of the new *Wochenschau* corporation consisted of six members, four of them UFA representatives, with one each from the Tobis and Bavaria film concerns. Fritz Hippler, head of the ministry's film division, was chairman of the board. At least two of the UFA representatives had to be employees of the Propaganda Ministry, and one of these was required by the charter of incorporation to be chairman of the board of directors. The managers responsible for newsreel production were Heinrich Roellenberg and Fritz Tietz, while Goebbels' close associate Dr. Max Winkler controlled financial aspects of production.[32]

The length and number of copies printed of each "German Weekly Newsreel" reflected the rise, decline, and collapse of the wartime Third Reich. The average 1939 *Wochenschau* was 300 to 400 meters in length, and took about twelve minutes to project. The demand for film footage of the conquest of France in June 1940 resulted in special *Wochenschauen* 1,200 meters in length, requiring a viewing time of forty to forty-five minutes. A similar situation prevailed in the summer of 1941 as the German public breathlessly awaited visual evidence of the Wehrmacht's successes in Russia. By August 1942 the *Wochenschau* was about 900 meters long, taking about thirty minutes of projection time. In 1943 the "Newsreel" reached its high point in terms of average length, 1,000 meters, necessitating a projection time of thirty-five minutes. Defeats at the front, Allied bombings, and technical problems combined to reduce the average "Weekly Newsreel" to 600 meters by the time of the Normandy invasion. When Hitler launched his desperate Ardennes offensive against Allies in December 1944, the *Wochenschau* was about 310 meters in length, a bit shorter than it had been just before the war.

The success of the *Wochenschau* was in part the result of the ministry's efforts to distribute the films widely and promptly. When war broke out, Goebbels wanted his *Wochenschauen* to be more up-to-date, so the DW Central Office ordered that films be circulated only for half as long a time as had earlier been the case. Production of each weekly edition was to be doubled. In August 1939 about 700 copies of each DW were printed and distributed. By the time of the fall of France that number had risen to 1,500. In August 1942 about 2 million meters of raw film were necessary to produce 2,000 copies of each "Weekly Newsreel." By D Day the average *Wochenschau* was only 60 to 67 percent as long as its predecessors of 1942–43, but more copies were being made, 2,500. The partial collapse of the German transportation network and the increasing scarcity of raw film caught up with the *Wochenschau* by the end of 1944. There was a precipitous decline in the length, distribution, and quality of films in 1945. Moreover, the DW of 1945 usually credited six or seven front-line cameramen; two years earlier the number had averaged fifteen to twenty-five.[33]

The "Newsreel" in 1938 was the product of the editing and cutting of about 3,000 meters of film; by the early wartime period that amount had increased to an average of 15,000 meters. During the fall of France *Wochenschau* editors and cutters had to work with an embarrassment of riches. Forty thousand meters of PK film arrived to be developed and analyzed, much of it top-notch material. Raw film reserves dropped drastically by December 1944; only 7 million meters a month were now available, instead of the customary 12 million. The *Wochenschauen* devoured the most raw film because of the work of both PK and civilian cameramen and also because of the enormous *weekly* printing of the "Newsreel." The film division of the ministry had a raw film reserve of 100 million meters, but this was meant to be relied upon only in the most extreme crises, for instance, during weeks when bombed film factories had not yet resumed full production. The reserve could also be drawn upon by the Wehrmacht to produce training films for the new Volkssturm, or people's militia, a task which required 1.6 million meters of raw film in 1944–45.

Economy was necessary, and major efforts in that direction were undertaken in December. The monthly raw film allocation for the armed forces as of January 1, 1945, was cut by 75 percent, while that which was exported dropped by 67 percent. The bulk of the monthly production of 7 million meters went to the Reich Film Chamber, which then provided the *Wochenschau* company with the necessary footage. The rationale behind the decreased Wehrmacht allotment may have been the belief that the armed forces needed raw film for special and nonrecurring missions. They were to obtain needed footage from the film division reserve rather than to accumulate it in storage for occasional crash programs. In storage, it would have stayed out of circulation—and out of Goebbels' hands. Transportation difficulties justified another economy in the use of raw film. Two "Newsreels" were released in late December and early January, rather than the customary three. This alone saved 465,000 feet of film.[34] These measures all contributed to the survival of a truncated but viable *Wochenschau* until the last weeks of the Third Reich.

Goebbels' continuing commitment to the *Wochenschau* placed him in increasing opposition to the manpower demands of the armed forces, particularly after 1942. Early that year, the director of the film division suggested that the minister obtain a Führer's decree placing the

"Newsreel" in the "decisive to the war effort" category, thus freeing it from the spector of mass conscription of technical personnel. This effort was unsuccessful, though the regime did officially consider the DW to be important to the war effort. When the government announced late in 1944 that all men aged sixteen to sixty capable of bearing weapons were liable to conscription into the Volkssturm, Goebbels reiterated his policy that materials and personnel necessary for *Wochenschau* production must be secured. Hans Hinkel, director of film, worked in tandem with the ministry's personnel coordinators to keep cameramen, narrators, and film cutters out of the clutches of the Wehrmacht and the Volkssturm. As late as February 1945, the *Wochenschau* staff learned that Goebbels had decided that the *Wochenschau* was to "continue under all circumstances" and that the personnel necessary were to be excused from Volkssturm service.[35] The minister was successful, for the Third Reich barely outlived the last, brief *Deutsche Wochenschauen.*

The catastrophe of the German Sixth Army at Stalingrad began on November 19, 1942, and ended on February 2, 1943. The contrast between the coverage of the battle and the propagandistic uses to which Goebbels put the results of the struggle was absolute. In one of the greatest cover-ups in *Wochenschau* history, Goebbels forbade any mention of Stalingrad or even of the "southern sector" of the eastern front during the final tragic weeks of the battle.[36] During the last weeks of January, *Wochenschau* audiences saw Hitler welcoming Marshal Ion Antonescu of Rumania, as well as scenes of fighting from the relatively quiet *northern* sector of the eastern front; but not a picture or even a map concerning the battle of Stalingrad appeared on the screen. Shrewd observers probably sensed the significance of the Antonescu visit, since the Rumanian marshal and chief of government might be particularly upset over Soviet successes in the southern sector, where the Red Army had destroyed much of the Third and Fourth Rumanian Armies. Yet almost as if this Antonescu scene gave too much away, the *Wochenschau* spent less time than usual on the visit of one of Hitler's favorite satellites. The silence about Stalingrad and the struggle of the German Sixth Army was almost deafening, since it contrasted so grotesquely with earlier statements by the OKW and especially by Hitler himself concerning supposed German successes in Stalingrad.

The *Wochenschau* dealing with events of the last week in January and the first days of February showed nothing about the Stalingrad sector but presented battle scenes drawn from other areas of the eastern front. The next two *Wochenschauen* were released in February, yet there was still nothing about Stalingrad. In a speech to factory workers Goebbels did allude indirectly to military setbacks, but he made no mention of the destruction of the Sixth Army. Goebbels' perception of the effect of different media upon the population played a role here. Between February 3 and February 18, Goebbels proclaimed three days of mourning for this army, used the press and radio extensively, and talked of "total war" before enthusiastic party faithful in the Sportpalast. Yet the minister made no use of the *Wochenschau* film medium to describe or to mourn the passing of the Sixth Army. Perhaps visual portrayal of the death of an entire German army in a *Wochenschau* would depress its audience and render it defeatist. Goebbels may also have been thinking of negative reactions among European allies and neutrals who received versions of the *Wochenschau* in their own languages. One might frighten a nation into resistance and victory, but one must take care not to depress it into apathy and defeat. The *Wochenschauen* of the period showed ice-skating rinks filled with happy vacationers, travelogues, and picturesque old towns and places such as Eisenach and the Wartburg castle.

The military catastrophes of the autumn and winter of 1942–43 changed the nature of the *Deutsche Wochenschau*. It would now have to adapt to setbacks and defeats without losing its triumphant, morale-boosting tone. Early in 1943 Admiral Dönitz replaced Grand Admiral Raeder as commander in chief of the German Navy. Dönitz was a submarine man, and the early months of his appointment coincided with tremendous U-boat successes against Allied convoys. Goebbels believed that these triumphs would strangle Great Britain and checkmate Anglo-American moves against Europe. Instead of dealing with Stalingrad, the *Deutsche Wochenschauen* showed Dönitz with Hitler and detailed footage on the struggle for the North Atlantic. In March, when the submarine campaign had reached its most successful point, Goebbels noted with approval that Dönitz wanted the Navy to receive more publicity. He snidely observed that Erich Raeder had lacked this propagandistic sense, but the minister was never one to praise a man who had fallen from Hitler's graces. Late in the summer Goebbels still saw Dönitz as a "very cool and realistic calculator," though the U-boat campaign in the North Atlantic had failed. Dönitz's starring role in the *Wochenschauen* passed by June, though he still appeared on the screen at funerals of war heroes and naval commanders and as a military voice pledging allegiance to Hitler while reaffirming his belief in victory.[37]

In 1943 the *Wochenschau* showed a great deal of Hermann Göring, because of Goebbels' belief that Göring, for all of his failures, was still a powerful and popular figure, a man who might be crucial to a total war program. Late in 1943 one *Wochenschau* showed Göring visiting a "sorely tried city" in western Germany. The phrase was a euphemism for a bombed or destroyed town. The city and its damage were never shown, but Göring was, one of the few top Nazis who occasionally visited bombed cities in 1943. By 1944 Göring had lost much of his appeal to Hitler, Goebbels, and to the German population, and insofar as he appeared on the *Wochenschau* screen it was mainly as a funeral orator for Luftwaffe dead.[38]

Two men emerged as "stars" of the German *Wochenschau* in the winter of 1943. One was Albert Speer, for the munitions minister was crucial to Goebbels' total war plans. He played a major role on the *Wochenschau* screen between late 1942 and early 1944. Speer appeared on January 30, 1943, at the tenth-anniversary celebration of Hitler's Seizure of Power. He was seen in the "Newsreel," sitting beside Himmler while Goebbels read Hitler's proclamation at the Sportpalast rally. The slogan "Führer, give us our orders, we will follow" dominated the occasion, and no allusion to Stalingrad was permitted to mar the scene for the German moviegoer. Speer was seen repeatedly thereafter, often inspecting factories, addressing industrialists and workers at gatherings of the Reich Labor Chamber, and attending major party rallies.

Nazi leaders, among them Himmler, Speer, and Ley, appear on "German Weekly Newsreel" screens at a party rally early in 1943.

CREDIT: The Library of Congress

When the war did not come to a conclusion in 1940 or 1941, Goebbels realized that propaganda about armaments production and devastating new weapons would raise German morale. Two staffs within his ministry worked in these areas, the "Schwarz van Berk office" and the "Working Staff for Armaments Propaganda." This staff was responsible for liaison with Albert Speer's ministry of armaments and munitions.[39] Speer's impressive armaments figures encouraged Goebbels. Contrary to impressions given by Speer at his trial and in two postwar books, he and his men worked closely with Goebbels and the RPL in armaments propaganda. Goebbels turned against Speer in 1944 because he felt that the munitions minister had misled him in regard to the imminent appearance of "wonder weapons." He was jealous of Speer's friendship with Hitler and worked with Bormann and Himmler to destroy Speer's credibility with the Führer. This tactic was partially successful.

The role allotted to Speer in the *Wochenschauen*, as important as it was, paled beside the screen part which Goebbels assigned to himself.[40] From Stalingrad until the end of the war, Joseph Goebbels was the major personality in the *Deutsche Wochenschauen*. Goebbels' total-war speech of February 18, 1943, was the rhetorical highpoint of his wartime career. The crowd stood at the end and sang a rousing chorus from "Deutschland über Alles." What the German movie audiences saw around March 1, 1943, was an ecstatic Goebbels, filled with fanatical will and hatred for the enemy, a man calling upon the nation to rise up and win the war. In the following weeks the minister continued to appear on the *Wochenschau* screen, for example, beside Hitler, interior minister Frick, and Göring as they paid tribute to past war dead on Heroes Memorial Day while a band solemnly intoned the sad, moving tones of the "Song of the Good Comrade." Even when Goebbels' image was not on the screen, his spirit could be felt by the audience, as in scenes in late 1944 showing women working in factories as part of the total war effort. By then most Nazi leaders, including Hitler himself, had long since been in hiding from the German people because of the disasters that confronted the Reich. Goebbels, however, continued to appear frequently before soldiers, workers, and party faithful. Late in the war the propaganda minister visited Field Marshal Model in order to hear his report about the western front. He also addressed workers in the threatened western provinces, speaking to them as a native Rhinelander. Goebbels' appearances were carefully orchestrated for impressive *Wochenschau* production. On the occasion of his visit to the west, the workers rose and sang "The Watch on the Rhine" at the end of his address.

Hitler became a virtual recluse from the German public after the Stalingrad debacle, but *Wochenschau* audiences saw him warmly greeting Marshal Antonescu during the winter of 1943. In March Hitler honored Germany's fallen on Heroes Memorial Day *(Heldengedenktag)* in Berlin and then greeted wounded soldiers of both world wars. The increasingly rare public appearances of Hitler made it important for the *Wochenschau* people to make the most of such "photo opportunities." [41] The attempted assassination of Hitler on July 20, 1944, presented a special challenge to the producers of the *Wochenschauen*. Only motion pictures could prove to a frightened, skeptical, or hostile German public that Hitler was alive if not well, that "Providence" had once again spared him for his "world-historical" tasks. Yet in showing Hitler as he looked in the summer of 1944, the "Newsreel" had to depict a prematurely aged man, one clearly not in the best of health. Despite carefully edited and staged scenes, the Hitler of July and August 1944 must have shocked the Germans who saw the Führer on their movie screens. The *Wochenschau* showed Hitler welcoming Mussolini to his East Prussian headquarters shortly after the attempt on his life and also permitted German audiences to see Hitler's farewell to Mussolini. Unbeknownst to the protagonists, this was to be their last meeting. A few weeks later Hitler visited badly wounded fellow victims of the July 20 bomb plot. The

Heroes Memorial Day 1943: Hitler greets wounded German veterans of two world wars.

directors of the *Wochenschau* emphasized the cheering bystanders and nurses as Hitler consoled his colleagues in their hospital, but this could not conceal his hesitant gait, puffy features, and prematurely aged appearance. Yet the *Wochenschauen* perpetrated the Hitler myth until the spring of 1945, when the last brief newsreel shots of Hitler appeared on German screens.

The *Wochenschau* played a major role in perpetuating the Nazi myth of heroic sacrifice. Late in 1944 one newsreel showed enormous numbers of Hitler Youths (HJ) volunteering for military service. The class of 1928 particularly distinguished itself by its commitment to Führer and nation.[42] In one of its more powerful scenes, the "Newsreel" captured a mood of youthful idealism and pathos. As thousands of boys stood in military formation, loudspeakers in a public square intoned statistics about the huge numbers of teenagers who had declared their readiness to fight for Führer and fatherland. This pledge unto death was the visual proof of the statement made by an anonymous *Wochenschau* narrator: "I can die, but to be a slave, to see Germany enslaved, that I cannot accept!" While a powerful march enveloped the square in heroic sound, the scene concluded by focusing on one young face, the symbol of National Socialist idealism and *Opferbereitschaft,* willingness to make sacrifices. This segment of the film was particularly poignant because the band played "Our Banners Are Waving Before Us," the moving anthem of the Hitler Youth, a memory of happier days.

Such groups of youthful volunteers prompted Hitler to dictate a widely disseminated proclamation, an appeal that recalled earlier, frighteningly prophetic professions of faith made by Adolf Hitler to German youth. In 1934 he had told the Hitler Youth that it was bound to him and to Germany, come what may, because this generation was, in his words, "flesh of our flesh and blood of our blood." [43] Hitler warned these youths that they must never fall apart in the face of adversity. At the 1936 Nürnberg rally he had told the HJ, "We are used to fighting, for we emerged in struggle. We will plant our feet firmly on the ground, and we will weather any storm. And you will stand beside me if such an hour should ever come." [44] Now, it was October 7, 1944: The hour was at hand.

The old rhetoric was once more on display, depicting the HJ's commitment to struggle in the vivid language of Nazi propaganda:

My Hitler Youth!

I have received the news of your registration as war volunteers of the class of 1928 with pride and joy. In this hour of danger to the Reich

HITLER'S CHANGING ROLE IN GOEBBELS' HITLER MYTHOS

A. "The Greatest Field Captain of All Time": Photographs and newsreel shots such as this one showed Hitler as the brilliant architect of German victories. He still looked relatively young and vigorous before 1942.   *CREDIT:* The National Archives

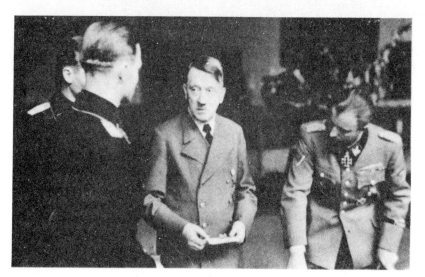

B. Adolf Hitler on his fifty-fifth birthday, April 20, 1944. By this time Hitler was clearly in a state of physical deterioration. The German media were not permitted to publish photographs such as this one.

CREDIT: The National Archives

Hitler Youth ca. 1937: the promise of heroism and victory.

Hitler Youth in 1944—the face of defeat. ("German Weekly Newsreel")

because of the menace of our hate-filled enemies, you have given a shining example of a fighting spirit and of the fanatical commitment to struggle, whatever sacrifices may be required. The youth of our National Socialist movement, both at home and at the front, has fulfilled the expectations of the nation. Your volunteers have given exemplary proof of their loyalty and unshakable will to victory by service in the "Hitler Youth," "Greater Germany," and Volksgrenadier divisions, and as individual fighters in all branches of the armed forces. Recognition of the necessity for our struggle fills the entire German nation today, but it especially fills our youth. We are

A year before the establishment of the Volkssturm, these children were taking part in the defense of the Reich. They operated flak batteries during enemy air attacks. These boys are attending the funeral of some of their teenage comrades who have fallen during such an air bombardment. The press received an order forbidding the use of this depressing photograph. A year later Goebbels encouraged the media to glorify the sacrifices of sixteen-year-old "volunteers."

CREDIT: The Suddeutscher Verlag. Munich, Germany

"We all help!" "War Mobilization of the Hitler Youth." Early in the war this was propaganda; by 1944 it was becoming reality.

aware of the merciless extermination plans of our enemies. For this reason we will fight on even more fanatically for a Reich in which you will be able to work and live in honor. You, however, as young National Socialist fighters, must do even more than the rest of the nation in terms of steadfastness, persistance, and unbreakable toughness. The sacrifices made by our heroic younger generation will result in a victory which will guarantee the proud, free development of our people and of the National Socialist Reich.

ADOLF HITLER
Führer Headquarters, October 7, 1944 [45]

Twelve days earlier Hitler had ordered the creation of a Volkssturm. It would be a "people's army," under Wehrmacht command in battle, but inspired by radical National Socialist ideology and leadership. The very name *Volkssturm* was supposed to recall memories of the reserve units and volunteers of 1813, when, according to popular legend, the people of Germany rose up against the French and expelled them from the Reich.[46] For this reason Heinrich Himmler proclaimed the establishment of the Volkssturm on October 18, 1944, the anniversary of the "Battle of the Nations," or *Völkerschlacht*, at Leipzig in 1813. Himmler read Hitler's decree, and this event inaugurated several months of intense Volkssturm propaganda in the German "public enlightenment" media. Disruptions caused by Allied bombings prevented the *Wochenschau* film crew from obtaining footage of Himmler reading the decree.[47] The embarrassed, almost apologetic tone of the Promi correspondence on this affair implies that some Nazi big shots, such as Himmler and Gauleiter Giesler of Munich, were angry about the *Wochenschau* omission. Whatever the *Wochenschau* failure upon that occasion, the "Newsreels" of the next three months amply covered the "rising of the nation, the eruption of the storm," as Goebbels called the *Volk* in arms, this Volkssturm.[48]

The *Wochenschau* presented the Volkssturm as an outburst of National Socialist enthusiasm and will to resist. It depicted huge, enthusiastic crowds taking the oath as Volkssturm men in an eastern Gau. High above the public square hung signs inscribed with the slogan "The Volk rises up, the storm breaks loose!" Himmler and Goebbels boasted that such rallies would show what Himmler called "our accursed enemies" that Germany still had great resources in men and materials. The Gauleiter, the SA, and the Hitler Youth marched with the Volkssturm men on the screen of neighborhood cinemas as visual proof of the nation in arms. In just two months of existence, the Volkssturm

The threat to the frontiers of the Reich gave SA members a chance to become active as instructors in the use of rifles and small arms. The old radical SA dream of a people's army was one of the sources of the Volkssturm idea.

"A nation rises up, the storm breaks loose!" Volkssturm men take the oath in Munich on November 9, 1944. This ceremony had special significance for the party, for it took place on the anniversary of the death of the martyrs of the Beer Hall Putsch of 1923. The men are taking the oath with hands placed upon the "blood banner," a flag carried on November 9, 1923, and supposedly spotted with the holy blood of the martyrs. In the far background: Himmler, Bormann, and Keitel.

CREDIT: The Suddeutscher Verlag, Munich, Germany

may indeed have encouraged the German people in their hopeless war effort. Older men could now feel useful; the idealism of youth was mobilized; the camaraderie of sporadic training tended to create an egalitarian mood. Yet grumbling soon began, especially after the failure of Hitler's Ardennes offensive in late December. The Wehrmacht was suspicious of the Volkssturm concept and did not have the weapons, training facilities, or even uniforms which new units required. "Newsreels" tried to claim the opposite to the German people. They implied that the Volkssturm was well equipped, but even the most gullible or fanatic moviegoer could see that these men wore armbands, not uniforms, and were often equipped with hunting rifles and small arms as they went off to fight the Bolsheviks or the Anglo-Americans. Their great

Volkssturm men with the *Panzerfaust* (antitank weapon), late in 1944 ("German Weekly Newsreel")

Propaganda for the German Volkssturm evoked memories of the uprising against Napoleon and the Nazi Era of Struggle. Here SA Chief of Staff Wilhelm Schepmann comments on the use of a rifle. Schepmann was inspector for this aspect of Volkssturm training. For years the SA had been instructing civilians in the use of carbines, pistols, and rifles.

service would supposedly be as antitank men against the Bolsheviks, and for this they were equipped with the *Panzerfaust.* Yet how could an old man or a young boy with a *Panzerfaust,* given a few weeks training, stop the Bolsheviks in the east when the mighty Wehrmacht had failed to do so since early 1943? The National Socialist answer would have been that fanatical will and the readiness to sacrifice would make up for deficiencies in training and arms.

The great moment of Volkssturm propaganda occurred on Sunday, November 12, 1944. On that day all new *Volkssturmmänner* were *vereidigt,* or took the oath of loyalty to Hitler and the Reich. The oath-taking ceremonies were originally scheduled to take place on November 9, the anniversary of the death of the Nazi martyrs of 1923, but Goebbels decided that Sunday (November 12) would be preferable from the viewpoint of organization and participation. The greatest of these ceremonies would occur in Berlin, where Goebbels was Gauleiter, the Conquerer of Berlin, Reich Defense Commissioner, and soon, the Defender of Berlin. This event was planned with great attention to detail.[49] The *Wochenschau* spent a good deal of time on this ceremony, which was set against the gloomy background of a dank, chilly Berlin day. Goebbels' face had a look of grim fanaticism as he gave the assembled Volkssturm men their oath of service. The minister was suffering from one of his colds, but he would not let that deter him from his starring role as the poet of the Volkssturm movement. The swearing in of the greater Berlin Volkssturm in 1944 was the closest thing to the prewar Nürnberg Rallies that the Reich had seen in years. Music, assembled masses, fanatical speeches, arms raised in holy oath, all of these factors were present on that long-ago day in Berlin.[50]

The ceremony began at 9:30 in the morning as Goebbels appeared on the balcony overlooking the Wilhelmsplatz while the band played "We Are Marching through Greater Berlin," a song of the Era of Struggle of the NSDAP. Trumpets sounded and the commands were given: "Berlin Volkssturm, at attention! Raise the standards and banners! Eyeş right!" The *Gau* SA staff leader, Obergruppenführer Gräntz, reported to Goebbels. The minister crisply replied, "Heil Volkssturm!" The answer was given: "Heil Hitler!" A brief musical interlude followed, the prelude to the honoring of those fallen in battle. The command was given: "Berlin Volkssturm, at attention! Raise the standards and banners! Lower the banners!" In this way the dead were honored as the band played the "Song of the Good Comrade." Temporarily presiding was the deputy Gauleiter. The full panoply of National Socialist romanticism reached its culmination when Goebbels took over at the ceremony. The command followed: "Raise the standards and banners! At ease!" The band then intoned the martial strains of the song "*Volk* to Arms." Then the second command: "Berlin Volkssturm, at attention for taking the oath! Raise the standards and banners!" Gräntz read the Volkssturm oath, whereupon Goebbels spoke to the assembled men, honoring the Führer, before the band played the two national anthems. The minister was particularly proud of the fact that the 4th company of the Berlin Volkssturm consisted entirely of Promi personnel, thereby demonstrating his personal commitment to the theme of total mobilization. Goebbels had begun to form his unit long before the Volkssturm itself came into being. Since Goebbels and his colleagues assigned such a high priority to their propaganda work, however, a contradiction arose, and as late as 1945 many of his people were still petitioning the Wehrmacht for Army and Volkssturm deferments.

Propaganda about the Volkssturm was an ideological expression of the fanatical German will to resist the Allies. The *Volksopfer,* or "People's Donation," movement was an attempt to collect clothing and other useful items for the Volkssturm men at the front. Wall placards and

„Nun habe ich meinem Fiffi die ganzen schönen Knochen vom Munde abgespart, und nu wollen Sie sie nicht!"

Wartime humor, early 1945. An old lady wants to contribute to the "People's Offering" for the Wehrmacht and Volkssturm. She offers one of Fiffi's best bones, ". . . and now you don't want it!" *(Illustrierter Beobachter)*

CREDIT: From *Illustrierter Beobachter*

posters were very much a part of all these appeals to the nation. Their message was always similar: "Hold out! *(Durchhalten!)*: "Save our women and children from the Red beasts!" "For freedom and life—German Volkssturm!" "Hard times, hard hearts!" Posters often showed an old man and a young boy with Volkssturm armbands, ready to resist the hated foe to the last—and perhaps only—bullet. The Volkssturm itself was a desperate ragtag militia which had no effect upon the course of the war. As a symbol, however, the Volksturm gave a new theme and opportunity to Goebbels and his propaganda people, especially in terms of press, posters, and newsreels.[51]

The Volkssturm represented a desperate return to themes of the German past in a last-ditch effort to fire the German people with renewed zeal for victory through resistance. The Nazi cult of death, transcendence, and commemoration, with its romanticism and morbid sentimentality, was at the root of the heroic pathos which enveloped scenes of old men and young boys going off to fight in a hopeless struggle. Yet this orchestrated euphoria failed, for it seems to have evaporated quite suddenly by early January 1945. Goebbels and the Security Service people were left with reports of civilians becoming frightened over the question as to whether Volkssturm men would be shot outright if captured by the Allies, since they were not wearing the military uniforms mandated by the Geneva Convention.

During the last three years of the war, the "German Weekly Newsreel" devoted much of its time and resources to a cult of death and commemoration. Heroic images of fallen leaders being saluted for the last time by the titans of the Third Reich often dominated the week's news. These state or party funerals were splendid opportunities for the *Wochenschau* to demonstrate the solemn unity of party, state, and Wehrmacht. They appealed to their audience through music that was thought to touch every true German soul, whether it was the heroic strains of the "Hohenfriedberger March" or that sad dirge, the "Song of the Good Comrade." By 1944 these deathly spectacles had become promises of transcendence and immortality through the eternal nation. "Victory through Faith," *Sieg durch Glauben:* The slogan achieved emotional power through a combined assault upon the mind and heart in picture and music. Harmony of all spirits within the fighting German nation became a theme almost religious in its confession and iconography. In this manner the Nazi elite created an appeal to past German traditions and to the many Germans who held dear those old symbols. The elite also created an image of its own immortality in these funeral spectacles, in this worship of the dead.

"For Freedom and Life: Volkssturm." One of Mjölnir's last posters for the RPL.

The first great instance of this wartime cult occurred in the autumn of 1939. On the evening of November 8, Adolf Hitler came to Munich to be with the "old guard" of party fighters in the Bürgerbräukeller, scene of the abortive 1923 coup. Soon after he left the building a bomb went off, and seven "Old Fighters" died in the rubble or soon thereafter. The DW newsreel devoted much of its time to the ceremony of November 9, a traditional holy day on the Nazi calendar. Rudolf Hess represented Hitler at the monument to the sixteen "martyrs" of 1923, laying a wreath at the site of their "Eternal Watch" at noon. The ceremony of November 9, 1939, seemed to have special meaning because of the Führer's "providential" escape the evening before. As Hess saluted the dead, the "old guard" assembled for the "last formation," and the dead men, "still marching in spirit" in the ranks, received the homage of the party as a band intoned the solemn, heroic tones of "Raise the Banner." The dead men represented the "eternal guard" of the movement: Near the names of the sixteen dead men was engraved the word "present" *(hier)*. The *Wochenschau* captured the spirit of the occasion, the theme of which appeared on another stone carving: "You have conquered after all." [52] The uncertain first winter of the war, which loomed ahead for the entire nation, gave its own special meaning to this commemoration.

The same "Weekly Newsreel" quickly turned to the funeral ceremony held two days later in the late morning. Hitler, wearing a black armband, had returned to Munich to pay tribute to the new martyrs of the movement. He extended his condolences to the loved ones of the dead Nazis, managing to convey that look of profound sorrow and heroic fortitude which he had mastered. The funeral procession filed through the streets of Munich to the cemetery; officers bore display trays containing the decorations of the victims before each casket, while a band played a slow, almost symphonic version of "Raise the Banner." The narrator concluded with a comment both commemorative and hopeful: These men were "blood witnesses to the struggle for a new, free Germany."

By 1942 the Propaganda Ministry and the *Wochenschau* crews achieved even greater effects by concentrating upon individual tragedies. On February 12, 1942, Hitler himself gave the eulogy for the fallen Dr. Fritz Todt, minister of armaments and munitions, killed in a suspicious plane crash. The Goebbels ministry had become a general contractor for all state and party funerals, and it wrote the guidelines for the farewell to Fritz Todt, which took place in the Mosaic Hall of the New Reich chancellory. Hitler consoled the widow and her children, a look of extreme anguish upon his face. The burdens of the harsh Russian winter made this a doubly tragic occasion. The audience was to perceive the deeds and death of Fritz Todt as symbolic of the efforts of German soldiers from the eastern front to Africa, from the English Channel to the North Atlantic. The propaganda ministry chose the music for the spectacle, which included the "Funeral March" from Wagner's *The Twilight of the Gods,* the "Song of the Good Comrade" (played while Hitler's wreath was placed before the sarcophagus), and the two national anthems, "Deutschland über Alles" and "Raise the Banner." [53]

Hitler made one of his last *Wochenschau* appearances as a funeral orator on May 7, 1943, when he addressed the mourners for Viktor Lutze, chief of staff of the SA, who had perished in an automobile accident. Lutze had little power, but Hitler remembered his loyalty before and during the purge of Ernst Röhm and other "dissident" SA leaders in 1934. Goebbels gave a long eulogy and placed the wreath of the Führer before Lutze's casket. Lutze received the "final salute" while an orchestra played "Siegfried's Funeral Music." [54] Goebbels never permitted words by the participants to mar these occasions, despite complaints from Germans who wanted to hear their Führer's voice. Images and music sufficed to achieve the effects which he sought.

Adolf Hitler's final tribute to SA Chief of Staff Viktor Lutze, spring 1943.

One of the most interesting death spectaculars of the regime appeared on the screens of German theaters late in the depressing year 1944. Suicides by major officers, particularly in the Luftwaffe, had occurred with depressing regularity since 1941. If the dead officer was of high enough rank, the state not only suppressed the true story of his death, but gave him an elaborate funeral, a show produced for the "Weekly Newsreel." Hitler suspected Erwin Rommel of complicity in the July 20, 1944, attempt on his life. Rommel, under prodding from the regime, killed himself on October 14, thereby sparing himself and his family a more gruesome fate. Goebbels and the *Wochenschau* had made Rommel great in the eyes of the nation; now Hitler had cast him down. How could the Nazis salvage something from the death of the popular general? They made their plans even before the death of Rommel: He would receive an elaborate, moving state funeral, which would in turn dominate a forthcoming *Deutsche Wochenschau.*[55] Secure in this knowledge, Hitler relaxed somewhat and sent a birthday telegram to the king of Afghanistan the next day.

The solemn state funeral for Field Marshal Erwin Rommel. ("German Weekly Newsreel")

Mourning became the national festive cult of the Third Reich during the last two and a half years of the war. This activity, perhaps more than the official slogans about will, faith, retaliation, and final victory, contained its own solace for many Germans and especially for their leaders. Victory was elusive, but in the celebration of heroic death an individual might transcend himself and become part of what Adolf Hitler called "national immortality." The great age of National Socialist mourning commenced with the three days of remembrance for the German Sixth Army of Stalingrad fame. A nihilistic cult of death was justified as a commitment to transcendent, eternal national greatness. Joseph Goebbels skillfully manipulated this mood through the mass media, and in this way contributed to the grim fatalism and determination of the German population. Yet Goebbels was also creating a monument to himself and National Socialism when he commemorated a martyr or filmed a state funeral. In his distorted vision of faith and salvation, Goebbels wrote his own epitaph every time his men combined music and image in a farewell ceremony, for he was promising himself what he thereby promised the German nation: victory in death.

7

The Feature Film as Nazi Propaganda:
Men, Organization, and Themes

Joseph Goebbels' interest in film as a medium of mass propaganda covered every form of film: documentaries, feature films, and short subjects and travelogues. His domination of the wartime German film industry was a perfect example of National Socialist "coordination" policy. Not only did Goebbels often choose topics, actors, and directors, but he occasionally wrote his own lines into scripts. Veit Harlan, one of the important men in Goebbels' stable of film people, wrote after the war, "The main role in the drama which I am describing was played not by me, but by Dr. Joseph Goebbels." [1] Harlan's comment was an attempt to protest his own innocence in regard to Nazi film propaganda, but, motive aside, it corresponded to the facts. As a close Goebbels aide noted during the war, "Before it is released, every German film is shown in the film room of the house on the Hermann Göring Strasse." [2] As early as 1933 Goebbels made clear to employees of the great UFA film corporation that coordination by the state meant National Socialist guidance.[3] From now on the cinema was to be in the vanguard of the struggle for "national culture." The emigration of Jewish film persons and other anti-Nazis made Goebbels' task of coordination easier. Looking back on six years of *Gleichschaltung,* the minister noted in 1939 that the regime could have contented itself with disinterest and censorship, but it desired more from the film industry.[4] The "total political structuring of the will of the German nation" required that the government come to grips with a medium that reached millions of citizens. Film had to be taken out of the hands of an anonymous group of people and made an educational instrument for building the new Reich.

The outbreak of war only confirmed Goebbels' belief in the national mission of film. In his words, "The war has demonstrated that man does not live by bread alone, that his mind and his spirit desire spiritual sustenance as well as reassurance." [5] The press constantly reaffirmed the theme: "In Germany cultural life continues without a hitch because the hard battles perpetuate its development." [6] In his ministerial conferences Goebbels insisted repeatedly that the press emphasize ". . . to the nation what significant work has been carried out in this artistic field in Germany during the war." [7] The minister restated his belief that the function of film was edification, diversion, and relaxation, but in a political sense. Even the diversion had as its purpose raising morale and enabling people to meet the hard challenges of wartime existence.[8]

A man filled with contradictions expresses such tensions in all aspects of his life and work. So too in the case of Dr. Goebbels. Privately, he sympathized with certain experimental tendencies in cinema: "We are loaded down altogether too much with tradition and piety. We hesitate to clothe our cultural heritage in a modern dress. It therefore remains purely historical or museumlike and is at best understood by groups within the party, the Hitler Youth, or the Labor Service." [9] Yet as a National Socialist, Goebbels railed against the decadence of Weimar culture and its "Jewish" practitioners, burned their writings, and drove them from the industry and from the land. Two sides of Goebbels were in conflict, the elitist and the manipulator of the masses. The propagandist triumphed over the film aesthete, for the attraction of power and the need to disprove accusations that he, too, was a "closet" intellectual led Goebbels to repudiate liberal concepts of the integrity of artistic work. Even when he used the screen to advance idealized versions of National Socialist ideology, Goebbels succumbed to a false and often awkward literalism, usually summed up in the claim that a historical film epic "was based upon historical facts." Goebbels' relations with more independent producers and directors were generally poor. He had been on bad terms with the famous actress, dancer, and director Leni Riefenstahl since 1934. His regime could be petty: Ms. Riefenstahl discovered in the winter of 1943 that Bormann and the propaganda ministry would not permit her the use of an automobile or a modest allocation of gasoline.[10]

The creation of a Reich Film Chamber (RFK) as part of the Reich Culture Chamber complex was one of Goebbels' early tasks as minister. The RFK had four official press organs: *Film, The German Film,*

Decisions of the Film Examination Office (the censorship list), and the official daily newspaper of the industry, the *Film-Kurier*. Early in 1942 Bormann claimed the right of prior approval of all important Reich Culture Chamber ordinances, but Goebbels maintained his control over film until the end of the war. The Reich Film Chamber was directed by men active in the film division of the ministry. All sections of the RFK were responsible for carrying out the orders which Goebbels gave to the personnel of his film division.[11] The film division was the head,[12] the Reich Film Chamber the body. The important film division was divided into several main offices for administration, film production, film dramaturgy, censorship, newsreels, and exports.

The film examination office of the division approved or rejected scripts and movies. Goebbels had achieved this total censorship control through a 1935 Hitler decree. The censorship office worked prodigiously, examining 355 films in December 1939 and January 1940 alone. Censorship under Goebbels took other forms besides the examination of films. He created new stamps of approval, for instance the description of a film as "valuable politically." After 1936 any film criticism worthy of the name was suppressed. The outbreak of war led the minister to inaugurate tighter forms of censorship.[13] No films could be begun before the propaganda division, the chief of staff of the RPL, and the censors of the film office had examined the scripts.

Goebbels did not have faith in the capabilities of German directors to produce good wartime "Nazi world view" films. He wanted products which were appealing and even humorous, not heavy-handed, boring sermons. It was for this reason that Goebbels ordered Gutterer and Fischer to work with the film division.[14] Goebbels warned producers to submit their final scripts to the film division a month before an approved film was to be made by a studio. Wartime censorship also presented tempting financial possibilities. Goebbels repeatedly instructed his subordinates to make sure American films were withdrawn from circulation, a policy inaugurated two years before Pearl Harbor. Goebbels was ever alert to the chance of driving out competition and dominating the German (and later, the European) film world.

The model of the National Socialist film administrator and producer was Dr. Fritz Hippler, director of the film division from 1939 to 1943, and Reich film intendant in 1942–43.[15] Hippler was another of Goebbels' young, fanatical, "convinced National Socialists." He assumed his high position at the age of thirty, having previously headed the important "Wochenschau Central Office." He had joined the NSDAP as a teenager in 1927. Hippler's father had fallen at the front during the war, and the ambitious young man had had to work with his hands to claw his way into the crisis-ridden German middle class. His chosen path was the university, and he studied in Berlin and Heidelberg before being expelled for Nazi activism. Hippler claimed that he got into trouble for mounting a balcony and giving a political speech against the backdrop of a Nazi banner. Intense and committed, Hippler had abandoned his hopes for an academic career and turned to full-time speaking and organizing within the party. He became a major Nazi student leader in Berlin, where he caught the eye of Reich Propaganda Director Joseph Goebbels. Hippler played a major role in the infamous book burnings of May 10, 1933, when German students in SA uniforms tossed works representative of the "un-German spirit" into the flames. Goebbels was building his new ministry around these young "Old Fighters," men who were ambitious, fanatical, and literate, and he may have encouraged Hippler to return to the now "coordinated" University of Heidelberg for his doctorate. The young man received his degree in 1934 for an essay on nineteenth-century political theory.

Hippler's social *ressentiment* turned him into a major combatant in the verbal struggle for the legacy of SA martyr Horst Wessel. Conservative students of the upper classes, dominant in the university "corporations," or fraternities, tried to defend their privileged position against Nazi "revolutionaries" by claiming that Wessel had been one of their own. Hippler sharply rejected this reactionary argument, declaring that Horst Wessel's death was that of a "freedom hero." He did not die because he had belonged to a "corporation," but because he had fought for a new Reich. Michael Siegert has argued that Goebbels may have temporarily withdrawn and altered a feature film about Wessel in September 1933 because it placed too much emphasis upon the man's "corporate" affinity.[16] This is a matter of some dispute, for it is possible that Goebbels feared that the film, *Hans Westmar, One of Many: A German Fate of the Year 1929,* would "demystify" the leading martyr of the movement.[17] Erwin Leiser has even suggested that the film may have been too sympathetic in its portrayal of the Communist opposition.[18] This is unlikely, for the film depicted the Reds as either scheming Jews or misled potential Nazis. In addition, Hugenberg's UFA people produced the film, and they were not noted for their Bolshevist leanings.

Fritz Hippler's "radical" Nazism was attractive to Goebbels, especially in his struggle against Rosenberg for control of the arts. Hippler and his friends, among them the Nazi painter O. A. Schreiber, rejected Rosenberg's "Wilhelminian," or reactionary, view of art. They wanted a campaign against "degenerate" contemporary abstract art but also some freedom for "moderate" expressionists. Rosenberg had enough power to deprive Hippler of his position in the NS Student League, but Goebbels'

HANS WESTMAR

PRODUCTION: Volksdeutsche Film GmbH.

DIRECTOR: Franz Wenzler

SCRIPT: Hanns Heinz Ewers

MAJOR PERFORMERS: Emil Lohkampf

Carla Bartheel

Paul Wegener

The SA of Berlin/Brandenburg

PREMIERE: December 13, 1933

---

patronage sufficed to guarantee a career to the young Nazi after his return from Heidelberg. Hippler's intellectual work indicated strong Marxist influence. His social resentment, in a different social milieu, might have led him to Communism. In the Germany of Hippler's era he became a Nazi, but he even sought to justify his anti-Semitism by giving it a "social" interpretation. The Jew was not bad in himself, but because he was rootless and deprived of community, hence "abstract and isolated." This was Hippler's view in 1934; by 1940 his treatment of the "Jewish question" was as obscene and vicious as that of Julius Streicher.

Goebbels had become a genocidal anti-Semite for Hitler; Hippler became one for Goebbels. Like Werner Naumann, whom he resembled in so many ways, Hippler became an active SS man. This furthered his career in the Propaganda Ministry, but could not save him from Goebbels' fury in 1943, when Hippler lost his position as director of the film section in a conflict over a script for the film *Münchhausen.* He was not merely an ambitious careerist; he was a fanatic National Socialist of the idealist persuasion. Hippler wanted to leave his mark on German film in both theory and practice, and was active in educating trainees at the Berlin Film Academy and creating a National Socialist film aesthetic. Hippler wrote the most important Nazi film treatise, *Observations on Making Films,* which went through at least six printings between 1940 and 1944. The president of the Reich Film Chamber, Carl Froelich, and Germany's most famous actor, Emil Jannings, wrote flattering prefaces to the book. Hippler had to tread a narrow path between his own sense of the artist's claims and the realization that he was working and writing for Joseph Goebbels. Hippler actually claimed that the state did not interfere in the "practical, artistic film work," but that the Third Reich, like every true "community" in history, did impress its needs and desires upon creative artists. Hippler's theoretical formulation allowed technical freedom to the director, but based his "inner freedom" upon identity with the goals of the state. In his own way the author was departing from Goebbels' method, which allowed the minister to interfere at will even in "practical, artistic film work," as Hippler well knew.

It is possible that by expressing slightly dissident attitudes, Hippler was trying to recapture his self-respect, never a commodity widely prevalent among Goebbels' employees. Fritz Hippler carried out some of the minister's most vile assignments, including the disgusting anti-Semitic "documentary," *The Eternal Jew*. Much of Hippler's treatise merely expressed in more theoretical language Goebbels' concept of film and its purpose—education of the masses, elevation of history through idealized presentation—and praised films made in the new Germany. "The film is and remains the most intensely effective applied art and the one which reaches the largest number of people," Hippler wrote. He believed that film was "a people's art." [19] In pious terms such as these, Hippler echoed Goebbels' aesthetic and expressed in thinly disguised terms Nazi intentions regarding film. It was thus fitting in 1939 when Goebbels announced that Hippler would henceforth direct the ministry's film division. His prior film experience had been confined to blatantly propagandistic newsreels.

Hans Hinkel steadily expanded his role in German cultural life during the Second World War. He eventually succeeded Hippler as director of the film division and as Reich film intendant. Because of his political reliability and his high SS rank (Gruppenführer, or "general"), Hinkel's career reached its peak after the attempted assassination of Hitler on July 20, 1944. Hans Hinkel was born in 1901 in Worms, the son of a wealthy manufacturer. Of a restless nature, Hinkel agonized over the defeat of Germany in 1918, and came to view the French with burning hatred. His studies led him nowhere, but his "national mindedness" and late-adolescent personality took him to Munich, where he joined the party in its very early days, in 1921. Hinkel gained some experience in newspaper work, becoming editor of various Nazi papers after 1928. He wound up on the editorial board of the *Völkischer Beobachter* and became a member of the Reichstag in 1930. After the Seizure of Power, Hinkel became Prussian state commissar for scholarship, art, and popular education.

Hinkel was a fanatic anti-Semite, and he viewed his work after 1933 as a mission to search out and destroy "Jewish" influence in German cultural life. In this capacity he became a handyman, or "special commissioner," for Joseph Goebbels. Hinkel was an ominous figure to Germans active in the arts, for one of his jobs as head of the "cultural personalities" division was to make constantly up-to-date political judgments about the reliability of thousands of men and women. Hinkel was particularly interested in the Jews he discovered in the course of his work, and he contributed to the "Final Solution" by turning this information over to various SS and police agencies. The name of Hinkel's office was changed to "Special Cultural Tasks" in 1939, then to "General Agency for Questions Concerning the Reich Culture Chamber." As Willi A. Boelcke put it, "Since Hinkel was business director of the RKK in his capacity as 'general secretary of the RKK,' the RKK in effect became a division of the ministry through the personal union of the two offices." [20] Goebbels appreciated his diligence and loyalty, not to mention his close relationship with Himmler, and the new director of the film division worked hard in the last months of the war to preserve the cinematic empire that Goebbels had established.

The key man in the economic and organizational workings of Goebbels' film empire was Dr. Max Winkler, officially Goebbels' advisor for finance and production. The wartime reorganization of the German film industry was complete by the winter of 1942. Goebbels and Winkler consolidated the various studios and distribution and production units into one "umbrella" corporation, the UFA Film Corporation, which came into being on January 10, 1942, with a capital base of sixty-five million Reichsmarks.[21] UFA now controlled seventeen German film studios and production centers, not to mention various concerns scattered throughout Europe. The German film industry had been entirely in the hands of the state for years, but an added quality of centralization and total control now emerged. The reorganization represented Goebbels' bid for European and even worldwide German film supremacy. UFA, Inc., was now a cartel controlling film production from the fabrication and production of raw film to the creation of movies and their distribution to cinemas. More and more of these theaters were owned by the same concern. The UFA studio itself, as one studio, was but a single German unit within the mother company, but it was a highly profitable concern, turning over a profit of ten million Reichsmarks in 1943-44. Branch directors of studios in Prague, Munich, and Vienna were somewhat annoyed at Winkler's centralizing policies, but there was little they could do about them. Since their dependency upon him was as absolute afterwards as it had been before, the grumbling soon died down and the provincial studios continued to carry out the tasks assigned to them. Their remoteness through most of the war from Allied bombers justified their location, aside from questions of local pride.

The Prague studio was unique in that it contained two units, one German and the other Czech.[22] This situation required cooperation between the propaganda ministry and the "protector" of Bohemia and Moravia, Reinhard Heydrich. Such an agreement was reached in the autumn of 1941, mandating collaboration in selecting personnel for high positions in the propaganda apparatus and the mass media within the Protectorate. One of the most lucrative units within the new UFA conglomerate was the Vienna Film Society, Inc., which reported a surplus of almost six million Reichsmarks as of November 30, 1942.[23] This studio specialized in producing films of a "Viennese" romantic nature—often musicals—always saccharine in their sentimentality: *Summer Love, Two Happy People, Late Love, Women Are No Angels.* The studio was capable of working on a dozen films simultaneously, but only by expending its energies to the breaking point.

Despite these successes, military conscription of technical personnel caused many problems for the Vienna unit by the summer of 1941, when 23 percent of the staff had already been inducted. The studio managed to sustain its hectic pace by attracting foreign specialists in large numbers. By the late spring of 1942 the percentage of conscripted personnel was only 25 percent, a bare rise over a year earlier despite the large increment in Wehrmacht conscription throughout the Reich. This apparent anomaly is accounted for when one looks at the large number of foreign technicians employed by the studio. Winkler and Goebbels viewed this unit as a borderland outlet for German domination of the film markets of southeastern Europe and, perhaps one day, of Italy. One of the specialties of the Vienna studio was the production of films such as *Heimkehr (The Return)* which dealt with the plight of "oppressed" ethnic Germans in hostile lands. Goebbels evidently believed that the Viennese, former Austrians who bordered on Hungarian, Slovene, and Italian territory, were the logical producers of such films. In the process of making these motion pictures they would strengthen their own suspect German ethnic consciousness and that of their fellow citizens in the former Austrian *Ostmark.*

During the final month of the great UFA reorganization, Joseph Goebbels gloated about his wartime film successes: "Movie production is flourishing almost unbelievably despite the war. What a good idea of mine it was to have taken possession of the films on behalf of the Reich several years ago! It would be terrible if the high profits now being earned by the motion-picture industry were to flow into private hands." [24] A high point of self-congratulation was reached on March 6, 1943, when German film luminaries celebrated the twenty-fifth anniversary of the creation of the original UFA.[25] Privy Councillor Alfred Hugenberg was there. According to Goebbels, the old man was flattered at receiving a medal from the regime. Veit Harlan and Wolfgang Liebeneiner became professors, while Ludwig Klitzsch gave the main address. The managing director of UFA, Klitzsch, did his best to link the present state monopoly to the firm founded by Emil G. von Strauss in 1917, a company which Hugenberg later took over. One wonders if any mixed feelings went through Hugenberg's mind as he heard the unctuous Klitzsch tell how proud he was that Goebbels had chosen the name UFA for his new film cartel in 1942. With Nazi eminences such as Funk, Ley, Hippler, and Gutterer looking on, the speaker launched into praise of Goebbels as "protector of the German film," a true patron of the arts in the struggle against Jewish and un-German influences.

Despite this apparent confidence and the fulsome flattery, there were ominous signs pointing to major problems for the German film industry. The production schedule which ended in 1940 had consisted of eighty-one films; that concluded in 1941 contained but forty-four titles.[26] By 1942 the average feature film cost almost three times as much to produce as in 1937-38. Goebbels exuded optimism, even privately, but he had to take note of some of the new problems. As he noted in his diary, "Winkler gave me a report on the movie situation. A number of personnel questions have to be discussed. The Finance Ministry is trying to soak us with new taxes, so that it will hardly be possible to build up any capital reserves for tasks after the war. But Winkler is himself a pretty shrewd financier who knows more about these things than the bureaucracy of the Finance Ministry." [27] High taxes on profits, a shortage of trainees for technical and performing tasks, disruptions in production and distribution caused by bombings, conscription of personnel into the Wehrmacht, inflation, and growing shortages of raw film and projection equipment presented Goebbels, Winkler, and Hinkel with major new problems during the last two years of the war. And even if the regime were to solve all these problems, what good would it do to produce a film if theaters were in ruins or if people were afraid to buy tickets for fear of being caught in an air raid? Goebbels therefore now gave much of his attention to keeping theaters functioning at all costs. He saw another possibility in the mobilization of the party film branches' equipment and organization. Nothing could distract the minister's attention from these tasks.

The Central Film Office (ALF) of the RPL, located in Berlin, was a National Socialist propaganda branch run by such reliable Nazi specialists as Eberhard Fangauf, Carl Neumann, and Curt Belling. In describing its function in 1937, publicist Belling wrote that the ALF made cinema available to millions who did not have film theaters in their small towns or rural communities. He estimated this potential audience at twenty-three million men, women, and children. Party film work was organized along NS hierarchical lines, from top to bottom, as follows: provincial film branch, *Gau* film branch, district film branch, local film branch. A problem endemic to Nazi organizational practices plagued party film work. The Gauleiter had disciplinary authority over the director of the *Gau* film branch, and the same situation prevailed at the district and local levels. Thus, however active the Berlin office might be, local film work depended upon the commitment of the political organization of the party at all levels. In 1937 there were 13 provincial branches, 32 *Gau* film offices, 771 district offices, and about 22,000 local branches of the ALF. By the eve of the war territorial expansion of the Reich and intensification of party film work had increased those figures by over 36 percent.

The party film division had two major tasks before the war, bringing movies to out-of-the-way areas and producing and distributing hundreds of party films for the Hitler Youth and other branch and affiliated Nazi organizations. "Village community evenings" sponsored by the party brought films to peasants and rural laborers. The party eventually owned over a thousand mobile motion-picture vans which contained equipment necessary for the projection of films. The films were shown in school-houses, in large rooms of inns or beer halls, or even outdoors—anywhere hundreds of spectators could be accommodated. The film branch brought movies to the Hitler Youth through the "Youth Film Hours." When the Nazis conquered a new territory with a large German population, the mobile film vans followed in the wake of the Wehrmacht occupation forces. The party was thus a key factor in the Germanization work of the Propaganda Ministry.[28]

In the months preceding the outbreak of war, the party film offices, Gauleiters, and office of the deputy Führer took steps to make sure that this film work would continue in the event of international conflict. These efforts were not entirely successful, for the Wehrmacht and its propaganda division often laid claim to technical personnel and equipment. The RPL proudly pointed to forty-five million admissions to its film programs in 1938, but it had to demonstrate its military function in order to carry on its work during an increasingly long and hard war. The film division did this by working with Goebbels on programs aimed at Wehrmacht personnel. Its main function during the war was the presentation of films for the education and relaxation of the armed forces. Charging the Wehrmacht nominal fees, the film division enabled the party to reach millions of troops by collaborating with the propaganda companies in the presentation of newsreels and feature films.

The film division continued its work of special screening for the Hitler Youth and other party groups as well as for isolated segments of the population, but the lack of projectors and trained personnel caused it to concentrate upon the needs of troops on leave. One advantage of the situation was the chance to influence the armed forces in a National Socialist direction, even through "nonparty" feature films and newsreels. Good examples of this work were the various film programs presented on the occasion of the tenth anniversary of the Seizure of Power, January 1943. Soldiers were the guests of the party at film shows presented in theaters throughout the Reich. The *Gau* film branches sponsored these events; film-distribution firms provided the movies to the theaters without charge. Soldiers received free tickets from their local party branch. Through such means the party hoped to convince the fighting troops that the struggle for Germany and the ideology of the party were identical causes.[29]

The party film organization might continue to reach soldiers on leave, party branches, and some Germans who did not have access to large urban centers. Goebbels knew, however, that the influence, prestige, and profits of his film industry depended upon the masses living in large cities and middling-sized towns. As early as the winter of 1940, the minister told his conferees that while the Führer had ordered that theaters and movie houses remain open during these wartime months of unusually cold weather, the closing of schools during the cold season could not be avoided. Goebbels also directed that if a lack of coal caused problems, private and state-owned legitimate theaters were to be closed before the movie houses shut their doors. A year later, during the winter of 1941, Goebbels told his film people to make sure that motion picture theaters were not closed because of a lack of heating fuel. New problems arose during the first Russian winter. In February 1942 the Army wanted to seize certain film theaters and turn them into field hospitals. Local party officials vigorously resisted these moves, citing party doctrine on the importance of film to the German racial community in wartime. Wartime conditions presented Goebbels with opportunities as well as problems. The Reich Film Chamber outlined a plan by which local, privately owned movie-house chains would be dissolved and rented or sold to politically reliable and technically knowledgeable wounded Wehrmacht veterans. This program did not get very far, but it would have been pursued if Germany had won the war, particularly where a Gauleiter had a personal or political grudge against private owners.[30]

Massive Allied bombings created a permanent emergency for German motion-picture theaters between 1943 and 1945. Goebbels believed that movies were more important to German morale and party propaganda than were plays. He therefore approved Hans Hinkel's efforts to turn legitimate theaters into motion-picture theaters in 1944, especially in cities which had suffered heavily from British and American bombings.[31] Because of lack of personnel and equipment, this was a slow process, with only nine theaters converted in September 1944, and fifteen or twenty in October. Hinkel pointed out that each of these theaters could accommodate an average of one thousand persons. Another difficulty arose when the government raised admission prices and the amusement tax. These measures were deemed necessary because of the inflationary costs confronting the entire German film industry between 1940 and 1945. One Reich propaganda office (Halle) informed the propaganda section that such increments were unfortunate, since they affected hard-working men and women who needed movies for relaxation. The main problem, however, continued to be the shortage of projectors, personnel, film prints for distribution, and the lost air war.

A macabre series of related incidents occurring during the first nine months of 1944 reveals a good deal about these problems and even more about Goebbels' mania for film propaganda. Berlin theaters were of special interest to the minister, and he was concerned about reports indicating that people were afraid to visit the movie houses that had survived the late 1943 Allied bombings. The Berliners feared being trapped in a burning, collapsing building while watching a newsreel or enjoying a feature film. Early in February Goebbels' ministry turned to General Reinecke of the Wehrmacht and asked him to provide troops for flak protection of individual theaters. The presence of the Army would calm the apprehensions of the civilian population, and they would presumably stream into the theaters again, secure in the knowledge that they were being protected against air raids, fires, and resultant chaos. The Army, alleging a "Führer order," turned down the request on February 9. Actually, the order merely stated that no further home-front burdens were to be placed on the Wehrmacht. Adolf Hitler, if anyone, would have sympathized with the ministry's request. Goebbels knew this, and he also sensed that if he and state secretary Gutterer pursued the matter, they would probably succeed, if not with the Army, then with the SS. This was not the type of matter about which Goebbels would bother Hitler directly, but Gutterer proceeded as if his authority stemmed from the highest sources. Reinecke told Gutterer that the most he could do was to suggest that theater managers and party personnel work with the Berlin police on emergency evacuation procedures. The police would notify Wehrmacht air-raid units in the Greater Berlin area in the event of Allied attack, and these units would devote some of their personnel to securing the safety of motion-picture houses.

The SS seemed more agreeable, and the ministry believed that coordination of SA, Hitler Youth, and Wehrmacht units might suffice to protect all the major theaters if new procedures were worked out. Von Behr, the SS contact, indicated that he would be happy to assist in assigning personnel to two major theaters, but stated that he could not do so unless he received the approval of his superior, Obergruppen-führer Jüttner, who was unfortunately away at the time. Von Behr, despite his protestations of sympathy, asked the ministry to put its request in writing. A ministry list of February 21 indicated that Goebbels wished to double the number of men and boys assigned to emergency duty in and around to theaters. Within a few days von Behr agreed to the ministry request, but asked that his men be guaranteed free admission. Bureaucratic confusion prevailed as the ministry talked of protecting eight theaters or ten or sixteen. The SS soon had reason to regret its approval, for Gutterer, desperately seeking to keep his position by impressing Goebbels, now had visions of extending this system to the entire Reich.

The SS assigned eighty extra men to special protective functions in Berlin, but it withdrew them on June 7, 1944, pleading the pressure of events in France (D Day). It promised more antiaircraft protection as soon as it was in a position to provide it. This crisis unleashed panic and confusion in the ministry. Should the theaters be closed down al-together? Such an action went against the grain of the ministry, for it would have represented a major blow against its entire reason for existing. Officials pleaded with the SS throughout the summer, asking for the return of their eighty men. The situation was finally clarified on September 20, when Himmler's office flatly rejected the ministry's request. As the Reich reeled under the combined blows of Allied air and land offensives in 1944, the propaganda ministry thus saw fit to devote much energy to the protection of Berlin movie houses. This episode said a good deal about Goebbels' mental set. As late as 1944 he was denying men to the front in order to produce film spectaculars. If he could have taken men from the front to protect major Berlin movie houses, he no doubt would have done so.[32]

The threat to the German film industry by 1944 was manifest in a number of other crises. Hans Hinkel received plenipotentiary powers in the summer to regulate the industry along the lines of total war. Did this mean shutting down most of its operations in order to release people for the front and for service in war industries or flak battalions? Hardly. It meant protecting and conserving the *minimal* forces necessary for the perpetuation of a *major* medium of propaganda. Early in 1945 the "command of the hour" for Hinkel and Goebbels was that the film industry must continue despite the "Mongol storm from the east," for the movie industry had important tasks to fulfill in the "decisive struggle" for the freedom and life of the Greater German Reich. Minor concessions to reality did occur. No feature films produced after January 1, 1945, were to be more than 2,200 meters in length; short features were to be confined to less than 300 meters.[33] The concession was a moot one, however, for the German film industry was in no position to produce anything from scratch in 1945. Distribution itself had become an almost insuperable problem by the end of 1944. The German Film Distribution Society did have over 26,000 prints of perhaps 650 feature films in its storage vaults, but these were mostly older productions, and in some cases the prints had begun to fade.[34] Nineteen newer feature films, including the lavishly produced *Opfergang,* were facing distribution difficulties. Raw film shortages meant that the more recent and relevant a film was, the fewer copies of it were available. Gorgeous color spectaculars such as *Opfergang* and *Kolberg* were indeed released (probably December 29, 1944, and January 30, 1945), but in extremely limited printings. Even if the towns of Germany had not been bombed, even if the theaters had been intact and the transportation system had functioned efficiently, shortages of raw film and personnel would have severely hampered Goebbels' film work by 1944.

Joseph Goebbels once stated, "We are convinced that films constitute one of the most modern and scientific means of influencing the masses. Therefore a government must not neglect them." [35] The Third Reich commissioned or approved over 1,300 films in the twelve years of its life.[36] Only about 15 percent of these movies might appear to be blatant "propaganda" films, but that is a misleading assumption. Even the most "apolitical" films served the purposes of the regime, or they would not have reached the German public. Escapist trite movies were approved because they permitted people to relax, thus preparing them to return to their workbenches or front lines with renewed commitments to labor and struggle. Movies that appeared to be pure entertainment often contained subtle applications of the regime's ideology, thus making doctrine more effective because it was less obtrusive. It is revealing that while certain postwar historians of Nazi film seem to believe that many of these movies were "apolitical," Nazis like Hippler and Ludwig Heyde believed just the opposite during the war. And these theoreticians of National Socialist cinema knew what they were talking about. Hippler believed that the "leadership function" of the state should permeate *all* films which reached production.[37] Heyde described the aim of the German film in terms of strengthening faith in the leadership and elevating the German national consciousness.[38]

What has caused some confusion is the fact that the propaganda ministry directly commissioned fewer than 10 percent of the German feature films produced during the life of the Third Reich. More relevant is the reminder that no film appeared on German screens without intense analysis of its contents by the censorship people of the ministry and the RFK. The context in which these less blatantly political films appeared is revealing. Short "cultural" features, such as *Magic of the Black Forest* and *Village Music*, may sound devoid of ideological underpinnings. Yet Leopold Gutterer included them in his propagandistic "Reich Week for the German Short Feature" in 1941, declaring of the German cultural film, "It has become a richly suggestive reflection of *the total* German life since Adolf Hitler's Seizure of Power." [39]

A few of the most successful wartime National Socialist films were heavy-handed in their reliance upon ideology. Others appear at first viewing to be more subtle politically. The sheer power and outstanding artistry of some of these films justified Goebbels' faith in the screen as a foremost means of ideological propaganda. These films fall into three categories of classification: the documentary, the war film employing occasional documentary techniques, and the feature film. A study of several of these wartime full-length motion pictures is extremely useful in furthering an understanding of the manner in which the regime employed this unique medium of expression to explain and justify the war to the German people. Some were great popular successes, others were never released. Four dominant approaches appeared and reappeared in these films, and they sometimes overlapped: (1) The documentary was used to give proof of German heroism, the greatness of the Führer, and the evil, repulsive nature of Nazism's enemies *(In Struggle against the World Enemy, Campaign in Poland, Baptism of Fire, Victory in the West, The Eternal Jew, Traitors before the People's Court).* (2) War films employing occasional documentary techniques humanized these themes by portraying the daily life and struggles of German soldiers, sailors, and airmen and thus brought the front and the homeland closer together as a fighting community *(U-boats Westward!, Fighter Squadron Lützow).* (3) Films gave graphic descriptions of the plight of ethnic

Germans at the hands of Slavic *Untermenschen (Return, In the Eye of the Storm)*. (4) "Light entertainment" feature films supported Nazi war ideology in unobtrusive ways *(Request Concert)*.

In Struggle against the World Enemy, narrated in a lively manner by famed actor Paul Hartmann, was an ideological documentary completed in 1939. Because of its anti-Soviet theme, the film could not be shown during the years of Nazi-Soviet détente, 1939–41. Subtitled *German Volunteers in Spain,* the movie was never widely distributed, but its contents make it a good example of the first category of German wartime films. *Im Kampf gegen den Weltfeind (In Struggle against the World Enemy)* was less a glorification of the exploits of the famed German Condor Legion than it was an anti-Communist diatribe in the spirit of the anti-Comintern pact of 1936–37. The film selected newsreel shots calculated to demonstrate the nefarious effects of Bolshevik activity in Spain between 1931 and 1939. Deserted churches, labor unrest, masses of miserable refugees, and a Communist-dominated popular front were the alleged results of the extension of the Jewish-Bolshevik conspiracy to Spain. One scene emphasized this connection by showing the arrival of "Moses Rosenberg," first Soviet ambassador to Red Spain. Hartmann melodramatically told his audience that 1936 might have been "Spain's last hour," had not Francisco Franco raised the banner of revolt and salvation. Thanks to the aid of General Sperrle and the Condor Legion, Franco was able to bring his forces to Spain from Morocco and begin the national struggle for Spain's soul. Throughout the film one sees the contrast between absolute good and total evil: the Jew Léon Blum of France aiding the Reds, heroic Italian legionnaires helping Franco. International brigades made up of the riffraff and the gullible are used by the Bolsheviks to decimate Spain, while the Nationalists and their German sponsors fight back for the good cause and triumph. One reason for the relatively small audience for the film may have been Franco's foreign policy after 1939. His friendly neutrality did not satisfy Hitler, and Germans seeing the film in 1941 or 1942 might well have asked a troublesome question: If German volunteers had died for the new Spain, why did Franco not aid the Axis in its struggle against Bolsheviks and Britons? Then, too, the picture contained intrinsic weaknesses; it was uneven and often dull in tone.

Two documentaries about the German victory over Poland were far more successful, especially during the early years of the war. *Campaign in Poland* and *Baptism of Fire* used the same basic materials and stressed identical themes. Some of these themes were apparent in a document circulated by the Reich propaganda office in Berlin even before Hitler began his war against the Poles. Poland was "the disturber of the peace of Europe." Its governing class was chauvinistic and expansionist and threatened the German "Free City" of Danzig. Since the spring of 1939, secret German propaganda directives to RPA offices had emphasized another theme that would play a major role.[40] They praised the late Polish dictator, Marshal Pilsudski, portraying him as reasonable and friendly to the Reich, while his successors were pygmies whose limitless ambition had led them to sell out true Polish interests to the West. These men had helped bring about war and were responsible for the plight of Poland.

CAMPAIGN IN POLAND

PRODUCTION: German Film Production and Sales Company, Inc.
DIRECTOR: Fritz Hippler
PREMIERE: February 8, 1940

Feldzug in Polen (Campaign in Poland) received its gala premiere in the Berlin Ufa-Palast am Zoo, the house usually employed by Goebbels for the first appearance of an important film. *Feldzug* was produced under the direction of Fritz Hippler, and represented the collaboration of the German Film Society, the Supreme Command of the Armed Forces, and the staff of the "German Weekly Newsreel." The dramatic photography was the work of various propaganda companies at the front, and *Feldzug* did much to enhance their prestige in the eyes of the German people. The early scenes of the film cleverly played upon popular historical consciousness. The audience saw shots of Danzig which emphasized its personality as a "primevally German town," its greatness in the days of the Hanseatic League, its role as a "bulwark of Germandom in the east." Hippler then focused on sources of German resentment against the Poles, antagonisms that were still present after the defeat of Poland: The Poland of Versailles was a *Raubstaat,* a state based upon robbery of other peoples' patrimony. It consisted of eight nationalities, all oppressed by the chauvinist Poles ruling in Warsaw. England was a villain in this motion picture, for the narrator described the British as egging on the Poles in an anti-German direction. This policy was part of Britain's attempt to encircle Germany once again, as she had done before 1914. Following the dictates of German propaganda at the time, France was spared criticism, for the audience was supposed to view gruesome shots of ethnic Germans fleeing the vicious Poles as part of England's work. Churchill, Eden, and Halifax were the criminals responsible, fighting to the last Pole. In this context the script justified the Hitler-Stalin pact, describing it as a way of avoiding British encirclement.

The next major segment of the film represented a pictorial and narrative attempt to prove Poland's hostile intentions. The script described a large Polish peacetime army of 300,000 men. This army was Warsaw's tool in advancing its "limitless goals of conquest," perhaps extending the western frontier of Poland to the Oder or even to the Elbe. The narrator described constant Polish provocations along the border, then the ruthless and destructive activities of Polish gangs in Danzig when war broke out. The script mobilized other media to demonstrate nefarious Polish intentions; a map was used indicating both the aggressive plans of the Poles and the effective countermeasures put into effect by the German Army High Command. The film then turned to its most effective and popular footage, a narrative, newsreel-like history of the *Blitzkrieg* in Poland. Polish forces were rarely shown, but were sometimes credited with bravery, if only to accentuate the heroic successes of the triumphant Germans. *Feldzug* showed the Wehrmacht taking Gdynia, whereupon the Nazis renamed it Gotenhafen, "Harbor of the Goths."

At this point the Führer made his entrance "at the front with his soldiers," the genius who headed the collective military leadership that made possible the most stunning victory in recent German history. *Feldzug* returned to the front in order to portray the isolation of huge Polish forces near Radom and Kudno, along with their vain attempt to break out to Warsaw to the east. "Not a single man" reached Warsaw from Kudno, the narrator proudly exclaimed, and the viewer saw the result on the screen: thousands of Polish POWs marching westward into captivity. This was an example of Nazi irony, for the government which had misled these men did tell them that they would be heading westward, towards the Reich, which is precisely what they were now doing—in a different context!

Feldzug did not miss the opportunity to demonstrate the superiority of National Socialism and the leadership of Hitler over the imperial German system of 1914–18. While Hitler and General Keitel stood at the banks of the San River, the audience learned that the Wehrmacht had conquered territory which it had taken its predecessor in the "Great War" a year to seize. The film built up the image of Hitler's greatness in the context of the achievements of his troops and, for this reason, was probably more effective than prewar epics such as *Triumph of the Will,* which centered entirely around a deified Hitler and left him devoid of human qualities. *Feldzug* cleverly turned from Hitler to "human" scenes of soldiers resting or sleeping in fields or cleaning their weapons; the narrator said little, but let the pictures speak for themselves against a background of dramatic music and beating drums. Refreshed and rested, the men resumed their "irresistible" advance, taking a total of 160,000 prisoners by September 21, the beginning of the campaign's fourth week.

The appearance of Germans and Soviets cooperating as the inexorable Wehrmacht rings closed in on Warsaw was meant to reassure the German people in regard to a two-front war. To the background of heroic music, Hitler greeted the men of his SS Leibstandarte before Warsaw, then watched the siege of the city, which capitulated on September 27. The script included a comment on the need for the siege, for even a few Germans may have had qualms, at least early in the war, about ruthlessly bombarding a huge civilian population. The audience learned that Hitler wanted to spare these people the agony of a siege, but the "criminal" decision of the Warsaw commandant to go on fighting necessitated the German attack. Taut, effective music accompanied the German entry into the city, depicted in powerful contrast to 120,000 more Polish troops marching off to captivity. The last scene of the film *Campaign in Poland* was shown in the context of the theme "the campaign in Poland has reached its conclusion." A military band played stirring Prussian marches as Hitler took the salute of his troops in the former Polish capital. Church bells rang in jubilation, a concession to German piety, and swastikas waved as strains of "Deutschland über Alles" accompanied a single word flashed on the screen—"Greater Germany."

Feldzug in Polen was part of a total media blitz in the Reich. The press gave it a great amount of attention while the film itself quickly became available throughout the nation. The *National Socialist Bibliography* advertised a new title published in Berlin in 1940, *Victory in Poland (Der Sieg in Polen),* a book introduced by Keitel that was the product of collaboration between the Wehrmacht and the SA. Over 200,000 copies were distributed in 1940. The approach of the book was very similar to that of the documentary, and was meant to appeal to the many Germans moved by what they had seen on the screen: They could learn more about the "boundless Polish plans" for conquest of German towns and provinces. Major personalities of party, state, and Wehrmacht were mobilized to publicize the film, including Goebbels, Keitel, Lutze, Heydrich, and Colonel-General Milch. The film was officially described as "valuable from a political viewpoint," "artistically valuable," "educational for the nation," and "a film of instruction." The party and all cinemas were encouraged to use the film on festive occasions and particularly for showings before youth groups. *Feldzug in Polen* was even used as an instrument of German foreign policy, for it was screened

Baptism of Fire

before the general staffs of neutral powers in the spring of 1940 as both a warning and a prediction.

Fritz Hippler took the same approach in hiring director Hans Bertram to make another documentary, *Baptism of Fire (Feuertaufe)*. This film used much of the footage that had appeared in *Campaign in Poland,* but it emphasized the contribution of the Luftwaffe to the lightning victory of the Germans.[41] Two factors contributed to the release of much the same footage in a new form. Hermann Göring was jealous of the role allotted to the Army in the first film, and the great popular success that *Feldzug in Polen* enjoyed encouraged Hippler to produce *Feuertaufe.* The beginning of *Baptism of Fire* informed the viewer that this was a "film about the Luftwaffe in action in Poland. The scenes were filmed during actual combat situations." The introductory script concluded, "This film is intended to serve as an example of the Greater German struggle for future generations. In creating this film the following [photographers of battle footage] fell for Führer and Fatherland." [The names of these men end the introduction.]

The young Luftwaffe is described by the narrator in *Feuertaufe* as "a sword in heaven." The narration is lively, at times almost ecstatic, as the glorification of Hermann Göring and his Luftwaffe unfolds. The film emphasizes the crucial role of the Air Force in saving lives, in providing reconnaissance information for the Army, and in destroying Polish rail and communications centers. One of *Baptism*'s most effective scenes shows the destruction of an enemy train concentration by low-flying dive-bombers. The narrator strongly implies that the Luftwaffe only attacked military installations, a false claim that was not abandoned by Luftwaffe spokesmen until the second stage of the Battle of Britain in late 1940. The sadism of the German bombers is actually glorified in *Feuertaufe,* Hippler evidently believing that it might be favorably received by the German people. Bombs fall on Poland as Luftwaffe fliers sing about flying through the Polish land and bombs raining "down from the sky, down there in smoke and flames." Hermann Göring, in total control of air operations, is shown with Hitler. The last scene of *Baptism of Fire* is entirely different from that of *Campaign in Poland.* In *Feuertaufe,* Göring himself addresses the theater audience, declaring, "What the Luftwaffe has promised in Poland, it will make good in England and France." The field marshal recommends this film, which concludes with a chorus singing anti-British songs. The final shot is of a map of the British Isles, the last sound, that of an exploding bomb. Audiences were exhilarated as they streamed out of the theaters.

Goebbels' propaganda machine mobilized all its resources to bring this film to the attention of private theater owners and potential audiences.[42] The reviewer for the *Berliner Morgenpost* described himself as overcome by "breathless tension" while experiencing *Baptism of Fire,* a "heroic epic." The *B.Z. am Mittag* called the movie "incomparable," "shattering," while the *Berliner Lokal-Anzeiger* saw in it a "powerful tempo," a warning to all the enemies of the Reich. Goebbels' film people in the ministry and the Reich Film Chamber prepared elaborate booklets for private theater owners, explaining why they should rent the film and how they should advertise it. The campaign for *Feuertaufe* represented a mobilization of several mass media to enable the regime to use film as a means of explaining and justifying the war. The packet prepared for theater owners included a one-page summary of the script, which could be duplicated and given to patrons or prospective theatergoers. The owners were told that it was their national duty to show this film. They were also warned against using placards or advertisements of their own design. Only materials provided by the official distributor, Tobis Studio, were suitable for such use. There was nothing original about their design, but they provide us with good examples of Nazi stylized heroism and wartime excitement in the cause of destruction. After in effect telling theater owners that they had to screen the film, the studio cheered them up by describing the great success that the film would enjoy, a film which contained scenes never before shown, not even in *Campaign in Poland* or in "German Weekly Newsreels."

Hippler's men suggested ways in which the cinema owners could attract a clientele and make the setting for the film more attractive and more stirring. If there was a Luftwaffe or flak unit stationed in the areas, why not have it on stage before the first showing of *Feuertaufe* so that the men might sing "Bombs over England" or other hit songs of the day, including the most popular song of all, "We Are Marching Against England"? Theater owners were encouraged to organize special screenings for schools, organizations, and party and Wehrmacht units. They could also arrange and pay for the printing of leaflets and handbills so long as these were designed along lines indicated by the studio. Many of the advertisements for the film *Baptism of Fire* included the complete text of "Bombs over England," almost encouraging audiences to sing along with their men. An advertising blitz for the film brought out another interesting fact: *Baptism of Fire* was considered too serious to be lumped together on the same page with the usual feature films. Its prominent notices appeared on newspaper pages devoted to the legitimate theater. Before the end of the year, Goebbels, heeding the growing shortage of paper, forbade advertisements taking up more than half a

Handbills and advertisements for the film *Baptism of Fire*. The mood of the publicity suggested a combination of heroism, sadism, and destruction. The UFA Palast am Zoo was one of Germany's great motion picture theaters, often used for the premiere of important films.

CREDIT: The International Museum of Photography, Rochester, New York page of a newspaper, even for "premieres of films of above average quality."

VICTORY IN THE WEST

PRODUCTION: German Film Society (introduction only) and
               Noldan Productions
DIRECTORS: S. Noldan and F. Brunsch
PREMIERE: Early 1941

A documentary which Goebbels did not consider above average in quality was *Victory in the West (Sieg im Westen)*, a work produced by the Army High Command with the collaboration of Fritz Hippler, the Army film office, and the propaganda companies.[43] This long film celebrated the conquest of France in June 1940. It was fundamentally a film made by the Army for the people, in effect circumventing the Goebbels operation. *Victory in the West* paid the obligatory homage to Hitler's genius as a field commander, but it gave little attention to the Luftwaffe. The film glorified the German soldier and his commanders. The OKH, or Army High Command, including Supreme Commander von Brauchitsch himself, sponsored the festive military gala premiere at Berlin's West End Theater. Embellishing the occasion were an orchestra and a military brass band with standard bearers. Germans wanted to see this film, for it celebrated, in a much more elaborate manner, a far greater event than the fall of Poland. The battle footage in *Victory in the West* was chosen from more than four times as much propaganda company film footage as that of *Baptism of Fire*. Goebbels had to go along with the Army, but he sabotaged this movie in as many ways as he could, once it was completed. Arguing that people would be too caught up in the January 30, 1941, celebration of eight years of Hitler, the minister postponed the premiere of the film until January 31, after having delayed publicity notices in the press and on radio. Within a day of its successful premiere, Goebbels told his conferees to tone down the publicity for the film, since it contained historical and psychological errors which could not be concealed. *Victory in the West* did not glorify National Socialism or the Third Reich in the manner of other documentary films commissioned by the party or the Propaganda Ministry. It was for this reason that Goebbels intervened; but despite his concerns, he could not ban the OKH film outright, and it enjoyed great popularity during the war years. Even Stalin may have seen it in the Kremlin, which received a copy by Soviet request.

The first part of *Victory in the West* was a classic German nationalist interpretation of modern German history. A Nazi like Goebbels would have found it unexceptionable, if incomplete, had it given Hitler a more central role. The film portrayed a peaceful, happy German Reich (between the Rhine, Danube, and Vistula) disrupted by the Thirty Years War. Britain and France then created the Treaty of Westphalia, which kept the Reich disunited while they built their world empires. The just victory of 1871 led to the anti-German encirclement policies of the Entente, which caused the First World War. The German Army conquered, but was stabbed in the back while the Allies were blockading and starving the German people. Shameful men signed the *Schandfrieden* of Versailles, a disgraceful peace that led the *Volk* to cry out for justice and revenge. The result was Hitler's Seizure of Power. Hitler broke the chains of Versailles, and this caused a frightened British government to take up its encirclement policies and to arm for a war against the Third Reich. This treatment of contemporary German history largely ignored the party and its struggles against the Weimar Republic, and this alone doomed the film in Goebbels' eyes.

The main part of *Victory in the West* was devoted to the *Blitzkrieg* against the Low Countries and France. Some background on the Polish campaign appeared, informing audiences that Poland had become the aggressive tool of the West. Germans trusted their Führer, in whose hands the fate of Germany lay, and Hitler justified this faith by his brilliant 1940 Ardennes offensive. The movie rationalized the German invasion of neutral Belgium, Luxembourg, and Holland by declaring that the Allies intended to march through Belgium on their way to the Ruhr, Germany's industrial heartland. As proof, the narrator cited Belgian cooperation with the Allied armies, and he implied that this collaboration antedated the German entry into Belgium on May 10, 1940. The film showed prominent army generals such as von Brauchitsch and Halder, chief of the general staff. Much of the battle footage of *Victory in the West* gave a greater sense of actuality than that of *Campaign in Poland.* It seemed less hurried and more balanced. The use of captured French newsreel film showing the Maginot Line and declaring, "We will conquer because we are stronger," made the German military achievement, which audiences were about to see, appear even more striking because of the technique of understated but ironic contrast.

German irony tends to boomerang, however, and snide references to the "wreckage" of an escaping British army at Dunkirk may have made Goebbels and other German film watchers uneasy during the winter of 1941. German documentaries of this period made little use of understatement, and their mocking use of the 1939 British song "We'll hang our washing on the Siegfried Line if the Siegfried Line's still there" may not have made the proper impression at a time when Britain was still very much in the war. The utter defeat of France was almost anticlimactic in *Victory in the West,* though it was in this last part of the film that certain themes dear to party propagandists made their appearance. Audiences were shown German munitions workers, the "best friends" of the German soldier (theme: unity of homeland and front); pious church scenes in Gothic cathedrals (theme: Germany the guardian of religion and culture); black colonial troops in the French Army (theme: France the racial poisoner of Europe); German soldiers saving the Rouen cathedral, set afire by retreating French troops (theme: France the fraudulent "grande nation" and self-proclaimed land of civilization).

The *Deutsche Wochenschau* unit produced its last full-length documentary in 1944, a grotesque item entitled *Traitors before the People's Court (Verräter vor dem Volksgericht).* The footage was filmed at the trial of some of the July 20, 1944, conspirators, officers who had attempted to kill Hitler. The psychotic and at times incoherent presiding judge, Roland Freisler, dominates the movie by screaming obscenities and denunciations at the helpless prisoners, who somehow maintain their "Prussian" dignity in the face of this madman. The existence of the film caused uneasiness in Army circles, especially among cadets, and the movie was never released for general viewing. The Reich Film Chamber supplied a print to Martin Bormann, who, of all people, should have enjoyed its contents. Bormann hesitated, however, and he ordered that *Traitors* not be sent out to individual Gauleiters even as a party film, since they might show it to unauthorized persons. This could lead to "undesirable" discussions about the manner in which the trial was carried out. Hinkel informed Naumann in August 1944 that the film would be screened before the assembled Gauleiters at their next

---

U-BOATS WESTWARD!

PRODUCTION: UFA
DIRECTOR: Günther Rittau
SCRIPT: Georg Zoch
MAJOR PERFORMERS: Ilse Werner
                       Herbert Wilk
PREMIERE: May 9, 1941

meeting.[44] Thus, the last full-length production of the *Wochenschau* staff was at once its most infamous and most unsuccessful film.

Goebbels and Hippler were aware that fictional stories could be more effective than pure documentaries in boosting civilian morale and transmitting an ideological message. Two productions of the 1940–41 period reflected this assumption, though one was a more skillful film. *U-boats Westward! (U-Boote Westwärts!)* glorified the fighting sailors of the German submarine fleets involved in a heroic attempt to break Britain's hold on North Atlantic sea lines and thereby bring the enemy to its knees. *U-boats* presented these German fighting men as human beings, tough and sentimental in turn, sailors who dreamed of their wives or girl friends, carried out their dangerous mission against the enemy, and listened to shortwave radio broadcasts beamed from the homeland. These were decent, brave men doing their duty for *Volk* and fatherland: Admiral Dönitz had a cameo role at the end of the film, thanking his men when they returned and awarding posthumous decorations and medals to fallen officers and men. The combat scenes were effective and the acting was adequate; these qualities attracted audiences to the film. Yet within this structure of a typical wartime film, ideology managed to make unobtrusive appearances. The clever way in which Nazi concepts were woven into the fabric of the plot without detracting from the human-interest aspects of a movie portraying combat is worth noting.

The musical part of the sound track is dominated by the song "We Are Marching Against England," and the portrayal of the British adversary is entirely negative, with one small exception. The British naval commanders are deceptive, employing wicked techniques to destroy the Germans: In one scene a supposedly innocent fishing boat is actually beaming signals to a British destroyer indicating the position of a surfaced U-boat. The perfidious British even make use of so-called neutral shipping to achieve their ends, in one instance using a Dutch ship to import propeller parts to Britain through a war zone. One scene does portray a British ship taking a wounded German sailor out of the sea to safety, but this was the film's only concession to traditional views of British probity and fairness. More typical is the craven British officer who screams "They'll kill us!" when a decent German submarine crew is about to rescue his men after their ship has been torpedoed. The German commander had made the decision to torpedo that boat even though German POWs were on board. Lest this action confuse the audience, a dying German sailor murmurs the words "It is beautiful and honorable to die for the fatherland." The National Socialist cult of transfiguration in death thus makes its triumphant appearance (realistic scenes of German war dead were forbidden, as they were in American wartime films). At the conclusion of *U-boats Westward!*, Admiral Dönitz, whose appearance gives the film a documentary aura, tells his men, "The fight goes on . . . ," and uses three crucial phrases in the German wartime vocabulary, "fighting, sacrificing, conquering." A rousing chorus of "We Are Marching Against England" brings the film to an end.

Hans Bertram's *Fighter Squadron Lützow (Kampfgeschwader Lützow)* was a far clumsier effort, one which interspersed documentary-style battle footage with a wildly improbable story.[45] The film glorified the fighting men of Luftwaffe combat crews and thanked in its credits the Army, Navy, and Air Force for their assistance. Bertram knew all about aviation, having made several flights around the world. His account of one of these voyages had been a best-selling book in the 1930s. The battle footage was shot in or over northern Germany, the General Government (formerly Poland), and "in numerous theaters of operations." The weakness of the film was not its combat scenes, but rather its absurd script. Hence its failure as a box-office attraction. The film represented, at least in part, an attempt to capitalize upon the success of the prewar production *Pour le mérite* (1938), but as a glorification of the Luftwaffe, it fell far short of *Baptism of Fire*.

FIGHTER SQUADRON LÜTZOW

PRODUCTION: Tobis
DIRECTOR: Hans Bertram
SCRIPT: H. Bertram, W. Neumeister, H. Orlovius
MAJOR PERFORMERS: C. Kayssler
                         H. Braun
                         Heinz Welzel
                         C. Loeck
PREMIERE: February 28, 1941

Lützow was, however, a fictional war film which contained ideological messages important to the regime and for this reason it retains some interest. The Nazis often claimed that they represented the authentic voice of the *breiten Massen*, of the broad masses of the *Volk*. The Luftwaffe, the youngest and presumably most National Socialist branch of the armed forces, aggressively reflected this camaraderie within the community of battle. In *Lützow* the new squadron commander is supposedly the opposite of the old "Prussian" military types who were still dominant figures in the Army. As in *U-boats Westward!*, the commander (Carl Raddatz) fraternizes with his men, bantering with them in a familiar manner, like a friendly guest of honor at a wedding. Yet the cultural and social chasm between the officer and his men never disappears. Other concepts dear to Nazi ideologists appear in *Lützow*. Two Luftwaffe men manage to slip through Polish lines in order to rescue ethnic Germans. When these men are not pursuing the same girl, in one of the more absurd love triangles of Third Reich cinema, they are helping to sink an eight-thousand-ton British freighter. One of the men is critically wounded in this attack, but in a gesture of ultimate heroism, he guides his crippled plane back to safety and thus preserves the lives of his fellow crewmen. The audience does not see much gore, only the heroic transfiguration of a fine young German. Lest this leave spectators somewhat depressed, the sound track of *Lützow* concludes with a chorus singing a Luftwaffe marching tune. Thus, an "apolitical" war film managed to support and convey Nazi ideological aims in three crucial areas: social egalitarianism in a common struggle, aid for *Volksdeutsche*, and heroic death as transfiguration. As the *Illustrierter Film-Kurier* wrote, "And his sacrifice will never be forgotten."

RETURN

PRODUCTION: Wien-Film GmbH.
DIRECTOR: Gustav von Ucicky
SCRIPT: Gerhard Menzel
MAJOR PERFORMERS: Paula Wessely
                        Peter Petersen
                        Carl Raddatz
PREMIERE: October 10, 1941

German wartime films which did not claim to be documentaries in any sense were often so larded with National Socialist ideology that they also defied the label "entertainment." An entire feature was often devoted to a single National Socialist message. These films were contemporary in their settings, but their themes were so heavy-handed that theatergoers generally avoided them, no matter how good the acting or direction might be. *Return (Heimkehr)* was elaborately produced in the Vienna studio by Gustav von Ucicky; the starring role was played by Paula Wessely, who no longer (1941) spoke of her years of apprenticeship with the Jew Max Reinhardt. *Heimkehr* was a caricature. Hans Hagge correctly called it "This unique song of hate," a "justification of the extermination campaign against the Poles." [46] Production began early in 1941. *Heimkehr* was one of the most vicious productions of the Goebbels-Hippler-Hinkel cinematic empire, a film totally lacking in subtlety. The setting was Poland in 1939; the story dealt with the fate of ethnic Germans in the district of Luzk in eastern Poland. The introduction informs us that "this film tells the story of a handful of German people whose forefathers emigrated to the east many decades ago because the homeland had no place for them. In the year 1939 they returned home, home to a new, strong Reich. What they experienced was true of hundreds of thousands of others who shared the same fate." [47]

The opening scene of *Heimkehr* is set in Luzk on March 27, 1939. Growing tension between Poland and the Reich is encouraging the excesses of chauvinistic, anti-German Polish "subhumans." These *Untermenschen* are enthusiastically whitewashing a sign which designates the local German school. A little German boy cries as the inhuman Poles pile up the school's furniture on the street and burn it. As a blackboard goes up in flames, we see that the words "Greater Germany" and some population statistics had been written on it by the diligent German teacher. Maria, a German woman, is a tower of moral strength for the German community, but even she receives no justice at the hands of Polish governmental officials. They will not order the school reopened. In one grotesque scene set in the town's little film theater, the predominantly Polish audience becomes menacing when they hear the Germans speaking their own language. When three Germans do not stand up while the Polish national anthem is being played in a newsreel, the Polish mob goes crazy and beats them up. A policeman arrives on the scene only to throw the Germans out of the theater! The owner will not even allow Maria's critically injured fiancé to lie on the sidewalk in front of his cinema until his ambulance arrives. Then the Polish attendant will not admit the man (Carl Raddatz once again) to the hospital. The shocked, furious Maria points to the crucifix on the wall over his head and tells him, "Think of God!" Her fiancé, a doctor himself, dies outside the hospital while this is going on.

It is obvious that there no longer is justice for *Volksdeutsche* in Poland, and Maria begins to despair. Polish troops are visible on every street, evidence of Poland's hostile intentions. Poles in official positions claim that the German minority still possesses all its rights, but we see the truth before our eyes: Poles stare approvingly at posters in the public square which show how the Polish Army will threaten Berlin; the German school remains closed; Germans lose their property on August 1 without compensation. An elderly German, a prominent member of the community, is blinded by a Pole using a slingshot, but the Polish official tells Maria that the regrettable incident had nothing to do with politics or the victim's ethnic identity. Polish Jews have a role in *Heimkehr;* though brief, it is characteristic. Maria walks by a stall run by an old Jew selling linen. He holds his wares before her, speaking Yiddish-sounding German as he praises the German people as a great nation. The Jew regrets only that Hitler does not like his people, to which Maria wittily responds, "You should write him a letter!" As she cheerfully walks off, we hear the Jew muttering horrible imprecations against the accursed German people.

As the story emerges, the time frame becomes the very eve of the Second World War. The German community is in danger of being exterminated. *Heimkehr* includes one scene of a Polish pogrom against the Germans that summarizes much of Nazi wartime ideology within a few minutes. Poles ransack and burn a German farmstead. They run about like crazed animals, and one ferocious "subhuman" tears a swastika necklace from the bosom of a terrified German woman, grunting in delight as he does so. Once again, the Nazis have projected their own crimes onto their victims. Just as the old Jewish merchant threatened the destruction of the German nation, so the Poles go berserk with lust as they kill and rob the poor oppressed ethnic Germans. When war breaks out, the Polish Army rounds up Maria and her fellow Germans, putting them in a crowded dungeon; the Poles plan to gun down every last man, woman, and child among them. Maria continues to be a beacon of hope, a stoic study in German courage. This was a favorite device; the Nazis loved to use idealized female figures as pure symbols of Germandom leading a troubled people back to salvation—in a man's world.

In despair and fear, Maria dreams of the German *Heimat*, of a day when she will no longer have to hear Yiddish or Polish, but only German. Many of the favorite Nazi wartime code words and expressions appear: "courage," "it is not in vain," "homeland," "faith." The strains of the "Deutschlandlied" are heard in the background, perhaps wafting down from heaven, as the whole group begins to sing of the homeland. Then a near miracle occurs, for the rumble of German tanks is heard. A Luftwaffe attack scatters the garrison which was about to murder the Germans. Maria screams, "The Germans are coming," reflecting an ecstasy not widely shared in Europe at the time. Perhaps a reading of Karl May's German novels about the American West influenced this ending. The Luftwaffe and the panzers were the cavalry, the Germans the white settlers, and the Poles the Indians. Hitler did recommend May's work to his generals when discussing future German policy in the east. The film has the ultimate happy conclusion for ethnic Germans. They return to the Reich, crossing the old German-Polish frontier as a large smiling photograph of the Führer welcomes them, thus blessing their *Heimkehr.*

Heimkehr was the contribution of the screen to a coordinated campaign undertaken by several German mass media after August 1939. Goebbels had begun talking about producing such a film as early as December 1939. The German press received orders to accuse the Poles of persecuting ethnic Germans as soon as Hitler's policy became openly anti-Polish. After war broke out on September 1, 1939, the Nazis accused the Poles of aggression and greatly increased their atrocity propaganda. The Germans claimed that Poles had murdered many German civilians at Bromberg on "Bloody Sunday," September 10.[48] Propaganda agencies of state and party published posters in remembrance of the terrible event. The message of *Heimkehr* was that these *Volksdeutsche* survived to return to the Reich, whereas brethren such as the Bromberg martyrs never made it home. Yet while the Bromberg incident and photographic "proofs" may not have been faked by the Germans, one German document supports a suspicious attitude about the "massacre." On August 30, eleven days *before* the alleged murders, the usually unreliable German News Agency made the following information available to its subscribers: "Ethnic German refugees who crossed the border overnight report that in the district of Bromberg the Poles instructed their women as follows: 'We will fight to the last drop of blood and destroy every German down to the last child. If things go badly, however, then you have to burn out the eyes of the Germans with boiling water.' " [49]

The propaganda surrounding *Heimkehr* emphasized the theme of stout German hearts enduring endless agonies in order to remain German and return to the Reich. One publicity notice called attention to those scenes in *Heimkehr* which evoked the joy of the righteous and the simple pride of those sacrificing for a great goal. Wilhelm Utermann, reviewing the film on October 24, 1941, for the *Völkischer Beobachter,* drew an even broader lesson from the motion picture. He believed that the theme of *Heimkehr* transcended the ethnic Germans in Poland. Utermann declared that the friends of those murderous Poles, the "plutocratic democracies," had intended to destroy Germany and the Germans, "To murder them, to exterminate them." [50] Maybe Utermann had in mind the Polish actor in *Heimkehr* who had been murdered in March by Polish nationalists for his pro-Nazi sympathies.[51]

Early in 1940 the German Foreign Ministry published a book containing atrocity photographs, allegedly of victims of Polish terror against ethnic Germans in Schulitz and Bromberg, 1939. Visual atrocity propaganda such as this was rare in Goebbels' use of the mass media. He objected to it until late 1944, fearing that photographs of this sort would undermine German home-front morale during the Russian campaign.

CREDIT: German Foreign Ministry

Another way of bringing the theory of Slavic subhumanity to the attention of the German people. A German woman found guilty of having had sexual intercourse with a Pole is bound to a post with him, as expiation for the sin of having committed *Blutschande,* or "racial disgrace." The Nazis shaved her head and forced her to hold a sign alluding to her "nefarious" deed.

CREDIT: University of Michigan Library, Ann Arbor, Michigan

The RPL and the propaganda ministry made sure that the anti-Polish campaign reached the intellectual and academic strata of the population. Tiessler and Berndt felt that too many people at home and abroad believed that the great sixteenth-century scientist Nicolaus Copernicus was a Pole, not a German. They decided to use the four hundredth anniversary of his death as a pretext for disproving this fallacy.[52] The ministry sent five confidential, schematic biographies of Copernicus to every Reich propaganda office for its own information. Tiessler pointed out that because of the war situation, major celebrations could not take place, though there would be a small-scale memorial service at the University of Königsberg on May 22–24, 1943. The major contribution of Nazi scholarship to these proceedings was the first volume of Dr. Fritz Kubach's edition of the complete works of Copernicus, which would contain texts in both the original Latin and in German translation. Writing "On the Four Hundredth Anniversary of the Death of the Great German Nicholas Copernicus," Kubach described the Pole as "a great German scientist" and disparaged Polish scholarship on Copernicus. Kubach argued that Copernicus had been born in Cracow, a town which owed its rise and prosperity to Germans.

The agony and salvation of the *Volksdeutsche* as a theme of German propaganda was not confined to a Polish setting. The theme could be taken up or suppressed, depending upon Hitler's foreign policy at the moment, but materials were assiduously collected for possible use. In 1939 Goebbels ordered that materials on "the oppression of ethnic Germans in Yugoslavia" be put together.[53] When Yugoslavia, under the regent Prince Paul, pursued a neutral policy increasingly friendly to the Reich, the materials were filed away but not forgotten. In March 1941 Paul joined the Tripartite Pact, but within a few days a military coup in Belgrade overthrew him and gave young King Peter plenary powers. The reversal of Yugoslav foreign policy in a pro-Soviet, pro-British direction infuriated Hitler, who vowed to crush the Yugoslav state. He planned to attack Yugoslavia and Greece with lightning blows on April 6, but until that time public calm must be maintained so as not to alert Germany's enemies. On April 1 Goebbels pretended that he was cautious about using reports regarding "acts of terror by Serbs against ethnic Germans," because they were not precise or substantial enough. Publishing uncon-firmed rumors, he claimed, would undermine "the credibility of our news policy."[54] Goebbels was not noted for deep research into the reliability of useful propaganda material, so another motive must have been behind his cautious attitude and policy. Goebbels realized that atrocity propaganda would be seen in Belgrade and elsewhere as the prelude to a German invasion. Why provide advance notice to the enemy in this hazardous situation which involved not only Yugoslavia, but also the war against Britain, and German-Soviet relations?

When the Germans invaded Yugoslavia, Goebbels' propaganda made use of material accumulated since 1939.[55] The German press emphasized the atrocities committed against *Volksdeutsche* by Serbs, and it began to differentiate between Serbs and Croatians, who were seen as an oppressed victims of pan-Serb nationalism and natural friends of the Germans. One cartoon showed a German peasant woman holding a baby while a ferocious dog labeled "Serbia" growled menacingly at her. It is interesting that a scene quite similar to this appeared in the film *Heimkehr.* German propagandists soon began to refer to Serbia's "blood guilt" in unleashing the First World War. A German lieutenant removed the tablet in Sarajevo which commemorated the assassination of Franz Ferdinand in 1914, and personally presented it to Hitler, who ordered that it be exhibited in the Berlin army museum. The major product of this 1941 propaganda blitz was the motion picture *In the Eye of the Storm,* which was released in December. *Menschen im Sturm* starred the popular Olga Tschechowa, but even she could not salvage the film from the melodramatic, uneven script and direction.

The plot of *Menschen im Sturm* is trite and obvious. A group of virtuous, hard-working ethnic Germans try to survive the increasingly vicious persecution of the Serbs. Heavy-handed symbolism conveys the eternal Nazi message of the struggle between light and darkness: A little girl cries while Serb beasts burn a German homestead. The heroine realizes that these pogroms are visited upon people because they are German, and she returns to her German ethnic consciousness. Her friend Alexander, a Yugoslav of Slovene origin, is carefree, rich, and cosmopolitan. There is a Nazi lesson in his fate, for Alexander is caught in the Serb police net and arrested. Any decent Yugoslav had to be friendly to the Germans, but a close social or personal relationship between German and Slav was bound to end in tragedy. Many scenes of *Menschen im Sturm* recall *Heimkehr:* the burning of the German library, the wrecking of the German school, the breathtaking escape to the border, the heroic role played by a German woman. The woman's role might be called the Queen Luise syndrome, after the romantic image of the queen of Prussia who saved the defeated land in 1807 by intervening with Napoleon and the czar of Russia. Without losing her dignity or her virtue, Olga Tschechowa flirts with the Serb commander and leads him to believe she shares his amorous desires. In this way she distracts him while some of her companion *Volksdeutsche* head for the border.

Some scenes symbolize the plight and heroism of the persecuted German minority. While the mother entertains the Serb officers, her daughter innocently turns on the radio. The station, probably Graz, is playing a Prussian march; the mother quickly turns off the radio, preserving her credibility with the Serbs even at the risk of alienating her German-conscious little girl. One scene justifies the Nazi wartime cliché of the decent, pro-German attitude of the Croatian people: A Croatian druggist aids the Germans ("Every decent Croat is friendly to the Germans, that is self-evident"), only to be murdered by Serb thugs. The conclusion of the film offers some excitement as the hunted Germans successfully flee through the woods to the border. It is also absurdly melodramatic when the radiant heroine admits to the vicious Serb commissar, "Yes, it is true, I have helped my fellow countrymen." She is proud and happy and will achieve National Socialist immortality. While escaping, she is shot by the Serbs. The martyr dies happily, yet another Nazi victory-in-death heroine, knowing that her fellow ethnic Germans are safe in the Reich. Her heroic death and transfiguration did not save *Menschen im Sturm,* however. It was too blatantly political in the most cliché-ridden manner to attract large numbers of theatergoers. The film was a testimony to the Nazi penchant for combining current events and wartime ideology; it was not popular entertainment.

REQUEST CONCERT

PRODUCTION: Cine-Allianz Tonfilmproduktion GmbH
DIRECTOR: Eduard von Borsody
SCRIPT: F. Lützkendorf, E. von Borsody
MAJOR PERFORMERS: Ilse Werner
                               Carl Raddatz
PREMIERE: December 30, 1940

In the eyes of Goebbels and Hippler a great film should be entertaining *and* substantial at the same time. They actually achieved this synthesis in *Request Concert,* one of the most popular "apolitical" films of the wartime Third Reich. *Wunschkonzert* borrowed its title from a popular radio program broadcast on Sunday afternoon throughout the Reich and occupied Europe. It was even beamed via shortwave to the officers and men of the German Navy. The format, structured by the master of ceremonies Heinz Goedecke, consisted of popular music, marches, classical pieces, and even comic sketches. The program was extraordinarily popular during the early war years, not because of its content, but because of its claim that broadcasts consisted of material requested by the fighting men of the German armed forces. The program thus seemed to unite homeland and front in a community of enjoyment. The sense of participation owed some of its strength to the presence of an enthusiastic audience in the studio during the live broadcast. Early in the war Goebbels realized how effective *Request Concert* was, and he insisted that all leading German performers be willing to contribute their talents to Goedecke's show. When famed actor Hans Albers declared that he had no time for such participation, the minister made it clear to him that he had two days in which to change his mind.[56]

The success of the radio program led to the publication of a widely distributed book of the same title, coedited by Heinz Goedecke and Wilhelm Krug.[57] It seemed logical to Goebbels and his film men that a movie making use of the "request concert" idea might attract millions of theater patrons. This assumption proved correct, and the film *Request Concert* became one of the most widely seen motion pictures in the wartime Third Reich. The seemingly innocent, purely entertaining radio program was a major success for Goebbels' radio propaganda, for it promoted the unity of party (Goedecke was a prominent Nazi, something not advertised by the ministry), nation, and Wehrmacht. It did so in a way that seemed nonideological and unobtrusive, and this was all to the good in Goebbels' eyes. The film *Request Concert* was an even greater success. Using the device of a touching love story, tragic and comic in turn, *Wunschkonzert* put several major themes of Nazi wartime ideology on a human level, thereby appealing to non-Nazis, the very people Goebbels needed to reach.

The story of *Request Concert* concerns a German officer, Herbert Koch (Carl Raddatz), and a young girl, Inge Wagner (Ilse Werner), who meet at the 1936 Berlin Olympics and immediately fall in love. He is suave, dashing, and decent; she is lovely and innocent. The couple is repeatedly separated by the officer's duty to the fatherland, for he serves in Spain, on the western front, and in the war against England. Because of the secrecy of his mission to Spain with the famed Condor Legion, they lose contact with each other. They are eventually reunited because Herbert has asked Goedecke to play the Olympic fanfare on his program, knowing that Inge will respond by asking the MC for the identity and location of the man who requested the music. After a series of misadventures and comic blunders, the couple is reunited in love, though in good National Socialist fashion the ending of the film implies that Herbert may once again be on the march, this time against England.

The average German who saw this film once, twice, or even three

An aspect of the multimedia propaganda for the *Request Concert* program. This is the cover of the book *We Begin the Request Concert for the Wehrmacht,* by Heinz Goedecke and Wilhelm Krug.

times ignored the improbable plot and enjoyed the love story, the good acting, and the fantasy world which the clever direction of Eduard von Borsody had created. Nazi wartime ideology made its appearance, but in a manner calculated to be fairly subtle. Inge's aunt and guardian, for example, muses sadly to the young girl about her own youth in the days of Wilhelmian Germany. She too has been in love, but with a young man of a higher social class. She could not marry him because her father was only an artisan. A surprised Inge, living in the "people's state" of the Third Reich, asks her aunt, "Is that possible?" and the aunt sadly replies, "In those days, yes." The Nazi ethos of heroic self-sacrifice in battle was manifest in *Request Concert* in many ways. Herbert and his men will suffer any privation in order to fight for the Reich, and this in turn means fighting for German culture. There are interesting juxtapositions in the film which bring out this theme. A soldier who is seen at home on leave plays Beethoven on the piano; the same man returns to the western front and dies while playing the organ in a church demolished by French artillery. So much for the French as guardians of western civilization! This soldier, by his heroism, saved his unit, for the French attack upon the church allowed them to escape to safety. The sound of the organ brought the shells of the enemy artillery battery down upon the building, since the French assumed that this was the base for a whole company of the Wehrmacht. The organist does not merely die a heroic death; he is transfigured, blazing faith in his eyes and German culture in his heart. Once again the Hitler motif appears: "He who has faith in his heart possess the strongest power in the world."

The portrayal of different social classes in the film is highly revealing. Despite all the talk about a "people's state" and the "masses" "Ordinary people . . . are shown in civilian life to be simple souls; and in war . . . they know their place and respectfully obey their superior officers." [58] The soldiers who are artisans and workers are devoted to their duty and to their orders at the front; at home they are real clowns. The hero, however, is never ridiculous and always knows how to live up to the excellence of his character and the status of his position. And for spectators devoted to high culture, there is a cameo appearance by a young conductor directing the orchestra in the *Marriage of Figaro* overture. The conductor is the famed Eugen Jochum, who today would probably just as soon forget his role in *Request Concert.*

The conclusion of the film cleverly combined a happy ending to the love story with a rousing chorus of "We Are Marching Against England." Thus, even love triumphant was not beyond the reach of National Socialist wartime propaganda.

8

Nazi Ideals and Demons in Feature Films: From Friedrich Schiller *to* Rite of Sacrifice

The most famous and infamous wartime German films all contained historical, political, and moral themes which reflected basic tenets of National Socialist ideology. Seven of these feature-length motion pictures were particularly effective in bringing the Nazi world view to the screen in a gripping manner. They fall into three major categories: (1) films treating great figures from the German past, in the process associating Hitler and his regime with cultural and political heroes familiar to the average German *(Friedrich Schiller, Bismarck, The Dismissal)*; (2) films attempting to alter German consciousness in a direction favored by the regime, preparing people for measures not yet openly discussed, such as the killing of the congenitally ill or the mass murder of the Jews *(I Accuse, The Eternal Jew, The Jew Süss)*; (3) feature films depicting lyrical, transcendent idealism, apparently escapist, but actually supportive of the social policies of the government *(Rite of Sacrifice)*.

The career of the actor Horst Caspar was that of a man whose manner reflected the tone and style of the "convinced National Socialist." Youthful, decisive, an inspired fanatic, these terms characterize Caspar in the German screen roles he played during the war, from *Friedrich Schiller* (1940) through *Kolberg* (1945). *Friedrich Schiller* was ostensibly a portrayal of the young poet and playwright, "the triumph of a genius" *(Der Triumph eines Genies)*, as the film's subtitle phrased it. This description was reminiscent of the title of Leni Riefenstahl's famous film about the 1934 party rally, *Triumph of the Will*. The similarity did not stop there. The young Friedrich Schiller is seen as a born genius, a striver for freedom and artistic integrity who confronts a hostile environment in military school. Schiller interrupts a debate before the grand duke of Württemberg to shout his belief that genius is born, not educated or cultivated. He rejects the Enlightenment belief in the potential equality of mankind through education. Moviegoers were supposed to see the young Schiller as a rebel against authority in the name of genius and fatherland; had not the young Hitler suffered similar agonies in his struggle for the triumph of *his* will? Goebbels himself brought out another dimension of the same theme when he spoke at the university of Heidelberg in 1943, declaring, "Leadership is born, education is acquired." [1] Despite these elements glorifying German genius, *Friedrich Schiller* contained themes which are surprising in the light of the censorship policies of the Third Reich. The young poet fights the oppressive grand duke in order to express freely his commitment to liberty on the stage. The poet Schubart, imprisoned by the grand duke and suffering in a dungeon, says, "In every corner of the world a strong man lords it over the weak. Where is freedom?" The writers and the director, Herbert Maisch, may well have included these and similar lines as a form of opposition to the regime, but the main theme of literary genius struggling for German freedom against a reactionary government was highly acceptable to National Socialists. The analogy with a political genius struggling for German freedom against the Weimar Republic was implicit.

FRIEDRICH SCHILLER, THE TRIUMPH OF A GENIUS

PRODUCTION: Tobis
DIRECTOR: Herbert Maisch
SCRIPT: W. Wassermann and C. H. Diller
MAJOR PERFORMERS: Horst Caspar
                       Heinrich George
PREMIERE: November 13, 1940

Goebbels and Hippler made much use of historical analogy in the wartime German cinema. No figure was more attractive to them than Otto von Bismarck, the German chancellor and minister-president of Prussia, the man who unified Germany by enabling Prussia to conquer the Reich. The wartime Third Reich produced two extravaganzas on the

Friedrich Schiller. The Triumph of a Genius: Horst Caspar as Schiller during a moment of inspiration.

Bismarck theme, *Bismarck* in 1940, and *The Dismissal* in 1942. Both were directed by the famed Wolfgang Liebeneiner, one of Goebbels' favorites. The films were purportedly based upon historical facts, and even though they took many liberties with history, they fell within Fritz Hippler's category of films which present historical truth "in a higher sense." [2] These movies not only embodied many of the clichés about the Iron Chancellor common in Germany, but, according to Hippler, they were successful in enveloping the past in the "national values" of the present. For these reasons, the Bismarck films became official "films of the nation."

   Bismarck stars Paul Hartmann as the Prussian minister-president and future German chancellor. Honest to the point of bluntness, this Bismarck of the 1860s is a paragon of national virtue, a good family man fanatically devoted to Prussia and Germany. These two entities are never permitted to clash, for the aim of the film is to present Bismarck as the

> ### *BISMARCK*
>
> STUDIO: Tobis
> DIRECTOR: W. Liebeneiner
> SCRIPT: R. Lauckner, W. Liebeneiner
> MAJOR PERFORMERS: Paul Hartmann
>   F. Kayssler
>   M. Koppenhöfer
>   Werner Hinz
>   Otto Gebühr
> PREMIERE: December 6, 1940

man who began the work completed by Adolf Hitler. Even the heroic trumpet fanfare which accompanies the credits as the film begins suggests this theme. The scene is Prussia in 1862, where a political battle with grave overtones is being waged between the old king, Wilhelm I, and the liberal majority in the Diet. While the *Volk* cries out for unification and the creation of a Reich able to defend Germany against rapacious neighbors, the liberals scheme to weaken the army and undermine the monarchy. The king even considers abdication, but in his despair turns instead to Bismarck and appoints the "hated man" minister-president: "He has courage," declares the king. Bismarck accepts this difficult task, and immediately confronts a pro-English court faction which is determined to create a parliamentary state on the model of Westminster. Liebeneiner's Bismarck is more than a Prussian patriot; he is a raving German nationalist, a man who declares, "Our goal is Germany!" Every German stereotype about this period appears in *Bismarck*. Napoleon III is portrayed as a scheming dilettante of little ability, a man who wants to preserve the "balance" between Austria and Prussia so that the French can steal German territory along the Rhine. Empress Eugénie, played by the beautiful Lil Dagover, is a frivolous courtesan who confuses Schleswig with Silesia.

Liebeneiner portrayed the parliamentary liberals as men obsessed with power, people who cared little about external threats to Germany so long as they could break the power of Bismarck and the king. The liberal leader Rudolf Virchow denounces the "Junker" reactionaries and describes the princes as the real scourge of the Reich. Bismarck tries to conciliate his parliamentary opponents, but to no avail. They are blinded by hatred, and they reject moderation, much as Hitler's enemies

Bismarck: A devious Napoleon III tries to make gains for France at Germany's expense, but is rebuffed and outmaneuvered by Otto von Bismarck.

supposedly did after 1939. Bismarck replies with his famous speech about "iron and blood," which throws the diet into an uproar: "You are violating the constitution!" "Who is this Bismarck anyway?" Virchow makes a statement defending the liberal position, a caricature of everything the Nazis despised about the liberal German tradition. He is proud of Germany's reputation as a land of poets and thinkers and lauds the unity of "heart and mind." Virchow goes so far as to accuse the Prussian war minister, von Roon, and Bismarck of being enemies of the people, "devoid of any patriotism." The resultant clash of words in the Diet leads Bismarck to dissolve it and call for new elections. He acts with sovereign equanimity, for "The newspapers are not the nation." Bismarck's convention with Russia, an anti-Polish move portrayed as foreshadowing Hitler's "brilliant" 1939 pact with Stalin, infuriates the press, which is pro-Polish. Bismarck, however, declares, "The convention with Russia means that our back is covered." There is an effective vignette of the old king, Wilhelm, enjoying tremendously a military parade. As in all Nazi epics, the selective use of military music is a key to establishing the tone of the film *Bismarck*.

Franz Joseph, emperor of Austria, schemes to recover the province of Silesia from Prussia: "If I can repay Prussia for what it did to Maria Theresa, it would be the happiest day of my life!" Almost everyone opposes the genius Bismarck, just as everyone seemed opposed to the genius Hitler in 1928. Bismarck is a lonely genius, as was the young Schiller, but like the poet he is sustained by his faith in himself and in his nation. Bismarck shores up the will of the old king, forcing Wilhelm to conform to the minister-president's concept of *raison d'état*. "Think of Prussia! Think of your forefathers, of your duty!" he prods. Bismarck leads Prussia into war with Denmark, justifiable to him on political grounds. The scenes depicting the Prussian victory are vintage Nazi cinema: battle diagrams, cheering crowds, artillery bombardments, military parades, and piety ("God has granted us victory"). Bismarck confronts the claims of Napoleon III like a good German, saying, "He won't get a single foot of German territory!" Napoleon, however, insists, "I'll take what I want." At this point Liebeneiner introduces an anti-Semitic theme, for Cohen-Blind, an English Jew, tries to murder Bismarck, but Bismarck is saved by "divine providence." This phrase, a favorite with Hitler, was used by the German press in 1944 to describe Hitler's survival of the Stauffenberg assassination attempt. The Cohen-Blind episode was a reminder of the assassination of German councillor Ernst von Rath by a Polish Jew in Paris in 1938. *Bismarck* thus makes a perfidious Jew the implicit agent of all of Germany's enemies. The film ends on a heroic, triumphant note. As a band plays "Watch on the Rhine," the Franco-Prussian war breaks out, leading to the unification of Germany in January 1871.

Bismarck cleverly took historical figures and situations and turned them into themes which justified Nazi ideology by relating them to the "work" of Adolf Hitler. This is what the "critic" Dr. Hans Bode had to say about *Bismarck* in 1941: [3]

> For old and young alike, it is possible to make certain comparisons with the present era. Bismarck began a new chapter of German history. He reunited the forces of Germany by alliances with its princes. Sixty years later our Führer Adolf Hitler succeeded in uniting the German people under central leadership. He too had to prevail over a world filled with enemies. At home as well as abroad, these enemies were at first stronger than the Führer. But he prevailed all the same, because he believed in his mission and was

convinced that his work would succeed. The merit of the film *Bismarck* is in bringing the past back to life and provoking such thoughts in the minds of its audience. It is so gripping, so striking, that after seeing it several members of the audience preferred ... to ignore the rest of the program in order to reflect at their leisure upon what they had just experienced.

The success of *Bismarck* led Goebbels, Hippler, and Liebeneiner to create a sequel in 1942, *The Dismissal (Die Entlassung)*, which dealt with Bismarck's fall from power in 1890. The old chancellor was portrayed by Emil Jannings, perhaps Germany's greatest actor. Famous to international audiences for his role as the schoolteacher in the screen version of Heinrich Mann's *Professor Unrat (The Blue Angel)*, Jannings was a powerful screen presence who dominated any film in which he appeared. If Goebbels and his men built a film around Jannings, it meant that the motion picture was a major priority of the Reich. Jannings was a difficult, tempestuous individual, so it was gratifying to Goebbels and Hippler when he cooperated to the extent of writing a little essay comparing Bismarck and Hitler as two men who struggled and prevailed against the main currents of their times. In *The Dismissal (Die Entlassung)*, Bismarck is an irascible old German nationalist who is destroyed by Wilhelm II and the dilettantes around the young kaiser, as well as by the evil "gray eminence" of the foreign office, Holstein. The script is not devoid of sympathy for the young emperor, who understands something about the plight of the proletariat, but it leaves the last word to old Bismarck: "Germany, Germany. Who will complete my work?" The audience was supposed to provide the answer in 1942: Hitler.

THE DISMISSAL

STUDIO: Tobis
DIRECTOR: W. Liebeneiner
SCRIPT: C. J. Braun, F. von Eckardt
MAJOR PERFORMERS: Emil Jannings
                 T. Loos
                 Werner Hinz
                 Werner Krauss
PREMIERE: October 6, 1942

The script presented the regime with certain problems, and these accounted for the long delay in releasing the motion picture to general audiences. The film was ready for public screening by July 1942, but it did not receive its Berlin premiere until the autumn. The major reason for the delay was its delineation of Bismarck's foreign policy. In the script Bismarck is a genius because he avoids the possibility of a two-front war for Germany by his Reinsurance Treaty with Russia (1887). Wilhelm II and Holstein overthrow Bismarck, and this turns Russia into an enemy. One final segment of *The Dismissal* even shows the Russian ambassador telling his coachman, "To the French embassy!" A scene of this sort was acceptable during the Nazi-Soviet period of collaboration (1939–41), but in 1942 it presented difficulties. How would audiences react to Hitler if Bismarck was a genius for *avoiding* a two-front war by his treaty with the Czar? Although Bismarck did not fall from power over a foreign-policy question, the Nazis knew that the average German was aware that the dismissal of the Iron Chancellor signaled a new and unhappy era in German-Russian relations. The question could not be avoided, so Liebeneiner and his writers tried to compensate for the unfortunate lack of analogy with Hitler's present Russian policy by portraying Bismarck as a man who forshadowed Hitler in the creation of Greater Germany.

The Dismissal was conceived early in 1941 in the wake of *Bismarck*'s great popular success. So much money and effort had been committed to the production by 1942 and so much hope placed in it that Goebbels did not consider abandoning the project, but Hitler's adjutant Schaub warned against public screenings until the Führer had decided that the time was opportune. Goebbels and Göring were greatly impressed by *The Dismissal,* but Hitler still had not made up his mind on August 20 about releasing the film. Hitler and Goebbels decided that the film would be tried out on a German audience in Stettin; the reaction of these spectators and those in other "secondary" German towns would determine its future. The foreign office was concerned about the impact of the film, since it was especially sensitive to negative comparisons between the Bismarck foreign policy and that of Hitler and Ribbentrop. The foreign office did not succeed in preventing the distribution of the film throughout the Reich, but Goebbels acceded to the request that the film not be exported.[4] Goebbels further ordered the press to discuss the film as a portrayal of a German tragedy: the great Bismarck overthrown by the foppish Wilhelm II. Goebbels wanted the press to review the film in the light of the contrast between German leadership after 1890 and the genius of the Führer in 1942. Even this bit of self-deception could not have blinded Goebbels to a frightening parallel, not a parallel between

Hitler and Bismarck, but between Hitler's war and that of Wilhelm II. *The Dismissal,* which received its gala Berlin premiere forty-seven days before the Russians isolated the German Sixth Army at Stalingrad, showed that the Nazi use of history for ideological purposes could back-fire in the light of contemporary military and diplomatic events.

Adolf Hitler had war aims far transcending the German domination of Europe. In the event of war he could carry out policies which peacetime conditions rendered difficult to conceal, even in a totalitarian state. Hitler believed that the German people were not yet hard enough to accept these policies, though he hinted at them in both his writings and in public speeches. Hitler wanted to eliminate from the national community the "racially unfit," individuals with hereditary diseases and the congenitally ill. In a secret decree of August 29, 1939, three days before the German invasion of Poland, Hitler ordered Reichsleiter Bouhler and Dr. Brandt to extend to qualified physicians the right to grant "a charitable death" to the incurably ill. The Nazi definition of "incurably ill" was a broad one; estimates of the number of "incurably ill" persons put to death between 1939 and the autumn of 1941 run as high as one hundred thousand. Medical commissions visited insane asylums and selected people who were to be put to death by oxide asphyxiation. Relatives were informed by the state that these individuals had died of cardiac arrest or of pneumonia. Suspicions grew wherever the "medical commissions" appeared, and the resultant public uproar, provoked in part by the courageous denunciations by Bishop Galen of Münster, caused the government to terminate the program in 1941. The risk of alienating segments of the nation while it was involved in a massive war effort made continuation of the "mercy killings" inopportune. The program was born by secret decree and came to an end in the same covert manner.

I ACCUSE

PRODUCTION: Tobis
DIRECTOR: W. Liebeneiner
SCRIPT: E. Frowein and H. Bratt
MAJOR PERFORMERS: Heidemarie Hatheyer
                      Paul Hartmann
                      Mathias Wiemann
PREMIERE: August 29, 1941

One of Goebbels' major tasks was the mobilization of the German media for justifying measures taken by the regime. In the case of the "euthanasia" program the Nazis had to be especially careful about popular sensibilities. The film produced to bring the nation to accept legal murders committed by the state was far more palatable to the average German than the actual murders would have been. *I Accuse (Ich klage an)* concerns a young woman stricken with multiple sclerosis, a disease which will turn her into a human vegetable before killing her.[5] There is no cure; the woman (Heidemarie Hatheyer) does not fear death, but she is afraid of the agony of dying, of turning into something less than a human being. Her husband (Paul Hartmann) accedes to her request that he kill her to spare her this suffering. He does so after the woman's physician has rejected her plea for death. The husband is put on trial, and the last, dramatic scene of *I Accuse* takes place in the courtroom, where he defends his action. With the well-written script and good acting of Wolfgang Liebeneiner's production, the concluding scene dramatically brings out the justifications for euthanasia that the regime had mobilized in its "educational" campaign. One juror argues that if the state has a right to demand that a soldier be willing to sacrifice his life for the nation, then it must also give the citizen the right to die at a time and under circumstances of his or her own choosing. The film presents euthanasia in the form with which we are familiar: death at a time chosen by the ill person to avoid further suffering. The physician, in defense of the woman's husband, now declares that he has changed his mind, that if had to do it all over again, he would kill the woman as she requested. The husband emotionally sums up his case by declaring that *he* is now the accuser, for there is something wrong with a law (Article 216 of the penal code) which puts a man on trial for saving his wife from needless torture. The dialogue in this scene is extremely effective, intellectual as well as emotional in its appeal, and apparently calculated to let the audience make up its own mind about the problem. No one is portrayed as a hero or as a villain, though audiences left the theater feeling sympathy for the accused and his action. Eliciting this reaction was precisely the aim of the regime when it urged Liebeneiner to direct a film about euthanasia.

The director knew of Hitler's 1939 decree, for the men responsible for implementing that order revealed it to him and asked him to make a film such as *I Accuse*. Goebbels was always concerned about German public opinion, and he sensed unease among many people over the regime's "secret" euthanasia policy. This may explain his violent reaction in April 1941 when the minister denounced the British for infamously asserting that the Reich would "kill its own wounded veterans after the war." [6]

Growing restiveness among Catholic laity and clergy in July was another concern.[7] Goebbels believed that *I Accuse* would be an effective first step in "educating" the German people, but he also hoped that the very human characters and situation portrayed in the movie would remove any fears or religious scruples preventing Germans from ascending to a higher level of National Socialist consciousness. Of course, the film had nothing to do with the real "mercy killing" policies of the regime. In the film the victim chooses to die; the patients in Hitler's asylums had no such choice. As in other potentially controversial areas, so here the regime was taking one cautious step at a time. Goebbels planned later films on this subject that would be more honest in introducing the masses to the real "euthanasia" policy of the government. The ultimate lack of success of *Ich klage an,* perhaps owing to the wordy script and the sense that the whole film was an intellectual exercise, precluded such sequels, as did the temporary halt to the program of "mercy killings."

THE ETERNAL JEW

DIRECTOR: Fritz Hippler
SCRIPT: Eberhard Taubert
PREMIERE: November 28, 1940

Two films of the early war years were less ambiguous and more honest in delineating another of the regime's murder policies, the far more massive program of annihilating every Jewish man, woman, and child in occupied Europe. Fritz Hippler used an idea suggested by the Propaganda Ministry's anti-Jewish expert, Dr. Taubert, and produced the notorious film *The Eternal Jew. Der Ewige Jude* opened in Berlin on November 28, 1940, and later appeared in dubbed versions in many parts of Europe.[8] *The Eternal Jew* is presented as a documentary about the role of the Jews in world history. The Jews are portrayed as lower than vermin, creatures akin to the rat, money-mad bits of filth devoid of all higher values, corruptors of the world: "They need a market and are not productive." "They carry disease." "They are ugly, cowardly, and move about in groups." Scenes of ritual animal slaughter, kosher style, underline the grotesque sadism of the Jewish "religion." The film does not conclude by urging the extermination of the Jews. But its message is clear: The only way to save the world is to murder the Jews. As Hitler put it in a conversation with Horthy in April 1943, "A healthy society can no more assimilate the Jew than a healthy organism can assimilate a tuberculosis bacillus." [9] Ludwig Heyde praised *The Eternal Jew* for making ordinary people understand the necessity for the measures undertaken by the government. The function of *The Eternal Jew* was to prepare the German nation and its occupied peoples and allies for the solution of the Jewish question. Those who saw *Der Ewige Jude* in 1941 and who by chance learned about Auschwitz in 1943 would rest easier in the possession, not of guilty knowledge, but of consolation.

THE JEW SÜSS

PRODUCTION: Terra

DIRECTOR: Veit Harlan

SCRIPT: L. Metzger, E. W. Moeller, V. Harlan

MAJOR PERFORMERS: Kristina Soederbaum

Ferdinand Marian

Heinrich George

Werner Krauss

Eugene Klöpfer

PREMIERE: September 24, 1940

One of the most infamous feature films produced in the Third Reich was *Jud Süss*, directed by Veit Harlan in 1940. Two film historians have referred to *The Jew Süss* as "the best propaganda film of the Third Reich." [10] It was certainly one of the most lavishly produced motion pictures of the year and one of the most hate-filled. The fictional story was based upon the life and death of the early-eighteenth-century Württemberg court Jew, Süss Oppenheimer. The cast included some of the most famous individuals in German cinema: Ferdinand Marian as Jud Süss, Heinrich George as the ruler Karl Alexander, Kristina Soederbaum as the ravished Aryan beauty, and Werner Krauss as Rabbi Loew (and as several other Jews). According to one account, Krauss was so taken with the script that he insisted upon playing no fewer than six Jewish roles in *Jud Süss*. Was this sadomasochism or perhaps a necessary personal effort to show his loyalty to the regime? Heinrich George, one of the great actors of the time, was the manager of the Berlin Schiller-theater. Upon one occasion he is reported to have screamed at his staff, "I'm talking about the Führer, do you hear? Get down on your knees, everybody!" [11] Again, was this ridicule or the sincere statement of a mind distorted by contact with and reliance upon men such as Goebbels,

Hippler, and Hinkel? The press gave *Jud Süss* a great deal of publicity.[12] The only question about the film was whether it was suitable for youth, for it did contain a rape scene in which the Jew deflowers Kristina Soederbaum. The film was often shown before audiences of the Hitler Youth and the SS, as well as in major motion picture theaters throughout the Reich and occupied Europe.

Süss Oppenheimer appears as a half-assimilated Jew who goes from ghetto to court within a few years. Through money and black magic he and his fellow Jews, such as Rabbi Loew, scheme to seize power by manipulating the corrupt, drunken duke, whom they see as the archetype of the pliable *goy*. The Jews who remain in the ghetto appear physically repulsive, but the message of the film is that they are less dangerous than Süss, who has acquired a veneer of court polish. Not content with his power at court, Süss wants the hand of the daughter of a

The conniving, "assimilated" Jew Süss Oppenheimer uses the dissolute, avaricious duke of Württemberg in one of his many schemes. Ferdinand Marian and Heinrich George played these roles in *Jud Süss*.

CREDIT: The International Museum of Photography at George Eastman House, Rochester, New York

local councillor of the realm. His fury knows no limit when the father informs Süss, "My daughter will never put any Jew children into the world." Süss Oppenheimer and his clique conspire to use the duke, Karl Alexander, to suck the blood of the good people of Württemberg. No infamy is too great if it serves the Jews in their quest for money, status, and power. When the duke dies of apoplexy, Süss's power base is gone, and the righteous wrath of the people causes him to be seized and tried. Protesting his innocence to the end, the slimy Süss Oppenheimer is ultimately hanged in a cage as snow blankets the newly tranquil Württemberg countryside. The lesson of *Jud Süss* was clear: The Jew is a parasite upon the body of society; the Jew must be killed. The only difference between the last scene of the film and Nazi genocide was that Jud Süss dies in public, while the Nazis (except in certain parts of the Ukraine and the Baltic region) murdered the Jews privately.[13]

The films *The Eternal Jew* and *The Jew Süss* represented the Nazi commitment to exterminating the Jews. Hitler had hinted at such a war measure during his speech of January 30, 1939,[14] but genocide did not become the official, actual policy of the regime until 1940; it was not until early 1942 that the final measures were taken for elimination of the Jews of Europe. These two motion pictures represented a Nazi synthesis, for they brought to mass audiences the murder policies formerly espoused by individuals and publications which lacked power and prestige beyond obsessed or psychotic anti-Jewish circles. Even after the "Crystal Night" pogroms of 1938, few Germans believed that the regime intended to murder the Jews. Only lunatics and degenerates like Julius Streicher and his associates at the newspaper *Der Stürmer* in Nürnberg called for such actions. Perhaps the Jews were being deported "to the east" or to "work camps," but to kill them? Hardly. The millions of Germans who saw these films in 1940 and 1941 must have realized what the government intended to do to the Jews and was doing to them. Only the individual possessing extraordinary powers of self-deception could leave *Jud Süss* thinking it was merely a historical tale with a moral twist, the triumph of good over evil. These films were a formula for action, not a denunciation of the Jews; this is why Goebbels insisted that *Jud Süss* *not* be described by the press as an anti-Semitic film. Anti-Semitism was traditional and harmless in the eyes of Goebbels and Hitler. What they had in mind was something far more radical. This is where the films linked up with the Streicher tradition, which was crude as well as murderous. "Respectable" Nazi leaders such as von Schirach and Fritzsche later claimed that they were repelled by *Der Stürmer* and had tried to have it banned, at least within their own areas of authority.[15] Their attempt to distance themselves from Streicher was an appeal to the

Werner Krauss as Rabbi Loew in *Jud Süss*, perhaps the greatest hate film ever produced in the Third Reich.

CREDIT: The Dartmouth College Library, Hanover, New Hampshire

International Military Tribunal to see them as deceived good Germans. Their anti-Semitism was that of 1919 or 1937, they claimed; they were trying to assert their innocence of the murder explicitly detailed in *Der Stürmer* and the two films.

By 1940 the regime had taken the final step; *Jud Süss* and *Der Ewige Jude* were advertisements for the "Final Solution." Streicher, a man deprived of real power since 1933, saw his crusade for murder vindicated by 1942, when Hitler declared, ". . . not Aryan humanity, but the Jew will be exterminated. Whatever the struggle brings with it, or however long it lasts, this will be its final result." [16] As the extermination of the Jews became a mass reality by 1942–44, Goebbels made sure that the German mass media constantly renewed their commitment to anti-Jewish policies. In the eyes of Hitler and Goebbels, Germany's military setbacks only proved their thesis that the Jew was the Reich's eternal enemy, that the Jew must be killed. As Streicher stated in 1946, "The Propaganda Ministry in Berlin had a National Socialist press service. In this service, in every issue, there were a number of enlightening articles on the Jewish question. During the war the Führer personally gave the order that the press, far more than previously, should publish enlightening articles on the Jewish question." [17]

Jud Süss and *The Eternal Jew* resembled the Jewish caricatures which played a dominant role in the pages of *Der Stürmer* since the 1920s. In the case of Jud Süss, the figure on the screen contained an element of the obscene sexuality so prominent in Streicher's newspaper. Streicher was a crude, unintelligent man whose personality reflected mental illness. Men such as Hans Fritzsche saw the Streicher types as an embarrassment. Fritzsche, who worked for a minister who did not conceal his desire that the Jews be murdered, later claimed that he wanted the government to ban *Der Stürmer,* since its crudities only fueled the anti-German cause. Alfred Rosenberg saw Germandom and Jewry as representative of two opposed forces, one of light, the other of darkness. He too had little use for the pornographic anti-Jewish psychosis represented by the Stürmer Verlag in its "struggle for the truth." Yet this same Rosenberg, a "philosopher," wanted to convene an international anti-Jewish congress in Cracow in June 1944. He received the cooperation of Ribbentrop and Goebbels but reluctantly gave up the idea in November after Bormann repeatedly indicated the time was not appropriate for such an event.[18] All these people, Veit Harlan and Fritz Hippler, Hans Fritzsche and Alfred Rosenberg, Goebbels and Ribbentrop, saw themselves as cultivated gentlemen and probably despised a lout like Streicher, but by their work they contributed mightily to the achievement of his ultimate aim, the "Final Solution." Hitler, who allowed him to continue publishing his

THE FINAL SOLUTION IN THE GERMAN MASS MEDIA

The Jew as profiteer and usurer, 1924. "The achievement of the [1918]
revolution! Stock market speculations, paper money, bank interest, peace
treaty."

The Nazi image of the Jewish-Bolshevik warmonger in a prewar book, *The Warmongers of Today as They See Themselves.*

CREDIT: The Dartmouth College Library, Hanover, New Hampshire

"Behind the Enemy Powers—the Jew": The Nazi explanation of the Allied coalition. A Jewish plutocratic banker hides behind the flags of Britain, America, and Soviet Russia.

CREDIT: The Suddeutscher Verlag, Munich, Germany

"The Jew—Purveyor of War, Prolonger of War": ca. 1943.

CREDIT: The Library of Congress

The Jew as the destroyer of Europe. A hate-filled maniac, the force behind Germany's enemies, goes wild with sick lust as the cities of Europe go up in flames. This poster was one of the products of the German Propaganda Studio, which carried out commissions of the Propaganda Ministry.

CREDIT: The Library of Congress

Streicher's consistency until the end. One of the last issues of *Der Stürmer*, September 7, 1944. The lead story was about the Jewish conspiracy to murder the best elements among the non-Jewish peoples. The pictures on page three are frightening in a different way. *Der Stürmer* shows several Hungarian Jews, including a young boy "who would like to become a rabbi." It is almost certain that they perished in Nazi death camps in the next few weeks.

CREDIT: "Der Stürmer"

newspaper until late 1944, was more sympathetic to Streicher, perhaps because of the naive purity of *Der Stürmer's* anti-Semitic idealism. As Hitler stated in December 1941, "Despite all his weaknesses, he's a man who has spirit. . . . I have a bad conscience when I get the feeling that I've not been quite fair to somebody. . . . Streicher had only one disease, and that was nympholepsy." [19] Even in 1945 Hitler expressed his fondness for Streicher—while talking to Joseph Goebbels. This in itself was a sign of Goebbels' "triumph." He, the "intellect" among thugs, should have, and probably did, most despise Streicher. Yet in 1945 he had convinced the man he worshipped that he too could appreciate Streicher, "a man who has spirit." This was a Goebbels victory—but at what a time, at what a cost!

Opfergang (Rite of Sacrifice), directed by Veit Harlan, received its Berlin premiere on or about December 29, 1944.[20] This interesting film was one of the last lavish "Agfacolor" spectaculars produced in the Third Reich. The settings are beautiful, the colors rich, the mood of the story far removed from the agonies of the dying Third Reich. But was this really a totally escapist film? Was its message unrelated to ideological propaganda and the world view of Joseph Goebbels? *Opfergang* actually reflected what Carl Hauptmann describes as the tendency among leaders of the Third Reich to confuse facts with possibilities, thereby ending up "believing their own phrases." [21] *Rite of Sacrifice* was based upon a novel of the same name by Rudolf Binding, though Harlan changed the story so as not to violate certain tenets of National Socialism.[22]

RITE OF SACRIFICE

PRODUCTION: UFA
DIRECTOR: Veit Harlan
SCRIPT: V. Harlan, A. Braun
MAJOR PERFORMERS: Kristina Soederbaum
                  Carl Raddatz
                  Irene von Meyendorff
PREMIERE: Probably December 29, 1944

Albrecht (Carl Raddatz) returns from a trip around the world and becomes involved in a tragic love triangle. His marriage to the beautiful

Octavia (Irene von Meyendorff) is in danger of breaking up, and the separation appears certain when Albrecht returns to the company of his former lover, the mortally ill Aels (Kristina Soederbaum). The film is filled with tragic overtones. Aels appears as the healthy outdoors type, the full blossom of Nordic (Finnish) womanhood. Yet her impending death from an incurable disease looms over the story. Sacrifices become a form of justification in *Opfergang*. When Octavia learns of the threat of an epidemic in the district where Aels' child is being raised, she urges Albrecht to rescue the little girl. He does so, but in the process he contracts the dangerous disease, and is no longer able to visit Aels, who is now dying. Octavia disguises herself as Albrecht and greets the dying Aels by continuing "his" daily rides on horseback before the window of the sick woman. Albrecht recovers, and learns from Aels, who knew of the well-meant deception, that Octavia's sacrifices showed a generosity of soul worthy of his love. Aels dies, the marriage is saved, and all three protagonists are justified in their behavior.

This "escapist," "romantic" film contained some of the final propagandistic statements of National Socialist ideology. There was not a "Heil" to be heard on the sound track, not a swastika in sight anywhere, yet *Opfergang* perfectly expressed Joseph Goebbels' character and world view. The film was not released for about a year after production had been completed, in part because Goebbels and Harlan had to make sure that the film conformed to the minister's view of the world. In the novel, for example, Aels does not die. But it was more acceptable to National Socialist tenets that an adultress be sacrificed to the preservation of a marriage.

The script portrays Albrecht as a man who dislikes Nietzschean tragedy, a man who says yes to life and loves the sea and the mountains. Yet this same Albrecht becomes aware of the tragic dimensions of life, and through them returns to a commitment to marriage, a social action acceptable to Goebbels' censors. In an early scene Albrecht finds one of Nietzsche's poems ("Remain strong, my brave heart") depressing, but through suffering, he becomes stronger, and his final return to Octavia represents not a rejection of Aels and her memory, but a return to reality and commitment after a life of travel, masked balls, and instability. Many scenes symbolic of other aspects of Nazi ideology appear in *Opfergang,* but usually in such a way as to avoid the vulgar trappings of National Socialist doctrine. One incident takes place in the Colonial Club in Hamburg, thus reminding the audience of the tradition of overseas German imperialism. Another briefly recalls the euthanasia theory of the Nazis, though in this case, a suffering dog is put to death.

The tragedy of Aels is that she is the Nordic embodiment of the will to live but is doomed to die young. This contradiction may have troubled Goebbels, but in the end the higher dictates of Nazi ideology made her death a necessity. Goebbels may have seen the story as analogous to his own love affair with Lida Baarova, for he too had saved his marriage (and possibly his career) by returning to Magda. Goebbels did so under duress, however, while Albrecht returns to Octavia out of rediscovered love and profound respect.

Goebbels was cynical and emotional by turn as he watched *Rite of Sacrifice* over and over again in 1944 and 1945. The most interesting and revealing aspect of *Opfergang* is its incredibly sentimental appeal to emotion. As Aels is dying, we hear a heavenly chorus preparing her for entry into heaven. The gates of eternity open for her to the accompaniment of romantic, transcendent music of a Lisztian sort. The beautiful colors become the joy of salvation; there is almost the sense of the Christian assumption into heaven. Goebbels was so moved by this scene that he saw it at times as a promise of his own immortality. As he noted with increasing frequency in 1944 and 1945, "I believe that man lives on in his deeds . . ." The conclusion of *Opfergang* is an allegory on the end of the Third Reich, on how commitment to an idea in the face of all adversity guarantees salvation or redemption through will, faith, and deed. In the last scene the gates of Aels' house, where Octavia has appeared before her window disguised as a consoling Albrecht, become the pearly gates of heaven. The entire scene is ludicrous, one might almost say cheap and vulgar, yet it is indicative of a certain mental state of Goebbels towards the end of the war. What is significant is not the trite reassertion of the Nazi concept of marriage, but the elevation of ideology to the level of transcendent, redemptive religion.

An analogous scene appears in the spectacle *Kolberg,* mainly filmed in 1944, where the queen of Prussia and a patriotic peasant girl (once again, Irene von Meyendorff and Kristina Soederbaum) are enveloped in angelic music suggestive of heavenly redemption. Commitment to fatherland *(Kolberg)* and commitment to proper social activity *(Opfergang)* had always been fundamental in the Nazi world view. But as the Third Reich crumbled, these yielded to a "higher" theme of personal redemption for the protagonists blessed with the grace of faith. By this time the films were speaking more to Goebbels than to the German nation: Lavishly produced at great cost, they reflected the romantic salvation of Joseph Goebbels, now a man inwardly beyond cynicism as he expressed a faith symbolically intended to outlive the physical destruction of Germany.

KOLBERG

PRODUCTION: UFA

DIRECTOR: Veit Harlan

SCRIPT: V. Harlan, Alfred Braun

MAJOR PERFORMERS: Kristina Soederbaum

Heinrich George

Horst Caspar

Irene von Meyendorff

Kurt Meisel

PREMIERE: January 30, 1945

What such films as *I Accuse, Jud Süss, The Eternal Jew, Rite of Sacrifice*, and *Kolberg* shared was a common commitment to death. Heinrich Himmler liked to differentiate between his "positive" and "negative" sides. Exterminating the gypsies, Jews, and other subhumans was unpleasant but necessary, he said, a page in German history which could never be written. The Reichsführer SS really enjoyed his "positive" work, such as planning peasant villages in Russia and selecting the Nordic elite upon which the future of Europe would depend. The first three films expressed Goebbels' negative but necessary National Socialist work: preparing the German people for conscious acceptance of measures taken by the regime against undesirable humans and subhumans. They appeared at a time when the victories of the Third Reich seemed to guarantee that this Greater Germany would indeed construct a new Europe. *Rite of Sacrifice* was also about death—indeed it glorified death—but it represented the "positive" or "idealistic" side of the Nazi character. The German screen offered incitement to murder in 1940. Now in 1943–45, it presented a vision of salvation in death. The nihilism of this orientation towards death embodied the spirit of National Socialism. A film such as *Jud Süss* was meant for the masses; *Opfergang* and *Kolberg* were visions of salvation for the Nazi elite.

IV

Plutocrats and Bolsheviks:

Two Views of Ideological and

Racial Enemies in the German

Mass Media

9

The War Against England in the German
Mass Media

When Great Britain became a hate object in the German mass media, National Socialist wartime ideology could find ammunition in popular tradition, the hatreds engendered by two wars, and the Nazi claim to social progress. Hitler viewed the English as Germany's racial brethren and the British empire as a potential ally of the Reich. When Britain became a foe rather than a friend, the Nazis denounced the empire as socially reactionary and oppressive of the masses. Some themes prominent during the First World War reappeared in this propaganda after 1939. German school children were taught to say "May God punish England!" after 1914, when Britain "surrendered" Germany and allied herself with alien Slavs and Gauls—Russians and Frenchmen. In 1940 German teachers entered classrooms and cried out "God punish England!" The pupils would reply "He will!" [1] Wartime Nazi propaganda about England drew upon concepts developed during the Great War by men such as Werner Sombart, Houston Stewart Chamberlain, and Oswald Spengler. Their slogans and insights had become broadly disseminated among the German people by 1920, and it was not difficult for Nazi propagandists to employ them in the mass media.

By 1914 the famed economic historian Werner Sombart had discovered that the English did not deserve to rank among the *Heldenvölker,* the nations of heroes. They were one more mercenary *Händlervolk,* or nation of traders. In this they were akin to the Jews rather than to the Germans. It was but a short step from this thesis to the later cry that the English were "the Jews among the Aryan peoples." Arthur Mitzman paraphrases Sombart: "War for the English was a capitalist enterprise; for the Germans it was a last defense against the onslaught of commercialism on the soul of modern man." [2] H. S. Chamberlain, a well-known theoretician on the role of race in history, was a convert to cultural and nationalistic Germanism. He received German citizenship during the First World War and wrote many essays intended to boost military morale and justify the German cause. In his essay "England," Chamberlain described his native land as a place where people worshiped money and as an antisocial country in which class lines were rigid and a deep gulf separated the privileged orders from the common people. In his somewhat awkward, archaic German style, Chamberlain denounced the institution of parliament as a plaything of the rich. He refused to acknowledge that the British made good sailors or that they were natural conquerors of other nations. They could oppress primitive peoples, but they were not heroic or creative in any sense. Chamberlain declared that the lust to make money had led Britain to the slave trade and to imperialism; the pursuit of wealth in the most immoral manner typified Great Britain. He described the Briton in history as hypocritical, arrogant, and devoid of idealism. Chamberlain grudgingly acknowledged that the average Englishman was brave, efficient, and honorable, but the class society and money-crazy state perverted decent people and turned them into a force worthy of contempt. Chamberlain provided many of the ingredients essential to the Nazi attack upon "plutocracy."

Oswald Spengler examined the British through the eyes of "Prussianism." He contrasted the Prussian sense of work and mission with the egotistical British notion of the free private individual: "It is typical of the Prussian way that the individual will merges into the common will," he wrote.[3] Spengler brought his enormous prestige as a philosopher of history to a denunciation of the British as inwardly unfree, lacking conscience and inner freedom. According to Spengler, the Englishman's materialism, rationalism, and liberalism rendered him incapable of appreciating the divine nature of work and other social obligations. Speaking of the influence of Calvinism and Cromwell upon the English character, Spengler argued that "To the pious Independent, work is the result of the Fall of Man; to the Prussian it is a divine commandment."

When the British government showed belated signs of resisting further German expansion in the spring of 1939, the Nazi propaganda apparatus assumed that many Germans shared the views of Sombart, Chamberlain, and Spengler. Party speakers received instructions to discuss the historic worthlessness of British guarantees. They were informed of the abandonment of Frederick the Great by the British in 1761 during his time of greatest need. Speakers in Bavaria learned that the British "balance of power" concept was merely a disguise for British hegemony in Europe. Party orators were to remind their audiences that Neville Chamberlain was repeating the "encirclement" policy of 1904–14, which led to the Great War. One series of hysterical instructions branded England as the murderer of men ranging from the French socialist Jean Jaurès to King Alexander of Yugoslavia and even Abraham Lincoln. Other topics for speakers' consideration were "Jews and Freemasons in English politics" and "Warmonger England." Propagandists received information about British hypocrisy and were told to apply this theme to alleged British ideals like "freedom of the seas," "self-determination," and the "European balance of power." Building upon the work of Sombart, Chamberlain, and Spengler, propagandists in the RPL urged speakers to emphasize that the British did not possess a profound spiritual world view as did the Germans. The British worshiped a "Jewish" materialistic God, and the Anglican Church was political, not spiritual in nature. The present struggle was one of "God against gold," for the English "world picture" had no place for the rights of other nations, only a lust for profits and exploitation.[4] In these ways the Nazis updated 1914–18 propaganda.

One strange convert to this view was the English renegade William Joyce ("Lord Haw-Haw"), who considered the Nazi movement to be a proletarian one which would "free the world from the bonds of the 'plutocratic capitalists.'"[5] Throughout 1940 Nazi propagandists worked hard in many media to develop the mature concept of "plutocracy."[6] Instructions for speakers drawn up by the RPL presented the British as a nation of Judaized moneylenders, as people who lived by the stock market and Freemason lodges. Even the British art and music were uncreative, repetitious, and sterile. Propagandists contrasted this alleged lack of culture with a Germanic world that had brought forth Meister Eckhart, Goethe, Beethoven, and Hitler. The theme that began to dominate this propaganda by early 1940, however, was the description of Britain as a retrogressive land of slums, unemployment, and social inequality. As Hitler put it in 1941, "Among the English, culture, like sport, is a privilege of good society."[7]

After the collapse of the French Army, Goebbels ordered a temporary halt to extreme anti-British statements in German propaganda. This pause lasted from late June to about July 22, 1940. Hitler hoped to persuade the British to accept his domination of the continent in return for an alliance which would guarantee the British Empire. Rudolf Hess may have already known of Hitler's plan to invade Russia. As he told

Felix Kersten around June 24, "I cannot imagine that cool, calculating England will run her neck into the Soviet noose instead of saving it by coming to an understanding with us." [8] The German press received instructions on June 25 that outlined new guidelines for the treatment of the British: "In treating our future policy towards England, it is important to emphasize that our struggle does not aim at the destruction of the British Empire, but rather at smashing British hegemony on the continent." [9] Actual or forthcoming feature films with anti-British themes, such as *U-boats Westward!* were no longer the objects of extensive discussions and promotions in the press.[10] Hitler made his "peace offer" to Britain on July 19; by July 22 Lord Halifax had clearly rejected the German concept of peace. Hess had another ten months in which to brood . . .

During the Battle of Britain Goebbels directed the German media to pursue a cautious line in dealing with Great Britain. He warned that an empire as great as that of Britain would not collapse in a moment. There were already signs of weakness, but the end would come suddenly, without warning.[11] Goebbels gave no dates, believing that it was a mistake to awaken false hopes among the German people. He also turned from prophecy to sarcasm, a technique which he loved to employ. In December 1940 he ridiculed British suggestions regarding the future political, social, and economic organization of Europe. He responded that England had had twenty years in which to make these contributions and had failed to do so. Now the British were plagiarizing German social accomplishments for their own purposes.[12]

Goebbels' anti-British propaganda suffered a severe setback in May 1941, when Rudolf Hess flew to Scotland in a last attempt to bring the British to their senses. The invasion of Soviet Russia was only six weeks away. The Luftwaffe and the U-boats, though delivering crippling blows, had not brought Britain to her knees. One biographer of Hess asserts, "Hess's historic flight to Britain was made with Hitler's full knowledge and approval." [13] This statement is difficult to prove or deny, but it is obvious that if Hess had brought the British government "to its senses," Hitler would not have spurned the results of his dramatic flight. Otto Dietrich tried to salvage something for German propaganda by declaring that Hess, realizing that Britain had been defeated, wanted to help the English "peace party" against Churchill, thereby terminating the war.[14] Albrecht Haushofer, son of the famous geopolitician and a man knowledgeable about British politics and society, had suggested to his friend Hess that he meet the Duke of Hamilton on neutral soil. The duke had access to both the king and the prime minister, Winston Churchill. Haushofer made this suggestion on September 8, 1940, and a week later he noted his belief that Hitler had personally approved the meeting between Hess and himself.[15]

The failure of the Hess mission strengthened the hand of Churchill and the British "plutocracy." German propaganda renewed its attacks on this nefarious phenomenon, often expanding it to "Anglo-American plutocracy."[16] As Karl Cerff phrased it, "German culture is the great moral qualification for waging this struggle! What do the parvenus England and American have to match it?"[17] Goebbels, noting the widespread discussion in Britain of the Beveridge Plan for postwar social planning, ordered the German media to denounce it as a sham. The minister stated that Germany had instituted social reforms as early as 1884 and had possessed since 1933 a state-directed socialist society. The German media were ordered to denounce the Beveridge Plan as a belated, false promise to carry out reforms that Germany had accomplished in Bismarck's time.[18]

Educational materials distributed by the Main Educational Office of the party contained massive amounts of material on British "plutocracy." The theme was a favorite of Robert Ley, who praised Germany in 1944 as "the only land on the face of the earth where the leadership has kept its promises" by creating a folk community and by establishing schools open to youths of all social strata.[19] Ley lauded the quantitative and qualitative accomplishments of German labor, making them the justification of the entire society. Such a statement was ironic, for it smacked of the capitalist exploitation that he denounced in "plutocratic" Great Britain. "Educational materials" used within party circles contained detailed information on the "class" nature of the British society.[20] One bulletin, using Marxist language, denounced the ruling class in Britain—high officials, military men, and parliamentarians—as mere tools in the hands of the omnipotent "plutocrats," great landlords and capitalists. The "educational materials" provided party members, officials, and future cadres with information about Great Britain drawn from a variety of German sources, including the works of the First World War generation. In the bulletins of the Ley office, England's ruling elite was represented as a materialistic, egotistical group which had spread the "poison gas" of its attitude to the Continent. One bulletin denounced the "Jew Ricardo" for his gift of laissez-faire economic theory and blasted Adam Smith and Jeremy Bentham for their contributions to the concept of a "materialistic national economy."

Goebbels knew that the apparent "totalitarian efficiency" and unity of the Third Reich were sometimes often chimerical. In their attitudes towards England, the German elite and the German media often reflected contradictory positions. In late April 1942, Goebbels noted that the British were careless about keeping state secrets, and commented, "I hope that isn't true also of our secret communications." [21] Yet ten days later Hitler praised the British for the opposite quality: "Up to the moment we have not heard a word about what occurred at these [parliamentary] sessions. This is a powerful tribute to the solidarity which unites the British people."[22] Later in the war, the minister noted, "I don't believe that England is now in danger of becoming Bolshevized. English mentality is anchored too much in the British tradition." [23] Yet at the same time, German propagandists in the RPL were beginning a media campaign designed to show that England was well on its way to being subverted by Bolshevism.[24]

German wartime propaganda confronted the task of explaining the hostility of Great Britain to the German people. The German media were consistent in their use of the "plutocracy" theme, though certain nuances of expression and emphasis appeared during the course of the war. Late in 1942 Hitler commented, "We must persist in our assertion that we are waging war, not on the British people, but on the small clique who rules them. It is a slogan which promises good results. . . ." [25] Perhaps Hitler had learned this technique from the hated Woodrow Wilson, who had "fooled" the Germans by declaring he was fighting Prussian militarism, not the German people. The "anti-plutocratic" theme was less effective than it might have been, largely because of Luftwaffe attacks on slums and working-class residential areas in Britain. Such bombardments hardly supported the Nazi assertion that Germany was fighting the plutocracy, not the people. As Goebbels belatedly noted in March 1943, "I proposed to the Führer in the future not to bombard slums but the residential sections of the plutocracy whem making air raids on England. . . . The Führer agrees with this." [26] March 1943! A belated insight.

Goebbels' public attacks on the "plutocrats" contained the sarcasm and denunciations of hypocrisy so characteristic of this vicious, witty, cynical, and often hypocritical man. As the French Army crumbled in June 1940, the minister denounced the British as "pious hypocrites" who were pietistic and Godlike in their own eyes, but brutal liars when objectively viewed by others. He asked, "What do we understand by plutocracy? Plutocracy is that form of political and economic leadership in which a couple of hundred families rule the world without any moral right to do so." [27] Goebbels was the inventor of the concept of "plutocracy," and the German mass media employed it until the end of the war.[28] The minister made many speeches in which he contrasted the German "social state" with the injustice perpetrated by the British upper class.[29] Goebbels even took up the cry, used so often by Mussolini, that the Axis powers were poor or proletarian nations trying to break the chains of British imperialism and achieve their place in the sun.

Goebbels argued that the British "plutocrats" would use and discard small nations in their quest for hegemony in Europe.[30] This is what they had done with Poles, Norwegians, Dutch, and Belgians, not to speak of the French. They had urged war upon unsuspecting peoples and their corrupt politicians. The results were tragic for these "victims" of the British policy of the encirclement of Germany. Goebbels was particularly annoyed by the piety and moral hypocrisy of the British leadership. He claimed not to care too much if the British behaved in an inhumane or bad way; what was most offensive was their pretense to morality and religion, their nerve in lecturing others with pious sermons.[31] In his know-it-all ignorance, Goebbels painted a highly misleading portrait of social London in 1941, one that must have confused the German audience at which it was aimed. The minister overlooked the heroic aspect of British resistance during the air blitz (which he privately appreciated) and described the "gilded youth" of British high society as dancing and reveling in luxury hotels while the city was in flames.[32] He did not explain how Britain could hold out against the German attacks if it was so corrupt. Yet the image fit Goebbels' world view concerning the inevitable decline of bourgeois, liberal society.[33] This approach was useful in mobilizing a new propaganda argument after the invasion of Soviet Russia: The choice for Europe was between German victory or Bolshevism.

Goebbels did not relent in his attacks upon British "plutocracy," even after Britain had clearly survived the worst of the German air and U-boat attacks. Late in 1943 the minister violated his own prohibition against media discussion of consumer shortages in Britain (Germans might wonder about their own privations, seeing the alleged problems of the British as foreshadowing further German cutbacks in rations). He described the British rationing system as one which favored the idle rich, whereas in Germany heavy industrial workers received extra rations. In combating British "plutocracy," Goebbels returned to his radical pose of 1926, describing the Second World War as a "social revolution" which precluded the return of the old order.[34] He predicted that the British workers would turn away from the collaborationist Labour party and would realize that only the "plutocracy," in its hatred for socially progressive Nazi Germany, wanted war over Danzig in 1939. By late 1943 Goebbels was declaring that an Allied victory would have the same destructive impact upon the "plutocrats" as would a German victory, only more so. The Bolsheviks would be at the Channel, and British imperialism would be strangled. Goebbels was correct (though he exaggerated) in sensing the decline of British imperialism and the problems confronting British society, and he predicted that Britain would emerge from the war without "money, without trade, with a decimated merchant marine and navy." [35] Goebbels refused to see that "plutocrats" and workers, Churchill and Roosevelt and Stalin, whatever their differences, would stick together until men such as himself had disappeared.

In 1940 Goebbels described the radio as the most modern and wide-ranging instrument for leading the people. Hans Fritzsche, already famous as a radio commentator for his *Political Review of Press and Radio,* collected some anti-British material from these media for his book *War Against the Warmongers.*[36] A cartoon from *Simplizissimus* showed Neville Chamberlain as the grim reaper, harvesting the bodies of the French *poilus.* Another cartoon, reproduced from the SS official newspaper, *The Black Corps,* showed the warmonger John Bull fire-bombing neutral Belgium and Holland. How did England wage war? By fighting to the last Pole and Frenchman. Fritzsche, whose power over the German radio was second only to that of Goebbels by 1943, often denounced the British for masking plutocratic war aims in social rhetoric. The arrogant sarcasm of Fritzsche and Karl Scharping lost some of its sting in 1943.[37] The commentators continued to gloat over the problems confronting Great Britain—Stalin, America, food shortages—but who were the Germans to laugh at these troubles? Many Germans realized that if Britain was having trouble with her allies, at least she had allies. And how could the German people enjoy Churchill's alleged fear of Stalin, since the Red Army was far closer to Berlin than to London?

An important medium of propaganda dissemination in National Socialist Germany was the party ceremony, or *Feierstunde.* These meetings were modeled upon church worship; they included songs, chants, incantations of the Führer, and a "sermon" containing a major National Socialist theme. Texts of proposed or actual *Feierstunden* provide useful examples of the manner in which the Nazi view of Britain reached the National Socialist public. The ceremonies held in Thuringia late in 1940 included denunciations of British imperialism, the declaration that Britain was finished as a world power, the reaction of the old line "England is to blame!" At the conclusion of these ceremonies, the "congregation" often rose and sang "We Are Marching against England." German power would presumably deliver the death blow to the reeling British Empire. Germany would be free, and the world would recover from the oppression symbolized by the "plutocratic" clique which had plunged Europe into another fratricidal war in 1939.[38]

The party mobilized Nazi journals and book publishers in its propaganda on the "England is guilty" theme. One journal, *Die Aktion,* had the explicit subtitle *Fighter against Plutocracy and Warmongering.*[39] The journal delighted in printing articles by pro-Axis foreigners from countries that had been "victimized" by the British (Norway, Ireland). Fritzsche contributed an occasional piece, filled with the usual wisdom of his endless sarcasm. *Die Aktion* even reprinted an anti-Semitic article by the noted British military historian J. F. C. Fuller, presumably written before the war. Journals reached a limited audience, but party and independent book publishers deluged Germany and much of Europe with books about Great Britain and her crimes, particularly during the first two years of the war. Some of these books were reprints of earlier works; most were the product of assignments commissioned after the war broke out.

Fritz Seidenzahl's *The Rule of Force of the British Pound: How England Misuses Her Economic Power* was a selective denunciation of the British lack of scruples in international affairs. Seidenzahl described a world about to break the tyranny of the pound, a world in revolt against manipulative British "subsidies" and British violations of the rights of other nations. Seidenzahl argued that British hatred for Germany arose as soon as it was clear in 1870 that the German people were becoming free and united. He described the last hundred and fifty years as a time during which England had acted ruthlessly against any power that appeared to be an actual or potential economic rival. Seidenzahl portrayed the British as exploitative imperialists, mere plunderers of raw materials who were incapable of organizing a productive economic imperium. He described British foreign policy after 1933 as a reaction against a Germany which had broken free of the tyranny of the pound sterling, and wrote "The overthrow of the pound and the fall of the sterling block are becoming the signal for the end of rule of force by the British pound and English plutocracy!"[40]

Pamphlets and books published by the German Labor Front and the Franz Eher Verlag appeared in huge editions throughout 1940 and 1941. Werner Morgenstern's *Under the Knout of Plutocracy: The Path of Suffering for Millions* went through several large printings in 1941. The long pamphlet, published by the German Labor Front, combined Robert Ley's attacks upon "plutocrats" with bragging about German social legislation.[41] The series "That Is England," Group V of the Franz Eher Verlag's "Series of Writings of the NSDAP," contained eleven books and booklets on the subject. Many of these publications went through several printings of ten thousand copies each, so they were a major factor in the dissemination of anti-British propaganda within Germany. The books were readable and usually brief, thus appealing to the mentality of the average Nazi. Walther Pahl's *British Power Politics* was a fervent denunciation of Britain's continuing bid for world rule. Pahl played another trick on Woodrow Wilson and described the British expulsion from the continent in 1940 as "the right to self-determination by the European continent." "Divide and rule," maintaining "the balance of power," and terror against weaker peoples typified the British technique, he claimed.[42]

F. O. H. Schultz concentrated his attack upon the retrogressive nature of British domestic policy. *In English Pity—English Social Policy* (1940) Schultz declared, "Even today the English worker is a plaything in the hands of corporations, a puppet held up by strings pulled by stock market and banking interests . . ." [43] Schultz denounced the "plutocrats" for allowing thousands of eastern Jews to pour into Britain in the late nineteenth century; he proceeded to explain British hatred of Germany as the result of Jewish intermarriage with the "plutocracy." The alleged tie between Jewry and British "plutocracy" became a major theme in Nazi wartime ideology as early as September 1939. Late in that month, Rosenberg's bulletin on ideology quoted General Fuller to prove that the Jews had decisive power in determining Anglo-Saxon foreign policy.[44]

The most interesting "book" on this subject was *Lord Cohn: The Judaization of the English Upper Class from D'Israeli to Hore Belisha,* the work of one Ernst Clam. This trashy book, which had the tone of a cheap novel and vulgar journalism, was one more striking proof of the degenerate nature of the Nazi world view. Clam begins his book by admitting that the title is false, for there is no "Lord Cohn." But there might as well be, for the love affair between Jews and British aristocrats, presumably consummated in Masonic lodges and Jewish synagogues, had long since produced the type symbolized in "Lord Cohn." Benjamin Disraeli is one of Clam's great interests, for he sees in that prime minister the slimy type who acquires prestige, power, and money to fulfil his "oriental dream" of domination through the British, the "dream of the Jews." Clam lovingly describes how Disraeli, at first rebuffed by Queen Victoria, wormed his way into her confidence. These passages read like a written version of *Jud Süss.* Just as Oppenheimer flattered and used Karl Alexander, so Clam's Disraeli manages to gain the confidence and affection of the queen. Clam even tells his readers that Disraeli the Jew invented the "encirclement" policy against Germany, ignoring the fact that if there were such a policy, it arose at least twenty-three years after the death of the "old Jew." Clam concludes by turning to contemporary Great Britain, where he sees the final fruits of Disraeli's work. Freemasons and German-Jewish émigrés dominate England through their close ties with the aristocracy. It is this unholy alliance that has pushed England and Europe into a second world war.[45]

As the war turned against Germany, as millions of Jews were put to death in camps such as Auschwitz and Treblinka, Hitler and Goebbels ordered that anti-Jewish propaganda become *more* intense. Fritz Sauckel provided one example of this policy in 1944 with his widely disseminated article, "The Fools of London." The tone was dominated by the apoplectic, fanatic fury of the "Old Fighter" allowing himself one last smirk at the expense of poor "Old England at the end of its glory." Sauckel connected the fall of the British Empire with London's rejection of the hand of "the greatest and most brilliant European of all times, namely, Adolf Hitler ..." The men who rejected Hitler's peace offers were fools being used by the Jews, especially Churchill, the "slave of the Jews and of alcohol." [46] One *Gau* propaganda central office distributed the Sauckel speech to all *Gau* and district speakers, informing them of the "valuable contents of its anti-Jewish propaganda"—on March 2, 1944.

Goebbels himself played a role in inducing the German press to give prominent space to praising certain propaganda works concerned with the British enemy. Wilhelm Ziegler's *A Documentary Work on English Humanity* and Giselher Wirsing's *A Hundred Families Rule England* were particularly attractive to the minister.[47] Goebbels understood the effectiveness of multimedia propaganda campaigns. He ordered Fritz Hippler to bring his material to the attention of Emil Jannings for possible use in his cinematic work. Two other books, somewhat more serious in tone than the junk produced by Ernst Clam or the smug idiocy later displayed by Fritz Sauckel, appeared in 1940 and 1941. Professor Bruno Raücker's *The Social Backwardness of Great Britain* and A. Reithinger's *The World Empire and the Axis: Great Britain's Strength and Weakness, the Appearance and the Reality of Her Economic Power* complemented each other. Raücker showed Britain to be a repressive and exploitative land, while Reithinger demonstrated how and why the British Empire was doomed.

Raücker, basing his book on the insights of the nineteenth-century sociologist W. H. Riehl and of Oswald Spengler, believed that each nation had a concept of work in harmony with its national character. The Englishman was an "adventurer" and "explorer," the prototype of the "pioneer." This meant that the British lacked any sense of a fair social policy, for labor was only a means to profit, not the highest national value. Raücker suggested that Britain's situation as an insular country may have accounted for this English characteristic. The result was an inability to overcome unemployment, in contrast to the success of the Third Reich in this area.[48] Reithinger took up the same theme in a different context, arguing that British power stemmed not from work and creativity, but from manipulation of other countries through brute force and financial corruption. British imperialism could not overcome the contradictions inherent in such a defective society, however, and the low British birth rate was but one contemporary sign that the days of the artificial British Empire were over. Reithinger pointed to unemployment and the "retreat of British industry from world markets" as signs of decline. He correctly predicted that the aftermath of the war would see Britain lose her central position in world commerce, shipbuilding, and currency exchange: "The world empire is already reduced to fighting for its very life, not for the preservation of its traditional form of life."[49]

During the first three years of the war, Nazi media propaganda used Winston Churchill as the symbol of this brutality and decay. Neville Chamberlain had not offered so convenient a target. He had been "reasonable" at Munich, and his appearance as a fatherly lover of peace made it difficult to switch gears and attack him as a vicious warmonger. Churchill, on the other hand, was a veteran Germany-hater in the eyes of the Nazis, and they turned him into a cigar-chomping, hypocritical, drunken gangster, the symbol of British "plutocracy." Max Domarus has catalogued some of the terms used by the Nazis in their descriptions of Winston Churchill: "crazy fool," "crazy," "whiskey-blissful boozer," "a big mouthed guzzler," "a liar," etc.[50] A German parody on "Our father who art in heaven" did refer to Chamberlain ("Father Chamberlain who art in London . . .") as a "bum for all eternity," but such attacks lacked the pungent quality of the Nazi portrait of Churchill.

Before Churchill became prime minister, the Nazi-controlled media described him in somewhat less personal terms, calling him the violator of Scandinavian neutrality, a warmonger, and an irrational hater of the Third Reich. As late as May 9, 1940, one day before Churchill assumed the prime ministership, Goebbels told his media people that they could dispose of a recent speech by Churchill "with a couple of witty observations." [51] As Churchill and his clique of "plutocrats" became the symbols of British resistance, Goebbels' tone changed.[52] He hoped that the attacks on Churchill would lead to his overthrow. Churchill now became a murderer of children because of RAF bombings, and the British urban population had to submit to devastating counterblows by the Luftwaffe, all because of one maniac.[53] In December Goebbels compared Churchill to a gambler who has lost 90 percent of his stake, only to raise the ante in a desperate attempt to recoup all his losses.[54] The attacks became more vicious when Goebbels gleefully quoted an alleged American account of how the sixty-seven-year-old whiskey

"Even the disguise was in vain!" Anti-Churchill cartoon, spring 1940. Churchill, defeated in Norway, orders his pathetic raft full speed ahead to the Mediterranean, where he and the moth-eaten British lion will no doubt meet with new catastrophes.

guzzler had been repeatedly outfoxed by the fifty-two-year-old tea-drinking Führer.[55]

Goebbels' essays and speeches of 1941 contained an enormous quantity of sarcastic, vindictive remarks about Churchill. In February he called Churchill a murderer of Boer women and children and described the prime minister the "first violinist" in the "infernal concert" produced by the "demoplutocratic" world.[56] Churchill was now a man who walked over piles of corpses in order to satisfy his perverted ambition. He was a cynic and voluptuary; the burnt-out stump of a cigar symbolized a corrupt life in total decline. He wanted war for the sake of war: This relatively mild statement may have contained an element of truth, but it disappeared in the piles of verbal manure with which Goebbels buried Churchill. Churchill was in league with Bolshevists in their common devastation of Europe. The attacks continued into November 1941: "As it is well known, the British Prime Minister Churchill enjoys an extraordinarily close relationship with alcohol. His relations with the truth are much more tenuous . . ." [57] Early in 1942 Goebbels noted, "Stalin's bust has been unveiled in the London Exchange. That's where it belongs. . . . England has sunk low. She is facing difficult times. She can thank Churchill. . . ." [58] However cynical his attacks, Goebbels had his private moments of insight. He noted in February that the British were a stubborn people, but concluded, ". . . possibly that is a national advantage rather than a disadvantage." [59] Of course, he refused (until 1944) to acknowledge that Churchill symbolized and fortified that "stubbornness." The growing military crisis caused the German propaganda apparatus to somewhat diminish the personal attacks on Churchill in the course of 1942. Hitler did not overrule this change in policy, but privately he continued to believe that Churchill should not be spared: He was "the undisciplined swine" drunk "eight hours of every twenty-four." "God help a nation that accepts the leadership of a Thing like that!" Hitler exclaimed.[60] By 1944 Goebbels had grudging respect for Churchill, even though he was the "fanatically rigid" half-American premier who was ready to hand Europe over to the Reds. If only he would die—but the old man seemed indestructible!

A major part of the Nazi attack upon Churchill rested upon his connection with Roosevelt. Churchill and his "plutocratic" clique were traitors to Europe, for they were ready to hand the British Empire over to FDR, and Europe to Stalin, in order to maintain their own shaky control over England. In a propaganda bulletin distributed to officials of the Reich Labor Service late in 1943, the noted journalist Otto Kriegk wrote, "It is altogether possible that Churchill can only continue the war that he started by his [sic] guarantee to Poland by surrendering this guarantee and handing Polish territories over to the Bolsheviks." [61] This statement did not lack insight into the future of Poland, but its imputation to Churchill of nefarious schemes and powers was vintage Nazi propaganda. The Nazi argument that Churchill was placing Britain in an inferior position in relation to the United States contained a valid insight, but the Nazis divorced this perception from its context of an English war for survival. Moreover, Hitler had seriously underestimated the ties of sentiment and interest that united Britain and America, and he did so because he typically ignored advice from "unreliable" sources.

Albrecht Haushofer had written a report for the prestigious *Journal for Geopolitics* which warned, "Whoever gets into a conflict with Britain should know that America too will be among his opponents, in spite of all neutrality laws." [62] By July 1939 Haushofer realized that Germany could not stand a long military struggle, yet American participation on the side of the enemy would ensure such a war. In October Haushofer was reaching the conclusion that the war would bring the Russians and the Americans into the heart of Europe. Haushofer was arrested for interrogation after the flight of his friend Rudolf Hess. He quoted Professor Carl Burckhardt, former League of Nations high commissioner in Danzig, to the effect that a continuation of the war would diminish the chances of the anti-Churchill "peace forces" in England, since power over the British Empire was passing into American hands at an accelerating pace. One of the reasons for Hess's desperate flight may have been a comment made to him by Haushofer late in 1940: "If the worst came to the worst, the English would rather transfer their whole Empire bit by bit to the Americans than sign a peace that left to National Socialist Germany the mastery of Europe." [63] Hitler hoped in July 1940 that the British would come to their senses when they realized that they "were losing their position as the leading maritime power to America." [64] When Churchill did not disappear, Nazi propaganda emphasized the theme of the abdication of empire, but more out of a sense of sadistic despair than diplomatic hope.

In 1942 Goebbels developed a theme that was to play a major role in Nazi ideological propaganda. While the Germans were building Europe and a just, new social order, British imperialists were losing their bases, leases, and empire to American imperialists. Their pitiful resistance was merely the discomfort of a dying man. "The Americans can hardly satisfy their appetites and no longer make any effort to camouflage their imperialistic aims with democratic phrases," he commented. "The English will someday realize how dependent upon Washington they have become throughout their alliance with the United States. . . ." Goebbels believed that in fact, the English had "already lost the war." [65]

Certain American "revisionist" historians have taken this line since about 1966, but Goebbels' motive was the cynical spite of a sore loser, not the intellectual inquiry of a scholar or journalist. Nevertheless, he was on to an interesting theme, one which reflected his flashes of intelligence in political matters.

The Main Educational Office of the party produced many materials which contained this thesis. It dredged up quotations from Friedrich List (ca. 1834) predicting, "England will lose its empire to the United States." [66] Throughout 1943 Goebbels and Scharping played upon this theme, though in different ways. After the Teheran Conference, Goebbels contemptuously noted that among the so-called Big Three, Churchill's name now was listed in third place on the official communiqués of the Allies. But of course, he commented, "We do not belong to those who consider ... Churchill to be a great statesman." [67] Scharping gloated after Stalingrad that the Americans were shutting out the English. As one German city after another fell victim to Allied bombings, Scharping continued to mock the weakness of Great Britain and its incapacity to lead or organize the postwar world. God had indeed finally punished England, and in the Nazi mental framework this alone was one vindication of the brilliance of Hitler's leadership, even if Germany was ruined. Victory in death ...

Hitler had profound misgivings about turning the British Empire into an ideological foe of Germany. Here, after all, was a largely "Nordic" nation which had brought the domination of the white man to places from Hong Kong to the Ganges. German mass media long hesitated about using anti-imperialist arguments when confronting Great Britain. By 1942 a decision had been reached, for it was clear that this war would be a long one, and one in which no mercy would be shown. The media followed Goebbels and Ribbentrop in emphasizing Germany's sympathy for oppressed India, but scarcely two months before Hitler received Subhas Chandra Bose, head of the pro-Axis "Indian Freedom Movement," the Führer still had misgivings. "If the English give India back her liberty, within twenty years India will have lost her liberty again," he believed. "If it's true that the English have exploited India, it's also true that India has drawn a profit from English domination." [68] Japan, Italy, and even Germany were trying to create new imperiums in an age of declining imperialism. Caught in this contradiction, Hitler sadly underestimated the force of Indian nationalism, over which he had no control, only to fall into the trap of supporting an opportunist without influence—Bose. Hitler did not feel comfortable in the role of liberator, especially of dark-skinned "natives." The result was a massive propaganda assault, not so much *for* national liberation, as *against* decadent British imperialism.

The massive intervention of German forces under Rommel in North Africa in 1941–42 increased German interest in India, since it appeared conceivable that the Japanese might move on India from the east, while Axis forces drove on the Middle East from the Caucasus and Egypt. In June 1941, while battles raged in the deserts of North Africa, the German press declared that British General Wavell wanted more Indians to bleed to death in the service of Britain.[69] Goebbels, at first hesitant about Bose, later used the Indian in his "Free India Central Office" within the ministry. Bose became prominent in the press-mobilization campaign of 1942, which was inaugurated at a time when it appeared that Rommel and Mussolini might soon be in Alexandria. The press was to counterattack the "Four Freedoms" and the "One World" propaganda by contrasting the realities of British rule in India with the grandiose proclamations of the Western Allies.[70] The Indian campaign in the press had a parallel in the mobilization of other media. Ludwig Alsdorf's book *India,* published in a series edited by Rosenberg, impressed Bormann, and he ordered the party chancellory to send copies to every Gauleiter for distribution to district officials.[71] The propagandists did not ignore the lecture circuit in their campaign. Bose himself made many speeches, praising German culture for its interest in Sanskrit and the ancient Aryans of India, and denouncing the British for imperialism in India. Professor P.T. Roy, an Indian associate of Bose, spoke in different places on topics such as "England the adversary of the Nordic spirit in India" and "On the most recent events in Asia." [72] The pages of party journals were open to contributions from these men; in August Bose wrote on "Free India and Its Problems" for *Will and Power,* the Hitler Youth journal published by Baldur von Schirach.[73]

The foreign office was particularly proud of Bose, taking credit for "putting the right man in the right place." Much of the anti-British "India" propaganda in the German media derived from men working directly or indirectly for the foreign office, where Adam von Trott zu Solz was the special advisor on Indian affairs.[74] The establishment of a German-Indian society in Hamburg in September 1942 was one expression of this wartime propaganda. Ribbentrop sponsored the "Indo-German Work Community," a center for Indian propaganda located in Dahlem. Bose had been honorary chairman of the Indian–Central European Society since its founding in Vienna early in 1934. Bose told his German collaborators what they wanted to hear, that Hitler and Mussolini were the best friends of the Indian people, and that the majority of the Indian people was leaning toward the Axis. German specialists on India argued among themselves throughout 1943 regarding the future of India. These disputes took place in an atmosphere of increasing unreality. German propaganda regarding India had no practical significance, but it was important as part of the total ideological framework within which the German media confronted Great Britain.

Ireland offered a more fruitful source of anti-British propaganda to the German ideologues. Many Germans had demonstrated their sympathy for oppressed Ireland before and during the First World War, sometimes to the extent of running guns to Irish nationalists. Ireland was neutral and anti-British when war broke out in 1939, and the republic stuck to this course until 1945. Here was an island of strategic importance to Great Britain that offered German propagandists rich material for demonstrating the perfidy of British rule. The German mass media directed an endless barrage of "Irish" propaganda at the German people, a campaign intended to stoke the flames of righteous wrath in both Ireland and Germany, but particularly in Germany. Hitler set the tone of this propaganda before the war, when he declared before the Reichstag (in his famous April 28, 1939, speech denouncing FDR), "I have to call Mr. Roosevelt's attention, moreover, to several historical errors. ... I have just read a speech of the Irish minister president De Valera, in which, strange to say, he does not accuse Germany of oppressing Ireland, but accuses England of continuing its aggression against his state." [75] The only time during the war when the German media avoided using the Irish theme was in late June and July of 1940, when Hitler hoped that the British would come to terms with him.[76]

Nazi publishers released enormous numbers of pamphlets and books dealing with the British oppression of Ireland, particularly in 1940 and 1941. In 1940 the press of the German Labor Front published "Ferdinand Gral's" (Heinrich Bauer's) *England's Wars—the History of British Wars on Five Continents.* Despite official misgivings about certain elements of Bauer's treatment of history, almost a million copies of the brochure were distributed by the Reich Ring for Popular Enlightenment and Propaganda in 1941. Bauer's thesis was that Britain had grown great by waging aggressive wars. Ireland played a prominent role as victim in his narrative.[77] The Franz Eher Verlag published Reinald Hoops' *Ireland and England,* a book in the "That Is England!" series. Hoops described the British presence in Ireland as one long tale of suffering, famine, and depopulation. He delineated the Irish struggle for freedom in some detail and with great sympathy.[78] The mentality of Nazi writers allowed them to denounce British "depopulation" policies in Ireland and to praise the Irish struggle for liberty without reflecting upon the human slaughterhouses in Poland or German starvation policies in Greece and the Ukraine. The "Information Series" of the Europa Verlag contributed a pamphlet entitled *Ireland in the English Hell,* which reprinted excerpts from the work *Is God an Englishman?* of one Meyer-Erlach. "For centuries the Irish people has fought a desperate battle for its vital rights in its own land against the robbery and murder of British greed," states one passage. "England's day will come." [79] Meyer-Erlach's intemperate prose led him to portray Ireland as a nation on the cross, asking in despair if God, too, was an Englishman. Meyer-Erlach promised revenge and stated his faith in the future of a fully liberated Ireland. German propagandists such as Fritzsche and Scharping declared that although Ireland was an extreme case, British policy there typified England's long history of violation of the rights of small nations and peoples.

THE FOX OF GLENARVON

PRODUCTION: Tobis
DIRECTOR: M. W. Kimmisch
SCRIPT: W. Neumeister and Hans Bertram
MAJOR PERFORMERS: Olga Tschechowa
                 Ferdinand Marian
PREMIERE: April 24, 1940

Goebbels' propaganda apparatus made ample use of the cinema in presenting the Nazi version of the Anglo-Irish relationship to the German people. The *Fox of Glenarvon (Der Fuchs von Glenarvon),* starring Ferdinand Marian and Olga Tschechowa, was an elaborate, well-acted production which received its premiere in April 1940. The statement which precedes the story indicates the intent and the nature of the film: "Ireland—the green isle—is one of the oldest victims of English oppression! For eight centuries betrayal, fraud, robbery, murder, and destruction have been the methods of British policy. The story of this people is the story of millions of starved, deported, and executed persons. But the pride and the love of freedom among the Irish could not be broken."

Ferdinand Marian, as usual, the villain, is a British justice of the peace, Philip Grandison, in an Ireland torn by revolution. His Irish wife, Gloria, played by Olga Tschechowa, is sympathetic to the revolutionaries, but married Grandison in the idealistic hope of mitigating British rule and aiding her people. The story is set in the turbulent year 1921. Sir John Tetbury, the "hangman of India," will soon arrive to assist Grandison in suppressing the Irish patriots, who are determined men. As one rebel puts it, "The struggle for our freedom has cost many lives." The portrayal of Ireland and its revolution conforms to the style of National Socialism more than to that of De Valera or Collins. The hymns sung by the Irish sound more like Lutheran chorales than Catholic liturgy. The attempted disruption of a revolutionary's funeral procession by two English constables is similar to the scene in *Hans Westmar* where the Reds and their stooges desecrate the final salute to Horst Wessel. The weird rituals and dances of the secret Irish revolutionary band could only have been the products of German script writers ignorant of their subject. An Irish revolutionary who argues against revenge for its own sake sounds like Joseph Goebbels in 1932: "We are political fighters!"

The *Fox of Glenarvon* utilizes other themes popular among wartime German film directors: the woman as savior-heroine *(In the Eye of the Storm, Rite of Sacrifice, Kolberg)*, the splendor of British "plutocratic" ritual contrasted with the misery caused by the English *(Ohm Krüger)*, the gruesome hanging of the evil party *(Jud Süss)*. Gloria rejects Philip, who works with the hated Tetbury to frame and kill the rebels. She falls in love with John Ennis, a devoted Irish revolutionary, and aids her people in their just struggle against Tetbury's "ruthless, hard measures." In the concluding scene the revolutionaries try Grandison before a secret tribunal and find him guilty. He dies by hanging before British troops can rescue him. Another traitor, an agent of Grandison, is swallowed up by the moor's quicksand as he tries to escape. John Ennis points the way to Ireland's future: "This night will be a sign for all Ireland."

The attack upon British imperialism in the German mass media drew strength from the history of another oppressed people, the Afrikaans-speaking Boers of southern Africa. German sympathy for the Boers went back to the time of their struggle against British imperialism at the turn of the century, and the Nazis made enormous use of this reservoir of good will. Soon after the Second World War broke out, Goebbels ordered his staff to prepare a book documenting English "concentration camps" and "colonial atrocities." Rosenberg's bulletin on Nazi doctrine repeatedly attacked the Anglican church for its hypocritical justification of British policy, no matter how atrocious the actions of the state might be.[80] Hans Fritzsche took up this theme in a radio commentary broadcast in 1942: "England ... entered this, her fateful struggle, once more in the part of the moralizing tea-drinking governess who faints if anyone treads on the tail of her lapdog, but would have thought the starving out of all the women and children of a whole nation ... as a deed particularly pleasing in the eyes of God ..."[81] One of Goebbels' wartime statements, "Our Socialism," contained a phrase reminiscent of the last words of Ohm Krüger in the anti-British film of the same name: "A better world will emerge from the sufferings of this war."[82] The wartime notes of the confused prisoner Rudolf Hess contained mumblings about *die Buren,* the Boers.[83]

In 1940 Stefan Schroeder published a booklet of cartoons and commentaries, dating from 1901, which exemplified the contribution of the publishing media to the pro-Boer campaign. *England and the Boers* depicted the British policy as one of extermination exacerbated by hypocrisy.[84] Schroeder described Cecil Rhodes as a tool of Jewish capitalism in southern Africa. The Nazi media campaign equated British gold pirates, vicious adventurers, Anglican hypocrites, and Jewish capitalists. Schroeder used the technique of publishing cartoons illustrating British atrocities during the Boer War (1899–1902) with appended commentary by British officials. For example, a cartoon depicting the starvation of children in British concentration camps preceded an "official war office communiqué" describing the healthy, happy condition of Boer children in the same camps. A picture of British officers beating up an old lady preceded the statement, "The humanity of our soldiers is a source of wonderment and is always the same."

OHM KRÜGER

PRODUCTION: Tobis
DIRECTOR: Hans Steinhoff, H. Maisch, and Karol Anton
SCRIPT: H. Bratt and K. Heuser
MAJOR PERFORMERS: Emil Jannings
                         W. Hinz
                         H. Wangel
                         Gustav Gründgens
                         Ferdinand Marian
PREMIERE: April 4, 1941

The most expensive and most powerful statement of the wartime Boer campaign in the German mass media was Emil Jannings' elaborate film *Ohm Krüger.* Goebbels himself commissioned and controlled this production. The film cost over five million Reichsmarks, or five times as much as was expended upon the average motion picture. Steinhoff described the film as political propaganda "intended to unmask England." The magazine *The German Film* saw Ohm Krüger as "the bearer of the destiny of a people, symbol of the struggle waged by a people of simple and pure peasants against capitalist exploitation and brute force." [85] Goebbels awarded *Ohm Krüger* the title "film of the nation" and had good reason to be pleased with the results of Emil Jannings' production. The acting was brilliant, the battle and crowd scenes spectacular, the settings impressive, and the dialogue taut. Emil Jannings received the title "artist of the state" for his efforts. *Ohm Krüger* carried off the honors of "best foreign film" at the Venice film festival, thus making Jannings the recipient of the Mussolini trophy cup. His enthusiasm led him to make some outspoken statements: "I played [Ohm Krüger] because he had been chosen to start that [the struggle which] will be concluded in our time." [86] Jannings' joy in the realism of the film even led him to brag about the number of extras killed during the production process. The entire motion picture revolved around the figure of the protagonist, played powerfully and yet humorously by the brilliant Jannings. He was supported by a talented cast, including Ferdinand Marian as the evil Cecil Rhodes and Gustav Gründgens as the wicked colonial secretary Joseph Chamberlain.

The film begins as an ailing, blind Ohm Krüger, president of the Boer republic, broods in a darkened hotel room in Switzerland. He has come to Europe during the Boer War in order to find support for the beleaguered Boer nation. The London press describes him as enjoying himself in luxury while his people suffer. Ohm Krüger comments, "When a lie is repeated over and over, then it is finally believed." A pushy Jewish photographer from the *Berliner Tageblatt,* one of Goebbels' great hate objects, manages to sneak into Krüger's room and take a flash photograph of the old man, thus gaining a scoop at the expense of Krüger's failing eyesight. Krüger later reflects on the history of his small, virtuous people, and through flashback technique the film offers the vision of a people enamored of peace and freedom who are forced to trek northward because of the relentless pressure of the English. The happy life of the Boers in their new home in the Transvaal is interrupted by the discovery of gold in their territory. Cecil Rhodes and his agent Jameson scheme to get their hands on this wealth and we have the setting for a classic Nazi conflict: blood against gold, honor against greed, race against capitalism.

Ohm Krüger is filled with caricatures, funny both intentionally and, one suspects, in ways unintended. Rhodes uses the willing Anglican Church to arm the black natives agains the Boers. In one of the most memorable and funniest scenes, two Anglican priests march down an aisle, one carrying copies of the Bible, the other a brace of carbines. As a band plays "God Save the Queen," one priest dispenses the weapons, the other the Bible. This image of British hypocrisy only confirmed an attitude widely held by many Europeans and Americans since the late nineteenth century. Even the caricatures in this film survive the heavy-handed intent of Joseph Goebbels, for the acting is superb and the film technique superior. Krüger resists British encroachments, forbidding foreigners to buy Boer land without the approval of the state council. There are traitors within the Boer "folk community," however, and some of these liberal types even sell sacred Boer soil to Jews. Krüger embodies the nature of his people, a warm paterfamilias with forty-five grand-children, a folksy character who acts firmly but sympathetically when dealing with the "natives." The blacks in the film are naive and childlike, playthings in the hands of the conniving Rhodes. By confronting the black chiefs with his knowledge of the source of their rifles, Krüger disarms the black men and leaves to the cheers of the assembled tribesmen.

The next major scene is one of the funniest in the film. It takes us to Buckingham Palace in London, where Colonial Secretary Joseph Chamberlain is trying to persuade old Queen Victoria to support English seizure of the Boer lands. Chamberlain is unctuous and hypocritical, justifying his plans by pointing to Boer "backwardness." The old lady is dubious, for, in her words, "people call us robbers." Chamberlain makes it a religious duty to steal the Boer lands. After the queen takes several swigs of her "medicine" (whiskey), Chamberlain hits her with an argument sure to convince: He mentions the word *gold.* Victoria, now slightly inebriated, replies, "Gold! If there is gold, then the Boer lands belong to us!" Chamberlain agrees, for he believes that only the English "are able to become so rich and yet remain so pious" at the same time.

Krüger comes to London, trying to avoid war. Chamberlain brings him there to impress him with the pomp and power of the Empire, thus hoping to force the old man to sign a treaty advantageous to British capitalist interests. The scene in which Krüger is received at court is one of the most powerful screen images of the wartime Third Reich. Heroic music sounds as old President Krüger walks slowly towards Victoria's throne, surrounded on all sides by generals and aristocrats in uniform. Krüger signs the treaty, though he knows that the powerful British will probably violate its terms. They do so, but the old man outfoxes Rhodes by charging a prohibitive tax on gold mining and exports on Boer territory. Rhodes confronts Krüger with unctuous flattery and offers of a huge bribe, but these tricks do not work on the sly old man. Krüger, who had resigned to protest the violation of the treaty, returns to office an angry, determined man. Another powerful scene appears on the screen: The Boer masses rise up as one nation; they mobilize for war by marching to the sounds of heroic, martial music, carrying banners inscribed "Down with England!"

British concentration camps in South Africa, ca. 1901. *(Ohm Krüger)*

CREDIT: The International Museum of Photography, Rochester, New York

The patriotism and enthusiasm of Krüger and his *Volk* contrast with another favorite Nazi theme, that of the traitor within the nation. Krüger's son Jan is thoroughly anglicized, a self-proclaimed "pacifist" (though in typically German style, Jan stands at attention when declaring to his angry father, "I am a pacifist!"). Jan, the pacifist, foreshadows the violinist Klaus in *Kolberg,* a young man who will not fight Napoleon's army because "one must be a citizen of the world." German propaganda instructions often contained denunciations of "cosmopolitan" Germans who despised their own nation and preferred foreign styles and ideas to German ones.[87] Krüger disowns his son, declaring that this "is a struggle of life and death" in which no one has the right to refuse to serve the cause.

Goebbels and Jannings portrayed the Boer War as a righteous form of guerrilla warfare against plutocracy and arrogance. The Boers raise a true *Volksarmee,* a people's army, which even contains an eighty-two-year-old unit commander. The Boers are courageous and righteous; the contrast with the Anglican missionaries is absolute. Jan bides his time, expecting to come to power under the beneficent protection of the British when the Boers are defeated. He drinks to peace with the British, the classic collaborator-traitor. Yet he, too, undergoes a change in the course of the film and in a most dramatic way. A British officer tries to rape Jan's wife, and the young man loses his pacifism while killing the intruder. He returns to his people a true patriot.

The great theme of *Ohm Krüger* was British cruelty. The British commanders, such as Lord Kitchener, are brutal: "Enough of this humanity drivel!" he cries. Kitchener, unable to subdue the tenacious Boers by traditional military methods, bombards the civilian population of Pretoria and uses Boer women and children to form a protective wall for his troops. The situation of the Boers becomes desperate as the English augment their brutal methods of war. Though delighted by the conversion of Jan, Ohm Krüger is saddened by the fate of his *Volk*. He travels to Europe in order to secure diplomatic and military help for his nation. Everywhere he is hailed as a hero, but despite universal sympathy, he does not obtain help, for no one wishes to anger the British lion. At this point Jannings includes a riotous scene typical of the Goebbels wit. While the dissolute Edward, Prince of Wales, enjoys a lewd burlesque review in Paris, he receives news that his mother, the queen, is dying. Edward visits her bedside, where Victoria croaks out a few last words of warning. She tells Edward that he must end this war, which is bringing upon the empire the "hatred of all peoples." She fears future retribution, which is precisely the German mission in 1940.

The situation of the Boers is desperate by 1901. The British institute concentration camps, one of which is presided over by a particularly sadistic commandant who looks much like Winston Churchill.[88] Women and children starve to death or are provided with spoiled rations. It is clear that this commandant has no use for the "false humanity drivel" that Goebbels continued to denounce in 1942. It is ironic but hardly atypical that Goebbels employed the very same words in criticizing the softness of *German* commandants of POW camps during the Second World War! [89] The English commandant makes an example of Jan, hanging him before the eyes of his own loved ones. Throughout the last scene, Krüger muses in his Swiss hotel about the moral retaliation which will one day be visited upon the British Empire. As in 1945 *(Kolberg)*, the suffering hero draws strength from the thought that all "was not in vain." England has won this war, but one day the great nations of the earth will rise up against British tyranny and create a better world. This is a thinly veiled allusion to the world that National Socialist ideology and the German media claimed to be creating in 1940: "And then the way will be free for a better world!"

10

"Jewish-Bolshevik Subhumanity": The Media War Against Soviet Russia

The German mass media attacked the British and their leader because they were "plutocrats" and "hypocritical imperialists." Within this structure there were nuances reflecting previous Nazi comments about the desirability of an English alliance. The British were human beings, even Nordics, with unfortunate moral and political characteristics; they were, however, human. Nazi media propaganda contained no such ambiguities when it dealt with Soviet Russia. The Bolsheviks were the archetypes of "Jewish criminality," the scum of subhumanity, an anti-world of loathsome hatred and perverted envy, committed to the destruction of everything good and beautiful.

Wartime Nazi anti-Communist ideology was built upon traditions which were securely in place by 1939, but which had to be shelved during the Hitler-Stalin period of rapprochement, 1939–41. Hitler's view of the Bolsheviks had emerged by 1923. His contact with White Russian émigrés and with the theoreticians Alfred Rosenberg and Dietrich Eckart, as well as his experiences in the turbulent Munich of 1918–19, had all contributed to the formulation of this murderous world view. Some of the elements of the Nazi concept of Jewish Bolshevism went back to the late nineteenth century—to "Darwinian" concepts of struggle, to Le Bon's theories about crowd manipulation, to Otto Seeck's view that the decline of Rome was the result of the "extermination of the best" in the racial cesspool of the fourth and fifth centuries A.D. H.S. Chamberlain contributed the insight that the czarist Russian state was the work of immigrant Germans; when the "Jews" and their tools swept it away in 1917, Russia had to grow weak and collapse. For Hitler, Stalin's Russia was both a temptation and a puzzle. It had to be basically weak, for it was the work of oppressive Jews; yet, it was dangerous, a sort of international bubonic plague that threatened to subvert the West. In its own way, Hitler's image of Bolshevism was but the Western middle-class view carried to the extreme of caricature.[1]

In his posthumously published *Bolshevism from Moses to Lenin: A Dialogue between Adolf Hitler and Me,* Dietrich Eckart gave the world a clear portrayal of the obsession shared by both himself and his friend Hitler.[2] Hitler excitedly told Eckart of his discovery that even in antiquity the Jews had turned one nation against another and cared only for themselves. He even "proved" their "Bolshevism" in the Book of Esther, where they allegedly murdered seventy-five thousand Persians. Years later Hitler built upon this "knowledge" to announce that the Armenians of today led a miserable existence because they were the descendants of intermarriage between Persians and Jews! Hitler saw the Jew as the intellectual and physical poisoner of the world, a creature who seduced Aryan maidens and managed to produce pure Jews through this union. The sexual element in Hitler's revulsion against Jewish Bolshevism was ever present, often consisting of accusations of incest and venereal disease, two of his manias. "The Jew has destroyed hundreds of cultures, but built none of its own," Eckart quotes Hitler as saying. "All social injustice in the world goes back to the subterranean influence of the Jews." Hitler believed that the Jews wished to conquer the world in order to destroy it. He added an incredible comment, namely, that the Jews would persist even unto their own destruction by Aryans, who were defending the world and themselves. The Jews sensed this coming destruction. They were thus "tragic" figures in the sense of Lucifer, for they could not act otherwise. As early as 1923, Hitler clearly outlined the coming destruction of the Jews, which he made the work of their own people. This was the ultimate projection of the Nazis' murderous impulses onto their victims. One sees this tendency in 1923 as in 1945.

Hitler and National Socialist ideology saw the Jews as the common tie between Christianity and Bolshevism. Both were leveling movements directed against race and excellence, movements of agitation which undermined and destroyed all greatness in the name of pity and equality. "The heaviest blow that ever struck humanity was the coming of Christianity. Bolshevism is Christianity's illegitimate child. Both are inventions of the Jew," Hitler commented in July 1941.[3] On another occasion Hitler found links between St. Paul, Trotsky, and the Jews, though he commented that a healthy reaction against this swamp of the anti-world was still possible. In order to save the world, men would have to deal with the problem ruthlessly and without Christian scruples. The Germans did indeed do so, and this was part of the success of Hitler. Every Jew carried the seeds of subversion and destruction, and all would have to be killed, down to the last babe in arms. Nazi ideologists often portrayed this struggle as the defense of Christianity, but Hitler and Himmler knew that only the elimination of the traces of the Christian ethic of pity could produce men capable of such "necessary measures." If the Jew were not destroyed, he would triumph, mobilizing the "plutocrats" of London and Wall Street and the Bolsheviks of Russia to achieve world rule through the extermination of the vanguard of the Aryan peoples.

Joseph Goebbels made his own wartime contributions to this ideology in his speeches and in the "German Weekly Newsreel." He commented late in 1941 that the German people were learning about the "atrocities of the GPU Soviet secret police and the Jewish gallows henchmen" from PK reports.[4] The "Newsreel" showed the torture chambers of the GPU, places where they murdered Lettish or Ukrainian nationalists. In March 1942, after the first hard Russian winter, the minister noted in his diary, "The situation is ripe for putting an end to Bolshevism in all Europe, and considering our position we can't give up that aim."[5] Goebbels took personal command of the famous "Soviet Paradise," or anti-Bolshevik exhibition, in the Berlin Lustgarten in April 1942, though Wächter was in charge of daily operations. This exhibition was intended to be proof to the German workers that Communism was not in their interests, for it rested upon misery, torture, and filth. As usual, Goebbels added his own twist, noting that actually the filthy stalls passing for workers' homes in the USSR had been cleaned up by his men before being opened to the public! A joke made the rounds of Berlin after the highly successful exhibition closed down: Question: "Why did they shut down the Soviet Paradise exhibition?" Answer: "Because the people of [working-class] north Berlin wanted their belongings back!" Goebbels maintained a certain consistency into 1945, writing in January that the Allied coalition was sticking together because of international Jewish glue.[6] Both Goebbels and Hitler repeatedly accused the Jews of genocide in 1945, after about six million Jews had perished at the hands of Germany and her allies.

As propaganda minister, Goebbels was particularly sensitive to the growing sense of unease among German civilians and soldiers late in 1941. The Bolsheviks had not collapsed; indeed, they were fighting tenaciously all along the front. Goebbels believed that Russian resistance might make Communism more attractive (or attractive once again) to many Germans. He therefore ruled out the Soviet commissar system as an explanation of Russian tenacity. Goebbels explained this resistance with a biological analogy: "A rat is also more capable of resistance than a domestic animal, because it lives amidst such terrible social circumstances that it must develop a healthy power of resistance if it is to exist at all." [7] Hitler described the Jew as a bacillus and Goebbels portrayed the Bolsheviks as rats. One did not treat such objects as human beings; one exterminated them in what Hitler called the "war of annihilation between doctrines." Goebbels returned to the problem of Soviet resistance in July, evidently dissatisfied with the results of his earlier reassurances. Now the Communists possessed "an almost animalistic persistence" and "contempt for death." [8] A few months later Hitler used the same theme: "If someone now says, 'But the Russian does get through after all'—yes, we have to admit that they are a type of swamp human and not European. It is more difficult for us to advance in this muck than it is for those people born in the morass." [9]

Goebbels' private thoughts about the Russians were somewhat more complex. He believed that the Russian was an eternal Pan-Slavist,[10] and that "great things" had been taking place in that land since the revolution. He claimed to have predicted this national upsurge twenty years before. Goebbels knew that Russian resistance was motivated not by a Jewish clique, but by what he called "the national creative spirit of the entire nation." The dictates of propaganda within Germany required, however, that the minister keep these ideas confined to a narrow circle of friends and employees. Goebbels actually admired the brutal determination of the Russian leaders and commissars. Referring to the German Communist leader of 1925-33, he told his colleagues that Germany required the same "Thaelmann types" if it was to defeat Russia.[11] Goebbels recommended to his subordinates that they view a Soviet film on the defense of Leningrad, for it demonstrated that the civilian population of the USSR was far more involved in a total war effort than was the case among the Germans. Goebbels' growing contempt for the German officer corps caused the minister to praise Stalin's extermination in 1937-38 of much of the Red Army elite.[12]

Joseph Goebbels did not believe in the Nazi propaganda which described the Slavs as subhumans, though he participated in its dissemination during the first year of the Russian campaign. He had misgivings as early as the spring of 1942, noting, "In the long run we cannot solicit additional workers from the East if we treat them like animals within the Reich." [13] Goebbels believed that public statements about the German exploitation of Russia were idiotic, resulting in harder Soviet resistance. His plan was to concentrate German propaganda against the Jews and the Bolsheviks, sparing the nationalities of the USSR. The permanent crisis on the eastern front from late 1942 on caused Goebbels to sound the alarm of victory or death, Bolshevism or triumph.[14] As early as November 25, only days after the initial Soviet success in the counterattack against the Axis armies on the Stalingrad front, Goebbels announced to his staff that propaganda would have to move into the breach and take the offensive once again.[15] Russian victories might be turned to good use, frightening the German people and its allies into renewed efforts towards final victory. "Our struggle against Bolshevism must be our propaganda slogan, used again and again," Goebbels stated, and he ordered his men to stop talking about conquests in the East and to shift to the crusade against Bolshevism.[16] The gains of the Red Army might not only lead to total war at home; they might have the pleasant side effect of bringing the Western Allies to the negotiating table with the Germans. For such reasons of state there was little room in Goebbels' propaganda for the "Slavic subhuman" nonsense so popular with Hitler and Himmler, and in somewhat different form, with Rosenberg.[17]

The anti-Bolshevik propaganda line of Goebbels' party and state agents during the wartime years was in some ways a return to theses advanced before 1939. Instructions for educational speakers distributed in 1937 and 1938 contained information about the "devil Stalin," the "Movement of the Militant Godless" in the Soviet Union, the role of the Jews in the GPU (Soviet secret police), the miserable standard of living prevalent in the USSR, and the part that the Japanese were playing in halting Soviet eastern expansion.[18] Goebbels was opportunistic, and he adapted, though with some displeasure, to the suppression of the anti-Soviet line during the years of the Hitler-Stalin pact, much as he had done during the years of the Hitler-Hugenberg alliance. The ministry and the RPL found it easy to return to their old outspoken anti-Bolshevism in 1941, when Hitler ordered the attack upon the Soviet Union.

A special issue of the RPL speakers' bulletin—"Germany Enters the Final Struggle against the Jewish-Bolshevik Murder System"—dredged up all the old ravings against the Bolsheviks.[19] It also contained a new element, the suggestion that the Jews were behind the unlikely yet natural (if you think about it) alliance between plutocrats and Reds. Party speakers were to explain to the people that Germany once again owed its salvation to Adolf Hitler, who at the last moment had saved Germany and Europe from a massive Communist invasion. Goebbels' experts on the Jewish-Bolshevik conspiracy, E. Taubert and W. Die- werge,[20] provided massive amounts of material for the Information

Service of the RPL: The Jews were using Russian Pan-Slavism; the Jew Kaganovitch pulled the strings for Stalin; the Jews were behind Soviet resistance, using the instrument of GPU terror to frighten Soviet soldiers into hopeless battles. In contrast to the later line, some instructions for party speakers emphasized that there was no Russian people, only thirty-eight ethnic groups in the "former" Soviet Union. Speakers were to point out, "The Jews and the plutocrats have sold Germany and the whole European world out to Bolshevism. Under the dictatorship of the mass murderer Stalin, millions of Germans, men, women, and children, would have been killed." [21] By 1942 the key RPL slogan was "Victory or Bolshevik Chaos," a variation on the "victory or death" theme. Propaganda against the plutocrats now receded behind the massive barrage directed against the Bolsheviks.

One "Propaganda Slogan" bulletin declared that Stalin had decided as early as 1923 that Berlin was to be the center of the Bolshevik world. It reprinted alleged quotations from Winston Churchill (1921) and Malcolm Muggeridge (1934) to the effect that the USSR was run by Jews who oppressed and exploited everyone else.[22] The renewed campaign against Bolshevism represented not so much a new attack upon *Marxism*, but rather the high point of Goebbels' crusade against the *Jews*. The last Jews were deported from his Berlin. In April 1943 the Information Service distributed a "Jewish School Calendar" which quoted statements allegedly made by Jewish authors, including the anonymous composers of the *Protocols of the Elders of Zion*. These quotations were "proof" that the Jews intended to take revenge upon the gentile world for its anti-Semitism, and seize power everywhere on the globe.

A front group subsidized by the ministry, the Anti-Semitic Action (ASA), had a library and files containing ammunition for the anti-Jewish murder campaign. Other ministeries and agencies made use of the materials contained in the ASA storage rooms, which included the files of the Institute for the Scientific Study of the Jewish Question. The Anti-Comintern (AC), a subordinate branch of the eastern division of the ministry, returned to life after a period of dormancy during the Hitler-Stalin pact. Its budget for fiscal 1942 was about RM 1.6 million, of which almost one fifth was devoted exclusively to anti-Jewish propaganda. This anti-Jewish division took over the files and responsibilities of the ASA. The AC was supposed to provide materials for anti-Bolshevik, anti-Jewish, and anti-Freemason propaganda, but all of its work, directly or indirectly, revolved around the "Jewish question." The organization contained five divisions, press, Soviet Union, foreign countries, anti-Jewish action, and administration. By 1943 it employed 124 men and women,

published the journal *The Jewish Question* twice a month in editions of
1,200 copies, maintained a library of 40,000 volumes, and planned a new
journal, *The Archives on the Jewish Question.* Auditors found its books in
good order. Unfortunately, the great Allied air raid on Berlin of
November 22, 1943, resulted in the destruction of all the valuable
treasures of the AC, thus depriving Goebbels' men of its "scholarly"
resources at a crucial time in Greater Germany's Freedom Struggle.[23]

Branches and affiliated organizations of the party often used materials
provided by the propaganda ministry and the RPL in their own internal
work. The SA, long a rather dormant organization, decided to activate its
internal propaganda along the lines of Goebbels' anti-Bolshevik approach. The result was a series of propaganda slogans and bulletins for
the SA membership, which contained every phrase that the RPL used, in
even cruder and more easily understood form. In 1941–42 this meant
describing the primitive animality of the Red Army soldier, a subhuman
devoid of all idealism. Lest readers or listeners make unfortunate
comparisons with the SA, say, of 1932, the authors of SA propaganda
bulletins emphasized the Soviet lack of any real *idealism.*[24]

During the last year of the war the propaganda division of the ministry
ordered the German press and radio to tell the nation what Bolshevism
meant in areas under Stalin's thumb. Alarming indications of satellite
attempts to break free of German control provoked specific instructions
concerning the future of such foolish, apostate nations and their leaders.
In March 1944 the German mass media indirectly warned wavering
Finland that a Western guarantee would be worthless to a would-be
neutral country confronted by Soviet advances in Europe.[25] The German
propagandists cleverly called the Finns' attention to the case of Italy,
which proved that a betrayal of the Reich could not get a nation out of
the war. The Germans described Italy as a battleground and a nation in
which chaos and Communism were the only alternatives to national
greatness (Mussolini) and an alliance with Germany. By the end of 1944
self-deception had become a motivating force within the propaganda
department's view of the world. Reports absurdly exaggerating the
potential of anti-Soviet partisan activity in the Baltic countries and the
Ukraine received much attention at the Wilhelmsplatz and were passed
on to the German press. *The New Day* (Prague) reported that a Swedish
newspaper had described a Soviet plan to build a gas line from Moscow
to Saratov with German and Axis slave labor.[26] Goebbels himself
indicated as late as February 24, 1945, that the German media should
continue to discuss the miserable living conditions that were prevalent in
the Soviet Union.

The German press began its concerted verbal and pictorial attack upon Bolshevism and its lackeys on June 24, 1941. A selection of headlines from the *National-Zeitung,* a party paper, gives some sense of the manner in which the press carried out the instructions of party and state: "Moscow Waited for London's Signal" (June 24); "Stalin and Churchill Arm in Arm" (June 25); "Europe Rises up Against Bolshevism" (June 28); "Jewish Agitation from Moscow" (July 10); "Roosevelt Is Looking for an Incident" (July 6). The press compared Hitler's invasion of Russia to the measures Hitler had taken to destroy German Communism after the Reichstag fire of 1933.[27] Newspapers received instructions from Otto Dietrich that they were to play up the horrified reactions of German soldiers to living conditions in the "workers' paradise." Many dispatches from the east emphasized the atrocities that the Jewish Reds had committed against Ukrainian and Latvian nationalists. Other reports, boastful in tone, tried to allay the fears of an older generation which had experienced great victories but final defeat in 1914–18. Early in July 1941 many newspapers pointed out that the German Army had reached points that it had taken three years to capture during the First World War.[28]

In the summer of 1941 the German press received instructions and materials relating to the historic role of the Soviet embassies in Paris and Berlin in murders, high treason, and sabotage. Rosenberg, the Gestapo, and the Security Service of the SS had approved use of this material, which allegedly dated back to 1924–25. The Propaganda Ministry claimed that reasons of state had earlier necessitated the suppression of these files, but that it was permissible to publicize them now, provided that the Foreign Office agreed. Some of the files recently seized in Germany and France supposedly corroborated Nazi assumptions based upon evidence offered at trials in the Weimar Republic. A few months later, in November 1941, the German press published a great deal of material "exposing" Soviet imperialism as the child of the old czarist imperialism going back to Peter the Great.

Hitler himself dictated the outlines of the "Peter the Great" press campaign, using the theme of the contemporary alliance between Jewish Bolshevism and Slavic imperialism. Hans Fritzsche of the Promi and Paul Schmidt of the Foreign Office ordered the press to follow this guideline, emphasizing that newspapers could quote the "Testament" of Peter the Great to substantiate their arguments.[29] This so-called testament had been exposed as a forgery by German scholars during the First World War, but Hitler did not care what a bunch of professors thought. Russian policy had followed the principles of the Testament, and that was all that counted. The forged testament may have dated back to Napoleonic officials in 1812.

An official party newspaper announces the invasion of Russia "From the North Cape to the Black Sea the Fighting Front against Bolshevism." "Moscow's Double Game Revealed." "Russia Was Ready at Any Time to Attack Us from the Rear." "Hostile Troop Concentrations and Unheard-of Border Violations." *(Bayerische Ostmark*, Regensburg and Bayreuth)

CREDIT: The Library of Congress

The Propaganda Ministry and the Foreign Ministry collaborated in this press manipulation, however unpleasant the relations between Goebbels and Ribbentrop might be. In 1942 the Foreign Ministry noted that the Paris weekly *Toute la Vie* had run an article which blamed Sir Stafford Cripps and Stalin for the anti-German coup in Belgrade in 1941.[30] Another ministry official suggested that the poor treatment of Polish prisoners by the Russians would make good anti-atrocity propaganda for the German side. These Polish troops were now (May 1942) in Iran, and some of them had talked openly about their grim treatment by Soviet Russia. In February 1942 sources in the Foreign Ministry decided that the glorification of female Soviet partisans in the Allied press could be used by the German newspapers to show how the Bolsheviks violated the rules of war.[31] The Foreign Ministry also collected Western press clippings designed to show that Russia wanted back all the territory she had seized in 1939–40, and that Anthony Eden had agreed to hand over eastern Europe to the Bolsheviks.[32] These were some of the suggestions passed on to the press control apparatus of Goebbels and Dietrich when they received Ribbentrop's approval.

Goebbels' Bolshevik scare campaign of the late winter and spring of 1943 involved the mobilization of magazines and journals, as well as the other mass media. The *Periodicals Service* provided editors with a "Slogan of Struggle" and materials relating to the theme "Europe's Mortal Enemy: Bolshevism." Bolshevism was the harbinger of annihilation, slavery, and misery, and the attention of editors was directed to the *German Weekly Service*, which provided more detailed information for potential articles.[33] The anti-Bolshevik campaign received a suspiciously propitious shot in the arm in the spring when the Germans claimed to have discovered twelve thousand graves of Polish officers taken prisoner and murdered by the Soviets between 1939 and 1941. The German News Service dispatch of May 3 was Hitlerian in tone, bearing a full measure of self-righteous indignation: "The Jewish-Bolshevik mass murder of Katyn, to which twelve thousand Polish officers fell victim, has, since its discovery, moved public opinion throughout the civilized world."[34] The German mass media continued to express sympathy for the Poles throughout the rest of the war, hoping thereby to split the Allied front. In August 1944 Otto Dietrich described Soviet policy as the attempt to exterminate "national Polish forces." [35] The "German Weekly Newsreel" described the end of the 1944 Warsaw uprising by the anti-Communist Home Army of General Bor in similar terms. The Reds had agitated among the Poles, then allowed Polish nationalists to rise up in a hopeless revolt against the German garrison, thus achieving Stalin's aim of exterminating non-Bolshevik Poles. Many Germans did not know about the genocidal nature of Germany's Polish policies in the General Government, so such propaganda may have been effective in certain sectors. Yet the Nazis were aiming this propaganda, which continued into 1945, at the Western Allies as much, and perhaps more, than at their own people.[36]

In 1941 Hanns Johst, president of the Reich Literature Chamber, declared, "Two books, *Mein Kampf* and *Das Kapital,* are in a state of war." [37] Books played an enormous role in the Nazi propaganda campaign justifying the war to the German people. Educated persons and intellectuals were the targets of "Vindex" (probably Giselher Wirsing) when he wrote *The Politics of the Oil Stain: Soviet Imperialism in the Second World War.*[38] Like all "serious" Nazi writers, Wirsing saw imperialism behind Soviet and American ideology, whereas Germany was simply trying to build a just new order. Wirsing, employing the language of the intellectual journalist, described the war as a struggle between faiths, a battle for Europe. The war had overcome its nationalist origins of 1939; it was now a war to save Europe from Soviet Russia, which was the dominant power in the enemy alliance (1944). Wirsing shrewdly and prophetically pointed to Soviet naval ambitions as a coming development of great importance, and he also showed insight in commenting that the British masses were moving sharply to the left. The sitting parliament and the Churchill government were out of step with public opinion.

The anti-Bolshevik crusade inspired some of the most vulgar National Socialist writings. J. von Leers, a demented Jew-hater noted for his study of the Weimar state, *Fourteen Years of the Jew Republic,* wrote a widely distributed pamphlet which exposed the "Jews behind Stalin." [39] Leers not only blamed the Jews for atrocities committed by the GPU, but he accused Jewish capitalists of financing the Bolshevik Revolution! In 1942 the Eher Verlag published a lurid account of the labor camps run by the GPU, Kajetan Klug's *The Greatest Slavery in World History,* and predicted that this book, available through any bookseller, would be a world sensation. [40] A pamphlet, "The Russian Door Is Pushed Open," portrayed the fate of workers and peasants in the Soviet Union, a story of torture and famine without end. In many instances *Gau* offices distributed books to district leaders, who were then expected to make copies available to interested persons in their districts. *I Saw Bolshevism* made the rounds of the Eisenach district in this way in 1942. [41] More widely distributed was a book published by Wolfgang Diewerge in 1942, *German Soldiers See the Soviet Union,* a work consisting of excerpts from letters written by German soldiers serving on the eastern front. Goebbels himself wrote the preface to this widely reviewed and praised book. Millions of copies of Diewerge's book appeared largely because of demand by party officials on all levels. The portrait of Soviet society contained in the book was that of a vast torture chamber of poverty and filth, a paradise for the Jews and a hell for everyone else.

Goebbels' "Soviet Paradise" exhibition in Berlin was the subject of the 1942 book *The Soviet Paradise: Exhibition of the RPL of the NSDAP, a Report in Word and Picture.* [42] This book brought the famous exhibition to many Germans who could not personally see it in Berlin. The government was just as considerate in disseminating news of the Katyn massacres, as can be seen in the publication *The Mass Murder in the Forest of Katyn: A Factual Account Based upon Official Files.* [43] The vital document in this account was the "Protocol" signed by medical experts representing twelve European nations. These men had visited the site of the murders in late April 1943, and their report confirmed German allegations about Soviet guilt. The horror stories about Bolshevism and its crimes always returned to the Jews; the Nazis delighted in accounts of GPU Jews murdering Polish patriots with the famous shot in the neck. In 1944 the Franz Eher Verlag published Heinrich Goitsch's *Never!*, an almost hysterical appeal to the German nation to resist the planned extermination of Germany by the Jews.[44] By this time most of the Jews in Europe had fallen victim to the German murderers, but Goitsch managed to return to Diewerge's 1941 claim that the Jews were planning to annihilate the Germans.

Alfred Rosenberg's twenty-four year struggle against Bolshevism made his "Rosenberg chancellory" a major source of anti-Soviet propaganda after 1941. Rosenberg was a true believer in National Socialism, and he was able to accept the 1939 agreement with Stalin only because he believed in Adolf Hitler. Rosenberg's muddled thoughts on the Stalin pact were a clear reflection of his confused mental state: "How can we continue to speak of the salvation and formulation of Europe when we have to ask the destroyer of Europe for help?" Poor Rosenberg arduously considered all possible justifications of the pact, even calling Ribbentrop a "joke of world history," but sadly concluded that only the need for freedom of action explained it.[45] Rosenberg felt relieved when Hitler attacked Soviet Russia, especially when he learned of his own appointment as minister for the occupied eastern territories. Years of frustration and administrative failure lay before him, but Rosenberg did not sense this on June 29, when he smugly referred to the "historic punishment about to be meted out to Russia for 'poisoning the European continent for twenty-three years.' "[46]

Rosenberg and his office spewed forth vast amounts of anti-Bolshevik propaganda after June 1941, much of it a classic formulation of the role of the war against Communism within the Nazi ideological framework. The "Action Staff" of Reichsleiter Rosenberg produced a great deal of ideological propaganda which party agencies published and distributed in editions of millions. Rosenberg's own "The Soviet Problem" (1943) was a typical production.[47] Rosenberg, who hated Great Russian nationalism and czarist expansionism, described the Russian empire as the oppressive reign of the czar over fifty "quite different peoples." This contradiction, when discovered and used by the Jews, led to the Bolshevik Revolution, which Rosenberg described as the rule of the *Lumpenproletariat*. In the same year the Reichsleiter spoke on the theme "The Soviets and their allies." In a passage that might have struck a responsive chord in some of his readers a year and a half later (if indeed, he had any readers by January 1945), Rosenberg thanked the Führer for invading Russia, arguing that if this genius had not done so, the Red Army might have broken into "East Prussia, Saxony, or Silesia"! Rosenberg, who wholeheartedly embraced the Nazi ideology of "Europe," accused Great Britain of betraying Europe and described the Second World War as a struggle pitting Goethe and Beethoven against black American bomber squadrons and Yankee gangsters. By May 1944 Rosenberg was referring to this "satanic world view" (Bolshevism) as the newest form of the wild hordes descending upon Europe from the steppes of Central Asia, a "perverted neo-messianism of the east." [48]

Men on Rosenberg's staff filled in details which gave substance to the Reichsleiter's concept of Bolshevism. Dr. Gerd Wunder was the expert on "The Jews in Bolshevism." His thought ran along these lines: "It is known that Jacob Schiff and other Jewish financiers of Wall Street financed the revolution of 1917. Even Churchill acknowledged the Jewish ties of Bolshevism . . ." Wunder "documented" the dominant role of the Jews in Soviet state, society, and economy, thus validating Baruch Levy's prophetic words, allegedly written to Karl Marx: "The rule of the Jewish people over the world will be achieved through the creation of a world republic . . ." [49] Wunder declared that the Jews had the most power when they let non-Jews like Stalin accept responsibility along with the appearance of authority. He believed that "typically Jewish" methods and law in the USSR involved fear, mistrust, revenge, and "Old Testament" hatred. Goebbels emphasized the national, Pan-Slavic, barbaric character of the Bolsheviks, while Rosenberg and Hitler continued to stress the Jewish-Bolshevik theme until the very end.

Bulletins and journals published by Rosenberg's staff contained vast amounts of ideological propaganda about Bolshevism. Even during the era of the Hitler-Stalin pact, the confidential *Bulletin on the Doctrinal Situation*—precisely because it was an internal publication—continued to study Communism and Soviet Russia.[50] The invasion of Russia meant that Rosenberg's ideological journal *The National Socialist Monthly* could now use this and related materials in expressing the attitude of the Nazis towards Bolshevism and the war in the East. A series of articles published early in 1942 gives a good sense of the scope of this journal's work:[51] Bruno Brehm wrote on "Russia," declaring, "Human life has never played a role there, it was never worth a penny." He quoted Dostoevski to prove that the human level of the average Russian was frighteningly low. Karl Rosenfelder, writing about "Europe's Eastern Front in History," tried to base Rosenberg's European ideology upon past history. In doing so, he referred to the Indo-Germans defending the East against the Scythians and Huns and Mongols: "Moscow is taking over the Mongol legacy." After 1918 old Moscow rose again under

Jewish auspices, taking the form of world revolution. The German attack upon Soviet Russia was thus a *counteroffensive.* The Rosenberg office contributed its views on the East to the German press through Dr. Taubert, the general advisor of the Propaganda Ministry and the liaison man between the "Eastern ministry" and Goebbels.[52] Hans Fritzsche began to receive materials for press publication after Rosenberg was appointed to his new ministry post.[53]

By 1944 Alfred Rosenberg was finished as a political force, though he continued to give speeches about the "European" idea and the struggle against Jewish Bolshevism. His ministry in shambles, the Reichsleiter expended his energies in futile denunciation of German agencies which encourage the "great Russian chauvinist" Vlasov in his quest for a Russian national army. Rosenberg was sympathetic to the aspirations of the Ukrainians and other national groups in Russia, but his opinions meant little even before 1944, at least in the practical sphere. His importance during the war centered upon his updating Nazi ideology in regard to the struggle against Bolshevism. One of his ideas, that Germany was fighting for Europe, and that the nations of Europe would have to prove themselves in this struggle against a common enemy if they wanted a secure place in the future New Order, received wide-spread attention in the German mass media.

Robert Ley's Party Main Education Office (HSA) provided Nazi cadres, speakers, and educators with crudely worded folders containing materials on "World Bolshevism," [54] "The Struggle of Destiny in the East," [55] and "The Essence of Bolshevism." [56] Ley set the tone for these materials with a style which he continued to use throughout the war: "It is inconceivable for a German mind to grasp how this wolf of the steppe leads his own people to the slaughter with such brutality in order to further his own fame." [57] So much for Stalin. The Ley educational materials, prepared by Wilhelm Loebsack and other "eastern experts," portrayed the Stalin regime as the tool of the Jews, who blessed the Soviets in the name of Jehovah and the Torah as an expression of their "Old Testament" hatred for Hitler. Ley's propaganda was for Nazis who dealt with the broad masses, while Rosenberg liked to formulate his ideas on a more "intellectual" plane. Ley's people made it easy for party cadres to absorb the message centering on (1) "The Jewish origins of the ideology of Bolshevism" and (2) "The Soviet state as center of Jewish power."

The ultimate statement of the theory of Jewish-Bolshevik "sub-humanity" logically occurred in the propaganda of Heinrich Himmler's SS, repository of National Socialist mystic racialism. *Struggle against Bolshevism: 28 Questions and Answers about Bolshevism,* published by

Himmler's SS Main Office, was a widely distributed handbook.[58] Some samples from the booklet prove informative: There is the question "Why do we struggle against Bolshevism until its annihilation? Answer: Because Bolshevism is an invention of the Jewish mind which tries to achieve the uprooting of all civilized nations . . ." The respondent added that the Bolsheviks had killed or deported all the Germans within the frontiers of old czarist Russia, except those who fled to the West. Another response declared, "Bolshevism is a doctrine which serves the world rule of the Jews." The booklet stated that Lazar M. Kaganovitch pulled the strings, and it asserted that the Jews ran the Communist party of the Soviet Union.

The most infamous product of SS propaganda was the booklet *The Subhuman (Der Untermensch)*, originally intended to serve as an introduction to the peoples of the east for German troops fighting in Russia.[59] This document achieved wide circulation within the Reich as well. *Der Untermensch* was a vicious hymn of hatred and loathing, viewing its object without pity as a vermin to be exterminated. In this sense it was similar to the motion pictures *Jud Süss* and *The Eternal Jew*, as well as to Wolfgang Diewerge's publication *The War Aims of World Plutocracy* (1941). The difference was that *The Subhuman* did not merely express hatred for the Jews, but it insulted all the peoples of the east as filthy, mongoloid, animalistic trash. This caused problems for German propagandists. As Goebbels noted, it was impossible to make good use of eastern labor within Germany or induce the peoples of the east to work for a German victory if this pamphlet circulated freely. Stalingrad lent a greater sense of urgency to the Propaganda Ministry's efforts to have *The Subhuman* banned, at least in the Reich. In February and March both Tiessler and Gutterer intervened on behalf of suppression, one with Bormann, the other with Himmler. *Der Untermensch* became rarer in Germany after the spring of 1943, but much damage had already been done.[60]

By the end of 1944, when it was too late, Goebbels' propaganda apparatus was making prominent use of the Russian general Vlasov and his Committee for the Liberation of the Peoples of Russia (KONR). Germans who had read *Der Untermensch* may have been surprised at the end of 1944 to see the general on the screen of their neighborhood theater, appearing in the "German Weekly Newsreel" as a hero. Goebbels had made his own contributions to *Untermensch* propaganda in 1941 and 1942, when he described Russian resistance as ratlike and animalistic. He changed abruptly, however, when he realized that the German war effort would suffer if this propaganda continued. Himmler altered his viewpoint far more slowly, Hitler not at all. By 1941 Nazi

"The Subhuman," a pamphlet which portrayed the Jews and the peoples of Russia as fit only for slavery or extermination.

CREDIT: The Dartmouth College Library (Myers Collection), Hanover, New Hampshire

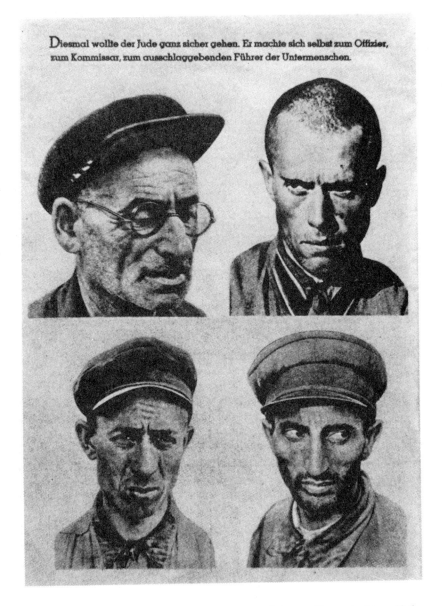

Diesmal wollte der Jude ganz sicher gehen. Er machte sich selbst zum Offizier, zum Kommissar, zum ausschlaggebenden Führer der Untermenschen.

"This time the Jew was not going to take any chances. He made himself the officer, the commissar, the crucial leader of the subhumans."

CREDIT: The Dartmouth College Library (Myers Collection), Hanover, New Hampshire

"God save us from this sort!"

ideological propaganda had expanded the theory of Jewish Bolshevism to include the "subhuman" masses of the East who were fighting tenaciously against the German armies. There was a certain logic in this progression, for as early as 1931, SA men referred to their adversaries as Communist *Untermenschen.* To Goebbels the core of wartime ideology was the Jewish connection; this was the cement that held "plutocrats" and Bolsheviks together. He could quickly modify his propaganda on eastern *Untermenschen,* since the concept of Slavic inferiority was not one of his more deeply held convictions, particularly after his love affair with Lida Baarova in 1938.

V

Conclusion:

Aspects of German Popular

Reaction

To Nazi Wartime Propaganda

11

German Reaction to Adolf Hitler's War

Joseph Goebbels believed that wartime propaganda must convince the largest possible segment of the population that every policy pursued by the leadership was correct and in the interests of the nation. People must believe in the leadership even when the government could not reveal its motives or purposes to the nation. When propaganda achieved this goal, it had succeeded, for the leadership was then free to act decisively without worrying about the moods and opinions of the nation. The government possessed at this point "freedom of action" and thereby enjoyed a tremendous advantage over more cautious and hampered parliamentary regimes.[1] Goebbels tried to protect Hitler from petty concerns such as public attitudes toward the war. Genius must be allowed to pursue its course of destiny with "sovereign equanimity." Goebbels realized that Hitler could not have this freedom of action unless his propaganda minister sensed the public mood. Only then could the German state prepare the public for Hitler's policies. Goebbels therefore required precise information about public attitudes and morale. Such material would inform him of the success or failure of various propaganda lines and campaigns and would enable the government to prepare the public for forthcoming policies and situations, whether these concerned curtailment of rations or a planned invasion of a neighboring country. Hitler's growing isolation was thus a guarantee of Goebbels' growing importance. In a totalitarian society propaganda often meant preparing the population for a *fait accompli* decided upon in secrecy: This was an operation requiring some subtlety.

There was no "public opinion" in the Third Reich, at least not in the sense familiar to citizens of the Western democracies, no clash of opinions in the mass media, no legal criticism of the regime or of its policies. In this totalitarian society Joseph Goebbels relied upon information about the attitudes of the nation which reached him through official, if clandestine, channels. He added his own imagination and intuition about the public mood to the material present in these reports and thereby arrived at major decisions within the broad framework of Hitler's policies. The minister carefully read the digests prepared from the "Activity Reports" of his forty-two Reich Propaganda Offices. These reports contained information about the weekly activities of the Offices in carrying out propaganda campaigns, but they also provided raw data about the mood of the people in the various German *Gaue.* Goebbels jealously guarded this material and warned the directors of the local offices not to provide any other agency or department with the "Activity Reports." [2] Goebbels supported this policy with the argument that the Security Service (SD) would resent such distribution, but the real reason was his desire to maintain a monopoly over all materials which gave insight into the mood of the nation and the success or failure of the Nazi propaganda apparatus. The state secretary and the head of the propaganda division in the ministry paid close attention to reports received from local propaganda offices. These men were concerned with the fundamental attitudes and morale of the population and repeatedly warned the directors of the Reich Propaganda Offices not to forward materials that merely delineated "isolated instances of perverse attitudes." [3] Gutterer told these directors early in 1943 that they were to take care of such cases with the methods of the Era of Struggle. Widespread grumblings about coal rations concerned Berlin; gripings which resulted from purely individual circumstances were of minor importance and could be either ignored or dealt with by the police.

The propaganda machine contained other channels of information feedback, including reports filed by party officials. These reports consisted of detailed questionnaires concerning local party meetings. They proceeded from the local, or *Ortsgruppen,* level to district and *Gau* party offices and became part of the information network controlled by the Reich Propaganda Central Office. The questionnaires consisted of the following inquiries: place and date of the meeting or rally, number of participants, manner in which the speaker handled the theme, impression made by the speaker upon the audience, total impression made by the speech, and suggestions or requests by local party officials. These questionnaires ostensibly were concerned with the effectiveness of a party speaker, but public reaction to a speech provided the RPL with valuable information about the public mood. If a given theme interested the audience in different parts of the Reich at the same time, this said something important about the concerns of the nation or at least about the National Socialist part of the nation. Once the party offices in Berlin and Munich sensed a pattern, they could use this data to make suggestions to local *Gau* propaganda offices about future propaganda themes and campaigns. These suggestions (or commands) were relayed to local offices through the *Gau* Information Service and other instructional channels.[4]

The "Reports from the Reich" produced by the Security Service of the Reich Security Main Office (RSHA) contained materials of vast importance to the Goebbels propaganda machine. The "SD Reports" contained specific information about the mood of the German people. They were often brutally frank, and for this very reason they excercised, according to Fritzsche, "a very favorable influence on propaganda . . ."[5] The reports were strictly confidential, intended only for the officials of the state and party to whom they were addressed, not for distribution within the agency or ministry of the addressee. These "Reports," originally entitled "Reports on the Internal Political Situation," reflected the desire of SS-Gruppenführer Otto Ohlendorf to create an organ which would bring the criticisms and concerns of the people to the attention of the Reich leadership. Ohlendorf headed the Domestic News Service of the SD, and it was in this capacity that he directed the production of the SD reports. When Ohlendorf was not editing these wartime reports, he headed one of the *Einsatzgruppen* in Russia, a unit which murdered 90,000 people in 1941–42. An American military court sentenced Otto Ohlendorf to death on April 8, 1948.

The SD reports represented a synthesis of materials provided in daily reports to Ohlendorf's agency by branch offices of the Security Service of the Reich Security Main Office. The SD selected the raw materials and passed the summary on to various state and party agencies about twice a week. In order to provide fresh and relevant material, Ohlendorf's office did not analyze and proofread the final report, since that would render the report less valuable and less contemporary by requiring more time. The SD reports contained six categories of information: general mood and situation, enemies, cultural areas, law and administration, economy, and folkdom and national health. A document dating from the winter of 1942 gives a good sense of the type of information which the Reich Security Main Office desired from local branches of various SS agencies. Berlin wanted to know the attitudes and mood of the German people in these areas: their sense of the war, their participation in the war effort, their belief in victory, their desire for peace, their view on the length of the war. The RSHA wanted its confidential agents to investigate the feeling of the community on the home front, the extent of courtesy and politeness in everyday life, and the attitudes toward the food supply. Inquiries were to be made about civilian views of the armed forces postal service, the manner in which survivors of fallen soldiers were being cared for, the closeness between homeland and front, and the distribution of the (civilian) War Merit Cross medal. The RSHA wanted its agents to investigate the reaction of the people to German propaganda. Did the masses believe that German propaganda was objective? Did it give people a sense of the front and of the enemy? The RSHA raised a fascinating question when it urged its agents to compare the effects upon people of German and enemy propaganda. Did many Germans listen to foreign broadcasts, exchange rumors, or in other ways prefer alien propaganda to that of the state? [6]

Adolf Hitler apparently did not pay much attention to the reports (if he read them at all), since they would have rudely interrupted his "tragic isolation." They might even have jarred his public pose of "sovereign equanimity." The precise distribution of the SD Reports is not clear, but Goebbels, Bormann, Göring, Rosenberg, Frick, and party Reichsleiters and cabinet ministers certainly received many or all of these typed reports. Many of the reports contained such blunt material, in raw form, that Goebbels, Bormann, and Himmler came to fear that they would have defeatist effects upon the ministries and agencies within which they were being irresponsibly and illegally circulated. One can well imagine the hunger which officials felt for such truthful information in the Third Reich, especially in the light of the monotonous and lifeless style of press and radio. As early as 1942 Goebbels spoke of putting an end to various confidential news reports. He wanted to replace this large-scale production of confidential reports with one single news report issued by the ministry itself. What Goebbels wished to do was combine the SD material with his own incoming reports from the RPA local offices, and pass this synthesis on to selected leaders in party and state. In April 1943 Goebbels noted, "If the material of the SD, which in itself is good, is sifted politically and brought into line with the political views of the Gauleiters and the Reich Propaganda Offices, it can develop into a good source of information." [7] In 1944 Goebbels' campaign was finally successful, at least in terms of halting the production of the SD Reports.

When war broke out there was little enthusiasm for a new conflict among the German people. Most Germans had believed that Hitler would solve the Danzig question, as he had earlier problems, by threats, bluff, and last-minute negotiation leading to victory. On September 1, 1939, Germans went about their usual routines, not even showing particular interest in the extra editions of the daily newspapers. People seemed stunned when they learned of the British and French declarations of war on September 3. "There is not even any hate for the French and British ... ," wrote Shirer in his *Berlin Diary*.[8] Goebbels' propaganda machine confronted this apathy and confusion in two ways. German propaganda emphasized that the successful war against Poland was defensive in nature and that vicious Britain had dragged hapless France into a war of encirclement and destruction against peace-loving Germany. The victory over Poland, so total and rapid as to be stunning, impressed the German people. No serious air raids ruined German towns, and the western front was quiet during the last months of 1939. The Germans now entered a period of watchful waiting, one not devoid of tension. There seemed to be a general yearning for peace based, of course, upon the conquest of Poland.

Rumors spread rapidly in the days after October 6, when Hitler appeared to have offered to the Allies precisely such a peace settlement.[9] Gossips declared that the king of England had abdicated, that Neville Chamberlain had resigned, even that an armistice had been concluded. The British and French rejection of the Hitler "peace offer" was quite useful to Goebbels, for he could portray Germany as peace-loving and Britain as a warmonger. A report written by the inspector of the security police in Defense District VI (Düsseldorf) reported that people in that western town were calm and confident, while hatred for Great Britain was growing.[10] Goebbels knew that the average German would work and fight for the Reich, but the minister wanted total control over minds and souls. Such control would insure that there would never again be another 1918, a "shameful capitulation" brought about by the subversive rumor-mongering of a few dissidents. He also realized that if the German people believed in the politics of their government, their commitment to total victory would be combined with an ethic of work and obedience, making that final triumph more certain and more imminent.

The continuation of the war into the winter of 1939–40 caused some anguish among the German people. The Reich had not prepared for a long war. Poor people did not react well to a statement by the Economics Ministry that they would have to make do with the shoes which they now had, since they would not be able to obtain new pairs for the time being. In Rostock citizens had to suffer through a cold winter with inadequate coal supplies, and they reacted adversely when the state supplied theaters and movie houses with adequate fuel stocks. Here was one instance in which the Goebbels policy of keeping theaters open at all costs backfired as propaganda. Advertisements in newspapers often contained phrases such as "closed for lack of food," at least until January 1940, when Goebbels put an end to such public admissions of shortages. Long lines appeared outside tobacco shops by the spring of 1940, another sign of import shortages and popular concern about future supplies of an important product. Queues were negative propaganda for the regime, so Goebbels ordered Gutterer and Wächter to make sure that the retail tobacco business adjusted its sales hours and practices so as to mitigate the situation. Goebbels could not do much about the cold weather and the fears which it caused, but he did order the press to note that the entire world was experiencing a particularly severe season.[11]

Goebbels sensed the impact which anti-British propaganda against "plutocrats" was having among the people, so he broadened this promising campaign. A foreign observer noted in February 1940, "No objective, dispassionate observer can deny that the propaganda is effective ... Men and women who, even last October or November, were by no means certain ... as to the causes and issues of the war with the western powers, now use identical language." He commented, "Dr. Goebbels and his alert young group of co-workers have truly succeeded in remaking the wartime thinking of the great majority of the German people." [12] By April 1940 Goebbels, wishing to maintain this momentum, ordered his broadcasters to stop ridiculing the rulers of Britain. They were to portray men like Churchill and Duff Cooper as "vengeful plutocratic enemies." [13] Goebbels was concerned about any British propaganda, such as leaflets dropped from airplanes, which might undermine the image of Britain which he had helped to create.

Despite all his boasting and all his success, Goebbels continued throughout the war to harbor doubts regarding the toughness and commitment of the German nation. Could the Germans survive setbacks? Here the minister's cynicism served him well, reflecting his brutal frankness within his inner circle. On April 22, 1940, the minister ordered that the *Request Concert* radio program of May 5 should only relay the German-Italian soccer match if the prospects appeared favorable for victory by the German team. Two days later Goebbels wanted an explanation as to why German wrestlers had competed against Czechs in Prague—and lost! [14]

The German people were concerned about shortages of consumer goods and by annoyances and anxieties engendered by British air raids. By 1940 British aircraft were dropping bombs rather than just leaflets on northwestern German towns. They did not yet do a great deal of damage, but they undermined some of Goebbels' propaganda about the vaunted Luftwaffe. The war was changing life-styles in ways which caused concern and frustration. Entertainment and social life were going into decline, partially because of the ration system that prevailed since the beginning of the war. Real coffee was hardly available, though one could still find some "German coffee," which actually contained a few real coffee beans. Wine was abundant, but beer was thin, prompting Berlin wits to compare it to the urine of a diabetic horse. Real tea could not be obtained. People were preparing their basements for air raids, or making sure that they knew where to hide if caught by an RAF raid. Families visited each other for days at a time, so as not to be caught in a raid while returning home late at night.[15]

Such concerns made Goebbels' task more difficult, for he had to inculcate the heroic Nazi ethic while at the same time inducing people not to get upset over shortages and annoyances. Some popular humor confirmed the efficacy of the propaganda machine, but other jokes could be seen as antiregime. By the spring of 1940 Germans were grumbling about the Italians, who were not marching with the Reich, despite years of pro-Fascist German propaganda. Italian military setbacks between June and December 1940 led to a spate of anti-Italian jokes. Goebbels knew the jokes, but he was not sure how to deal with them. Some other current jokes were treasonous, such as one passed by word of mouth in the autumn of 1940: Question: "An airplane carrying Hitler, Göring, and Goebbels crashes. All three are killed. Who is saved?" Answer: "The German people." More to the regime's liking was the following question-and-answer joke, dating from the late summer of 1940, and probably much more popular: Question: "Who is the greatest electrician of all time?" Answer: "The Führer!—He has coordinated Germany, turned off Poland, grounded Röhm and his comrades, isolated the Jews, electrified England, put the world into a state of high tension, and never had a short circuit!"[16]

The great German victories in the Low Countries and France during May and June had a tremendous impact upon German opinion, not merely because of the defeat of France, but because of the euphoric sense that the war was ending in a German victory of unheard-of proportions. The "France Song," a stirring march, blared forth from radios and loudspeakers.[17] German reaction to defeated France was of great interest to the regime. Since August 1939 Goebbels had portrayed France as the slave of British aggression, dragged into a war forced upon the Reich by British connivance with corrupt, unrepresentative French politicians. Anti-French propaganda had largely consisted of recalling past French depredations on German territory. This changed during the campaign of May–June 1940, when Germans heard a great deal about black colonial troops, French atrocities against German POWs, and France as a biologically corrupt and dying nation. When France collapsed but Britain insisted on remaining a remote annoyance during the time of euphoria following the German victory, many Germans soon became confused.

Germans sensed that a great turning point in history had occurred, the overcoming of a millennium of Franco-German enmity. This sentiment had been present at the Olympic Games in 1936, when German spectators wildly cheered the French team as it marched by Hitler's box and saluted the Führer. In 1940 Hitler wanted to use France against Great Britain; hence, his propaganda machine quickly diminished its output of anti-French hate propaganda. The widespread sympathy for France and the defeated French Army was not to Goebbels' liking, however, and Germans read in July of French atrocities. What confused many Germans was the contrast between this hate propaganda and abundant PK reports from the front, which acknowledged the bravery and decency of the French soldier. The German press dredged up older atrocity stories, some of them in the spirit of early June articles alleging that colonial troops had tortured German soldiers. Many citizens of the Austrian town of Innsbruck demanded that France pay in blood for these "atrocities." The SD reported that the German people had created a new unity of front and homeland during these great weeks of victory.[18]

German euphoria was partially the result of a premonition of the immediate cessation of all hostilities. Rumors about peace circulated throughout the nation; this concerned Goebbels, who knew better, and he forbade the media to use the word "peace." As an RPL bulletin had stated on May 15, the phrase "after the victory" was permissible, the terms "after the conclusion of peace" or "after the war" were not. In June and July many Germans shared the opinion, widespread in France and in neutral lands, that the war would soon be over. Goebbels knew that possible British resistance (Churchill's policy) rendered such optimism dangerous. He sensed that a long war, including heavier aerial bombardment of German cities, could have a disastrous moral effect upon a population which hungered for peace. For this reason, the minister concentrated during the last five months of 1940 upon preparing the nation for the air war. As early as May 20, during the time of the decisive German breakthrough in the west, Goebbels ordered the German media to give accurate statistics on the number of victims of British air raids. Falsification would undermine the credibility of the media, while statements of the truth might harden the German people and make them even better haters. Goebbels repeated his admonition in August, during the Battle of Britain. Of course, he could afford to be frank when the momentum lay with the German side, but his propaganda had some effect upon German opinion.[19] A foreign correspondent noted at the end of August that many Germans believed Goebbels when he declared that the British were murderers because they bombed the homes of Germans, while the Luftwaffe only struck at "military targets." [20] The minister made indignation and self-righteousness a key part of German propaganda. He knew his people.

In early September Goebbels ordered his men to work with the Air Defense people on a placard to be posted throughout the Reich. The theme was "It's Up to You," and it would involve the masses in the air war through advisement of the location of shelters and procedures to be followed during air raids. Twelve days later Goebbels made it clear that references to unsatisfactory air shelters in Britain were to be avoided by the German press. They would only call attention to German preparations, which themselves were incomplete and often inadequate. Goebbels had reason to be pleased with his work in 1940; after initial mistakes and popular misgivings during the early months of the war he sensed his growing power. A foreigner noted in December, "After a year and a half ... German morale is still good." [21]

When Britain survived the relentless onslaught of the Luftwaffe in 1940–41, the German people realized that the war would be a long one. Goebbels had been correct in attempting to dispel any mood of premature optimism. He now tried to dissipate any undue pessimism by declaring that time was working for Germany and her allies. Many Germans doubtless remembered the years 1917–18, when time had worked against the Reich. The average German continued to react most strongly to announcements that affected his or her personal life and standard of living. There was grumbling when beer breweries reduced production. The rationale behind this unpopular move was that much of the one million tons of cereals used in annual grain production for beer could be put to better use fattening pigs. This would increase the amount of pork available to the German consumer. Many Germans missed that second or third beer, though the watery, false taste of the first gulp may have brought some people around to approval of the government's move.[22]

During the early part of 1941 Germans, beer drinkers or not, continued to complain about the Italian military performance, or the lack thereof. They also showed disturbing signs of respect for British powers of resistance. In February Goebbels ordered the German media to drop references to visits to bombed areas by the English royal family. Such reports had not had anti-English effects; rather they caused many Germans to respect the king and queen, as well as to make unpleasant comparisons with the absence of German leaders from bombed German towns. By April Germans were often voicing sentiments such as "The

English are tougher than we are!" "Imagine if we had to experience what the English are enduring." "We keep conquering, and in the end the British will win." Even the German successes in the Balkans did not dispel this disquieting mood. Germans showed anxiety over American aid to Britain, and they speculated about whether German victories over Yugoslavia and Greece would cause Roosevelt to increase or decrease his aid to the British. Many Germans overestimated the power of American antiwar isolationists such as Charles Lindbergh, a man popular in the Reich. Leaflets dropped over Germany by the RAF were of great concern to Goebbels, for their theme of massive American aid for ultimate British victory was a disquieting one—as it had been in 1918.[23]

The flight of Rudolf Hess to Scotland in May 1941 caused an uproar everywhere in Germany, but especially among party members. The SD reported that no other recent event had so shocked people. Some party members compared the flight to Ernst Röhm's SA "revolt" in 1934. For at least ten days Germans discussed Hess and little else. No one seemed to believe the story about his "mental illness." One rumor stated that Hess had planned to fly to his parents in Egypt; another, that he had really intended to fly to Russia. Hess was popular among some segments of the population, and discussion about his flight took place at newsstands, barber shops, beer tables. The British did not help matters, for by their silence and understatements they gave the Nazis little information or ammunition for counterattack. In addition, the RAF dropped leaflets announcing, "Hess knew something. He saw the defeat coming." The government mobilized the party at all levels to reach out to the people in order to calm their apprehensions. This worked to an extent, but the damage to party prestige was extensive. The one good thing about the Hess uproar, from the Nazi viewpoint, was that it drove a politically dangerous rumor from the minds of people during the second half of May, a rumor which returned to circulation by the middle of June: Hitler was going to attack Soviet Russia.[24]

There was no "public opinion" in Nazi Germany, only official policy, the "truth," and private opinion, which could be antiregime. In this totalitarian atmosphere, Goebbels could not directly deny rumors without lending them a semblance of truth. Fortunately for the Nazis, the regime's control over communications fostered ignorance and caused contradictory rumors to come into being on the same issue. These contradictions canceled each other out, making it unnecessary for the government to worry about the formation of a single block of sullen opposition among the people. Rumors circulated in the late spring of 1941 that (1) Hitler was going to invade Russia around May 20 and (2)

Stalin was going to join the Tripartite Pact and allow German troops transit through the Ukraine in order to reach Iraq, where Nazi sympathizers were briefly in power. When the German people learned of the attack upon Soviet Russia, there was both surprise and a tremendous hunger for news. The Wehrmacht was stingy in its early reports, preferring to wait for overwhelming successes before giving the public details of its eastern operations. During this tense period of watchful waiting, many Germans speculated about the duration of the war in the East. There was little doubt about ultimate German victory, the consensus being a war lasting from three to twelve months.[25]

Goebbels, who had long been concerned about leftist tendencies within Germany, felt quite competent to deal with the changed relationship with Soviet Russia. Some Germans were cheered by reports that Europe, including little Slovakia, was marching with Germany; most believed, however, that satellite contributions were more propagandistic than military. The news that Mussolini was contributing a motorized division met with cool and sarcastic response. Many Germans felt that the retreat of the Red Army into the vast spaces of Russia might mean that the war would last a bit longer than earlier campaigns. By July few people doubted that Germany would win, and no one gave much thought to a Russian winter which seemed far off, both in time and space. Germans now made wagers about how long the campaign would last, a popular estimate being six weeks. While the German armies were advancing, seemingly at will, the regime cleverly announced that the vast armaments captured by the Wehrmacht proved that Stalin had intended to attack Germany. The combination of Wehrmacht victories, captured booty, and the self-righteousness of a "defensive war" was good propaganda and had a powerful effect upon German attitudes. In July few Germans were making comparisons with Napoleon's ill-fated 1812 invasion of Russia. Some Germans took pride in the fact that the Reich was defeating Russia without abandoning its war against Great Britain. But in one small town two men were overheard discussing media reports about the eastern front. There was an ominous note: They commented that the Russians seemed to fight to the death rather than surrender as had the Poles and the French. Such insights were rare at the time, late June 1941, but became more common by August.[26]

By August, Goebbels and Tiessler were becoming concerned about British propaganda, which was asserting that the eastern campaign had been a mistake. Goebbels could call Churchill a liar again and again, but by late August the popular reaction to the eastern war indicated widespread belief that the conclusion of the campaign in Russia would not occur in the near future. Goebbels moved to quash other disquieting rumors, gossip which demoralized relatives of men fighting in the east. These rumors concerned Soviet atrocities against captured German soldiers. Goebbels inaugurated a media policy which remained in effect until the last desperate months of the war. There was to be no specific mention of such atrocities by the media. The Bolsheviks were to be described as beasts, but Germans were not to see or hear of specific bestial acts unless they were committed against non-Germans, for example, against Lithuanian nationalists. When the Soviets occupied certain towns in East Prussia in October 1944, Goebbels reversed this policy and did report Soviet atrocities against German civilians.[27]

The resumption of the German advance against Moscow in the autumn of 1941 by Army Group Center combined with two other factors to unleash a wave of optimism. Hitler and Dietrich declared in early October that the campaign in the east had already been decided. The German people, fearing the imminent unknowns of the fabled Russian winter, clutched at these straws and gave vent to dangerous illusions. Goebbels tried to combat this giddiness, but this was difficult to do when Adolf Hilter himself had been the perpetrator. By the middle of November it was clear to the nation that a Russian winter would indeed be the fate of the Wehrmacht. Optimism gave way to fatalism and grim determination, in addition to outbursts against foreign POWs in the Reich, who were often clothed in warm coats while their German captors had no winter clothing. A thorough report on the mood of the people at this time indicated widespread concern over the increased British bombings; the shortages of food, heating resources, winter clothes, and shoes; the lack of doctors, many of whom were serving in the greatly expanded Wehrmacht. Goebbels resolved to change this mood, but he continued to rave against "intellectuals," whom he suspected—along with religious types and people of property—of spreading the bacteria of pessimism and subversion.

Increased griping about deferred men, and the continued ostentatious life-style of Nazi big shots, troubled the minister. Part of Goebbels' answer was to increase propaganda about the merciless "sadistic, and hate-filled enemy," since he found that he could do little about Army deferment policy, and still less about the conspicuous consumption syndrome. The Germans would have to understand that this was a struggle for the existence of their nation. It also might be useful to remind them of the degradation and misery of the Reich after 1918. The party must become more active in caring for armed-forces widows and orphans and for the relatives of the men at the front. These were Goebbels' guidelines for the winter propaganda campaign of 1941-42.[28] The German declaration of war upon the United States on December 11,

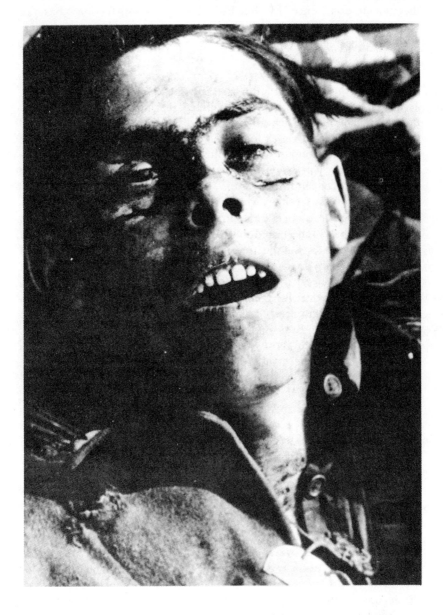

The Propaganda Ministry suppressed photographs such as this—until late in 1944.

CREDIT: The National Archives

1941, did not have a great effect upon the German public. People viewed the Japanese advance in the Far East with satisfaction; besides, Germany had really been in a state of war with the United States for many months. Russia was more important than remote America, which Japan could deal with.[29]

One journalist, Rudolf Pechel, openly criticized Goebbels' propa-aganda and the policies of the government, in January 1942. Pechel argued that the Reich should have offered real peace to its enemies in the summer of 1940, when all fronts were holding. He drew a parallel with the First World War (a forbidden comparison), and mentioned the potential military strength of the United States.[30] His was a courageous and lonely voice. This essayist for the *Deutsche Rundschau* spent the rest of the war in a concentration camp.

The plight of the German Army in Russia during the winter of 1941-1942 unleashed a tremendous spirit of sacrifice among the German people. Goebbels orchestrated this campaign, which consisted mainly of donations of clothes for the freezing troops in the east. This spirit of sacrifice was itself good propaganda. It gave the people a sense of participation in the struggle against Bolshevism and prevented wide-spread depression over the great Soviet counteroffensive. People in rural areas and small towns seemed as concerned about the military situation as about consumer-goods shortages, while individuals in the big cities continued to grumble about the lack of potatoes, shoes, and tobacco products. When the German Army's winter lines held in the east and the immediate crisis was overcome, anxieties about future shortages and curtailment of rations once again occupied the minds of the nation. Goebbels ordered the media to stop gloating about consumer goods shortages in England, since these stories led the German people to suspect that they were deceitful preludes to new German curtailments of rations. Despite this order, the press continued to print stories about cutbacks and rations in England. People were skeptical about yet another aspect of Goebbels' propaganda. He was once again, as a year earlier, using the cold weather as an excuse for German difficulties and shortages. People wanted more of the unvarnished truth.[31]

By the summer of 1942, Germans living in large cities and heavily industrialized regions were complaining loudly and often about the limited supply of fruits and vegetables. The conquest of large areas of sourthern Russia during this summer alleviated some consumer fears, for the regime promised large-scale imports of wheat and raw materials from the Ukraine. The tensions and shortages that were emerging in the course of a long war caused Goebbels to reflect that the state should never use the words "assassination" and "sabotage" in any of its news

A Nazi *Wandzeitung,* or wall poster, 1940. It shows an obese woman screaming because she will "starve" unless she can find some (unavailable) bananas. The abundance of vegetables does not appease her hunger. Doesn't she know that there's a war going on? Goebbels referred to this kind of griping as "the bowel movement of the soul."

CREDIT: The Imperial War Museum, London, England

media, since the terms might give certain people evil ideas. He was concerned about signs of demoralization, the increasing boorishness and lack of politeness among the people. Goebbels wanted to restore a sense of "German decency" by a campaign for more politeness and more consideration of others, with prizes for people who suggested the best ideas. Despite his growing commitment to the idea of total mobilization, Goebbels continued to oppose closing down barber shops, beauty parlors, and manicurists' establishments. His view was that the people were suffering many privations; why deprive them of the rewards of their vanity, especially when this particular industry did not employ many men eligible for the Wehrmacht? Goebbels himself made a humorous contribution to public morale: His comment that griping was the "bowel movement of the soul" was widely quoted.[32]

The prolongation of the war and the growing demoralization of many Germans led to a revival of interest in the churches. This concerned Goebbels and Bormann, especially when they learned that people were saying that Adolf Hitler had brought about a renewal of Christianity, that thanks to him the churches were now filled! A report from the Sudetenland indicated that people did not consider it proper to honor those who had fallen at the front outside a Christian setting. The party was at the time engaged in a massive campaign to take over and secularize such memorial services, but opposition from the churches and many believers blocked its attainment of that goal. The Nazis viewed filled churches and opposition to National Socialist memorial services as rejections of German propaganda. The growing number of reports concerning sexual relations between German women and foreign workers and POWs caused even more anguish in state and party circles. These reports indicated that many of the women were not peasants or of "inferior race," but came from socially and biologically "spotless" families. Such activities reflected both loneliness and demoralization; though carried out in secret, they were a clear, albeit pleasurable, rejection of Nazi racial propaganda.[33]

German perceptions of the Soviet Union changed in the course of the winter of 1941–42. The party attempted to combat the growing popular belief that this war would last a long time, perhaps ending in something less than a total victory. Party agencies distributed millions of copies of the anti-Soviet pamphlet *German Soldiers See the Soviet Union,* particularly during the first three months of 1942. Yet on March 13, Dr. Werner Holle, an agent of the SD branch office in Bielefeld, reported that while people still believed in a German victory, they were worried about the war in the east and doubted that the Soviet Union was on the verge of collapse.[34] Some people were depressed and believed that war might even last into 1944. Devout Catholics saw the long war as divine retribution. Others, who had lost men at the front, were bitter about the long delay between the time of a soldier's death and the date on which the grim news reached his family. Even more disturbing were reports that many Germans no longer believed that the Russians fought so hard because of their fear of "Jewish" commissars or their "animalistic" nature. Some people now believed that the Red Army soldier was a convinced Bolshevik, fighting for an ideal. This was a particularly dangerous thought, since the Nazi party claimed a monopoly upon idealism unto death. Goebbels could take some satisfaction from reports indicating that anti-Jewish propaganda had been effective. One survey not published until after the war indicated that this was indeed the case: Party members who had largely disapproved of the 1938 pograms or who had been indifferent to the "Jewish question" now cared little about the fate of the Jews. Sympathy for the Jews seems in fact to have been inversely related to the extent of suffering among Germans.[35] Goebbels drew two major conclusions: He would have to intensify anti-Bolshevik propaganda, and anti-Jewish propaganda should remain a ubiquitous constant in the German mass media.

Many Germans complained about military coverage in the mass media. PK reports, the radio, and newsreels often were vague about the precise location and time frame of battles which they described or filmed. The people still had confidence in the official Wehrmacht communiqué, but mistrusted much of the political reportage, particularly that of German newspapers. Letters from soldiers at the front had a great effect upon German attitudes towards the war. Their comments on coldness, losses, and suffering caused concern at home, though such fears often led to harder work and grim determination on the home front, rather than to demoralization. A wave of optimism—which Goebbels viewed as dangerous—swept through the nation during the summer of 1942 as German armies advanced towards Stalingrad and the Caspian Sea. One rumor foresaw a stabilization of the eastern front along a line stretching from Astrakhan to Archangel.[36] The virtual cessation of the advance during the last weeks of the summer proved Goebbels' point: Undue optimism could only be followed by demoralizing pessimism.

During the last five months of 1942, Germans were asking disturbing questions about the Bolsheviks and the peoples of Russia. How could such "primitive people" have built huge, modern factories? How could "subhuman" workers from the East be so intelligent, so technically skilled? Was the commitment of the Russian soldier the result of mere contempt for death, or did it reflect fanatical commitment to the Communist ideal? It is interesting that one important question was not often asked: Were German atrocities hardening Societ resistance? By September many Germans showed a certain war weariness, even a sense of resignation, summed up by questions and statements such as these: "Who would have thought after the great victories at the beginning of the war that the war would take this course and would last so long?" "How long will the war last? One cannot foresee its end!" "What lies before us?" More disturbing were widely circulating rumors concerning a compromise peace with the Soviet Union, rumors which often met with the response "It's too good to be true." SD reports indicated that many Germans had no clear sense of German war aims in the east, indeed, that they believed that the Wehrmacht could not defeat Russia.

Disquieting stories about the disturbances in the occupied territories were circulating throughout Germany by the autumn of 1942. "We are as far away from a 'new Europe' as were were a year ago" was a common reaction. Even the successes in the German U-boat war against the Anglo-Americans in the North Atlantic did not cause unqualified rejoicing among the German people. Disturbing questions did not elicit satisfactory answers from the mass media: "How many enemy convoys reach their destination without serious losses? What percentage of enemy tonnage has been destroyed? What is the approximate relationship between the current sinkings and enemy ship production?" [37] Although the U-boats would achieve even greater successes early in 1943, truthful answers to these questions would have undermined Goebbels' U-boat propaganda.

The north German *Gau* of Weser/Ems was the subject of an "Activity Report" sent to Berlin early in November. People there were increasingly concerned about the fate of Rommel's Afrika Korps. There was grumbling that rations were too low and that foreign workers were getting too many of them. People had reacted well to recent speeches by Hitler, Goebbels, and Göring, as they had to pamphlets containing articles by the propaganda minister. The party and its related agencies were active in a number of ways in this *Gau*. The Hitler Youth held song contests to cheer up the population of bombed towns. The local propaganda office cooperated with the Reich Music Chamber in putting on concerts for the blind. Reports such as this reflected the self-interest of the men who worked in the *Gau* propaganda central offices. It was in their interest to stress the successful and popular mobilization of the party when writing to Berlin. Yet even these reports could not conceal the decline of the party. Fewer than 30 percent of the boys eligible for membership in the Nazi party showed up for the induction ceremony. Some could not be contacted; others were serving in the Reich Labor Service.[38] Despite these excuses, the authors of the report were aware of the poor impression that such a statistic would make upon the RPL.

On December 8, Dr. Schaeffer summarized the most recent reports of the Reich propaganda offices. He placed his condensation before the minister. Schaeffer acknowledged that popular opinion was depressed over the seemingly endless, indecisive course of the war. Yet despite concern over events in the east and in North Africa, "the basic attitude of the population has become more stable," he wrote. Schaeffer touched upon a crucial point early in his report. He declared that people were impressed by the frankness and rapidity with which the government acknowledged the evacuation of Tobruk by Axis forces. People were less enchanted about the vagueness of German reports concerning "the Soviet breakthrough west of Stalingrad." Rumors were circulating everywhere, since news of this breakthrough did not appear in the German media. People wanted the truth, or so Schaeffer told Goebbels.[39] The German civilian population would have been shocked had it known the truth: The German Sixth Army had been surrounded at Stalingrad since November 22. This fact accounted for the disappearance of the word "Stalingrad" from the German mass media. Schaeffer and Goebbels hoped that recent increments in certain civilian rations would improve the public mood and prepare the nation for a winter of possible crises in North Africa, Russia, and the North Atlantic.

Even in January, when the position of the Sixth Army drastically deteriorated, few Germans had a clear sense of the crisis in the southern sector of the eastern front. Military affairs specialists could read between the lines of increasingly deceptive and vague Wehrmacht communiqués, but the average German could not. People did not comprehend why the Wehrmacht had not evacuated the Sixth Army. They sensed an impending crisis, but were without orientation, helpless and depressed. It was at this time that Goebbels decided to launch his new two-pronged propaganda campaign for "total war" and "victory or Bolshevism." People were ready to make sacrifices if they understood what was happening and what was expected of them. Goebbels intended to appeal to fear and self-sacrifice. Without giving up his propagandistic use of "the genius of the Führer," Goebbels turned to the nation for support. People reacted sarcastically to the first "total war" measure, the announcement of the labor plenipotentiary Fritz Sauckel on January 27 that men sixteen to sixty-five and women seventeen to forty-five were liable to labor conscription and assignment. There were so many loopholes in this decree that it soon became the object of widespread derision. The contrast between Goebbels' campaign of "scare tactics" and the mild measure of Sauckel did nothing for German civilian morale. People recalled with bitterness and even hatred earlier communiqués which announced German victories on the Stalingrad front, or slogans which had confidently stated, "Time is working for Germany." Yet a key sentence in one SD report confirmed Goebbels' sense that the majority of the population was "open to manly, soldierlike talk." [40]

Goebbels incorporated such "talk" into his speeches and knew a new wave of popularity between New Year's Day and late February, 1943. The Security Police report from Stuttgart on January 3 reported that people had responded well to a recent Goebbels speech, though there was some criticism, particularly in regard to the *person of the speaker*. An SD report on February 22 described an overwhelmingly enthusiastic response to the Sportpalast speech.[41] But this favorable reception soon turned into a new disappointment, not so much with Goebbels as with the failure of the government to commit itself to real total war measures. In March an SD report indicated that the population had fallen back into apathy and skepticism. The storm of a nation rising as one man, promised by Goebbels, was not to be seen on the German horizon. Some Germans seized upon a symbolic point: The government had lifted the ban upon women's hair permanents, put into effect as a labor-saving "total war" measure.

Goebbels' anti-Bolshevik campaign, intended to harden the will of the nation in its struggle for victory, was successful. Goebbels believed that it was necessary, even aside from its practical utility for the war effort, in order to counteract growing public confusion about the Bolsheviks. Reports from the Wartheland *Gau* indicated that many people believed that the Soviet collective farm system could not be surpassed in terms of productivity. German soldiers spread stories such as this and even described the population of the Crimea as well-off and content. Some individuals asserted that a defeat "would not be too bad"; others showed a certain nostalgic (Weimar Republic) fondness for "Communism." Small merchants, resenting some of the regime's tepid attempts to augment the labor force by closing down a few of their shops, grumbled that Nazism was becoming like Bolshevism, that it would destroy the lower middle class, so why worry about the Reds? Yet the overwhelming majority of Germans believed, according to an SD report, that the defeat of Germany would mean the end of the nation. Even this was not enough for Goebbels; he wanted *everyone* to believe that and to work and fight accordingly. He knew that many Germans felt, "The English and the Americans will prevent Bolshevization," or "The Bolsheviks will only hang the Nazis." [42] People had to realize that the Allies would destroy Germany, not just kill the Nazis, that the Western Allies were prepared to hand Europe over to the Bolsheviks. Allied propaganda regarding "unconditional surrender," a formula enunciated in January 1943, assisted Goebbels in his tasks, but more in 1944–45 than in 1943.

Goebbels' campaign of "toughening" the German nation was not contingent upon any military success except the final one. In fact, crises and defeats played into his hands, for it was he, not Hitler, who was demanding cutbacks in meat rations. His was the voice for total war, and he knew that he was waging the one war that Hitler was winning. Yet Goebbels also realized that he could not change the mood of the nation overnight. German opinion was taking on a quality of despair by April. There was a feeling that (1) the summer offensive in the east would have to be decisive; (2) in Tunisia, Germany faced its own "Dunkirk"; (3) Germany was helpless when confronting the Allied air attacks. This mood of anxiety was useful to Goebbels, so long as it did not turn into apathy and despair. Some Germans had, after all, responded "incorrectly" to his anti-Bolshevik atrocity propaganda, arguing that the Germans, who had massacred enormous numbers of Poles and Jews, had no right to get upset about the Bolsheviks' measures.[43]

There was growing concern in the population about the possibility of a "second front" in France. To allay this fear the government ordered the media to publish articles and pictures showing effective German fortifications from Norway to Spain. This propaganda campaign seems to have quieted some of those fears. The long-awaited collapse of Axis resistance in Tunisia unleashed a wave of bitterness about German news policy. Goebbels argued that the press and radio were to blame; he implicitly accused Hitler and Otto Dietrich of causing the propaganda apparatus to produce unrealistic estimates of the German chances in North Africa. By May 1943 a shrewd SD agent noted a general sense of calm in the population. This was the result, not of inner confidence in victory, but of a certain sense of exhaustion and helplessness. People seemed to be turning away from discussions of the war, paying heed only to their own work and concerns.[44] They were doing their duty, but with a sense of pessimism.

Joseph Goebbels believed that the answer to this pessimism was more power for himself. Why were people listening to Russian radio programs? Because German news policy had completely "obscured" the truth about Stalingrad, thereby causing relatives of missing men to listen to Bolshevik stations—which gave out some of their names. The growing apathy of the population did not undermine *resistance* to the enemy, but it was hardly conducive to an *offensive* will to final victory. Goebbels sensed that people needed a successful offensive to cheer them up.[45] While some Germans cursed the Reds, and others the "plutocrats," one observer noted little hatred for the enemy, even after air raids. That was early in 1943; by the middle of the summer there was growing hatred for the enemy because of the terror bombings of German cities.[45] A cry for "retaliation," at first encouraged by Goebbels, went through the nation. Goebbels orchestrated and increased the hatred, though he came to regret his use of the "retaliation" theme.

By May Goebbels noted that he had received more than fifteen thousand letters in a few weeks offering suggestions for the total war program. Many Germans wanted to contribute, but the regime refused to make the transition to a total war economy. Goebbels had his own blind spots—he believed that theaters and beauty parlors must be kept open for purposes of morale—but the refusal of the state to give him plenipotentiary total war powers was maddening. Many Germans began to look to Goebbels for this new type of leadership, especially since Hitler was disappearing from public view, forever the "lonely hero," the "tragic figure." Some Germans hungered for a glimpse of the Führer; others now ignored his occasional radio speeches. New elements of cynicism appeared, and without total war Goebbels could do little about them. A ditty sung at the front went something like this: "Everything passes away, everything passes away./Retreat in December, offensive in May." At home some wits changed the last part to "First goes the Führer, and then the party." A tendency on the part of some Germans to put their own survival above that of the nation was apparent in another bit of doggerel, recited by miners in an industrial region of the Reich:

> Dear Tommy, keep on flying,
> We're all miners down here,
> Keep on flying to Berlin,
> They're the ones who screamed "Ja." [46]

The last line referred to the hysterical enthusiasm which had greeted Goebbels' February 18 "total war" speech in Berlin.

Growing fear produced wild rumors during the summer of 1943. Some Germans claimed that the Reich was preparing to attack Britain with rockets containing atomic bombs; others said that a thousand Japanese fliers would assist in the invasion. Yet another rumor declared that the Soviet Union would permit the Japanese to fly over its territory in order to help Germany against England! The air war produced vengeful thoughts. Many Germans heard the mass media brand English bomber pilots as the murderers of helpless women and children; yet, they also saw German officers treat captured Allied fighters as officers and gentlemen. Ugly thoughts of lynching such "assassins" surfaced in isolated parts of the Reich. Goebbels would soon encourage such murderous activities; many Germans heard that the Japanese had executed captured bomber pilots and admired them for doing it.[47]

The military crises of 1943 produced a wave of anti-Berlin feeling in different parts of the Reich, particularly among people who liked to think of themselves as different from the "Prussians." The Nazis, who had produced Germany's first truly centralized administration, were nervous about these destabilizing tendencies. As early as the winter of 1942 Goebbels had alluded to the problem of German unity in a speech. He declared that Churchill would like nothing better than to see urban dweller opposed to peasant, entrepreneur to worker, Protestant to Catholic, Bavarian to Prussian. The Nazis claimed to have buried the German class struggle and caste differences, but they were sensitive to the reemergence of old hostilities. By 1943 some of these dangerous tendencies had surfaced, despite ten years of Goebbels' propaganda. People had written the hateful numbers "1918" on walls at various points in Vienna.[48] Anti-Prussianism was apparent in that former Austrian capital. People were saying, "If we win the war, we're Germans; if we lose, we're Austrians."

Jokes making the rounds of the Reich in 1943 expressed a sort of gallows humor. Even employees of the Propaganda Ministry were not immune to this type of subversive laughter: Question: "What's the difference between Germany and Russia?" Answer: "In Russia it's colder." Question: "What's the difference between Germany and India?" Answer: "In India one goes hungry for all." Cynics now referred to the North African city as "Tunisgrad." Another sick joke concerned a man who is dug out of some bombed rubble after two days underground. His wife and his son have been killed in the air raid, but he raises his aching right arm in salute, declaring, "Heil Hitler! Danzig is German, and that's the main thing!" One story concerned a man who had lost his home in a bombing raid. He needed to buy a suit, but because of the bombings and the wartime shortages, he could not find one. He exclaimed in disgust, "And all this on account of one single man!" Hauled before a Nazi judge, the man was asked whom he had had in mind when he made that remark. The man raised his head and stared straight at the judge: "Churchill. Whom did *you* have in mind?" Nazi big shots were often the victims of these jokes: Twenty years after the war Goebbels is selling newspapers on the street, while Göring makes a living selling medals and decorations. A stranger asks them what they are doing; after they explain their new professions, they ask his name. "Don't you recognize me? I'm Lord Hess!" Even Propaganda Ministry employees were telling such jokes.[49] And Rosenberg's office, which assembled its own intelligence dossiers on popular attitudes, noted that recent jokes did not spare Göring, Goebbels, Ley, and others. Who was telling these stories? People from Hamburg, Berlin, and Düsseldorf and individuals who had been resettled elsewhere after bombing raids were often the purveyors of subversive anecdotes.

The extensive movements of vast numbers of people also facilitated the circulation of rumors. In some places small numbers of people argued that Germany could only be saved by a military dictatorship: "The Führer can stay at the head of the state, but the party and all its branches and affiliates must be dissolved." [50] Evidently, comments such as this one had been floating around for quite a while, but the collapse of Italy in the summer of 1943 accelerated their dissemination.

The contrast between the fanaticism of the Nazi message and the growing crisis at the front produced the following reaction in the newspaperwoman Ursula von Kardorff: "Even a compromise peace is quite unthinkable for people of this kind. Death or victory! Fight on until the last round but one, and save the last one for yourself. Has there ever been a nation so determined to destroy itself?" [51] She wrote those prescient lines in June 1943. People who lacked this fanaticism did their duty, told grim jokes, turned away from discussions of the war as much as possible—and were frightened out of their wits. No wonder that Goebbels ordered his men to drop the word "mood" and only talk about popular "attitudes." [52] A man who did his duty in a bombed city had a healthy attitude; one could not expect his mood to be a cheerful one.

Goebbels' victory-or-death propaganda achieved notable successes despite the complaints and the jokes, the apathy and the despair. People feared the consequences of defeat, and that was the main thing. Hitler had so involved the nation in his own destiny that the only alternative to Hitler appeared to be destruction. This unity of fate was one of Goebbels' major wartime achievements, if that is the correct term for such a morbid victory. As he wrote, "Nobody doubts any longer that this is a war to be or not to be." [53] Heinrich Himmler and the SS cooperated in his campaign to make the German people see that this was a war for the Reich, not for the party or the SS. If the party was doomed, so was the nation. By November 16, Goebbels was commenting to posterity, "Morale among our people at present is excellent. This is partly owing to our good propaganda, but partly also to the severe measures which we have taken against defeatists . . ." [54] Himmler helped carry out such measures. Goebbels believed that the people were frightened enough to fight to the end; now he needed total war powers and a victory at the front. Certainly, there was a traitor here and there, an occasional mood of dangerous resignation, but by and large his work had succeeded: "We shall never lose the war for reasons of morale," he stated.[55] A turning point in his own popularity came in November, when Goebbels brought personal solace and administrative relief to the many victims of the great Allied raids upon Berlin. In July 1943, Gottlob Berger had told Himmler that Goebbels was unpopular; within a year and a half he would tell him that the people only believed in Hitler, Goebbels, and Himmler.[56] Goebbels summarized his success in "The new stage of the war," an article published in *Das Reich* on October 16, 1943: "The moral attitude of the German nation does not give its enemies the slightest hope that it will yield." [57] This proved to be a prophetic comment, but Goebbels could not have made it nine months earlier.

The success of Goebbels' propaganda meant that the worsening course of the war was working in his favor. A Swedish observer had noted some time earlier, "Goebbels is unpopular and even hated." [58] All this was changing by early 1944 as Goebbels became a sort of "tribune of the common people" in their struggle against the air terror. "This disaster, which hits Nazis and anti-Nazis alike, is welding the people together," wrote Kardorff in February 1944.[59] Goebbels reached his peak in power and moral prestige between late 1943 and early 1945. There was a good deal of griping; in October 1943 one concierge noted, "Let the Russians come, that's what I say. They wouldn't do anything to little people like me and at least the war would be over." [60] More useful to Goebbels, and more common, were stories about eastern workers who had assured their masters that the Bolsheviks would only shoot the Germans, not torture them, if they had treated their eastern help decently.[61] Goebbels had called for total war, and everyone could now perceive that total war was a necessity. He alone of Nazi leaders had taken over real responsibility in the frightening air war. The propaganda minister had constantly warned of the horrors of Bolshevism, and by October 1944 some Germans were experiencing these nightmares. Goebbels' success ultimately made him the logical successor to Hitler, which he became for a few hours from April 30 to May 1, 1945.

In February 1944, Goebbels spoke to the Gauleiters about the worsening air war. He turned the occasion into a celebration of the party and of the will of the German nation to hold out. Goebbels compared the stalwart behavior of the German people with the craven panic in other Axis capitals during and after far less serious air attacks.[62] He had discovered that a community of suffering and of shared destiny now united the nation as people from all social classes used the same air-raid shelters and cooperated in putting out flames caused by aerial bombardments. An anti-Nazi noted of Goebbels' men, "How cleverly they exploit every human feeling for purposes of propaganda." [63] Nazi propagandists took no chances. As losses on the eastern front mounted, Schaeffer ordered the Reich propaganda offices to stop using the word "cannon fodder" when speaking of the enemy.[64] Denunciation of partisans as "bandits" stopped late in 1944, as the regime considered guerrilla warfare against Allied occupation forces. By the spring of 1944 party propagandists seemed convinced that people understood the menace of Bolshevism; they would have to better appreciate the reasons for holding out until victory against the capitalist democracies. The German radio listening service, which reported on foreign broadcasts, provided some material for this campaign in May: "Enemy voices: fight against all Germans, not only against the Hitler party." [65] This campaign took place at a crucial time, for an Allied invasion in the west was only days or weeks away.

The period from June to September 1944 was a critical one in terms of Nazi perceptions of German opinion. The successful Allied onslaught upon France, the increasingly disastrous air war, and the Bolshevik destruction of Army Group Center, exposing German territory to a Red Army invasion, sorely tested Goebbels' propaganda machine. Some people were once again heard expressing the opinion that the Bolsheviks were not so bad. Propagandists feared the reemergence of pro-Communist sympathies among German workers and banned the publication of an anti-Marxist "dialogue" written by Kurt Blank because one worker-protagonist articulated too many Marxist and pacifist thoughts. Rome fell; Paris fell; the Bolsheviks neared East Prussia. One top Nazi told a journalist that his life was already "played out." As the Americans neared German territory around Aachen, rumors circulated that seventy party badges had been found in garbage cans, that the administration, police, and party were the first to flee the threatened city. Even SS men were not immune to the new and sudden demoralization. Gottlob Berger, chief of the SS Main Office, wrote to Himmler on September 26, regretting that he had not died a soldier's death while recently engaged in the pacification of rebellious Slovakia. He also reported that Goebbels had "tremendous credibility in the western part" of Germany.[66]

Trains filled with refugees fleeing west German towns bore subversive slogans: "We are coming from Cologne, Aachen, and Trier, thanks to you, Führer!" and "We thank our Führer!" A frustrated party chancellory informed the Propaganda Ministry that it would be nice if these graffiti were erased before the trains departed, not when they reached Westphalia. Germany's last European allies surrendered. Grasping at straws, one party propaganda sheet told its cadres to inform the people that this meant that the Reich would no longer have to feed Finland! Another anxious propagandist suggested that party members punch defeatist types in the mouth. Himmler reported to Bormann that the population in the district of Düren was so hostile to the party that no one raised his arm in the German greeting, not even party officials.

In September, the V1, or buzz bomb, attacks upon Britain "temporarily" ceased after three months of bombardment. People had placed a great deal of faith in such weapons, and the evident failure of the V1s produced a wave of sarcastic comments. Some people called the weapon *Versager* Number One, or "failure number one"; others named it *Volksverdummung* Number One, "national stupidization number one." The disappearance of Rumania, Finland, and Bulgaria from the Axis coalition caused many Germans to note that "the rats were leaving the sinking ship." [67] Within a few months people would apply the same term to Gauleiters and other Nazi big shots who fled threatened towns after ordering the population to hold out until the end.

Late in 1944 the director of propaganda in the *Gau* Halle-Merseburg described his recent experiences and used them as suggestions that might be useful to other party propagandists. He admitted that popular opinion was depressed and asked how party and state could strengthen the will to resist. The director pointed to the difficulty of holding meetings and rallies under the present circumstances. Such occasions made little impact anyway. He argued that the cadres closest to the people, block leaders and Nazi factory men, should logically be the persons to counteract enemy radio and leaflet propaganda. The director argued that the approach must be realistic, that the gap between actual circumstances and party propaganda had been too broad. He might have also added (but did not) that the misleading Wehrmacht communiqués of the post-Stalingrad period had widened this gap. Ideological propaganda of the type which had inundated the Reich for years was no longer of any use: "I emphasize that this form of training and informing must be limited to *questions of today*—any attempt to educate the population in a schoollike manner is *pointless today.*" The director concluded that the proclamation of the Volkssturm, or People's Militia, offered new possibilities for effective propaganda.[68]

The proclamation coincided with the beginnings of a temporarily successful defense of East Prussia, thus calming fears that the Red Army was about to march to Berlin. Many people greeted the inauguration of the Volkssturm with doubts and grumblings. Germany's plight must indeed be extreme if old men and young boys had to go to the front. The tremendous emotional barrage of propaganda with which Goebbels surrounded the new institution soon produced more favorable reactions. The Volkssturm included men of all social classes and all ages; it seemed to promise total mobilization and meaningful contributions by all to the defense of the Reich. Those not inducted were put to work digging antitank ditches and building fortifications. The heroic fanfare surrounding the oath-taking on November 12 produced many enthusiastic comments, but disillusionment set in during December and January. The promised modern weapons were not placed in the hands of the Volkssturmmänner, organization of the new force was chaotic, and fears grew about whether these men would be treated by the Allies as POWs or would be shot as partisans. A nation disillusioned by earlier promises of "wonder weapons" now showed little confidence in this newest gimmick of the beleaguered state and party. In some areas Germans tore down Volkssturm posters. People grumbled about spending their free time training for combat under party officials who lacked military competence. The Volkssturm bought some time for the regime because, however briefly and incompetently, it demonstrated a commitment to solidarity and action. In this way it served Goebbels' purposes and was one of the factors accounting for a last tremendous burst of confidence in Hitler during November.[69]

At the end of this hard year Joseph Goebbels reviewed German propaganda and believed that it had achieved a great deal. In late December he declared that Allied propaganda had failed because it had not succeeded in driving a wedge between the German nation and the German leadership.[70] Moreover, the "Atlantic Wall" bluff may have delayed the Allied invasion of France, no matter how sarcastically "apolitical intellectuals" in Germany ridiculed it after D Day. Despite the overwhelming Allied military superiority, the will of the people to resist had hardened during the last months of the year. Goebbels believed that his propaganda had made possible the stabilization of the threatened fronts, particularly in the west, during the autumn of 1944. Although two million German soldiers were dead by 1945, although over three hundred thousand civilians had perished during the Allied bombings by Christmas 1944, although there was pessimism, griping, and doubt among the people, the nation was ready to resist until the end. Goebbels sensed that this proved he was the one man winning a war for Adolf Hitler. People were afraid of the consequences of defeat, since this would mean a Bolshevik victory. As Martin Broszat has noted, even people who no longer believed in a German victory refused to think of defeat.[71] They continued to fight, work, and suffer, mainly to avoid a Bolshevik victory. And this was not the least of Goebbels' successes. In this context Helmut Heiber's observation is a shrewd one: "And this propaganda without sense or point, which orbited madly around phantoms, was against all reason successful and did enable the threatening and overdue collapse of intellect and morale to be postponed by several months. In spite of their unbelievable burdens, the German people held solidly to their faith and their madness to the very end." [72] And Hitler gave Goebbels his fondest wish. He could prove his devotion by sacrificing his own life and family to Hitler as a final blood tribute.

But by March 1945 signs of this impending collapse were everywhere. Horoscopes consulted by party and SS figures sometimes offered the same type of consolation provided by Goebbels' propaganda: "... a considerable number of favorable constellations, so that if these critical months are overcome, better times will follow." More typical were readings like the following: "There is no advantageous constellation visible which would signal a complete victory and a great success for the Greater German Reich." [73] The destruction of Germany in a long war was indeed possible.

The Propaganda Ministry was the last holdout in this world of fantasy. Officials such as governmental councillor Spengler managed to combine objective reports about morale with suggestions that German poets and writers could be useful (March 1945!) if they published their professions of faith in the Reich.[74] Spengler reported that people wanted more objective military news. They wondered why old Volkssturm men were sent to the front while young soldiers remained on garrison duty. Reports sent to the ministry from Reich Propaganda Offices now contained some of the greatest understatements ever written: "The mood of the people remains grave" (March 16, 1945), and "The development of the military situation is, according to the unanimous reports of the Reich propaganda offices, not one which will contribute to raising the generally depressed morale of the population" (March 21, 1945).[75] Wilfred von Oven noted on March 17 that the German nation was finally "burnt out," sunken into a torpor or "mass stupor from which it can never again emerge." [76] Seven weeks later, but only after Hitler and Goebbels were dead, the German Armed Forces High Command surrendered to the Allies.

German Reaction to the Wartime Mass Media

There was no public opinion or open exchange of differing views in the Third Reich, but an underground people's mass media emerged which disseminated both illegal opinions and information suppressed by the government. This counterpropaganda took many forms. Among the most prominent were anonymous hate letters to Nazi leaders, wall graffiti attacking the regime, distribution of enemy leaflets, and rumors passed along by word of mouth. The government, seriously underestimating its control over the German people as a whole, reacted to this dissent with increasing alarm. It relied upon two major factors in opposing such popular resistance, the Gestapo and "word of mouth" propaganda of its own.

The leaders of the Third Reich proclaimed that they were rulers of a "people's state." They wanted every German to have access to newspapers, books, radio receivers, and motion pictures. Through the media, Nazi propagandists could disseminate both their ideology and their version of the latest news. Radio was a unique medium in that through it the leaders of the Third Reich could most quickly reach tens of millions of Germans. The slogan "Every fellow citizen a radio listener" had come close to fulfillment by the end of 1942. The number of radio subscribers had risen from about four million in 1933 to over sixteen million. While a subscription cost a modest amount of money, the party often provided free licenses to those citizens unable to afford even that small fee.[1]

Before the war Goebbels had intensely promoted the "people's receiver," or *Volksempfänger,* a small, inexpensive radio set. Most German families had a radio receiver and a subscription license by the time the Second World War began.

The war increased the importance of the radio as a means of almost instant propaganda, but it also caused new difficulties for the medium. Germany lacked powerful transmitters, since propagandists, including Goebbels, had not foreseen the enormous territorial expansion of the Greater German Reich after 1938. During the war the shortages of spare parts for radio receivers reached alarming proportions. In the Warthegau alone, reports indicated that twenty thousand receivers were silent owing to a lack of basic replacement parts.[2] These shortages may have been partly caused by a growing concern among propagandists as to the listening habits of the German people. It is possible that spare parts were being withheld from areas in which many listeners tuned in to illegal broadcasts from Switzerland, England, and Soviet Russia.

Popular reaction to radio broadcasting appears to have been favorable during the first nine or ten months of the war. Once it appeared that the war would last a longer time than anticipated, there was growing popular annoyance at the evasions and repetitiveness of German programming. A foreign correspondent noted in October 1940, ". . . of late I have noticed more than one German shut off a news broadcast after the first couple of minutes with that expressive Berlin exclamation: 'Oh, Quatsch!' which is stronger than 'Oh, nonsense!' " [3] Of course, Berliners tended to be more skeptical than most of their fellow countrymen. By 1942 illegal reception of enemy broadcasts had reached crisis proportions in many regions.

Adolf Hitler had foreseen this possibility even before the war. He had requested that Goebbels produce a radio receiver so wired as to prevent reception of broadcasts from abroad. During the war Goebbels blamed others for the failure to carry out this suggestion, but Hitler held him personally responsible for that serious omission. As soon as the Germans invaded Poland, Goebbels drafted an ordinance on "extraordinary radio measures." This decree outlawed unauthorized listening to foreign radio broadcasts and proclaimed stiff penalties for violations, even death in extreme cases. For the next three years Goebbels fought a running battle with other Nazi leaders as to who would receive permission to listen to foreign broadcasts. Hitler himself had to make this decision early in 1942.[4] Four cabinet ministers who had sought permission were turned down, though Rosenberg received approval. Goebbels angrily noted, "It is disgusting how many big shots are now trying to prove to me that they can't continue their work unless they receive permission to listen to foreign radio broadcasts. In almost all cases I deny their requests." [5] The minister characteristically failed to add the phrase "where I have the authority to do so."

Goebbels took it as a personal insult when he learned of the widespread violation of the September 1, 1939, ordinance. He raved against Germans who were so "common" as to listen to Churchill's voice rather than accept an account of a Churchill speech from Fritzsche or the propaganda minister. Goebbels branded illegal listening as "ingratitude, contemptible, low," since it showed a lack of confidence in the German leadership.[6] He was overreacting. Many Germans who listened to the BBC at this time wanted more military news; they did not necessarily reject the Nazi leadership, but rather, its news policy.

A wave of mass revulsion against German radio policy occurred during the winter of 1942–43. People were sick and tired of hearing tirades about "Roosevelt, puppet of the Jews," when they craved news of Stalingrad and North Africa.[7] There existed a general hunger for specific military accounts of the front, and articles or broadcasts by military men such as Oswald Zenkner, General Paul Hasse, and First Lt. Soldan were widely popular. Families worried about the fate of loved ones in Russia secretly tuned in to Soviet broadcasts, which mentioned names and places absent in the German mass media. There was little that Goebbels could do about these Soviet broadcasts. Jamming was out of the question, for the present state of German broadcast technology meant that such a measure would have seriously impeded the reception of broadcasts produced by the Greater German radio network.[8] Goebbels' response to the great increase in illegal radio reception was apparent in a number of areas. His total war program promised a new frankness. Party propaganda campaigns against listening to enemy transmissions and the dissemination of rumors based upon such programs greatly intensified throughout the last two and a half years of the war.

Goebbels' radio people confronted another type of problem in enemy shortwave broadcasts, which disguised themselves as underground German transmissions. "SA Man Max Schroeder" broadcast his anti-Nazi version of the war to the German people: "And no one believes any longer that Poland intended to attack us. Even the greatest swindler of all times, our Doctor of Lies, admits that Poland cannot be considered to be a cause of the war, that Poland was only a welcome pretext." "SA Man Schroeder" told his listeners that Hitler had been preparing for war since 1933, whereas England had consistently shown its goodwill towards Germany. This type of "black propaganda" was monitored by the radio section of the Propaganda Ministry. Reports based upon such illegal broadcasts were another source of concern to Goebbels. He discovered that monitors had been distributing their reports to unauthorized persons, thereby contributing to the spread of rumors of enemy origin.[9]

Hans Fritzsche was the most prominent wartime commentator on the German radio. At Fritzsche's Nürnberg trial, the defense attorney Heinz Fritz admitted of his broadcasts, "Without any doubt, they greatly contributed toward the formation of political opinion in Germany . . ." [10] This was true into 1943, but after Stalingrad, Fritzsche, whose style had often evoked negative reactions before that time, met increasing hostility among his listeners. The Security Service of the SS kept Fritzsche informed about reaction to his weekly political broadcasts. During the death struggle of the German Sixth Army, Fritzsche's broadcasts often elicited admiration. His moving praise of the heroism of the Army impressed some Germans, though others decried his whining voice as the typical phrase mongering of a nonsoldier. Even when mourning a dead army, Fritzsche could not overcome his cynical, supercilious tone, which was more apt in times of victory than after Stalingrad. Listeners criticized Fritzsche for having too little to say. He sometimes seemed embarrassed by the irrelevance of his material. Fewer Germans were listening to him.[11] SD reports which described Fritzsche's problems often coupled this analysis with the frank admission that more and more Germans were listening to foreign broadcasts. People respected the military analyses of General Dittmar, but had turned against the political addresses of Fritzsche and Karl Scharping by 1944.

Letters to Fritzsche and Goebbels between 1941 and 1945 provide fascinating evidence of the growing popular hostility to Greater German radio programming. An early 1941 letter from one Elisabeth Hentze to Fritzsche was typical of the admiring response which Fritzsche broadcasts often elicited from people before the Russian campaign. Frau Hentze told Fritzsche that the English deserved destruction for unleashing the war and bombing Hannover, killing innocent people. "The main purpose of my letter is that retaliation also be carried out on behalf of Hannover!" she wrote. This long letter, which must have taken hours to compose, was certainly comforting to Fritzsche. He wrote to Frau Hentze offering his "best thanks" for her letter. Fritzsche assured his correspondent that Hitler was working day and night to make sure that Germans were protected against such terrible air raids. In a second letter Hentze had complained that Fritzsche did not devote any words on his radio program to expressions of sympathy for the Hannover dead. His reply that he had followed instructions in expressing general sympathy for *all* civilian victims did not satisfy her, though she was an ardent admirer of the commentator. She concluded by happily telling Fritzsche, "Tonight I will listen to you again, and I am already happy at the thought!" Implicit in her praise were criticisms that would later become widespread: His words were too vague, and the media people did not realize the extent to which the air war was affecting civilians. Even fanatic Nazis were getting restless. One A. Knoch wrote to Hitler, suggesting massive retaliatory bombardment of British homes and hospitals.[12] Fritzsche could not tell his correspondent that the Luftwaffe had been carrying out that sort of raid since late 1940, since he had always declared that the British, not the Germans, were practitioners of air terror.

Problems such as how to handle the story of the Hess flight undermined Hans Fritzsche's credibility. He hewed to the party line, declaring that Hess was a "confused person" who had wanted to bring the British to their senses so as to save them. Party loyalists wrote in, complaining about this account. Was not Hess an undisciplined traitor who deserved to be shot? One correspondent compared the shock of the Hess flight to the Röhm "revolt" of 1934. Many party members had liked Hess, but for those who did not, it was not enough to say that he was "deluded." "One of thousands" wrote to Fritzsche that party members wondered how a mentally ill man could have been Hitler's successor? This writer managed a jibe at the "escapades" of Robert Ley, a man who told German married couples that they "could get by on 48 marks a month" while he picked up girls on the street and "plunked down 148 marks!" And how about the "devil with the club foot!" The correspondent condemned Goebbels' "repulsive sexual forays" and his sudden wealth, and concluded with a significant comment, "Can you understand it, therefore, that thousands of people now listen to the English news broadcasts?" "A good German" recommended to Fritzsche during the Hess uproar that he keep his mouth shut because "at least 70 percent of the listeners" were turning off their radios when he came on the air. He continued, "As for Hess, anyone who thinks honorably must pay homage to this man. He was the only man who would not go along with someone who is driving all humanity to ruin. And this person dares to say that Hess is crazy. I believe that Hess is more normal than Hitler, for only a maniac can lead entire peoples to their doom in this manner." This anonymous writer condemned the nouveau riche Nazi big shots, including that "fat pig," Göring, and expressed the hope that Hess would give England Hitler's military plans, thereby leading to the defeat of Nazi Germany. "And you, you bum . . ." The writer, clearly not one of

Goebbels' success stories, concluded by asking Fritzsche to show his letter to Hitler so he could see "that all Germans are not as dumb as he would like to think!"

Goebbels himself received many letters which contained hostile or negative reactions to the mass media. One such letter, signed "public opinion," expressed respect for Hess's morality and sense of justice. Using the sadistic terminology even many anti-Nazi letters contained, the writer referred to the "Nazi straitjacket" and blasted Hitler and the Nazi clique as criminals: Hitler, Goebbels, Ribbentrop, Rosenberg, Himmler, and Ley must be "whipped, tarred and feathered, tortured on the wheel, and then burned . . ." "Public opinion" concluded by expressing the wish that all victims of Nazi criminality could take part in this act of revenge—priests, concentration camp prisoners, Englishmen and other invaded peoples, "and last but not least, Jews." Goebbels viewed such correspondents as sick traitors. Yet in the Nazi world of inverted values, what an extraordinary testimony they were to the endurance of truth, at least in some Germans!

In becoming the major political commentator of Third Reich radio, Hans Fritzsche brought down upon himself the wrath of an increasingly unhappy public. When he declared that Germany, which had freedom of religion, was fighting Bolshevism, a correspondent called a discrepancy to Fritzsche's attention: ". . . in theory there is freedom of religion, freedom of faith in Germany. But in practice things look quite different." The writer, Ernst Meir, recalled years of Nazi pressure to induce people to leave their churches. "I have written to you as an inwardly free person," he concluded. This sort of anti-Nazi "inward emigration" was anathema to the National Socialists. Fritzsche lamely replied on October 3 that freedom of religion meant the freedom of an ecclesiastic to impart his message to his flock, even if he used his authority in an antistate manner, such as "mentioning the Jews as a chosen people." This was vintage Fritzsche, managing to sound like an anti-Semite without directly attacking the Jews.

After the invasion of Russia, Fritzsche's main supporters among letter writers appear to have been vindictive, self-promoting Nazis of little intelligence. Some of their letters are useful evidence when they discuss rumors circulating among the people. One such letter, written on August 31, 1941, is significant because it indicates a growing lack of confidence in Hitler's leadership. The writer, Ida Kayser-Insinger, mentions a rumor to the effect that the Gestapo was killing mildly mentally ill people. She also alludes to a lack of understanding of the regime's Jewish policy: Some people were even saying that the Jews did not deserve the harsh fate meted out to them. Such people did not "understand" that the Jew was behind England, Russia, and America, the writer commented. In answering these letters, Fritzsche received the assistance of Dr. Albrecht of the ministry's propaganda division.[13] He responded with more alacrity to favorable than to unfavorable ones.

Correspondents occasionally addressed both Fritzsche and Goebbels, and other leaders as well. One such writer, who obviously knew whereof he spoke, declared that the Nazis, because of massacres carried out by the SS in places like Lemberg (in eastern Galicia) , were to blame for the "hatred of the Jews of the world." Another correspondent, writing to Fritzsche in September 1944, recalled, "It was about two years ago that I informed you of my firm conviction that Germany must lose this war, and that in the coming year almost every German would agree." The writer noted that Fritzsche was one of the few Germans who still seemed to disagree and prophetically stated that some top Nazis would continue to predict victory when the enemy was at the very gates of Berlin! Who had brought about this grim state of affairs? "A blind, crazy, unscrupulous leadership." The correspondent turned Fritzsche's irony against him by noting the difficult task which confronted the commentator: He had to reverse every concept of truth, justice, and ethics in order to blind the German people to reality. The letter alluded to the coming era of justice, for the Third Reich world would last twelve years, not one thousand, and those who had committed crimes in its name were now shaking in their boots.[14]

Even the cool, ironic Fritzsche might have broken out into a cold sweat when he read the following scrawled note:

Dear Hans!

You have spoken enough,
Much nonsense occurs in your words—
Now get on the next train,
Keep your mouth shut and go to the front,
And become a hero!

(Signed) From a hospital for severely wounded soldiers.[15]

By late 1944 more letters of complaint were pouring into the Propaganda Ministry, a large number of them addressed to Fritzsche and Goebbels. One writer sarcastically quoted Hitler's line, "Give me ten years and you won't recognize your cities." Another correspondent foresaw posthumous revenge for the anti-Hitler officers murdered by the Nazis after July 20, "as sure as there is a God in heaven." Letters containing hysterical expressions of hatred now reached Fritzsche and

Goebbels, letters denouncing "Prussians" as "robbers and murderers," while prophesying that Germany's name would be stained until thousands of murdered Jews, Russians, Serbs, Poles, and dissidents were avenged. Other letters alluded to earlier propaganda campaigns and asked disquieting questions: What about the vaunted "Atlantic Wall"? Why did total war have to be proclaimed a second time, after July 20, 1944, when Goebbels had proclaimed it after Stalingrad? Some notes sounded like political placards, turning Nazi techniques against the Nazis: "Down with the bloodhound Hitler and death to all Prussians." "We don't hate the plutocrats, but the Nazis . . ." A woman dreamed that Hitler and Goebbels were stuffed exhibits in the British Museum. Another wrote, "One thing is clear to everyone, Germany will only have peace when the madman from the Obersalzburg disappears."

The degree of knowledge about mass murder in the east revealed in these letters is fascinating. One writer mentioned a good source—drunk SS big shots. Another correspondent denounced Hitler as a Bohemian criminal type, predicting (falsely) that the nation would indeed rise up, but not in the manner desired by Goebbels. It would revolt against Hitler and take revenge upon the Nazi criminals. This letter contained an interesting variation: The Nazis, who were so enthusiastic about racial purity, had themselves turned German women and girls over to a "foreign mob" of millions of workers and POWs! It was apparent to many writers that the real "plutocrats" in Germany were in the Nazi elite. Such outpourings of hatred dominated many of the notes and cards mailed to Hans Fritzsche.[16] These signs of opposition bear moving testimony to the incorruptibility of some human spirits. Goebbels was not unduly alarmed by such letters, however. He saw as his main task the prevention of another 1918. So long as the masses kept working and fighting for the Nazis, he was winning the war, however infamous his tactics might be.

The sharp drop in German morale during the summer of 1944 resulted in attacks upon Fritzsche even by Nazi propagandists. The director of the RPA office in Bochum noted that people no longer cared for Fritzsche's irony. They did not want sarcastic dialogue with the enemy; they wanted straight talk to the German people. This report wounded Fritzsche deeply, since Bochum was his home town. He learned nothing from the criticism, being above and beyond it, and only responded by weakly alluding to his difficult task in hard times. Some Nazis continued to try to be helpful, one sending Goebbels a detailed report about the advances made by Communism in Vienna, another mailing Fritzsche a poem that might be used as the Volkssturm anthem. One masochistic or demented woman even wrote to Fritzsche in late

February 1945, after the destruction of her hometown of Dresden, requesting a copy of his beautiful words commemorating her dead city. She had not been able to hear his words firsthand because of the destruction of her radio. . . . Other encouraging voices came from people with "occult gifts," including a letter in 1944 from a woman who claimed to have foreseen the rise of Germany's "savior" in 1921.[17]

Growing lack of confidence in the radio and other mass media encouraged the spread of rumors. From 1940 the dissemination by civilians of information gleaned from enemy leaflets dropped over Germany was of major concern to Heinrich Himmler. The Nazis believed that the enemy sought to demoralize the population and bring about a 1918 type of German capitulation. Despite explicit police instructions about handing in dropped leaflets, many cases occurred in which persons passed the illegal fliers to second and third parties. Enemy leaflets were most effective when they provided specific military information that was lacking in the German mass media. Himmler's attempt to combat rumors of enemy origin by cooperating with relevant state and party offices was one of the government's antirumor actions. The secret bulletin "Defense against Lies" *(Lügenabwehr),* published jointly by several state and Wehrmacht offices, was another aspect of the antirumor struggle. This interesting bulletin actually published false rumors that were making the rounds among the population. It then provided information to counter the rumors, thus facilitating the suppression of "wrong" facts and ideas. Example: "Japan–USSR. The announcement on a North American transmitter about the recall of the Japanese ambassador in Moscow is false." The Special Service of the RPL published its own "Mirror of Rumors," using the same method as that employed by the *Lügenabwehr.*[18] The "Mirror of Rumors" was more thorough, however, for it also published the alleged origin of specific rumors.

By 1942 the Third Reich was fast becoming the rumor center of the world. Police records contain fascinating case studies of how rumors spread—and how dangerous it was to disseminate them. Two nurses, Hildegard Wolf and Ingeborg Neumann, met two Wehrmacht soldiers who promptly began a political discussion. One of the men noted, "Greater Germany bears the main burden of guilt for the war." The soldiers also mentioned that the Russians had in no way been armed for an aggressive war and that the Germans had behaved brutally towards the Russian civilian population. When the women countered by alluding to Soviet atrocities against German soldiers, the Wehrmacht men "smiled ironically." They even defended the Jews as innocent of causing the war. The good women went to the police to report the incident, since denunciation was encouraged by the regime as a good antidote to rumormongering. This incident, like others of the kind, came to Goebbels' personal attention.[19]

Rumors that the war would last a long time often took the form of antiregime humor: "When will the war end? In twelve years, when Adolf Hitler retires." Other rumors were passed around as factual accounts of recent events. One alleged that there had recently been disturbances in Berlin which had to be suppressed by the Waffen SS. Another declared that someone had displayed a Soviet flag in Leipzig and that enemy slogans had appeared in windows and on the sidewalk. One of the prevalent types of rumor concerned a lowering of bread and meat rations. A report written by Tiessler acknowledged that in the town of Gera on May 11 and 12, 1942, "coarse slogans" had appeared on display windows and sidewalks, denouncing the party and the Führer. The Gestapo immediately took measures to locate the culprits, but exaggerated rumors about the incident spread to neighboring districts. What had these "criminals" scrawled on the walls? "Hitler is our murderer," "Red Front," and a symbol (three arrows) of the old republican Reichsbanner organization. Also "Hitler is a pig" and "Hitler is shit." The Nazis had been using the walls for their own propaganda since the 1920s. Now their enemies were doing so in increasing numbers. The party concluded that enemy radio broadcasts were the origin of most political dissidence, especially that concerning lowering of civilian rations.[20]

By 1943 Robert Ley was using the pages of a bulletin of the Reich organization leader to fight rumormongering. In July this bulletin made the startling admission that the main task of instruction at that time was to ward off rumors.[21] But rumors would not die; there were more of them and they grew wilder as the war lasted into 1944. People in Schleswig-Holstein were saying that Hermann Göring had been arrested for making contact with the Allies.[22] During the last eight months of the war the government mobilized all its resources to counter the dissemination and effect of dangerous rumors. The Reich Propaganda Office of Düsseldorf requested a special paper allotment so that it could print one million leaflets by November 2, 1944.[23] By this time the enemy was on German soil, as was much of the Wehrmacht. The gap between civilians and the military was narrowing as the armed forces and the population came into closer contact. Men were being rushed into the Wehrmacht and trained rapidly. In this setting, leaflets and other forms of antirumor action were aimed at both civilians and military personnel. Party and state propaganda offices, the Wehrmacht propaganda staff, and National Socialist leadership officers worked together on antirumor campaigns between October 1944 and April 1945.[24]

The state's most formidable weapon during this last stage of the war was intensified "whisper," or "word-of-mouth," campaigns *(Mund-propaganda)*. An agent, whether civilian or military, would talk in a loud voice to a companion, expecting to be overheard by news-hungry Germans. The agent was planting an authorized rumor, which spread among the people. The government hoped that its rumor would counteract and ultimately suppress the hostile rumor. Official rumor-mongers were also to report anything they heard to the *Gau* propaganda office. After years of combating rumors in more orthodox ways, the Nazis were now using the methods they had always attributed to enemy agents and radio broadcasts. The guidelines for *Mundpropaganda* were the responsibility of each *Gau* propaganda office, but Werner Naumann insisted that he had the right to inspect all slogans before local agents disseminated the counter-rumor.[25] Examples of "word-of-mouth" propaganda, or counterpropaganda, reveal a great deal about the attitudes of the German people during the last months of the war.

Rumor: The Bolsheviks are behaving decently in the occupied territory.[26]

Counter-rumor: They are committing numerous atrocities.

Origin of rumor: Enemy agitation working for the collapse of German morale.[27]

Counter-rumor: We have reached the high point of the war. We have to win time now in order to equip new armies with new weapons for the counterblow.

Rumor: The German Seventh Army is surrounded in Normandy.[28]

Counter-rumor: It is not, but the Allies have to lie because of successful German V1 bombardments and differences between Russia and the West over Poland.

Slogan number 29 (Saxony): "He who is disloyal to Germany falls victim to Bolshevism." [29]

Slogan number 32 (Saxony): "General Time cannot fulfill English hopes!" [30]

Slogan number 7 (Magdeburg-Anhalt, October 6, 1944): "Northern sector of the eastern front stable." [31] "Southern sector of the eastern front is being strengthened." "Our fighter wings are having an effect!" "The Anglo-Americans are as bad as the Bolsheviks!"

Slogan number 8 (Magdeburg-Anhalt): "The public must not make the mistake of noting daily losses of territory on a map and using them as a guide to the military situation." ". . . in the end the victory will be ours." ". . . our enemies have but one goal, THE EXTERMINATION OF OUR NATION." "In another village drunk Negro soldiers threw three hand grenades into a group of playing children." "The German

Volkssturm is the great demonstration of the armed community of the nation!" "Better dead than a slave!" (Variation in the "German Weekly Newsreel": "I can die, but be a slave and see Germany enslaved—Never!") "Volunteers forward! Into the Volkssturm for honor, freedom, and bread!"

Slogans in Danzig on October 10, 1944 ("Only for personal information and for transmission by word of mouth!"): America is a land of prostitution and injustice.

Slogan number 12 (Chief of the propaganda staff, December 22, 1944): "Traitors will be liquidated. In three towns near Aachen occupied by the Anglo-Americans, honor-conscious German comrades have liquidated swine who place themselves at the disposal of the enemy . . ." [32]

The Viennese were particularly fond of rumormongering. During the autumn of 1944 local Nazis under Eduard Frauenfeld decided to launch a press campaign against rumors. Their slogan was "The enemy speaks here!" Largely identical articles bearing this title appeared in the Vienna edition of the *Völkischer Beobachter,* the *Neues Wiener Tageblatt,* and the *Wiener Neueste Nachrichten* between October 4 and December 1.[33] Local authorities claimed that the press campaign had been effective. Schaeffer in the Propaganda Ministry was not so sure, since these articles spread the very rumors they were denouncing. Nazi antirumor campaigns used the technique of creating counter-rumors; they did not believe in publicly denouncing and identifying a rumor, since that would only further disseminate enemy disintegrative propaganda. Schaeffer ordered Vienna to stop the campaign on December 12, telling the head of the local Reich Propaganda Office to counteract rumors with other rumors.[34] Such bureaucratic confusion frustrated the Berlin ministry in its propaganda campaigns and was a factor in Naumann's insistence that he review and approve all word-of-mouth propaganda campaigns.

The bulletin "The Propagandist" published a list of popular rumors and concerns, with recommendations on how to counter those sources of potential trouble. "The Propagandist" called attention to enemy leaflets and radio broadcasts which spread disturbing, false rumors among the people, such as "The Führer is in danger." Rumors of this sort were aimed at German unity, at the will to fight, because, it was stated, ". . . our enemies hope to bring about a moral collapse of the German people, just as they did twenty-five years ago." [35]

Popular response to radio became increasingly negative during the last two years of the war, as both Fritzsche and Goebbels learned. The National Socialist press enjoyed little credibility (except in the vital area of provoking fear of the Bolsheviks), a fact reflected in the relatively small amount of time and energy devoted to it by Joseph Goebbels, particularly after 1941. He used the press for specific purposes and wrote his highly influential column for *Das Reich*, but his real interests were directed to other media. The popular appeal of the German film industry, on the other hand, justified the amount of time and money which German propagandists devoted to it. People flocked to the motion picture theaters in record numbers through the first four years of the war. Some went for edification and inspiration, others sought escape and entertainment. Whatever their motives, Germans responded positively to many films, making this industry more important than ever as a mass medium. Destruction of theaters in Allied bombings and technical shortages and problems combined to cause sharp decreases in attendance during the last year of the war.

The party continued its own film programs during the war, building upon measures which had been in effect since the advent of the Third Reich. In 1935 the Party Film Office, in its drive to bring film to rural as well as urban areas, had about 350 mobile projection vans, in addition to more traditional facilities. It projected films which attracted about 20 to 30 million total admissions, or about 6 to 9 percent of the motion picture patrons of the Third Reich in that year. By 1937 the figure had risen to 37 million admissions. Late in 1938 the *Gau* Film Office in Munich reported that it had offered almost 4,000 film presentations during the year, and had drawn 870,000 admissions. Party propagandists believed that "more is better," so they intensified their work during the early wartime period. By January 1941 the RPL boasted that it had been sponsoring up to 45,000 film evenings a month during the war. The Party Film Office offered both NSDAP and general films to its audiences, either free or at nominal admission fees. The *Gau* propaganda central office in Bayreuth noted that in 1940 the party there had presented 11,000 film shows, attracting over 2 million admissions. This represented a 60 percent rise over the figures for 1939; the figure for admissions was higher by about 600,000 than that for the preceding year.

The Party Film Office for the entire Reich claimed that the NSDAP had sponsored about 243,000 film shows in 1940, which had drawn almost 50 million admissions. Propagandists probably inflated their figures—which were sometimes contradictory—and made no attempt to clarify the difference between admissions and patrons. One patron may have visited these "party film evenings" many times during a given year and the party preferred to count him or her as an individual statistic each time. By 1940 the party possessed over 800 mobile film projection vans, though it later lost some of these to Wehrmacht propaganda company training centers.[36] Despite the impressive statistics, one must keep in mind that they represented under 10 percent of total film attendance in the Reich.

In many areas the party was preying upon captive audiences, whether party members and cadres who were expected to show up, or rural residents who had few alternatives if they wished to see a motion picture. By 1941 most party film presentations were directed at rural residents or troops stationed in the Reich and the occupied territories. The Party Film Office claimed that it had reached 55.6 million admissions in small towns and rural areas and 31.5 million Wehrmacht admissions. Problems caused by the war seem to have impeded party film work by late 1942. The boastful statistics disappear, and in their place one finds complaints such as that recorded by an SD official in Bielefeld. People were grumbling that the *Gau* Film Office, even if it brought rural residents a film every month, did not present the motion picture under ideal conditions. Proper screens could no longer be found, and the party often projected the film in a church, or even in a barn. The benches were uncomfortable, and patrons often viewed a great film like *Ohm Krüger* or *I Accuse* in a setting dominated by stables, cow stalls, and horse· manure.[37] What kind of an environment was that for an epic film?

The RPL worked with the Hitler Youth and other party youth organizations in offering "Youth Film Sessions," the first of which took place in 1934. Youth was one of the more promising objects of Nazi propaganda. Once again, the party played the primary role of bringing film to residents of towns without permanent motion picture theaters. In Nazi Germany, as in most other parts of the world, the great theaters were located in the big cities. Here, too, the party played the role of bringing culture and politics to the "broad masses." Much of its success before 1933 had rested upon its ability to look like it was bridging the gap between widely different geographical and social segments of the "Aryan" German population. It built upon this role after 1933. In 1934–35 the Youth Film Sessions attracted 300,000 youth-group patrons. A year later the figure had risen to 1 million. By 1937 it was up to 3 million; by 1940 it had reached 3.5 million. The figure claimed for 1941 was 5.5 million admissions, followed by a high point of 11.2 million for 1942–43.

By 1942–43 almost half of the Youth Film Sessions were taking place in villages and rural areas devoid of permanent theaters. The party required that teachers and staff involved in the Hitler Youth movement attend these sessions. Goebbels had widened the scope of the Youth Film Sessions soon after the outbreak of the war, when he ordered that film theaters be made available for these Youth Film Sessions once or twice a month on Sunday mornings. The timing was not accidental. The theaters were not being used, and anyone who attended these sessions would find it difficult to participate in church services. Goebbels turned these Sunday morning sessions into solemn celebrations of National Socialist film, boasting that in the autumn of 1941 on one Sunday 900,000 boys and girls had attended the presentations. The Third Reich was preparing for a totalitarian intensification of control of youth through motion pictures. The changing course of the war prevented the full realization of this plan, best expressed in the words of the Reich youth leader Axmann in 1942: "Are not films such as *The Great King* or *The Dismissal* the best form of education through experience for youth?" [38]

The enormous interest in film among the German people was a major source of Goebbels' power. Statistics give some idea of his success:

Admissions	*Income*
1932–33: 238 million	RM 176 million
1934–35: 280 million	RM 205 million
1935–36: 317 million	RM 237 million

Nazi film people took particular satisfaction in another set of statistics, one which showed that they were reaching the "broad masses" of people who had not been accessible to the film industry during the days of the Weimar Republic. Before the war, film admissions had been growing at the rate of 17 percent in the large cities, but at the rate of 33 percent in the small towns and rural areas.

The war itself did not bring about a decrease in film attendance, at least not until its latter stages. On the contrary, people crowded into the theaters as never before:

Admissions	*Income*
1939: 623.7 million	RM 477 million
1940: 834 million	RM 650 million
1941: 892 million	RM 726 million
1942: 1.065 billion	RM 896 million
1943: 1.129 billion	RM 971 million

Goebbels, speaking during the high tide of German media expansion, boasted that these statistics ran parallel to figures drawn from other media. One hundred million more copies of books and pamphlets were printed in 1941 than in 1940. Twenty thousand new titles had appeared in 1941 alone. Goebbels was extraordinarily proud of such statistics, and he ordered subordinates such as Gutterer and Hippler to make speeches about them throughout the Reich.[39]

Confidential statistics prepared by the German Film Distribution Society late in 1942 are extremely useful in studying the apogee of the wartime German film industry. They are also a prelude to decline. By the summer of 1942, Greater Germany possessed 7,043 movie theaters, as compared to 5,446 theaters in 1938. Most of the increment was the result of the annexation of new territories after March 1938, though there is evidence by 1942 that 200 new movie theaters had opened, mostly during the first years of the war. Berlin possessed 400 theaters, almost four times as many as its nearest competitor, Hamburg. The average German *Gau* had somewhat fewer than 2 million residents and possessed about 1 theater for every 12,000 persons. In this regard Berlin does not seem to have maintained an undue advantage. The capital possessed about 1 movie theater for every 10,000 residents. The average theater in other German cities of over 50,000 inhabitants averaged larger audiences during August 1942 than did the Berlin houses. This is somewhat misleading, however. Berlin had the most theaters in the Reich per square mile. The number of films was, moreover, limited. This meant that the proximity of large numbers of theaters to residents made for smaller crowds, especially since many of the theaters offered the same motion picture. Audiences in Halberstadt or Schwerin had to crowd into their 3 theaters to see whatever was available.[40] Greater Berlin and Potsdam had only 6.5 percent of the functioning motion picture theaters, but they provided 9.5 percent of the total German film audience during August 1942 and 10.1 percent of the gross income from ticket sales. How could this be, if the Berlin theaters drew smaller audiences than their urban counterparts elsewhere? The apparent discrepancy disappears when one compares greater Berlin to rural or small-town regions. Areas such as Pomerania, eastern Brandenburg, and Carinthia contained respectable *numbers* of theaters, but they were small and far from regions of great population density. They attracted fewer patrons than the number of theaters would lead one to believe. They also contained poorer populations than Greater Berlin or Hamburg, persons less likely to go to the cinema several times a month.

Berlin was the crowning summit of Goebbels' cinematic edifice, the administrative, financial, and prestige center of his film world. If Berlin crumbled under Allied air attacks, the German film industry would no longer have to worry about dominating European and world markets; it would be reduced to fighting for its life.

In November 1942 the officials of the German Film Distribution Society prepared their "strictly confidential" statistics for August. Goebbels read them with great satisfaction; he had reason to feel smug. From June to August 1941 German theaters attracted 214.6 million paid admissions, realizing a net ticket sales income of 163.4 million Reichsmarks. During the same period a year later the figures were 254.8 million admissions and 202.5 million net Reichsmarks. If one took into account and compensated for territories listed in 1942 but not in 1941, the statistics still gave sound reason for satisfaction, with admissions up 15.8 percent, income up 21.4 percent. Only one ominous sign appeared in these reports, and the statisticians chose not to mar the total effect of their work by emphasizing it. Almost three hundred theaters—a mere 4 percent of the total—were no longer functioning because of "war-related circumstances." This meant that they had been bombed or were unable to replace essential equipment or personnel.[41]

The geographical distribution of German cinema audiences in August 1942. The survey, prepared by the German Film Distribution Society, dealt with towns of 50,000 or more inhabitants.

Communities	Number of theaters included in the survey	Paid Admissions	Gross Theater Income (in Reichsmarks)
Berlin	400	7,278,383	6,653,226.51
Potsdam	7	164,868	153,545.30
Königsberg	21	540,876	538,957.65
Danzig	22	323,442	324,899.35
Bromberg	4	116,123	111,318.30
Bialystok	2	31,681	24,755.50
Tilsit	3	116,030	101,933.45
Thorn	5	68,715	56,216.35
Graudenz	3	42,784	34,656.40
Allenstein	4	109,715	111,394.10
Elbing	5	123,904	127,188.10
Gotenhafen	3	87,552	85,706.10
Grodno	2	20,485	18,366.20
Litzmannstadt	13	283,000	224,771.70
Posen	7	197,118	165,812.75
Leslau	1	17,515	13,832.35
Kalisch	2	37,675	29,921.50
Stettin	27	489,643	403,764.85
Frankfurt/O.	5	149,147	131,480.70
Cottbus	3	78,601	69,057.95
Stralsund	3	85,643	88,511.75
Stolp	2	80,725	86,638.30
Magdeburg	30	724,004	550,340.30
Dessau	7	178,107	183,983.65

Communities	Number of theaters included in the survey	Paid Admissions	Gross Theater Income (in Reichsmarks)
Brandenburg/H.	4	144,044	132,477.95
Halberstadt	3	93,937	81,506.45
Hamburg	117	2,825,187	2.358,643.--
Kiel	17	477,201	393,012.90
Lübeck	12	183,714	163,851.70
Rostock	7	188,406	183,189.--
Flensburg	5	119,855	102,299.--
Schwerin	3	107,226	121,669.30
Neumünster	4	92,996	80,802.85
Hannover	30	701,937	646,838.45
Bremen	27	497,683	433,739.35
Braunschweig	8	287,687	278,169.20
Wilhelmshaven	4	137,978	106,815.--
Wesermünde	8	157,012	132,774.20
Osnabrück	5	85,819	85,450.90
Oldenburg i./O.	5	102,027	90,186.39
Hildesheim	3	102,019	93,362.50
Göttingen	3	99,208	107,326.85
Totals 42 communities	846	17,749,672	15,887,394.10

No report written in 1943 or 1944 could ignore these "war-related circumstances." Discussions took place starting in 1943 concerning payment of compensation so that war-damaged theaters might be rebuilt.[42] Most of the motion-picture theaters in Germany were the property of the eighty companies, theater groups, and chains which comprised the UFA organization. This centralization might have facilitated reconstruction, but the lost air war rendered such discussions purely theoretical. Disastrous signs appeared everywhere. In July 1943 paid admissions in towns of over 50,000 persons had comprised 54 percent of total patronage; a year later the figure was 47 percent. Attendance at large city cinemas, the backbone of the German industry, dropped precipitously during the second half of 1944. Even towns in southern Germany, largely immune to the worst of the air war before the spring of 1944, now suffered extensive damage from Allied aerial bombardment. By July 1944 total film attendance began dropping at an accelerating rate, falling by 5 million paid admissions from June to July alone.[43]

How far away the great days of August 1942 seemed when the Propaganda Ministry took stock of the damage in June 1944! Five hundred theaters had been completely obliterated as a result of the terror attacks. "Numerous others" had suffered extensive or substantial damage. Since enemy attacks concentrated upon densely populated areas, the theaters that fell victim to enemy bombs were among the larger ones in the Reich. UFA had lost its most prestigious Berlin "premiere" theaters, the UFA-Palast, the Gloria-Palast, and the Capitol. In some *Gau* capitals, such as Kassel, every theater was either in ruins or out of commission.

Goebbels and his men inspired and directed massive efforts to make up for some of the damage. Between June 1943 and June 1944 they restored or were in the process of restoring 174 film theaters in Berlin alone. The authorities improvised throughout the Reich, converting legitimate theaters and industrial meeting places into ersatz movie houses.[44] A decision made by the "total war" Goebbels of 1942 now came back to haunt him. In order to mobilize more men and resources for the armaments industry, Goebbels had ordered an end to the production of projectors. Although 70 percent of the projectors survived the destruction or devastation of the theaters in which they were located, massive imports of projectors proved necessary after 1942. By 1944 the sources of such imports were fast shrinking. Germany possessed few effective air defenses after the summer of 1944. By the end of the war probably no more than 35 percent of her motion picture theaters were capable of functioning.[45] Even then, a lack of technicians and films, as well as the disastrous military and communications situation, rendered the surviving houses irrelevant as well as empty. A few weeks before Goebbels' suicide, the last brief "German Weekly Newsreels" occasionally appeared on screen, but the preoccupied population had more pressing concerns than finding an intact theater.

The decision to continue producing these "Newsreels" almost until the end of the Third Reich was based upon their overwhelming importance during the first two years of the war. By 1944 the *Deutsche Wochenschauen* had taken on an increasingly unreal, symbolic aura. Their music and pathos expressed a form of National Socialist heroic desperation. To Goebbels and his media men these newsreels recalled earlier days of glory; they continued to employ all their tested technical and symbolic tricks in producing the newsreels, though the reels were much shorter than they had been in better days. Goebbels believed that the newsreels were proof of the unity of homeland and front.[46] In 1940 they had celebrated German greatness through victory; they now created a myth of heroic resistance unto death. In 1940 the "Newsreels" had spoken to the German people. In 1945 they were a testament to the faith and will of Joseph Goebbels and the Nazi leadership.

The early wartime "German Weekly Newsreels" seem to have made little impression upon their viewers. Complaints poured in that many people were forced to view *Wochenschauen* that were up to two months old, and thus irrelevant except as history. The "Newsreels" devoted to the victory over Poland were less effective than later documentaries on the same subject, *Campaign in Poland* and *Baptism of Fire,* which used PK material not shown on newsreel screens. The great military events of the spring of 1940, the victories in Scandinavia and France, led to an enormous growth of interest in the newsreels. Goebbels was not content to let this enthusiasm take its own course. He ordered Fritzsche to make sure that the press publicized the enthusiastic public reaction to the latest newsreels.[47] The minister himself wanted useful information about this public reaction. Where would he find such material? Certainly not from the press, which reported what he wanted it to about popular opinion. Goebbels told Gutterer to request information from all *Gau* propaganda directors.[48]

Public interest in the *Wochenschauen* reached a peak between May 1940 and August 1941, the era of German victory. The long "special edition" *Wochenschauen* of 1940 gave German spectators a gripping, powerful picture of the Wehrmacht's "victory in the west." Most Germans were enthusiastic about the victory because they thought it was a prelude to peace. When peace did not come and victory over Great Britain remained a hope, disillusionment with the "Newsreels" set in. By November the SD reported that during the last few weeks interest in the films had declined. People complained that the newsreels were too long. They were interested in pictures of Hitler ("Was he serious? Was he laughing?"), but they were disappointed that they could not hear his voice on the sound tracks. This was a recurring complaint throughout the war. Regions which had not yet seen the "victory 'Newsreels' " viewed them with great enthusiasm. In some places these older films excited more interest than did recent *Wochenschauen.*[49]

The invasion of Soviet Russia unleashed a new wave of interest in the "German Weekly Newsreel." People responded well to the sight of European volunteers marching with the Wehrmacht against Russia, yet they wondered if and when these troops were to reach the front. There was special enthusiasm for the Finnish Army. *Wochenschau* scenes of Soviet prisoners and "proof" of Soviet atrocities seemed to have made a powerful impression upon some segments of the population. The "Newsreels" emphasized "criminal-looking types" among Soviet POWs. They also portrayed atrocities committed against Lettish nationalists by "Jewish-Bolshevik" commissars and GPU police sadists. During this same month, July 1941, some Germans expressed concern about events in North Africa. Did the absence of this front from the newsreel screen imply that the Axis offensive had come to a standstill? There was an interesting change in attitude in August, when disturbing rumors about powerful Soviet resistance began to circulate. Many people now reacted negatively to scenes of Bolshevik atrocities, allegedly because children and young people were exposed to these pictures in German theaters.[50] The real reason may have been growing unease over the Soviet refusal to collapse, an unease exacerbated by atrocity pictures. If a nation has to fight a long *offensive* war, such pictures demoralize the home population, which fears for its men at the front. Goebbels realized this, and the atrocity scenes generally disappeared, only to reappear late in 1944, and especially in 1945, as Germany engaged in a *defensive* war—now involving the civilian population in a more intense way. Fear was useful. Goebbels' anti-Bolshevik fear campaign had commenced in February 1943. It now culminated in this atrocity campaign.

During the early months of the Russian campaign many Germans found reassurance in the sight of their Führer. They saw him flying over Minsk (some Germans worried about danger to Hitler: "It is inconceivable what could take place if something happened to the Führer while he was at the front!") and consulting with Field Marshal Gerd von Rundstedt. Scenes which showed volunteers from other European nations in action on the Russian front brought satisfaction to some Germans. Scenes of the Rumanian siege of Odessa evoked enthusiasm, as did the sight of Italian contingents in the east. Many Germans wondered what the Italians had been up to in the summer of 1941. In early October, when it was clear that the struggle in the east was a hard one, some Germans took solace from the sight of the German encirclement of Russian armies around Kiev.[51] It was shortly thereafter that Hitler declared that the Red Army was finished, that the campaign in the east had basically been "decided." Nervous Germans, fearing a winter in Russia, looked at these *Wochenschauen* in a desperate search for a clue that would prove Hitler right once again.

A general crisis of confidence in the German mass media developed soon after Hitler's "decision in the east" statement (October 1941). By January the German armies were facing violent Soviet counteroffensives. Men were retreating or dying by the thousands every day. Goebbels believed that the German public was not ready for the stories of the winter in Russia. The hunger for news drove honest soldiers to tell stories even more grotesque than their experiences merited. The shock of defeat, however temporary, contrasted so greatly with past media statements that many Germans flatly rejected radio, press, and *Wochenschau.* People looked at newsreels showing thousands of furs and overcoats on their way to the east, shook their heads, and declared,

"That is not right; our soldiers are freezing. They're only receiving horse meat." [52] Reaction to the newsreels improved somewhat in March, when the front became stable and expectations of a great spring offensive ran high. Youth appears to have reacted less traumatically to the winter crisis than did the older generation.

The recovery of interest in the "German Weekly Newsreel" did not restore confidence and hope to the levels of June 1940 or July 1941. The final phase of the Battle for Stalingrad (November 19, 1942–February 2, 1943) saw Goebbels and the *Wochenschau* staff make a major miscalculation. German opinion was not prepared for the encirclement of the German Sixth Army, which took place between November 19 and November 22. Earlier Wehrmacht communiqués and Hitler's own comment about the city ("We have it!") had given rise to general confidence about the outcome of the great battle for the city on the Volga. Moviegoers watched PK film accounts of the battle in the October *Wochenschauen*. When the situation of the Sixth Army grew desperate, nothing about it or its fate appeared on *Wochenschau* screens. Goebbels feared defeatist reactions if he showed the public what was happening in the east. He would later use *other* media to call the nation's attention to the crisis in the east, but not the "German Weekly Newsreel," for it was too graphic, too emotional for this topic. There is a fascinating sentence confirming this interpretation in an SD Bericht of February 4, 1943: "The spectator gains the impression from the newsreels, in contrast to press and radio, 'That we are victorious on all fronts.' " [53] Another aspect of this disillusionment was the refusal of people to stand in line for tickets to uninteresting films solely to see the *Wochenschauen*. Such an occurrence had been common in 1940 and 1941.

The appeal of the *Wochenschau* never again reached the levels of earlier days, though occasional renewals of public interest could be perceived. People no longer seemed as interested in the excellent PK battle footage. They wanted a sense of the entire front, not isolated shots of victorious individual German efforts. The *Wochenschau* avoided such strategic information, since the front was shrinking and coming closer to home. Goebbels would use German defeats for his own plans, but he had no intention of letting maps or films speak objectively for him. His Sportpalast "total war" speech, impressively filmed for the *Wochenschau,* made a favorable impression, but disillusionment with "total war" also led to negative comments about *Wochenschau* coverage of the home front. Scenes which showed everyone making a contribution through labor brought snickers and sarcastic comments, since people knew that total mobilization was a myth. Soldiers on leave further undermined confidence in the post-Stalingrad "Newsreels," for they laughed out loud and made negative comments when the narrator showed how German retreats were all carried out "according to plan." On the other hand, a popular desire for reassurance through scenes of Hitler and heroes like Rommel persisted. The cynicism was growing, though. People were referring to the "Newsreel" as "Rumpelstiltskin's fairy-tale show" (*Märchenschau*).[54]

A revealing incident occurred in a theater in Vienna one day in March 1943. The audience could not yet have seen the new *Wochenschau,* yet 40 percent of the patrons departed after the feature film to avoid seeing the "German Weekly Newsreel." In Kattowitz the figure of prematurely departing persons was about 20 percent. The newsreels never recovered their earlier prestige, though their technical level remained high. To whom did they appeal during the last year of the war? Convinced National Socialists still found sustenance in the heroic music and deification of the leadership, in the enunciation of struggle unto death against Bolshevism and plutocracy. As one shrewd observer noted late in 1944, "There are still plenty of people who believe that victory is imminent and that we must not slacken our pace during the last few yards of the race." [55] During the last months, Goebbels intensified the "Newsreel" atrocity propaganda, but one wonders how the survivors of the Dresden firebombing reacted to these reports. How did audiences react when the *Deutsche Wochenschau* showed them evidence of misery and fear in Finland as the Reds approached, when they knew of the mass exodus from East Prussia during the last weeks of 1944? Much of the German propaganda of the last stages of the war was a vindication of the Nazis, who were in effect telling the German people that although the Reich was in desperate straits, Britain was losing her empire, America faced social unrest, and the Soviet Union was a living hell. To the average German trying to survive, all this meant very little, but to the Nazi elite it signified justification. "We will never capitulate," Goebbels and his colleagues were screaming to the world as they emphasized that there were no victors in this war. Their sadistic nihilism reflected a total lack of concern regarding the fate of the German nation. Goebbels took credit for the resistance offered by the German people, but he ultimately would have contempt for the nation if it lost the war. He had won a war for Hitler. Could they not do the same?

The packed motion picture theaters of the early and middle war years offered vivid proof that feature films of the Third Reich attracted Germans on a scale surpassing that of previous times. Goebbels declared that two functions of the German film were "relaxation" and "spiritual recuperation." [56] He made this public comment during the last stages of the Battle of Stalingrad, when an agitated German public was badly in need of both experiences. Statistics offer valuable evidence regarding the moviegoing tendencies of the German people during the war. They do not, however, tell us much about reactions to the great *themes* of Nazi-made and Nazi-commissioned films. What films succeeded, and which failed, and why? Police intelligence reports, plus confidential comments made by other state and party agencies, are helpful in forming a tentative picture of German popular reaction to wartime film.

Campaign in Poland opened in Berlin to great popular approval. In February 1940, theater owners and managers presenting the film noted that their houses were consistently sold out. In some movie houses the audiences erupted into spontaneous applause during especially powerful scenes. Some persons believed that such demonstrations were not worthy of the "earnest attitude" which the film required of an audience. Others became angry if the whole theater did not go wild with applause at the sight of the destruction of a Polish train convoy. Since several parts of the film were based upon previously screened *Wochenschauen,* certain blasé Berliners were disappointed by *Campaign in Poland.* Persons who had not seen those "Newsreels," however, often commented that *Campaign in Poland* had been their most powerful film experience since the beginning of the war. *Campaign in Poland* particularly impressed Germans who lived in areas which bordered upon formerly Polish territory. The much longer film *Victory in the West,* of which Goebbels was not fond, played throughout the Reich in 1941. An American correspondent reported that the "Great documentary film *Victory in the West* is playing week after week before sellout crowds all over the Reich." [57]

The reaction to *Jud Süss* is of great interest, for this film totally embodied the National Socialist world view in its most extreme form of extravagant hatred. SD reports about reaction to the film in late 1940 noted an "extraordinarily affirmative reception" by the German public. Perhaps too affirmative: Some teachers and elderly persons worried that the film, precisely because it was so powerful, would psychologically affect youth in a negative manner. These people were concerned about the evil and violence portrayed in *Jud Süss,* not its central anti-Jewish theme. It is possible that some Germans who objected to the film's "song of hate" used this alleged effect upon youth to cover the real reason for their revulsion, the film's anti-Jewish theme. The rape scene seems to have had a powerful effect upon the public, as did the segment where the Jews ominously trudge into Stuttgart. Some people were so moved by the film that they emerged from Berlin theaters screaming curses at the Jews: "Drive the Jews from the Kurfürstendamm! Kick the last Jews out of Germany!" [58]

When *Ohm Krüger* appeared on German screens in the spring of 1941, one report noted that it caused greater interest than any other recent film except *Jud Süss. Ohm Krüger* was so powerful that some persons did not even seem interested in discussing the "German Weekly Newsreel" when they left the theaters. In Bielefeld the film excited great interest for about ten days, then attendance dropped precipitously.[59] One cause of this decline may have been a rumor that the film was for people with strong nerves (because of the concentration camps scenes?). A more likely cause was a problem which plagued other Nazi ideological and historical epics. These films were "heavy," no matter how great the acting and the direction; they were political and contemporary, not offering much opportunity for relaxation or spiritual recuperation. On the contrary, they took the past and plunged it into the present, denying the audience any sense of detachment from the world of war and bloodshed. Such films were more appealing to Youth Film Session audiences or to party cadres, though they had their followers among the general public. People spoke of them with respect—but often without enthusiasm. Tremendous publicity campaigns prepared audiences for the appearance of *Ohm Krüger* in their hometowns. Its premiere always excited great interest and sellout crowds, but attendance often dropped off after a week or so. But one SD report noted: "The reports from the various areas of the Reich all confirm that the general response to this film among all sections of the population has far exceeded the exceptionally high expectations aroused by a strong press campaign. The film is considered the *outstanding achievement of the current year in the cinema,* and particular mention is made of its superlative blending of political message, artistic construction and first-class performances . . ." [60] This is precisely what Goebbels and Hippler wished to hear. The film continued to attract audiences through 1944, but it barely made the list of the ten most profitable wartime German films, though it was one of the most expensive.

The mass reaction to *I Accuse* is of special interest, since the regime used it to introduce the theme of "mercy killings" to the public. Cadars and Courtade note that the Nazis had some reason to be disappointed, despite the reasonably good attendance figures. People reacted most emotionally to the illness and death of the heroine, not to the question of the rights and wrongs of "euthanasia." The churches rejected the theme of the film, and the SD noted, "There are reports that Catholic priests have used house visits to try to stop individual members of the population from going to see the film on the grounds that it is an inflammatory film directed against the Catholic Church or a state propaganda film designed to justify the killing of people suffering from hereditary illness." [61] Equally unfortunate in the eyes of Goebbels was the tendency of many people who had seen *I Accuse* to approach the "mercy killing" question, not from the viewpoint of the film, but from that of the Catholic Bishop Clemens August Galen of Münster.

One SD report distorted the public reaction so as to make it sound favorable to the regime. It declared that most Germans believed that hopelessly ill people should have a way out as provided by the state—death. The report omitted mention of the "many reservations" expressed by the people, and its discussion of the "positive" public reaction made it appear that people saw beyond (or behind) the film and approved Nazi killing policies. What they may have approved of was death by one's own decision. The *Gau* office of Hannover East made a more honest report to the party chancellery in January 1942. It first described a strong positive reaction to *I Accuse,* but soon admitted that the message of Galen had ruined this effect.[62] The party was now on the defensive on the "euthanasia" question as the Church continued to dissipate the effects of the film throughout the winter.

Galens triumphed over the Nazis at least in part because *I Accuse* provoked discussion which backfired against the regime. The state fared better with "entertainment" such as *U-boats Westward!* and *Request Concert. Request Concert* did more than earn enormous amounts of money. It fulfilled a major ambition of the regime, that National Socialist values appear on the screen in an unobtrusive manner so as to influence the general, non-Nazi public. The SD commented, "According to reports received to date from all parts of the Reich, the film *Request Concert* has had a very *sympathetic response* and has been enthusiastically *approved* by the public. . . . It is precisely these *church scenes* and the organ music which particularly appeal to those sections of the population who are still influenced by the church." [63] The reader will recall that this church scene involved German valor and German piety in a classic Nazi death-and-transfiguration trick. The gimmick appears to have been successful. People were moved, and they did not see the party badge looming over the whole scene.

THE GREAT KING

PRODUCTION: Tobis
DIRECTOR: Veit Harlan
SCRIPT: Veit Harlan
MAJOR PERFORMERS: Otto Gebühr
                 Kristina Soederbaum
                 Gustav Froehlich
                 Paul Wegener
PREMIERE: March 1942

The Nazis devoted tremendous efforts toward publicizing one of their major historical efforts, *The Great King.* This massive spectacle about Frederick the Great during the Seven Years War starred Otto Gebühr (the most famous "Frederick") in the title role. Frederick was portrayed as the lonely genius who overcame adversity and subversion in fulfilling his mission of Prussian greatness. This film earned more money than *Ohm Krüger,* though it received its premiere only in March 1942, before an audience of war heroes and munition workers. Hitler, the great Frederick worshiper, was evidently pleased—though it is possible that he followed Goebbels, the critic, in this—and he named Otto Gebühr "state actor." The movie itself was awarded the honor of becoming a "film of the nation," thus receiving the highest accolade of the Ministry for Popular Enlightenment and Propaganda.[64] It even won the Mussolini Trophy as the best foreign film at the 1942 Venice film festival. The Propaganda Ministry saw the film as "especially valuable from political and artistic viewpoints, culturally valuable, valuable as folk art, educational for the nation, good for youth." After the war, Allied occupation authorities in Western Germany saw it as a "Very elaborate production with some fine battle scenes, good acting, rather heavy, North German type of film with militarist and nationalist propaganda." [65] The film is somewhat tedious and wordy, but the reception which it received in the Germany of 1942 encouraged Goebbels in his use of the Frederick the Great myth.

Reports came to Goebbels indicating that *The Great King* was a great popular success.[66] The SD reported that it was doing well in Paderborn. The National Socialist Teachers' League in Regensburg noted that *The Great King* had run for two full weeks, and people were enthusiastic about it.[67] By 1944 this production was an established commercial and political success. It attracted good audiences in Danzig as late as October 1944.[68] The party there provided a speaker who discussed the film for ten or fifteen minutes before the screening. The Danzig RPA office suggested that such a procedure might well be followed throughout the Reich. In November *The Great King* played for a week in Berlin and attracted almost 15,000 patrons, as compared with a turnout of 8,000 for *Friedrich Schiller* and almost 7,000 for *The Dismissal.*[69] Yet even during this era of the last burst of Nazi enthusiasm and heroic rhetoric, more than twice as many people attended the screenings of lighter, romantic, or comic motion pictures. "Serious" films such as *The Great King* owed some of their success to massive publicity by the regime. One wonders if they would have attracted as many patrons had it not been for such saturation advertising.

Request Concert attracted over 23 million patrons during the war, far more admissions than great epic films could claim. One party bulletin noted in 1943 that people usually wanted films "which have nothing in common with our Idea.... Problem films (such as *Bismarck)* do not arouse much enthusiasm and are anything but box-office successes." [70] The type of film which Rosenberg wanted would not have had much popular appeal in 1943. Yet some political films attracted large audiences. How can one account for this discrepancy? A good part of the audience of films such as *Ohm Krüger, The Great King,* and *The Dismissal* consisted of party members, Wehrmacht personnel, and members of Nazi youth organizations. The *general* public responded well when such films opened, for massive publicity aroused interest and anticipation. Many, perhaps most, later screenings of the same films, however, played before politically responsive, or "captive," audiences. It may be true that "... political films like *Ohm Krüger* and *Jud Süss* left a deeper imprint on the minds of movie goers than a score of romances or comedies." [71] Yet if this was true, it was valid only for politically conscious audiences who shared the Nazi view of the world. Massive publicity, selected audiences, and the continued circulation of "epics" inflated admission figures and accounted for their financial success or at least for their avoidance of financial disaster. Youth provided huge audiences for such films during the war.

Youth was susceptible to the themes embodied in such motion pictures, so the regime encouraged parents to permit their children to attend many of the films presented "free to youth," which they often confused with films which were *Jugendfilme,* or films for young people. Or perhaps the regime intentionally confused parents to attract their children to National Socialist epic films. Many had other things, such as survival, on their minds by 1942, and were only too happy to permit troublesome Hans or bratty Inge to go to the movies. Numerous towns contained only one or two theaters, and the regime saw to it that they often offered "serious" films, that is, films of a political or ideological nature. People noted that the influx of noisy children kept adults away from theaters much of the time.[72] A situation thus arose often from 1942 on, in which young people, party members and officials, and Wehrmacht men on leave comprised much of the audience for the great Nazi epic films. This was not necessarily unfortunate from Goebbels' viewpoint. Let the general public receive its Nazi message in a more subliminal manner, in "escapist" films such as *Request Concert.* Those ready for stronger themes, those who comprised the present and future elite of the National Socialist nation, were the targets of more serious films.

Dr. Paul Joseph Goebbels still wanted to justify himself before the German people, even as Berlin burned around him. True to his character, he combined a profession of faith with a desperate attempt to escape condemnation by the "whore," history. Like Hitler, Goebbels attempted to evade responsibility for his action. As he addressed his colleagues during his last ministerial conference, the minister's voice rose, for the moment overcoming the noise of the Berlin streets. This was no longer the speaker pounding on the rostrum with calculating emphasis. Here was a man desperately trying to vindicate the National Socialist ethic of heroism by imputing it to the German people. In so doing he made himself the agent of the nation and of its honor, thus returning to the original claim of the National Socialist movement. Now, on April 21, 1945, Goebbels sought vindication in the shared destiny of nation and leadership, a community of fate which he had done so much to create. Firmly convinced that the Allies would destroy both the Nazis and the nation, Joseph Goebbels perversely sought hope and justification in this shared community of despair and death:[73] The German people fought on to the end. Thus Hitler and Goebbels won their war against the "shame" of 1918. "After all, the German people did not want it otherwise. The German people by a great majority decided through a plebiscite on the withdrawal from the League of Nations [in 1933] and against a policy of yielding, and chose, instead, a policy of courage and honor; thereby the German people themselves chose the war which they have now lost."

Notes

The following abbreviations or shortened names have been used:

ADPR	Enlightenment Service for the Political Speaker
B.A.	Bundesarchiv (West German Federal Archives)
DAF	German Labor Front
DAZ	*Deutsche Allgemeine Zeitung*
DNB	German News Service
DPA	German Propaganda Studio
DW	German Weekly Newsreel
GPL	*Gau* Propaganda Central Office
H.I.A.	Hoover Institution Archives
IMP	International Museum of Photography
IMT	International Military Tribunal
KPL	District Propaganda Office
KPMB	*Cultural-Political Communication Bulletin*
LOC	Library of Congress
Michigan	Weinberg Collections, University of Michigan
N.A.	National Archives
PK	Party Chancellory
RKK	Reich Culture Chamber
ROL	Reich Organization Leader
RPA	Reich Propaganda Office
RPL	Reich Propaganda Central Office
RS	Circular Letter or Instruction
RSI	Speakers' Information
⁻/B	*Völkischer Beobachter*
YIVO	Institute for Jewish Research

Introduction

1. Henri Michel, in *Politics and Strategy in the Second World War,* ed. Arthur L. Funk (Manhattan, Kan.: 1976), Preface.
2. Gerhard Jagschitz, in *Filmbestände. Verleihkopien von Dokumentar-und*

Kulturfilmen sowie Wochenschauen 1900–1945, comp. Hans Barkhausen (Bundesarchiv: 1971).

3. From the film *Triumph of the Will,* 1935.

1

1. Karena Niehoff and Boris von Borresholm, eds., *Dr. Goebbels nach Aufzeichnungen aus seiner Umgebung* (1949), p. 187. Most sources give the date of the last ministerial conference as April 21, 1945. By this time Goebbels' Berlin residence was also the "ministry."

2. Erich Schneyder, "The Fall of Berlin," trans. L.P. Lochner, *Wisconsin Magazine of History,* L (1967): 418. Cf. Helmut Heiber, ed., *Goebbels-Reden* (Düsseldorf: 1972), II: 452, n. 6.

3. Heiber, ibid.

4. Schneyder, p. 419.

5. Wilfred von Oven, *Mit Goebbels bis zum Ende* (Buenos Aires: 1949-50) I: 123.

6. Von Oven, II: 212.

7. Ibid., p. 213.

8. Ibid., p. 224.

9. Ibid., p. 236.

10. Ibid., pp. 304–5. Some or all (1924–45) of these valuable diary entries have been recovered and will soon appear in print. See also *Frankfurter Allgemeine Zeitung,* November 21, 1974, "Goebbels Tagebücher," and October 12, 1973, "Die Goebbels-Kommentare."

11. Heiber, *Reden,* II: 448.

12. Schneyder, p. 424.

13. Ibid., pp. 422–27.

14. Cf. Willi A. Boelcke, ed., *Kriegspropaganda 1939–1941: Geheime Ministerkonferenzen im Reichspropagandaministerium* (Stuttgart: 1966), p. 43.

15. This phrase appears in the typescript of Frau von Oven's account of her husband's diary, Mass Communications Center, Wisconsin State Historical Society.

16. Rudolf Semmler, *Goebbels—The Man Next to Hitler* (London: 1947), p. 24. The man's name, unless legally changed, was *Semler.*

17. Ibid., p. 29.

18. Louis P. Lochner, trans. and ed., *The Goebbels Diaries 1942–1943* (Garden City: 1948), p. 56.

19. Heiber, *Reden,* II: 208, n. 99.

20. Helmut Heiber, *Goebbels* (New York: 1972), p. 149.

21. Frau von Oven account.

22. Ministerial conference of September 16, 1942 (Luther, based on Todenhoefer notes for foreign office) in N.A. T-120/736/339707. See also Joseph Goebbels, "Wofür Kämpft der Deutsche Soldat?" in *Das eherne*

Herz. Reden und Aufsätze aus den Jahren 1941/42 (Munich: 1943), pp. 334–35.

23. Hans-Leo Martin, *Unser Mann bei Goebbels. Verbindungsoffizier des Oberkommandos der Wehrmacht beim Reichspropagandaminister 1940–1944* (Neckargemünd: 1973), p. 136.

24. Boelcke, *1939–1941*, p. 276.

25. Willi A. Boelcke, ed., *"Wollt Ihr den totalen Krieg?" Die geheimen Goebbels-Konferenzen 1939–1943* (Stuttgart: 1967), p. 338. See also p. 344.

26. Von Oven, II: 156.

27. Lochner, *Diaries*, p. 320; Frau von Oven (August 4, 1943).

28. Martin, *Unser Mann*, pp. 32–33.

29. N.A. T-580/644 (no frame numbers for this series).

30. Lochner, *Diaries*, pp. 88, 153.

31. Von Oven, I: 87.

32. Semmler, p. 43.

33. Boelcke, *1939–1941*, p. 301.

34. Semmler, p. 48.

35. Ibid., pp. 48–49.

36. Ibid., p. 63.

37. Lochner, *Diaries*, p. 35.

38. Adolf Hitler, *Hitler's Secret Conversations 1941–1944* (New York: 1953), pp. 452–53.

39. Heiber, *Reden*, II: 267 (Goebbels' italics).

40. Heiber, *Goebbels*, p. 22.

41. See Von Oven, I: 238–46, for this account by Goebbels of his early life.

42. Ibid., pp. 231–32.

43. See Julien Benda, *The Betrayal of the Intellectuals* (Boston: 1955), passim. Italics in quotations are Benda's.

44. Joseph Goebbels, "Deutsches Schrifttum im Lärm der Waffen," in *Der steile Aufstieg: Reden und Aufsätze aus den Jahren 1942/43* (Munich: 1944), p. 21.

45. See Joseph Goebbels, *Michael. Ein Deutsches Schicksal in Tagebuchblättern* (Munich: 1929), passim. In the Third Reich at least one editor changed the title to give the work a more Nazi tone. Cf. *Michaels Weg zum Volke* in the series "Das Reich im Werden," ed. Dr. Rudolf Ibel (Frankfurt-am-Main: 1941).

46. Norman Cohn, *Warrant for Genocide. The Myth of the Jewish World-conspiracy and the Protocols of the Elders of Zion* (New York: 1967), p. 197.

47. Joseph Goebbels, "Gelobt sei was hart macht!" in *Die Zeit ohne Beispiel: Reden und Aufsätze aus den Jahren 1939/40/41* (Munich: 1941), p. 244.

48. See Heiber, *Goebbels*, p. 51.

49. Carin Kessemeier, *Der Leitartikler Goebbels in den NS-Organen "Der Angriff" und "Das Reich"* (Münster: 1967), pp. 279–80.

50. "Mjölnir" and Joseph Goebbels, *Das Buch Isidor, Ein Zeitbild voll Lachen und Hass* (Munich: 1931).

51. Semmler, pp. 56–57.

52. Joseph Goebbels, *Kampf um Berlin. Der Anfang* (Munich: 1937), p. 18.
53. Hans Schwarz van Berk, ed., *Der Angriff. Aufsätze aus der Kampfzeit* (Munich: 1936), pp. 14–15.
54. Heiber, *Goebbels,* p. 57.
55. Albert Krebs in *The Infancy of Nazism: The Memoirs of Ex-Gauleiter Albert Krebs 1923–1933,* William S. Allen, ed. (New York: 1976), pp. 191–205.
56. Ibid., pp. 196–97.
57. Kessemeier, p. 259.
58. Hitler, *Conversations,* p. 603.
59. Quoted by Heiber, in *Goebbels,* pp. 75–76.
60. Goebbels, *Der Angriff,* in *Aufsätze aus der Kampfzeit* (München: 1935), p. 21.
61. Goebbels, ibid., "Der Führer" and "Wenn Hitler spricht," pp. 214–17.
62. Ibid., p. 218.
63. Ibid., "Wir gedenken der Toten!" pp. 250–52.
64. Ibid., "Kütemeyer," pp. 256–59.
65. Ibid., "Die Fahne hoch!" pp. 268–71.
66. Ibid., "Gegen die Reaktion," pp. 291–94. This piece was also a thinly disguised appeal to radical workers furious at the Social Democratic government for unleashing the police against an illegal Communist May Day demonstration in Berlin.
67. Albert Speer, *Spandau: The Secret Diaries* (New York: 1976), p. 82.
68. Lochner, *Diaries,* p. 139.
69. Ibid., p. 205.
70. Goebbels, "Adolf Hitler als Staatsmann," speech of April 1, 1932.
71. Joseph Goebbels, "Aufruf zum Befreiungskampf," in *Wetterleuchten. Aufsätze aus der Kampfzeit* (Munich: 1939), p. 307.
72. Joseph Goebbels, "Der Sturm bricht los," in *Signale der neuen Zeit. 25 ausgewählte Reden* (Munich: 1934), pp. 82–89.
73. Joseph Goebbels, *Vom Kaiserhof zur Reichskanzlei. Eine historische Darstellung in Tagebuchblättern (Vom 1. Januar 1932 bis zum 1. Mai 1933),* (Munich: 1935), p. 196. This work was one of Goebbels' best sellers.
74. Goebbels, "Der Nationalsozialismus führt," in *Signale,* pp. 91–107.
75. Ibid.
76. Ibid.
77. Ibid.
78. Semmler, *Goebbels,* p. 75.
79. See Gustave Le Bon, *The Crowd: A Study of the Popular Mind* (New York: 1960), passim.
80. Adolf Hitler, *Mein Kampf* (Boston: 1962), pp. 180, 183.
81. Goebbels, "Erkenntnis und Propaganda," in *Signale,* pp. 28–51, passim.
82. Krebs, p. 205.
83. Semmler, p. 17.
84. In articles such as "Die Juden sind Schuld!" and "Mimikry," Goebbels employed Yiddish phraseology. See *Die Zeit ohne Beispiel,* pp. 526–27, for some good examples.

85. Cohn, p. 258.
86. I was tempted to write "a twist of foot," but that would be intolerable self-indulgence.
87. Cf. Semmler, p. 30.
88. See "Isidor" and "Angenommen" in *Der Angriff,* pp. 308–11, passim.
89. "Der Jude" in *Der Angriff,* p. 322.
90. Ibid., p. 324.
91. "Ist das preussisch?" and "Die Juden sind schuld!" in *Wetterleuchten,* pp. 129, 323.

2

1. Quoted by Cohn, p. 204.
2. Goebbels, "Die Deutschen vor die Front!" in *Die Zeit,* pp. 535–36.
3. Goebbels, "Die Juden sind schuld!" and "Wann Oder Wie?" in *Das eherne Herz,* pp. 81, 85.
4. Quoted by Cohn, p. 206.
5. Goebbels, "Das eherne Herz: Rede vor der deutschen Akademie," pp. 34–37.
6. Quoted by Cohn, p. 207.
7. Lochner, *Diaries,* p. 377.
8. "Die Judenfrage als inner-und aussenpolitisches Kampfmittel," *Redner-Schnellinformation,* Lieferung 57 (NSDAP Reichspropagandaleitung, May 5, 1943).
9. Ibid., *"Judendämmerung in aller Welt!"* May 18, 1943.
10. Heiber, *Reden,* II: 235.
11. Von Oven, II: 10.
12. Heiber, *Reden,* II: 433. Cf. Adolf Hitler, "Mein politisches Testament," in *International Military Tribunal, Proceedings* (Nürnberg: 1947–1949), 41: 548 ff.
13. Boelcke, *1939–1941,* p. 537.
14. Semmler reports that Goebbels gave Hitler credit for this observation.
15. Semmler, pp. 35–36.
16. Boelcke, *1939–1941,* p. 724.
17. Goebbels, in *Die Zeit,* p. 479.
18. Ibid.
19. Goebbels, in *Das eherne Herz,* p. 171.
20. Heiber, *Reden,* II: 101.
21. Ibid.
22. E. H. Gombrich, *Myth and Reality in German War-Time Broadcasts* (London: 1970), p. 12.
23. Hitler, *Conversations,* pp. 399–400.
24. Goebbels, "Schwarze Wolken über England," in *Das eherne Herz,* p. 300.
25. Heiber, *Reden,* II: 162.
26. Lochner, *Diaries,* p. 536. See also Boelcke, *1939–1943,* p. 335.

27. Hans-Guenther Seraphim, ed., *Das politische Tagebuch Alfred Rosenbergs, 1934–1935, 1939–1940* (Munich: 1964), p. 81.
28. Ibid., p. 83.
29. Ibid., p. 88.
30. Ibid., pp. 110–11.
31. Ibid., p. 117.
32. Ibid., pp. 138–39.
33. William L. Shirer, *Berlin Diary* (New York: 1941), p. 588.
34. Hitler, *Mein Kampf*, pp. 176–83.
35. Hans Thimme, *Weltkrieg ohne Waffen: Die Propaganda der Westmächte gegen Deutschland, ihre Wirkung und ihre Abwehr* (Berlin: 1932), pp. 182–83.
36. Eugen Hadamovsky, *Propaganda and National Power: The Organization of Public Opinion for National Politics* (reprinted New York: 1954).
37. Harold D. Lasswell, *Propaganda Technique in the World War* (Cambridge, Mass.: 1971), p. 200.
38. Hans Baehr, "Die englische Weltkriegspropaganda und das deutsche Volk" (August 1939), in *Unser Wille und Weg*, pp. 177–92.
39. Von Oven, I, 36: 216–17.
40. Goebbels' clichés as early as the late 1920s. Cf. Goebbels, in *Signale*, p. 52.
41. Cf. Jay W. Baird, *The Mythical World of Nazi War Propaganda, 1939–1945* (Minneapolis: 1974), pp. 58–59, 64.
42. Steinkopf AP dispatch from Oslo, November 28, 1940. Louis P. Lochner papers, Box #19, Wisconsin State Historical Society, Mass Communications Center.
43. Goebbels, "Was denkt sich Churchill eigentlich?" in *Die Zeit,* pp. 346–49.
44. Lochner, *Diaries,* p. 235 (December 8, 1942): By the end of the month Goebbels had changed his mind about the Russian winter. See also Semmler, pp. 44–45. On optimism regarding Balkan and Soviet campaigns: Boelcke, *1939–1941,* p. 658 and Boelcke, *1939–1943,* p. 182.
45. Cf. on Brusilov: Boelcke, *1939–1943,* p. 319; on Churchill: Von Oven, I: 19.
46. Goebbels, "Wandlung der Seelen," in *Das eherne Herz,* p. 191.
47. Boelcke, *1939–1941,* p. 240.
48. New York *Times,* "Goebbels Sees '39 as a 'German Year,'" January 1, 1940, p. 11.
49. Baird, pp. 91–92.
50. Boelcke, *1939–1941,* p. 307.
51. Fritz Sauckel, instructions for *Gau* propaganda director of August 7, 1940, B.A.
52. Boelcke, *1939–1941,* p. 668.
53. Ibid., p. 723.
54. Boelcke, *1939–1943,* p. 184.
55. Semmler, p. 51.
56. Boelcke, *1939–1943,* pp. 196.
57. Cf. Goebbels, "Verändertes Weltbild," in *Das eherne Herz,* p. 126.

58. Boelcke, *1939–1943,* p. 317.
59. Semmler, p. 73.
60. Boelcke, *1939–1943,* p. 185.
61. Lochner, *Diaries,* p. 288.
62. Heiber, *Goebbels,* p. 232.
63. Von Oven, I: 23, 27, 36, 47, 50–51, and Frau von Oven (October 18, 1944). In 1941 Goebbels claimed that Roosevelt's agent, Col. Donovan, was a drunkard. See William Stevenson, *A Man Called Intrepid: The Secret War* (New York: 1977), p. 226.
64. Semmler, p. 13.
65. Von Oven, I: 84.
66. Quoted by von Oven, I: 14.
67. Cf. on Lanke, Frau von Oven typescript.
68. Niehoff and Borresholm, pp. 146–49.
69. Boelcke, *1939–1941,* p. 441.
70. Ibid., p. 40.
71. Cf. Semmler, p. 43; von Oven, I: 128; Hans Speier, *Social Order and the Risks of War. Papers in Political Sociology* (Cambridge, Mass.: 1969), p. 377.
72. Cf. Kessemeier, pp. 137, 169, 172–75, 257; von Oven, I: 262.
73. Cf. Frau von Oven typescript; von Oven, I: 197.
74. Heiber, *Reden,* II: 31.
75. Goebbels, "Verändertes . . .," in *Das eherne Herz,* p. 134.
76. Semmler, p. 28.
77. Schwarz van Berk, in *Die Zeit,* p. 9.
78. Lochner, *Diaries,* p. 129. Cf. *ibid.,* pp. 154, 242, 376; see also Heiber, *Reden,* II: 159; Boelcke, *1939–1943,* pp. 269, 323–24, 336; N.A. T-120/5/13324-13328 ("Handakten Kruemmer" for conferences of January 24–26, 1943).
79. January 31: *Berliner Boersenzeitung, Berliner Morgenpost;* February 1: *Nationalblatt* (Koblenz) and *Westfälische Landeszeitung.*
80. Heiber, *Reden,* II: 208, n. 99.
81. Cf. Günter Moltmann, "Goebbels' Rede zum totalen Krieg am 18. Februar 1943," *Vierteljahrshefte für Zeitgeschichte,* XII (1964): 13–43. See on press coverage: February 19: *Völkischer Beobachter* (Berlin); *Berliner Volkszeitung; Der Angriff.*
82. Hans-Georg von Studnitz, *While Berlin Burns. The Diary of Hans-Georg von Studnitz* (Englewood Cliffs, N.J.: 1964), pp. 22–23, 232. Lochner, *Diaries,* p. 296.
83. Goebbels, *Der geistige Arbeiter im Schicksalskampf des Reiches* (Munich: 1943), p. 21.
84. Goebbels, *Dreissig Kriegsartikel für das deutsche Volk* (Munich: 1943).
85. Cf. N.A. T-580/590 (no frame designations).
86. Lochner, *Diaries,* pp. 532–33, 537.
87. On plans for total war, see Lochner, *Diaries,* pp. 482, 532; von Oven, I: 96.
88. Von Oven, II: 57.
89. Lochner, *Diaries,* p. 493.

90. Von Oven, II: 189.

91. N.A. T-175/225/2763887. Cf. Heiber, *Reden,* II: 419.

92. Boelcke, *1939–1941,* p. 497. Cf. Boelcke, *1939–1943,* p. 238.

93. Heiber, *Reden,* II: 226–28, 293.

94. Von Oven, I: 29–30.

95. Goebbels, "Das Denkmal der nationalen Solidarität," in *Das eherne Herz,* p. 348; von Oven, I: 169.

96. Frau von Oven (January 5, 1944).

97. Von Oven, II: 22.

98. Heiber, *Reden,* II: 336 (Goebbels' italics).

99. Helmut Sündermann, *Tagesparolen. Deutsche Presseweisungen 1939–1945, Hitler's Propaganda und Kriegsführung* (Leoni: 1973), p. 272.

100. Cf. Martin Broszat, *Der Staat Hitlers: Grundlegung und Entwicklung seiner inneren Verfassung* (Munich: 1969), pp. 382–95.

101. Lochner, *Diaries,* p. 268.

102. Frau von Oven typescript.

103. Speer, *Spandau,* p. 236.

104. Lochner, *Diaries,* pp. 260, 262, 264, 266; Frau von Oven (November 11, 1943).

105. Lochner, p. 277.

106. Ibid., p. 512.

107. Von Oven, II: 146–47.

108. Seraphim, pp. 32, 37, 45, 48, 49, 52.

109. Krebs, p. 202.

110. Lochner, *Diaries,* p. 85.

111. Von Oven, I: 113–14.

112. Boelcke, *1939–1941,* p. 507.

113. Lochner, *Diaries,* p. 277.

114. Von Oven, II: 172. See also Frau von Oven (February 5, 1945).

115. Semmler, pp. 53–54.

116. Von Oven, II: 23–27. Cf. Lochner, *Diaries,* pp. 443, 475; Baird, p. 31.

117. Semmler, p. 26.

118. Lochner, *Diaries,* p. 277.

119. Ibid., p. 429. Cf. pp. 435–37.

120. Ibid., pp. 477–78.

121. Von Oven, I: 145–46.

122. Cf. Martin, pp. 134–35; Niehoff, *Dr. Goebbels,* pp. 182–84; von Oven, I: 180, 219, 265–66; von Oven, II: 11.

123. Lochner, *Diaries,* p. 512.

124. Speer, *Spandau,* p. 142.

125. Shirer, p. 522.

126. Lochner, *Diaries,* p. 547. Cf. Von Oven, II: 14–15; Frau von Oven (October 18, 1944).

127. Von Oven, II: 8, 56.

128. Von Oven, II: 132–33, 150–51.

129. Von Oven, II: 241, 252–53.

130. Helmut Heiber, ed., *Reichsführer! Briefe an und von Himmler* (Munich: 1970), pp. 362–66.

131. Schneyder, pp. 417, 422.

132. Von Oven, II: 309.

133. Hitler, *Conversations,* p. 127.

134. Heiber, *Reden,* II: 12. Cf. Goebbels, in *Die Zeit,* p. 293.

135. Cf. Boelcke, *1939–1941,* pp. 587, 601; Boelcke, *1939–1943,* pp. 204, 216; Goebbels, "Die überlegene Führung," in *Das eherne Herz,* pp. 311–13; Lochner, *Diaries,* p. 61.

136. Heiber, *Reden,* II: 127–32.

137. Ibid., II: 191 (Goebbels' underlining).

138. Lochner, *Diaries,* p. 359. On the Rhineland, see Goebbels in *Der steile Aufstieg,* p. 323.

139. Lochner, *Diaries,* p. 360. Von Oven, I: 89, 94.

140. Von Oven, I: 98.

141. Ibid., I: 99.

142. Lochner, *Diaries,* pp. 488–89.

143. Von Oven, I: 134–37.

144. Cf. von Oven, I: 192, 274; *Archiv der Gegenwart,* pp. 6324–25. Heiber, *Reden,* II: 264, 326–28.

145. Cf. Heiber, *Reden,* II: 355, 372–74; von Oven, II: 108–9.

146. Frau von Oven (March 9, 1945).

147. Heiber, *Reden,* II: 149.

148. Ibid., II: 160 (Goebbels' italics).

149. Ibid., II: 451.

150. *Archiv der Gegenwart,* pp. 5897–98. Cf. Goebbels, "Das Denkmal . . .," in *Der steile Aufstieg,* p. 354.

151. Goebbels, "Von den nationalen Pflichten im Kriege," in *Der steile Aufstieg,* p. 454.

152. Heiber, *Reden,* II: 288 (Goebbels' italics).

153. Von Oven, II: 46.

154. Heiber, *Reden,* II: 384.

155. Goebbels, "Um die Entscheidung," in *Die Zeit,* p. 541.

156. Heiber, *Reden,* II: 435.

157. Heiber, *Reden,* II: 48.

158. Ibid., II: 65.

159. Von Oven, II: 237.

160. Ibid., II: 300.

161. *Goethes Faust,* ed. Trunz (Hamburg: 1961), p. 348.

3

1. Cf. N.A. T-81/675/5484403; Boelcke, *1939–1941*, pp. 46–47; IMT, XVII, 236 (Schirmeister testimony of June 28, 1946).
2. See also Boelcke, *1939–1941*, pp. 27, 36–39, 43, 49, 54, 192–93, 330, 428; von Oven, II: 308; N.A. T-120/9/15325; IMT, XVII, 237, 238 (Schirmeister); IMT, XXXII, 328 (Fritzsche affidavit of January 7, 1946); Martin, p. 30; Boelcke, *1939–1943*, p. 253.
3. Boelcke, *1939–1941*, pp. 57–59, 749.
4. Derrick Sington and Arthur Weidenfeld, *The Goebbels Experiment: A Study of the Nazi Propaganda Machine* (New Haven: 1943), pp. 49–50.
5. Von Oven, I: 43.
6. Lochner, *Diaries*, p. 122.
7. Von Oven, I: 14, 20–21.
8. Ibid., II: 252–53, and Boelcke, *1939–1941*, pp. 54–56.
9. Cf. Boelcke, *1939–1941*, pp. 105–6.
10. See on Semler: Boelcke, *1939–1941*, pp. 52–53, 60.
11. Cf. Boelcke, *1939–1941*, pp. 51–54.
12. Cf. Frau von Oven typescript, p. 1.
13. Boelcke, *1939–1941*, pp. 51–54.
14. N.A. T-580/643.
15. C. Brooks Peters, "Nazis Make Science of Propaganda," New York *Times*, November 19, 1939.
16. IMT, I, 182.
17. Cf. Heiber, *Goebbels*, p. 123; Boelcke, *1939–1941*, pp. 138–41; N.A. T-70/1/3503298-431.
18. Mueller's book cited in IMT, XXX, 484–85.
19. Examples of *Kreisleiter Information* may be consulted in Rare Books Dept., University of Michigan Library.
20. Cf. N.A. T-580/644.
21. Cf. N.A. T-70/123/3651286, T-580/579.
22. Hitler, *Mein Kampf*, p. 583.
23. Heiber, *Goebbels*, p. 119.
24. See on youth cult: Boelcke, *1939–1941*, p. 117.
25. See N.A. T-120/1015/401506; N.A. T-70/10/3514753 through 759; T-70/123/3650749 through 901; T-81/24/21710; T-580/982.
26. See N.A. T-580/671.
27. See Boelcke, *1939–1941*, pp. 121–22; Heiber, *Goebbels*, p. 121; N.A. T-580/643.
28. See Otto Neuburger, *Official Publications of Present-Day Germany* (Washington: 1942), p. 9.
29. See Lochner, *Diaries*, p. 523; N.A. T-580/657 (Oldenburg RPA to Abt. Pro. January 6, 1945); Von Studnitz, p. 262.
30. Goebbels, "Richard Wagner und das Kunstempfinden unserer Zeit," in *Signale*, p. 191 ff.

31. Goebbels, "Die deutsche Kultur vor neuen Aufgaben," in *Signale*, p. 323 ff.

32. Cf. Neuburger, p. 12; N.A. T-580/964, T-580/973; Boelcke, *1939–1941*, pp. 182–83.

33. N.A. T-580/950.

34. N.A. T-81/674/5482961 et passim.

35. N.A. T-81/675/5483729.

36. N.A. T-580/588.

37. N.A. T-580/592.

38. N.A. T-81/671/5479787 et passim. Joseph Wulf, ed., *Theater und Film im Dritten Reich* (Gütersloh: 1973), pp. 85–86; N.A. T-580/606; T-580/592; T-120/2474/E255447; T-81/675/5484029ff.; T-580/587.

39. N.A. T-81/675/5483936 ff., N.A. T-580/657; *Kulturpolitisches Mitteilungsblatt der RPL der NSDAP*, September 25, 1943, pp. 1–5.

40. Wulf, pp. 52–53.

41. N.A. T-580/589.

42. *Nachrichtenblatt* 1944, # 107, p. 68.

43. T-580/671; T-580/670; Boelcke, *1939–1941*, pp. 101-2, 184–85.

44. See Boelcke, *1939–1941*, p. 281; N.A. T-580/656; T-70/123/3651237-249; T-580/672; Boelcke, *1939–1941*, p. 46.

45. Cf. N.A. T-580/644; T-580/658; T-81/24/21867; T-580/660.

46. Cf. N.A. T-580/643 (programs of these meetings).

47. Cf. N.A. T-580/589.

48. See on *Volkstum* work: N.A. T-580/586 (1940–41); T-580/641 (programs and budget for 1941); T-580/586 (subsidies to border territories); T-580/671 (RPAe budget for fiscal 1943); T-580/589 (Mainfranken, Styria, Brandenburg, 1942); T-580/589 (fiscal 1941 budget, esp. *Grenzländern);* T-580/586 (Danzig); T-580/586 (Ostmark and Niederdonau, 1939–1941); T-580/589 (budget for 1942); T-580/589 (RPA Wien, fiscal 1943); T-580/669 (East Prussia, 1944, Bolshevism); T-580/671 (Kulturarbeit, 1941-1942).

49. N.A. T-580/669. Cf. T-580/671. This last point was a favorite Goebbels theme.

50. N.A. T-580/589.

51. Cf. IMT, XXXI, 204 ("Organization Plan"); Friedrich W. Lampe, *Die Amtsträger der Partei* (Stuttgart: 1944), pp. 92–93, 98–99; Hans Volz, *Daten der Geschichte der NSDAP* (Berlin: 1943), pp. 150–53.

52. See on Fischer, Hadamovsky, and Wächter: Sington and Weidenfeld, p. 50; Boelcke, *1939–1941*, pp. 97, 99–100; *Archiv der Gegenwart,* May 25, 1941 and June 8, 1942 (5033A, 5524C); N.A. T-81/671/5479327.

53. KPMB, February 15, 1944; Boelcke, *1939–1941*, p. 317.

54. See on slogans and campaigns: N.A. T-81/673/5481685 ff., 696 ff., 468 ff.; N.A. T-580/671; T-81/672/5480895.

55. See *Sonderdienst* in N.A. T-580/644; T-81/24/21865 (on its various editions); T-120/5/13306 (contains a Goebbels article); *Die Lage* (Michigan, Weinberg Collections); *Propaganda-Parole* in T-81/672/5480795 ff.; *Propaganda-Anweisung* Nr. 23 in T-81/675/5483976; T-81/672 (July 19,

1943); "Die parteiamtliche Propaganda-Zeitschrift der NSDAP," in *Unser Wille und Weg: Monatsblätter der RPL der NSDAP.* LOC.

56. See on the speaker system: Sington and Weidenfeld, pp. 37–38; Ross Scanlan, "The Nazi Party Speaker System," *Speech Monographs,* XVI (1949): 90–97; on mobilization and speakers, exchange between Hess's office and *Gau* mobilization commissioners, August–October 1939, H.I.A.; M. Grimm, *Massenpsychologie und Propaganda im dritten Reich* (Vienna: 1949), p. 48; *Aufklärungsdienst für den pol. Redner* (ADPR) (Koblenz: 1939), Folgen 3, 6.

57. See ADPR, Folge 4; *Informationsdienst* #17; "Lichtbildvorträge und Lichtbildabende," in *Unser Wille und Weg,* January 1941, p. 4; *Redner-Schnellinformation* (RSI) nos. 30, 43 (April 16, May 15, September 30, December 28, 1942, and March 17, May 3, May 18, and June 8, 1943). B.A.

58. N.A. T-81/673/5481122 ff., 117 ff.

59. Questionnaire may be consulted in N.A. T-81/672/5480521 ff.

60. See on Tiessler and Gauring system: Walter Tiessler, "Der Reichsring . . . als Instrument des Propagandaleiters," in *Unser Wille und Weg,* June 1939, p. 126 ff.; list of Tiessler's political positions in N.A. T-81/673; Boelcke, *1939–1941,* p. 98; N.A. T-81/671/5479242, 328; on Saxony, N.A. T-81/675/5483847 ff.

61. See Tiessler memos in N.A. T-81/673/5482074-97.

62. Martin Broszat, *Der Staat Hitlers: Grundlegung und Entwicklung seiner inneren Verfassung* (Munich: 1969), p. 392.

63. IMT, XVII, 200.

64. N.A. T-580/979.

65. See Louis E. Schmier, "Martin Bormann and the Nazi Party, 1941–1945" (Ph.D. diss., University of North Carolina, 1969), pp. 112, 119; *Stabsamt* of the Thuringia *Gauleitung,* January 10, June 20, 1942 (Michigan); Dietrich Orlow, *The History of the Nazi Party: 1933–1945* (Pittsburgh: 1973), pp. 343, 350.

66. See on the colonial issue: *Propaganda-Parole* Nr. 17 (Weimar), February 10, 1943, p. 9; N.A. T-81/676/5484461.

67. N.A. T-81/671/5479395-6.

68. *Verordnungsblatt der Reichsleitung der NSDAP* (Munich), January 1943.

4

1. *Schulungsdienst der Hitler-Jugend* in N.A. T-81/677/5485569 et passim.

2. See on Ley and the *Schulungsamt:* Sington and Weidenfeld, *Experiment,* p. 39; Rundschreiben der DAF Gau Thüringen (Michigan); IMT, XXXI, 207 *(Organisationsbuch),* 64 *(Der Hoheitsträger);* Neuburger, *Publications,* p. 94; Orlow, p. 274; *Der Schulungsbrief* 1942–1943 (YIVO). On the Redner: circular bulletin of Schulung division of the Kreisleitung Eisenach, November 18, 1941. *Politische Auslese aus Buch und Zeitschrift* (Ausgaben

A and C) in N.A. T-81/683/4721511 ff., Michigan; *Mitteilungen, Schulungsunterlagen, Sammelsendungen,* and *Sprechabenddienste* may be consulted in the same excellent collection.

3. *Redner-Schulung des Gauschulungsamt Thüringen,* October 15, 1943, pp. 1, 13-14; *ibid.,* November 25, 1943, and August 10, 1944 ("Zwei jüdische Aufsätze" and "Die Judenfrage").

4. See on Fritzsche: IMT, XVII, 230; Nürnberg judgment: IMT, I, 182.

5. See on Rosenberg: Seraphim, pp. 9-10; IMT, XXXI, 252.

6. Krebs, pp. 217-20.

7. Ibid., pp. 215-17.

8. See Seraphim, p. 14; IMT, XXXII, 388-89; Constantin Graf Stamati, "Zur 'Kulturpolitik' des Ostministeriums," in *Vierteljahrshefte für Zeitgeschichte,* VI, no. 1 (January 1958), pp. 78-81.

9. Cf. N.A. T-120/780/371115.

10. Heiber, *Reichsführer!,* p. 206.

11. Cf. Neuburger, p. 96; Reinhard Bollmus, *Das Amt Rosenberg und Seine Gegner: Studien zum Machtkampf im NS Herrschaftssystem* (Stuttgart: 1970), p. 293; Cohn, pp. 217-18.

12. Cf. IMT, 385; Ley, *Organisationsbuch,* p. 312; *NS Jahrbuch* (1942), pp. 185-86; IMT, XLI, 211-13; *Idee und Tat; Mitteilungen zur weltanschaulichen Lage* in N.A. T-81/21; *NS Monatshefte* (LOC) for 1942 and 1943; *Aufklärungsdienst* 1939, Folge #6; *Die Gestaltung der Lebensfeiern* (1942) in N.A. T-81/674/5482611 ff.

13. Cf. Schulung department of Kreisleitung Eisenach, November 18, 1941 (to speakers), Rundschreiben of July 29, September 3, 1942; Rosenberg to party educators on May 11, 1944, in *Archiv der Gegenwart,* p. 6370; Gauschulungsamt Thüringen, *Redner-Schulung,* August 15, 1944, "Sinn und Aufgaben der Reichsthemenschulung."

14. Cf. Bollmus, pp. 134-39. I believe that Bollmus exaggerates Rosenberg's success in augmenting his power through use of the Reich themes.

15. Cf. on *NS Kulturgemeinde;* Wulf, p. 64.

16. Seraphim, p. 139.

17. Ibid., p. 199.

18. Cf. N.A. T-120/1056/423552; T-120/734/693; Lochner Papers, Box #20 (June 27, 1941); T-120/1070/425771-91; Tiessler to Goebbels, October 29, 1941 in T-81/671/5479437; T-120/2474/E255269-272; T-120/5/13218; T-120/9/15322; T-580/682.

19. Lochner Papers, Box #20 (June 24, 1941).

20. Von Oven, II: 10.

21. N.A. T-81/674/5482673-745.

22. Gutterer: N.A. T-70/123 (October 9, 1941).

23. N.A. T-81/672/5480996-7.

24. Goebbels, "Nachrichtenpolitik," in *Die Zeit,* pp. 514-19.

25. Lochner, *Diaries,* p. 210.

26. Ibid., p. 459.

27. Cf. Boelcke, *1939-1941,* pp. 130-32; Jeffrey R. Willis, "The Wehrmacht

Propaganda Branch: German Military Propaganda and Censorship During World War II" (Ph.D. diss., University of Virginia, 1964), pp. 125–26; Shirer, p. 344; Erich Murawski, *Der Deutsche Wehrmachtbericht 1939–1945* (Boppard: 1962), pp. 27–60, 103, 135–155.

28. Cf. N.A. T-580/644 (July 29, 1943, August 23, 1943); Joseph Goebbels, "Neujahrsgruss an unsere Soldaten," in *Der Blick nach Vorne: Aufsätze aus den Jahren des Krieges* (Munich: 1943), January 1, 1943.

29. Franz Six, "Die politische Propaganda der NSDAP in Kampf um die Macht" (Ph.D. diss., University of Heidelberg, 1936), pp. 48–54. The author, a good example (along with Naumann, Rüdiger, and Hippler) of the young Nazi activist intellectual, later became dean of the political science faculty of the University of Berlin. Rapid advancement was Six's hallmark. He was slated to play an important role in the extermination of Jews and intellectuals in England. Cf. Stevenson, p. 128.

30. Cf. Hans L. Zankl, *Zeitungsbild und Nationalpropaganda: Die Politik der Aufmachung* (Leipzig), pp. 23–31.

31. Oren J. Hale, *The Captive Press in the Third Reich* (Princeton: 1964), p. 86.

32. Ibid., pp. 83–91, 275–76, 289; N.A. T-70/131 (German newspapers in 1943); T-176/24 (guide to records of the Reich Association of the German Press); T-70/131 (materials on penalties assessed against the *Frankfurter Zeitung);* Heiber, *Goebbels,* pp. 138–39; Boelcke, *1939–1941,* p..145.

33. Cf. Boelcke, *1939–1941,* pp. 30, 64–69, 145, 562–63; Sington and Weidenfeld, pp. 59, 66–67; Ley (ROL), *Organisationsbuch* (München: 1937), pp. 303–6; Sündermann, pp. 7, 13–14, 252–53; Baird, p. 30.

34. IMT, XXX, 485; IMT, I, 352; IMT, XVII, 206–207, 239 et passim.; IMT, XIX, 333–334; IMT XXXII, 310–313; Boelcke, *1939–1941,* pp. 148–52, 272.

35. Cf. RPA Berlin, Presse-Rundschreiben of August 30, 1939, and Sonderrundschreiben of November 22, 1939, H.I.A.; IMT, XXXII, 318–322.

36. Cf. *Bayrischer Ostmark,* May 13, 14, 1941; Lochner Papers, Box #20 (May 14, 15, 1941).

37. IMT, XVII, 170.

38. *Stettiner General-Anzeiger/Ostsee-Zeitung,* November 29, 1941 (N.A. T-580/963); T-120/5/13219.

39. Cf. Christoph Peters, "Stilforman der NS-Bildpublizistik" (Ph.D. diss., University of Vienna, 1963), p. 168; N.A. T-580/638 (budget); T-580/979 (PK and DNB photos); T-580/638 (list of illustrated weeklies, 1943); Willis, p. 50.

40. Herbert Schmidt, "Der Propagandist und die Presse," in N.A. T-580/656, pp. 9–11.

41. Cf. Krebs, pp. 304–307; Boelcke, *1939–1941,* pp. 110–13.

42. Cf. Baird, p. 25, Boelcke, *1939–1941,* p. 359; Hale, p. 278; N.A. T-580/656 (Sondermann to Redeker of RPA Hannover, October 5, 1944); on the difficulties confronting *Das Reich:* T-580/964 (December 25, 1942).

43. IMT, XVII, 241.

44. Goebbels, "Der Rundfunk als achte Grossmacht," in *Signale,* p. 197 ff. (italics in original).

45. See on radio directors: Boelcke, *1939–1941*, pp. 78–83, 90–92; on the Rundfunkabteilung: IMT reprint of Mueller, Doc. 2434-PS.

46. Hans Fritzsche: IMT, XXXII, 305–309, 316–317, 326–327; IMT, XVII, 139; IMT, XXXI, 427–428.

47. See N.A. T-580/677; "Die Tendenz der Hetze im feindlichen Rundfunk," "Die Lage in der Sowiet-Union," "Die Entwicklung im Mittleren Osten," T-580/676 (March 10, 1945).

48. See Ernst Kris and Hans Speier, *German Radio Propaganda: Report on Home Broadcasts During the War* (London: 1944), p. 53; Boelcke, *1939–1941*, pp. 94–96; Sington and Weidenfeld, pp. 153–54.

49. Kris and Speier, p. 60; Boelcke, *1939–1941*, p. 383; Sington and Weidenfeld, pp. 250–61.

50. N.A. T-81/671/5479746-59.

51. See Heiber, *Goebbels,* p. 196; N.A. T-580/608 ("Entspannung").

52. See Boelcke, *1939–1941*, p. 290; Lochner Papers, Box #20 (April 6, June 23, 1941).

53. See Boelcke, *1939–1941*, p. 237; Lochner Papers, Box #20 (March 11, July 17, 1941).

54. N.A. T-81/671/5479793.

55. See on Dittmar: Kris and Speier, p. 76; N.A. T-120/5/13303.

56. IMT, XVII, 153, 216.

57. Von Oven, I: 138.

58. IMT, XIX, 347.

59. IMT, XXXII, 323–25.

60. IMT, XVII, 140–41; IMT, XXXII, 71.

61. Boelcke, *1939–1941*, p. 65.

62. Hans Fritzsche, "Politische Zeitungs-und Rundfunkschau vom 20.4.40," H.I.A.

63. December 6, 1942 ("Das neue Kampfjahr") B.A.; see also January 18, 1943 ("Zehn Jahre"); March 31, 1943 ("Der Bombenkrieg"); March 9, May 8, July 17, July 24, July 31, August 14, August 28, September 11, November 20, December 27, 1943; January 3, January 8, January 15, March 18, 1944.

64. Many of Scharping's addresses (carelessly filmed in reverse chronological order) may be consulted in N.A. T-70/123/3651410-685.

5

1. Hermann Liese, ed., *Das deutsche Hausbuch* (Berlin: 1943), preface by Goebbels.

2. Goebbels, "Buch und Schwert," in *Das eherne Herz,* p. 65.

3. Sington and Weidenfeld, p. 236; Boelcke, *1939–1941*, p. 178.

4. Cf. on Rosenberg's office: *Bücherkunde: Monatshefte für das deutsche*

Schrifttum; Deutsche Bücher (1940), Michigan; "Buch-Hinweise" in N.A. T-81/21/19023.

5. *Hausbuch* (Liese, ed.) reviewed in the *Kulturpolitisches Mitteilungsblatt,* September 25, 1943, B.A.

6. "Bibliothek des Reichstags: Ausgewählte Neuerwerbungen" (32. Jahrgang/March-August 1944), YIVO.

7. *Aufklärungsdienst,* Munich/Upper Bavaria, Folge 3 (1939), B.A.

8. Six, pp. 56–57.

9. N.A. T-81/24, May 24, 1943 ("Universum-Verlag").

10. Cf. Boelcke, *1939–1943,* p. 276; N.A. T-81/24/21878 et passim.

11. N.A. T-81/672/5480061-82.

12. N.A. T-580/671.

13. N.A. T-81/674/5482796-819 ff.

14. Ley, Anordnung 14/39, *Rundschreiben der DAF* (Thuringia).

15. N.A. T-580/587 (October 5, 1942). See also *Unser Wille und Weg* (January 1941).

16. Heiber, *Reichsführer!* pp. 266–67.

17. Party Chancellory, *Vertrauliche Information,* January 17, 1944, Beitrag: 8; PK, January 26, 1942 (to all *Gauleitungen* on Alsdorf's book).

18. Sington and Weidenfeld, p. 238; KPMB, October 20, 1941, p. 2.

19. See on censorship forms: Boelcke, *1939–1941,* p. 178; Bouhler, "Parteiamtliche Prüfungskommission zum Schutze des NS.-Schrifttums," in Neuburger, *Publications,* #213; Ley, *NS Jahrbuch* (1942), p. 187; Amt Schrifttumspflege (Rosenberg), Neuburger, #220; on Bouhler's office describing its view of its authority: N.A. T-81/672/5480546; on censorship of *Our Hitler Youth:* N.A. T-81/672/5479986 (May 26, 1941); on Kraeger book: T-580/601 (March 27, 1944).

20. Cf. *NS Jahrbuch* ("Der Reichsleiter für die Presse"); F.X. Schwarz, *Anordnung* as *Reichsschatzmeister der NSDAP,* 34/42.

21. Boelcke, *1939–1941,* pp. 295, 598.

22. See on Hess: N.A. T-81/675/5484215 (January 12, 1942).

23. Ibid., 5483318-328.

24. Goebbels, *Vom Kaiserhof,* pp. 48–49 (February 20–22, 1932).

25. Boelcke, *1939–1941,* p. 614.

26. Cf. Six, pp. 50–57.

27. Cf. on "Parole der Woche": Neuburger, *Publications,* #216 B; Tiessler to GPL Danzig, August 12, 1940 (N.A. T-81/672); "Bild der Woche": Reichsamtsleiter Davidts, RPL *Rundschreiben,* in T-81/24/21989-90; display of placards: T-81/24/21814 (RPL, Boetticher to all GPL, January 14, 1944); poster slogans, ibid., Promi to all RPAe, March 18, 1943; end of "Parole der Woche": T-81/24/21886 (May 5, 1943); cooperation with Speer: ibid., RPL to all GPL, May 13, 1943; examples of the "Weekly Motto" in H.I.A. (among them "The Führer Is Always Right," possibly borrowed from the "Decalogue" of Italian fascist youth); DAF on the "Motto": *DAF Rundschreiben,* Thuringia, February 15, 1940; Frowein, February 13, 1943 in T-580/592.

28. Cf. on the DPA: Sondermann to Abt. H, March 24, 1944, in N.A. T-580/592; rejection of proposal by RPA Franconia, April 6, 1944, ibid.; budget and exhibition of DPA work: T-580/605, March 31–May 15, 1941; elimination of smaller studios and presentation of claims by them, ibid., August 28, 1944.

29. See on maps and charts: N.A. T-580/589 and T-81/671/5479394 (February 22, 1943); use of cartoons and loudspeakers in Linz, October 1940: T-580/586 (from the *Volksstimme*); withdrawal of "picture of the week": RPL measure described in RS 36/42, August 29, 1942, *Kreisleitung* Eisenach. Michigan.

30. Ibid., RS 40/41 (September 29, 1941).

31. Cf. N.A. T-81/674/5482252-505.

32. Cf. "Kurzparolen für die Vorder-oder Rückseiten der Speisekarten," N.A. T-81/672/5480312/345.

33. Ibid., 517.

34. Cf. T-81/24/22004-043 (March–July 1943).

35. See on cancellation marks and postage stamps: T-580/657 (RPAe Graz/Vienna/Munich, 1942–1944); T-70/123/3651235 et passim.

36. Cf. N.A. T-580/656 (December 16, 1944 and January 15, 1945).

37. Ibid. (December 1944).

38. Cf. on *Metallspende:* Eisenach KPL RS 11/40 (March 27, 1940); Mother's Day: Ibid., RS 22/40 (May 15, 1940), Michigan.

39. Ibid., RS 39/40 Schu. (July 31, 1940).

40. Ibid. (December 2, 1940).

41. Cf. KL Eisenach, RS 35/41 (August 6, 1941).

42. Ibid., RS 41/41 Schu. (September 30, 1941).

43. Ibid., "An alle Kassenleiter," (March 17, 1942).

44. Ibid., KPL, "An alle Redner" (May 27, 1942).

45. See on Christmas program, "Der Gegner Lügt!" and "Grüsse aus der Heimat: Soldatenbriefe": N.A. T-580/657.

46. *Die Parole* (Munich), "Monatsdienst der GPL," May 1943, pp. 7–8. Michigan.

47. Tiessler to all *Gau* Circle Directors, June 18, 1943 (N.A. T-81/672/5480433).

48. "Der Gauring," (April 1943) in N.A. T-580/669, pp. 3, 5–7.

49. *Der Gauring,* "Was unsere Gegner als Kriegsziel herausstellen . . ." (May 1943); ibid., "Stabschef Viktor Lutze" (June 1943). For good examples of the pictorial quality of this bulletin, see October and November 1943 in N.A. T-81/663/5470911-65. Many of these *Gau* publications of the *Reichsring* only commenced publication in 1941 and 1942 to strengthen the wartime propaganda apparatus when it had become clear that the war would not be over quickly.

50. Cf. the *Gauarchiv der NSDAP Gau Magdeburg-Anhalt,* still in skeletal form in 1942–1943. N.A. T-81/674/5482564 ff.

51. Cf. N.A. T-81/24.

52. GPL to Promi state secretary Werner Naumann, N.A. T-580/672.

6

1. Siegfried Kracauer, *From Caligari to Hitler: A Psychological History of the German Film* (Princeton: 1947), p. 275.
2. Quoted by Richard M. Barsam in *Filmguide to* Triumph of the Will (Bloomington, Ind.: 1975), p. 42.
3. Von Oven, I: 57–58.
4. *Unser Wille und Weg* (1940), p. 103.
5. Goebbels, "Der Film als Erzieher," in *Das eherne Herz,* p. 43.
6. Hitler, *Secret Conversations,* pp. 69, 75.
7. Cf. Boelcke, *1939–1941,* pp. 358, 360, 366, 375 (all 1940), and p. 672 (1941).
8. N.A. T-120/5/13310.
9. Quoted by Wulf, p. 363.
10. Boelcke, *1939–1941,* p. 718.
11. The ban was lifted on September 29, 1941, but press reviews were still subject to censorship. See RPA Berlin, Presse-RS II/117/41 in Wulf, p. 364.
12. Boelcke, *1939–1941,* p. 336.
13. N.A. T-580/584.
14. Cf. A. Fredborg, *Behind the Steel Wall: A Swedish Journalist in Berlin 1941–1943* (New York: 1944), p. 3; Boelcke, *1939–1941,* p. 715.
15. H. Koch and H. Braune, *Von Deutscher Filmkunst* (Berlin: 1943), on the "Kriegswochenschau."
16. Eric Borchert, *Entscheidende Stunden: Mit dem Kamera am Feind* (Berlin: 1941), p. 5.
17. Goebbels, "PK," in *Unser Wille und Weg* (June 1941), p. 74.
18. Ibid., p. 73.
19. Lochner Papers, Box #19 (probably June or July 1940).
20. L. Heyde, *Presse, Rundfunk und Film im Dienste der Volksführung* (Dresden: 1943), pp. 32–33.
21. Cf. Boelcke, *1939–1941,* pp. 128–129; O. Buchbender and H. Schuh, eds., *Heil Beil! Flugblattpropaganda im zweiten Weltkrieg: Dokumentation und Analyse* (Stuttgart: 1974), pp. 13–14; Stab des Stellvertreter des Führers, Abt. M, May 26, 1939, and March 10, 1939 (motorized reserve unit), H.I.A.
22. Ibid., June 26, 1939, p. 1.
23. Cf. on ministry and PK personnel: Promi (Wentscher) to RPAe, June 12, 1939, point 5; ibid., point 6 (Luftwaffe PK); ibid., point 12 (responsibility of RPA offices); maintenance and supplying of technical equipment: Advisor for Defense of the Reich in Promi to RPAe, July 12, 1939, pp. 1–2; shortages of personnel in 1942, PK to mobilization commissioners in all *Gaue:* January 26, April 17, May 11, August 6, 1942, H.I.A.
24. Cf. Boelcke, *1939–1941,* p. 286.
25. Ibid., p. 292.
26. Cf. on organizational plan: N.A. T-70/3503324-431 (Promi); contents: T-580/621/Ordn. 258.

27. Willis, p. 94.
28. Cf. N.A. T-580/983 (December 7, 1944).
29. Lochner, *Diaries,* p. 347.
30. N.A. T-580/984 (July 13, 1944).
31. Richter, *NS-Filmpublizistik,* pp. 39–56. Cf. also pp. 90–99.
32. See on establishment of *Deutsche Wochenschau G.m.b.H.:* N.A. T-580/621/Ordn. 258; Boelcke, *1939–1941,* p. 170; *Auslandstonwochen: Die Lage,* June 24, 1944, p. 6.
33. Cf. on length and average number of prints: Boelcke, *1939–1941,* p. 382; records of the RKK, N.A. T-580/940; Heyde, p. 33; *Die Lage,* June 24, 1944, p. 6; Leiter Film to Goebbels, December 20, 1944 in T-580/983; Richter, *NS-Film.,* pp. 90–108.
34. Cf. on raw film requirements and shortages: H. Barkhausen et al., *Propaganda und Gegenpropaganda im Film 1939–1945* (Vienna: 1972), pp. 31–32; Leiter Film Abt. to Dr. G., December 5, 12, 20, 1944, in N.A. T-580/983.
35. Cf. N.A. T-70/121/3648960; T-580/983 (Leiter F to G., December 20, 1944); T-70/121/3648924.
36. Cf. DW #646-650, LOC.
37. Cf. on Dönitz in the "Newsreel": DW #649, 679, 686; Goebbels on Dönitz: Lochner, *Diaries,* pp. 312, 436.
38. Cf. Göring: DW 687, 737.
39. Cf. Boelcke, *1939–1943,* p. 296.
40. Cf. DW 651, 655, 686, 733, 735, 736, 754.
41. Cf. DW 646, 655, 725, 754, 755.
42. See DW 737.
43. Quoted by Barsam, p. 48.
44. Quoted by Barkhausen et al., p. 36.
45. From Max Domarus, *Hitler: Reden und Proklamationen 1932–1945, Kommentiert von einem Deutschen Zeitgenossen* (Munich: 1965), II: 2153–54. Domarus believes that Hitler's statement was made on October 8; an original print of the document bears the date October 7. The German News Agency disseminated the text on October 10.
46. Cf. on the Volkssturm and the legend of a popular uprising: R.E. Herzstein, "Goebbels et le mythe historique par le film, 1942–1945," *Revue d'histoire de la 2e guerre mondiale,* no. 101 (1976): 52–53, 60–61.
47. Cf. N.A. T-580/983 (Leiter F to Naumann, November 18, 1944).
48. DW 738.
49. Cf. N.A. T-580/667.
50. DW 741.
51. DW 755.
52. DW 480. The coordinated press developed the same themes. Dietrich suggested to reporters that they write, "Providence has held its protective hand over the Leader of the German nation." Sündermann, p. 85. The November 11, 1939, *Angriff* described "Adolf Hitler at the caskets of the seven victims of the assassination attempt." Michael Siegert, speaking of

the DW, refers to the secularized national church, the supreme rite of sacrificing one's life in war: Barkhausen et al., p. 62.

53. Cf. Hitler's eulogy for Todt: Domarus, II: 1836–40, and DW 598; photograph of Hitler at Todt's funeral: R.E. Herzstein, *Adolf Hitler and the German Trauma* (New York: 1974), p. 167.

54. DW 662; a tape containing Goebbels' eulogy is available in N.A. Audio-Visual Section.

55. DW 738; cf. on Goebbels' building up Rommel image: T-120/5/13286 (December 22, 1942).

7

1. Veit Harlan, *Im Schatten meiner Filme: Selbstbiographie,* ed. H. C. Offermann, p. 6.
2. Von Oven, I: 58.
3. Wulf, p. 268.
4. Ibid., p. 290.
5. Quoted by H. Blobner and H. Holba, "De Morgenrot à Kolberg: le cinéma allemand au service du Nazisme," *Cinéma 64,* No. 87, p. 57.
6. Ibid., p. 58.
7. Boelcke, *1939–1941,* p. 618.
8. Quoted by Erwin Leiser, *Nazi Cinema* (London: 1974), p. 61.
9. Lochner, *Diaries,* p. 203.
10. N.A. T-81/671/5479234.
11. Cf. on Reich Film Chamber: Wulf, p. 283 (quoting Gerhard Menz); information on RFK official organs and Bormann's role, N.A. T-580/949.
12. Cf. Boelcke, *1939–1941,* p. 169.
13. Cf. Barkhausen et al, p. 50; Boelcke, *1939–1941,* p. 169.
14. Ibid., p. 219.
15. Boelcke, ibid., pp. 83–85.
16. Michael Siegert, "Fritz Hippler—Goebbels' Reichsfilmintendant," in Barkhausen et al., pp. 51–60.
17. Cf. on *Hans Westmar:* Wulf, p. 350.
18. Leiser, p. 35.
19. Hippler, *Betrachtungen zum Filmschaffen* (Berlin: 1942, 4th printing), pp. 2–5, 104–7.
20. Boelcke, *1939–1941,* pp. 85–87.
21. Cf. Wolfgang Becker, *Film und Herrschaft: Organisationsprinzipien und Organisationsstrukturen der nationalsozialistischen Filmpropaganda* (Berlin: 1973), pp. 191–94, and Hans Hagge, *Das Gab's Schon Zweimal: Auf den Spuren der UFA* (Berlin: 1959), pp. 55–61.
22. Cf. report for Goebbels, November 15, 1941, "Verhandlungen mit . . . Heydrich," H.I.A.
23. Cf. N.A. T-580/626 on "Wien-Film Geselleschaft," and the *Wien-Film-Band* (Material for the period June 1941–December 1942).

24. Lochner, *Diaries,* p. 38.
25. Cf. Wulf, pp. 321–22, and Goebbels on UFA: Lochner, *Diaries,* p. 273.
26. Boelcke, *1939–1941,* p. 171.
27. Lochner, *Diaries,* p. 158.
28. Cf. Curt Belling, *Der Film im Dienste der Partei (Die Bedeutung des Films als publizistischer Faktor),* LBB Schriften No. 2 (1937), pp. 8–19, 30–31, 48; Sington and Weidenfeld, pp. 48–49; Belling, "Der Film-Propagandawaffe und Kulturgut (Betreuung der Volksgenossen durch die Partei Filmarbeit)," in *Unser Wille und Weg,* pp. 5–7.
29. Cf. on securing film work in the event of war: Staff of the Deputy Führer, Abt. M., "Vorbereitung der personnellen und materiallen Mobilmachung der Gaufilmstelle," February 2, 1939, H.I.A.; admissions in 1938: Carl Neumann, "Die Filmarbeit der Partei," in *Unser Wille und Weg,* p. 130; party film work for troops: Willis, pp. 88–90; general public: RPL outline drawn up late in 1941 ("Propagandaaktion") in N.A. T-81/673, 5481696 ff. (IId), and records of Kreis Eisenach, March, June 1942, Michigan. Tenth anniversary: instructions from RFK, "Der deutsche Film am Jahrestag der Machtergreifung," (December 15, 1942).
30. Cf. on winter 1940: Boelcke, *1939–1941,* pp. 263, 274; winter 1941: ibid., p. 610; field hospitals: Kreis Eisenach, December 17, 1942, *Gau* personnel office on RFK decree, Michigan; confiscation of privately owned theaters: Kreis Eisenach, February 23, 1942, *Landesleiter Film to Kreisleiter,* Michigan.
31. Cf. N.A. T-580/682 and 983; Halle: T-580/660 (September 29, 1944).
32. N.A. T-580/579.
33. N.A. T-580/944 (Ordner #30).
34. N.A. T-580/983 (Hinkel to Goebbels, October 27, 1944).
35. Quoted by Leif Furhammer and Folke Isaksson, *Politics and Film* (New York: 1971), p. 41.
36. Barkhausen et al., p. 33.
37. Hippler, *Betrachtungen,* p. 29.
38. Heyde, pp. 18–19.
39. Gutterer: N.A. T-580/584 (September 16, 1941).
40. RPA Berlin, Presserundschreiben Nr. I/198a/39 (August 30, 1939), H.I.A.; *Aufklärungsdienst,* München/Oberbayern (late April or May 1939), Folge 4.
41. Pierre Cadars and Francis Courtade, *Le Cinéma nazi* (Paris: 1972), p. 216, improperly criticize an author who believed that *Feuertaufe* and *Feldzug in Polen* were two different films.
42. There is an excellent collection of promotional materials for *Feuertaufe* in the IMP; some of these are reproduced above on p. 280.
43. Cf. Furhammer and Isaksson, p. 174; Lochner papers, Box #20 (January 27, 1941); Boelcke, *1939–1941,* pp. 607, 610; Kracauer, pp. 279–305.
44. N.A. T-580/983.
45. Cf. Cadars and Courtade, pp. 208–209; Leiser, p. 32.
46. Hagge, p. 59. R. Manvell and H. Fraenkel, *The German Cinema* (New York: 1971), p. 91, mistakenly locate the setting of the story in Lodz.

47. Introduction to *Heimkehr.*

48. *Die polnischen Greueltaten an den Volksdeutschen in Polen* (Berlin: 1940).

49. "Volksdeutsche Flüchtlinge . . ." DNB Nr. 240, p. 1, August 30, 1939. See illustrations on p. 290 above.

50. Quoted by Wulf, p. 355.

51. Cf. Boelcke, *1939–1941,* p. 639.

52. Cf. N.A. T-81/671/5479609-640 et passim.

53. Boelcke, *1939–1941,* p. 253.

54. Ibid., p. 653.

55. Cf. Lochner papers, Box #20 (April 7, 1941, ff.).

56. Boelcke, *1939–1941,* p. 293.

57. Heinz Goedecke and Wilhelm Krug, *Wir Beginnen das Wunschkonzert* (Berlin, 1940).

58. Leiser, p. 63.

8

1. Joseph Goebbels, *Der geistige Arbeiter im Schicksalskampf des Reiches* (München: 1944), p. 7.

2. See on historical films: Hippler, pp. 28, 76–80.

3. Quoted by Cadars and Courtade, p. 72.

4. Cf. on release of *The Dismissal:* Luther in foreign office to Ribbentrop, July 25, 1942, N.A. T-120/738/858; Hitler, *Conversations,* p. 601; Boelcke, *1939–1943,* pp. 273–74.

5. Cf. Cadars and Courtade, pp. 138–41. Leiser analyzes the movie on pp. 90–93 and reproduces some of the crucial dialogue on pp. 143–49.

6. Boelcke, *1939–1941,* p. 711.

7. Lochner papers, Box #20 (July 7, 1941).

8. Cf. Furhammer and Isaksson, pp. 116–19; Heyde, p. 22. For an example of the gruesome sort of poster which promoted the film throughout Europe, see Blobner and Holba, p. 53.

9. Domarus, II: 2005.

10. Blobner and Holba, p. 54.

11. Cf. Richard Grunberger, *The 12-Year Reich: A Social History of Nazi Germany* (New York: 1971), pp. 416–17.

12. The promotional campaign included reprinting selected documents relating to the Jews in Württemberg ca. 1730–40. Cf. O. Gerhardt, *Jud Süss: Mätressen und Judenregiment in Württemberg vor 200 Jahren* (Stuttgart: 1940).

13. Ferdinand Marian evidently had qualms about portraying Jud Süss. After the war he was killed in an automobile accident which some investigators believed indicated suicide. Heinrich George died in Russian captivity. Veit Harlan made no major films after the war and was continually in legal trouble over *Jud Süss.* See David S. Hull, *Film in the Third Reich* (Berkeley: 1969), p. 269.

14. Domarus, *Reden,* II: 1058.
15. IMT, XIX, 316, and IMT, XIV, 421.
16. Hitler, February 24, 1942, "Des Führers Botschaft zum Parteigründungstag," IMT, XLI, 544.
17. Ibid., XII, 319.
18. Cf. Orlow, pp. 455–56; Bollmus, pp. 123, 293.
19. Hitler, *Conversations,* pp. 168–69.
20. Cf. N.A. T-580/983.
21. Carl Hauptmann, "Der Film in totalitären Staaten," *Politische Studien,* Heft 124 (1960): 538.
22. Cf. Harlan, p. 164; Grunberger, p. 422.

9

1. Shirer, p. 277.
2. Cf. on Sombart: Arthur Mitzman, *Sociology and Estrangement: Three Sociologists of Imperial Germany* (New York: 1973), pp. 254–61, et passim.
3. Oswald Spengler, *Preussentum und Sozialismus* (Munich: 1921), pp. 32–41, et passim.
4. Cf. *Aufklärungsdienst,* nos. 5 and 7 (May–Summer, 1939); *Gau* München/Oberbayern: *Kriegsinformationsdienst,* Folgen 4 through 6.
5. "Lord Haw-Haw": Shirer, p. 525.
6. Cf. Boelcke, *1939–1941,* pp. 247 and 279; *Informationsdienst* (München), Folgen 9–13 (early 1940).
7. Hitler, *Conversations,* p. 42.
8. James Douglas-Hamilton, *Motive for a Mission: The Story Behind Hess's Flight to Britain* (London: 1971), pp. 120, 130–31.
9. Sündermann, p. 47 (June 25, 1940).
10. N.A. T-580/979 (July 2, 1940).
11. Boelcke, *1939–1941,* pp. 551, 558.
12. *Ibid.,* p. 585.
13. J. Bernard Hutton: *Hess: The Man and His Mission* (New York: 1971), p. 21.
14. Quoted by Sündermann, pp. 147–149.
15. Cf. Douglas-Hamilton, pp. 46, 120, 137.
16. Boelcke, *1939–1941,* p. 207.
17. KPMB of March 1, 1942, in N.A. T-81/683/4721888.
18. "Handakten Kruemmer," N.A. T-120/5/13244.
19. *Archiv der Gegenwart,* p. 6360.
20. Schulungs-Unterlage Nr. 33 ("Das System der Plutokraten"), Schulungsmaterial Nrs. 1, 4 (ROL).
21. Lochner, *Diaries,* p. 195.
22. Hitler, *Conversations,* p. 440.
23. Lochner, *Diaries,* p. 461.
24. RPL bulletin of April/May 1944 ("Bolschewismus"), Blatt 1/5.
25. Hitler, *Conversations,* p. 638.

26. Lochner, *Diaries*, p. 313.
27. Goebbels, "Von der Gottähnlichkeit der Engländer," in *Die Zeit*, p. 301 ff.
28. Cf. *Die Zeit*, p. 248.
29. Cf. Lochner Papers, Box #20 (February 11, March 12, 1941).
30. Goebbels, "Das alte Lied" (April 8, 1941), in *Die Zeit*, p. 453.
31. Goebbels, "Der Frömmste unter uns allen," March 23, 1941 *(Die Zeit*, p. 437).
32. Goebbels, "England und seine Plutokraten" (January 5, 1941), in *Die Zeit*, pp. 359–60.
33. Goebbels, "Die Vision . . .," in *Die Zeit*, p. 66.
34. Goebbels, "Der Sieg wird unser sein," in *Das Reich*, November 6, 1943. This phrase was the caption appearing on a widely distributed poster in 1943.
35. Goebbels, "Das neue Stadium des Krieges," in *Das Reich*, October 16, 1943.
36. Hans Fritzsche, *Krieg den Kriegshetzern: Acht Wochen politische Zeitungs- und Rundfunkschau* (Berlin: 1940), with Goebbels' foreword on pp. 5–7.
37. N.A. T-70/123/3651321-541.
38. "Feierstunde am Sonntag, den 1. September 1940," Michigan.
39. *Die Aktion: Kampfblatt gegen Plutokratie und Völkerverhetzung* (Erstes Jahr, 1939–1940).
40. Fritz Seidenzahl, *Die Gewaltherrschaft des englischen Pfundes: Wie England seine Wirtschaftsmacht missbraucht* (Berlin, n.d.), pp. 5, 6, 57–59, passim.
41. Werner Morgenstern, *Unter der Knute der Plutokratie: Der Leidensweg von Millionen* (Berlin: 1941).
42. Walther Pahl, *Die britische Machtpolitik* (Berlin: 1940), pp. 116–17.
43. F.O.H. Schulz, *Englisches Mitleid-Englische Sozialpolitik* (Berlin: 1940), pp. 7–11, 86–89.
44. Rosenberg, *Mitteilungen*, September 25, 1939.
45. Ernst Clam, *Lord Cohn: Die Verjudung der englischen Oberschicht von D'Israeli bis Hore-Belisha* (Leipzig: 1940), pp. 3–27, 110–17.
46. Fritz Sauckel, "Die Narren von London," B.A.; cf. on distribution: GPL Thüringen, March 2, 1944 (Michigan).
47. Wilhelm Ziegler, *Ein Dokumentenwerk über die englische Humanität* (Berlin: 1940), and G. Wirsing, *100 Familien regieren England* (Berlin: 1940). Goebbels mentioned these books during his conference of April 20, 1940: Boelcke, *1939–1941*, p. 325.
48. Bruno Rücker, *Die soziale Rückständigkeit Grossbritanniens* (Berlin: 1940), pp. 5–7, 43, 61.
49. A. Reithinger, *Das Weltreich und die Achse: Grossbritanniens Kraft und Schwäche, Schein und Wirklichkeit seiner Wirtschaftsmacht* (Stuttgart: 1941), pp. 7–9, 19, 77–79.
50. Domarus, II: 1006. Cf. on Chamberlain: File 1939, State Historical Society of Wisconsin.
51. Boelcke, *1939–1941*, p. 343.

52. Ibid., p. 417.
53. Shirer, p. 509; Boelcke, *1939–1941,* p. 490.
54. Ibid., p. 579.
55. Ibid., p. 680.
56. Goebbels, "Winston Churchill" (February 2, 1941), in *Die Zeit,* pp. 380–83.
57. Goebbels, "Der tönerne Koloss" (November 23, 1941), in *Das eherne Herz,* pp. 92, 97.
58. Lochner, *Diaries,* p. 53.
59. Ibid., p. 64.
60. Hitler, *Conversations,* p. 353.
61. Otto Kriegk, "Offener Kampf" (October 1, 1943), in *Führen und Erziehen,* p. 13.
62. Douglas-Hamilton, p. 74.
63. Ibid., p. 134.
64. Domarus, II: 1561.
65. Lochner, *Diaries;* p. 273. Also see pp. 183, 211, 212, 219, 235, 248.
66. *Mitteilungen der ROL, HSA,* April 1943, pp. 18–19.
67. Goebbels, "Der fallende Koloss," *Das Reich,* December 18, 1943.
68. Hitler, *Conversations,* p. 340.
69. Lochner Papers, Box #20 (June 17, 1941).
70. Party press office directives, N.A. T-81/671/5479380 ff.
71. PK, January 26, 1942 (Michigan).
72. KL Eisenach to OG, May 28, 1942 (Michigan).
73. S.C. Bose, "Das freie Indien und seine Probleme," *Wille und Macht: Führerorgan der NS Jugend,* issue 8/42 (LOC).
74. Cf. N.A. T-120/765/349587-350485 (June 1942–May 1943).
75. Domarus, II: 1174.
76. N.A. T-580/979 (July 11, 1940, RPK).
77. F. Gral, *Englands Kriege—Die Geschichte der britischen Kriege in fünf Erdteilen* (1940), N.A. T-81/671/5479854 ff.
78. Reinald Hoops, *Irland und England* (Berlin: 1940), pp. 5–9, 61–65, 79–85.
79. *Irland in der englischen Hölle* (Berlin: 1940), pp. 12–14 (reprint of Meyer-Erlach, "Ist Gott Engländer?").
80. Cf. on Goebbels: Boelcke, *1939–1941,* p. 217; Rosenberg: *Mitteilungen,* November 1, 1940.
81. Quoted by Gombrich, p. 19.
82. Goebbels, "Unser Sozialismus," N.A. T-70/123/3651498.
83. See on Hess: Hutton, p. 165.
84. Stefan Schroeder, *England und die Buren* (Berlin: 1940).
85. Cf. Cadars and Courtade, p. 84 ff.; Furhammer and Isaksson, pp. 120–123.
86. Grunberger, p. 417.
87. *Informationsdienst,* Folge 15 (summer 1940).
88. Manvell and Fraenkel, p. 92, make this observation.
89. Lochner, *Diaries,* p. 190.

10

1. Cf. Furhammer and Isaksson, p. 39.
2. Dietrich Eckart, *Der Bolschewismus von Moses bis Lenin: Zwiegespräch zwischen Adolf Hitler und mir* (Munich: 1924), pp. 5–7, 49–50, passim.
3. Hitler, *Conversations,* pp. 37, 156.
4. Goebbels, *Das eherne Herz: Rede vor der deutschen Akademie* (Berlin: 1941), p. 22.
5. Lochner, *Diaries,* p. 113.
6. Goebbels, "Die Urheber des Ungluecks der Welt," *Das Reich,* January 21, 1945.
7. Boelcke, *1939–1943,* p. 257.
8. Goebbels, "Die sogenannte russische Seele" (July 19, 1942), in *Das eherne Herz,* p. 399.
9. Quoted by Baird, p. 177.
10. Cf. on Pan-Slavism: Niehoff, pp. 178–80.
11. Boelcke, *1939–1943,* pp. 320–21.
12. Frau von Oven (November 3, 1943).
13. Lochner, *Diaries,* p. 186.
14. Boelcke, *1939–1943,* p. 324.
15. Ibid., pp. 304–305.
16. Ibid., p. 324.
17. Goebbels, "Damals und Heute" (March 7, 1943), in *Der steile Aufstieg,* p. 213.
18. RPL *Redner-Informationsdienst,* B.A.
19. "Deutschland zum Endkampf mit dem jüdischbolschewistischen Mordsystem angetreten" (1941), pp. 3–5.
20. Taubert put his expertise on Communism at the service of the West German government after 1949. Diewerge became a successful businessman.
21. *Informationsdienst* no. 18: *Redner-Schnellinformationen* nos. 22, 26, 27, 30, 51 (1942). RPL Hauptamt Pro, "Anweisung" of February 20, 1943, N.A. T-81/24/22074 ff.
22. Cf. *Propaganda-Parole Nr. 18,* Thuringia (March 6, 1943), p. 6.
23. "Jüdischer Schulkalender," *Informationsdienst,* April 28, 1943. Cf. N.A. T-580/601 (1940–42, reports of Vorprüfungsstelle, and report of AC general secretary to Stuckenberg, February 7, 1944).
24. "Propagandaparole für die SA," N.A. T-81/673/5481481 ff.
25. N.A. T-70/123/3651276 ff. (instructions for press and radio).
26. Cf. N.A. T-580/646 (Abt. Pro), *Der neue Tag,* December 30, 1944.
27. Sündermann, pp. 167, 171–172.
28. Lochner Papers, Box #20 (July 6, 1941).
29. N.A. T-120/757/346472 ff. (Schmidt memo of November 30, 1941).
30. N.A. T-120/9/14905 ("Anregung" nr. 147, July 4, 1942).
31. Ibid., 15073 (Anr. nr. 83, February 28, 1942).

32. N.A. T-120/757/346103 (Anr. nr. 41, January 3, 1942).
33. *Zeitschriften-Dienst,* February 5, 1943. The Hoover Institution Library possesses an outstanding collection of these guides for the periodical press.
34. DNB report of May 3, 1943, in *Archiv der Gegenwart,* p. 5923.
35. Sündermann, p. 249.
36. *Ibid.,* p. 250.
37. Quoted by Hildegard Brenner, *Die Kunstpolitik des Nationalsozialismus* (Rowohlt: 1963), pp. 207–8.
38. *Die Politik des Ölflecks: Der Sowjetimperialismus im zweiten Weltkrieg* (Berlin: 1944), pp. 10–17, 137–47.
39. J. von Leers, "Juden hinter Stalin," Michigan.
40. Klug, *Die grösste Sklaverei der Weltgeschichte: Tatsachenbericht aus den Strafgebieten der GPU* (Berlin: 1942), pp. 1–16.
41. Cf. *Gau* Organization Office to district leaders, Eisenach, October 14, 1942 (Michigan); W. Diewerge, ed., *Deutsche Soldaten sehen die Sowjet-Union* (Berlin: 1942).
42. *Das Sowjetparadies: Ausstellung der RPL der NSDAP: Ein Bericht in Wort und Bild* (Berlin: 1942).
43. "Der Massenmord im Walde von Katyn: Ein Tatsachenbericht auf Grund amtlicher Unterlagen."
44. Goitsch, *Niemals!* (Berlin: 1944), pp. 40–44, 59. At least three hundred thousand copies of this pamphlet had appeared by early 1945.
45. Seraphim, pp. 89–95.
46. Lochner Papers, Box #20 (June 29, 1941).
47. *Das Gesicht des Bolschewismus* (Berlin: 1943) contains Rosenberg's "Das Sowjetproblem" and his "Die Sowjets und ihre Verbündeten."
48. Rosenberg speech (May 11, 1944) in *Archiv der Gegenwart,* p. 6371.
49. Gerd Wunder, "Die Juden im Bolschewismus," in *Das Gesicht des Bolschewismus,"* p. 26 ff.
50. *Mitteilungen,* August 20, 1940.
51. *NS-Monatshefte,* Heft 142 (January 1942), XIII, 10–30.
52. Taubert: *"Generalreferent"* for All Eastern Questions," N.A. T-580/672 (November 18, 1941).
53. IMT, XIX, 326 (Heinz Fritz, July 24, 1946).
54. Robert Ley, "Schulungs-Unterlage: Weltbolschewismus," in *Der Weg zum Deutschen Sieg* (Munich: 1943), pp. 8–9.
55. Ibid., "Kurzthemen zu dem Schicksalskampf im Osten."
56. Ibid., "Vom Wesen des Bolschewismus."
57. Ibid., pp. 8–9.
58. *Kampf dem Bolschewismus: 28 Fragen und Antworten über den Bolschewismus* (Reichsführer SS Hauptamt).
59. *Der Untermensch:* see illustrations on pp. 366-68 below.
60. See Tiessler to Witt, February 20, 1943, N.A. T-81/672; and Taubert/ Gutterer to Himmler, March 5, 1943, quoted by Baird, p. 163.

11

1. Von Oven. II: p. 14.

2. See on the ministry's rejection of a request for RPA reports by Hagemaier of the Dienstselle Rosenberg: N.A. T-580/670.

3. N.A. T-580/644 (Gutterer to all RPAe, February 27, 1943).

4. See on questionnaire: Kreisleitung Eisenach, Rundschreiben Nr. 48/40 and 24/40 (Michigan); Information Service: GPL München/Oberbayern, Folge 8, B.A.

5. IMT, XVII, 201. Cf. Heinz Boberach, ed., *Meldungen aus dem Reich: Auswahl aus den geheimen Lageberichten des Sicherheitsdienstes der SS 1939–1944* (Neuwied: 1965), pp. ix, xv, xvii, xxvi–xxvii.

6. RSHA "Sonderbericht" of February 5, 1942 in N.A. T-175/267/2762548-553.

7. Lochner, *Diaries*, pp. 333–34.

8. Cf. Shirer, pp. 191, 200–201, 218–19.

9. Boberach, p. 8.

10. N.A. T-175/272/2768895.

11. Cf. Boelcke, *1939–1941*, pp. 213, 264, 268, 341; Boberach, p. 35.

12. Lochner Papers, Box #19A (February 1940).

13. Boelcke, *1939–1941*, p. 328.

14. Boelcke, ibid., pp. 326, 329.

15. See L.P. Lochner, "Round Robins from Berlin: Louis P. Lochner's letters to His Children, 1932–1941," *Wisconsin Magazine of History,* L (1939): 326, and Lochner, "Entertaining in Reich Difficult," AP dispatch in Lochner Papers, Box #45.

16. Cf. Boelcke, *1939–1941*, p. 582; Shirer, p. 563; File 1939, Wisconsin State Historical Society.

17. Lochner Papers, Box #19. Cf. Boberach, p. 40.

18. Cf. Boberach, pp. 77, 85; Baird, p. 105.

19. Cf. Boelcke, *1939–1941*, pp. 300, 358, 382, 396, 476; "Redner-Schnell-information," No. 43 (May 15).

20. Shirer, p. 492.

21. Shirer, p. 581. Cf. Boelcke, *1939–1941*, pp. 494, 514.

22. Lochner Papers, Box #20 (May 5, 1941; June 20, 1941).

23. Cf. Boberach, pp. 134, 142; Boelcke, *1939–1941*, pp. 615, 699; N.A. T-81/691, 629.

24. Lochner Papers, Box #20 (May 14, 1941).

25. Cf. Boberach, p. 152; N.A. T-175/269/2764964 (Paderborn, June 24).

26. Cf. Boelcke, *1939–1941*, p. 455; N.A. T-175/269/2764975-980; Boberach, pp. 158–59; SD Bericht (Bielefeld and Detmold), June 30, T-580/963; Lochner Papers, Box #20 (June 26, 1941); T-175/269/2764982 (Hoexter, June 27).

27. See Tiessler Vorlage on "Propaganda," July 31, 1941, N.A. T-81/673/5481668 ff., and Baird, p. 173; on Russian resistance: "Redner-Schnellin-

formation," September 19–20, 1941, B.A.; on atrocities: N.A. T-580/646 (Dr. Prause in Pro V, October 8, 1942); on 1944 change: Sündermann, pp. 296–97.

28. Cf. Boberach, p. 184; Boelcke, *1939–1943*, p. 195; RPL, N.A. T-81/673/5481673 ff.

29. Cf. Boberach, p. 198.

30. Rudolf Pechel, *Zwischen den Zeilen: Der Kampf einer Zeitschrift für Freiheit und Recht 1932–1942* (Würzburg: 1948), pp. 338–40.

31. Cf. Boberach, pp. 202, 228, 245; Boelcke, *1939–1943*, p. 207.

32. Cf. Boberach, pp. 267, 270; Lochner, *Diaries*, pp. 93, 168, 181, 196.

33. Cf. Boberach, pp. 238, 310; N.A. T-81/673/5482014 ff. (Albrecht to Tiessler, March 20, 1942).

34. Cf. GPL Weser-Ems, report on "Druckschriften-und Plakat-Propaganda" for December–January 1941–42, in N.A. T-81/672/5480193; ibid., 5480029; T-175/267/2762660.

35. Cf. Boelcke, *1939–1943*, p. 261; Cohn, pp. 210–11 (on Müller-Claudius' investigations of German anti-Jewish opinion, 1938–1942). Goebbels may have left a permanent mark: See the *Boston Globe*, May 26, 1976, "German poll finds 50% are anti-Semitic."

36. N.A. T-175/267/2762580-592 (Dortmund, Bielefeld, March 1942); "Redner-Schnellinformation" No. 38 (August 25, 1942); Boberach, p. 273.

37. Boberach, pp. 286–295, 314.

38. N.A. T-81/675/5483543-570 (Report of November 9, covering September–October 1942).

39. N.A. T-580/963. One problem with the SD and the RPAe reports was that they often included contradictory expressions of popular mood and attitudes without attempting to analyze the relative strength of the differing sentiments. This allowed one's superior to confirm his own subjective or politically motivated interpretations.

40. Walter Hagemann, *Publizistik im Dritten Reich: Ein Beitrag zur Methodik der Massenführung* (Hamburg: 1948), pp. 427–30; Boberach, pp. 344–47.

41. N.A. T-175/271/2767997; Boberach, pp. 359, 373.

42. Cf. N.A. T-81/673/5481102 (Buehler to Tiessler, March 13, 1942); Boberach, pp. 369, 343, 358; Boelcke, *1939–1943*, p. 537.

43. Lochner, *Diaries*, pp. 364, 367; Boberach, pp. 382–83.

44. Boberach, pp. 386–87; Lochner, *Diaries*, p. 389.

45. Lochner, *Diaries*, p. 396; Studnitz, p. 25; Boberach, p. 413.

46. Lochner, *Diaries*, pp. 367, 373; Boberach, pp. 382, 390; Studnitz, p. 113. Listening to a Hitler radio speech on September 10 in the Hotel Adlon, Studnitz noted that few guests paid any attention, while cooks, waiters, and maids comprised most of the audience. In Goebbels' eyes, this type of effect upon the "masses" justified his admittedly "primitive propaganda."

47. Cf. Boberach, p. 414; memo in Tiessler's files, "Behandlung englischer Kriegsgefangener," N.A. T-81/673/5482127.

48. Cf. Goebbels' speech of March 15, 1942, Heiber, *Reden*, II: 106. Boelcke, *1939–1943*, p. 335; Fredborg, p. 181.

49. Cf. Von Oven, I: 24–25; Ursula von Kardorff, *Diary of a Nightmare. Berlin 1942–1945* (New York: 1966), p. 54; Fredborg, p. 194 and p. 167 (adapted). The versions of the jokes differed in detail, not in sentiment.

50. "Bericht zur weltanschaulichen Lage," October 6, p. 8.

51. Kardorff, p. 50.

52. Boelcke, *1939–1943*, pp. 345–46.

53. Lochner, *Diaries*, p. 443.

54. Ibid., p. 514.

55. Ibid., p. 533.

56. Heiber, *Reichsführer!*, p. 283.

57. Goebbels, "Das neue Stadium des Krieges," *Das Reich,* October 16, 1943.

58. Fredborg, p. 221, appears to be referring to late 1942 or early 1943.

59. Kardorff, p. 101.

60. Ibid., p. 69.

61. Boberach, p. 363.

62. Goebbels, "Rede vor der Tagung der Reichs-und Gauleiter," February 23, 1944 (Munich: 1944), pp. 6–11.

63. Kardorff, p. 110. She heard a sailors' choir singing in the Berlin underground: "It was eerie, but for a moment I felt moved."

64. Schaeffer to RPA Württemburg, March 14, 1944, N.A. T-580/671.

65. N.A. T-580/678.

66. Cf. "Propagandaführung in der Presse," Elsner to Promi, September 6, 1944, N.A. T-70/123/3651383; Dr. Schlösser in Abt. Schrifttum to Abt. Pro. re: Blank ms., T-580/657; Kaltenbrunner to Ribbentrop in regard to Veesenmayer, September 6, 1944, T-120/712/329951; Aachen: Frau von Oven (September 13, 1944); Berger to Himmler, September 26, 1944: Heiber, *Reichsführer!*, pp. 362–66.

67. Cf. PK to Abt. Pro. (Sondermann), September 28, 1944, N.A. T-580/660; "Mitt. des GSAs" (Thuringia), October 1944, p. 9; Düren: Himmler to Bormann, December 2, in Heiber, *Reichsführer!* p. 378; V1: Marlis G. Steinert, *Hitlers Krieg und die Deutschen: Stimmung und Haltung der deutschen Bevölkerung im Zweiten Weltkrieg* (Düsseldorf: 1970), p. 497.

68. Leiter RPA Halle-Merseburg, "Vorschlag für die Propagandaarbeit auf Grund von Erfahrungen im Gau'H-M" (written after October 23), N.A. T-70/123/3651231-4.

69. Cf. Hagemann, p. 438, Steinert, pp. 502–10, and summary Activity Report of October 23, N.A. T-580/682. The reports through November 21 describe increasing enthusiasm for the Volkssturm idea.

70. Cf. N.A. T-84/160/1527440-1; Frau von Oven, p. 9; von Oven, II: 182–83.

71. Broszat, p. 388.

72. Heiber, *Goebbels*, p. 317. Cf. essays in Daniel Lerner, ed., *Propaganda in War and Crisis* (New York: 1951): S.K. Padover, "A Folio of German Types," M.I. Gurfein and M. Janowitz, "Trends in Wehrmacht Morale," and the U. S. Strategic Bombing Survey Morale Division, "Social and Psychological Factors Affecting Morale." The latter observes, "The persons who became extremely frightened were no more willing to give up than were those who remained calm" (p. 355). What a triumph for Goebbels!

73. Some horoscopes are undated; most are unsigned. The one quoted was cast by Wilhelm Wulff. N.A. T-84/349/966-1005.
74. N.A. T-580/660.
75. RPA Main/Franconia, N.A. T-580/682; for "Activity Report" summary of March 21: ibid., p. 1. Like most reports, this declared that Goebbels' speeches in Lauban and Görlitz had had a wonderful effect upon morale. One detects a contradiction here!
76. Von Oven, II: 273.

12

1. See Kris and Speier, p. 57; N.A. T-580/643.
2. Cf. Werner Stephan, *Joseph Goebbels, Dämon einer Diktatur* (Stuttgart: 1949), p. 214; Kris and Speier, p. 56; "Meldungen aus dem Reich," December 16, 1942, N.A. T-580/963.
3. Shirer, p. 542. Cf. Boberach, p. 60.
4. Hitler, *Conversations,* pp. 538-39; "Verordnung über ausserordentliche Rundfunkmassnahmen," para graph one, in N.A. T-120/2474/E255274; ibid., E255406-407.
5. Lochner, *Diaries,* pp. 77-78.
6. For police files on illegal listening, see N.A. T-175/577; Goebbels, "Die Sache mit der Leichenpest," in *Das eherne Herz,* p. 34.
7. Cf. Boberach, pp. 334-39; Redner-Schnellinformation No. 63 (June 28, 1943).
8. N.A. T-70/123/3651286.
9. Sonderdienst Seehaus monitored "SA Mann Schroeder," N.A. T-580/962 (August-September 1942); Goebbels' statement to various Reich authorities, supported by Lammers, in T-120/2474/E255486-489 (October 1944).
10. Fritz: IMT, XIX, 319.
11. Cf. "Meldungen aus dem Reich," in N.A. T-580/963.
12. Hentze, February 12, and March 25, 1941; Fritzsche reply of March 28, 1941; Knoch to Hitler in a letter turned over to Fritzsche, March 24, 1941. These and letters subsequently discussed are in H.I.A., unless otherwise noted.
13. Fritzsche response, September 4, 1941; Albrecht to Fritzsche, September 9, 1941.
14. Some of the letters referred to in this paragraph may be found in N.A. T-580/964 and 965.
15. N.A. T-580/965.
16. By the autumn of 1944 Fritzsche found reading his mail an unpleasant task. T-580/975 (file 188) contains interesting anti-Nazi postcards and notes.
17. Cf. report of RPA Bochum, September 25, 1944, N.A. T-580/963; Fritzsche's response, ibid.; Vienna: Hans Jirsa to Goebbels, September 16,

1944; Volkssturm poem: Fritzsche to Richard Lange, October 21, 1944, in T-580/965. This file contains a copy of Lange's mediocre but passionate Volkssturm poem. Annemarie Reutsch to Fritzsche, February 27, 1945, N.A. T-580/965; "occult gifts": Theresa Süss to Goebbels, August 27, 1944, and report to Goebbels about her from RPA Westphalia/North, November 23, 1944, N.A. T-580/671.

18. Cf. on enemy leaflets and their impact: Klaus Kirchner, *Flugblätter: Psychologische Kriegsführung im Zweiten Weltkrieg in Europa* (Carl Hanser Verlag, 1974), pp. 27–35, and Buchbender and Schuh, p. 21 ff.; *Lügenabwehr:* N.A. T-120/9/15664 ff. (1942 issues). Rumors: "Der Gerüchtespiegel," *Sonderdienst der RPL,* T-580/644.

19. Report on the incident, April 14, 1942, N.A. T-81/673/5481542 ff. Cf. Tiessler to Bühler, June 1, 1942, ibid., and Tiessler, "Vorlage für den Herrn Minister," ibid., fr. 5481537 ff. (May 27, 1942).

20. "Vermerk für Pg. Tiessler," September 17, 1942, N.A. T-81/673/5481534-535.

21. "Mitteilungen der ROL," July 1943, page 8.

22. Kiel RPA, September 28, 1944, and Promi to RPA, October 2, 1944, N.A. T-70/123/3651379 ff.

23. N.A. T-580/656.

24. Willis, pp. 221, 225.

25. "Rundschreiben" to all GPL, November 17, 1944, N.A. T-580/672.

26. N.A. T-580/672, Mundpropaganda Parole Nr. 16.

27. Ibid., Mundproparole Nr. 28 (August 31, 1944).

28. Ibid., Mundparole Nr. 27 (August 24, 1944).

29. Ibid., Mundparole Nr. 29 (September 7, 1944).

30. Ibid., Mundparole Nr. 32 (September 28, 1944).

31. N.A. T-580/656, Mundparole Nr. 7 (October 6, 1944), and N.A. T-580/672, Mundparole Nr. 8.

32. N.A. T-580/672, Mundparole Nr. 12, distributed directly by the chief of the propaganda staff, Berlin, December 22, 1944. The timing of this whisper campaign was particularly important, since the Ardennes counteroffensive was in progress. Atrocity propaganda about the Americans intensified in 1945. See Mundparolen 21, 27, and 28, in N.A. T-580/673.

33. *Völkischer Beobachter* (October 4), *Neues Wiener Tageblatt* (December 1), and *Wiener Neueste Nachrichten* (December 1), in N.A. T-580/656.

34. Schaeffer to RPA Vienna, November 30; Frauenfeld to Schaeffer, December 6; Schaeffer decision, December 12; all in N.A. T-580/656.

35. "Fragen aus dem Volk," pp. 2–8, N.A. T-580/656. Promi tried to counteract defeatist propaganda by intensifying its distribution of leaflets among Wehrmacht personnel on German soil. See an interesting example of the genesis of such leaflets in N.A. T-580/659, "Worum es jetzt geht!" and "Kamerad, das musst du wissen!" (both still in the drafting stage as of March 28, 1945, Promi to RPA Oberdonau, ibid.).

36. Belling, pp. 14–15; see Belling in *Unser Wille und Weg* (January 1939), p. 8, where he appears to contradict the figure he gave in *Der Film,* p. 14; on

Munich: *Redner-Informationsdienst* (Autumn 1938), B.A., and "Propaganda in Zahlen," in *Unser Wille und Weg* (January 1941); on Bayreuth: *Bayrische Ostmark* (January 27, 1941), p. 5; on 1940 statistic: Boelcke, *1939–1941*, p. 172.

37. Hauptamt Film, N.A. T-580/940; SD Hauptaussenstelle Bielefeld, October 19, 1942, N.A. T-175/271/2767197-8.
38. Goebbels and Axmann, "Die deutsche Jugend im Krieg" (zur Eröffnung der HJ-Filmstunden 1942/43), p. 5. See also Richter, pp. 78–83; Belling, p. 33; Goebbels, "Filmarbeit," in *Das eherne Herz,* p. 44. The tremendous movie campaigns aimed at youth during the last years of the war also reflected concern over hostility to the regime among different groups of young people. Cf. Scheffler to Goebbels, August 18, 1941; Tiessler to Bormann, August 22, 1941; Tiessler to Goebbels, October 1942; all in N.A. T-81/675/5484203-208. Youthful alienation assumed forms such as dancing to forbidden "Nigger music," English dress styles, homosexuality, promiscuity, "racial disgrace," and acts hostile to Nazi youth group members. See the highly interesting article by Daniel Horn, "Youth Resistance in the Third Reich: A Social Portrait," *Journal of Social History,* Fall 1973, p. 26 ff.
39. Belling, pp. 42–43; Goebbels (1942 speech in Posen), N.A. T-580/669; Boelcke, *1939–1941*, p. 172 (Boelcke may have overestimated the number of theaters functioning in 1942). *Deutsche Allgemeine Zeitung,* August 1942; "Film und totaler Krieg," report for Hinkel (August 1944), N.A. T-580/944. Statistics become more sparse toward the end of 1943. For typical Gutterer speeches, see *Deutsche Allgemeine Zeitung,* September 16, 1941, and *Film-Kurier,* August 8, 1942.
40. Cf. "Filmtheater-Statistik" (Grundsätzliche Bemerkungen zur 'Aufteilung nach Ortsgrössenklassen'). N.A. T-580/620. DFVG report to Getzlaff, November 2, 1942.
41. Ibid., "Inland-Vertrieb" List A.
42. N.A. T-580/643.
43. Hinkel's office (Bacmeister) to Goebbels, November 20, 1944, N.A. T-580/983. Figures for late 1944 are spotty.
44. *Die Lage,* June 9, 1944, on "Film Theaters and Terror Attacks," pp. 7–8.
45. A survey carried out in 1947 indicated that Germany then possessed over 3,000 picture houses. This compared to about 7,000 in late 1941. See Manvell and Fraenkel, p. 144.
46. "Die Propaganda der NSDAP im Kriege," N.A. T-81/671/5479290.
47. Cf. Boberach, p. 10; Boelcke, *1939–1941*, p. 323. Goebbels reiterated his orders to the press on July 10, 1941. See Hagemann, p. 64.
48. Boelcke, *1939–1941*, p. 369.
49. Boberach, pp. 116–17; Boelcke, *1939–1941*, p. 630.
50. Boberach, pp. 164–65; Lageberichte der SD, Auss. Bielefeld (July–August 1941), N.A. T-175/272/2768615-625.
51. Ibid., 610–617; SD Bericht zur Aufnahme der DW, October 9, 1941, N.A. T-580/963.

52. Boberach, p. 213.

53. SD Bericht on DW, November 1942, N.A. T-580/963. Cf. Boberach, pp. 364–65, n. 1.

54. Boberach, pp. 332, 365, 367; Hagge, pp. 62–63.

55. Studnitz, p. 203. Boberach, p. 368. See on Finland: DW #735. Goebbels was still nervous about scenes of *German* victims of Bolshevik atrocities, since they might induce panic and mass surrender to the *Western* allies.

56. Goebbels, "Die Optik des Krieges," January 24, 1943, in *Der steile Aufstieg,* pp. 130–31.

57. Thuermer, March 11, 1941, Lochner Papers, Box #20. Cf. Boberach, p. 47.

58. Boberach, pp. 114–15.

59. SD Auss. Bielefeld, May 2, 1941, N.A. T-175/272/2768670-675.

60. Quoted by Leiser, p. 159. (Leiser's italics.)

61. Boberach, p. 207. See also Cadars and Courtade, p. 142; Leiser, p. 146.

62. Gauleitung Hannover/Ost to PK, January 10, 1942; Bayr. Ostmark to PK, February 17; both in N.A. T-81/674/5482986-989.

63. Quoted by Leiser, pp. 158–59 (italics in original). Cf. Leiser, p. 62, and Hauptmann, p. 536.

64. Such an honor was not unique to *The Great King,* contrary to the implication of Ernest K. Bramsted, *Goebbels and National Socialist Propaganda, 1925–1945* (1965), p. 279. Both *Die Entlassung* (1942) and *Kolberg* (1945), for example, were so honored. Cf. Alfred Bauer, *Deutscher Spielfilm Almanach 1929–1950: Das Standardwerk des deutschen Films herausgegeben aus Anlass des 20. jährigen deutschen Tonfilm-Jubiläums* (West Berlin: 1950), pp. 559, 562, 662.

65. "The Catalogue of Forbidden German Feature and Short Film Productions Held in Zonal Film Archives of Film Section, Information Services Division, Control Commission for Germany" (mimeographed by the British authorities), p. 27. Cf. Herzstein, "Goebbels et le mythe historique par le film, 1942–1945," pp. 45–51, 62.

66. The Main Cultural Office of the RPL was delighted by the early success of the film: KPMB, #9, May 1, 1942, B.A.

67. NS Lehrerbund to NSLB Bayr. Ostmark, N.A. T-81/675/5484063-064.

68. N.A. T-580/682 (October 16, 1944, two days before the proclamation of the Volkssturm).

69. N.A. T-580/983, Leiter Film to Goebbels, November 24, 1944. During this same month *Bismarck* played in Worms for three days and attracted 2,573 patrons: communication from Johanna Mueller to Promi, November 26, N.A. T-580/947.

70. "Bericht zur welthanschaulichen Lage," August 6, 1943, p. 26.

71. Grunberger, *Social History,* p. 418.

72. Cf. SD Bielefeld, October 26, 1942, N.A. T-175/271/2767131-132.

73. Hans Fritzsche recalled these words fourteen months after Goebbels uttered them. He waxed indignant at his Nürnberg trial when he spoke of his realization that Hitler and Goebbels "had deliberately lied to the people..." IMT, XVII, 187.

Sources

I. There is no single comprehensive guide to archival resources relevant to subjects studied in this book, but the following compilations have been extremely useful:

Barkhausen, Hans, comp. *Filmbestände. Verleihkopien von Dokumentar—und Kulturfilmen sowie Wochenschauen 1900-1945.* Bundesarchiv: 1971.

Boberach, Heinz. "Das Schriftgut der staatlichen Verwaltung, der Wehrmacht und der NSDAP aus der Zeit von 1933-1945. Versuch einer Bilanz." *Der Archivar,* XXII, No. 2.

Booms, Hans. "Die 'Sammlung Rehse,'" *Der Archivar: Mitteilungsblatt für deutsches Archivwesen,* XXII, No. 1 (1969): 1.

Granier, G., Henke, J., and Oldenhage, K. *Das Bundesarchiv und seine Bestände.* Boppard: 1977.

"Guide to German Newsreel Series Entitled Deutsche Wochenschau (Inland Reihe, 16 and 35 mm.) made by UFA, Berlin." In Hoover Institution Archives, Stanford University.

Hoover Institution Archives. "Third Reich Collection." Mimeographed: 1973.

Kent, George O., comp. and ed. *A Catalog of Files and Microfilms of the German Foreign Ministry Archives 1920-1945,* Vol. 3. Stanford: 1966.

National Archives. "Guides to German Records Microfilmed at Alexandria, Va." Mimeographed: 1958.

Rothfeder, Herbert P. *Checklist of Selected German Pamphlets and Booklets of the Weimar and Nazi Period in the University of Michigan Library.* Ann Arbor: 1961.

Weinberg, Gerhard L. "German Archival Material in the Rare Book Room of the University of Michigan Library." Mimeographed.

Wolfe, Robert, ed. *Captured German and Related Records.* Athens, Ohio: 1974.

II. Archival materials:

Anonymous. *Schmähbriefe* to Fritzsche, Goebbels, and Hitler, 1941. Hoover Institution Archives, Stanford University.

"Bibliothek des Reichstags: Ausgewählte Neuerwerbungen." March–August 1944. Mimeographed. YIVO Institute for Jewish Research, New York.

"Deutsche Bücher." Weinberg Collection, University of Michigan.

"Die Lage." Weinberg Collections, University of Michigan.

Eher Verlag brochure, "Schriftenreihe der NSDAP."

Fritzsche, Hans. "Politische Zeitungs-und Rundfunkschau vom 20.4.40." Hoover Institution Archives, Stanford University.

Gau Thüringen. "Feierstunden der NSDAP." Weinberg Collections, University of Michigan.

———. "Kreisleiter Informationen." Weinberg Collections, University of Michigan.

———. "Rundschreiben der DAF." Weinberg Collections, University of Michigan.

———. Stabsamt records, 1942. Weinberg Collections, University of Michigan.

Gral, F. *Englands Kriege—Die Geschichte der britischen Kriege in fünf Erdteilen.* 1940. National Archives, Washington, D.C.

Hess, Rudolf (Office of the Stellvertreter des Führers), correspondence with the Gaupropagandaleitung, Berlin, on mobilization questions. August–October 1939. Hoover Institution Archives, Stanford University.

Hitler, Adolf. Proclamation of October 7, 1944. Library of Congress, Prints and Photographs, Washington, D.C.

Lochner, Louis P. Papers. Boxes 19, 19A, and 20. Mass Communications Center, Wisconsin State Historical Society, Madison.

Oven, Frau Wilfred von. Account of and selections from the Wilfred von Oven diaries. Typescript. Mass Communications Center, Wisconsin State Historical Society, Madison.

Partei-Kanzlei, "Vertrauliche Informationen" and "Rundschreiben." 1941–1944. Bundesarchiv, Koblenz, and Weinberg Collections, University of Michigan.

Reichsleitung der NSDAP. "Verordnungsblätter." 1943. YIVO Institute for Jewish Research, New York.

Reichsministerium für Volksaufklärung und Propaganda. "Nachrichtenblatt." YIVO Institute for Jewish Research, New York.

Reichsorganisationsleiter der NSDAP, Hauptschulungsamt. "Der Schulungsbrief." 1941–1942. YIVO Institute for Jewish Research, New York.

———. "Mitteilungen." Weinberg Collections, University of Michigan.

———. "Sammelsendungen." Weinberg Collections, University of Michigan.

———. "Schulungsunterlagen." Weinberg Collections, University of Michigan.

———. "Sprechabenddienste." Weinberg Collections, University of Michigan.

Reichspropagandaamt, Berlin. "Presse-Rundschreiben." August–November 1939. Hoover Institution Archives, Stanford University.

Reichspropagandaleitung der NSDAP. "Aufklärungsdienst fur den politischen Redner," in files of Gaupropagandaleitung München/Oberbayern. Bundesarchiv, Koblenz.

———. "Informationsdienst." Bunedesarchiv, Koblenz.

———. "Kriegsinformationsdienst," Gau München/Oberbayern, 1939–1940. Bundesarchiv, Koblenz.

———. "Kulturpolitisches Mitteilungsblatt." Bundesarchiv, Koblenz.

———. Materials from the records of the Kreisleitung Eisenach, 1940–1942. Weinberg Collections, University of Michigan.

———. "Redner-Schnellinformationen." Bundesarchiv, Koblenz.

———. "Sonderdienst." Bundesarchiv, Koblenz.
———. *Unser Wille und Weg.* 1939–1941. Library of Congress, Washington, D.C.
Sauckel, Fritz. Instructions for *Gau* Propaganda Director, August 7, 1940, *Gau* Thüringen. Bundesarchiv, Koblenz.

III. Microfilmed records available at the National Archives, Washington, D.C., especially:

T-70: 1/10/121/123.
T-81: 21/24/671–677/683.
T-84: 160.
T-120: 712/734/738/757/765/780/1015/1056/2474.
T-175: 225/267/269/271/272/577.
T-580:   579/584/586/588/589/592/601/605/608/621/626/641/643/644/646/
     656–660/663/667/669–673/676/677/683/940/944/949/950/962–965/975/
     979/982–984.

IV. Newspapers and journals:

Bayrische Ostmark
Berliner Börsenzeitung
Berliner Morgenpost
Berliner Volkszeitung
Das Reich
Der Stürmer
Deutsche Allgemeine Zeitung
Die Aktion: Kampfblatt gegen Plutokratie und Völkerverhetzung
Keesings Archiv der Gegenwart
NS-Monatshefte
Nationalblatt (Koblenz)
National-Zeitung (Essen)
Stettiner General-Anzeiger/Ostsee Zeitung
Westfälische Landeszeitung
Wille und Macht: Führerorgan der NS Jugend

V. Films:

A. *Deutsche Wochenschauen* or *UFA-Tonwochen:* 480, 598, 646–651, 662, 679, 725, 733, 735–738, 741, 754–755.
B. Feature Films (all in Library of Congress, unless otherwise noted):
Bismarck
Der Fuchs von Glenarvon
Der Grosse König
Die Entlassung
Feldzug in Polen
Feuertaufe (International Museum of Photography)

Friedrich Schiller: Der Triumph eines Genies
Heimkehr (International Museum of Photography)
Ich klage an
Im Kampf gegen den Weltfeind
Jud Süss (National Archives)
Kampfgeschwader Lützow (International Museum of Photography)
Kolberg
Menschen im Sturm
Ohm Krüger
Opfergang
U-Boote westwärts!
Verräter vor dem Volksgericht

VI. *Published sources:*

BÄHR, HANS. "Die englische Weltkriegspropaganda und das deutsche Volk." *Unser Wille und Weg,* August 1939.

BARSAM, RICHARD M. *Filmguide to* Triumph of the Will. Bloomington: 1975.

BAUER, ALFRED. *Deutscher Spielfilm Almanach 1929-1950: Das Standardwerk des deutschen Films herausgegeben aus Anlass des 20. jährigen deutschen Tonfilm-Jubiläums.* West Berlin: 1950.

BELLING, CURT. *Der Film im Dienste der Partei (Die Bedeutung des Films als publizistischer Faktor),* LBB Schriften No. 2 (1937).

BENDA, JULIEN. *The Betrayal of the Intellectuals.* Boston: 1955.

BOBERACH, HEINZ, ed., *Meldungen aus dem Reich: Auswahl aus den geheimen Lageberichten des Sicherheitsdienstes der SS 1939-1944.* Neuwied: 1965.

BOELCKE, WILLI A., ed. *Kriegspropaganda 1939-1941: Geheime Ministerkonferenzen im Reichspropagandaministerium.* Stuttgart: 1966.

———, ed. *"Wollt Ihr den totalen Krieg?" Die geheimen Goebbels-Konferenzen 1939-1943.* Stuttgart: 1967.

BOLDT, GERHARD. *Hitler: The Last Ten Days.* New York: 1973.

BORCHERT, ERIC. *Entscheidende Stunden: Mit dem Kamera am Feind.* Berlin: 1941.

CLAM, ERNST. *Lord Cohn: Die Verjudung der englischen Oberschicht von D'Israeli bis Hore-Belisha.* Leipzig: 1940.

DIETRICH, OTTO. *Hitler.* Chicago: 1955.

DIEWERGE, WOLFGANG, ed. *Das Kriegsziel der Weltplutokratie.* Berlin: 1941.

———. *Deutsche Soldaten sehen die Sowjet-Union.* Berlin: 1942.

DOMARUS, MAX, ed. *Hitler: Reden und Proklamationen 1932-1945, Kommentiert von einem Deutschen Zeitgenossen.* Vols. I, II. Munich: 1965.

ECKART, DIETRICH. *Der Bolschewismus von Moses bis Lenin: Zwiegespräch zwischen Adolf Hitler und mir.* Munich: 1924.

FREDBORG, A. *Behind the Steel Wall: A Swedish Journalist in Berlin 1941-1943.* New York: 1944.

FRITZSCHE, HANS. *Krieg den Kriegshetzern: Acht Wochen Zeitungs-und Rundfunkschau.* Berlin: 1940.

GERHARDT, O. *Jud Süss: Mätrassen und Judenregiment in Württemberg vor 200 Jahren.* Stuttgart: 1940.

GERMAN FOREIGN OFFICE. *Die polnischen Greueltaten an den Volksdeutschen in Polen.* Berlin: 1940.

GOEBBELS, JOSEPH. *Michael. Ein Deutsches Schicksal in Tagebuchblättern.* Munich: 1929.

———. *Revolution der Deutschen: 14 Jahre Nationalsozialismus.* Oldenburg: 1933.

———. *Signale der neuen Zeit. 25 ausgewählte Reden.* Munich: 1934.

———. *Vom Kaiserhof zur Reichskanzlei. Eine historische Darstellung in Tagebuchblättern, Vom 1. Januar 1932 bis zum 1. Mai 1933.* Munich: 1935.

———. *Der Angriff. Aufsätze aus der Kampfzeit,* ed. H. Schwarz van Berk. Munich: 1936.

———. *Kampf um Berlin. Der Anfang.* Munich: 1937.

———. *Wetterleuchten. Aufsätze aus der Kampfzeit.* Munich: 1939.

———. *Die Zeit ohne Beispiel: Reden und Aufsätze aus den Jahren 1939/40/41.* Munich: 1941.

———. *Der geistige Arbeiter im Schicksalskampf des Reiches.* Munich: 1943.

———. *Dreissig Kriegsartikel für das deutsche Volk.* Munich: 1943.

———. *Der Blick nach Vorne: Aufsätze aus den Jahren des Krieges.* Munich: 1943.

———. *Das eherne Herz. Reden und Aufsätze aus den Jahren 1941/42.* Munich: 1943.

———. "Rede vor der Tagung der Reichs-und Gauleiter." February 23, 1944. Munich: 1944.

———. *Der steile Aufstieg: Reden und Aufsätze aus den Jahren 1942-43.* Munich: 1944.

GOEDECKE, HEINZ, AND KRUG, WILHELM. *Wir Beginnen das Wunschkonzert für die Wehrmacht.* Berlin: 1940.

GOITSCH, HEINRICH. *Niemals!* Berlin: 1944.

HARLAN, VEIT. *Im Schatten meiner Filme: Selbstbiographie,* ed., H.C. Offermann. N.p., N.d..

HEIBER, HELMUT, ed. *Goebbels-Reden.* Vol. II. Düsseldorf: 1972.

———, ed. *Reichsführer! Briefe an und von Himmler.* Munich: 1970.

HEYDE, LUDWIG. *Presse, Rundfunk und Film im Dienste der Volksführung.* Dresden: 1943.

HIPPLER, FRITZ. *Betrachtungen zum Filmschaffen.* Berlin: 1942.

HITLER, ADOLF. *Mein Kampf.* Boston: 1962.

———. *Hitler's Secret Conversations, 1941-1944.* New York: 1953.

HOOPS, REINALD. *Irland und England.* Berlin: 1940.

IBEL, DR. RUDOLF, ed. *Michaels Weg zum Volke,* "Das Reich im Werden" series. Frankfurt-am-Main: 1941.

KARDORFF, URSULA VON. *Diary of a Nightmare. Berlin 1942-1945.* New York: 1966.

KLUG, KAJETAN. *Die groesste Sklaverei der Weltgeschichte: Tatsachenbericht aus den Strafgebieten der GPU.* Berlin: 1942.

KOCH, H., and BRAUNE, H. *Von Deutscher Filmkunst.* Berlin: 1943.

KREBS, ALBERT. *The Infancy of Nazism: The Memoirs of Ex-Gauleiter Albert Krebs 1923-1933,* ed. W.S. Allen. New York: 1976.

KRIEGK, OTTO. "Offener Kampf." *Führen und Erziehen,* October 1, 1943.

International Military Tribunal, Proceedings. Vols. 1, 12, 13, 14, 17, 19, 30, 31, 32, 41. Nürnberg: 1947–1949.

LANDES, HANNS. *Wofür kämpft der deutsche Soldat?* Berlin: 1940.

LE BON, GUSTAVE. *The Crowd: A Study of the Popular Mind.* New York: 1960.

LIESE, HERMANN, ed. *Das deutsche Hausbuch.* Berlin: 1943.

LOCHNER, LOUIS P. "Round Robins from Berlin: Louis P. Lochner's Letters to His Children, 1932–1941." *Wisconsin Magazine of History,* L, No. 4 (1967).

———, trans. and ed. *The Goebbels Diaries 1942–1943.* Garden City: 1948.

MARTIN, HANS-LEO. *Unser Mann bei Goebbels. Verbindungsoffizier des Oberkommandos der Wehrmacht beim Reichspropagandaminister 1940–1944.* Neckargemünd: 1973.

MEYER-ERLACH. "Ist Gott Engländer?" Reprinted in *Irland in der englischen Hölle.* Berlin: 1940.

"MJÖLNIR," and GOEBBELS, JOSEPH. *Das Buch Isidor, Ein Zeitbild voll Lachen und Hass.* Munich: 1931.

MORGENSTERN, WERNER. *Unter der Knute der Plutokratie: Der Leidensweg von Millionen.* Berlin: 1941.

NEUBURGER, OTTO. *Official Publications of Present-Day Germany.* Washington: 1942.

NIEHOFF, KARENA, and BORRESHOLM, BORIS VON, eds. *Dr. Goebbels nach Aufzeichnungen aus seiner Umgebung.* 1949.

OVEN, WILFRED VON. *Mit Goebbels bis zum Ende.* Vols. I, II. Buenos Aires: 1949–1950.

PAHL, WALTHER. *Die britische Machtpolitik.* Berlin: 1940.

PECHEL, RUDOLF. *Zwischen den Zeilen: Der Kampf einer Zeitschrift für Freiheit und Recht.* Würzburg: 1948.

RAÜCKER, BRUNO. *Die Soziale Rückständigkeit Grossbritanniens.* Berlin: 1940.

REICHSFÜHRER SS, HAUPTAMT. *Das Gesicht des Bolschewismus.* Berlin: 1943.

———. *Kampf dem Bolschewismus: 28 Fragen und Antworten über den Bolschewismus.* N.p. N.d.

———. *Der Untermensch.* N.p. N.d.

Reichsorganisationsleiter der NSDAP (Ley).

———. *Organisationbuch.* München: 1937 and 1943.

REITHINGER, A. *Das Weltreich und die Achse: Grossbritanniens Kraft und Schwäche, Schein und Wirklichkeit seiner Wirtschaftsmacht.* Stuttgart: 1941.

SCHNEYDER, ERICH. "The Fall of Berlin," trans. and ed. L.P. Lochner. *Wisconsin Magazine of History,* L (1967).

SCHOCKEL, ERWIN. *Das politische Plakat: Eine psychologische Betrachtung.* Munich: 1939.

SCHROEDER, STEFAN. *England und die Buren.* Berlin: 1940.

SCHULZ, F.O.H. *Englisches Mitleid—Englische Sozialpolitik.* Berlin: 1940.

SEIDENZAHL, FRITZ. *Die Gewaltherrschaft des englischen Pfundes: Wie England seine Wirtschaftsmacht missbraucht.* Berlin: n.d.

SEMMLER, RUDOLF. *Goebbels—The Man Next to Hitler.* London: 1947.

SERAPHIM, HANS-GUENTHER, ed. *Das politische Tagebuch Alfred Rosenbergs, 1934–1935, 1939–1940.* Munich: 1964.

SHIRER, WILLIAM L. *Berlin Diary.* New York: 1941.

SPEER, ALBERT. *Inside the Third Reich. Memoirs.* New York: 1970.

SPENGLER, OSWALD. *Preussentum und Sozialismus.* Munich: 1921.

STEPHAN, WERNER. *Joseph Goebbels, Dämon einer Diktatur.* Stuttgart: 1949.

STUDNITZ, HANS-GEORG VON. *While Berlin Burns. The Diary of Hans-George von Studnitz.* Englewood Cliffs, N.J.: 1964.

SÜNDERMANN, HELMUT. *Tagesparolen. Deutsche Presseweisungen 1939-1945, Hitler's Propaganda und Kriegsführung.* Leoni: 1973.

THIMME, HANS. *Weltkrieg ohne Waffen: Die Propaganda der Westmächte gegen Deutschland, ihre Wirkung und ihre Abwehr.* Berlin: 1932.

VINDEX [pseud.]. *Die Politik des Olflecks: Der Sowjetimperialismus im zweiten Weltkrieg.* Berlin: 1944.

VOLZ, HANS. *Daten der Geschichte der NSDAP.* Berlin: 1943.

WIRSING, GISELHER. *100 Familien regieren England.* Berlin: 1940.

WULF, JOSEPH, ed. *Theater und Film im Dritten Reich.* Gütersloh: 1973.

ZIEGLER, WILHELM. *Ein Dokumentwerk über die englische Humanität.* Berlin: 1940.

VII. Secondary works:

BAIRD, JAY W. *The Mythical World of Nazi War Propaganda, 1939-1945.* Minneapolis: 1974.

BARKHAUSEN, HANS ET AL. *Propaganda und Gegenpropaganda im Film 1939-1945.* Vienna: 1972.

BECKER, WOLFGANG. *Film und Herrschaft: Organisationsprinzipien und Organisationsstrukturen der nationalsozialistischen Filmpropaganda.* Berlin: 1973.

BLOBNER, H. and HOLBA, H. "De Morgenrot à Kolberg: le cinéma allemand au service du nazisme." *Cinéma 64,* no. 87.

BOLLMUS, REINHARD. *Das Amt Rosenberg und Seine Gegner: Studien zum Machtkampf im NS Herrschaftssystem.* Stuttgart: 1970.

BRAMSTED, ERNEST K. *Goebbels and National Socialist Propaganda, 1925-1945.* 1965.

BRENNER, HILDEGARD. *Die Kunstpolitik des Nationalsozialismus.* Hamburg: 1963.

BROSZAT, MARTIN. *Der Staat Hitlers: Grundlegung und Entwicklung seiner inneren Verfassung.* Munich: 1969.

BUCHBENDER, O. and SCHUH, H., eds. *Heil Beil! Flugblattpropaganda im Zweiten Weltkrieg: Dokumentation und Analyse.* Stuttgart: 1974.

CADARS, PIERRE, and COURTADE, FRANCIS. *Le Cinéma nazi.* Paris: 1972.

COHN, NORMAN. *Warrant for Genocide. The Myth of the Jewish World-conspiracy and the Protocols of the Elders of Zion.* New York: 1967.

DOUGLAS-HAMILTON, JAMES. *Motive for a Mission: The Story Behind Hess's Flight to Britain.* London: 1971.

FURHAMMER, LEIF, and ISAKSSON, FOLKE. *Politics and Film.* New York: 1971.

GOMBRICH, E. H. *Myth and Reality in German War-Time Broadcasts.* London: 1970.

GRIMM, M. "Massenpsychologie und Propaganda im Dritten Reich," Ph.D. dissertation, University of Vienna, 1949.

GRUNBERGER, RICHARD. *The 12-Year Reich: A Social History of Nazi Germany.* New York: 1971.

HADAMOVSKY, EUGEN. *Propaganda and National Power: The Organization of Public Opinion for National Politics.* New York: 1954.

HAGEMANN, JÜRGEN. *Die Presselenkung im Dritten Reich.* Bonn: 1970.

HAGEMANN, WALTER. *Publizistik im Dritten Reich: Ein Beitrag zur Methodik der Massenführung.* Hamburg: 1948.

HAGGE, HANS. *Das Gab's Schon Zweimal: Auf den Spuren der UFA.* Berlin: 1959.

HALE, OREN J. *The Captive Press in the Third Reich.* Princeton: 1964.

HAUPTMANN, CARL. "Der Film in totalitären Staaten." *Politische Studien,* Heft 124 (August 1960).

HEIBER, HELMUT. *Goebbels.* New York: 1972.

HORN, DANIEL. "Youth Resistance in the Third Reich: A Social Portrait." *Journal of Social History.* (Fall 1973.)

HULL, DAVID STEWART. *Film in the Third Reich: A Study of the German Cinema 1933-1945.* Berkeley: 1969.

HUTTON, J. BERNARD. *Hess: The Man and His Mission.* New York: 1971.

KESSEMEIER, CARIN. *Der Leitartikler Goebbels in den NS-Organen "Der Angriff" und "Das Reich."* Münster: 1967.

KIRCHNER, KLAUS. *Flugblätter. Psychologische Kriegsführung im Zweiten Weltkrieg in Europa.* Hanser Verlag: 1974.

KRACAUER, SIEGFRIED. *From Caligari to Hitler: A Psychological History of the German Film.* Princeton: 1947.

KREUZBERGER, HANS. " 'Das Reich.' Ein Beitrag zum Versuch der Deutung der Propagandapolitik Goebbels im zweiten Weltkrieg." Ph.D. dissertation, University of Vienna, 1950.

KRIS, ERNST, and SPEIER, HANS. *German Radio Propaganda: Report on Home Broadcasts During the War.* London: 1944.

LAMPE, FRIEDRICH W. *Die Amtsträger der Partei.* Stuttgart: 1944.

LASSWELL, HAROLD D. *Propaganda Technique in the World War.* Cambridge: 1971.

LEISER, ERWIN. *Nazi Cinema.* London: 1974.

LERNER, DANIEL, ed. *Propaganda in War and Crisis.* New York: 1951.

MANVELL, R., and FRAENKEL, H. *German Cinema.* New York: 1971.

MERKL, PETER H. "Violence and Propaganda in the Third Reich." *Reviews in European History,* II, No. 4.

MITZMAN, ARTHUR. *Sociology and Estrangement: Three Sociologists of Imperial Germany.* New York: 1973.

MOLTMANN, GÜNTER. "Goebbels' Rede zum totalen Krieg am 18. Februar 1943. *Vierteljahrshefte für Zeitgeschichte,* XII (1964).

MURAWSKI, ERICH. *Der Deutsche Wehrmachtbericht 1939-1945.* Boppard: 1962.

ORLOW, DIETRICH. *The History of the Nazi Party: 1933-1945.* Pittsburgh: 1973.

PETERS, CHRISTOPH. "Stilformen der NS-Bildpublizistik." Ph.D. dissertation, University of Vienna, 1963.

RICH, NORMAN. *Hitler's War Aims: The Establishment of the New Order.* New York: 1974.

RICHTER, HORST. "Die nationalsozialistische Filmpublizistik." Ph.D. dissertation, University of Vienna, 1963.

RIESS, CURT. *Joseph Goebbels, a Biography.* Garden City, N.Y.: 1948.

———. *Das Gab's Nur Einmal.* 1957.

SCANLON, ROSS. "The Nazi Party Speaker System." *Speech Monographs,* XVI, no. 1.

SCHMEER, KARLHEINZ. *Die Regie des öffentlichen Lebens im Dritten Reich.* Munich: 1956.

SCHMIER, LOUIS E. "Martin Bormann and the Nazi Party, 1941–1945" Ph.D. dissertation, University of North Carolina, 1969.

SINGTON, DERRICK, and WEIDENFELD, ARTHUR. *The Goebbels Experiment: A Study of the Nazi Propaganda Machine.* New Haven: 1943.

SIX, FRANZ. *Die politische Propaganda der NSDAP im Kampf um die Macht.* Ph.D. dissertation, University of Heidelberg, 1936.

SPEER, ALBERT. *Spandau: The Secret Diaries.* New York: 1976.

SPEIER, HANS. *Social Order and the Risks of War. Papers in Political Sociology.* Cambridge, Mass.: 1969.

STAMATI, GRAF CONSTANTIN. "Zur 'Kulturpolitik' des Ostministeriums." *Vierteljahrshefte für Zeitgeschichte,* VI, no. I.

STEINERT, MARLIS G. *Hitlers Krieg und die Deutschen: Stimmung und Haltung der deutschen Bevölkerung im Zweiten Weltkrieg.* Düsseldorf: 1970.

SYWOTTEK, JUTTA. *Mobilmachung für den Totalen Krieg. Die Propagandistische Vorbereitung der Deutschen Bevölkerung auf den Zweiten Weltkreig.* Opladen: 1976.

WILLIS, JEFFREY R. "The Wehrmacht Propaganda Branch: German Military Propaganda and Censorship During World War II." Ph.D. dissertation, University of Virginia, 1964.

ZANKL, HANS L. *Zeitungsbild und Nationalpropaganda: Die Politik der Aufmachung.* Leipzig.

ZEMAN, Z. A. B. *Nazi Propaganda.* New York: 1964.

Index

Taubert, Dr. Eberhard, 22, 123, 309, 355, 364
Thaelmann, Ernst, 104
"That Is England" series, 333–34
Thielscher, Corporal, 34
Thimme, Hans, 73, 74
"Thirty Articles of War" (Goebbels), 86, 195, 209
Tiessler, Walter, 142, 144, 148–50, 151, 153, 180, 181, 197, 198, 212, 218, 219, 292, 365, 383, 412
Toute la Vie (weekly), 359
Training Bulletin, 156
Traitors before the People's Court (Verräter vor dem Volksgericht) (film), 283–84
Triumph of the Will (film), 276, 300
Trott zu Solz, Adam von, 341
Tschechowa, Olga, 293
Tusca (Gruenwedel), 160

U-boats Westward! (U-Boote Westwärts!) (film), 273, 283, 284, 328, 428
Ucicky, Gustav von, 286
Under the Knout of Plutocracy (Morgenstern), 333
United States, 147, 150, 174, 339–40, 382, 384–86
UFA (Universum-Film Aktiengesellschaft) 231–33, 259, 265
"Unknown SA Man," 46
Untermenschen, 32–33
Untermensch, Der. See *Subhuman, The*
Utermann, Wilhelm, 289

Victory in Poland (Der Sieg in Polen) (book), 277
Victory in the West (Sieg im Westen) (film), 273, 281–83
"Victory or death," 13, 77, 356, 396
"Victory through faith," 252
Vienna Film Society, 266
Village Music (film), 273
"Vindex," 360
Vlasov, General, 365

Volk idea *(Volkstum),* 74, 128, 137–40, 154, 231, 285
Völkischer Beobachter (newspaper), 50, 159, 170–71, 264, 289
Volksdeutsche (German colonials), 289, 292–93
Volkssturm, 90, *205,* 234, 235, *243,* 244, 246–52, *253,* 399–400; and the oath-taking ceremony, 250–51
Volk und Reich (journal), 166
V1 (Vergeltung-1) bomb, 92, 398
Vossische Zeitung (newspaper), 170–71

Wächter, Werner, 134, 141, 142, 148, 181, 194, 196, 225, 229, 353, 378
Wagner, Richard, 128, 255
Wangel, H., 345
War Against the Warmongers (Fritzsche), 332
War Arms of World Plutocracy, The (Diewerge), 365
Warmongers of Today, The (book), 316
Wassermann, W., 300
Wavell, General, 341
"We Are Marching Against England" (song), 179, 180, 279, 284, 285, 297, 332
We Begin the Request Concert . . . (Krug and Soedecke), 295, *296*
Weber, Dr., 80
Wedel, Gen. Hasso von, 170, 231
Wegener, Paul W., 90, 263, 428
Wehrmacht, 145, 150, 157, 215, 226, 228, 246, 248, 250, 266, 276, 383, 412; propaganda department of, 169–70, 229, 268. *See also* Supreme Command of the Armed Forces (OKW)
"Wehrmacht (WB) Report," 169–70
Weimar Republic, 48
Weiss, Bernhard, 63–64, 199
Welzel, Heinz, 285
Wenck, General, 30
Wenzler, Franz, 263
Werner, Ilse, 283, 294
Wessel, Horst, 41, 42–43, 262, 344